PSYCHOLOGY
From Research to Applications

Dennis P. Saccuzzo
San Diego State University

Allyn and Bacon, Inc.
Boston ▪ London ▪ Sydney ▪ Toronto

To my parents, Paul and Rose,
my wife, Lorraine,
and my children, Jennifer and Jason.

Series editor: *John-Paul Lenney*
Developmental editors: *Allen Workman and Tom Mancuso*
Production administrator: *Peter Petraitis*
Senior editorial assistant: *Leslie Galton*
Copy editor: *Diana Gibney*
Cover coordinator: *Linda Dickinson*
Cover designer: *Design Ad Cetera*
Text designer: *Glenna Collett*
Photo research: *Laurel Anderson/Photosynthesis*
Illustrators: *Pat Rossi & Assoc./Kriebel Arts*

Library of Congress Cataloging-in-Publication Data

Saccuzzo, Dennis P., 1947–
   Psychology: from research to applications.

   Includes bibliographies and index.
   1. Psychology.   I. Title.   [DNLM: 1. Psychology.
BF 38 S119p]
BF121.S22   1987   150   86-25960
ISBN 0-205-08842-2

Printed in the United States of America

10 9 8 7 6 5 4 3 2 1   91 90 89 88 87 86

PHOTO CREDITS

Chapter One   Page 2, 4, Pablo Picasso, "The old and the new
year" 1953, Musée d'Art et d'Historie de Saint-Denis. Photo P.
Douzenel. © 1975 Picasso by S.P.A.D.E.M. Paris. 7, Ken R.
Buck/The Picture Cube. 11, Paul Johnson. 12, Historical Picture
Service. 13, Brown Bros. 15, Archiv/Photo Researchers, Inc. 17,
Historical Picture Service. 19, UPI/Bettman Newsphotos. 20,
The Bettman Archive. 21, Robert Eckert/Stock, Boston. 27,
Monkmeyer Photo Service.

Chapter Two   Page 34, 36, Ira Berger/Woodfin Camp & As-
sociates. 37, Courtesy of Harry F. Harlow, Primate Laboratory,
The University of Wisconsin. 40, UPI/Bettman Newsphotos. 41,
Bonnie Griffith/The Picture Cube. 43, AP/Wide World Photos.
44, Elizabeth Crews/Stock, Boston. 48, Yves Debaire/Black Star.
50, Don Fawcett/Photo Researchers, Inc. 51, Fred Bodin. 53,
Alan Carey/The Image Works. 55, Science Library/Photo Researchers, Inc. 56, Margaret Thompson/The Picture Cube. 59,
David Linton. 60, Topham/The Image Works. 64, Burk Uzzle/
Woodfin Camp & Associates. 69, Alan Carey/The Image Works.
73, Ted Cordingley.

Chapter Three   Page 78, 80, Richard Wood/The Picture Cube.
87, David Strickler/The Picture Cube. 91, Martha Stewart/The
Picture Cube. 103, David Witbeck/The Picture Cube. 107, Dr.
Monte Buchsbaum, California College of Medicine.

Chapter Four   Page 114, 116, Fred Bodin. 117, Stephen Dalton/
Photo Researchers, Inc. 120, F.W. Binzen/Photo Researchers,
Inc. 127, Martha Stewart/The Picture Cube. 129, Andrew Bril-
liant/The Picture Cube. 131, Ellis Herwig/Stock, Boston. 139, Joe
Demaio/The Picture Cube. 143, Fred Bodin. 144, Robert Frerck/
Odyssey Productions. 146, Robert Frerck/Odyssey Productions.
148, M.C. Escher Heirs c/o Cordon Art-Baarn, Holland.

*(Credits continue on p. 653, which constitutes a continuation of the
copyright page.)*

Contents

Chapter 3
The Nervous System and Behavior   79

Preface

The primary purpose of this book is to bring the mainstream of modern psychology to the diverse body of students who enroll in introductory psychology. These students deserve a book that is not only interesting and accessible, but accurate and intellectually honest. With this in mind, I have developed a description of psychology around the following major theme: *The science of psychology seeks to understand behavior (defined in terms of thoughts, feelings, and actions), and in doing so uncovers information of everyday practical significance.* Thus, each chapter includes methods and findings as well as practical implications that give the material personal meaning. In addition, because many beginning students lack effective study skills, I have tried to improve on the pedagogical strategies of comparable texts. My goal has been to make the entire book an integrated learning device; the findings of science are applied in their everyday relevance, and much of this knowledge is further applied to innovative learning techniques carried out in the book.

The first objective here is to give students a solid ground in psychology as well as a sense of what the current issues of interest are. I have strived to make the chapters conceptually up-to-date rather than to give that impression with a sprinkling of current citations. I have attempted to provide details that make the basic concepts in psychology meaningful and relevant so that students are not just faced with an endless series of conclusions supported only by names and dates. Rather, for central or exemplary ideas, I attempt to give enough detail to show how scientists arrived at their conclusions with the evidence used to support them. Students learn that the generalizations and conclusions offered in a book must be based on more than the opinion of one or two authors.

COVERAGE

This book provides substantive, in-depth discussions and, at the same time, gives a strong overview of the field. Because the scope of psychology makes it impossible to cover everything, the challenge for an introductory text is to avoid becoming diluted with too many topics or distorted by biased selectivity. The material in this book is set up to provide a thorough, accurate coverage of all the basic introductory-level topics, concentrating on key concepts and avoiding the blinding array of terms often found in similar texts. I have attempted to provide a thorough discussion of central, illustrative concepts that are developed with everyday examples and demystified by clear, thorough, explanations. From this, the student should get an even balance between breadth of coverage and depth of understanding.

The chapters are arranged to provide a balance, not only among the important areas of psychology, but also between the student's expectations or interests and the need for a logical unfolding of topics. In my own teaching I like to encourage students at the beginning of the course with a broad view of psychology. For this reason, the human development chapter has an early position in the book and has been written without assuming prior knowledge of other topics. Teachers who wish to take advantage of this sequence can find a solid logic to beginning with development—a field that crosscuts others in psychology—as much as they could for the more conventional beginning with physiology. I personally feel that this developmental beginning is nearer to most students' expectations of what psychology is about. Nevertheless, the development chapter is written to permit its being conveniently scheduled at any point in the term, and the other standard fundamental topics are placed early.

In the middle of the text, central concepts in learning, cognition, and neurophysiology are brought together in the chapter on Motivation and Emotion (Chapter 9); this is quickly followed by the two more applied topics on Sexuality (Chapter 10) and Life-style and Coping (Chapter 11), which also bring together several central aspects of psychology. These and other later chapters help students to appreciate how the different aspects of human behavior can fit together, forming a whole that is something more than the sum of its individual parts.

LEARNING AIDS

The learning aids in this book include features that appear in other books, features other books claim to have but do not, and features that, to my knowledge, are unique in introductory psychology texts. They are as follows:

1. A running glossary of key terms lists and defines each new important term in the margin as it first appears; this should help students learn a definition as quickly as possible and locate it easily for review. Running glossary items stand out clearly and look like this:

   Chromosomes: Particles containing genes, which are found in the nucleus of every cell in the body.

2. Schematic diagrams—"family-tree"-type diagrams showing relationships among ideas—are scattered throughout the text. They are used whenever an important cluster of concepts can be shown in a significant hierarchy. The visual cluster can help students group together key ideas and remember them better. In this way students can deal with a large number of related concepts in psychology and also acquire a new learning tool that can be applied to work in other subjects. Schematic diagrams have a distinctive appearance in this text:

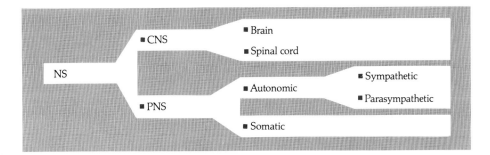

3. "Learning Clues" and "Learning Checks" are two devices that are spaced through each chapter to facilitate active, thoughtful reading. They are, in fact, variations on the familiar SQ3R learning technique: the "Learning Clue" is a survey device that gives readers an alert to look ahead for key ideas, formulating questions in advance as basis for active reading. Here is an example of a Learning Clue:

■ Learning Clue ■

As you read about sleep and dreams, remember that there are two main stages of sleep—one associated with rapid eye movements and one in which such eye movements do not occur.

The "Learning Check" is a rehearsal and review device. It consists of questions to be matched with answers, directions to review key figures, and terms, definitions, and other brief items that students can read, cover, and recite for review. Both the "Clues" and "Checks" are placed in chapters at irregular intervals and do not try for a comprehensive reviewing effect. At these irregular spacings they serve as an "intermittent reinforcement" device; thus they encourage a high, steady rate of response and a form of learning that resists extinction. A brief Learning Check looks like this:

■ Learning Check ■

Read the right side, then cover and try to recite. Repeat.

The hypothalamus plays a role in: 1. Homeostasis.
                                        2. Motivation (for example, thirst).
                                        3. Regulation of the endocrine system.
                                        4. Emotional behavior.

---

4. The "Learning Framework" is an outline-like summary review that occurs at the end of the chapter. Unlike the usual summary, it provides the students with a hierarchical grouping of key ideas in the chapter that they can use for review. The idea of the "Learning Framework" is to provide a means of tying ideas and facts together to help recall key relationships and concept clusters. As its title suggests, it provides a framework or structural connection for the chapter's key ideas. As a reviewing device, it emphasizes ideas and their relationships rather than simply stating definitions, names, and factual details. A portion of a Learning Framework looks like this:

LEARNING FRAMEWORK

III. Two theories try to explain social and personal motivation.
   A. Murray's theory describes social motivation in terms of needs acquired through learning (such as the need to affiliate or the need to excel). (Review: *Psychogenic Needs; n. Ach.*)
   B. Maslow's theory describes personal motivation in terms of an inborn urge for fulfillment. (Review: *Self-Actualization; Figure 9.5*)

5. The *Programmed Learning Guide* is a study guide written by Theron Stimmel and Edward Scholwinski, both of Southwest Texas State University, and myself. We refer to it as a "Programmed Learning Guide," since it was developed as part of the integrated learning devices in the text. It provides a challenging and effective means of learning the text material, as well as a structured program that takes excellent advantage of the learning aids in the text. Included are Learning Objectives based on the text's Learning Frameworks; Key Terms in Matching Format; Programmed Chapter Reviews and Programmed Unit Reviews consisting of summaries in paragraph format with key terms and concepts left blank; Multiple Choice Self-Test Questions; and Essay and Short-Answer questions. Students are given frequent opportunities to quickly check learning progress based on their performance in the learning guide.

STYLE

I have attempted to involve all students in the material by giving them an appreciation of psychology as an exciting, expanding science and profession. While I refuse to sacrifice accuracy and coverage to be interesting, I have tried to underscore the relevance of psychology to readers with a variety of current interests and future goals. The writing style, like other major aspects of the book, revolves around the goal of achieving the appropriate level of presentation for the target audience and topic. The vocabulary has been carefully selected to meet the needs of a majority of students; definitions are concise and concepts carefully articulated. The tone is relaxed and personable. I have tried to speak directly to students in sharing my knowledge of psychology, sometimes from personal experience; yet I have tried to maintain a style that is respectful to the views of the many psychologists who have contributed to this field. Thus I have attempted to combine scholarship with warmth and empathy for the uninitiated.

ACKNOWLEDGEMENTS

Writing a book may be a lonely process, but nobody writes a book alone. I owe a sincere debt of thanks to numerous people, without whom I could not have written this book.

Virginia Anderson assisted in obtaining suitable figures and permissions and conducted extensive library research to uncover new topics of interest. Bill Barke, editor-in-chief of Allyn and Bacon, encouraged and inspired me to continue at a very critical point in which I thought I might not complete the project. Allen Workman and Tom Mancuso, developmental editors, worked hand in hand with me in completing the final manuscript. Leslie Galton, editorial assistant, played a key role in the art package and aided Alicia Reilly in coordinating the works that supplement the text. John-Paul Lenney, psychology editor, was a constant source of inspiration, support, and wisdom from the time that he first became involved with the book through all of its final phases. Peter Petraitis kept the production running smoothly and on schedule.

Special thanks to my family who put up with me, endured with me, and supported me throughout the entire six years from start to finish. Words cannot express my appreciation for the efforts of my wife, Lorraine. Lorraine contributed to every draft of every chapter, providing insightful suggestions, locating new sources of information, and helping me to obtain the perspective of an individual with no prior background in psychology. In addition, Lorraine typed every word from first to final draft and contributed her editorial skills throughout.

Reviewers

I am also indebted to the reviewers of the various versions of the manuscript. Each provided a unique expertise and had an important input on the final manuscript. All final decisions, and alas any errors, are mine, of course, but these individuals deserve credit for their insightful and helpful comments:

Michael Aamodt
Radford University

Leslie Arberman
Kingsborough Community College

William Calhoun
University of Tennessee

John L. Caruso
Southeastern Massachusetts
University

Russell Clark
Florida State University

William O. Dwyer
Memphis State University

Jeffrey D. Fisher
University of Connecticut

Harry Frank
University of Michigan, Flint

David Griese
State University of New York
at Farmingdale

Don Hall
Radford University

Robert W. Herrmann
Christopher Newport College

Sidney Hochman
Nassau Community College

Irwin Kantor
Middlesex Community College

Harold O. Kiess
Framingham State College

James M. Knight
Humboldt State University

Larry La Voie
University of Miami

Phil Lau
De Anza Community College

Shay McCordick
San Diego State University

Jane Pirkle
Bentley College

Steven Prentice-Dunn
University of Alabama

Kathleen Preston
Humboldt State University

Byron D. Robinson
Technical College of Alamance

Ed Scholwinski
Southwest Texas State University

Leo Spindel
Centennial College

Theron Stimmel
Southwest Texas State University

Ursula M. White
El Paso Community College

D.P.S.

Introducing Psychology

3.12.58.

Psychology: Its Origins, Methods, and Personal Relevance

Chapter Outline

Since the dawn of civilization there has been a mystery. What causes people to act, feel, and think as they do? Until just over a century ago, those who considered this question relied mostly on common sense, personal opinion, or guesswork. Then a new branch of science was born. A handful of people began to study the nature of the human mind, using scientific methods as their tools. This science became known as psychology. From humble beginnings, psychology has blossomed into a vast and ever-expanding field of study. Have you ever wondered how you might improve your memory? What causes you to dream? Why is it so difficult for some people to stick to a diet? These are just a few of the questions psychologists are attempting to answer. Psychology is all about you, and many of the questions that you have about yourself will appear throughout the chapters of this book.

Psychology: The science that studies behavior—the actions, mental processes, and experiences of humans and other organisms.

Behavior: Any activity of an organism, whether shown outwardly or experienced inwardly—actions, feelings, and mental processes.

Psychology is the science that studies behavior—the actions, mental processes, and experiences of humans and other organisms. Any personal activity, whether shown outwardly or experienced inwardly, qualifies as a **behavior.** Kissing, arguing, blushing, eating—all are behaviors, as are loving, hurting, and planning. Taking alcohol at a party is a complex behavior that involves the act of drinking the alcohol, an expectation as to its effects, and the actual experiences of the effects of alcohol. Psychology studies behaviors such as alcohol and drug use in an effort to understand how and why they occur. Consider, for instance, binge eating—a behavior that may occur in as many as two out of every three college students (Halmi et al., 1981). Most of us can relate to the problem of "pigging out," that is, eating far more chocolate cake, french fries, ice cream, or whatever than we really need or want. Binge eating can make us overweight, feel bad about ourselves, or experience that overstuffed feeling. Why then is the behavior so common? Psychologists who study binge eating attempt to understand how such factors as basic physiological urges, learned or inherited dispositions, expectations, the influence of others, the tantalizing smell, taste, and looks of certain foods, and other factors contribute in whole or in part to one's eating behaviors. As one would expect, there is no simple explanation. Some psychologists believe that a major cause of binging is, surprisingly, dieting, which deprives the body and causes the person to think so much about food that it becomes too much to resist (Polivy & Herman, 1985). (Many of the topics that you will encounter in this chapter will be discussed in greater depth in the chapters ahead. For example, you will learn more about dieting and weight problems in Chapter 11 on Life Style and Coping.)

THE PSYCHOLOGISTS IN OUR LIVES

The study of our eating habits is just one of many examples of the personal relevance of psychology—the study of behavior. Psychology has found its way into just about every facet of modern life. Perhaps you can identify some way in which **psychologists**—the scientists who study behavior—have influenced you or someone in your family. Let's look at the many different types of psychologists and see how their work might be of personal relevance. (See Figure 1.1.)

Psychologists: The scientists who study behavior.

Psychologists in the Schools

Perhaps you have already encountered a school psychologist. **School psychologists** apply their understanding of behavior in primary and secondary schools. They engage in a number of activities, including vocational counseling for students who seek guidance in selecting an occupation and psychological testing to assess the mental abilities, personality traits, or aptitudes of students. School psychologists work with teachers, school administrators, and parents to help some schoolchildren overcome problems and

School Psychologist: A psychologist who works in the primary and secondary schools. Duties include counseling students and administering and interpreting psychological tests that measure abilities and interests.

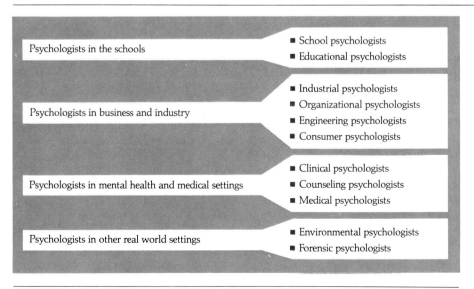

Figure 1.1 Schematic Overview of the Psychologists in Our Lives.

difficulties and others to achieve their potential and pursue goals consistent with their abilities, needs, and interests.

Behind the scenes, the **educational psychologist** conducts research into techniques of teaching, student learning and motivation, and curriculum development. Unlike the typical school psychologist, the educational psychologist conducts research and teaches college and university courses for education students and others who aspire to a career in the school system.

Educational Psychologist: A psychologist who conducts research into techniques of teaching, student learning and motivation, and curriculum development.

Psychologists in Business and Industry

Psychologists also affect our lives in the workplace. An **industrial psychologist** may have developed the test or interview procedure used in selecting you for your job. In so doing, the industrial psychologist helps the company find the most qualified applicants. He or she also helps ensure that you are placed in a position suitable to your abilities, interests, and goals. After you have been selected for a job, you may be trained in a program developed or designed by an industrial psychologist. And after you have been trained, whether you are retained, promoted, or transferred may depend, in part, on a performance evaluation test developed by the industrial psychologist.

Industrial Psychologist: A psychologist who works in business and industry. Duties include development of tools for employee selection, training, and evaluation.

When too many people quit, or when productivity sags, the industrial psychologist investigates. Through surveys of employees, systematic observation, and careful analysis of the available **data** (singular—**Datum**), the industrial psychologist tries to find a solution. Perhaps the position is too demanding; maybe it's not challenging enough; or maybe it doesn't offer enough pay or opportunity for advancement. To correct matters, the industrial psychologist may revise the duties, split the job in two, recommend raising the salary range, or suggest some incentive system whereby a worker can earn a bonus or promotion.

Data (singular—Datum): Evidence. The facts—usually numbers based on measurements that a psychologist uses to study behavior.

Industrial psychologists don't work alone. They work directly with company executives, middle managers, and even front-line supervisors. Often the role of the industrial psychologist is to make recommendations; it's the job of those in authority to make use of the psychologist's input in carrying out their duties.

The work of an industrial psychologist often complements or overlaps with that of an organizational psychologist. **Organizational psychologists** concentrate on the overall organization of a company. Are there too many managers in the production department, so that workers aren't sure whose orders to follow? If so, the organizational psychologist might suggest some changes in the reporting structure, to clarify the lines of authority and communications.

Organizational Psychologist: A psychologist who works in business and industry. Duties include making recommendations concerning the organizational structure of a company.

Another type of psychologist in business and industry is the engineering psychologist. **Engineering psychologists** work with designers and engineers to make machines and goods suitable for the people who use them. An engineer may have a brilliant idea for a new high-speed airplane with over one hundred separate control systems, but the engineering psychologist knows that no person can adequately attend to one hundred things at a time. The two therefore work together to develop a new airplane that is compatible with human abilities. Engineering psychologists are involved in everything from the instrument panels of automobiles and washing machines to high-

Engineering Psychologist: A psychologist who works in business and industry, often in collaboration with engineers to make machines and other mechanical products suited for the humans who use them.

Engineering psychologists may work with airplane engineers in order to design a cockpit that a pilot can operate competently.

technology radar screens and suits for space exploration. Even the push-button phone was the result of the work of an engineering psychologist, who determined that people make fewer errors when they push rather than dial. And the seven-digit phone number is no accident. It is based on psychological findings on the limits of human recall for a string of digits.

Also involved with business and industry are **consumer psychologists.** These psychologists try to make the products and services we use attractive, appealing, and marketable. Everything from the way a product is packaged to the way it is displayed in stores and depicted in advertising may be traced to the work of a consumer psychologist. Consumer psychologists also conduct surveys for political candidates, to help them with their campaign strategy.

Since everyone is a consumer—of automobiles, television programs, toothpaste, and promises from political candidates—consumer psychologists' work affects all of us. But like other psychologists they don't work alone. Advertisers, marketing specialists, political campaigners, fund-raisers, and television programmers all work with the consumer psychologist in carrying out their duties.

Behind the scenes, the university-based psychologists create and refine the knowledge used by industrial, organizational, engineering, and con-

Consumer Psychologist: A psychologist who works in business and industry. Consumer psychologists are involved with activities such as product selection and packaging, marketing, advertising, and television programming.

Social Psychologist: A psychologist who studies behavior in the social context. Social psychologists study such topics as the way people influence and affect each other in groups.

sumer psychologists. These university psychologists supply the fountain of new knowledge that helps psychologists in business and industry keep up-to-date and responsive to the needs of the times. Among these psychologists, social psychologists are perhaps the most active. **Social psychologists** are primarily interested in behavior in the social context—how the presence of others affects individual behavior. For example, they study how the individual behaves in a group setting and how the group's structure and interaction influence the individual. Social psychologists also participate in training those psychologists who venture into business and industry settings.

Psychologists in Mental Health and Medical Settings

Clinical Psychologist: A psychologist who functions in mental health settings and is involved with the diagnosis, treatment, and understanding of problems of adjustment.

Psychotherapy: Techniques for helping people cope more effectively and deal with their problems.

Psychiatrist: A medical doctor who specializes in the treatment of abnormal behavior and engages in psychotherapy.

If you or someone close to you has ever sought professional help for a personal problem, there is a chance that you have encountered a clinical psychologist. **Clinical psychologists** are involved in the diagnosis, treatment, and understanding of mental disorders and other behavioral problems. They help people adjust, solve personal problems, and overcome the stresses of life. Clinical psychologists develop and administer tests to evaluate a person's emotional functioning, personality dispositions, and problem areas. They also conduct **psychotherapy**—techniques for helping people cope more effectively and deal with their problems. As a psychotherapist, the clinical psychologist is often confused with a **psychiatrist,** a medical doctor who specializes in the treatment of abnormal behavior and who also engages in psychotherapy.

The difference between the psychiatrist and the clinical psychologist is that the psychiatrist holds an M.D. degree and, as a medical doctor, can prescribe medications. Clinical psychologists hold the Ph.D. degree (Doctor of Philosophy). They are trained to treat emotional problems just as the psychiatrist is but, by law, are not permitted to prescribe medication. Clinical psychologists work with children, adolescents, adults, and the elderly. They work with families and groups. They can be found in mental hospitals, outpatient mental health clinics, and private practice. Some clinical psychologists restrict themselves to the research and teaching activities of a university position. They train others to become clinical psychologists.

Counseling Psychologist: A psychologist who works in mental health settings. Counseling psychologists administer occupational and interests tests and conduct vocational counseling to help people plan career goals.

Closely related to the clinical psychologist is the **counseling psychologist.** The activities of the counseling psychologist overlap with those of the clinical psychologist as well as with other applied branches of psychology. The major difference is that the counseling psychologist tends to work with less disturbed individuals—for example, a student in a crisis over family or drug problems or a recent graduate searching for a job that best suits his or her interests. But the distinction between the clinical and counseling psychologist isn't always clear, and both can be found performing similar duties.

Developmental Psychologist: A research psychologist who studies how people develop and change over the life span.

Behind the scenes, new knowledge and techniques in clinical and counseling psychology spring from the work of university-based psychologists. **Developmental psychologists** contribute new knowledge about how we grow and change from the moment of conception to the moment of death. Developmental psychologists are interested in studying what is called the life course—the character of a person's life as it unfolds over time, from beginning to end (Levinson, 1986). **Physiological psychologists** conduct research into the relationship between biological processes and behavior. Such information has relevance for clinical psychologists who work with brain-injured persons. It has also led to important findings on the role of biological factors in behavioral problems. **Personality psychologists** study how and why people differ in their dispositional tendencies and reactions to situations; they work hand in hand with clinical psychologists in unraveling the secrets of the human personality.

Clinical psychologists also obtain knowledge from experimental psychologists. **Experimental psychologists** study how people learn, remember, solve problems, and perceive the world about them. They attempt to understand what motivates people and how emotions are activated. Experimental psychologists are also concerned with developing new methods and approaches to psychological research. The work of experimental psychologists is of relevance to all applied areas of psychology. Indeed, experimental psychology is the very core of almost all areas of psychology. What is more, experimental psychology, like developmental, physiological, and personality psychology, stands alone as an independent field of psychology in its own right.

Medical psychologists apply knowledge from the various research areas of psychology, such as experimental and social, to the treatment of medical problems. Traditionally, the treatment of such problems was the exclusive domain of the medical doctor. But recently psychologists have become increasingly involved in almost all aspects of health and medical care (Maddux et al., 1986). It has become evident that many health problems—ulcers, high blood pressure, obesity, heart disease, lung disease, even cancer—are related to behavior. For example, smoking and overeating are behaviors that are dangerous to one s health and have been implicated in many diseases. No matter what medicine a physician prescribes, a patient often can't be cured without making significant changes in behavior—smoking less and eating right. Medical psychologists work hand in hand with medical doctors and other health professionals (nurses, physical therapists, paramedics) to help both children and adults change their behavior for good physical health.

Psychologists in Other Real World Settings

Psychologists are involved in a vast array of real world settings. **Environmental psychologists** study how the physical environment affects an individual's behavior—for example, how the impact of pollution, noise, and crowding affects aggression and work performance. Environmental psychologists also work on artificial environments, such as submarines and skylabs, to make them suitable for humans. These psychologists work closely with government officials and military personnel.

Psychologists also apply their knowledge to the law and our legal system. **Forensic psychologists,** for example, are concerned with all aspects of the criminal justice system. They study crime and how to prevent it. They work with police to understand and eventually help capture dangerous criminals. They work with prison guards and officials, probation workers, and parole officers in rehabilitating offenders. They work with lawyers and

Physiological Psychologist: A research psychologist who studies the relationship between biological processes and behavior.

Personality Psychologist: A research psychologist who studies how and why people differ in their dispositional tendencies and reactions to situations.

Experimental Psychologist: A research psychologist who studies how people learn, remember, solve problems, and perceive the world. These psychologists also study motivation and emotion, and they are concerned with developing new methods and approaches to psychological research.

Medical Psychologist: A psychologist who functions in medical settings. Medical psychologists are concerned with the behaviors that play a role in the development or maintenance of problems of physical health and in helping people alter these behaviors.

Environmental Psychologist: Psychologists interested in the impact of the physical environment on the individual and behavior. These psychologists study such topics as the impact of pollution, noise, and crowding on health and behavior.

Forensic Psychologist: Psychologists who work in the criminal justice system. These psychologists study all aspects of crime from working with police to catch criminals to rehabilitation and prevention of crimes.

Box 1.1 PSYCHOLOGY IN ACTION: How to Study

Helping students study is of deep concern to all psychology teachers. One technique that has proven to be effective for improving reading comprehension and efficiency is called the SQ3R technique. The S and Q of the formula refer to Survey and Question. The 3R's are read, recite, and review. Let's look at each of these steps in more detail.

1. *Survey.* Your survey of the material begins before you start reading. To survey, read the chapter outline, headings and subheadings. Scan the boldface type. Examine the drawings, photos, and diagrams. The five minutes you spend surveying will give you a valuable forward look at the chapter. It will help create mental frameworks or "schemata" that form the structure on which you can file and organize new facts. Psychological research, as we will see in Chapter 7, has revealed the importance of such mental frameworks in long-term memory. The schematic overviews and summaries that appear throughout this book, such as Figure 1.1, are also designed to help you acquire mental frameworks and facilitate your study and long-term retention of the material.

2. *Question.* Questioning is also done before you read. As you begin a new section or subsection, try to turn its heading into a question. For example, if the heading is *Freudian Psychology*, you might ask yourself,

"What is Freudian Psychology?" Questioning not only helps arouse interest, it guides you. It gives you a specific direction, a goal—to find the answer to your question. Questioning also helps you to organize your thoughts, to pay attention to the headings, and to concentrate on a topic.

3. *Read.* This part of the formula is simple. Read the material as you normally would. Having done your survey and asked your questions, however, you might be pleasantly surprised to find that you read more actively—as if you are searching for rather than passively acquiring facts. Because you stop and ask a question at each new heading, you are forced to read the material in smaller units or chunks, which also aid your studying

4. *Recite.* After you have read a section or subsection, recite what you have learned. Ask yourself, "What have I learned?" or "What did I just read?" Then note the answer mentally, out loud, on paper, or all three. As you will see when we study memory in Chapter 7, people retain as much or more when they recite, rather than reread. If you study for two hours, you will generally be better off spending about half your time reciting than if you simply use the time to reread. When you recite, you fix what you have learned in your memory. Reciting also provides feedback, allows you to check yourself, makes you a more active partic-

judges in assessing the competence of suspects to stand trial and in jury selection.

In colleges, psychologists apply their knowledge to such problems as how to study effectively and make the best use of one's time. Indeed, such knowledge has even been put to use in the design of this book and the learning aids it provides. (See Box 1.1.)

Psychology proliferated into a broad and diverse variety of settings over time as individual scientists wrestled with specific questions. To get a better

■ Learning Check ■

For each type of psychologist listed on the left, read the information provided on the right. Then cover the right side and try to recite. Repeat.

	Setting and Some Duties:
Consumer Psychologist	Business and industry; marketing and advertising.
Clinical Psychologist	Mental health; diagnosis and treatment of mental disorders.
Forensic Psychologist	Criminal justice system; crime and rehabilitation.
Engineering Psychologist	Business and industry; designing machines for human use.

Box 1.1   *(cont'd.)*

ipant in the learning process, and helps prepare you for exams.

5. *Review.* Reviewing can make the difference between an A and a B or even between a B and a D. After you have finished reading, it is important to go over what you have learned. Reviewing helps fix the information firmly in your brain so that you can access it when you need it, as during an exam. It also helps you to integrate your knowledge—to tie together what you have learned—and, in so doing, increases your understanding.

The SQ3R is not a rigid set of rules to be followed like some ritual. There are, in fact, many approaches to studying. What works for one person may not work for you. In this text, you will be given a variety of learning aids. At various intervals throughout the text, you will encounter learning clues and learning checks. The clues tell you what to look for. The checks consist of questions with answers, terms and definitions, or other brief material that you can read, then cover and recite. The purpose of these clues and checks is to aid and reinforce your learning of the material, not to review everything. They provide examples of the various approaches you might take to studying and may help you to adapt the ideas of the SQ3R technique to suit your own personal style and approach to studying. The learning framework at the end of the chapter

Reciting to each other in a study group is one approach to the recitation part of the SQ3R.

will then help you as you review the entire chapter. The learning framework is an outline-like review that you can use as a base for paging through and rereading selectively during study. It is not a comprehensive list of definitions, names, and details—those are available elsewhere. Instead, it presents the "bare bones" of the chapter, to which you can tie and relate the details.

---

understanding of the science of behavior, let's take a brief look at psychology's roots.

THE HISTORICAL DEVELOPMENT OF PSYCHOLOGY

There were no parades, no fanfares, not even a modest ceremony to mark the birth of psychology in 1879. A forty-seven-year old person simply moved his scientific equipment to a small room at the University of Leipzig in Germany and began a determined effort to discover the basic structure of the human mind. His name was Wilhelm Wundt (1832–1920). (See Figure 1.2.)

Wundt, of course, was not the first to try to penetrate the depths of the human mind. A string of philosophers, beginning with the ancient Greeks and continuing through the great minds of the seventeenth and eighteenth centuries—Descartes, Hobbes, Locke, Kant—had accepted the same challenge. Experiments of a psychological nature had also been conducted prior to the late nineteenth century. But it was Wilhelm Wundt who championed a scientific approach, and it is he who is generally credited with establishing psychology as a formal science (Hearst, 1979).

Figure 1.2 Wilhelm Wundt (1832–1920). Founder of the first psychological laboratory in 1879 and leader of the school of thought known as structuralism.

Physiology: A branch of science concerned with how the body and its organs (e.g., the brain) function.

Wundt was trained in **physiology,** or the scientific study of how the body and its organs function. It was his dream to apply the experimental methods used in physiology and other sciences to the study of the mind. Could the complicated tangle of human consciousness be broken down into basic components that combine and build into complex ideas and thoughts? Wundt thought so; his goal was to identify the most basic structures of human consciousness. The approach that Wundt and colleagues took to the study of human consciousness grew eventually into a school of thought known as **structuralism.**

Structuralism

Structuralism: The name for Wundt's approach to psychology, whose aim was to analyze conscious experience in terms of its basic elements or structures.

Wundt wanted to identify the basic building blocks that fit together into the complex ideas and thoughts the human mind produces: the elements of consciousness. His idea, to break down consciousness into its most basic parts, was a natural approach to the study of the mind. In solving a problem, it often helps to break it down into smaller, more manageable parts. Language can be approached in this way. The English language can be broken down into paragraphs, which can be further broken down into sentences, which can be divided into words, which can ultimately be divided into the twenty-six letters of the alphabet. Wundt's goal, in a sense, was to discover the alphabet of consciousness.

Introspection: Looking inward. A method for analyzing consciousness by having observers report their experiences in response to a specific type of stimulation.

Wundt went about his ambitious task using a technique known as **introspection,** in which he asked his students to report their experiences in response to specific types of stimulation such as the sound of a bell (Danziger, 1985). Wundt would then compare the reports of different subjects to the same types of stimulation. He eventually proposed that human consciousness could be reduced to three basic elements, or structures: sensation (the product of external stimulation), images (sensation-like experiences produced by the mind), and feelings (the emotional element of experience). A specific idea, for example, might be reduced to one or more images, or to some combination of sensations, images, and feelings. The three basic structures could be reduced no further, however. They were the indivisible letters of the alphabet of consciousness.

What separated Wundt from those who preceded him, philosophers who contemplated the human mind, was his insistence that phenomena be studied in a highly controlled laboratory situation. Wundt and colleagues believed in experimentation as the only path to truth. Though modern psychologists no longer identify with structuralism, an emphasis on experimentation continues to be a major characteristic of psychological research. We will discuss it in greater detail later on (page 24).

Wundt's structuralism was the first pillar in building the new science of psychology. But it wasn't long before other scientists began to advance schools of thought of their own. While endorsing Wundt's emphasis on a scientific approach to the mind, some objected to his use of introspection. Others, such as William James, viewed psychology from a different perspective.

Functionalism

In 1890 an American named William James (1842–1910) initiated a new school of thought with the publication of his classic book, *The Principles of Psychology* (1890). In it he advanced his belief that psychologists should study the functions of the mind rather than its structure—an approach that Wundt criticized as "ganz Amerikanisch" (typically American). James's approach to psychology came to be known as **functionalism.**

What are the practical uses (that is, functions) of the mind? James believed that over the ages the human mind has played an important role in our very survival. He was familiar with Darwin's theory of evolution (1859),

Functionalism: The term used to describe James's approach to psychology, which attempted to discover the functions or practical uses of the mind.

William James. Founder of the school of thought known as functionalism.

specifically the concept of the survival of the fittest. Darwin had proposed that all forms of life had changed gradually over the millennia, as the result of the "natural selection" of those creatures best fitted to their environment. Put simply, the fit members of a species had survived, according to the theory, so that their superior characteristics would be passed on to future generations; the unfit had died off. Perhaps some creatures had survived because of their superior ability to defend themselves with their claws; others because of their ability to outrun their enemies on their long, sturdy legs. James believed that those humans who had survived had done so because of their mental abilities. Their higher degree of consciousness, logic, power of invention, intelligence, and learning ability had enabled them to adapt successfully to a rapidly changing, frequently hazardous environment.

James's functionalism played a major role in psychology's early development, and many of its ideas have been incorporated into modern psychological theories and research. Although psychologists no longer specifically identify themselves as functionalists, they do pursue research in areas such as intelligence and learning, which can be applied in teaching and counseling. James and the functionalists provided psychology with one genuine alternative to Wundt's structuralism. Another approach, known as the Gestalt School of Psychology, provided a second.

Gestalt Psychology

The evolution of a new science is never smooth and steady. Independent lines of thought often develop at about the same time. New ideas clash with the old. New positions emerge. Such a new position was being developed in the early part of the twentieth century, about the same time that functionalism was becoming popular in the United States. A small group of German scientists, among them Max Wertheimer (1880–1943), Wolfgang Kohler (1887–1967), and Kurt Koffka (1886–1941), were opposed to Wundt's general notion of studying the mind in parts. These scientists argued that breaking consciousness down into its basic components would not help in understanding it. The properties of the parts they said, depend on their relation to the whole. For example, one cannot fully understand the family by studying only each of its members as individuals. Each has a place, a role, and a function in relation to the entire family. The premise that the whole cannot be reduced to so many individual elements was the foundation for what was to become the **Gestalt School of Psychology.**

Gestalt Psychology: The school of thought that emphasized the importance of studying the whole—that the properties of the parts depend on their relation to the whole.

To understand what gestalt means, look at Figure 1.3a. What do you see: three dots or a triangle? If you are like most people, you will see a triangle. Take the same three dots and put them in a row (Figure 1.3b) and you perceive a line instead. What you perceive is the configuration, the pattern, the form, or—to use the German word—the gestalt. Taking their cue from perceptual experiences such as these, the Gestalt psychologists argued that human consciousness and behavior must be studied as a *whole* phenomenon, not in terms of its individual elements. Studying just the parts, they believed, was like looking at the trees in an attempt to understand the forest, or like studying two lovers separately in an attempt to understand their relationship.

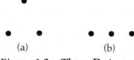

(a)　　　　　(b)

Figure 1.3　Three Dots or a Triangle?

Gestalt theory continues to influence psychological thought, especially on the subjects of perception, problem solving, and social interaction. But just as few modern psychologists specifically identify with the structuralist or the functionalist school of thought, few call themselves Gestalt psychologists. Like those of other early schools, the ideas of Gestalt psychology have been absorbed into a much broader context. Although the relatively narrow scope of these early schools led to their abandonment, the ideas and research of the psychologists who founded them continue to have a significant impact on modern psychology.

Freudian Psychology

While the structuralists, functionalists, and Gestalt psychologists were debating each other's ideas and developing their own, Sigmund Freud (1856–1939), a Viennese physician, was independently developing a theory of his own. (See Figure 1.4.) Freud's interest in the mind stemmed from his efforts to understand and treat mental disorders—such as persistent, nagging, and highly disturbing thoughts and extreme, unrealistic fears. Freud's major method was not experimentation but rather the careful observation and analysis of case studies—the life histories of the individual patients who went to him for treatment. Based on his patients' dreams and slips of the tongue and the connection he observed between a patient's problem and his or her description of early childhood experiences, Freud began to emphasize the hidden forces of the mind—mental processes that operate without the awareness of the person controlled by them. He referred to such mental processes as the unconscious. The **unconscious**, according to Freud, is the repository of fears, wishes, thoughts, desires, and other mental processes of which the person is unaware, but which still affect behavior.

Have you ever done something you couldn't explain—forgotten about a lunch date, or said no when you really meant yes? Your forgotten lunch date, according to Freud, was probably due to the workings of your unconscious. Perhaps, deep down, you really wanted to miss the lunch. You were angry with your friend, but the idea of expressing your anger was unacceptable to you on a conscious level. So your unconscious went to work and

Unconscious: According to Freud, mental processes that govern behavior without the individual's awareness; the wishes, thoughts, desires of which the person is unaware but which still affect behavior.

Figure 1.4 Sigmund Freud (1856–1939).
Founder of psychoanalysis.

Free Association: A technique used in Freud's psychoanalytic approach to treatment to uncover unconscious content. In free association, a person is asked to express his or her feelings, experiences, and thoughts without evaluation or censorship.

Psychoanalysis: The technique of treatment for psychological disorders and the psychological theory developed by Sigmund Freud.

found a way to hurt your friend without causing you a conscious feeling of guilt—by "accidentally" standing him up. A fundamental idea of Freud's was that a person's actions are motivated and determined by mental activities and processes that are hidden from conscious awareness.

He believed that the mind is the major influence on behavior, and that unconscious mental processes are the most powerful of all. He also believed that people are driven by unconscious animalistic impulses, which are kept out of awareness in order to avoid crippling conflicts with prevailing moral and social codes, conflicts that would create anxiety if they entered into consciousness.

Freud's observations also led him to believe in the importance of early experiences in determining behavior. According to his theory, many childhood problems and conflicts wind up in the unconscious, as a psychological defense against anxiety. There they remain inaccessible to conscious awareness and hence cannot be dealt with constructively. Consequently they continue to affect the person throughout the life span. Say, for example, that a four-year-old boy is sexually abused by his father, an experience that causes him intense, crippling anxiety. To deal with this anxiety, the boy's psychological defenses operate to remove the experience from awareness and place it in the unconscious. If he does not have an opportunity to relieve himself of his unconscious anxiety, he may suffer a lifelong disgust of sex or deep-seated resentment toward his father. Later in life, his unconscious conflict may impair his sexual functioning, preventing him from achieving a normal penile erection. Consciously he may desire to have sexual relations, but his unconscious prevents him from doing so. To treat this problem, Freud would try to make the man aware of the early experience through techniques such as **free association** (thinking out loud without censoring anything) and dream analysis. Once brought out into the open, the problem can be dealt with from an adult perspective.

Today, as in the past, many psychologists do not completely accept Freud's notion of the unconscious. Many would allow, though, that there are degrees of awareness, and that behavior may be in part the result of factors of which the person is unaware (Shevrin & Dickman, 1980). Freud had a major influence on the treatment of emotional problems. His was the first comprehensive theory of the causes of mental disorders and the first systematic approach to the treatment of the mentally ill. The term **psychoanalysis** applies to both his theory and his method of treatment.

In contrast to the three other approaches we have discussed—structuralism, functionalism, and Gestalt psychology—Freudian psychology is more of a theory about human personality, abnormal behavior, and treatment than an approach to science. In Freud's theory one can find a comprehensive explanation of the factors that underlie behavior. Many of his ideas have worked their way into modern psychology, and during the late 1940s and early 1950s Freudian psychology was generally considered to be one of the two major forces in psychology. (The other major force, Behaviorism, is discussed in the next section.) Today Freud's position is still accepted by a core of committed followers. However, his theory has been difficult to prove. In Chapter 2 we look at Freud's views concerning the different stages of development that he believed each person goes through from infancy through early adulthood. Then in Chapters 12, 14, and 15 we consider other aspects of his theory of personality and psychoanalytic approach to treatment.

Behaviorism

In sharp contrast to the emphasis on hidden mental forces and the workings of the mind, an American psychologist, John B. Watson (1878–1958), led a school of thought that restricted itself to the study of observable actions. Watson's main concern was to make psychology a truly scientific discipline. In this regard, he pointed to the limitation in Wundt's technique of introspection. In asking a person to look inward and describe his or her experiences, Wundt and colleagues had been relying on private reports of a subject's own experiences and mental processes, evidence that could not be scientifically verified through direct measurement (Watson, 1913). Wundt's method of gathering data had a fatal flaw, from the standpoint of a new discipline trying to establish itself as a science.

Watson's approach, which he called **behaviorism,** asserted that the proper object of study in psychology is observable, or overt, behavior, which can be directly measured and verified. Behaviorism fulfilled psychology's need to establish itself as a true science based on the accumulation of objective evidence. It soon became a major force on psychological thought and remained so from the late 1920s through the 1960s (Hearst, 1979).

The goal of behaviorism was to predict and thereby control behavior. To achieve their goal, Watson and other behaviorists concentrated on understanding the relationship between two factors: an observable behavior, known simply as a **response** (**R**); and the environmental condition that triggers, or gives rise to, the response, known simply as the **stimulus** (**S**).

Because of the complexity of human behavior, Watson's approach to psychology included the study of the behavior of relatively simple organisms, such as the rat. Today the study of animal behavior is a very important pursuit in psychology. Although generalizations about animal behavior may not always apply to humans, animal experiments provide a means for obtaining objective information about behavior under highly controlled conditions (Higgins & Morris, 1984). Indeed, though the use of animals in research is a sensitive topic for many people, animal experiments are sometimes the only ethical or moral way many questions can be studied. Animals are used to study the effects of modern urban living, such as crowding and prolonged exposure to noise, on humans. They are also used to study the effects of a new drug or the consequences of prolonged sleep deprivation. The psychologist who uses animals in experiments is not insensitive or cruel. Rather, the psychologist believes that the undesirable aspects of such experiments are justified by the potential benefits to people and to society. And, to protect animals, the American Psychological Association has a formal set of ethical guidelines for the care and use of animals in research. Universities have committees to see that such guidelines are enforced.

Watson fully endorsed the method of experimentation for both human and animal studies; in addition, he advocated the use of other important ways of studying behavior objectively, including the simple technique of observing and recording events as they occur in a natural setting (Hearst,

Behaviorism: A perspective in psychology based on J. B. Watson's position that the proper objects of study in psychology should be observable or overt behavior.

Response (**R**): The behavior of an organism. In behaviorism, an observable and directly measurable behavior.

Stimulus (plural—**stimuli**) (**S**): According to the behaviorists, the environmental condition that triggers or gives rise to a response.

John B. Watson. *Founder of behaviorism.*

1979), a technique known as naturalistic observation. Most of all, though, behaviorism brought to psychology an aura of scientific respectability that it had not had. This aura attracted psychologists of all persuasions to join the ranks of behaviorism, thus elevating it to its long-held position of importance in psychology.

Two main premises of behaviorism—that psychology must restrict itself to the study of observable behavior and that the forces that maintain or modify behavior exist exclusively in the environment—came to be viewed as ironclad rules by a small army of psychologists. These psychologists, most notably B. F. Skinner, whose work will be discussed in detail in Chapter 6, conducted many investigations that supported their beliefs, and behavioristic concepts soon found their way into nearly every major area of psychology.

Today the concepts of behaviorism have been expanded and applied to working with people in therapeutic ways, such as treatments to help people control anxieties and fears, programmed learning, and a technique known as biofeedback. In **biofeedback,** an individual is taught to control a behavior not normally under voluntary control by being given information (feedback) about it. A machine that monitors blood circulation, for example, can be used to provide a person with feedback about the flow of blood. Using such feedback, the person might learn to control the flow of blood from the head and neck muscles to the hand and arms, to treat migraine headaches. Recently, biofeedback has been used to help hundreds of patients recover from nerve damage. In one case, for example, a child lost the use of his hand through an injury. Electrodes were placed on the child's arm to record the activity of the muscles the child could no longer control. When the signal gets through to the correct muscles, those that control movement, dots appear on a TV screen. Such feedback helped the boy learn to control his muscles. In a similar case, a man who had been crippled by nerve injury in his legs learned to correctly contract all the leg muscles involved in walking (Miller, 1985).

As a school of thought, though, behaviorism is no longer the dominant force it once was. As psychology's status as a science became less of an issue, and as newer and more sophisticated techniques of measurement became available, mental processes were gradually brought back into psychology's mainstream. Most psychologists today include mental processes and other unobservable experiences in their definition of behavior and consider such covert behaviors legitimate topics of scientific inquiry. Though the con-

Biofeedback: A technique for allowing people to gain control over bodily functions that are normally involuntary by providing them physiological feedback.

■ Learning Check ■

Read the right side, then cover and try to recite—repeat.

Three important facts about behaviorism:

1. It insists that psychology restrict its studies to observable (overt) behavior.
2. Its founder, J. B. Watson, encouraged animal experimentation and other techniques such as naturalistic observation.
3. It brought to psychology an aura of scientific respectability.

cepts of behaviorism continue to play an important role in psychology, only a relatively small handful of psychologists identify with behaviorism as it was originally formulated. Indeed, those who continue to restrict psychology to observable behavior and who insist that behavior is maintained and altered exclusively by environmental forces are referred to as **radical behaviorists.** The radical behaviorists believe that mentalistic concepts that cannot be anchored to some overt, reliable expression never had and never will have a place in a genuinely scientific psychology. Their position is in sharp contrast to still another major root of psychology's historical development, humanistic psychology.

Radical Behaviorist: Psychologists who believe that psychology should restrict its inquiry to observable and directly measurable behavior.

Humanistic Psychology

The rise of behaviorism on the one hand and Freudian theory on the other created what some psychologists saw as a major distortion. In an effort to correct for this distortion, a group of psychologists led by Carl Rogers (1902–) and Abraham Maslow (1908–1970) founded the **humanistic school,** which emphasizes the individual, personal awareness and those qualities that distinguish humans from animals. The goal of these humanistic psychologists was to correct for what they viewed as two extremes: the overemphasis on unconscious processes and on mentally disturbed persons (Freudian psychology) on the one hand and on observable actions (behaviorism) on the other. Both viewpoints seemed to them to undermine the person, casting the person as subject to the whims of environment or as motivated solely by hidden mental processes.

Humanistic Psychology: A perspective in psychology that emphasizes the individual, personal awareness, and human qualities—characteristics that distinguish people from animals.

The humanistic psychologists wanted to bring the person back into psychology—the whole person; not, as they saw it, some behavior machine or mindless slave to unconscious forces—and to reveal the positive side of human nature. They focused on the importance of growth, freedom of choice, personal responsibility, and personal experience as determinants of human

Carl Rogers. One of the two major founders of humanistic psychology.

Abraham Maslow. *One of the two major founders of humanistic psychology.*

behavior. In contrast to the Freudian view that people are basically evil, driven by animalistic impulses, the humanistic thinkers argued that people are basically good and that the primary human impulse is a striving for growth. In contrast to the behaviorists, who sought general laws that could apply to all organisms and who minimized differences between humans and simpler organisms, the humanistic psychologists emphasized those differences and focused on the uniqueness of each individual. In fact, it is because they emphasized those qualities that distinguish humans from animals that these theorists are called humanistic.

In emphasizing personal responsibility and other uniquely human characteristics, the humanistic psychologists expanded the scope of psychology. Like the theorists who preceded them, however, they tended to overemphasize one factor at the expense of others—for the humanistic psychologists, this was the person at the expense of the environment. They also created a philosophical dilemma. Their belief that behavior is freely willed by the individual implied that human behavior is not necessarily lawful and predictable—a basic assumption of science. Many critics concluded that humanistic psychology was inherently unscientific.

The issue of free will versus determinism is, of course, philosophical. The problem for humanistic psychology was that of reconciling a belief in personal responsibility and free will with the basic assumption that behavior is governed by orderly principles and laws. If people have free will, then how can their behavior be predicted? But if their behavior can be predicted, how can they be free? And if they are not free, then how can they take personal responsibility for what they do? In resolving the dilemma, humanistic psychologists maintain that people are more than passive observers of the world about them; they react to their environment and in so doing can influence the forces that govern their behavior. This idea, that people play an active role in relation to their environment, has become a central premise of a relatively recent historical development in psychology, social learning theory and cognitive psychology.

Social Learning Theory and Cognitive Psychology

Social Learning Theory: A viewpoint in psychology that focuses on learning in the social context through observation and emphasizes the importance of cognitions.

The term **social learning theory** derives from the assumption that much human learning takes place in a social context through observation. (See Figure 1.5.) A child learns to be helpful by watching others being helpful; a student learns to turn assignments in on time by watching another student being scolded for not doing so. Social learning theory stresses that it is possible for a person to learn without ever making an overt response or receiving an actual reward or punishment. The person learns by watching others and seeing what happens to them. Other people serve as models for their behavior. An alcoholic parent provides a model for how to act like an alcoholic. But, though the child of an alcoholic runs a greater risk of becoming one than does the child of a nonalcoholic, mere exposure to an alcoholic model is not what causes a child to become an alcoholic. The outcome is not predetermined by the models in one's environment—it also depends on one's reaction to them (Bandura, 1978).

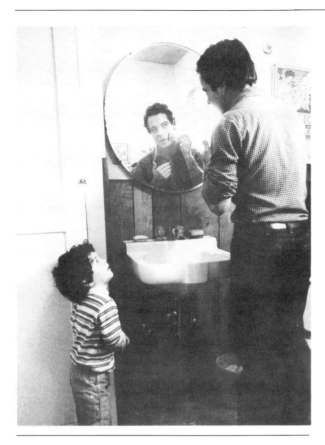

Figure 1.5 Social Learning Theory. *According to social learning theory, much of human learning takes place in a social context through observation.*

A fundamental notion of social learning theory is that behavior is the product of a continuous interaction between environment and personal factors (Bandura, 1977; 1986). The environment may affect the individual, but the individual also affects the environment. A child of a parent who uses drugs might react to the parent's drug-taking behavior with such fright, disappointment, or disgust that the parent stops using drugs. The child's reaction thus worked to alter the nature of the home environment. A second child might react to a parent's drug abuse in the home by attempting to justify it—seeking reassurance from the parent that such behavior is acceptable. In this case, the child's reaction might actually increase the odds of subsequent drug abuse, in that it did nothing to discourage the parent from displaying such behavior and may have encouraged the attitude that there is nothing wrong with abusing drugs.

There is a personally relevant implication in the social learning notion that behavior is the product of a continuous interaction between environmental and personal factors. That is, the outcome of any given circumstance is not necessarily a foregone conclusion. Instead, it depends, at least in part, on the actions and reactions of the individual. Being fired from one's job may be the first step to disaster, or it may be a stepping-stone to success, de-

Cognitions: The mental aspects of behavior such as thoughts, images, evaluations, ideas, beliefs, expectations, and our awareness of these mental processes.

pending on whether the individual responds by giving up or by seeking an even better job.

The way an individual reacts to a situation, according to social learning theory, depends strongly on the individual's beliefs and expectations. In emphasizing beliefs and expectations, social learning theory helped to underscore the role of **cognitions**—thoughts, memories, beliefs, expectations, images—and their manipulation by the mind, in behavior. Indeed, this emphasis on cognition was a major factor in reintroducing the study of mental functioning and of various aspects of consciousness—emphasized by the structuralists, functionalists, and Gestalt psychologists—into the mainstream of psychology. This internal—not directly observable—aspect of behavior is once again a respectable object of scientific inquiry in psychology. For example, psychologists have studied the expectancies of college students regarding alcohol use and the perceptions of the college environment by freshmen. Students' expectations about alcohol are an excellent predictor of their drinking patterns (S. A. Brown, 1985). Those who believe drinking alcohol will lead to pleasant experiences, for instance, are more likely to drink than those who expect to be embarrassed by drinking. And, regarding the expectations of freshmen, psychologists have identified a pervasive myth. Entering college students typically anticipate far more from the college envi-

Figure 1.6   Schematic Summary of Psychology's Historical Development.

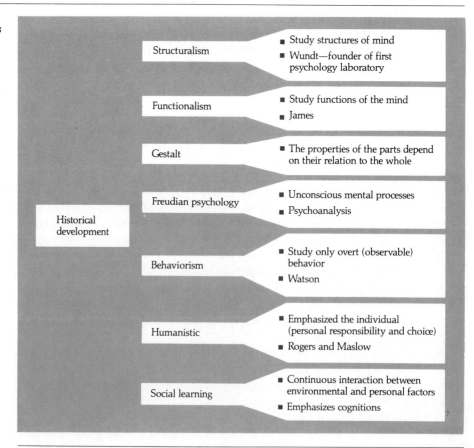

■ Learning Check ■

Figure 1.6 contains a schematic overview of the material we have just covered. It lists each of the seven major viewpoints and an important fact or two about each. Scan the figure for about thirty seconds. Then try to reconstruct as much as you can without looking. Check yourself and try again. Repeat this process for about five minutes.

ronment—romance, adventure, and excitement—than is subsequently realized (Baker et al., 1985). For the naive, the realities of college life can be a rather rude experience.

Social learning theory and **cognitive psychology**, which specializes in the study of cognition, are still evolving and growing, however (White, 1985). They do not represent a single viewpoint, but rather are based on the work of many psychologists. Variations on social learning theory go by different names, such as "cognitive social learning theory" and "cognitive behavior theory." Three of its most important architects are Albert Bandura (1925–), Walter Mischel (1931–), and Julian Rotter (1916–).

Cognitive Psychology: The study of memory, consciousness, thought processes, and other cognitions.

METHODS OF PSYCHOLOGICAL RESEARCH

In this last section, we examine how psychologists study behavior. In the preceding discussion of historical development, you were briefly exposed to some of the major methods in use today—experimentation, naturalistic observation, case studies, and others. If you don't remember these terms, don't worry. We are now going to examine each of them more closely and learn about the methods psychologists use in gathering information and drawing conclusions. Each method has unique advantages. We begin with

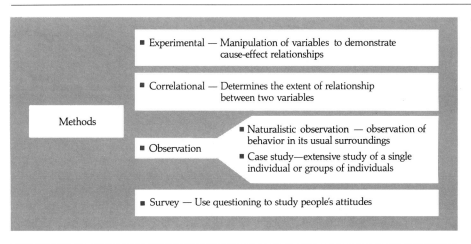

Figure 1.7 Schematic Overview of Psychology's Methods.

the experimental method, which has been called the cornerstone of psychological research. (See Figure 1.7.)

■ **Learning Clue** ■

As you read, keep in mind that the experimental method is the *only* method that allows a psychologist to demonstrate *cause-effect* relationships.

The Experimental Method

Experimentation has held a special position among methods of research in psychology right from the beginning. In fact, as we have seen, an emphasis on experimentation is what distinguished the work of Wilhelm Wundt and his colleagues from early philosophical speculations about the human mind. Let's examine how experimentation works.

Variables. The principal technique in experimentation is the systematic variation of one factor in order to observe its effects on another factor (Calfee, 1985). These factors, called **variables,** are best thought of as any characteristic that can differ either in quality (e.g., degree of liking another person) or in quantity. For example, hours of sleep is a variable that varies in quantity. In conducting an experiment on sleep and memory, a researcher would systematically vary the number of hours of sleep subjects are allowed to have to examine how changes in quantity of sleep affect memory. The goal is to answer a specific question: Does the amount of sleep a person has affect his or her memory? This question is called the hypothesis. More specifically, a **hypothesis** is an expected relationship between two or more variables.

To demonstrate a relationship between two variables, one is systematically varied by the experimenter. The other is expected to change as a result. Sleep is systematically varied; memory recall is expected to change as a result. The variable that is systematically varied is called the **independent variable.** The variable that is expected to change as a result is called the **dependent variable.** You can think of the independent variable as the one that is under the experimenter's control. It is called the independent variable because it is changed by the experimenter, *independently of what the subject does.* You can think of the dependent variable as the variable that the experimenter observes to see whether its value changes in response to changes in the independent variable. The experimenter observes how much subjects recall (the dependent variable) in response to changes in amount of sleep (the independent variable). The dependent variable is so called because it *depends* on what a subject does. In sum, the independent variable is the one the experimenter changes; the dependent variable is the one the experimenter observes to see whether it changes.

Control. In the experimental method, a major challenge is to avoid confusion among all the possible variables. The experimenter must find a way to control, or hold constant, all variables other than the ones being studied. Otherwise there would be no way of telling which variables had caused the effect the experimenter observed. For example, a researcher studying the ef-

Variable: Any measurable aspect of behavior that can take on two or more values. Any characteristic that can be observed dependably to differ in either quality (for example, good-bad) or quantity.

Hypothesis: The expected relationship between two or more variables. An assumption about why something occurs or how things are related, which represents the end of a careful process of observation and thinking about behavior.

Independent Variable: The variable that a scientist manipulates or varies in an experiment, so called because it is changed independently of what a subject does.

Dependent Variable: A variable that is presumed to be affected by the independent variable; the variable the scientist observes to see whether it changes, so called because it depends on what a subject does.

fects of sleep on recall memory would want to hold constant all variables other than amount of sleep that might affect recall. Since it is known that caffeine improves recall, the researcher would not let some subjects have two cups of coffee, others three, and still others none, because there could then be no way of knowing if differences between subjects were actually due to differences in sleeping or to differences in the amount of caffeine in their systems. Variables other than the independent variable that may affect the results—in this case, caffeine—are called **confounding variables.** When such variables are not controlled, the experiment is a failure, because any observed change in the dependent variable could be due to the confounding variable.

One strategy scientists use for ruling out the effects of possible confounding variables is to study two or more randomly selected groups. In **random selection,** each individual has an equal chance of being assigned to a particular group. For example, if sixty subjects are available for an experiment, the experimenter could divide them into two groups by putting each of their names on a separate card, shuffling the cards, then dealing them into two equal piles. The assumption is that errors due to confounding variables will split evenly between the groups. The experimenter then exposes only one group to the independent variable. The group that is exposed to the independent variable is called the **experimental group**; the other is the **control group**.

Confounding Variable: A variable that, if not controlled, might affect the results of an experiment. Variables other than the independent variable that might affect the dependent variable.

Random Selection: A method for selecting subjects in which each individual had an equal chance of being chosen or assigned to a specific group.

Experimental Group: The group in an experiment that is exposed to the independent variable. For example, if the effect of a drug is being studied, only the experimental group would receive the drug. A second, control group, would not be given the drug.

Control Group: The group in an experiment that is not exposed to the independent variable and provides a reference point against which the experimental group can be compared.

■ Learning Check ■

Read the definition, then cover the right side and try to recite. Repeat.

Dependent Variable | Depends on what subject does; the variable presumed to be affected by the independent variable.

Confounding Variable | A variable other than the independent variable that might affect the dependent variable.

Control Group | The group in an experiment that is not exposed to the independent variable.

The experimental method is known as the cornerstone of psychological research because it is the only method that allows a researcher to demonstrate cause-effect relationships. By testing a subject's ability to recall a string of ten different numbers, after some have had four hours of sleep and others eight hours, we might find that those with more sleep recall an average of two or three more items than those who slept for four hours. Assuming we had adequate control of possible confounding variables, we could conclude that having less sleep *caused* the subjects who slept for four hours to recall less.

The Correlational Method

■ Learning Clue ■

Remember, correlation does not prove causation.

Correlation: A statistical method that is used to determine the extent to which two variables or events are related.

Correlation Coefficient: A mathematical index between −1 and +1 that describes the direction and magnitude of the relationship between two variables.

Though psychologists have proved ingenious at devising experiments to test all sorts of hypotheses, there are certain questions that defy experimentation. Scientists cannot manipulate the IQ, personality, or age of individual human subjects. Even if it were possible to do so, it could hardly be considered ethical. When it is not feasible or ethical to manipulate one variable to determine its effect on another, a researcher at least can determine if the two variables are related in some systematic way by correlating them. **Correlation** is a statistical method for determining the extent to which two variables are related.

The extent to which two variables are in fact related is expressed as a number called the **correlation coefficient**. Correlation coefficients vary between +1 and −1. The closer the number is to +1 or −1, the stronger the relationship. Thus, a correlation of −.87 would indicate a stronger relationship than +.5.

If your instructor gives a midterm and a final exam, she or he could use correlation to determine the relationship between the two tests. A strong positive correlation—say, anything above +.75—would indicate that students tended to maintain about the same relative position on both tests. Those that got high scores on the midterm also did well on the final; those that got low scores on the midterm also did poorly on the final. A correlation close to zero—say, anything between +.25 and −.25—would indicate little relationship between the two tests. A student's score on the midterm tells us nothing about how she or he did on the final. Finally, a strong negative correlation—say, −.75—would indicate that students showed a reversal in their relative position for the two tests. Those that got high scores on the midterm tended to get relatively low scores on the final, while those that did poorly on the midterm did well on the final.

Correlations can be used for predictive purposes. Suppose, for example, your instructor knows that over the past ten years there has always been a correlation somewhere between +.71 and +.85 between the midterm and final. In such a case, the instructor can roughly predict who will do well (and who will not) on the final.

In considering the correlational method, you should keep in mind that correlational analysis can be used to determine the degree of relationship between any two variables. For example, an experimenter can, and often will, calculate the correlation between an independent variable and a dependent variable. The main difference between a correlational study and an experimental one is that the former does not involve the manipulation of an independent variable. Consequently, unlike the experimental method, the correlational approach cannot demonstrate cause-and-effect relationships. Correlations tell us only that two variables change together in some systematic way. Though being outgoing may in fact be related to being a good salesperson, that does not mean that being outgoing *causes* one to be a good salesperson, or that being a good salesperson *causes* one to be outgoing. It simply means that people who are outgoing also tend to be good at sales—that the two qualities are related in some way.

To give another example, geese begin flying south about the same time children go back to school in the fall. The two events are correlated in that they vary together: when the geese fly, the children go back to school. But the children obviously do not cause the geese to fly south, nor do the geese cause the children to go back to school. For quite different reasons, the geese and the children exhibit a change in behavior about the same time each year. (For more on correlation, see Appendix A.)

The Observational Method

The observational method is often used to support the results of controlled experimentation. It is also used for the many cases where experimentation in a controlled laboratory setting is impractical. As its name suggests, the observational method involves careful and objective observation. Two major techniques, naturalistic observation and the case study method, illustrate the strengths and limitations of the observational method. In **naturalistic observation,** events are observed and recorded in their usual surroundings. To study the behavior of people at a wedding reception through naturalistic observation, one would carefully observe and record what people do. The relationship between drinking champagne and the eating of junk food might be studied, for instance, by recording how many glasses of champagne a person has and how many potato chips, nuts, pretzels, and other goodies a person eats. In such a study, one sacrifices the degree of precision and control of the laboratory but is able to obtain data in the actual situation in which it occurs. Behavior in the sterile lab might not be the same as when it occurs in the natural setting. On the other hand, measurements in the natural setting usually are not as precise as those that can be obtained in the laboratory. What is more, because there is no systematic manipulation of an independent variable in the naturalistic study, cause-effect relations cannot be ascertained.

Naturalistic Observation: A method of psychology in which behavior is studied by observing or watching events as they occur naturally.

In naturalistic observation, a psychologist observes and records events as they occur in a natural setting. Here the psychologist is observing through a one-way mirror so as not to interfere with the behavior of the individuals being observed.

■ Learning Clue ■

For each question: read, cover, try to recite. Repeat.

What do naturalistic observation and case studies have in common?

1. Both involve careful observation and recording of behavior.
2. Neither can be used to demontrate cause-effect relationships.

How do naturalistic observation and the case study differ?

1. In the case study, behavior is not necessarily observed in the natural setting.
2. In the case study, the observer actively interacts with subjects.

Case Study: A method of psychology that intensively explores the behavior of a single individual or specific group of individuals in great depth.

Psychologists in business and industry use naturalistic observation to study the behavior of employees without disrupting their work schedules and sacrificing productivity. Psychologists in the military use it to observe soldiers in combat. They have learned, for example, that in the heat of a battle most new recruits forget to fire their weapons. It is now well known that new recruits need considerable training, preparation, and simulated experiences if they are to be more than sitting ducks on the battlefield.

As an alternative to simply observing behavior in the setting in which it occurs, psychologists take a more active role by asking detailed questions and making extensive recordings of a single individual or a well-defined group of individuals in the **case study** method. There are two major differences between naturalistic observation and the case study. First, in the case study behavior is not necessarily observed in the natural setting. Instead, the subject or subjects may be observed in the psychologist's office, as Freud observed his patients in formulating his psychoanalytic theory. In a well-known case study of multiple personality, in which a young woman named Eve was found to have at least three distinct and very different personalities, practically all observations took place in the therapist's office. Although the therapist was able to observe Eve's different personalities during her therapy sessions, most of the data were obtained from Eve's statements and her response to careful questioning. A second major difference between the case study and naturalistic observation is that in the case study the observer actively interacts with the subjects of study, whereas in naturalistic observation the observer makes every attempt not to interfere with the behavior and events under study. And because the researcher does the questioning in the case study, what is asked and the information obtained may depend on the researcher's biases.

Survey Research

Survey Method: A research method in which a representative sample of individuals are asked to respond to a set of questions, so that the opinions, attitudes, and the like of a population can be studied.

Whereas the case study method uses careful questioning and observations to study a specific individual or class of individuals, the **survey method** uses questioning by telephone, mail, or face-to-face interviews to study people's beliefs, opinions, preferences, and attitudes. Surveys allow the researcher to collect a large amount of information quickly and efficiently. Asking people what they will do, especially if their only task is to respond to a preprinted questionnaire that asks them to circle "yes" or "no" or respond briefly to a series of questions, is a lot easier than observing how they actually behave. By surveying attitudes and the like, the psychologist often gains important insights into why people behave as they do. The relative ease with which survey questionnaires can be constructed makes them ideal for measuring a reaction to some event immediately after it has occurred. And, if done correctly, a survey study can allow a psychologist to make predictions: What products will people purchase? What television programs will they watch? What candidates will they vote for? How will they react to a new tax proposal?

A good example of the survey method can be found in a study of attitudes toward different styles of women's clothing (Harris, 1983). Subjects, 149 men and 184 women, were used to rate five pictures of a model wearing five clothing styles: formal skirt, formal pants, casual skirt, casual pants, and jeans. The subjects rated each style on each of the following dimensions: happy to sad; successful to unsuccessful; feminine to unfeminine; boring to interesting; attractive to unattractive; active to passive; intelligent to unintelligent; someone you would want as a friend to not want as a friend. Results revealed that a model was viewed by both male and female subjects as most happy, successful, feminine, interesting, attractive, intelligent, and wanted as a friend when she was wearing a formal skirt outfit and as least when wearing jeans. The model was also seen as most active when wearing pants as compared with a skirt.

The biggest problem for the psychologist using the survey method is determining which people to question. A survey of the driving attitudes of people who do not drive, for example, would be misleading. The first thing that must be done is to identify a **population** of interest—a group of individuals who can be classified together because they have certain characteristics in common—such as all people who drive, or all people who are married, or all who believe in God, all union members, all small business owners, all single people between eighteen and thirty-five, all rock fans, and so on. The survey is then given only to individuals in the population of interest.

It is not necessary to study an entire population, however. A good-sized **sample,** or selected subset of the population, if chosen carefully, can yield almost the same results as a whole population. (See Figure 1.8.) The important step is to ensure that the sample is **representative** of the larger population. One way of doing this is to use random selection in which each individual in the population has an equal chance of being selected. Another is to select individuals so as to achieve the same proportion of all important characteristics of the population. If the population of voters contains 45 percent women and 15 percent blacks, then the sample should also contain 45 percent women and 15 percent blacks, randomly selected from all women voters and black voters.

Surveys are used in business, industry, advertising, and politics. A supermarket chain conducts a survey of the shoppers in a local neighborhood to see whether they are satisfied with existing stores. The survey shows people are dissatisfied with the available selection of fruits and vegetables. The chain opens a new store in the neighborhood and puts an ad in the local paper claiming to have the widest selection of fresh fruits and vegetables.

A company that puts its money on the results of a survey can, however, lose it. The major problem with the survey approach is that what people say they will do and what they actually do are often not the same. Sometimes

Population: A group of organisms that can be categorized together because they hold certain characteristics in common.

Sample: A subset or portion of a population.

Representative Sample: A sample that reflects all the major characteristics of the population from which it was drawn.

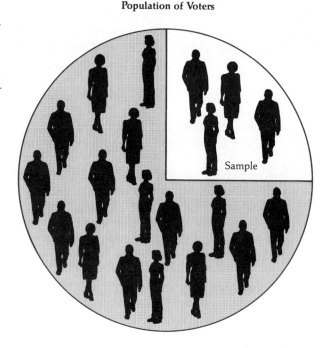

Figure 1.8 Population and Sample. A sample is a carefully selected subset of a larger population—a group of individuals who can be classified together because they hold certain characteristics in common.

Population of Voters

Sample

people respond to a survey item according to their preferences, rather than the way things actually are. Sometimes they try to please the interviewer by responding the way they think the interviewer would like them to. The prospective automobile buyer says he prefers the larger, more luxurious model, but then goes and buys the smaller one for economy. After all, he thinks, they can't hold you to your word, and anyway, surveys are supposed to be confidential. Survey results can also be wrong because people sometimes simply change their minds. Today they prefer luxury, tomorrow economy. Although surveys of well-selected samples are accurate more often than not, they can be wrong.

In the chapters ahead, we will explore, in detail, psychology's theories, findings, and methods. We will explore many new ideas as well as expand on many that were covered in this chapter.

LEARNING FRAMEWORK

I. The work of psychologists touches our lives in many ways. (Review: *Figure 1.1*)
   A. In the primary and secondary schools, some psychologists work directly with students, teachers, administrators, and parents; others conduct research and participate in the training of educators. (Review: *School Psychologist; Educational Psychologist*)
   B. In business and industry, psychologists play a role in job selection, company organizational structure, product design, marketing, and advertising. (Review: *Industrial Psychologist; Organizational Psychologist; Engineering Psychologist; Consumer Psychologist; Social Psychologist*)

    C. Some psychologists work in mental health settings—participating in the treatment and diagnosis of mental disorders; others apply their knowledge to problems of physical health; and still others conduct research that has implications to a variety of practical problems. (Review: *Clinical Psychologist; Experimental Psychologist; Medical Psychologist*)

    D. Psychologists also study how our physical environment affects the individual and apply their knowledge to the law and the criminal justice system. (Review: *Environmental Psychologist; Forensic Psychologist*)

II. Seven viewpoints have played a major role in psychology's development as a science from 1879 to the present. (Review: *Figure 1.6*)

    A. The structuralists tried to discover the basic structures or elements of consciousness. (Review: *Introspection; Wundt*)

    B. Functionalists emphasized the mind's function in survival. (Review: *James*)

    C. Gestalt psychologists believed it was incorrect to view the mind in terms of an assembly of structures or functions. (Review: *Gestalt School of Psychology*)

    D. Freudian psychology focused on mental processes of which the individual was unaware. (Review: *Unconscious*)

    E. Behaviorism rejected the mind as a legitimate object of scientific study. (Review: *Watson; Radical Behaviorism*)

    F. Humanistic psychologists said that in their studies of hidden mental forces and observable behavior, psychologists had lost sight of the person. (Review: *Humanistic School*)

    G. Social learning played a major role in the reintroduction of mental processes into mainstream psychology. (Review: *Cognitions; Cognitive Psychology*)

III. The different psychological methods have unique advantages and disadvantages. (Review: *Figure 1.7*)

    A. Experimentation allows one to demonstrate causal relationships, but it is not always feasible to manipulate variables in a controlled laboratory setting. (Review: *Independent Variable; Dependent Variable; Confounding Variable*)

    B. Correlation can't demonstrate cause-effect, but does allow one to determine the degree of relatedness between two variables. (Review: *Correlation Coefficient*)

    C. Naturalistic observation has the advantage of studying behavior in its usual surroundings but sacrifices the precise control of the laboratory. Case studies involve in-depth study of a single individual or group. What is obtained from them may represent a researcher's bias. (Review: *Naturalistic Observation; Case Study*)

    D. Surveys sample people's attitudes and preferences. They can provide a lot of information quickly, but great care must be taken in selecting an appropriate sample. (Review: *Population; Sample*)

PART

II

Developmental and Biological Processes

CHAPTER 2

Human Development

Chapter Outline

Which is more important for the infant to receive from its mother, nourishment or cuddling? The answer, provided by research, might surprise you. Baby monkeys were taken from their mothers shortly after birth and placed in a cage with artificial mothers. Each baby monkey received two "mothers," one made of bare wire and one covered with soft terrycloth (see Figure 2.1). Some of the monkeys were fed from baby bottles built into the wire mother; the others from bottles attached to the cloth mother. Both groups were permitted to spend as much times as they wished with either mother. The researchers found that both groups of monkeys spent more time with the terrycloth mother, no matter which mother fed them. When they were frightened, monkeys who were fed by the wire mother ran to the terrycloth mother. Apparently the warmth and pleasant feel of the soft cloth was more important to them than the nourishment they got from the wire mother. It appears that in the formation of emotional ties, pleasant physical contact is more important than food (Harlow, 1958). Indeed, human babies tend to form their strongest **attachments**—an enduring affectional bond between two people that produces a desire for close contact—to caretakers who cuddle, talk, and interact with them. The person who merely feeds or cares for a baby's basic needs is less important (Bowlby, 1969; Sroufe, 1985).

Attachment: An enduring affectional bond between two people that produces a desire for close contact.

Attachment is one of the many fascinating topics in **developmental psychology**, the study of how people develop and change with age. Developmental psychologists are interested in all the changes—physical, personality, social, and cognitive—that occur with age, from the moment of conception to death. Their subject cuts across just about every area of psychological inquiry that you will read about in this book. Many of the questions developmental psychologists ask may also be questions you have asked, or will ask at some time in your life. What are some of the factors to consider in choosing an occupation? How important is an intimate relationship for adults? Is one method of raising children better than another? When does a person reach the prime of life? How can older adults lead productive

Developmental Psychology: The study of how individuals develop and change with age; the scientific study of how individuals and psychological processes develop over the life span, and the factors influencing their development.

Figure 2.1 Harlow's Monkeys. No matter which mother fed them, baby monkeys spent more time with the soft, terrycloth mother. Apparently, the warmth and pleasant feel of a soft cloth was more important to them than the nourishment they received from the wire mother that fed them.

and rewarding lives? The changes you will experience with age will have a deep impact on your daily life.

Developmental psychology also is of relevance to a number of occupational pursuits outside of psychology. Teachers in the primary and secondary schools are interested in how children grow and develop during the school years, so that, among other reasons, they can present material when a child is ready and capable of learning it. Developmental psychology is relevant to nurses and physicians, especially those who specialize in the treatment of children (Masek et al., 1985). In fact, any worker involved in the care of the very young or the very old—from those that staff nurseries to those that staff nursing homes—can benefit by understanding the unique problems and abilities of the age group with whom they work (Birren, 1983). In business and industry, it is important for a supervisor or a manager to understand the unique needs of employees as they develop and change from young adulthood through the preretirement years (Dennis, 1984). Developmental psychology is also of interest to legislators and policy makers in government who are concerned with the best interests of children and their families, maximizing productivity in adults, and dealing with the problems of an aging population (Miller, 1983; Neugarten, 1983).

Studying human development may help you to better understand yourself and others, to anticipate future problems, and perhaps to solve some of your current difficulties. But developmental psychology will not give you hard and fast rules or formulas for living. In fact, just as people change over the life span, theories of development change over time—in response to new research findings, shifts of emphasis within the discipline, or changes in the perceived needs of society. Just as change is a normal part of growth, change is also a part of scientific progress.

In this chapter we consider both traditional and modern views of how people change over the entire life span, from conception to death. In so doing we will examine human development from two perspectives. From one perspective we will learn about the changes that belong to different periods of stages of life. From the other we will learn about the changes that belong to different aspects of living: developmental changes of the body, of personality, of thinking, of social relationship, and of moral development.

MAJOR THEORIES OF HUMAN DEVELOPMENT

Developmental theories provide an overall perspective and a framework for understanding the changes that occur over the life span. Prominent among these are Sigmund Freud's theory of personality development, Erik Erikson's theory of social development, and Jean Piaget's theory of cognitive development. Also important is Lawrence Kohlberg's theory of moral development. Each of these theorists believed that development proceeded in **stages**—a specific ordered sequence. They believed that all people go through the same sequence of age-related changes and that each stage in this fixed sequence involves a unique set of challenges.

Stage: A distinct period of development within a sequence of levels.

Freud's Stages of Psychosexual Development

Freud's belief that early experiences have lifelong effects on a person's personality was briefly presented in the first chapter. Freud also believed that unconscious, animalistic impulses are the origin of a person's potential conflicts with everyday reality. In Freud's view, each person, in the first years of life, passes through stages of development that address these impulses and their consequences. From these basic assumptions, Freud evolved a complete theory of human personality, to be discussed in Chapter 12.

Freud was the first theorist to emphasize the idea that development occurs in a fixed sequence of separate stages. He argued that there are five stages through which each person passes in the course of personality development. He called these the oral, anal, phallic, latency, and genital stages.

The Oral Stage. Like anyone who carefully observes the behavior of babies, Freud noticed how much an infant's mouth serves as focal point for exploring and enjoying the world. A baby uses its mouth to experience food, toys, fingers, and noises for self-expression; from this, Freud saw a period of basic need for oral gratification that drives an infant to interact with the environment. This first stage he called the **oral stage,** spanning the first eighteen months of life. During this period an individual seems dominated by the need to obtain pleasure through sucking, biting, and other activities with the lips, mouth, or gums.

Oral Stage: The first of Freud's stages of psychosexual development (first eighteen months of life), which is dominated by a need to obtain gratification of the mouth, tongue, and gums.

Freud also observed that some people seemed to get stuck—or *fixated*—

at one of these stages, through having had too much or too little success with these gratifications. (For instance, a baby might have been fed too much, or been denied food in a very frustrating fashion.) In later life, long after they had outgrown a focus on this form of gratification, these people might be inwardly, or unconsciously, focused on the pleasures of that stage. For example, they might focus on food, on making mouth noises, on aggressive biting behavior, or on a dependent need for constant emotional nurturing, as standard ways of comforting or defending themselves against moments of anxiety.

The Anal Stage. Freud also observed very young children focusing, in a comparable way, on bowel movements as a primitive form of self-assertion; this also involves the child in further conflicts arising from the family's and society's pressure on the child to control bowel movements (Freud, 1925). This second stage, from about two to three years of age, Freud called the **anal stage**—the years of toilet training. He theorized that a child having trouble outgrowing or successfully controlling the challenges of this stage might later be inwardly focused on "anal" behavior; he or she might hold back on performance of various kinds, hoard personal goods with excessive protectiveness, or seek a life of excessive cleanliness.

Anal Stage: The second of Freud's stages of psychosexual development (ages two to three), which is dominated by a need to obtain gratification through bowel movements.

The Phallic Stage. During the **phallic stage** (ages three to five or six), Freud saw the individual becoming acutely aware of sex differences and learning that manipulation of the genitals, the focus of this stage, can provide pleasurable sensations. The major growth challenge at this stage is to lay the foundation for the development of an appropriate sexual identity, as defined in relation to one's mother and one's father.

At this stage, according to Freud, the child becomes aware of bodily gratification from contact with parents; the child also learns to accept bodily similarities to and differences from both parents, as appropriate to his or her sex. In this process—described in more detail in the chapter on personality—the child learns to take the appropriate parent as a model for a personal role in life, and to be comfortable with the guidance and authority offered by either parent. To Freud, problems with resolving these challenges seemed to be the origin of sexual identity confusions and of excessive concern for sexual activity and vanity (self-love).

Phallic Stage: The third of Freud's stages of psychosexual development (ages three to five or six), in which the individual becomes acutely aware of sex differences.

The Latency Period. In Freud's system, the ages of six to twelve are a quiet and relatively unchallenging **latency period,** a time of consolidating previous experiences. Since expressive energy in this period is not focused on any center of physical gratification, Freud did not see the latency period as a source of later "hang-ups" in itself, rather, he considered it a time of growth based on how successfully a child had resolved earlier challenges. A person with what Freud saw as sexual identity problems might be reluctant emotionally to leave this period for the next one, however.

Latency Period: The fourth of Freud's stages of psychosexual development (ages six to twelve), which is a period of crystallization of the personality.

The Genital Stage. The period of the awakening of mature sexuality, from 12 to adulthood, Freud named the **genital stage**—the time when a person accepts a sexual identity and interacts with a sexual partner (Freud, 1933). In Freud's personal view, this would lead to maturity in the form of a relatively stable love relationship, leading to marriage and having children.

Genital Stage: The fifth and last of Freud's stages of psychosexual development (ages twelve to adulthood), which is characterized by an awakening of sexual interests and mature sexuality.

Table 2.1 Freud's Stages of Psychosexual Development

Stage	Focus	Age Range	Problems That May Result
Oral	Mouth, tongue, gums	0–18 months	Aggressive biting behavior (including verbal biting such as sharp sarcasm) and immature dependency.
Anal	Anal area	2–3	Hoarding; excessive cleanliness.
Phallic	Genitals	3–5 or 6	Sexual identity confusion.
Latency	Consolidating previous experiences	6–12	None, as this period is not a center of physical gratification.
Genital	Genitals	12–adulthood	Failure to develop mature love and sexual relationships.

Any problems in achieving this Freud attributed to difficulty with the challenges of the first three stages, complicated by the complex demands of adult life. Freud had no systematic theory of stages describing passage through the adult years. (Table 2.1 provides a summary of Freud's stages.)

Erikson's Stages of Psychosocial Development

Many early students of human development were guided by Freud's theory of cumulative stages. Indeed, Erik Erikson, who began his career by studying the work of Freud, extended the theory by focusing on the social forces in the environment. Erikson developed a theory of psychosocial stages, as he called them, that shape the individual's development at different periods of the life span (Erikson 1950, 1963, 1972). He also went beyond Freud's genital stage, which described only the transition to early adulthood: he emphasized that developmental changes continue throughout the life span, stretching from birth all the way to death. Erikson proposed as his main idea that there are eight major developmental crises associated with each of eight major stages of development. The crisis for each stage represents a collision of conflicting motives; facing and resolving these creates a turning point in the life of the individual. Meeting the crisis paves the way for a successful entry into the next stage. Failure to resolve a crisis at any stage impedes the individual's progress to a more mature level of development and may lead to enduring personality problems. For example, if a helpless young child cannot develop a basis for trusting the adults on whom he or she is dependent, it may prove very difficult in later years to trust another person in an intimate relationship.

Because the way one handles a crisis at one stage may affect the quality of life at another, the stages of development are interconnected. And with each new stage, crises from the past may reappear. Thus, inability to form a trusting relationship with a parental figure may make it difficult for an older child to learn from other adults at school.

Erikson's theory helps us to understand the impact of early stages of development on those of the later years of life. Table 2.2 summarizes his eight stages of psychosocial development and the unique crises that each stage entails.

Erik Erikson. Proposed eight major stages of development spanning birth through old age.

Table 2.2 Erikson's Stages of Psychosocial Development

Stage and Approximate Age	Crisis or Challenge	Consequences of Failure to Meet Challenge
1. First year	Develop a sense of trust	Mistrust of others
2. Second to third year	Develop a sense of autonomy	Shame and doubt
3. Third to fifth year	Develop a sense of initiative	Guilt
4. Sixth to twelfth year	Develop a sense of industry (competition)	Feelings of inferiority
5. Twelfth to eighteenth year	Develop a sense of identity (Who am I?)	Identity confusion
6. Early adulthood	Develop an intimate relationship	Isolation
7. Middle adulthood	Provide for future generations	Self-absorption, stagnation
8. Later maturity	Develop a sense of integrity	Despair

Source: Adapted from E. H. Erikson, *Childhood and society* (New York: Norton, 1963).

The first crisis, which spans the first year of life, is that of learning to trust others. Helpless and totally dependent, the infant must learn to rely on others for nourishment, love, and protection. If let down by parents who are inconsistent or unreliable, the infant may develop an attitude of mistrust— an enduring tendency to suspect and fear others. The supervisor who watches over the shoulder of every employee is an example of such a person. But with consistent and dependable care from an adult, the infant develops a sense of trust, which provides the foundation for later stages of growth.

Having learned to trust others, the next challenge for the developing two- to three-year-old infant is to develop a sense of self-trust or autonomy during the second stage of development. A child who is "overprotected," prevented from standing on his or her own two feet and not allowed to function independently, even if it means an occasional stumble, may develop a sense of shame and doubt. But given the freedom to try and fail and function independently insofar as she or he is capable, the child develops a

The challenge for the 2–3 year old, according to Erikson, is to develop a sense of self-trust and autonomy.

sense of autonomy and the foundation for greater levels of independence in the future.

In the third to fifth year, the child faces the challenge of learning to initiate activities on his or her own—to develop a sense of initiative. Thwarting the child's efforts to choose what to play or how to explore the world can crush a budding initiative. The child develops an enduring tendency to passively wait for direction from others and experiences a sense of guilt. But with enough freedom to choose and decide, the child develops a foundation for assertiveness and self-confidence.

Then, from age six to twelve, the child meets the challenge of acquiring basic life skills (e.g., academic, social, athletic) in order to develop a firm sense of self-competence, or industry as Erikson called it. Feeling competent then paves the way for mastering the issues of adolescence. One of Erikson's most noted concepts is the "identity crisis" faced by adolescents. In looking beyond the family, a young person compares his or her behavior patterns with those of peers and others in the outside world. Erikson sees this process as forcing a young person to make decisions about where to "fit in" and about "who I am"—thus constructing a formal identity for dealing with the world. Most young people are still left with some indecisions about independence and trust, carried over from earlier periods; depending on their severity, these can create conflicts and a crisis of confidence about what identity or role seems appropriate. Difficulties in reaching a settlement on this can lead a person to question his or her role, purpose, or sense of self-worth in facing new crises of adulthood.

The young adult's primary task (Stage 6) is to find intimacy with others, without which one faces the pain of isolation and loneliness. Successful resolution of the intimacy crisis, giving oneself to another in an interdependent relationship, paves the way for a new level of giving of oneself in the middle adult years. The individual may raise a family, participate in community functions, or contribute to society through productive work. Success or difficulty in one's immediate family relationships will impact on how a person copes with the challenge of middle adulthood—that of contributing to the next generation or to one's society as a whole. If the individual becomes self-absorbed and preoccupied with personal concerns, this can be a poor foundation for meeting the last of the eight crises of development. In the final crisis, that of later maturity, the individual reviews his or her life for good or bad, attempting to gain satisfaction from the challenges successfully met. Here one may find despair or a sense of success, which gives him or her the strength to accept death and a life well lived. An individual who has faced and met earlier crises can face the later years with the feeling that his or her life has been fruitful. The last years of life can be experienced with a sense of satisfaction and accomplishment.

From Erikson's theory, one can see the continuity of development over the life span. The theory also reveals the dramatic changes and transitions that occur during the years of adulthood.

Piaget's Theory of Cognitive Development

Of the major developmental theories, perhaps none has generated more research than that of Piaget. Piaget's cognitive theory focused on the devel-

Jean Piaget. *Proposed four stages of cognitive development.*

opment of the mental processes—logical thought, problem-solving, and understanding the physical world (Piaget, 1952, 1970). Because psychologists are interested in the growth of these cognitive processes, we will examine Piaget's theory in detail. Fundamental to Piaget's theory is the assumption that cognitive development provides the foundation for the development of other types of behaviors. For example, to develop give-and-take skills in a social relationship requires the ability to see the thinking pattern that emerges from another person's point of view. This ability, according to Piaget, requires an advancement to a new stage of cognitive maturity beyond simple egocentric thinking (which assumes that others view the world as does oneself), characteristic of two- and three-year-old children.

For Piaget, cognitive development begins with an inborn tendency to organize experiences into meaningful patterns, which he called **schemata** (singular—**schema**). A schema is an organized pattern of behavior or thought. For the infant, such a pattern can best be seen as a mental representation of a sequence of related behavior—a mental program for action. For example, the infant reflex action of sucking a nipple becomes organized into a schematic sequence of behavior. Thumb sucking soon becomes possible due to the program for action established by the mental representation of sucking for food. In a sense, a schema is like a mental filing system in which related information is organized together. A schema is also like a set of mental instructions for responding in a particular way in a given circumstance. For example, events may be organized into those that bring comfort and those that bring discomfort. When those that bring discomfort are encountered, the infant reacts with a programmed sequence of avoidance or withdrawal responses—crying or wiggling, for instance.

According to Piaget, schemata can be acquired or modified in two ways. The learner might integrate new experiences into an existing schema, a pro-

Schemata (singular—Schema): Organized patterns of behavior or thought; a cognitive framework or mental representation of a sequence of related behaviors.

Assimilation: Incorporating new experiences into existing organized patterns of behavior or thought (schemata).

Accommodation: The development of a new schema (organized pattern of thought or behavior) or modification of an existing one.

cess called **assimilation.** For example, the infant may apply his innate sucking reflex to a fingertip or corner of a blanket or any object touching the lips. Or using the process of **accommodation,** the learner might develop a new schema or modify an existing one. An object too large to fit the infant's mouth may force the infant to open wider, or to grasp or nuzzle it in some new kind of action. Thus, a new schema may be formed or the existing schema may be expanded to permit actions with a wider range of objects or situations. The infant's experiences with colors also illustrate assimilation and accommodation. For example, orange may be assimilated into a schema that includes all shades of red. Or it may become the basis for a new schema into which shades of orange can be filed independently of red.

Through assimilation and accommodation, cognitive development occurs in what Piaget believed to be a definite ordered sequence of four qualitatively different stages, each building upon the previous one. These he called sensorimotor, preoperational, concrete operations, and formal operations.

Sensorimotor Stage: Piaget's first stage of cognitive development (zero to two years) in which organized patterns of behavior and thought (schemata) are acquired through sensory impressions and motor activities.

Object Permanence: The ability to be aware of the existence of objects even when they are not within the range of immediate sensory experience.

The Sensorimotor Stage. During the first stage of cognitive development, the **sensorimotor stage** (through approximately age two), the infant acquires schemata through sensory impressions—sights, sounds, tastes, and the like—and motor activities—grasping, holding, sucking, and so on. The infant responds to sensory sensations, but does not interpret them, and defines experience through motor activities; hence the term, sensorimotor.

One important milestone in the sensorimotor stage is the point at which an infant will search for a hidden object. At first, infants seem to be aware of only thoses objects within the range of their immediate experience. If they can't see, hear, feel, smell, taste, or touch an object, they act as if it doesn't exist. Thus, they show surprise, as Piaget (1929) observed in his own children, when a hidden object is brought into view, and take great delight in games of peek-a-boo. But before the sensorimotor stage is complete, the infant develops the concept of **object permanence:** the idea that objects continue to exist even when not directly seen or heard.

The notion of object permanence is supported by experimentation. In a standard experimental procedure, an infant is shown an object, which is

Figure 2.2 Object Permanence. In a game of peek-a-boo, this child searches for his mother's hidden face, indicating that he has developed the concept of object permanence—the idea that objects continue to exist even when not directly seen or heard.

then hidden behind an upright screen or cloth (see Figure 2.2). Infants five months or younger will not search for the hidden object, suggesting that they cease to be aware of its existence as soon as it disappears from view. By the age of eight or nine months, infants will respond to this same maneuver by reaching and searching for the hidden object, indicating that they can represent it mentally, without the aid of an immediate sensory impression (Dunst et al., 1982). With this discovery of object permanence, the infant begins to develop a concept of self as separate from others. Instead of everything being merged into one, the notion of an "I" or "me" that exists as a stable entity, independent of the rest of the world, begins to emerge.

The Preoperational Stage. Following the sensorimotor period comes the second or **preoperational stage,** which begins about age two and lasts approximately until age six or seven. During this stage, the child acquires images (i.e., mental representations for objects) but lacks operations (i.e., the mental activities that allow for manipulation and coordination of schemata and images). Thus the term, preoperational. The child has imagination, but no logical reasoning. The child can think about horses, though none are in sight. And without logical reasoning, a broomstick becomes a horse for exploring the pretend wilderness in the front yard.

It is during this preoperational stage when children are **egocentric** in their thinking, unable to see things from another's perspective. It is also during this stage when they become afraid of the dark or of their own shadows: an imaginary monster can be just as frightening as some real threats. Even the dreams of a preoperational child seem real. Given their vivid imaginations, it is not surprising that preoperational children engage in **animistic thinking,** or the attribution of life and consciousness to inanimate objects. I (your author) can recall a personal experience as a preoperational lad of four and a half years of age. I was deathly afraid of my father's electric car polisher, thinking it was alive and might buff me on purpose. One Saturday afternoon I noticed it motionless on the floor, taking a rest. My father had decided to grab a sandwich. Devilishly, I decided to kick it. In so doing, I accidentally turned it on causing it to move directly toward me! My scream was so bloodcurdling my father must have thought the sky had fallen.

Despite their fertile imaginations, preoperational children lack the ability to think in terms of abstractions. Their representations are **concrete**. That of a horse is a specific horse, not the general idea of a horse. The former is real and tangible; the latter, an abstract idea. Thus, the child can mentally represent a horse and a car, but not deal with them in terms of the abstraction: means of transportation. The concrete quality of a preoperational child's representations can lead to some difficult questions for parents.

Concrete Operations. During the third stage of cognitive development, **concrete operations,** which roughly spans ages seven to twelve, the child's thinking continues to be concrete, but subject to mental activities that allow for manipulation and coordination of schemata and images (i.e., operations). And, with the ability to think logically, the concrete operations child can begin to master imaginary fears of monsters and goblins (and electric polishers that chase little children). The child can perform mental tasks such as interpreting a simple map (Anooshian & Young, 1981). In this stage, too,

Preoperational Stage: Piaget's second stage of cognitive development (ages two to six or seven), during which the individual has difficulty taking the vantage point of others (i.e., is egocentric).

Egocentric Thinking: Assuming others view the world as oneself, and an inability to take the view of another.

Animistic Thinking: Attributing life and consciousness to inanimate objects or natural phenomena.

Concrete Thinking: Thinking in terms of specifics rather than in terms of abstractions.

Concrete Operations: Piaget's 3rd stage of cognitive development (ages seven to eleven or twelve) in which the individual learns the principle of conservation.

the child gains a better understanding of other people's points of view, realizing that not everybody sees things in the same way.

One of the major advances in the concrete operations stage is the development of the concept of **conservation:** the idea that certain properties of objects, such as volume or mass, remain constant, despite transformations in the object's appearance. In the typical demonstration of conservation, a child is shown two equal-sized glasses of water (see Figure 2.3). After acknowledging that the two are equal, the child is asked to pour the contents of one glass into a third taller, slimmer glass. A child in the concrete operations stage will quickly recognize that the tall glass contains the same amount of water as the short glass. But the preoperational child will usually insist that the tall glass has more water. Similarly, a child in the concrete operations stage will realize that there are just as many pennies in a row of twelve, spaced two inches apart as in a row of twelve spaced one inch apart. The preoperational child, by contrast, will almost always insist that the more spaced-out row has more (McLaughlin, 1981).

One possible explanation for the older child's ability to grasp the principle of conservation is that, in being able to manipulate representations, the older child can visualize the object in its earlier condition, an ability that Piaget referred to as **reversibility.** For example, the older child can mentally reverse the process of moving the pennies closer together or farther apart. Preoperational children may not be able to perform such mental tricks. A second explanation is that the older child has the ability to consider more than one characteristic of an object at the same time, a skill Piaget called **decentration.**

One thing children in the concrete operations stage still cannot do, due to their limited ability to abstract, is apply general rules to specific situations. Thus, parents and teachers should not try to teach general problem-solving strategies or moral concepts to children of this age and expect them to be able to apply such ideas in their daily lives. To cite one case in point, a teacher wanted students not to become discouraged at occasional bullying from older children. To encourage them, the teacher read the class stories of

Conservation: In Piaget's theory, the ability to recognize that certain properties (e.g., weight, volume) of an object or group of objects remain the same despite changes in the object's shape, length, or position.

Reversibility: The capacity to mentally reverse an operation and understand what a condition was like before it was changed.

Decentration: The ability of a child to consider more than one characteristic of an object at the same time.

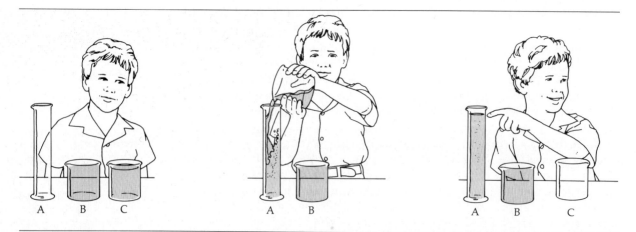

Figure 2.3 *During the stage of concrete operations, the developing child learns that certain properties of objects (for example, volume or mass) remain constant despite transformations in the object's appearance. In thinking that the taller glass has more water, this child has not yet acquired the concept of conservation.*

■ **Learning Check** ■

For each type of thinking listed on the left, read the definition and associated stage of cognitive development. Then cover the right side and try to recite. Repeat.

Animistic Thinking	Attribution of life and consciousness to inanimate objects (preoperational).
Decentration	The ability to consider more than one characteristic of an object at the same time (concrete operations).
Reversibility	The capacity to mentally reverse an operation and understand what it was like before it was changed (concrete operations).

how the faster, stronger person isn't always the winner. Nobody seemed to get the point. Then in a history lesson the teacher told of how the mighty Spanish armada, 140 ships strong, was defeated by 30 small English ships. "Though greatly outnumbered and outgunned," explained the teacher, "the English ships chased the giant armada across the seas until it was no more." Then the teacher asked, "What are we talking about here?" "Battleships and wars," was the reply.

Formal Operations. By the final stage of cognitive development, the stage of **formal operations,** children develop the capacity to think in terms of abstraction and apply the formal rules of logic. For example, a formal operations child can deduce from the general to the specific, as follows: Dogs have four legs. Fido is a dog. Therefore, Fido has four legs. During this stage, mental operations become conventional, or formal, from the standpoint of the adult. Indeed, formal operations is the stage in which the child finally thinks and reasons in the same way as does an adult.

The stage of formal operations also brings the capacity to think hypothetically—of conceiving possibilities beyond those of present reality. The adolescent can wonder, "What if?" and explore the various alternatives. For instance, she or he can realistically evaluate the negative effects of drugs and alcohol or the consequences of having sexual intercourse without a contraceptive. Table 2.3 summarizes Piaget's four stages of cognitive development.

Formal Operations: Piaget's fourth and final stage of cognitive development, which begins by age eleven or twelve and in which the individual develops the ability to deal with abstractions, form hypotheses, solve problems systematically, and consider hypothetical possibilities.

Table 2.3   Piaget's Stages of Cognitive Development

Stage	Approximate Age Range	Cognitive Functions
Sensorimotor	0–2 years	Innate reflexes (capacity to move around; elementary communication; mental images); object permanence.
Preoperational	2–6 or 7 years	Development of speech; beginning of the ability to use language symbolically; animistic thinking (objects seen as alive or awake); egocentric orientation (inability to adopt the perspective of others).
Concrete Operations	7–12 years	Basic calculations (multiplication, etc.); development of logical reasoning; conservation; reversibility; decentration.
Formal Operations	12 years and beyond	Ability to reason from general to specific and vice versa; ability to consider hypothetical possibilities.

Piaget's work in cognitive development led him to consider a similar approach to how people develop a sense of morals. It was from some of Piaget's ideas that Lawrence Kohlberg worked out a theory concerning stages of moral development.

Kohlberg's Stages of Moral Development

If your parents were sick and starving, would it be morally wrong to steal food for them? If an untested drug seemed to hold promise in the treatment of your terminally ill grandfather, but it was banned in the United States, would you be wrong to smuggle it into the country? These are among the questions that Lawrence Kohlberg (1963, 1969, 1976) asked young people in an effort to determine how humans develop morally. Kohlberg's studies led him to propose that moral development proceeds according to a specific sequence of stages.

Kohlberg identified three major stages of moral development. Each stage in turn was divided into two levels. In the first and lowest stage, **preconventional morality,** rewards and punishments are the primary determinants of morality. At level one of this stage, moral behavior is that which avoids punishments; at level two it is that which gains rewards. During this preconventional morality stage, acts that are rewarded are considered good; acts that are punished are considered bad. Turning in homework is good because teachers praise such behavior; fighting is bad because it gets one in trouble. By the end of the first stage, children have learned to follow rules, but they obey them only out of self-interest. ("If I follow the rules, I'll get rewarded.")

After passing through the preconventional level, the child moves on to the stage of **conventional morality,** a stage in which he or she begins to take the intentions and opinions of others into account. Children at the first level of this stage evaluate behavior based on good or bad intentions and approval and disapproval from others rather than consequences: moral behavior is well-intended behavior that meets with approval from others. During the second level of conventional morality, individuals interpret rules rigidly and literally, without regard to fairness. They follow rules not out of fear of punishment, but because "that's the rule."

As individuals mature from later childhood to the period of adolescence and adulthood, they may move on to Kohlberg's third and final stage of

Preconventional Morality: According to Kohlberg, the first stage of moral development (typical of children up to about age nine), in which rewards and punishments are primary determinants of morality.

Conventional Morality: The stage in Kohlberg's theory of moral development (ages eight or nine to twenty) in which society's rules are followed because they are the rules.

Lawrence Kohlberg. *Proposed three major stages of moral development.*

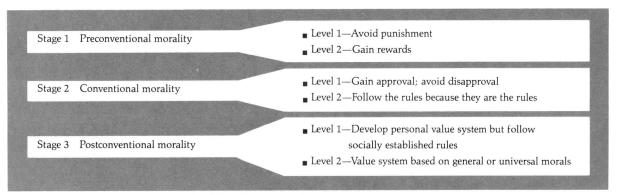

Figure 2.4 Schematic Summary of Kohlberg's Stages of Moral Development.

morality. They begin to challenge the validity of rules. During the first level of this **postconventional morality,** the person develops a definite system of values, one that is not necessarily consistent with formal law. While most postconventional adults feel bound to obey the socially established rules, they may hope to see many of them changed legally. Kohlberg believes that a few adults reach even beyond this to the second level in which they formulate a new value system based on general or universal morals. At this point a person may develop a basis for disobeying a bad law in the name of a higher one. Moral guidance now comes from within rather than from without (Kohlberg, 1976). (Figure 2.4 summarizes Kohlberg's stages.)

Although the idea that moral development is age-related is generally accepted, Kohlberg's contention that it unfolds in a specific sequence has come under heavy fire (Ferguson & Rule, 1982; Grueneich, 1982). The methodology of his work is accused of bias and unnecessary complexity, making it difficult for other researchers to repeat Kohlberg's findings (Kurtines & Greif, 1974). And, as is the problem with all stage theories, the idea that people pass through the same sequence of stages in an orderly fashion has been challenged, due to a number of contradictory findings (Smillie, 1982; Walker, 1982). A possible factor in such contradictions is that there may be differences in the morality of men and women at the higher levels (Gilligan, 1982). Nevertheless, like each of the other major theories, Kohlberg's has helped to provide an overview of certain major aspects of human development. With these organizing perspectives to help us focus on some key questions, we can proceed to some of the particulars for each of the major periods of the life span from conception to death.

Postconventional Morality: According to Kohlberg, a level of moral development in which the individual begins to challenge the validity of rules and develops a personal value system.

DEVELOPMENT FROM CONCEPTION TO BIRTH

Heredity, environment, and the interaction between them shape development from the moment of **conception,** or fertilization of the female egg (*ovum*) by the male sperm (see Figure 2.5). The single cell that results from

Conception: The union of sperm and egg.

Figure 2.5 The Moment of Conception.

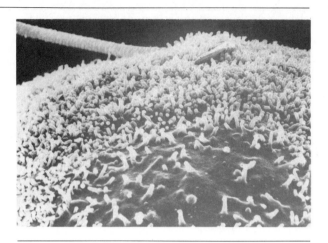

this union of egg and sperm, called a *zygote*, soon begins to divide into two, then four, then eight cells, and so on to make a complete organism. Yet this growth takes place within an environment that depends on the mother's health, nutrition, and behavior and so varies from mother to mother. In this section we look first at the biological foundations of human development. We will then examine environmental influences during the nine months of development between conception and birth, called prenatal development.

The Genetic Foundations of Development

Through heredity our biologically based characteristics are transmitted to new generations. The basic unit of heredity is the **gene,** a microscopic structure composed of a biochemical substance called **deoxyribonucleic acid (DNA).** DNA contains the information, or code, that governs the functioning and growth of the cell. Genes are carried on larger bodies called **chromosomes** (see Figure 2.6), which are found in the nucleus of every cell in the body. In humans, all cells, except for the female egg and male sperm, contain twenty-three pairs of chromosomes—a total of forty-six.

Gene: The basic unit of heredity composed of a biochemical substance called deoxyribonucleic acid (DNA).

Deoxyribonucleic Acid (DNA): The chemicals of which genes are made.

Chromosomes: Particles containing genes, which are found in the nucleus of every cell in the body.

Figure 2.6 This figure illustrates the 23 pairs of human chromosomes. In males the 23rd pair consists of an X chromosome and a Y (XY); while in females, the 23rd pair is an X and an X (XX).

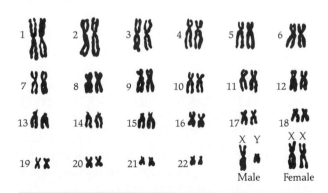

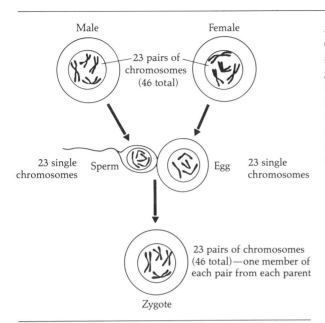

Figure 2.7 *Unlike other cells, the sex cells (egg and sperm) contain only 23 single chromosomes, rather than 23 pairs. At conception, the 23 unpaired chromosomes from each parent unite to form 23 pairs containing the full 46 chromosomes.*

In normal cell division, each of the forty-six chromosomes forms a replica of itself. The cell then divides in half, leaving two virtually identical cells, each with forty-six chromosomes. The sex cells, however—the egg and the sperm—contain only twenty-three single chromosomes, rather than twenty-three *pairs*; that is, half the normal number of chromosomes (see Figure 2.7). At conception, the twenty-three unpaired chromosomes of the egg unite with the twenty-three unpaired chromosomes of the sperm to form a complete cell containing forty-six chromosomes; this is the **zygote.** The zygote then begins to divide in the usual way—by doubling its chromosomes and dividing in half. Each of the twenty-three pairs of chromosomes in the zygote consists of one chromosome from the mother and a matching one from the father.

Zygote: A fertilized egg.

A person's characteristics depend on the genetic information contained in the genes from both chromosomes in a pair. The chromosomes that contain the genetic instructions for a particular characteristic pair up and together determine, say, the size and the structure of a feature such as the

A person's characteristics depend on genetic information from the parents; sometimes the resemblance between parent and offspring can be striking.

face. If the instructions contained in the chromosome contributed by the mother are different from those contributed by the father, the information is combined to form a new face that is different from either parent's. Thus, the size of someone's nose may be determined by instructions from the mother's chromosome; the size of the ears may derive from the father. The mother might have a large nose and large ears, while the father might be small in both features, yet their offspring may inherit a large nose and small ears or a small nose and large ears. The new combination may be an advantage or a disadvantage in any given society.

Some genes are **dominant;** that is, their message wins out when paired with other genes for the same characteristic, or trait. The gene for brown eye color is dominant over the gene for blue eyes. An individual who receives one gene for brown eyes and one for blue will have brown eyes, not light brown or one brown and one blue. In contrast to the dominant brown-eyed gene, the gene for blue eyes is **recessive.** Recessive genes yield to dominant genes when they are present. An individual will inherit blue eye color only when the eye color genes from both parents are of the recessive blue type (see Figure 2.8).

Genetic defects sometimes result from an unfortunate pairing of two recessive genes as in phenylketonuria (PKU), a disorder that can lead to mental retardation. Some characteristics are the result of genetic errors. **Down's Syndrome,** another form of mental retardation, may result when the female egg ends up with two chromosomes no. 21. When the egg is fertilized, it re-

Dominant Gene: A gene whose effect on a trait is dominant over another (recessive) gene's and that will be manifest in the individual.

Recessive Gene: A gene whose effect on a trait is only seen when there is no dominant gene.

Down's Syndrome: A form of mental retardation caused by a genetic abnormality, usually an extra chromosome no. 21.

Figure 2.8 The male's dominant gene (brown eyes) may unite with either the dominant or recessive female gene. In either case the child will be brown-eyed. Or the male's recessive gene (blue eyes) may unite with either the dominant or recessive female gene. In the first case, the child will be brown-eyed. In the second, the child will have two recessive (blue-eyed) genes and will therefore have blue eyes.

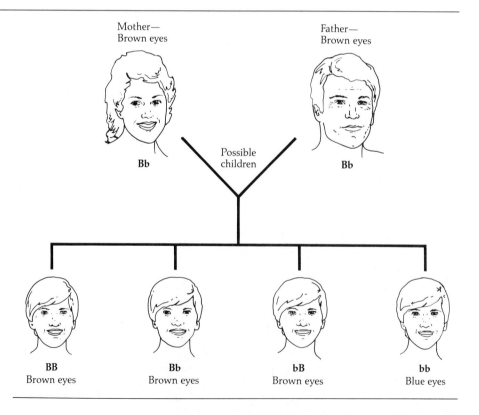

Mother—
Brown eyes

Father—
Brown eyes

Bb

Possible children

Bb

BB
Brown eyes

Bb
Brown eyes

bB
Brown eyes

bb
Blue eyes

Though Down's Syndrome usually results in impaired intellectual functioning, it does not prevent these children from enjoying a tennis lesson.

ceives a third matching chromosome, so that the individual winds up with a total of forty-seven instead of the usual forty-six.

The primary feature of Down's Syndrome is impaired intellectual functioning. The individual typically learns at a slower rate and has a below-average memory (e.g., can recall only about four or five digits after a single presentation instead of six to eight). Thus, the differences in intellectual functioning are quantitative: their capabilities are similar to others', only less. It's like the difference between two computers with different memory capacities. Both work on the same principles, but the one with the large capacity can handle far more information and manipulate it more efficiently (Saccuzzo & Michael, 1984).

The chances of having a child with Down's Syndrome increase substantially for women as they age from thirty to forty-five. For women between twenty and thirty, the probability is about 1 in 1,500. For women between thirty and thirty-five, the chances are 1 in 600; for those between thirty-five and forty, 1 in 300. In women forty to forty-five years of age the probability is 1 in 70. However, the cause of Down's Syndrome is far more complicated than these figures might suggest. Older men also have an increased risk of passing on Down's Syndrome, as do certain families. Moreover, Down's Syndrome does not always result from an extra chromosome 21 in the female egg. It can also be—and often is—caused by an error of **translocation** (the attachment of all or part of one chromosome to another), in which an extra piece of chromosome 21 is added to one of the members of the pair during cell division.

Translocation: A genetic error in which all or part of one chromosome becomes attached to another during cell division.

It should be kept in mind, however, that genetic defects of all kinds are relatively rare: the majority of newborns are perfectly normal. There is a relatively simple test for genetic abnormalities that an expectant mother can undergo about ten to fifteen weeks after conception. In a procedure called

Amniocentesis: Withdrawing and analyzing amniotic fluid from a pregnant woman to determine if the fetus has a genetic defect.

amniocentesis, a long, hollow needle is inserted into the womb in order to draw off a sample of the *amniotic fluid* that surrounds and protects the developing organism. The fluid contains cells that the tiny organism has shed during growth, cells whose genetic makeup can be analyzed for Down's Syndrome or other genetic problems. The procedure is relatively safe, though there is a very slight danger of injuring or infecting the mother or the fetus, a risk the woman must agree to take before the procedure is used. A study of about two thousand women showed no significant difference between infants born to mothers who had the test and infants born to mothers who had not (Brody, 1977). If the test detects a genetic abnormality, the mother can make an informed judgment on whether to proceed with the pregnancy. Even if all she does is prepare herself emotionally for a genetically impaired infant, her feeling of being in control, rather than a passive victim, can greatly enhance her ability to cope with the situation.

Prenatal Development

Heredity and environment interact throughout prenatal development. About four to seven days after conception the zygote travels down the mother's Fallopian tube and implants itself in her uterus. Responding to a genetic code, certain cells begin to specialize, to create a more suitable environment for the zygote. Some form a sac to hold the amniotic fluid. Others interlock with the tissues of the uterus to form the **placenta,** the membrane through which the growing organism is nourished. With the formation of the placenta, the developing organism is referred to as an **embryo.**

Placenta: A membranous organ that lines the uterine wall and partially envelops the embryo.

Embryo: The earliest stages of growth. In humans it begins about four to seven days after conception and lasts to the end of the second month.

Fetus: Prenatal organism from end of second month after conception until birth.

Within its sac, the embryo continues to develop according to the preprogrammed blueprint contained in its genes. About the eighth week after conception the blood vessels, internal organs, eyes, nose, arms, and heart have taken shape. At this point the developing organism is recognizably human and is referred to as a **fetus,** a term that is used to describe it until birth (see Figure 2.9).

As this genetically determined sequence unfolds, environmental forces are also at work. Because the nutrients the embryo receives are brought by the mother's blood, the mother's physical condition can affect the developing organism for good or ill, fostering or distorting the child's genetic endowment (see Figure 2.10). If the embryo is to receive the proper nourishment, for instance, so must the mother. Poor maternal diet has been linked to an increased risk of miscarriage, premature birth, prolonged labor, and in extreme cases long-term intellectual deficiencies (Committee on Maternal Nutrition, 1970). Exposure to environmental pollutants can extract a similar

Figure 2.9 Schematic Summary of Prenatal Development.

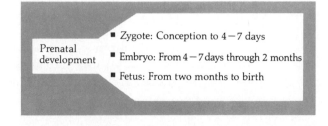

Prenatal development
- Zygote: Conception to 4–7 days
- Embryo: From 4–7 days through 2 months
- Fetus: From two months to birth

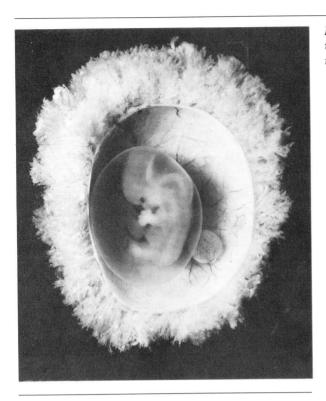

Figure 2.10 Prenatal Environment. *Fetus surrounded by amniotic fluid.*

toll (Fein et al., 1983). Infectious diseases such as rubella (German measles), syphilis, and gonorrhea can cause permanent defects.

Just about any drug is a potential danger. Expectant mothers who smoke run an increased risk of premature birth. Those who use alcohol heavily or even moderately during pregnancy may bear children with permanent, irreversible, physical and mental defects (Hanson et al., 1976; Rosett & Sander, 1979). In one study, women who drank the equivalent of 2 ounces of 100-proof alcohol per day both before and during pregnancy bore children with six times the number of defects as the children of women who drank lightly or not at all (Hanson, 1977). Pills can be just as harmful. During the 1960s a tranquilizer called thalidomide caused numerous deformities of the limbs, heart, and digestive system among the unborn.

Another important decision of the expectant mother is what anesthetic medication to use, if any, in delivery. The contractions of the uterus that result in the expulsion of the child through the birth canal can become extremely uncomfortable for the mother. She must consider the possible effects of a painkilling drug on her unborn, however. The use of anesthetics in delivery may be harmful, and some research suggests that infants delivered with anesthetics may differ in responsiveness from infants delivered without anesthetics for up to four weeks (Brazelton, 1979). However, there are also cases in which the mother's unwillingness to use anesthetics resulted in a very prolonged labor (instead of a cesarean section) and an asphyxiated infant. Expectant mothers are well advised to discuss the pro's and con's of anesthetics with their doctors before the delivery.

As you read about the characteristics of newborn children, keep in mind that they are better equipped than most people realize.

THE NEWBORN CHILD

Reflex: Automatic behavioral reactions to a stimulus that occurs without previous learning or experience.

Grasp Reflex: Inborn reflex found in the neonate characterized by tightening of the fingers around an object placed in the palm.

Rooting Reflex: Neonate's reflexive turning of its head toward the side on which its cheek is touched.

Officially, birth occurs the moment the newborn's entire body is outside the mother's. After nine months in a safe, secure, relatively painless environment in which all needs are automatically provided for, the newborn is suddenly thrust into comparatively harsh surroundings. To deal with the rigors of the world outside the womb, the newborn possesses a number of life-sustaining **reflexes**—automatic behavioral reactions to stimulation that occur without previous learning or experience—like sucking and swallowing. Less well known is the **grasp reflex:** many first-time parents are amazed to discover that if they place an object in a newborn's hand, the child will grip it ferociously (see Figure 2.11). The grasp reflex allows the newborn to cling to the mother and may play an important role in the development of the mother-child relationship. Another reflex that delights and surprises new parents is the **rooting reflex.** Touch a newborn's cheek and the child will turn its head to that side. The rooting reflex helps the newborn to find the breast or bottle with its mouth.

The newborn, in fact, is better equipped than most people realize. At birth or soon after, infants can smell most odors, respond to most of the ma-

Figure 2.11 Grasping Reflex. Place an object in a newborn's hand and the child, thanks to the grasp reflex, will grip it with considerable power.

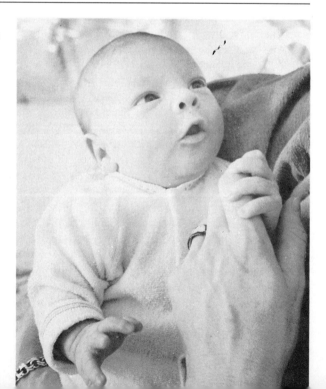

jor tastes, experience pain, and hear a wide range of sounds (Lipsitt, 1977, 1979). The newborn's reflexive crying also provides important signals to the outside world. A shrieking, energetic pain cry often (but not always) signals hunger (Wolff, 1969; Zeskind & Lester, 1981). In addition, newborns frequently synchronize their movements with those of a speaker, a phenomenon known as **interactional synchrony.** For example, in response to a soft-spoken word, the infant may nod her head or alter her facial expression. Thus, the newborn is far from a passive recipient of parental care (Whitt & Casey, 1982).

Interactional Synchrony: The synchronization of a newborn's movements with the words and voice tone of others.

Newborns differ in their temperaments. Some are easily soothed; they respond quickly to gentle rocking and cuddling, reinforcing the caretaker's efforts. Others are not so easily calmed and may frustrate or anger the caretaker, sometimes eliciting a negative response that only increases their tension (Bell & Harper, 1977; Simpson & Stevenson-Hinde, 1985). Researchers have identified a number of temperamental styles among American infants (Garrison et al., 1984). Infants of easy temperament, for example, are positive in mood, regular in their bodily functions, and moderate in their reactions. Infants of difficult temperament are irregular in their bodily functions and intense in their reactions. One thing the parents of such infants can do is to recognize the need for unusually painstaking care, and treat the infant as patiently and consistently as possible. Infants of slow-to-warm-up temperament need to be encouraged and stimulated, for they react cautiously, are likely to withdraw from new situations, and adapt poorly to new situations. If parents do not respond to their cries, their responses may weaken further (Thomas et al., 1970). Because environment usually interacts with heredity to influence behavior, by responding consistently to such children parents can help to strengthen their responses.

EARLY CHILDHOOD

The constant give-and-take between nature and nurture, heredity and environment, continues through early childhood. But perhaps the most striking feature of early childhood development is the transition from total dependency to ever-increasing independence. In this section we will see how the child's rapidly improving motor, perceptual, cognitive, and social skills foster that transition.

Motor Development

All humans enter the world totally dependent on others for nourishment, protection, love, and survival. At birth newborns lie in the position they are put in. They must learn to master their bodies. They cannot so much as roll over by themselves. But by one month most infants gain sufficient muscular control to lift their heads at the shoulder. By about five or six months the typical infant can sit alone for a brief time and has discovered how to roll over. In another five or six months he or she can stand alone and will soon be walking without help (see Figure 2.12). Before long the developing child will be hiking up and down stairs, rummaging through

Figure 2.12 *This figure shows the approximate age ranges for early motor development. The ranges given are based on typical averages, and some children progress faster than others, though the sequence of development remains fixed.*

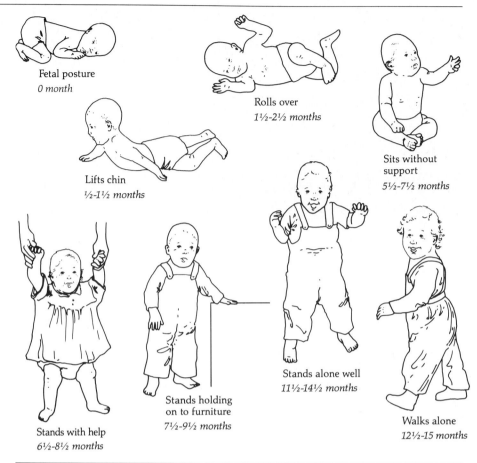

Fetal posture
0 month

Rolls over
1½-2½ months

Lifts chin
½-1½ months

Sits without
support
5½-7½ months

Stands with help
6½-8½ months

Stands holding
on to furniture
7½-9½ months

Stands alone well
11½-14½ months

Walks alone
12½-15 months

closets, and inspecting the contents of the medicine cabinet. Most parents don't take long to realize the need to "baby-proof" the house—to put all medicines, household cleansers, and breakable knickknacks safely out of reach.

One of the striking features of infant motor development is the fixed sequence in which it unfolds. Although the rate of motor development may vary, all infants seem to follow the same sequence: they learn to sit up before standing and to stand before walking. One may sit alone at five months, another not until six months, but both will sit before they stand. Environmental factors may speed up or slow down the process, but they cannot alter the basic sequence (Bayley, 1965).

Perceptual Development

Perceptual development also takes place in stages. The study of early motor development involves a straightforward process of observation and recording—when the child sits, walks, and so on. The study of early perceptual development is a much more difficult challenge because of the child's limited ability to understand instructions, remain alert, and respond. How-

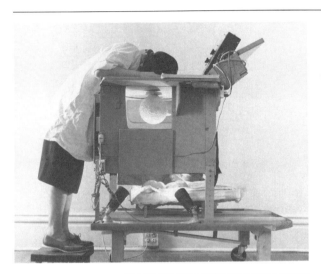

Figure 2.13 The Franz Looking Chamber. This device is used to study infant perceptual development.

ever, researchers have devised a number of ingenious procedures and devices, such as *Fantz's looking chamber*, to investigate the perceptual capabilities of infants (see Figures 2.13). The basic idea behind Fantz's procedure is that an infant's pattern of looking reflects his or her innate capabilities and preferences. The infant is seated comfortably in front of two or more stimuli—a circle and a square, for example. A camera records the infant's eye movements and an observer records the amount of time the infant spends looking at each stimulus (Fantz, 1958, 1965).

Studies using such devices have revealed that infants definitely prefer some stimuli over others. They will spend more time looking at a circle filled with lines and contrasting colors, for example, than they will looking at a solid red one. They also seem to favor stimuli resembling the human face (Flavell, 1977; Nelson & Dolgin, 1985).

As infants develop, their ability to analyze faces increases. Figure 2.14 shows the eye movement patterns of one- and two-month-old infants as

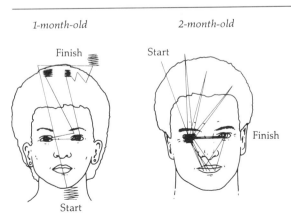

1-month-old   2-month-old

Figure 2.14 The pattern of eye movement can be seen in the lines drawn over these representations of a human face. The figure on the left illustrates the eye movement pattern of a one-month-old; the figure on the right, the pattern for a two-month-old. (Adapted from Philip Salapatek, Pattern Perception in Early Infancy. In L. B. Cohen and P. Salapatek (Eds.), Infant Perception: From Sensation to Cognition, Vol. 1, Basic Visual Processes. New York: Academic Press, 1975, p. 201.)

they watched an adult leaning over them. The younger infant concentrated on the top and bottom edges of the head; the older one focused on the more complicated internal facial features, particularly the eyes (Salapatek, 1975). An infant's eye movements also provide clues to their color vision and their ability to distinguish patterns (Bornstein, 1975, 1979). An infant will eventually become bored with any stimulus. But if a new stimulus is introduced, the infant will perk up and direct his or her gaze toward it. If an infant who has become bored with a blue circle fails to perk up and gaze at a green circle, then we might conclude that she or he cannot discriminate between the two. If the child does perk up, we assume he or she can tell the difference between the two colors (Wood, 1983). By three months of age infants do show evidence of normal adult color vision in their response to such stimuli. In addition, their color preferences appear to be similar to those of adults— like adults, for example, they would rather look at pure red than orange-red (Bornstein, 1975, 1979). Their preferences appear to be inborn and independent of their language development (Bornstein & Marks, 1982). That is, the child has not yet learned the words for colors and therefore must be responding to the colors themselves rather than to the words or any concepts related to color.

Other studies have shown that infants can perceive depth as early as two months. To investigate infant depth perception, scientists developed a device called the **visual cliff,** a tabletop that is half checkerboard and half glass (see Figure 2.15). The mother stands near the glass side and calls to the infant, urging the child to leave the checkerboard and crawl out onto the glass. Presumably, if the infant perceives depth, he or she will note that the floor beneath the glass is dangerously lower than the tabletop and will shrink from it. And that is just what happens. As long as the checkerboard pattern is clearly perceptible, infants will not cross the cliff (Gibson & Walk, 1960). Unfortunately, because it takes several months before infants are able to crawl, researchers have been unable to determine conclusively if depth perception exists from birth in humans. Animals that *can* walk at birth— chickens and goats, for instance—will not cross the cliff (Campos et al., 1978).

Visual Cliff: A research apparatus designed to produce the optical illusion of a drop-off used to test depth perception in infants.

Figure 2.15 Visual Cliff. Studies with the "visual cliff" technique indicate that infants can perceive depth as early as two months of age.

■ Learning Check ■

Read the right side, then cover and try to recite. Repeat.

Two methods for investigating perceptual development.	1. Fantz's looking chamber (records eye movements and scanning behavior). 2. Visual cliff (investigates depth perception).

As suggested by Piaget, up to the age of two the child acquires much of his or her understanding of the world through sensory activities like looking and motor activities like crawling. After that time, language becomes the most important tool in the developing child's quest for independence.

Language Development

Like motor activities and at least some aspects of perception, language appears to develop in an ordered sequence. Though individual children differ in the way they express themselves, some preferring single words and others more complex expressions, there is a general pattern that applies more or less to all children.

In the first phase of the language development sequence the child begins to vary the pitch, duration, and rhythm of its cries. Next, in the second half of the first year, the infant emits the basic sounds of language more or less at random. At the beginning of this so-called babbling stage, infants produce a wide variety of sounds; it appears that they are capable of producing all the basic sounds, or **phonemes,** of all the languages of the world (Brown, 1973). Eventually, though, they voice only those of their native language, signifying the child has entered a new level in the language development sequence. This preference for sounds of their own language is no accident. For one thing, the parents attend more carefully to the child's sounds that are phonemes of the parent language and tend to ignore other sounds. For another, the parents' language behavior provides a model for the child to imitate.

Phoneme: The smallest unit of sound that indicates a difference in meaning in a particular language (e.g., pit–bit).

As the sequence of language development continues to unfold, the one-year-old finally combines phonemes in a very special way to utter the first word. This is an event of great importance to the parents and the attention baby receives for the utterance rewards the response and helps to insure that baby will say it again. And as the baby utters "ma-ma" or "da-da," the word comes to acquire meaning. Ma-ma comes to be associated with the appearance of mother. The child utters "da-da" and soon sees father, smiling or holding a small toy. Eventually the infant also learns that certain utterances have instrumental value in that they lead to the satisfaction of a need or desire. The infant looks at a ball on the floor, says "ba-ba," and big sister tosses the ball into the crib.

The first word is like the small ice pebble rolling down a snow covered mountain slope. New words are added very quickly and soon the child's vocabulary grows like a rolling snowball. From about age one to two, the infant acquires a vocabulary of approximately fifty words. A year later, at age three, the toddler has picked up the meaning of about a thousand words. One word utterances are soon replaced by two: "All gone," "Mike fall," "ma-ma funny." Such two-word utterances are referred to as **telegraphic speech** because they resemble telegrams in which simple verbs and auxiliary words are omitted.

Language development is more than a process of learning new words. As the sequence continues to unfold, the child also learns new ways to combine words to produce meaning. However, for quite some time their ability to understand words exceeds what they can say.

By the age of five, children can understand the meaning of about two thousand words. By age six they seem to have absorbed the rules of grammar and word inflections or combinations. Though they cannot actually state the rules (as many adults cannot), they know how to use them (Bowerman, 1976). If the meaning of a new word is explained to them, they can often use it correctly in a sentence.

The common pattern of language development and the apparent ease with which children acquire language suggest that its acquisition is the result of genetic programming. Nevertheless, environment plays an important role, for children always learn the language of their social group, no matter what their heritage. A Korean child raised by French parents in a French town will learn French, not Korean. Again, heredity and environment interact to produce behavior. (Theories of language acquisition and usage processes are discussed further in Chapter 8.) The objects and events a child is most likely to encounter in the environment are those for which the child will find having a word useful. For example, a child whose parents own a computer will probably acquire the word computer before a child in an impoverished rural area where computers are all but nonexistent.

Personality and Social Development

Besides learning to communicate, young children gain a personality—dispositional tendencies and a sense of self as separate and distinct from others. This they gain from interacting with others, developing personal connections and a concept of individuality through the process of social development. These processes begin in infancy with their first experiences of others.

Attachment. According to Freud and Erikson, the extreme dependence of the infant on others is the key to personality and social development in the first year. An important element in the infant's development at this time is the creation of a special bond, or attachment, between parent and dependent child.

Attachment, as we've seen, involves mutual desire for physical contact between two individuals—parent and child, husband and wife, and so on. It is critical to a helpless infant's survival to encourage attachment behavior in parent or caregiver. Fortunately, the newborn comes equipped with behaviors that foster attachment (Ainsworth, 1974). Reflex responses, such as the rooting reflex, cause the newborn to burrow her little head in the shoulder, breasts, or what else is pushing against it, creating a feeling of closeness between infant and parents. Through its smiles and cries, the infant communicates to the parents. And because infants cannot get around for themselves, they must be held and carried.

A secure bond or attachment is also very important to a child's later development. Infants who have developed a secure attachment have been found to adapt more readily to a variety of situations—exploring the environment, interacting with strangers, and the like—than infants with weak or insecure attachments (Ainsworth, 1979; Ainsworth et al., 1978). In dozens of research reports based on a wide variety of samples, secure attachment to a parental figure (mother, father, guardian) has been related to self-esteem, curiosity, coping with novelty or failure, ability to interact with peers, and independence (Sroufe, 1985).

While much of an infant's behavior seems designed to promote attachment, a parent's behavior can both foster attachment and discourage it. Mothers who appear to enjoy bodily contact with their babies, for example, and who have a good sense of timing in their response to the child's signals (playing when the child wants to play and letting the child sleep when tired) tend to have strong, secure attachments with their infants (Donovan & Leavitt, 1985). Their children are less distressed by the presence of strangers, more cooperative, and more active in exploring the environment than infants whose mothers lack this sense of timing. Such mothers might enjoy bodily contact with their infants but be awkward in responding to the infant's signals; for example, feeding the infant when he or she just wanted to be picked up and reassured, or trying to interest the infant in a toy long after she or he has become bored with it. Mothers who neither enjoy physical contact with their infant nor have a good sense of timing in their responses tend to have the least well-adjusted infants. Such mothers typically show little emotional expression and are impatient, resentful, or angry when the baby interferes with their activities (Ainsworth, 1979).

However, although the mother's behavior in interacting with a child can affect the mother-infant attachment, some infants may inherit a disposition to be more responsive to bodily contact and to convey their signals more clearly than others (Schaffer & Emerson, 1964). Thus, the formation of attachments depends on how the infant's inherited disposition interacts with the mother's behavior. A very responsive mother might produce a better attachment for a difficult infant than an unresponsive mother might with an easy infant. Moreover, a mother might learn to be more effective in developing an attachment by observing other mothers and imitating those who seem to be most successful in responding to a baby's signals.

Independence. With the normal development of attachments come new sources of anxiety. By about six months, the infant begins to show signs of anxiety and distress if separated from the mother, a phenomenon known as **separation anxiety.** The infant also exhibits a similar distress if picked up by anyone other than the mother—**stranger anxiety.** Thus, with the formation of attachments, the baby seems to become highly dependent on the mother (or parent) for support and reassurance and becomes noticeably upset in her absence. Even when she is present, the baby becomes upset if approached by the relatively unfamiliar face of a grandparent, relative, or friend of the family. To function, the baby must learn to operate independently of the parents.

The rapid physical growth and developing language skills of the second and third year of life prepare the youngster for greater independence from

Separation Anxiety: The tendency of infants less than one year old to display discomfort and signs of anxiety when separated from their mothers.

Stranger Anxiety: The tendency of infants less than one year old to show marked fear of strangers.

Box 2.1 PSYCHOLOGY IN ACTION: Being a Parent of a Young Child

Human needs are many during each of the first three years of development. The infant requires consistent nourishment, love, cuddling, and encouragement, as well as protection, challenge, and limit-setting. Since so many skills are developing at once—motor, perceptual, cognitive, language, and social—parents must be on guard not to overemphasize or to neglect any single aspect of development. Flexibility and the realization that no one approach is best for all children seem to be important at this stage of parenting.

Some probably worry too much about the effects of a working mother's absence on her children; some not enough. But psychologists have learned that multiple caretakers—for example, stepfather, working

mother, and babysitter—can, if they are consistent in their treatment of the infant, provide a workable alternative to the traditional mother-child model. Though attachment and trust are important in early development, it does not seem to make a great deal of difference to whom a child attaches. As long as children learn that they will be cared for warmly and consistently, one or many people may supply the care (Leiderman & Leiderman, 1974; Rutter, 1979).

To foster attachment, caregivers can try to respond to activities initiated by the child (Stern, 1977; Schaffer, 1977). The child who looks your way and smiles is very possibly asking to be picked up or played with. The child who is absorbed with a toy is perhaps best left alone, at least for the time being.

Talking to children frequently and in understandable terms helps them to develop their language and social skills as well as attachments (Levine et al., 1985). Letting them know that help and encouragement will be supplied most of the time (but not all the time) helps, according to Erikson (1972), to encourage trust in self as well as others. And arranging things so that the child feels a sense of control over what happens also seems to foster healthy development (Ainsworth & Wittig, 1972; White & Watts, 1973). For example, there are many situations in which the child can be given a choice (e.g., "Would you rather have juice or milk?"). There are also situations in which the child can be made to feel helpful (e.g., "Can you get me the screwdriver over there on the table?"). Having choices and feeling helpful help the child feel a sense of importance; that what she or he does matters and can make a difference. But there is no one right way to rear a child. Flexibility is the key. As children grow and mature, their needs change, and effective caretakers change accordingly. (For more on parenting, see Chapter 6.)

Allowing a child to be helpful fosters a sense of importance in the child.

the parent. The child's dual need for attachment and independence, however, poses a number of difficult problems from the standpoint of parenting. (See Box 2.1.)

Gender Differences. An important aspect of personality and social development concerns the development of male-female differences in behavior. Curiously enough, up to about the first month after conception, the only detectable difference between males and females is the presence of the Y chromosome in the male; the genital organs are identical (Wilson et al., 1981). In the second month, the male embryo responds to genetic instruc-

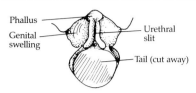

Figure 2.16 Sexual Differentiation during Prenatal Development.

Phallus
Genital swelling
Urethral slit
Tail (cut away)

First month after conception

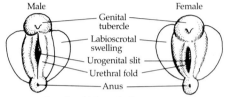

Male   Female
Genital tubercle
Labioscrotal swelling
Urogenital slit
Urethral fold
Anus

Second to third month after conception

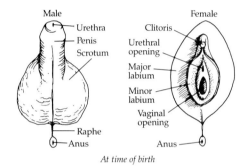

Male   Female
Urethra
Penis
Scrotum
Clitoris
Urethral opening
Major labium
Minor labium
Vaginal opening
Raphe
Anus   Anus

At time of birth

tions carried on the Y chromosome by manufacturing male hormones, and the male sex organ begins to emerge (see Figure 2.16).

But the effects of male hormones are not restricted to the genital organs. In fact, some studies indicate that exposure to male hormones before or even shortly after birth can permanently affect an infant's brain (MacLusky & Naftolin, 1981). In the 1950s, well-meaning doctors sometimes administered the hormones to pregnant women to prevent miscarriage. Some of the female infants of these women were born with a small penis. Though the organ could be removed surgically, the girls still tended toward boyish behavior, despite their XX chromosomal makeup. They showed much less interest in dolls than a control group and little interest in having babies, were more active and competitive, and were described by adults as "tomboys" (Money & Ehrhardt, 1972).

Animal studies have produced similar results. For example, female monkeys exposed to male hormones before or just after birth were more active and aggressive than a control group (Rubin et al., 1981). And cross-cultural studies have shown that, in just about every culture of the world, males are more aggressive than females (see Feshbach, 1970 for a review). Such evidence would seem to suggest that some male-female differences—particularly aggression—are biologically determined rather than due to environmental factors such as parenting styles (Maccoby & Jacklin, 1974; Ehrhardt & Meyer-Bahlburg, 1981).

Other researchers have argued, however, that the biological differences between the sexes are minor compared to the cultural influences on children. Numerous studies have shown that, though there are few identifiable differences among newborn girls and boys, parental attitudes toward their newborns vary sharply with the sex of the child (Condry & Ross, 1985). Long before infants are old enough even to realize that there are two sexes, parents treat them differently. Fathers play more vigorously with boys and generally spend more time talking to them than to girls. Mothers tend to cuddle their daughters more than their sons. Parents dress their children in "sex-appropriate" colors—pink for girls, blue for boys—and give them sex-appropriate toys—dolls for girls, trucks for boys. Soon the children have acquired a personal preference for the appropriate toys, as revealed in their letters to Santa Claus (Richardson & Simpson, 1982).

It is fairly well established that girls perform better than boys on language-related tasks. On the average, girls express themselves with greater ease, spell and read better, and achieve better grades, at least until high school (Yarborough & Johnson, 1980). By contrast, boys generally outperform girls in mathematics and on tasks requiring spatial visualization (Sanders, et al., 1982). The exact cause of these differences is unknown.

But though numerous studies have confirmed the importance of gender differences in cognitive development, the fact is, age-related changes in cognitive development are far more profound than gender differences. A twelve-year-old boy's reasoning is far more similar to a twelve-year-old girl's than to a six-year-old boy's. A six-year-old, male or female, is in the preoperational stage, tending to focus on only one aspect of a problem at a time. The twelve-year-old, male or female, has gone through the concrete operations stage and is on the threshold of the highest level of cognitive development—only a step away from adult power of reasoning. (For more on gender-related issues, see Chapter 10 on Human Sexuality.)

ADOLESCENCE

Adolescence: The period of development that begins about the time the individual becomes biologically mature and ends by young adulthood (usually twelve to eighteen years).

Adolescence—the period of development that begins about the time an individual becomes biologically mature and ends by young adulthood—is fraught with change (Kohn, 1984). The drive for independence accelerates as the young person, now almost an adult, strives to achieve a sense of personal identity. Cognitively, the adolescent moves into Piaget's formal operations stage and is suddenly able to think from a variety of perspectives—an ability that encourages self-evaluation and self-doubt (Eisert & Kahle, 1982). But perhaps most dramatic is the adolescent's physical growth and development, accompanied as it is by hormonal changes that bring on a heightened sexuality and new emotions.

Puberty: The period during which the individual becomes physically capable of reproduction.

Physical Maturation

Early in adolescence the young person reaches **puberty,** the period in which one becomes physically capable of reproduction. At this time increased secretion of hormones, triggered by a signal from the pituitary gland (see Chapter 3), brings on menstruation in females and the production of sperm in males. **Secondary sex characteristics** also appear at this point: in females, development of the breasts and hips; in males, broadening of the shoulders, deepening of the voice, and growth of facial hair. Over the next few years, both sexes experience a rapid growth spurt: three to six inches in females, four to eight inches in males.

Girls reach puberty faster than boys, at about twelve years, nine months. (The average for boys is fourteen years, six months.) By age thirteen, most girls can become pregnant—and in the next six or seven years, 40 percent do (Zelnick & Kantner, 1980). Indeed, there has been a veritable explosion in teenage pregnancies—nearly a million a year, most of them unwanted (Wallace et al., 1982). In Chapter 10 we will discuss adolescent sexuality and the problem of teenage pregnancy further.

Herein lies one of the major difficulties of adolescence. Adolescents are at a stage of cognitive development (the formal operations stage) in which they are keenly aware of the consequences of their actions (see page 47). They can explore various ways of handling their sexual urges and of avoiding pregnancy before they become financially independent or complete their education. But the huge gap between their cognitive maturity and their emotional and social development frequently prevents them from acting in their own best interest (Melton, 1983).

Personality and Social Development

Due to differences in genetic makeup and nutrition, some girls and some boys reach physical maturity much sooner than others of their own sex (see Figure 2.17). These individual differences in the rate of maturation influence personality and social development. You will be able to see, as we discuss this influence, the interrelationship that is typical among different areas of development.

Early-maturing boys tend to be physically stronger, better at athletics, and more popular with peers than late-maturing boys. As a result, the male who matures quickly has a tendency to become self-confident and develop a high level of self-esteem. His self-satisfaction may make him resistant to growth and change, however, causing him to become more rigid, conforming, and inflexible in his response to new situations in later life than the boy who matures late. Late-maturing boys are often unpopular with peers; they are prone to clowning and other attention-getting behaviors. But the adjustment problems they face in high school often pay off later on in the form of greater maturity (Livson & Peskin, 1980). Having to face and overcome problems apparently prepares them to deal with subsequent challenges.

Unlike early-maturing boys, early-maturing girls tend to be unpopular with their peers, less confident and self-assured than late maturers. The girl who matures early seems to cope well with new situations later in life, however. The late maturer often has difficulty adapting to stress, compared to the early maturer (Livson & Peskin, 1980).

These findings on differences between early and late maturers are generalizations, of course; there are many exceptions to the overall trends. They do illustrate, however, the interrelationship of physical and personality de-

Secondary Sex Characteristics: Physical characteristics that accompany the maturation of the sex organs, such as appearance of pubic hair, voice change, and breast development.

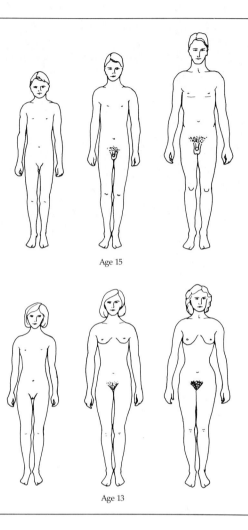

Figure 2.17 *As this figure illustrates, dramatic differences in physical maturity can be found for adolescents of the same age.*

Age 15

Age 13

velopment and also how heredity and environment interact to produce long-term behavioral patterns. The rate at which an adolescent matures physically influences the way peers respond and the amount of emotional struggle the adolescent endures. These experiences, in turn, can affect adjustment in later life.

For all adolescents, no matter how early or late they mature, the major challenge is to establish a sense of **identity,** of purpose and direction. Adolescents must define themselves and their role in society, independently of their parents' role. At the same time, they must accept and like the face they see in the mirror.

The importance of developing an identity during adolescence was a central theme of Erikson's, who believed that establishing a satisfying sense of personal identity and meaningful goals was the single most important challenge of adolescence. Failure to meet the challenge, he believed, results in role confusion—feelings of worthlessness, lack of purpose, an inability to relax around or find intimacy with others, and self-defeating behavior (e.g., cutting classes excessively, reckless driving, abuse of drugs and alcohol).

Identity: Recognition of continuity and sameness in one's personality across situations and experiences; having a degree of self-understanding and self-acceptance.

Asserting a satisfying sense of identity is an important part of meeting the challenge of adolescence.

The establishment of an identity is a pivotal point in the life of the individual. Childhood interests are subordinated to a new kind of identification as an emerging adult. Once cherished possessions—toys, comic books, Raggedy Ann and Andy, now seem like "kid's stuff." The adolescent's interests turn toward socializing and competing with peers. Of particular importance is the establishment of a gender identity—a sense of being male or female, which helps the adolescent feel more self-assured when dealing with peers of either sex.

Parental attitudes toward their children's drive for independence can make a huge difference in the adolescent's ability to meet the challenges of this stage of life. Democratic parents who allow adolescents to participate in family decisions and permit them a degree of freedom can help their children to become self-reliant and acquire a sense of control over their lives. Authoritarian parents who set rules without consulting adolescents, limit their freedom, and employ physical discipline are likely to add to their children's problems (Baumrind, 1975). Fortunately, most adolescents somehow survive, indeed thrive.

ADULTHOOD

Adulthood is the longest period of the life span, extending from about age twenty to sixty-five. Yet, until recently, this forty-five-year period was largely neglected by psychologists (Levinson, 1986). One recent approach has attempted to divide this period into meaningful stages, each with its own developmental tasks (Levinson, 1986). During the early adult transition

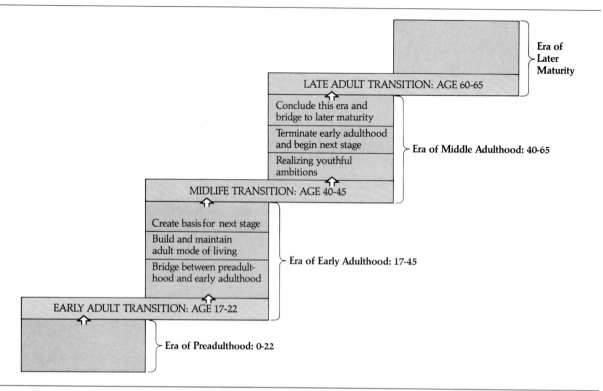

Figure 2.18 Developmental Periods during Early and Middle Adulthood. (*After D. J. Levinson, 1986 and D. J. Levinson, C. N. Darrow, M. H. Levinson, and B.* McKee, The Seasons of Man. *New York: Alfred A. Knopf, 1978.*)

stage (age seventeen to twenty-two), the task is to bridge the period between preadulthood and early adulthood. Then, during the early adulthood period, the individual builds and maintains an initial mode of adult living.

Although adulthood does appear to have its own stages and developmental tasks, it differs from earlier stages of development in several respects. Physical and cognitive changes take place much more slowly. The person's independence reaches its peak, and the major developmental challenge becomes that of making good use of what one has achieved. More than ever before, the individual is faced with decisions, perhaps none more important than those involving love and work (Erikson, 1974; Levinson et al., 1978; Levinson et al., 1976; Gould, 1978).

Throughout adulthood, love and work provide the basis for the individual's sense of happiness and fulfillment as well as pain and sorrow. When intimacy turns sour, as it sometimes does, the adult faces loneliness and uncertainty. If work does not lead to success and fulfillment, adults experience disappointment and self-doubt (Menaghan & Merves, 1984). Sometimes the two forces collide: people become consumed by their work and neglect their families, or sacrifice a career for love. The double-edged sword of love and work has become especially sharp in contemporary times, cutting into traditional male-female roles and family patterns. Divorce and remarriage, single parenthood, working mothers, dual-career families, mid-life career changes, childless marriages, and long-term nonmarital relationships—these are the new realities of adult life.

Love and Intimacy

According to the results of a forty-year study, one's mental health, happiness, and satisfaction with life are linked directly to the capacity to love. Mutual caring, mutual giving, and mutual fulfilling of needs appear to be essential ingredients of adult development (Vaillant, 1977).

Erikson ranked the task of establishing an intimate relationship as the first major challenge of adulthood. He defined *intimacy* as a close caring relationship, usually involving strong physical, social, and emotional attachments. The two individuals care for each other as much as they do for themselves and are willing to compromise and sacrifice for the other's good (Erikson, 1974).

Marriage continues to be the most common way in which people form intimate relationships. **Cohabitation**—two people living together in a nonmarital relationship—is becoming relatively common in the 1980s, however. But, according to most experts, at least nine out of every ten Americans will marry at some point in life, most during their early adult years (Masnick & Bane, 1980). However, about four out of every ten marriages in the United States end in divorce (Norton & Glick, 1979; Parish & Wigle, 1985). Considering that at least 90 percent of Americans marry, about two out of every five individuals will face the trauma of divorce at some point in their lives. Terminating what was once an intimate relationship, especially a marriage, is painful and disrupting. In the thick of their pain, ambivalencies, and anger, the couple must decide how to divide their belongings and bank accounts. If they own a home they may be forced to sell it.

Cohabitation: An unmarried adult couple living together.

The situation becomes even more complicated when children are involved—and about half of all divorcing couples have children (Cassetty, 1983; Gardner, 1970). Divorce may free a child from the stress of his or her parents' unhappy marriage or, in extreme cases, prevent the child from becoming a victim of child abuse. In some cases, then, the overall impact may be positive. But an extensive study of sixty families found that only about one out of four children of divorce seemed better off than those children still caught in the strife of an unhappy marriage. Four years after their parents' divorce, about half the children were still struggling, and one in four had yet to recover (Wallerstein & Kelly, 1980).

Given all the trauma of a broken marriage, it is remarkable how many people remarry. About 80 percent of divorced men and 75 percent of divorced women remarry. Though some also end in divorce, the majority of these second marriages are, reportedly, more successful than the first. Perhaps divorced people learn from their negative experiences and select for their second partner a person they can respect and accept, shortcomings and all, an important factor in a successful marriage (Kimmel, 1974). Perhaps they work harder at achieving some of the critical ingredients in an intimate relationship: good communication (sharing feelings, being open); good sex (being tender, overcoming inhibitions, pleasing one's partner); and good times (engaging in mutually satisfying activities, or taking turns doing what the other wants to do) (Williams & Long, 1983).

Work

Work, the second major force in adult development, also has its complications. Most careers have a price in terms of money or satisfaction—between security and independence, between aspirations and reality (Rice, 1985). For example, one may have to choose between what appears to be a less interesting but higher paying job in the computer field and the lower paying but perhaps more personally satisfying field of high school teaching. Moreover, traditionally men have been the breadwinners, women the unpaid, hardworking stewards of the home. But times have changed, and dual-career families are now commonplace, due to such factors as the women's liberation movement and current economic realities (see Chapter 10). Today's woman must decide whether and when to have a career instead of, or in addition to, a family. And, if the latter, when—before, during, or after her family is established.

Though women can now choose to combine work and marriage, custom has not changed the burdens they bear at home. The working mother typically is still expected by her husband to assume most of the housekeeping duties and is saddled with about ten more hours of work per week than he is (Hackman, 1977; Hansen & Darling, 1985). Thus, a new challenge for many women is to find a personally satisfying compromise between family and work. A new challenge for men is to adjust to the new opportunities for women. Some men are dismayed to discover that their wives earn more money or advance further in an occupation or profession than they. Others may meet resentment from their wives if they do not compromise and share family responsibilities equally (Krause & Geyer-Pestello, 1985; Shaw, 1983).

The need to establish oneself in a career may lead to conflicts between the forces of work and love. This is especially so in dual-career families. A husband may feel obligated to devote most of his effort to his work, though reserving some time for leisure. A wife might feel that she is not getting enough recognition or help from her husband, whose Saturday golfing or Sunday football-watching habits appear selfish to her. Unless a compromise is reached in such conflicts, the relationship could be in jeopardy.

The work-love conflict is especially pressing on mothers, who may feel caught between their careers and their families. More than half of all women with children at home are employed, including a large segment of single and divorced parents (Hansen & Darling, 1985). Many worry that their employment will have negative effects on their children (Clarke-Steward, 1978). The mere fact of employment, however, does not have to be detrimental.

■ Learning Check ■

Read the right side, then cover and try to recite. Repeat.

Three differences between adulthood and other developmental periods.	1. Physical and cognitive changes take place more slowly. 2. Independence reaches its peak. 3. The theme of life shifts from gaining independence to making use of what one has achieved.

Maternal employment does not necessarily weaken the mother-child attachment, nor does it appear to have a negative impact on a child's intellectual or social development (Etaugh, 1980). It may benefit the child by fostering independence and responsibility (Hoffman, 1979). (For a discussion on coping with the problems of the life span, see Chapter 11, Life Style and Coping.)

LATER MATURITY: AGE 65 AND BEYOND

With the passing of adulthood, physical and cognitive changes once again occur more rapidly. When strength and endurance begin to decline and health problems emerge, the maturing adult becomes increasingly aware that his or her body is aging and declining. Both sexes experience a slowing down in cognitive functioning: thinking speed, learning speed, and the like (Birren & Renner, 1977). Memory functions may also decline (Jackson & Schneider, 1985). The mature adult is still able to learn and create, but not as rapidly as before. Emotionally, aging adults face retirement and the loss of loved ones, events that tend to make them acutely aware of the inevitability of death.

Later maturity can be a time of growth and enrichment as well as decline, however. The challenges and rewards of life continue as always, and the individual continues to change. Assuming the role of grandparent and finding new recreational outlets after retirement are among the many challenges of later maturity (Swensen, 1983).

One of the most unfortunate myths about aging is that it brings about a serious decline in intelligence. Feeble memory and dramatic decline in intelligence occur in less than 10 percent of the elderly, due to diseases such as **dementia** and *Alzheimer's disease,* in which there is a premature degeneration of the brain. The great majority of the elderly experience a gradual decline in body functioning, called **senescence,** and a small decrease in immediate memory—the amount of information that can be recalled after a single presentation. Most sustain no more than a very slight decline in intelligence

Dementia: A disease of old age involving losses of concentration, attention, and memory.

Senescence: Sensory and bodily declines with aging; growing old.

Later maturity can be a time of growth and enrichment.

(Birren & Schaie, 1977), a loss that is often compensated for by the wisdom and knowledge accumulated through experience.

Some of the decline observed in the aging individual may be more apparent than real. What a person does—his or her performance—and what the person can do—his or her competence—are not the same. With increasing age, a person may be less motivated to perform, even though still competent. Aging persons may also have less confidence or exercise more caution than their younger counterparts (Botwinick, 1973). Thus, they may perform less well on cognitive tests because they are less willing to risk errors rather than because they have less actual ability (Birren, 1974).

Many of the observed age differences may also be due to poor health. With aging comes greater susceptibility to sickness and disease. Indeed, according to a major investigation, health is the single most important factor in an aging person's psychological well-being (Birren et al., 1963). Differences in performance between the old and the young are far less dramatic when healthy old people are compared to healthy young people (Birren, 1974).

Productivity may actually increase with age in some fields. In a study of workers in the humanities, arts, and sciences, people in their seventies outperformed those in their twenties. In general, productivity peaked between ages thirty and forty and then declined only slightly through the seventies (see Labouvie-Vief, 1977).

A number of investigators have argued that creativity increases in later life (Gruber, 1973; Arlin, 1975). Rejecting Piaget's contention that cognitive development reaches a point of equilibrium in young adulthood, they have proposed new stages such as the "postchildrearing, preretirement stage" or the "postretirement stage" (Schaie, 1982; Swensen, 1983). Each of these stages presumably has its own crises, problems, and opportunities for growth.

According to Erikson, if, at the end of a normal life span, individuals can look back on their lives with approval and satisfaction, they can face death with the knowledge that they used their time on earth meaningfully. Everyone makes mistakes, suffers setbacks; no one is perfect. Bearing that in mind, can the elderly feel that they have done about as well as they might have?

Carl Jung (1963) believed that facing death at the end of the life span can be a healthy, positive experience if viewed in its proper perspective. Jung emphasized that death is a normal part of the life span, one that all organisms face. He believed that, as part of the challenge of later maturity, one must develop a philosophy of death as well as of the meaning of life, or at least think about these issues. Is death something to fear, or is it a welcome relief from the struggle of life? Is old age a time when one might rejoice at having been alive? Later maturity is a time of reflection.

Because of this last reckoning, advanced age brings an increased risk of depression. Moreover, age takes many people by surprise—we grow older faster than we think (Fischer, 1977). Unfortunately, some elderly people spend their last years tormenting themselves with their mistakes, their shortcomings, and their failures. They grieve to discover that it is too late to tell their loved ones how much they cared; too late to help their old friends in need. But the elderly need not fall into this trap. Old age need not be a

---

Box 2.2 PSYCHOLOGY IN ACTION: Death and Dying

One challenge of aging which can't be ignored is that of facing death. A study of the problems of the terminally ill by Kübler-Ross (1969) provides some insights on how people cope with **death.** Kübler-Ross maintained that terminally ill individuals who are given advanced warning of death go through five stages. In the first stage there is "denial," in which the individual has difficulty believing that he or she is, in fact, going to die. In the second stage the individual experiences "anger." In the third stage the individual begins to "bargain," primarily with God. The individual might, for example, make some promise or commitment to God in exchange for a longer life. In the fourth stage the individual experiences "depression." However, in the fifth and final stage the individual "accepts" the reality of the situation. Like other stage theorists, Kübler-Ross has been criticized on the grounds that the stages don't necessarily follow an orderly sequence. The stages may overlap and the individual may move back and forth between stages. Furthermore, her results apply to terminally ill individuals and may not have the same relevance to individuals facing death at the end of a normal life span.

---

time of passive decay, but of a renewed commitment to make the best of the precious gift of life.

In Box 2.2 we briefly discuss something that everyone must face—**death** and dying.

Death: The moment at which life ends.

Because development covers every major aspect of life, its study provides an overview of the entire field of psychology. In the chapters ahead we will elaborate on topics covered in this chapter.

LEARNING FRAMEWORK

I. Four major theories view development in terms of the unfolding of a specific ordered sequence of events.
   A. Freud's theory proposed five stages of personality development. (Review: *Table 2.1*)
   B. Erikson's theory included eight stages of social development. (Review: *Table 2.2*)
   C. Piaget's theory broke cognitive development into four stages. (Review: *Table 2.3*)
   D. Kohlberg's theory divided moral development into three major stages, with two levels at each stage. (Review: *Figure 2.4*)
II. Development is shaped by heredity, environment, and the interaction between them from the moment of conception.
   A. Biologically based characteristics are transmitted through the genes and chromosomes. (Review: *Zygote; Dominant Gene; Recessive Gene; Translocation*)
   B. Although the instructions for the growth of a newly conceived organism are contained in the genes, its development is influenced by the prenatal environment in which the growth takes place. (Review: *Figure 2.9* and *2.10*)
III. The newborn child is equipped with a set of reflexes and a distinctive temperament. (Review: *Grasp Reflex; Rooting Reflex; International Synchrony*)

IV. Early childhood is characterized by a transition from total dependency to greater and greater degrees of independence.
  A. Motor development unfolds in a fixed sequence as the newborn gradually gains control over his or her body from head to toe. (Review: *Figure 2.12*)
  B. Perceptual development also unfolds in sequences. (Review: *Fantz's Looking Chamber; Visual Cliff*)
  C. The young child's independence is further enhanced by the rapid acquisition of language between ages two and five. (Review: *Phoneme; Telegraphic Speech*)
  D. In the course of personality and social development, the child forms close bonds with his or her parents and acquires a sense of being male or female. (Review: *Attachment; Separation Anxiety; Gender Differences*)
V. During adolescence, physical changes and a striving for increasing independence combine to characterize development. (Review: *Puberty; Secondary Sex Characteristics; Identity*)
VI. During adulthood, the theme of development changes. Physical changes slow down considerably; independence is at its peak. (Review: *Love and Intimacy; Work*)
VII. Later maturity is a time of growth and enrichment as well as physical decline. (Review: *Senescence*)

CHAPTER 3

The Nervous System and Behavior

Chapter Outline

The human nervous system performs feats unparalleled by any machine ever invented, or ever likely to be invented. It enables us to interact with our environment and to learn from those interactions. Through it we dream, wish, hope, love, and remember. Without it we could not see, hear, smell, taste, or feel. It is the seat of reason and passion, beauty and ugliness. It is, in the end, the human nervous system that makes us *human*.

Because the nervous system underlies our actions, mental processes, and experiences, its study is fundamental to the science of behavior. The nervous system mediates learning, memory, and emotion. It governs our basic drives—hunger and thirst, for instance, as well as more complicated motivated behaviors such as those involving sex and aggression. Many forms of mental illness and disorders such as Alzheimer's disease are intimately linked to the functioning of the nervous system (Grimes et al., 1985). And discussions of such personally relevant topics as stress and anxiety, sleep and dreams, chronic pain, and the behavioral effects of drugs and alcohol would not be complete without reference to the nervous system. Thus, the mastery of the many new or unfamiliar terms and concepts you are about to encounter is well worth the effort, for you will be paid back with interest, in terms of understanding yourself and others.

The human nervous system can be compared to a modern metropolitan airport. In such an airport, radar and other instruments gather information on incoming planes and relay it to the central control tower. There, this information is quickly analyzed and integrated with other data on weather, scheduled take-offs, and runway conditions. After determining the best course of action, air traffic controllers tell pilots what to do. Sometimes they put an incoming plane into a holding pattern while they give special attention to a distressed plane that is about to land. The airport functions through the efforts of many parts, each doing a highly specialized job. Yet the entire operation is carefully coordinated so that it works as a unit.

Although the airport analogy does not fully capture the complexity of the nervous system, it does illustrate some of its important characteristics. Like the airport, the nervous system has various instruments, the sense organs, which gather information and carry it to a control tower, the brain and spinal cord. There, this information is quickly analyzed and integrated with other data. After determining the best course of action, the brain and spinal cord send a message to the muscles and glands, which tells them what to do. Although the various parts of the nervous system have specialized functions, the system as a whole is highly coordinated, so that it works as a unit.

How does the nervous system accomplish this? In this chapter we attempt to answer this question. We begin by considering the cells that make up the nervous system. Then we examine the overall structure of the nervous system, and end with a detailed examination of the brain, the principal organ of the nervous system. Let us begin by examining the nervous system in miniature.

THE NEURON: THE NERVOUS SYSTEM IN MINIATURE

The nervous system consists of billions of individual cells called **neurons** (see Figure 3.1). Neurons are the basic unit of the nervous system. Each, with its three main parts, can be seen as a model in miniature of the entire nervous system. It has receivers, called **dendrites,** which pick up information and carry it to the cell body. The **cell body** is a kind of central command post; it collects and integrates input information, which, in turn, may cause it to send a message to other neurons along its output cable, the **axon.** Like the nervous system itself, the neuron performs three main functions: picking up information (through the dendrites), analyzing information (in the cell body), and sending messages (along the axon). Figure 3.2 provides an overview of the three main parts of a neuron and the function of each part.

Neuron: A nervous system cell; the functional or basic unit of the nervous system.

Dendrites: The receiving component of a neuron.

Cell Body: The information analysis component of a neuron, which contains the nucleus and carries out the life-sustaining functions of the cell.

Axon: The transmitting component of a neuron.

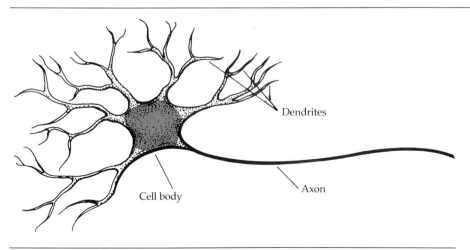

Dendrites

Cell body

Axon

Figure 3.1 A Basic Neuron. A neuron has three main parts: dendrites, cell body, and axon.

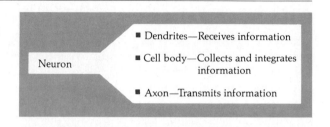

Figure 3.2 Schematic Summary of the Parts and Functions of a Neuron.

Neuron

■ Dendrites—Receives information

■ Cell body—Collects and integrates information

■ Axon—Transmits information

Receptor Sites: Large molecules scattered across the surface of the dendrites and cell body of a neuron, which respond to chemical messages sent by other neurons.

Neural Transmission: The sending and receiving of information by neurons.

Synapse: The very tiny space between neurons; the area of functional contact between neurons.

Neurotransmitters: Chemical substances that a neuron releases in transmitting messages to other neurons.

Both the cell body and the dendrites have **receptor sites** scattered across their exterior surface, the cell membrane, which means that they can receive messages from other neurons at many different locations. The dendrites, of which a neuron may have many, are actually extensions of the cell body. Each neuron has only one axon, however; this is a slender tube that sometimes branches at the end. (Figure 3.3 illustrates the various types of neurons that can be found throughout the body.)

Communication among neurons is a two-step process called **neural transmission.** The first step is electrical in nature: when sufficiently stimulated, either by other neurons or by direct sensory input, the neuron sends an electrical impulse, similar to that of an electric battery, jetting to the end of its axon. The second step is chemical and takes place at the **synapse,** the very small space between the end of one cell's axon and the dendrites or cell body of its neighbor. Neurons manufacture and store chemicals called **neurotransmitters.** When the electrical impulse reaches the end of the axon, it causes the release of a chemical neurotransmitter into the synapse. The action of a neurotransmitter on the dendrite or cell body of the neighboring

Figure 3.3 Neurons Differ in Size and Shape.
Neurons throughout the body differ in size and in shape, but each can be identified by its three main parts—dendrites, cell body, and axon.

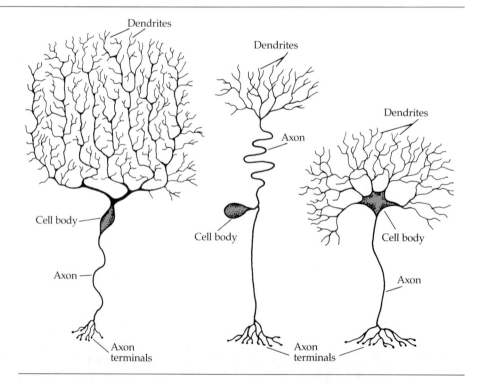

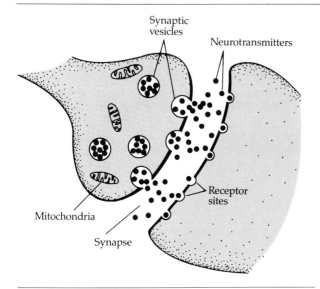

Synaptic vesicles

Neurotransmitters

Mitochondria

Synapse

Receptor sites

Figure 3.4 Neural Transmission is a Two-Step Process. Stimulation received by the dendrites passes through the cell body and along the axon and causes the neuron to "fire." This electrical impulse triggers the release of a chemical neurotransmitter into the very tiny space between neurons, the synapse.

neuron, in turn, determines whether or not the neighboring neuron will fire an electrical impulse of its own. If it does, the process will start again, with *this* neuron sending an electrical impulse jetting to the end of *its* axon. In short, communication among neurons is **electrochemical,** a combination of electrical and chemical processes. Electrical messages trigger the release of chemical messages, which in turn initiate electrical messages. Figure 3.4 illustrates this two-step process of neural transmission.

The first step in the process, transmission of the electrical impulse within the neuron, is called **axonal transmission.** The second step, the relaying of an impulse from one neuron to another through the release of a chemical neurotransmitter into the synapse, is called **synaptic transmission.** Let's take a close look at both.

Axonal Transmission

Within the fluids that fill and surround the neurons are tiny electrically charged particles, called **ions.** When a cell is in its normal non-excited or **resting state,** the ions inside give it a slight negative charge compared to the fluid outside. This difference in charge occurs because the neuron's membrane is **semipermeable**—capable of being penetrated by some, but not all, chemical substances. It allows negatively charged chloride ions (Cl^-) to enter, but keeps out the larger, positively charged sodium ions (Na^+). The smaller positively charged potassium ions (K^+) do find their way in, but not in sufficient quantity to balance all of the negatively charged Cl^- ions. The difference in charge between the inside and the outside of the cell membrane of a neuron in the resting state is called the **resting potential.**

Stimulation pickup at the receptor sites on the dendrites and cell body is relayed to the point where the axon joins the cell body and has the effect of decreasing the cell's resistance at that point to the positively charged sodium ions. This weakening of resistance allows some sodium ions to pass through

Electrochemical: Involving both electrical and chemical processes. Transmission of information in the nervous system is electrochemical.

Axonal Transmission: Refers to the coordination of the neural impulse within a neuron. Axonal transmission begins with stimulation of receptor sites on the dendrites and cell body of a neuron.

Synaptic Transmission: Refers to the transmission of information between neurons (i.e., from one neuron to another).

Ion: An atom or molecule having a net positive charge or a net negative charge.

Resting State: The slight negative charge within a neuron compared to the outside when the cell is not firing. In its resting state, the cell membrane is said to be polarized.

Semipermeable: The condition of something that allows some things through but not others, as in a semipermeable cell membrane.

Resting Potential: The difference in charge between the inside and the outside of the cell membrane of a neuron in the resting state.

the cell membrane. If the number of sodium ions entering the cell reaches a certain level, a sudden change occurs: the inside of the cell membrane at that point now becomes positively charged relative to the outside. This sudden change is called an **action potential** (see Figure 3.5). The action potential starts a chain reaction that proceeds like a wave along the length of the axon. An action potential on one part of the axon stimulates adjacent areas of the axon to produce one at that point. As if a running garden hose had been snapped at one end, the action potential is systematically propelled along the axon. Sodium ions enter into the axon all along its length and reverse the balance between positive and negative ions on either side of the cell membrane. This sequence of electrical change along the axon is the electrical impulse.

The degree of stimulation a neuron receives may vary considerably. A typical neuron picks up chemical messages from several neighboring neurons. If the combined strength of these messages is sufficient, they will cause an electrical impulse to be transmitted along the axon. However, the electrical impulse along the axon does not vary in intensity. A neuron either fires or it does not, and its intensity is the same each time it fires. This phenomenon is known as the **all-or-none principle.** It is similar to the firing of a gun: if the pressure on the trigger is sufficient, the gun fires; but when the gun fires, the bullet travels at the same speed and with the same force, regardless of how hard the trigger was pulled.

When stimulation is strong enough to start the electrical impulse along the axon, the neuron is said to have reached its **threshold** for firing. You might think of the threshold as the point at which the semipermeable membrane becomes permeable to the sodium ions and the action potential be-

Action Potential: The measurable change in voltage that occurs with the sudden influx of sodium ions which reverses the imbalance of charged particles on both sides of the cell membrane.

All-or-None Principle: The principle that either a neural impulse will occur or it will not, with no levels in between, and that its intensity is the same each time it occurs.

Threshold: The point at which the amount of stimulation is sufficient to cause a neural impulse.

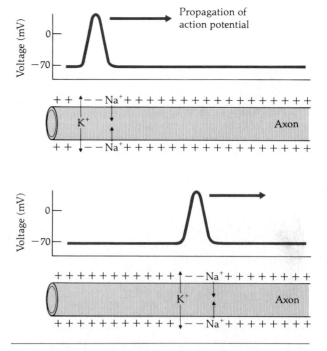

Figure 3.5   The Action Potential.   Stimulation of the neuron causes it to become more permeable to Na$^+$ until finally the inside of the cell becomes positively charged relative to the outside. This sudden change in charge is called the action potential. Like a chain reaction, the action potential propels systematically along the entire axon.

gins. In terms of the all-or-none principle, if the threshold is not reached, there will be no electrical impulse; if the threshold is reached, the impulse occurs, but increases above the threshold have no additional effect. The range of experience we feel is due to the number of cells firing and the frequency with which they do it. As more cells fire, and as they fire more frequently, an experience becomes more intense.

The electrical impulse of axonal transmission ends at a tiny knob called the **axon terminal.** Within some axon terminals are small structures known as **synaptic vesicles.** The force of the electrical impulse causes the synaptic vesicles to open and release their neurotransmitter. At that point, synaptic transmission takes over.

Axon Terminals: Tiny knobs at the end of the axon that bear small structures called synaptic vesicles (the storage bins for the cell's chemical neurotransmitter substance).

Synaptic Vesicles: Tiny storage bins inside the axon terminals that contain a neuron's neurotransmitter.

Synaptic Transmission

With the release of the neurotransmitter into the synapse, the electrical impulse of the action potential triggers a chemical signal. The receiving neuron is able to read the signal because the neurotransmitter's molecules fit the receptor sites exactly, as a key fits a lock. When a neurotransmitter finds its way to a compatible receptor site, it activates the cell. The process is analogous to putting the right key into your car's ignition and turning the key to start the car.

The neurotransmitter can influence the cell in one of two main ways: by increasing the cell membrane's permeability or by reducing it. This variation of neurotransmitter substance is referred to as the more-or-less principle and is in reality the decision-making function of the neural cell. If it increases permeability—that is, weakens the cell membrane—it increases the chance that an action potential will occur. Neurotransmitters that increase permeability, and hence a cell's tendency to fire, are said to have an **excitatory** effect. Excitatory impulses are like turning a door key to the right, opening the door to the cell. Impulses that reduce the cell's permeability and tendency to fire are said to be **inhibitory.** Inhibitory impulses are like turning the key to the left, locking the door and making it more difficult for a burglar to break in. Whichever effect a neurotransmitter has, after it has done its work, it is absorbed back into the axon terminals and used again or broken down by other substances.

Excitatory Stimulation: Stimulation that reduces permeability of a neuron's membrane, thus increasing its potential to fire.

Inhibitory Stimulation: Stimulation that increases the permeability of a neuron membrane, thus decreasing its potential to fire.

Brain researchers have identified some six dozen different neurotransmitters, though the action of all but a handful remains a mystery (Snyder, 1984). Among the neurotransmitters that play an important role in behavior are serotonin, acetylcholine, and the catecholamines.

Serotonin has an inhibitory effect. When serotonin is released into the

---

■ Learning Check ■

Read the definition, then cover the right side and try to recite it. Repeat.

Neural Transmission	The two-step process of communication among neurons.
Axonal Transmission	Neural transmission within a neuron.
Synaptic Transmission	Neural transmission between neurons.

Box 3.1 PSYCHOLOGY IN ACTION: Midafternoon Drowsiness

Have you ever experienced the throbbing pain of a toothache or tried to fight off that midafternoon drowsiness that seems to strike just when you need to be alert? These and many other personally relevant everyday experiences are intimately linked to the functioning of our nervous systems and neurotransmitter substances.

An important breakthrough in our understanding of neurotransmitters came in 1973 when two Johns Hopkins University scientists, Solomon H. Snyder and Candace Pert, discovered that a number of neurons in the brain had receptor sites specifically engineered to bind with morphine and other opiate drugs. The pain-relieving properties of opium and its derivatives, heroin, morphine, and codeine, had long been known. But why did the human brain have receptors just made for opium? The inescapable conclusion was that the body must be capable of manufacturing its own opium-like substance.

In 1975, Hughes and Kosterlitz of the University of Aberdeen in Scotland confirmed this conclusion. They located a neurotransmitter that is manufactured by the brain when a person is in pain and found that the neurotransmitter binds with opium receptors (Fincher, 1981). They named this substance enkephalin (en-keff-uh'-linn'), meaning in the head. A few months later, Snyder and Pert reported the same discovery.

The discoveries of enkephalins and related substances have shown that the nervous system has its own control system for dealing with pain. So, the next time you are in pain, it might help you to realize that, through release of its own morphine-like substances, your nervous system is working to control it.

Painkilling narcotic drugs such as morphine and codeine relieve pain by occupying the receptor sites usually filled by the brain's own painkilling enkephalin and related substances. The drug keeps the receptors saturated and reduces the body's need to manufacture its own natural painkiller. Consequently, the administration of narcotic drugs suppresses the brain's own pain control system. Eventually, the receptors are occupied by and dependent on narcotics. Then, when the drug is withdrawn, the body undergoes a withdrawal response—a heightened sensitivity to pain, cramps, nausea, and other very uncomfortable effects.

Neurotransmitters have also been linked to the so-called gambler's high and compulsive gambling

---

brain, it hastens the onset of sleep, decreases alertness, and depresses the appetite. Acetylcholine is an excitatory neurotransmitter. Acetylcholine is the transmitter that activates the skeletal muscles and permits voluntary movements. The poisonous botulinum toxin (present in improperly preserved foods) prevents the release of acetylcholine and results in complete paralysis and, ultimately, death.

The catecholamines are a group of chemically related neurotransmitters whose net effect may be either inhibitory or excitatory. Among the catecholamines are the neurotransmitters dopamine, epinephrine, and norepinephrine. These neurotransmitters activate the individual and increase alertness. In Chapter 5 we will see how these transmitters affect everything from sleep to consciousness. They affect perception, memory, and self-awareness. In Chapter 14, we will see how certain forms of mental illness have been linked to the catecholamines. Box 3.1 presents some insights into how neurotransmitters can affect such experiences as pain and midafternoon drowsiness.

Neuron Networks: The Two Main Branches of the Nervous System

Central Nervous System (CNS): The brain and the spinal cord. All the neurons that lie within the bony structures of the skull and backbone.

Billions of neurons work together to form the extremely complex network that is the human nervous system. The largest of these networks make up the two main branches of the nervous system.

The neurons in the brain and spinal cord make up the **central nervous system (CNS).** The central nervous system may be thought of as the control

Box 3.1 *(continued)*

(Rosenfeld, 1985). Recently, psychologists have found in compulsive gamblers abnormally high levels of a natural brain opiate known as beta-endorphin. Theoretically, the risk and excitement of gambling causes a

The "runner's high," like the so-called gambler's high, appears to be due to the release of beta-endorphins.

release of beta-endorphin, whose narcotic-like effects produce the "high" experienced by compulsive gamblers. When the individual tries to stop gambling, withdrawal symptoms occur, which urges the gambler back to the race track, card room, or dice table in spite of its ruinous effect on marriage, career, and pocketbook.

And what about that pesky midafternoon drowsiness? Research conducted by psychologist Bonnie Spring (1983) indicates that certain types of foods have different effects on the brain because of their effect on the balance of brain levels of certain neurotransmitter substances. A lunch high in carbohydrates (Twinkies, french fries, breads, pastas, and the like) that is not balanced by proteins from meat, poultry, fish, dairy products, and the like, causes an increase in brain levels of serotonin after about one to three hours. Serotonin, in turn, induces calmness and drowsiness, and impairs concentration. And the degree of sleepiness experienced by women, it seems, is even greater than that experienced by men. If you've been afflicted by the midafternoon slump, you might try eating a lunch that is high in protein and low in carbohydrates (Revkin, 1985).

tower of the nervous system; it analyzes incoming information and decides how to handle it. All the neurons that lie outside the brain and spinal cord form the second major branch of the nervous system, the **peripheral nervous system (PNS).** The peripheral nervous system serves to connect the central nervous system with the rest of the body and the external environment. It is the input-output part of the system, so to speak; it carries messages back and forth to and from the control tower. Figure 3.6 illustrates these two main branches of the nervous system.

Peripheral Nervous System (PNS): All the neurons and neuron groupings that lie outside the central nervous system.

Sensory Neurons: Neurons that carry information from the body to the central nervous system (the input cables).

Types of Neurons

Neurons in the peripheral nervous system that carry information from the body to the brain and spinal cord are called **sensory neurons. Motor neurons** are those that carry information from the brain and spinal cord to muscles and glands (see Figure 3.7). Sensory neurons can be viewed as the

Motor Neurons: Neurons that carry information from the central nervous system outward to the body (the output cables).

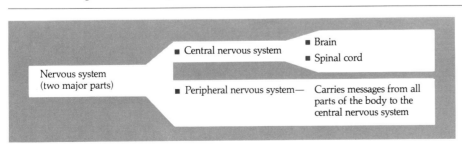

Figure 3.6 Schematic Summary of the Major Divisions of the Nervous System.

Try to remember that sensory neurons carry afferent impulses to the CNS and motor neurons carry efferent impulses from the CNS: *sensory/afferent; motor/efferent.*

Afferent Impulses: Neural impulses going to the central nervous system (afferent means directed inward toward a center).

Efferent Impulses: Neural impulses from the central nervous system going outward to the body (efferent means conducted outward from a center).

input cables; motor neurons as the output cables. Messages going to the brain and spinal cord, along the sensory neurons, are called **afferent impulses;** messages going from the brain and spinal cord to the body, along the motor neurons, are called **efferent impulses.** Afferent impulses keep the central nervous system informed about what is going on in the body and in the environment, just as an airport radar system keeps air traffic controllers informed on conditions outside the control tower. Similarly, efferent impulses control muscles and glands, just as an airport's control tower regulates air traffic.

To get a better idea of the role of sensory and motor neurons in everyday behavior, consider what happens when someone taps you on the shoulder. The touch stimulates sensors in the skin, and these trigger afferent impulses in sensory neurons. The sensory neurons carry the impulses to the spinal cord and up the spinal cord to the brain, where you become aware that someone has touched your shoulder. Your brain then sends efferent impulses down the spinal cord to the muscles in your neck and back. Motor neurons then release the neurotransmitter acetylcholine, allowing you to turn toward the person who touched you. The two main branches of the nervous system thus work together. The PNS sends input information to the CNS along its sensory neuron input cables; the CNS processes the input and

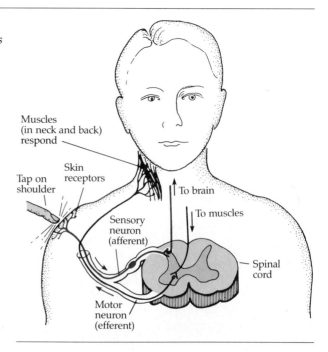

Figure 3.7 Sensory and Motor Neurons. Messages going to the CNS (afferent) are carried along sensory neurons; messages going to the muscles and glands of the body (efferent) are carried along motor neurons.

sends a command; and the command is carried to the muscles along the PNS motor neuron output cables. To further understand how the neurons carry information to and from the CNS, let's take a closer look at the two main branches of the peripheral nervous system.

THE SOMATIC AND AUTONOMIC SYSTEMS

The peripheral nervous system, like the nervous system itself, has two main branches. The **somatic system** is the branch of the PNS that connects the central nervous system with **striated muscles,** which are attached to the bones and, for example, allow you to walk and talk. The neurons of the somatic system also carry information back and forth between the central nervous system and the joints and skin. The **autonomic system,** the second branch, connects the central nervous system with the smooth muscles of the stomach and other internal organs, with the heart, and with the endocrine glands (see below). The autonomic system is so-called because its activities are, under normal circumstances, carried out automatically. As a general rule, you are not aware of, nor can you voluntarily control, the neural impulses that cause your heart to beat or your stomach to digest. That is fortunate, for heartbeat and digestion are essential to the normal functioning of your body; they must continue whether or not you are thinking about them. Imagine what would happen if you had to think to digest or to keep your heart running. You probably wouldn't last long because you'd soon forget to do it or get lazy and skip it or fall asleep.

The Autonomic System: Sympathetic and Parasympathetic Branches

The autonomic system is still further divided into two branches: the sympathetic and parasympathetic systems. The **sympathetic system** generally prepares the body for action. Its neurons, which lead from the central nervous system to the internal organs and glands, carry commands that rouse the body for action. The impulses it carries stimulate the heart, cause sugar to be released into the bloodstream, and slow digestion and other bodily processes that might interfere with the ability to meet danger either by fighting or fleeing. You feel the full force of the sympathetic system when you step into a street and find you must jump out of the way of an on-rushing car. After such an incident, your heart pounds and you may tremble—but you are alive! The sympathetic system contributes to our survival. Unfortunately, it also may go into action when there is no real physical danger, as when you speak in public. On those occasions, the racing of your heart, the butterflies in your stomach, and other sympathetic effects may actually hamper your performance. In extreme cases, an individual may experience a panic attack—a crippling fear accompanied by a wildly pounding heart, choking sensations, and a dreadful feeling of impending doom. (For more on panic attacks, see Chapter 14.)

Somatic System: The division of the peripheral nervous system that includes all the input nerves that carry information from the skeletal (striated) muscles, joints, and skin to the central nervous system, plus all the output nerves leading to the skeletal or striated muscles, which control voluntary movement.

Striated Muscles: Muscles attached to the skeletal system that are involved in voluntary movement.

Autonomic System: The division of the peripheral nervous system whose nerves lead from the CNS to the heart, smooth (generally involuntary) muscles of the internal organs, and glands. The autonomic system consists of two divisions, the sympathetic and the parasympathetic.

Sympathetic System: A division of the autonomic system that generally prepares the body for action. It is usually active during excitement, threat, or fear.

The ready-alert state of this Lacrosse player is due, in part, to the sympathetic nervous system, which prepares the body for action.

Parasympathetic System: A division of the autonomic system that is concerned with recuperative life-sustaining functions. It is active during quiescence and often acts to counter the arousal-producing functions of the sympathetic division of the autonomic system.

The **parasympathetic system** (*para* means "along" or "beside") is primarily concerned with recuperative and life-sustaining functions, such as digestion and the slow, steady beating of the heart. Neurons in the parasympathetic system lead to many of the same organs as the sympathetic system, but the impulses they carry serve to balance or counteract many of the sympathetic impulses. It is the parasympathetic impulses that help you calm down after a close encounter with a speeding car, or the sometimes harrowing experience of a public talk. It also goes into action after you have had a large meal.

Color Plate 3A shows both the sympathetic and parasympathetic systems and the body parts they are connected to. Figure 3.8 presents a schematic overview of the major divisions of the nervous system.

Figure 3.8   Schematic Overview of the Divisions of the Nervous System.

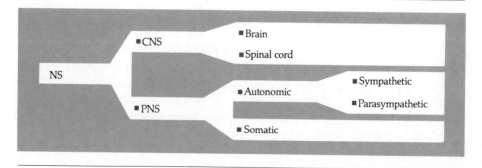

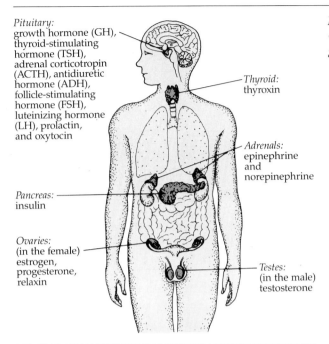

Pituitary:
growth hormone (GH),
thyroid-stimulating
hormone (TSH),
adrenal corticotropin
(ACTH), antidiuretic
hormone (ADH),
follicle-stimulating
hormone (FSH),
luteinizing hormone
(LH), prolactin,
and oxytocin

Thyroid:
thyroxin

Adrenals:
epinephrine
and
norepinephrine

Pancreas:
insulin

Ovaries:
(in the female)
estrogen,
progesterone,
relaxin

Testes:
(in the male)
testosterone

Figure 3.9 The Endocrine Glands. *The endocrine glands and the hormones they secrete.*

The Autonomic System: Interaction with Glands

The autonomic system influences not only smooth (involuntary) muscles, but also **glands.** Glands are organs that manufacture and release chemical substances.

There are two types of glands. **Duct glands** release substances into body cavities or onto the surface of the body. Examples are the salivary glands in your mouth, the digestive glands in your stomach, and the tear glands in your eyes. The effects of duct glands are, for the most part, restricted to the area where the chemical is released. The ductless or **endocrine glands** release chemicals into the bloodstream and have more widespread effects. Examples include the adrenals, the thyroid, and the sex glands (Figure 3.9).

The chemicals the endocrine glands secrete are called **hormones.** This term comes from a Greek word meaning "urge on"; they are well-named, as their function is to stimulate activity in various organs. Because the endocrine glands have a powerful influence on behavior and work in concert with the nervous system, they merit a close look.

THE ENDOCRINE SYSTEM

The endocrine system consists of four paired glands—the adrenals, the thyroids, the sex glands (ovaries and testes), and the parathyroids—and

Gland: An organ capable of manufacturing and releasing chemical substances.

Duct Glands: Glands that release their chemical substances into body cavities like the mouth or onto the surface of the body.

Endocrine Glands: Glands that release chemical substances called hormones into the bloodstream.

Hormones: Chemical messenger substances produced by the endocrine glands or brain which are released into the brain or bloodstream and can have a powerful effect on bodily functions and behavior.

Table 3.1 *Endocrine Glands and Their Hormones*

Gland	Hormone	Effect
Adrenals	Epinephrine (adrenalin)	Increases heart rate, elevates blood pressure, stimulates breakdown of sugar and glycogen for energy.
Ovaries	Estrogen	Stimulates development of female secondary sex characteristics; maintains condition of uterus and birth canal.
	Progesterone	Maintains condition of uterus.
Pituitary	Adrenocorticotropin (ACTH)	Stimulates adrenal gland to release stress hormones.
	Antidiuretic Hormone (ADH)	Stimulates kidneys to preserve water to counteract dehydration.
	Growth Hormone (GH)	Stimulates tissue growth, fat breakdown for energy, protein metabolism.
	Luteinizing Hormone (LH)	Stimulates ovulation in females and secretion of testosterone in males.
	Prolactin	Stimulates production of breast milk.
	Thyroid-Stimulating Hormone (TSH)	Stimulates thyroid to secrete hormones for fat breakdown and for energy.
Testes	Testosterone	Maintains male sex drive.
Thyroid	Thyroxine	Increase burning of sugar.

Box 3.2 PSYCHOLOGY IN ACTION: How Hormones Affect Our Moods and Behavior

Endocrine glands are involved in the emotions you feel. Whether you feel angry or frightened in response to a threat may depend, for example, on the levels of certain hormones in your bloodstream; (McGeer & McGeer, 1980). Studies show that fear is associated with increased levels of epinephrine, anger with increased levels of norepinephrine (Ax, 1953; Davis, 1977). Other research shows that people with too much norepinephrine tend to be irritable or angry much of the time, while people with excessive amounts of epinephrine are constantly anxious (Cohen et al., 1980). Low levels of norepinephrine have been linked to depression. In fact, antidepressant drugs (drugs that combat depression) work by raising blood levels of norepinephrine (Merrell-National Laboratories, 1985). The point is that how we behave and feel has much to do with the actions of our endocrine glands, glands that are largely under the control of the autonomic nervous system.

Recently, hormones secreted by the sex glands—the ovaries in females, which secrete estrogen and progesterone; and the testes in males, which secrete testosterone—have been indirectly linked to aggression and even family arguments. Changes in estrogen and progesterone levels that follow a woman's menstrual cycle play an important part in the irritability as-sociated with the so-called premenstrual syndrome (PMS) that some women experience just before and during menstruation. Studies have revaled that some women are particularly prone to violence during this time of hormonal change; and, in England, as a result of such studies, PMS is considered a legitimate legal defense in criminal cases (Ingber, 1982; Sommer, 1984). Aggression in males has similarly been linked to increased levels of testosterone.

Some scientists believe that testosterone may also be the basis for math genius (Kolata, 1984). According to one theory, increased levels of testosterone during the fetal period of development (see Chapter 2, p. 65) can cause a permanent change in the structure of the brain so that areas of the brain related to mathematical talent become overdeveloped. Although testosterone is found in both males and females, it is secreted in far larger quantities in males. Thus, males are more likely to be affected, which Geschwind (1982) believes explains why males are far more likely than females to obtain extremely high scores on standard measures of mathematical ability, such as the math section of the Scholastic Aptitude Test (SAT). The theory is, of course, speculative, but again illustrates how hormones can have a profound effect on behavior and experience.

four unpaired glands—the pituitary, the pineal, and special cells in the pancreas and kidney. (See Table 3.1.)

The **pituitary** is called the master gland because of its influence over other endocrine glands. Located at the base of the brain, the pituitary secretes hormones that, among other things, affect growth and regulate the amount of water the body retains. The pituitary gland also plays an important role in the body's reaction to stressful events (Axelrod & Reisine, 1984). (For more on the stress response, see Chapter 11.)

Another endocrine gland, the **thyroid,** secretes a hormone that influences the rate at which the body burns energy. Too little of this hormone can make a person prone to obesity; too much, and a person is apt to be the sort who "can't sit still."

The **adrenal glands,** located on top of the kidneys, produce two hormones, **epinephrine** (also known as **adrenalin**) and **norepinephrine** (also called **noradrenalin**). Epinephrine and norepinephrine are sometimes called **neurohormones** because they also function as neurotransmitters (see page 82). As neurotransmitters, epinephrine and norepinephrine affect only neighboring neurons. But when released into the body via the adrenal glands, epinephrine and norepinephrine have a much more pervasive effect on the individual; that is, they can affect nearly every organ in the body. Together, epinephrine and norepinephrine affect the body in much the same way as activation of the sympathetic nervous system (see page 89). The primary function of epinephrine is to mobilize the body to meet emergencies: it speeds up the heart, slows digestion, and activates the sweat glands. Norepinephrine also prepares the body for action: it increases blood pressure and slows the burning of sugars. (Box 3.2 presents some insights and some speculations concerning the role of hormones on everyday behaviors such as anger and irritability.)

Speculations aside, the peripheral nervous system, together with the endocrine system, plays a vital role in both physiology and behavior by linking the brain and spinal cord with the muscles and glands of the body. But the impulses controlling those muscles and glands do not originate in the peripheral nervous system; they come from the "control tower," the central nervous system. In the sections ahead we will examine this control tower beginning with the spinal cord, which serves as a major link between the peripheral nervous system and the brain.

Pituitary Gland: An endocrine gland located at the base of the brain attached to the hypothalamus. Sometimes known as the master gland of the endocrine system, the pituitary gland releases hormones that influence other organs to release hormones.

Thyroid Glands: A pair of endocrine glands located in the neck that release thyroxin, a hormone that influences the rate at which the body uses energy.

Adrenal Glands: A pair of endocrine glands located just above the kidneys consisting of the adrenal medulla, which releases epinephrine and norepinephrine, and the adrenal cortex, which releases hormones known as cortical steroids.

Epinephrine (Adrenalin): A hormone released by the adrenal medulla that mobilizes the body for action, especially in fear situations.

Norepinephrine (Noradrenalin): A hormone released by the adrenal medulla that mobilizes the body for action, especially in anger situations.

Neurohormones: Hormones released into the brain that act only on neurons.

THE SPINAL CORD: GATEWAY TO THE BRAIN

Except for impulses from the eyes, ears, and nose, all afferent impulses from the peripheral nervous system travel to the brain by way of the spinal cord. (Impulses from the eyes, ears, and nose go *directly* to the brain.) Similarly, efferent impulses travel down the spinal cord on their way to muscles and glands. The spinal cord is thus a major link between the brain and the peripheral nervous system.

But the spinal cord is more than a highway, and that is one of the main reasons it is classified with the brain as part of the central nervous system.

Figure 3.10 The Spinal Reflex. In the spinal reflex, an impulse from the body is integrated by interneurons in the spinal cord, which send a message back to the body via motor neurons, without instructions from the brain.

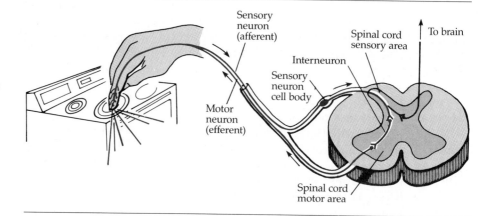

Spinal Reflex: A reflex coordinated by the spinal cord in which neural impulses travel a circuit from sensory neurons to the spinal cord and back again to the motor neurons, without first going to the brain.

Interneurons: Neurons that carry messages from one neuron to another. Interneurons integrate the activities of incoming sensory input and coordinate outgoing messages.

For, in addition to collecting and relaying impulses between the brain and the peripheral nervous system, the spinal cord can initiate muscular movements on its own through what is known as a spinal reflex. In a **spinal reflex,** impulses travel from the sensory neurons to the spinal cord and from there to the motor neurons, without first going to the brain (see Figure 3.10). The impulse also travels to the brain, but only after the efferent impulse has gone on its way. Thus, spinal reflexes do not require processing by the brain. In fact, spinal reflexes are so fast that a person often responds before being aware of what happened, as when you remove your hand reflexively from a hot iron before it burns you.

The spinal reflex is possible because of **interneurons,** neurons that carry messages from one neuron to another. In the case of a spinal reflex, an im-

Figure 3.11 The Major Structures of the Brain. This drawing shows the major structures of the brain. Each of these structures will be discussed in detail in the text.

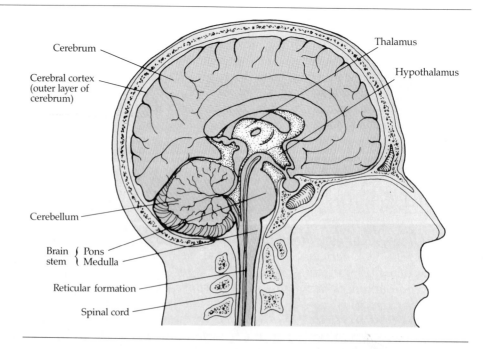

pulse passes from sensory neurons to interneurons in the spinal cord, and from these same interneurons to motor neurons. However, interneurons in the spinal cord do not always pass messages directly to a motor neuron; in fact, the incoming impulse is usually sent to the brain. Only when the interneurons receive intense input, as when you accidentally touch a hot stove, do they send messages directly to the motor neurons.

The spinal cord, important as it is, is no rival to the brain in complexity and in the sophistication of what it does. For our convenience in studying it, we will divide the brain into three "levels." First, we will discuss the brain stem, the part that controls life-sustaining processes such as breathing and heartbeat. We will then move to the limbic system, a set of structures that affect emotional and motivational behaviors. Finally, we will reach the most highly developed part of the brain, the cerebrum, which is responsible for the higher mental processes. Figure 3.11 provides an illustration of each of the major structures to be discussed.

THE BRAIN, LEVEL ONE: THE BRAIN STEM AND RELATED STRUCTURES

At the base of the brain, extending from the spinal cord, is the **brain stem** (see Color Plate 3B), which is responsible for essential life-sustaining processes. The brain stem functions automatically, whether you are awake or asleep. It performs virtually the same duties in humans as it does in reptiles and fish (Restak, 1984). Its activities generally take precedence over those of the rest of the brain, for if it ceases to function, death soon follows. The brain stem includes a number of structures with specific functions, including the medulla and pons. And attached to the brain stem is the cerebellum, which plays a critical role in coordination.

Brain Stem: The inner core of the brain that begins where the spinal cord leaves off and continues like a stalk to the highest level of the brain, the cerebrum. The brain stem contains the structures responsible for most life-sustaining behaviors such as breathing and heartbeat.

■ **Learning Clue** ■

The higher the level of the brain, the less essential are the functions it governs.

The Medulla, Pons, and Cerebellum

The first inch of the brain stem is called the **medulla.** Located immediately above the spinal cord (see Color Plate 3B), this structure contains neurons that govern reflexes such as sneezing, swallowing, and vomiting. The medulla also sends the signals that keep your lungs working and your heart beating twenty-four hours a day. Drugs such as heroin and alcohol taken in large doses are extremely hazardous because they interfere with the functioning of the medulla. In addition to its life-sustaining and reflex-governing responsibilities, the medulla connects the spinal cord with the rest of the brain. Damage to the medulla or suppression of its functioning due to drug overdose can cause death.

Medulla: The first structure of the brain stem, which governs reflexes such as swallowing and a number of life-sustaining activities like heartbeat.

Figure 3.12 Schematic Summary of the Functions of the Medulla, Pons, and Cerebellum.

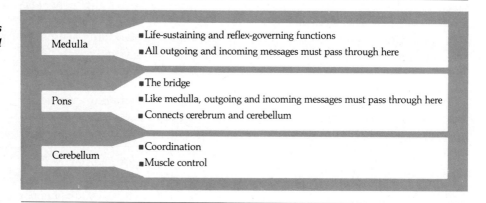

Medulla	■ Life-sustaining and reflex-governing functions ■ All outgoing and incoming messages must pass through here
Pons	■ The bridge ■ Like medulla, outgoing and incoming messages must pass through here ■ Connects cerebrum and cerebellum
Cerebellum	■ Coordination ■ Muscle control

Pons: A structure of the brain stem above the medulla, which connects the outer layers of the cerebrum with the cerebellum.

Cerebellum: A brain structure attached to the brain stem that cooperates with other brain structures to permit muscular coordination and timing.

Arching over the medulla is the **pons** (Latin for "bridge"), which connects the outer layers of the cerebrum—the highest brain structure, to be described later—with a lower brain structure called the **cerebellum.** The cerebellum is a bulb-shaped structure attached to the rear of the brain stem (see Color Plate 3B). It is not actually part of the brain stem.

Thanks to connections through the pons, the cerebellum is capable of cooperating with the highest centers of the cerebrum—the cerebral cortex (the outer layers of the cerebrum); together the two structures, the cerebrum and the cerebellum, govern muscular coordination. The cerebrum initiates specific movements, and the cerebellum coordinates them by inhibiting action in uninvolved muscle groups. Damage to the cerebellum results in jerky movements, because muscles that normally would be inhibited while others move instead compete with those that are in motion. The function of the cerebellum is revealed by the effect of alcohol, which, by impairing the cerebellum's functioning, tends to make movements difficult and awkward. (See Figure 3.12 for a schematic summary of the medulla, pons, and cerebellum.)

The Thalamus and Hypothalamus

The uppermost portion of the brain stem merges into the thalamus and hypothalamus (see Figure 3.11). These two structures have interconnections throughout the brain and technically are not structures of the brain stem. The **thalamus** is a complex brain structure that interconnects the brain stem and the higher brain centers (including the cerebral cortex). It collects incoming sensory information from the brain stem and sends it on to the appropriate higher structure. The thalamus is also a relay station for incoming visual and auditory input from the eyes and ears. Messages from the eyes go to one area, messages from the ears to another. Thus, the thalamus acts as a major relay station for all incoming sensory information. It has other functions as well.

Thalamus: A large complex brain structure that interconnects the brain stem and cerebral cortex and participates with other structures of the brain in carrying out such activities as relaying sensory information and participating in sleeping and waking behaviors.

Damage to the thalamus can affect a person's sleeping, waking, and attention patterns. It also can impair learning ability. In one experiment rats were repeatedly given five seconds to run from a box before an electrical current was turned on. After a few such experiences, normal rats learned to escape the shock well within the five seconds. Those with a damaged thalamus did not (Vanderwolf, 1962, 1963).

Just under the thalamus (see Figure 3.11) lies the peanut-sized **hypothal-amus** (the prefix *hypo* means "below"). But don't let its size fool you; the hypothalamus has connections throughout the nervous system. In fact, it participates in a wide range of behavior—eating, drinking, sleeping, temperature control, rage, and sex. It is sometimes called the brain's brain.

The hypothalamus keeps the body functioning smoothly by calling for adjustments in one process to offset irregularities in another. If the temperature of your blood rises above normal, for example, the hypothalamus detects it and takes appropriate countermeasures. It might, for example, activate your sweat glands by sending an impulse to them through the autonomic nervous system. The sweat reduces the temperature of your body and hence of the blood, and your condition returns to normal. This tendency of the body to maintain its internal stability through a complex system of checks and balances is called **homeostasis** (*homeo* means "the same"; *stasis* means "standing"). The hypothalamus maintains homeostasis by monitoring the body's internal state and directing or cooperating with organs throughout the body to correct any imbalance.

The hypothalamus also helps to regulate basic needs such as hunger and thirst. To give an example, a large loss of body water will lead to an increase of salt in the fluids surrounding the cells throughout the body. Though all body cells are affected, it is the hypothalamus that detects the change and initiates activity that ultimately leads to drinking behavior. When drinking has reduced the concentration of salt outside your body cells, your hypothalamus detects the change and, scientists believe, you cease to be thirsty (Malmo, 1975). (For more on the role of the hypothalamus in motivational processes, see Chapter 9.)

The hypothalamus regulates activity in the endocrine glands through its interconnections with the autonomic nervous system and its control of the master gland, the pituitary (Schally et al., 1977). You might recall that the pituitary lies at the base of the brain (page 93); it is actually attached to the hypothalamus. The hypothalamus stimulates the pituitary both directly, through neural impulses, and indirectly, through the secretion of hormones. In response, the pituitary secretes hormones that trigger other glands to release their hormones. And, in addition to all these functions, the hypothalamus plays an important role in emotional behavior through its connections with the second level of the brain, the limbic system. We discuss this level next, but first let's look at an important network that interconnects with all three of the brain's levels.

The Reticular Formation

Unlike the hypothalamus, the **reticular formation** is not a single structure but a complex network of neurons running through the core of the brain stem and stretching into the areas above (Figure 3.13). It thus interacts with structures on all levels of the brain. Though the reticular formation is not yet fully understood, scientists do know a few of its functions. It prepares the higher brain centers to receive incoming signals, as when you perk up at the smell of smoke or the sight of danger. It facilitates concentration by blocking out distracting noises, preventing them from reaching those parts

Hypothalamus: A peanut-sized structure below the thalamus that plays a critical role in emotional and motivational behavior and regulates the endocrine system.

Homeostasis: Processes that maintain internal stability by a system of checks and balances that correct for any deviation from an optimal or set level.

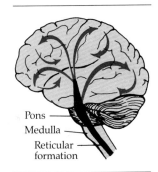

Pons
Medulla
Reticular formation

Figure 3.13 The Reticular Formation. This drawing shows the reticular formation, a complex network of neurons running through the core of the brain stem and stretching into the areas above.

Reticular Formation: A complex network of cells extending through the brain stem that participates with structures throughout the brain in carrying out their functions and that plays a role in waking and sleeping.

of the higher brain centers where they would register in your consciousness. And it may help coordinate the thinking activities of higher brain centers with the emotional activities of lower centers by funneling information between them (Weil, 1974).

Studying the Reticular Formation and Other Parts of the Brain

Electrical Brain Stimulation: A method of studying the brain in which a mild electric current is sent through a tiny wire called an electrode implanted inside the brain.

Electrode: A tiny wire used in electrical brain stimulation and in obtaining electrical recordings of brain activity.

Electroencephalograph: A machine that records the brain's electrical activity through electrodes placed on the scalp.

Electroencephalogram (EEG): A record of the electrical activity of the brain, recorded from the scalp.

Lesion: An injury or loss. The brain can be studied by observing the behavioral effects of accidental injury (lesions) in specific parts of the brain or by systematically destroying certain parts of an animal's brain and observing the effects on behavior.

Study of the reticular formation has provided some good examples of techniques scientists use to study the brain. Brain researchers obtained some of their first clues to the function of the reticular formation by using the method of **electrical brain stimulation,** in which a thin wire called an **electrode** is inserted into the brain so that it can be stimulated by a low-voltage current.

In a classic study, Moruzzi and Magoun (1949) inserted an electrode into the reticular formation of an anesthetized cat and stimulated it by switching on an electric current. They measured the effects of the stimulation by recording the cat's brain waves with an **electroencephalograph,** a machine that records the brain's natural electrical activity, which it detects through electrodes placed on the scalp. The cat's brain wave pattern, called an **electroencephalogram (EEG),** changed from the slow wave pattern typical of a sleeping or anesthetized animal to the fast wave pattern typical of wakeful animals. The researchers hypothesized that the reticular formation plays a central role in the control of sleeping and waking. To further test their hypothesis, the researchers used electrical brain stimulation to stimulate the brains of waking and sleeping cats. They found that such stimulation could cause a wakeful animal to suddenly fall asleep, or a sleeping animal to awake. Converging evidence for the role of the reticular formation in waking and sleeping was then found using another major technique of brain study, the ablation method.

In the ablation method, experimenters destroy certain areas of an animal's brain, creating a brain **lesion.** What is learned can then be compared to observations of the behavior of humans who incur a similar brain lesion through accident or necessary surgery. The rationale for the ablation technique is that the function of a particular part of the brain can be evaluated by determining how behavior is affected following destruction of that part. Surgical destruction of the reticular formation of animals, for example, produces coma; and humans who sustain accidental damage to their reticular formation also often fall into a coma, going into a deep sleep from which they may never return.

The ablation technique and electrical brain stimulation have also helped

---

■ Learning Check ■

Read the right side, then cover and try to recite. Repeat.

The hypothalamus plays a role in:

1. Homeostasis.
2. Motivation (for example, thirst).
3. Regulation of the endocrine system.
4. Emotional behavior.

researchers uncover information about the limbic system and its role in emotion. In the next section, we see how some of these techniques have been put to work in the search for an anger switch.

THE BRAIN, LEVEL TWO: THE LIMBIC SYSTEM

The **limbic system,** a set of structures that form a collar (Latin *limbus*) around the brain stem, is concerned with such functions as emotional responses and memory (see Figure 3.14). It includes the **hippocampus,** which is thought to play a role in learning and memory (Milner, 1959); the **amygdala,** a center for rage (Mark & Ervin, 1970); and the **septum,** which seems to be associated with pleasure (Heath, 1972). These and other parts of the limbic system are linked with each other and with the rest of the nervous system by neural pathways. In fact, the limbic system cooperates so closely with the hypothalamus that many researchers consider the hypothalamus part of the limbic system. While the exact functions of the limbic system are not completely clear, there is no question that it, in conjunction with the hypothalamus, plays an important role in emotional behavior. Probably the best example is its role in rage.

Switching on Rage

Did you ever "blow a fuse"—lose your temper and say or do something you later regretted? Maybe you threw an ashtray at a friend, or got into a heated argument over a parking space. For years researchers have been tantalized by the possibility that there are in the brain, fuse-like switches or circuits that, if activated, will lead to sudden swings in mood.

Limbic System: A group of brain structures that form a collar around the brain stem and that play an important role in emotional and motivational behavior like rage and sex.

Hippocampus: A structure of the limbic system believed to play a role in learning and memory.

Amygdala: A structure of the limbic system believed to play a role in feelings of rage.

Septum: A structure of the limbic system believed to play a role in pleasure.

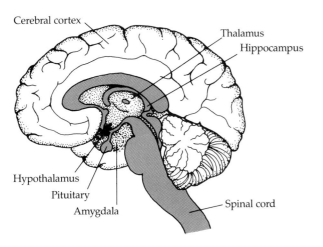

Figure 3.14 The Limbic System. The limbic system is not a specific area; rather, it is a circuit covering many areas with interconnections throughout the brain. Together with the hypothalamus, the limbic system plays an important role in motivation and emotion.

In 1927 the pioneer brain researcher Walter R. Hess reported that he could induce a full-blown rage in a cat by electrical stimulation of its hypothalamus. By turning on the current for an electrode implanted in the cat's hypothalamus, Hess could elicit rage and attack behavior in a previously friendly, affectionate animal. At the flick of a switch the cat would hiss, spit, and even assault him.

Hess's experiments in electrical stimulation of the brain, for which he later won the Nobel Prize, vividly illustrated the relationship between brain and behavior. His findings have been replicated time and time again, not only with cats but also with other animals. Stimulation of specific brain regions in the hypothalamus or limbic system will elicit aggression in rats, monkeys, dogs, and hamsters, while stimulation of other areas in these brain structures will inhibit aggression (Potegal et al., 1981). It is as if these animals are programmed to produce certain kinds of behavior when certain parts of their brains are activated. But the human brain is far more complex. Can findings obtained from cats or monkeys apply to humans?

About the same time Hess was working with cats, Wilder Penfield, a **neurosurgeon,** began using the technique of electrical stimulation of the brain with humans. Normally it is considered unethical to stimulate a human's brain for research purposes, but Penfield was working with patients who required brain surgery for severe uncontrolled **epileptic seizures,** a sudden firing of brain cells that often causes uncontrollable convulsions of the body. By stimulating a certain part of a patient's brain just before the operation, Penfield hoped to map the brain, so that he could avoid accidental damage to normal areas during surgery and identify the area causing the seizures. If stimulation of one part of the brain produces arm movement, for example, Penfield deduced that injury to that area might result in paralysis.

Penfield eventually learned that patients would actually see and hear past experiences when their brains were stimulated. Thus, his work, like Hess's, indicated a relationship between brain and behavior. Producing simple movements and even sounds and visions as Penfield did is a long way from switching on attack behavior, however. Not until a case study of a young girl named Julia was published by Mark and Ervin (1970) did scientists find support for the notion of a human attack switch.

When Julia was only two years old, she contracted a disease that causes swelling of the brain. Following her recovery, she began to experience sudden unexplained "spells," or moments of confusion and fear. Sometimes during a spell she would make wild attacks on her schoolmates, seemingly without reason. Afterward she would experience depression and remorse; four times she attempted to kill herself. On other occasions she would run frantically for miles, then emerge from confusion lost in some strange part of town. For protection, she purchased a pocketknife. (See Figure 3.15.)

Julia was only sixteen years old when she almost killed someone with that knife. She was at the movies with her parents when she began to feel sick. She went quickly to the restroom, where she was horrified by what she saw in the mirror. The entire left side of her body seemed to her to have become shriveled and disfigured. When another girl entered the restroom, the distraught Julia pulled out her pocketknife and stabbed her. Not long after the stabbing incident, she attacked a nurse with a pair of scissors. By the time the neurosurgeons Vernon Mark and Frank Ervin became aware of her case, Julia was clearly a danger both to herself and to others.

Neurosurgeon: A physician specializing in brain surgery.

Epileptic Seizure: A sudden abnormal firing of brain cells that may result in uncontrollable convulsions of the body.

Figure 3.15 Limbic System and Rage. Julia suffered from limbic system damage and bouts of rage.

Extensive examination of Julia's brain revealed a small amount of scar tissue buried deep within the limbic system, on the amygdala. Because normal surgical methods of removing scar tissue might damage other parts of Julia's brain, Mark and Ervin instead implanted an electrode in the scar tissue, with the idea of burning it off electrically. Before attempting this new procedure, however, they wanted some reassurance that Julia's spells were related to the scar tissue. So, after they implanted the electrode, they first determined the effect of a mild electrical current on Julia's behavior. Almost immediately Julia became violent, attacking a physician in the room without warning (Mark & Ervin, 1970). The surgeons' suspicion had been confirmed. Like Hess's cats, Julia's brain seemed to be preprogrammed for rage. The surgeons later sent a stronger current through the electrode, which burned off the scar tissue and drastically curtailed Julia's episodes of violence.

Julia's case alone does not prove that humans have an attack switch, either in the amygdala or anywhere else. Julia's brain was damaged; normal brains may not respond the same way. But there is some rather tantalizing evidence that many of our most basic feelings do originate in the limbic system and that stimulation of that region produces predictable responses. Much of that evidence comes from studies in which stimulation of the brain seemed to produce feelings of pleasure, rather than rage.

Switching on Pleasure

In the 1950s, two psychologists added a new dimension to brain research by giving a rat the opportunity to stimulate its own brain. First they implanted electrodes in the animal's hypothalamus, as Hess had done with cats. Then they connected the electrodes to a lever in the rat's cage so that, by pressing the lever, the rat could turn on the current and stimulate its own brain (see Figure 3.16).

The rat pressed the lever incessantly (Olds & Milner, 1954), a response that intrigued the researchers so much that they repeated the experiment many times, each time changing the conditions of the experiment slightly. They found that some of the animals would pump the lever a hundred times a minute, hour after hour, until they were finally overcome by exhaustion. When given a choice between food and the opportunity to stimulate their brains, even starved rats, they observed, would choose stimulation—provided that the electrode was in just the right spot. And, though a rat would not cross an electrified grid to get to its food, it would do so to get to the lever. What did the rats find so appealing about this brain stimulation?

Of course, nobody can really know whether rats experience pleasure, a subjective experience that cannot be observed directly. But, because the rats went to such great lengths and even endured severe shock to press the lever, the researchers proposed that there must be a **reward mechanism** in the rat's brain. Excitation of this reward mechanism, or pleasure center as it came to be called, was apparently more rewarding even than eating.

It wasn't long before researchers began to wonder whether humans too had a reward center in their brains. Some had hopes of treating severe mental illness through brain stimulation. At Tulane University, a team of experimenters began implanting electrodes in the limbic systems of victims of schizophrenia, a severe mental illness (see Chapter 14). The implants were only used on the most severely disturbed patients, those who had failed to

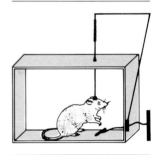

Figure 3.16 Self-stimulation of the Brain. This drawing shows the bar-pressing apparatus by which a rat can administer an electric current to electrically stimulate its own brain.

Reward Mechanism: A central nervous system process whose excitation is rewarding.

respond to conventional treatment. Though the implants did little to cure the patients of their mental illness, the attempt was not a complete failure. The results of more than twenty years of work with more than sixty patients pointed strongly to the existence of a pleasure center in the human brain (Heath, 1972). Nearly every patient tested reported feeling pleasure, alertness, and a sense of well-being following electrical stimulation of the *septum* and other structures of their limbic system. Many patients also reported sexual arousal much like the build-up preceding orgasm. Again the evidence suggested that pleasure, like rage, originated in the limbic system.

The limbic system is more than an on-off switch, however. It has a far more complicated influence on behavior. Unlike the structures of the brain stem, its activities are neither as routine as breathing nor so fixed and automatic. In fact, stimulation of one part of the limbic system might produce pleasant arousal on one day and unpleasant irritation on another (Heath, 1972). Apparently the higher the level of the brain, the more variable the response to incoming impulses. Note too that the higher the level, the less essential are the functions it governs. Limbic system functions such as feeding, fighting, fleeing, and reproduction, the so-called four F's, are certainly essential to the survival of the species, but they do not affect individual members of the species moment by moment the way breathing, heartbeat, and other activities of the brain stem do. Increasing flexibility can also be seen in the highest level of the brain, the cerebrum.

THE BRAIN, LEVEL THREE: THE CEREBRUM AND CEREBRAL CORTEX

Cerebrum: The highest level of the brain; the center for higher mental processes.

Cerebral Cortex: The outer covering of the cerebrum composed of deep infoldings called convolutions. Most complex human functions are carried out in the cerebral cortex.

The **cerebrum** overlays the limbic system and is the center for higher mental processes. Its outermost layer plays such an important role in reasoning, planning, and other complex mental processes that it has a specific name, **cerebral cortex** (see Figure 3.11). Our discussion of the cerebrum will focus on its outer layer, the cortex.

The cerebral cortex is more highly developed in humans than in any other animal. And, while the brain stem and limbic system respond only to basic needs and emotions, the cerebral cortex responds to a variety of higher concerns, from the pursuit of money and power to the quest for spiritual awareness. The cortex is thus highly flexible. As the seat of reasoning and planning, it provides humans with a most effective tool for satisfying their needs, whether they are basic survival needs or personal needs for self-fulfillment.

Global and Localization Theories of Brain Function

We have seen that separate structures in the brain may interact as they affect behavior: the cerebellum and cerebral cortex work together in controlling muscular coordination; the reticular formation and cerebrum cooperate in blocking out distracting noises when you wish to concentrate. This interaction has led some scientists to propose that the brain works as a whole,

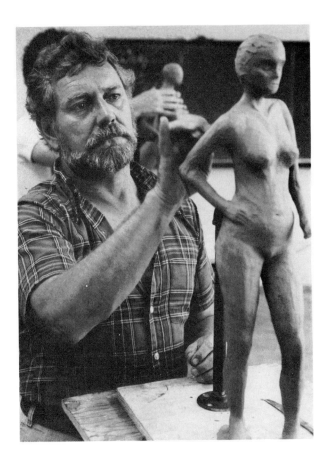

It is the highly developed human cortex which allows us to respond to higher concerns such as personal fulfillment and artistic creativity.

a theory known as the **global theory** of brain function. The theory became popular in the 1920s and 1930s after psychologist Karl Lashley performed some impressive experiments. Lashley trained rats to perform a variety of tasks and then systematically removed portions of their cerebral cortex. He found that, while certain functions such as sensory and motor abilities could be destroyed, he could not completely wipe out an animal's memory—as evidenced by their ability to run previously learned maze patterns—no matter how much cerebral cortex he removed.

Lashley concluded that memory was not located in any one specific region of the cerebral cortex; nor were, he believed, any of the highest mental functions such as judgment, planning, and reasoning (Lashley, 1929). He proposed instead two general principles of brain function. According to his principle of **equipotentiality,** all parts of the cerebral cortex are equal in their potential to assume any of the higher mental processes of the cortex—memory, reasoning, planning, and so on. If one area of the cortex is destroyed, another can take over the functions it used to perform. This would help explain the rats' ability to hold onto their memories despite their extensively damaged cortexes. Specifically, Lashley believed that the entire cortex participates in behavior (Kolb & Whishaw, 1980). And, according to Lashley's principle of **mass action,** the critical factor in learning and other higher mental processes is the total amount of cortex tissue involved in the activity, not which part of the cortex is involved.

Global Theory: A theory of brain functioning that emphasizes the workings of the brain as a whole and the interplay among the various structures of the brain.

Equipotentiality: A principle of how the brain works, proposed by Karl Lashley, which states that different regions of the cerebral cortex are equal in their potential to assume any given function.

Mass Action: A principle of how the brain works, proposed by Karl Lashley, which states that the critical factor in learning ability and other higher mental processes is the total amount of tissue involved, not its location.

Localization Theory: A theory of brain functioning that views the cortex as an array of discrete regions, each governing a different and specific behavioral output. That is, control of each kind of behavior is governed by a different but specific region of the brain.

Autopsy: The dissection and examination of a dead body and its various parts.

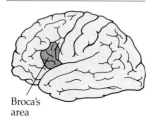

Broca's area

Figure 3.17 Broca's Area. Broca's area is responsible for programming the muscles in the face, tongue, and larynx to speak. Patients with damage in this area can understand language but cannot speak it.

Sensory Cortex: Neurons in the cortex that receive incoming information including the visual areas, the auditory areas, and the sensory strip that spans across the brain like earphones.

While Lashley was arguing for a global theory of brain function, proponents of the **localization theory** held that specific regions of the cortex governed specific behaviors. The localization theory originated in 1861, when a terminally ill man was referred to the French surgeon Paul Broca. Broca observed that, although the patient could understand and obey commands, he was unable to speak or write. After the man died, Broca did an **autopsy** and found brain damage on the left side of the cortex. He concluded that this area of the brain must be involved in the production of language. Further studies confirmed Broca's conclusion: damage to a specific area on the left side of the cerebrum's outer layer, the cortex, consistently produced speech impairment. This region is now referred to as Broca's area (see Figure 3.17).

Localization theorists reasoned that, if speech were governed by one area of the brain, then problem-solving should be governed by a second, memory by a third, and so on. They envisioned the cortex as a mosaic of specific areas associated with specific functions. And they predicted that damage to a specific area of the brain would produce a specific loss. But years of painstaking research have shown that, like the global theory, the localization theory is only partially correct (Crockett et al., 1981).

While certain behaviors can be localized, others cannot. A closer look at the cortex will illustrate the problems with both theories.

■ Learning Check ■

Read the definition, then cover the right side and try to recite. Repeat.

Equipotentiality	The theory that all parts of the cerebral cortex are equal in their potential to assume higher mental processes.
Mass Action	The theory that the critical factor in higher mental processes is the total amount of cortical tissue involved.
Localization Theory	The theory that specific regions of the cortex govern specific behaviors.

The Three Types of Cortex

As Lashley discovered, the most clearly localized functions of the cortex have to do with input and output. Incoming sensory information from the body—touch, heat, cold, and pain—is registered in the **sensory cortex.** Other parts of the cortex can receive stimulation from the sense organs but cannot give rise to appropriate sensation. Destruction of the part of the sensory cortex that receives sensory information from the left hand, for instance, will result in a loss in the sense of touch for that hand. The hand and all the neural pathways between the hand and the brain may be intact, but if the small part of the brain that registers touch is not, a person will not feel the roughness of sandpaper or the smoothness of fine silk. Figure 3.18 illustrates the sensory cortex—where sensory information is registered in the brain. It also shows the points at which outgoing messages are sent—the motor cortex.

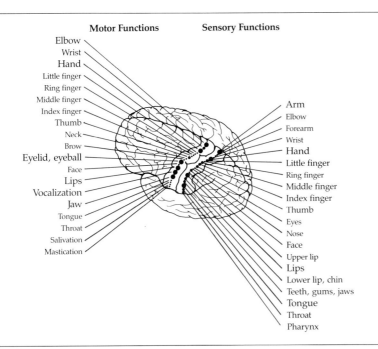

Figure 3.18 Sensory and Motor Cortex. *This drawing shows the location of various input and output functions on the sensory cortex and motor cortex.*

Outgoing impulses issue from the **motor cortex,** which is responsible for all voluntary movements, from walking to smiling. Damage to the part of the motor cortex corresponding to hand movement will result in paralysis of the hand, even if the hand and all the neural pathways from the hand to the brain are completely intact. However, the hand would still be able to feel the roughness and smoothness. Moreover, through physical therapy, other parts of the cortex can restore some movement, as in the case of victims of stroke.

Wilder Penfield, the neurosurgeon who studied brain functions by stimulating his patients' brains electrically (page 100), suggested that it might be possible to construct a detailed map of the brain. Though this goal has never been realized, Penfield and others have been able to sketch out a map of the sensory and motor cortexes and the body parts they govern, as shown in Figure 3.18. Penfield found many parts of the cortex where stimulation did not produce a specific sensory or motor response, however. The parts of the cortex that are not specifically related to the senses or to movement are called the **association cortex.** The association cortex, which is far bigger than the sensory and motor cortex combined, performs the information-processing (i.e., decision making and data analysis) functions of the brain. Judgment, reasoning, and even consciousness appear to reside there.

Motor Cortex: Neurons in the cortex that execute output and are responsible for every voluntary movement.

Association Cortex: All the areas of the cortex that are not concerned with sensory or motor functions but instead coordinate these two activities and are responsible for higher mental processes such as judgment and reasoning.

The Four Lobes

The entire cerebral cortex, including all sensory, motor, and association cortex, is physically divided into two hemispheres, or halves. Each hemisphere is further divided into four roundish lobes, which are shown in Figure 3.19. Using case studies of brain-damaged patients and maps made by electrical stimulation, scientists have located certain functions in the outermost layer (cortex) of each of the lobes (Rothi et al., 1985; Stuss & Benson, 1984).

Parietal Lobes: A region of the cortex that receives information from the body concerning touch sensations.

The **parietal lobes,** which lie at the crown of the head (behind the central fissure), is where the sensory cortex that registers sensations from the body is located (see Figure 3.19). Damage to the cortex of these lobes may produce distortions of a person's body image. Patients with lesions in this area may not even recognize parts of their body as their own. Parietal damage also may prevent a person from recognizing an object by touch, or it may produce reading and writing disabilities (Rothi et al., 1985).

Temporal Lobes: A region of the cortex that receives auditory information and transforms sounds into recognizable patterns.

The **temporal lobes** (everything below the lateral fissure), so-called because they lie at the temples, receive auditory information from the thalamus and transform sound into recognizable patterns (see Figure 3.19). Damage to the temporal lobes can result in an inability to recognize familiar melodies (Milner, 1971). Though these lobes are not the exclusive seat of memory, electrical stimulation of the area may produce thoughts which patients identify as memories (Penfield & Rasmussen, 1950) or impair performance on memory tests (Fedio & Van Buren, 1975).

Figure 3.19   The Four Lobes.   The cerebrum can roughly be divided into four major areas or lobes—parietal, temporal, occipital, and frontal. Researchers have associated a number of important functions with each of the outermost layers (the cortex) of each of the four lobes.

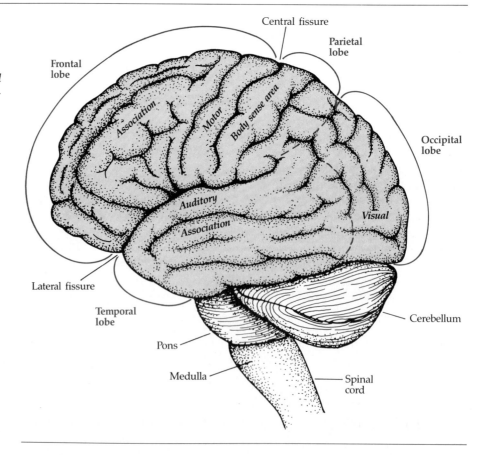

The **occipital lobes,** located at the rear of the brain, behind the parietal lobes, receive visual information from the thalamus and transform it into recognizable images (Figure 3.19). If lesions in this lobe are not extensive enough to produce total blindness, they may still interfere with a person's ability to perceive visual input as a whole. For example, a person with a small lesion in this lobe might be able to recognize the letters in a word, but not the word's meaning, or fail to recognize familiar objects (Larrabee et al., 1985).

> **Occipital Lobes:** A region of the cortex lying at the rear of the brain that receives visual information.

The **frontal lobes,** everything in front of the central fissure, at the front of the brain, are the largest part of the cerebral cortex (see Figure 3.19). They include the motor cortex, which governs voluntary movement. Many investigators suspect that these lobes are responsible for most higher mental processes.

> **Frontal Lobes:** The largest region of the cortex (in humans), lying at the front of the brain, which includes the motor strip involved in voluntary movements and may be the site of most higher mental processes.

A dramatic case study of quadruplets born in 1930 (see Figure 3.20) revealed a possible link between frontal lobe damage and schizophrenia. The quadruplets shared more than an identical genetic makeup. All four developed schizophrenia—a severe mental illness that causes disturbances in logical reasoning and other higher mental processes—in their early adult years. The chances of this occurring, scientists estimate, are about one in two billion. What made this case even more remarkable was that each of the four had a different degree of severity of the mental illness, ranging from Nora and Hester, who had the most severe and persistent symptoms, to Iris and Myra, who had the same symptoms but to a lesser extent (Buchsbaum, 1984).

Using a modern method of brain study called PET, or positron emission, which produces computer-generated color pictures of the brain (see Color Plate 3C), researchers found that the sisters with the most severe cases also had the most extensive damage to the frontal lobe areas. While it is not clear how the damage occurred, the study helps explain why the sisters all had

Figure 3.20 Schizophrenia. Schizophrenic quadruplets—all four suffered damage to the frontal lobes of the cerebral cortex.

Figure 3.21 Schematic Summary of the Types of Cortex and the Four Lobes.

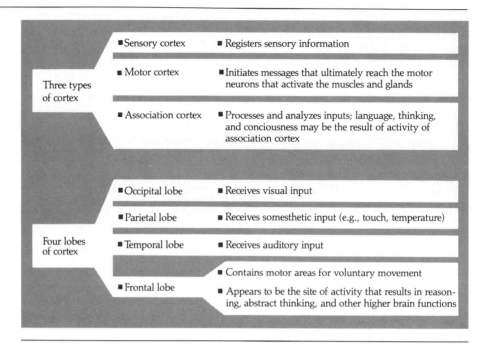

Three types of cortex	■ Sensory cortex	■ Registers sensory information
	■ Motor cortex	■ Initiates messages that ultimately reach the motor neurons that activate the muscles and glands
	■ Association cortex	■ Processes and analyzes inputs; language, thinking, and conciousness may be the result of activity of association cortex

Four lobes of cortex	■ Occipital lobe	■ Receives visual input
	■ Parietal lobe	■ Receives somesthetic input (e.g., touch, temperature)
	■ Temporal lobe	■ Receives auditory input
	■ Frontal lobe	■ Contains motor areas for voluntary movement ■ Appears to be the site of activity that results in reasoning, abstract thinking, and other higher brain functions

trouble planning and anticipating events, a major problem in schizophrenic patients (Hamer, 1982; Endicott, 1986).

The frontal lobes have long been implicated in schizophrenia, and during the 1930s and 1940s, prior to the discovery of effective drugs for the disorder, many patients were treated with a radical procedure known as prefrontal lobotomies. In a prefrontal lobotomy, the frontal lobe fibers on each side of the brain are cut off from the rest of the brain through surgical lesions. The technique produced what seemed to be impressive results, in that patients given to excitement, agitation, and physical assaults showed dramatic behavioral change. Their violence ceased; indeed, they seemed to become relatively unconcerned about events around them. However, subsequent study revealed some very serious and irreversible side effects.

Patients who underwent prefrontal lobotomies experienced severe difficulties in their mental processing. For example, some showed an inability to alter their approach to problem solving, repeating an old approach over and over, despite numerous failures. Given two tools to work with, such patients would continue to use the one that was too large, never trying the smaller one that lies next to it. People given lobotomies also suffered socially. They had trouble telling when their behavior offended or pleased others. To many relatives, the personality changes seemed so great that they felt the patient wasn't the same person. Today, given the known irreversible side effects, lobotomies would be unthinkable except under rare circumstances. (For more on lobotomies, see Chapter 14.) Figure 3.21 provides a schematic overview of the three types of cortex and the four lobes.

Right Side/Left Side

In general the human brain is **bilaterally symmetrical** in structure, which means that its left side is almost a mirror image of the right. You have

Bilaterally Symmetrical: The same on both sides; as the right half of the body is almost a mirror image of the left, the right half of the brain is almost a mirror image of the left half.

two cerebellums, a right one and a left one. You also have two cerebral cortexes, referred to as the **right hemisphere** and the **left hemisphere**. Similarly, each of the four lobes has a near mirror image twin in each hemisphere.

The human brain's access to the environment and control over behavior is also **contralateral,** which means that the left side of the brain receives input from and controls the right side of the body, and vice versa. As illustrated in Figure 3.22, your right hand is controlled by the left side of your brain. Moreover, sensory information from your right hand goes to the left side of the brain.

In recent years researchers have marshalled considerable evidence in support of what had been suspected for quite some time: that the two hemispheres of the cerebral cortex, the right and left hemispheres, specialize in different functions (Hines et al., 1985; Segalowitz & Plantery, 1985; Tan, 1985). This means that certain attributes may not only be localized in a particular lobe, but may be further localized only in the right or left side of the brain, represented in one side but not the other. Thus, it may be an oversimplification to say that the temporal lobes have one function and the parietal lobes another. Instead, we have to look at the right temporal lobe versus the left temporal lobe, the right frontal lobe versus the left frontal lobe, and so on.

The term **lateralization** refers to the phenomenon that certain attributes may be represented more strongly or exclusively in one hemisphere, and that the two hemispheres specialize in different functions. The possibility of lateralization first became known when Broca found that damage in the left hemisphere produced language deficits but that damage to the comparable areas in the right hemisphere did not for right-handed subjects. There soon emerged the concept of **cerebral dominance,** the notion that one hemisphere

Right Hemisphere: The right half of the cerebrum or cerebral cortex, which is a near mirror image of the left half.

Left Hemisphere: The left half of the cerebrum or cerebral cortex, which is a near mirror image of the right half.

Contralateral: Refers to the fact that the left side of the brain receives input from and controls the right side of the body, and vice versa.

Lateralization: Refers to greater representation of some functions in one cerebral hemisphere than in the other.

Cerebral Dominance: An old concept that suggested that one hemisphere was superior to and dominated the other. Generally, the left hemisphere was believed to be the dominant one in right-handers.

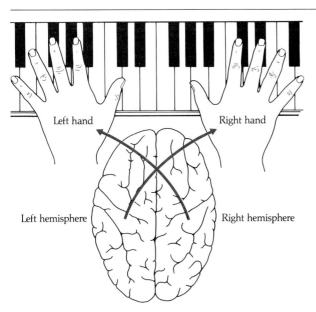

Figure 3.22 The Contralateral Nature of the Right and Left Hemispheres. *Due to the brain's contralateral structure, the left side of the brain receives input from and controls the right side of the body; the right side of the brain receives input from and controls the left side of the body.*

is superior to another. It was commonly accepted, for example, that the left hemisphere, which controls the right side of the body and contains the primary language areas for most right-handed and many left-handed people, was superior to and dominated the right hemisphere in such individuals. For some left-handers, the right hemisphere specializes in language and was thought to dominate the left hemisphere.

But the real truth did not become known until the early 1960s, when Roger Sperry initiated a series of investigations at the California Institute of Technology for which he was later to win the Nobel Prize in 1981. Sperry's work suggested that one hemisphere didn't really dominate the other. Rather, each seemed to have its own area of expertise.

Split-Brain Experiments

The story of Sperry's work actually began in the 1930s, when some neurosurgeons tried a new technique for treating patients with severe epileptic seizures (see p. 100) that produced massive uncontrollable convulsions of the body. It had been known that, in many cases of epilepsy, a seizure would begin when neurons in the brain started firing. If the motor cortex that controlled the right arm suddenly started firing, the right arm would begin to jerk. Once a seizure began, it would spread across the entire brain, causing the entire body to jerk and wiggle out of control.

Some 1930 neurosurgeons believed that it might be possible to prevent the spread of a seizure by severing the major fibers that connected the right and left hemispheres, the **corpus callosum** (see Color Plate 3D). If the two hemispheres could be disconnected, then the seizure could not spread across the brain.

Corpus Callosum: The major fibers that connect the right and left cerebral hemispheres and allow information to be passed back and forth between them.

After a large number of animal experiments, the neurosurgeons began their work on only the most severely impaired patients, because no one knew how splitting the two hemispheres might affect a person. The surgery proved to be effective in controlling seizures for many patients, but, to the surprise of the neurosurgeons, they found almost no other detectable changes in their **split-brain patients.**

Split-brain Patients: Individuals who have had their corpus callosum severed, disconnecting the right and left hemispheres, in an effort to control severe epilepsy.

If severing the corpus callosum had no apparent effect on behavior, what could this four-inch body of densely packed fibers be for? Sperry and colleagues devised an ingenious series of experiments to solve the riddle (Sperry, 1961, 1974, 1982).

In the general procedure the split-brain patients' hands were hidden from view by one screen, and they were seated in front of another screen on which images could be flashed. Patients were asked to look at a central point on the screen. The visual system is structured such that all the information in the left visual field travels to the right hemisphere and all the information in the right visual field travels to the left hemisphere (see Figure 3.23). Thus, Sperry could flash images to just one hemisphere by projecting them to the right or left of the central fixation point. Normally, information projected to one hemisphere would be transferred to the other through the corpus callosum. But, because the corpus callosum had been severed in these patients, there was no communication between the two hemispheres.

Sperry and colleagues found that if words were projected to the right hemisphere, the split-brain patient could not recognize them. They would

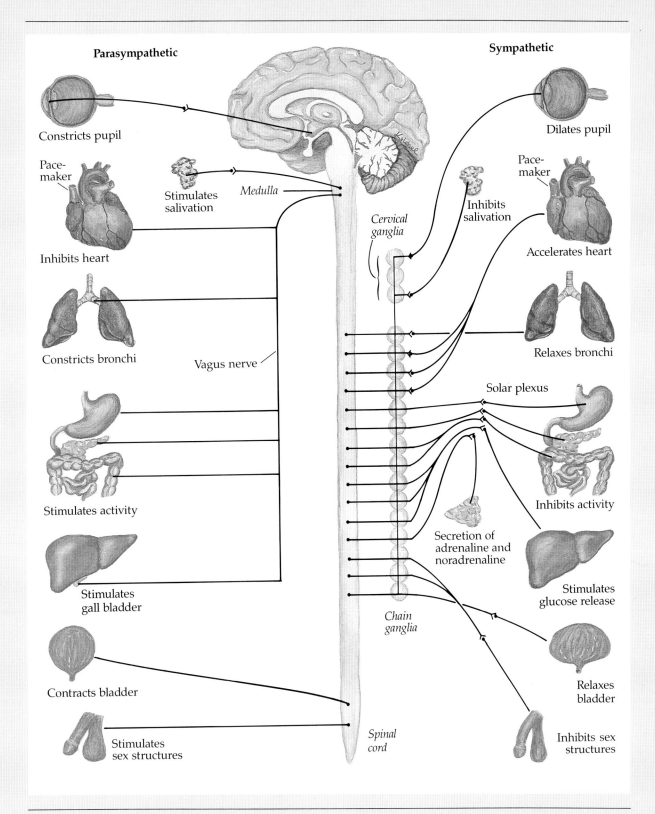

Parasympathetic

Constricts pupil

Pace-maker

Stimulates salivation

Medulla

Inhibits heart

Constricts bronchi

Vagus nerve

Stimulates activity

Stimulates gall bladder

Contracts bladder

Stimulates sex structures

Sympathetic

Dilates pupil

Pace-maker

Inhibits salivation

Cervical ganglia

Accelerates heart

Relaxes bronchi

Solar plexus

Inhibits activity

Secretion of adrenaline and noradrenaline

Stimulates glucose release

Relaxes bladder

Inhibits sex structures

Chain ganglia

Spinal cord

Color Plate 3A   The Sympathetic and Parasympathetic Branches of the Autonomic Nervous System.   The sympathetic branch (right) serves to arouse the body—inhibiting salivation, accelerating the heart, and so on. The parasympathetic branch is primarily involved with recuperative and life-sustaining functions—inhibiting the heart, stimulating digestive activity, and so on.

The human nervous system is an incredible machine, which governs all of our abilities, mental processes, and interactions with our environment. Due to its intricate workings, the nervous system provides us with a broad range of experiences, all dependent upon the firing of individual neurons within the system.

When we experience strong stimulation, more neurons fire with greater frequency than when we experience weak stimulation. Thus, we shrink from the intense heat of a burning building, though we enjoy the cozy warmth of a campfire.

Billions of firing neurons work together in this system, allowing us to respond quickly to incoming stimuli. Due to the rapid interaction between sensory and motor neurons, a ball player can catch a baseball and then throw it immediately to complete the play.

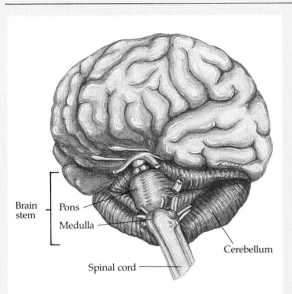

Color Plate 3B   The Brain Stem and Related Structures.   *This drawing shows the brain stem and two of its main structures, the medulla and pons. Also shown is the cerebellum, which is attached to the brain stem.*

Brain stem

Pons

Medulla

Cerebellum

Spinal cord

The nervous system does more than control our responses to the world around us; it controls our internal body states as well. Structures in the brainstem govern many life-sustaining processes; others, in the limbic system, regulate our body's internal stability, reminding us, for example, to stay cool on a hot day.

Color Plate 3C   PET Studies of Schizophrenia. *These positron emission (PET), or computer-generated, color pictures of the brain, show a normal brain (left) and a schizophrenic brain (right) revealing frontal lobe damage. In the case of the schizophrenic quadruplets, the sisters with the most severe cases also had the most extensive damage to the frontal lobes.*

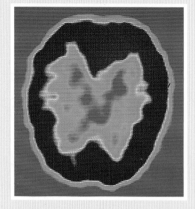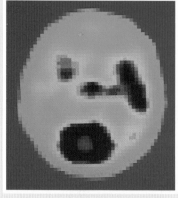

Color Plate 3D   The Corpus Callosum. *This photograph of a medical view through the center of the brain illustrates the corpus callosum—the major fibers that connect the right and left cerebral hemispheres.*

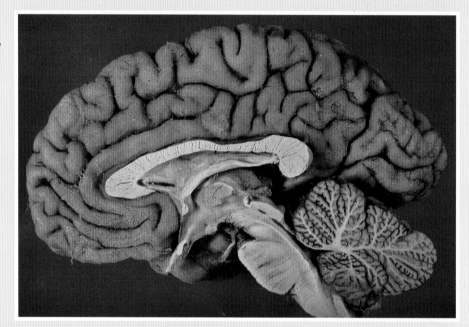

While the brainstem and limbic system respond to our basic needs and emotions, the highly developed cerebral cortex is responsible for more elaborate mental activity. Through the workings of the cerebrum's convoluted lobes, we are able to reason logically and to fulfill our desire for creative expression.

By understanding the intricate structures and processes of the nervous system, we are better able to understand ourselves. It is, after all, the complex workings of this system that make us human.

only recognize words if they were projected to the left hemisphere, which specializes in language for most people. In one experiment they projected the word HEART on the screen such that the HE was in the left visual field (and hence went to the right hemisphere) and ART was in the right visual field. The subject only reported seeing ART. In other experiments the researchers would place familiar objects like a fork or a toothbrush in the subjects' hands that were hidden behind the screen. If the object was placed in the left hand, the subjects could not name it. The subject could only name the object when it was placed in the right hand. (See Figure 3.24) The message seemed clear. The left hemisphere specialized in language (Sperry, 1970; Gazzaniga, 1970).

But that wasn't all. If designs were projected to one hemisphere at a time and copied by the opposite hand, the left hand always did better, even though subjects were right-handed! This suggested that the right hemisphere was superior in analyzing spatial patterns. Subsequent research seemed to suggest that each hemisphere had its own particular strengths, with skills such as reasoning and writing specialized in the left hemisphere and skills such as pattern recognition, art and music appreciation, and mental imagery in the right hemisphere (Berent, 1981).

More recently, researchers have learned that many of the differences attributed to the two hemispheres are not as clear and simple as once believed (Hass & Whipple, 1985; Myers, 1985). Mental imagery and facial recognition, both once thought to be lateralized in the right hemisphere, have shown to be represented in the left hemisphere as well (Farah et al., 1985; Jackson, 1985; O'Boyle, 1985). A new consensus is now emerging. Simply stated, although one hemisphere may be better than another at performing certain functions, for the intact brain, the two hemispheres almost always work together (Levy, 1985). For example, Zatorre (1985) found that discrimination and recognition of tonal melodies actually involves at least two steps: stor-

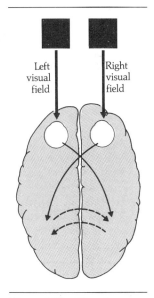

Figure 3.23 Visual Fields. *The visual system is structured in such a way that all the information in the left visual field travels to the right hemisphere and all the information in the right visual field travels to the left hemisphere. When the corpus callosum is severed, information projected to the right or left visual field goes to the corresponding hemisphere, but is not transferred to the other hemisphere.*

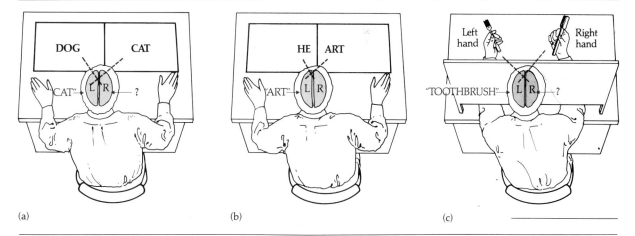

(a) (b) (c)

Figure 3.24 Split-Brain Experiments. *(After Sperry, 1970)*

■ Learning Check ■

Read the right side, then cover and try to recite. Repeat.

Three important facts about the brain.	1. It is bilaterally symmetrical (the right side is almost a mirror image of the left).
	2. It is contralateral (the left side of the brain controls the right side of the body and vice versa).
	3. Its right and left cerebral cortex (right and left hemisphere) are connected by a structure called the corpus callosum.

---

age of the tones in memory, which is primarily under left hemisphere control; and identification of the stored tonal information, primarily a right hemisphere function.

Our study of the human nervous system has helped to reveal how our actions, mental activities, and experiences are intimately linked to the structures of the nervous system and its innumerable electrical and chemical processes. Understanding the nervous system helps to give us a better understanding of ourselves and a host of personally relevant topics, ranging from pain and midafternoon drowsiness through drug addiction and mental illness. In the next chapter we will take a closer look at how our brain interacts with the environment in activities such as seeing, listening, feeling, smelling, and tasting.

LEARNING FRAMEWORK

I. The neuron has three main functions—receiving, integrating, and sending information. (Review: *Figure 3.1; Figure 3.2; Receptor Sites; Neurotransmitters*)

A. Axonal transmission involves communication within the neuron. When the level of stimulation reaches a certain point, a battery-like electrical message is sent along the neuron's axon, which causes the neuron to release its neurotransmitter substance. (Review: *Action Potential; All-or-None Principle; Threshold; Figure 3.4; Figure 3.5*)

B. Synaptic transmission involves communication between neurons. (Review: *Synapse; Excitatory Stimulation; Inhibitory Stimulation*)

C. Neurons group into complex networks for sending, analyzing, and receiving information. (Review: *Central Nervous System (CNS); Peripheral Nervous System (PNS); Figure 3.6*)

D. Some neurons send messages to the brain; others carry messages from the brain to the muscles and glands. (Review: *Sensory Neurons; Afferent Impulses; Motor Neurons; Efferent Impulses; Figure 3.7*)

II. The peripheral nervous system has two main branches, the somatic system (connected to the voluntary muscles) and the autonomic system (connected to the internal organs, heart, and endocrine glands)

A. The autonomic system also has two branches, one that operates during arousal (sympathetic system), the other concerned with recuperation (parasympathetic system).

B. Through its interconnections with the endocrine glands, the autonomic nervous system can send neural messages that cause hormones to be released into the bloodstream.

III. Hormones released by endocrine glands provide chemical signals that profoundly affect behavior. (Review: *Epinephrine; Norepinephrine; Figure 3.9; Table 3.1*)

IV. The spinal cord provides a major link between the peripheral nervous system and the brain. (Review: *Spinal Reflex; Interneurons; Figure 3.10*)

V. The brain is structured in levels, with the lower brain centers at the bottom and highest centers at the very top. (Review: *Figure 3.11*)

   A. Structures at level 1 govern life-sustaining functions and coordination. (Review: *Brain Stem; Medulla; Cerebellum; Color Plate 3B; Figure 3.12*)

   B. The thalamus acts as a major relay station for incoming sensory information. The hypothalamus serves so many functions it is sometimes called the brain's brain. (Review: *Homeostasis*)

   C. The interconnections of the brain are vividly seen in examining the reticular formation. (Review: *Figure 3.13*)

   D. Efforts to study the reticular formation have revealed its role in sleeping and waking. (Review: *Electrical Brain Stimulation; Lesion*)

VI. At level 2, the limbic system is involved with emotion. (Review: *Amygdala; Septum; Case of Julia; Reward Mechanism; Figure 3.14*)

VII. At level 3 (the cerebrum) are the brain structures involved in interpreting incoming messages and sending commands. A number of theories have been proposed and some rather ingenious experiments conducted in an effort to understand the workings of this level.

   A. Some theories emphasize cooperation among the various brain structures; others the relationship between specific areas and specific functions. (Review: *Cerebral Cortex; Global Theory; Localization Theory*)

   B. Three different types of cerebral cortex have been identified that specialize in receiving information (sensory cortex), integrating information (association cortex), and sending commands (motor cortex).

   C. Scientists have identified specific functions in the outermost layer (cortex) of each of the four lobes of the cerebrum (Review: *Figure 3.19*)

   D. The cerebral cortex also can be divided into two halves or hemispheres. (Review: *Left Hemisphere; Right Hemisphere; Lateralization; Figure 3.22*)

   E. Split-brain studies supported the idea of lateralized brain function. (Review: *Corpus Callosum; Split-Brain Patients; Color Plate 3D*)

C H A P T E R

4

Sensation and Perception

Chapter Outline

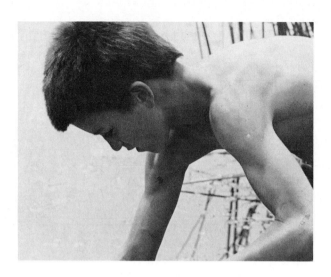

Several years ago an imaginary being from another world came to life in one of the most remarkable illusions ever created on film. E.T., or the Extra Terrestrial, was a creation of Hollywood, but for those who saw him on the screen, he seemed real as life. He walked, he talked, he helped himself to a few cans of beer and became intoxicated. He developed a close bond with an eleven-year-old boy, who sheltered him from unsympathetic humans. When the innocent little creature appeared to be dying, many people in the audience cried. Others rejoiced when he regained his strength and escaped to the safety of his spaceship.

Like all films, *E.T.* was no more than a series of still photographs pieced together in sequence and projected on a screen at the rate of 24 frames per second (see Figure 4.1). Its lovable hero lived because of the filmmaker's skills in exploiting the peculiarities of the human sensory-perceptual system. Without realizing it, people experience similar **illusions**—discrepancies between perception and reality—every day. This common phenomenon reveals much about how people gather, organize, and interpret the various forms of energy that bombard the senses.

Illusions also have practical significance in fields as diverse as engineering and advertising. Natural, or unplanned, illusions are of great concern to those who design, build, and maintain the expressways that crisscross the nation. They strive to design roads that will prevent accidents by minimizing illusions. The military also takes a great interest in the kind of illusion that allows a huge tank to blend into the surrounding terrain. The advertising industry uses illusions to increase the desirability of its clients' products. How many times have you seen TV ads for a dessert that looks so good, you can practically taste it; a pain reliever so effective, you can almost see it work; a detergent that gets clothes so clean, you can smell its freshness? By piecing together shots of headache sufferers, first in pain and then smiling and pain free, the advertiser suggests that the sufferers have been relieved of their distress by the latest over-the-counter painkiller. The success of the

Illusion: Discrepancy between what a person perceives and the physical world; perception that does not represent a stimulus as it exists in reality.

Figure 4.1   The Illusion of Motion.   *The illusion of motion is produced by a series of still photographs pieced together in sequence, similar to this time-delay photograph of a fly jumping from a leaf.*

product, like that of the surprise military operation, depends on the effectiveness of the illusion.

Artists and musicians are also masters of illusion. Those who make musical recordings and stereo equipment strive to produce sound that seems live; through illusion, they recreate performances long past. Using various techniques, painters create the illusion of depth on flat canvas. Photographers manipulate lighting and sets to their subjects' best advantage. Beauticians and fashion designers use cosmetics and clothing to create the illusion of glamour, status, or sexiness.

Still other specialists are concerned not so much with making use of perceptual distortions as with correcting malfunctions in the sensory-perceptual system. As teachers of reading and special education know, a trouble-free information-gathering system is vital to the learning process. A child who cannot see or hear properly is going to have problems in school. Thus educators, counselors, clinical psychologists, and rehabilitation specialists seek to identify children whose sensory-perceptual systems are not working well, and to correct their problems when possible (Porter & Kirby, 1986).

Innovators in the electronics industry study the sensory-perceptual system in order to imitate it. Already we have computers that respond to the sound patterns of the human voice or the visual pattern of a price code on a box of cereal. One day, no doubt, someone will develop a machine that can read handwritten zip codes. To accomplish feats such as this, engineers, technicians, and scientists are taking a careful look at the sophisticated equipment they are trying to replace: the human senses.

Thus, for a variety of reasons it is useful to understand how energy is translated into meaningful mental patterns. In this chapter we examine each of the major sensory-perceptual systems—how it works, and how the brain makes sense of its input. Theories of the process provide a good starting point for our understanding.

Figure 4.2 Destination of Sensory Information. *Neural impulses from the sense organs travel through the nervous system until they reach a specific area of the brain. Visual inputs are relayed to the occipital lobes, auditory information to the temporal lobes, bodily sensations to the parietal lobes.*

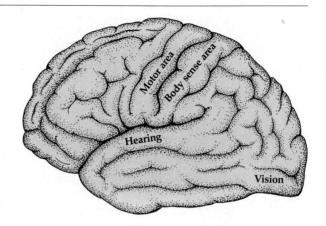

THEORIES OF SENSATION AND PERCEPTION

Sensation and perception are two sides of the same coin. The senses gather information and produce sensations that we experience as light, sound, or warmth. The brain evaluates those sensations and translates them into meaningful perceptions. In this section we briefly discuss four viewpoints of how sensory experience is converted to perceptual experience: traditional theory, Gestalt theory, Gibson's theory, and modern views.

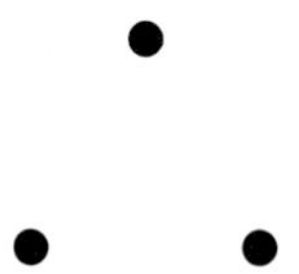

Traditional Theory: The Point as the Unit of Perception

According to traditional theory, still widely held today, for each kind of sensation there are specialized **receptor cells** designed to detect specific kinds of physical and chemical energy. Receptor cells in the eye respond to light; receptor cells in the skin respond to changes in temperature and pressure. These cells convert the energy into neural impulses, translating it into a form the nervous system can understand and use—a process known as **transduction.** The impulses then travel through the nervous system until they reach a specific area in the brain, where they are analyzed and interpreted (see Figure 4.2). Thus, the eye doesn't see; the ear doesn't hear. What one experiences takes place in the brain, not in the receptors, or receptor cells.

To explain how incoming sensory information becomes a perception, traditional theorists proposed a point-to-point correspondence between a stimulus and the neural message that goes to the brain. For example, the three dots shown in Figure 4.3 would stimulate three separate messages, which the brain would then organize and interpret as a triangle. More complicated stimuli would be relayed to the brain in basically the same way, point-to-point. Imagine the brain as a neon billboard made of countless light

Figure 4.3 Pattern of Three Dots. *According to traditional theory, the three dots shown here would be sent to the brain point-to-point, where the information would be organized and interpreted as a triangle.*

Receptor Cells: Specialized cells found in the eye, ear, tongue, and other sensory organs designed to detect physical and chemical energy and convert it into a neural impulse.

Transduction: The translation of energy into neural impulses by sensory receptors; to change energy into a neural impulse.

bulbs, each of which individually lights up when a corresponding receptor in the eye is stimulated. The message, "DON'T WALK" would be translated, Times Square fashion, into the pattern shown in Figure 4.4. Though logical, the traditional theorists' view of a point as the unit of perception has been challenged by the Gestalt psychologists.

Figure 4.4   Neon Sign Analogy. *According to the traditional view, the brain can be likened to a neon billboard made of countless light bulbs, each of which corresponds to a receptor in the eye and lights up when a receptor is stimulated.*

The Gestalt Perspective: Form as the Unit of Perception

Consider the drawings in Figure 4.5. The two middle circles are exactly the same size. If perception were simply the sum of individual points of stimulation, viewers would have no difficulty seeing that the two are equal. But most people don't. Instead, they see the middle circle on the left as larger. Why? Because the one on the right, being ringed by large circles, occupies a smaller proportion of its surrounding area than the one on the left, which is ringed by small circles. Thus, a figure's apparent or perceived size depends not just on the figure itself, taken in isolation, but on the entire visual pattern or context of which it is a part. The nervous system responds to points of stimulation in relation to their context, and the pattern, or form, said the Gestalt psychologists, is the basic unit of perception. (See Color Plate 4A, an example of an art style known as pointillism.)

Figure 4.5   The Perceived Size of Circles. *The perceived size of the circles depends on the entire pattern. The middle circle on the left appears larger because it is surrounded by relatively small circles. In fact, the two middle circles are identical.*

Gibson's View of Complex Perceptual Units

The Gestalt theory of perception dominated psychological thinking between 1925 and 1950 (Hochberg, 1979). But in the late 1940s a researcher named J. J. Gibson proposed the existence of perceptual units less complex than an entire form or pattern, though more complex than a point (Gibson, 1950, 1966). Gibson believed that specific visual features such as angles, curves, and depth were perceived whole by clusters of receptor cells in the eyes that respond directly to those patterns as a unit. Though his theory is still a controversial one, researchers have identified some receptor cells, known as **feature detectors,** that respond only to specific features of the environment such as horizontal lines or movement (Hubel & Wiesel, 1962). The major difference between Gibson and the traditional theorists is that Gibson believed that our perception of certain patterns takes place at the receptor level, rather than in the brain. Such an arrangement obviously increases the brain's efficiency in analyzing visual input. To detect a vertical line, the brain need not wait for information from a multitude of tiny points; instead, it receives the input whole.

Feature Detectors: Receptor cells in the eye that respond directly to certain visual patterns (such as a curve) as a unit.

Modern Approaches: Perception as an Active Process

More modern theories of sensation and perception emphasize the active nature of the process (Haber, 1978, Lindsay & Norman, 1977). People are not passive recipients of sensory input; instead, they use current information to predict what they might experience next. When you go to the movies or watch a television program, notice how often the story jumps ahead a couple of steps. In one cut someone is handing a present to another; in the

Perception is an active process. Thus, while this diver is experiencing the rush of air on the body and the pull of gravity, he can, at the same time, predict the feeling of plunging into cool water.

next, the ribbon and wrappings have been removed and the box is being opened. You have little trouble filling in the missing step; no doubt you predicted it as soon as you saw the package change hands. When you make such a prediction, you are actually participating in the construction of a perception.

■ Learning Check ■

Read, try to recite, repeat.

Theory	Basic Unit of Perception
Traditional Theory	A point.
Gestalt Theory	A form.
Gibson's Theory	Specific visual features.

constantly being replaced. At birth people are equipped with about as many taste buds as they will ever have; the number decreases with age (Geldard, 1972).

Despite its limitations, the sense of taste serves a number of important functions. It discourages us from swallowing potentially harmful substances, for many poisonous substances are bitter, a taste that most people, children and infants in particular, have a natural dislike for. Try dissolving an aspirin in your mouth; you'll see how its bitter taste would discourage most children from eating another. Infants also have a natural dislike for sour tastes, and usually will spit out sour milk that might upset their digestive systems. They have a natural inclination toward the sweet taste of mother's milk and baby formula.

Later in life this apparently inborn preference for sweet tastes can prove a mixed blessing, at least in the opinion of dieters. Even so, it helps to ensure adequate levels of blood sugar, essential in day-to-day functioning. In the same way, the natural love of salt helps to keep the body's salt level up, preventing dehydration. If you crave sweets or salt, your body may have a specific need for that chemical, though admittedly, most cravings for sugar and salt are learned preferences and not the result of nutritional deficiencies.

A number of industries take a special interest in the sense of taste. Companies that market coffee, tea, cola, wine, beer, and distilled alcohol depend on skilled professional tasters to select the blends most pleasing to customers. Taste is also of concern to the food industry. People are not likely to buy TV dinners or frozen vegetables unless they taste good. But, in the process of their research, experts in the food and beverage industries have learned that taste depends on the nose as well as the tongue. The reason is that, when taste receptors are stimulated, the information that is relayed to the brain is integrated with information from the other senses, most notably smell.

Taste and smell are closely related. Thus, when tasting their chicken cacciatore, these chefs also sample the aroma.

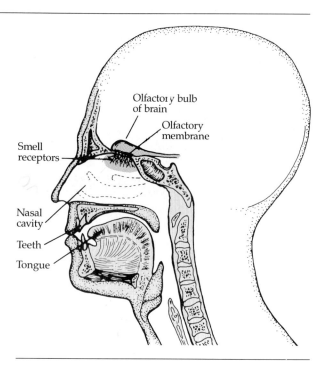

Figure 4.8 The Anatomy of the Human Nose.
Receptors for smell are located high in the nasal cavity on the olfactory membrane.

Smell. Anyone suffering from a head cold knows how important smell is to taste. Were it not for the sense of smell, an onion would taste no different from an apple, a broiled steak no different from an old piece of leather. That is why packagers of foods that release few gaseous molecules (the physical stimulus for smell) often lace their products with sugar and salt. Look at the ingredient list on almost any box of cold cereal and you will find that sugar and salt are among the most important.

The receptors for smell are located high in the nasal cavity, on a structure called the **olfactory membrane** (see Figure 4.8). From the millions of receptor cells in each cavity, information on smell is transmitted directly to the olfactory bulbs of the brain. There, just below the brain's frontal lobes, it is processed in one step.

Researchers have been unable to agree whether, like the four basic tastes, there are fundamental smells, or even categories of smells. According to one idea, the **stereochemical theory,** smell receptors are sensitive to molecules of similar shape and electrical charge; the two fit together much as a key fits a lock (see Figure 4.9). Just like brain cells that bind with specially shaped neurotransmitters, smell receptors may fire when gaseous molecules of similar shape bind with them (Amoore et al., 1964). Although the stereochemical theory is probably at least partially correct, it cannot account for all of what we know about smell (Hubert et al., 1980; Schiffman, 1974). One of the problems with it is that the way people perceive and categorize an odor depends on more than the shape and electrical charge of its gaseous molecules. Language—the labels we have for various odors—as well as culture and learning influence the way odors are categorized and interpreted (Cain, 1979). Consider, for example, how the advertising industry has taught many Americans to attach a negative label to common house and body odors.

Olfactory Membrane: A layer of tissue high in the nasal cavity which contains the receptors for smell.

Stereochemical Theory: The theory of smell that states that smell receptors are sensitive to molecules of similar shape and electrical charge.

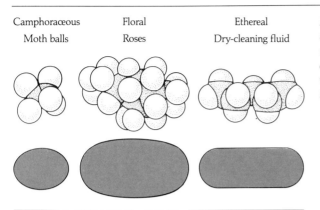

Camphoraceous	Floral	Ethereal
Moth balls	Roses	Dry-cleaning fluid

Figure 4.9 Stereochemical Theory. Examples of the molecular shape of three odorous substances along with their hypothesized similarly shaped receptors.

Air fresheners and carpet deodorizers are just two of the many products that didn't seem necessary until recently, when Madison Avenue advertising agencies began raising the public's consciousness of odors. Now, in addition to perfume and colognes, we have mouthwashes, breath fresheners, breath deodorants (for people with more serious mouth odor problems), antiperspirants, roll-on, stick, and spray deodorants for the underarms, foot deodorants (liquid or handy spray), and even feminine hygiene sprays. Our sense of smell, which once served us mainly in food selection and food avoidance and warned us of danger, has become a matter of social concern. Perhaps the fragrance of flowers is preferable to that of boiling broccoli, but are cooking and other common household odors really that embarrassing? For most smells, sensory adaptation occurs quickly. A guest may detect an odor as she walks in the door, but her smell receptors will soon become accustomed to it. And though a breath mint may be called for now and then, is it really vital to mask all our body's natural odors? If recent speculation that humans may communicate through body odors proves correct, we might want to reconsider the need for these products.

The Skin Senses

Skin-to-skin contact, or gentle stroking, can be one of the most intimate forms of human communication. Like other kinds of touch, this pleasurable sensation results from stimulation of several kinds of receptors at once: cold and warmth receptors, pressure receptors, and pain receptors. Even the relatively simple sensation of heat does not result from stimulation of a single kind of receptor, but from simultaneous stimulation of the cold and warmth receptors.

The strength of a sensation varies, depending on the rate of change in stimulation and what part of the body is stimulated (Pertovaara & Kojo, 1985). Skin receptors are unevenly distributed: there are pressure spots where receptors for pressure concentrate, cold spots, and warm spots. Pain receptors are densely packed in the vulnerable neck and back of the knees, but only sparsely distributed on the sole of the foot, which takes a daily beating without causing too much discomfort (see Figure 4.10).

Although skin receptors of clearly different structure have been identified, it is not always possible to find a consistent relationship between specific receptors and specific sensations. Consider, for instance, the **free**

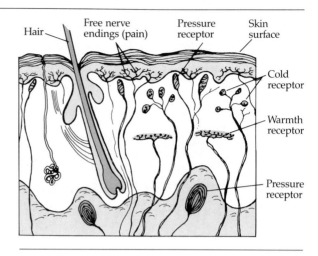

Figure 4.10 Receptors in the Skin. A cross section of the skin showing cold and warmth receptors as well as pressure receptors and the free nerve endings.

Free Nerve Endings: Receptors that terminate in the outer layer of the skin, which are believed to produce painful sensation if stimulated.

Basket Cells: Receptor cells located at the bottom of each hair cell on the skin. Stimulation of these cells produces pressure sensations and indicates that something has come into contact with the skin.

nerve endings, receptors that terminate in the outer layer of the skin. Unlike **basket cells**—skin cells attached to the hairs on the skin that, when stimulated, produce pressure sensations—free nerve endings are not anchored to any particular place. Stimulation of the free nerve endings can cause sensations of both pain and pressure (Geldard, 1972). Yet free nerve endings are not the only kind of skin receptor involved in pain perception. Overstimulation of any kind of skin receptor, as previously noted, can cause pain. Furthermore, under certain conditions, such as hypnosis or acupuncture, stimulation of these cells apparently will not cause pain—or at least subjects do not respond as if they are in pain (see Box 4.1).

One possible explanation for our ability to ignore pain under certain conditions lies in the way in which pain is conducted from the body to the brain. According to one theory, called the gate control theory, pain impulses travel through one of two major pathways of nerve fibers in the spinal cord. One, made of large fibers, is believed to relay sharp pain, such as a pinprick or a burn, to the cortex. The other, made of small fibers, is thought to relay dull aches, like a backache, to a second area of the brain (the limbic system). Presumably, only one of these two pathways to the brain can be opened at a time, and that is whichever one is carrying the heaviest traffic (Melzack, 1973; Melzack & Wall, 1965). Thus, if you are accidentally jabbed by a pin when you already have a backache, your backache will be blocked temporarily as the large-fiber path opens up to the sharp pain of the pinprick. And if an acupuncturist inserts needles in your skin to relieve you of chronic pain, the same result should occur.

To test the gate control theory, researchers used a mild electric current to stimulate the large-fiber path of a patient with chronic low back pain. As predicted, the patient experienced considerable relief, though the shocks were administered for only two minutes, and were not strong enough to be painful (Wall & Sweet, 1967). Other explanations may be made for the result of this experiment, however. The patient's expectation that the treatment would work; the activation of the body's own painkilling substances (see Chapter 3); or a shift of attention from one part of the body to another could

Box 4.1 PSYCHOLOGY IN ACTION: Applying Psychology to Understanding Pain Control

Pain treatment centers, such as the one founded by psychologist David Corey, utilize the power of perceptions to help people cope with chronic pain (see Stark, 1985). One primary goal of Corey's approach is to help the sufferer feel in control of his or her pain, rather than be a passive victim of it. Patients are encouraged to identify the kinds of situations and behaviors that seem to increase pain or seem to reduce it, and then, as much as possible, act accordingly. For example, if sitting at a desk for more than an hour causes lower back pain, individuals might purchase an inexpensive alarm wristwatch and set it to go off every forty-five minutes or so to remind them to get up and walk around. Patients are encouraged to learn to focus on something other than pain—music, a conversation, a pleasant experience. They are also taught to change their attitudes and thinking about pain. For example, thoughts like, "I feel miserable," can be replaced with thoughts like, "The discomfort I may be experiencing is small compared to the joys of being with people I love."

Just as a sense of control can have an important effect on the outcomes we achieve (see Chapter 1, Box 1.x), so too, feeling that we exercise some degree of control over unpleasant sensations can overpower our experience of them.

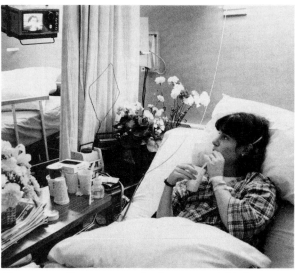

The way we direct our attention has a powerful influence on our experience of pain. Thus, being preoccupied by the sights and sounds of the television, the taste of a cool drink, and the smell of the flowers, this patient probably expriences less pain than she might in a darkened, quiet room.

also account for the temporary relief from pain. The fact is, pain is more than a sensation; a person's perceptions can have a powerful influence on the degree of pain experienced (Stark, 1985). In the heat of a championship game, a player may be completely unaware of a painful wound. Even when the game is over she may struggle to hide her distress, believing it a sign of

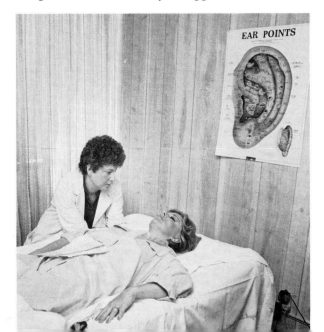

Stimulation of skin receptors through acupuncture can help relieve chronic pain.

■ **Learning Check** ■

Read the right side, then cover and try to recite, repeat.
Skin receptors associated with:

Pressure	Basket cells.
Heat	Cold and warm receptors.
Pain	Free nerve endings; overstimulation of any receptor.

weakness. The same wound may cause a victim of an automobile accident extreme agony.

HEARING

Much more is known about hearing than about the motion, chemical, and skin senses. Both sound—the physical stimulus for hearing—and its receptors, located in the ear, have been studied in detail. In this section we will first examine the physical properties of sound and how they are detected by the ear. We then speculate on how sounds are translated into meaningful codes that the brain can understand and interpret.

The Nature of Sound

Sound is energy produced by vibrating objects. It travels in waves of compressed air molecules. If you strike a piano key, the vibrating string in-

Figure 4.11 Characteristics of a Sound Wave.
This figure illustrates the characteristics of the sound wave, and shows how frequency and amplitude vary independently of each other.

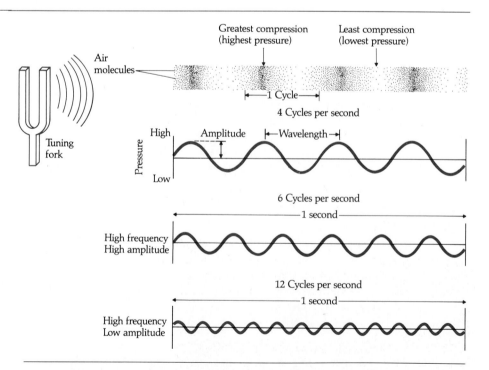

side the piano will alternately squeeze and let up on the surrounding air molecules—much as you might squeeze a rubber ball and then release it. The tightly squeezed molecules form the crest of the sound wave, the released molecules, the trough (see Figure 4.11). It is this alternating compression and expansion of molecules that provides the physical stimulus humans perceive as sound.

The two most important characteristics of a sound wave are its amplitude and frequency. **Amplitude,** or the height of the wave from base to crest, or base to trough, is perceived as the intensity or volume of a sound. The higher the amplitude, the louder the sound. When you turn up the volume on your radio or stereo, you increase the intensity of its vibrations, which in turn increases the amplitude of the sound waves it produces.

For purposes of human hearing, the amplitude of a sound is measured in units called **decibels (dBs).** Normal speech has a volume of about 60 dB; a loud shout, a volume of about 100 dB. The takeoff of a jet plane when heard from a distance of 200 feet produces about 120 dB, and rock concerts sometimes produce sounds as loud as 125 to 130 dB (Dey, 1970). When the amplitude of a sound wave reaches about 140 dB, the hearer begins to feel pain. In fact, prolonged exposure to any high-amplitude sounds—90 dB or more—can cause permanent hearing damage (Lipscomb, 1969a, 1969b). To prevent permanent hearing loss, people who are exposed to high-intensity sounds should wear protective devices like earplugs.

The **frequency** of a sound wave, or the number of crest-trough cycles per second, is perceived as the pitch, or tone, of a sound. The higher the frequency, the higher the pitch. Frequency is measured by a unit called the **hertz (Hz),** which is exactly equal to one cycle per second. The range of frequencies that the human ear can detect runs from about 20 to 20,000 Hz. The lowest note on a piano is about 25 Hz, the highest, about 4,500.

Amplitude and frequency vary independently of each other. A sound can be of low amplitude and low frequency or low amplitude and high frequency; of high amplitude and high frequency or high amplitude and low frequency. Figure 4.12 summarizes the main points relevant to amplitude and frequency.

Sound waves have much more to them than amplitude and frequency, of course, as any musician or music lover knows. The complexity of a sound wave—its richness, texture, or quality—is called **timbre.** If you strike just one key on a piano, the tone you hear will contain remnants of higher tones as well as the basic one you struck. These higher tones, called **overtones,** are actually multiples of the basic frequency. They differ from one instrument to

Amplitude: A physical property of a sound wave determined by the height of the wave from base to crest, or base to trough, which is perceived as loudness or intensity of sound.

Decibels (dBs): The units of measure for the amplitude or energy of sound.

Frequency: The number of cycles per second of a sound wave, which is perceived as pitch.

Hertz (Hz): The unit of measure of the frequency of a sound wave which specifies or indicates the cycles per second of a sound wave. One hertz equals one cycle per second.

Timbre: The quality or richness of a sound; the quality that distinguishes one musical instrument from another.

Overtones: Multiples of the basic frequency of a sound wave, which result from vibrations in a musical instrument and are of a higher frequency than those played.

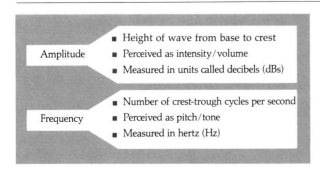

Figure 4.12 Schematic Summary of the Nature of Sound: Amplitude and Frequency.

the next, so that the same note played on two different instruments will sound different. That is why you can discriminate between a piano and a guitar, both playing the same note. Although the sound wave produced by these instruments may be of exactly the same amplitude and frequency, they differ in complexity. Timbre even distinguishes two guitars, pianos, or violins, as you know if you have ever shopped for a musical instrument.

The Structure of the Ear

The structure that detects these fine distinctions, the human ear, is more marvelous than even the finest violin or piano. It can be divided into three main parts—outer, middle, and inner. The first of these essentially collects raw sound waves (see Color Plate 4B). The *pinna,* the skin-covered cartilage that projects from the head, traps the waves and sends them down a narrow passage called the *auditory canal.* At the end of the canal, the waves reach the **tympanic membrane,** or eardrum, which responds to their pressure by moving in and out. Thus, air pressure is converted into physical vibrations.

On the other side of the eardrum, in the middle ear, lie three small bones called the hammer, anvil, and stirrup, known collectively as the **ossicles.** Acting like levers, these three bones react in sequence, amplifying the vibrations from the eardrum and transmitting them to the inner ear.

In the inner ear, a snail-shaped bony structure called the **cochlea** receives the amplified vibrations. At its entrance lies a structure called the **oval window,** which holds back the fluid inside. When the stirrup strikes the window, its vibrations create pressure changes in the fluid, which cause movements in another spiral structure (within the cochlea) called the **basilar membrane.** These movements, in turn, jar the *organ of Corti,* attached to the basilar membrane, which houses more than a million tiny hair cells, the actual receptors for sound. It is the movement of the hair cells that creates a neural impulse, which eventually reaches the brain via the auditory nerve. Figure 4.13 provides a schematic summary of the structure of the ear.

Theories of Auditory Perception

Though scientists have been able to determine how sound waves in general are converted to neural impulses, they are still trying to discover how

Tympanic Membrane: The eardrum.

Ossicles: Three small, connected bones in the middle ear, known as the hammer (malleus), anvil (incus), and stirrup (stapes), that act like levers to make sounds louder.

Cochlea: A snail-shaped structure of the inner ear.

Oval Window: A structure in the inner ear that holds back the fluid that lies inside.

Basilar Membrane: A layer of tissue in the inner ear that vibrates in response to sound.

Figure 4.13 Schematic Summary of the Structure of the Human Ear.

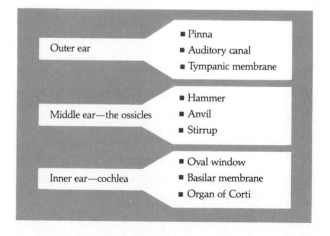

some specific properties of sound are perceived. There is general agreement that loudness varies according to the number of hair cells that are stimulated. Quite simply, loud sounds put more pressure on the basilar membrane than soft ones, stimulating more hair cells to send more impulses to the brain. There is some dispute about how humans perceive pitch, however.

According to one theory, sound waves of different frequency, or pitch, concentrate their effect on different parts of the basilar membrane (Von Békésy, 1928, 1957, 1960). High-frequency waves have their greatest effect on the outer part of the membrane, near the oval window. Low-frequency waves concentrate on the inner membrane (see Figure 4.14). This theory of pitch perception, called the **place theory,** provides some explanation of pitch perception (Simmons, 1970), but it does not account for the fact that very low frequencies cause the entire basilar membrane to vibrate.

According to a second theory, the **frequency theory,** the hair cells on the organ of Corti on the basilar membrane fire at the same rate, or frequency, as the sound wave that stimulates them. If stimulated by a wave of 400 cycles per second, they will fire 400 times per second. The only problem with this theory is that neurons can't fire faster than 500 cycles per second—yet humans can hear frequencies higher than that. To explain the perception of high frequencies, most psychologists rely on the **volley theory,** according to which groups of cells fire in quick succession to achieve a faster-than-normal rate of firing. First one group fires, then another, and so on in volleys. While the second group fires, the first recharges.

Theories of auditory perception have helped to give psychologists a new perspective on everyday problems such as childhood speech disorders. For example, work conducted by Paula Tallal (1981) indicates that many speech disorders are due to a failure in the process of sensation and perception, rather than to low IQ. Children who have speech problems are more often than not just as intelligent as other children. For some reason yet to be discovered, their sensory or basic perceptual processes fail to properly analyze incoming information. Their normal-functioning higher brain centers are thus deprived of the information needed to properly interpret sounds

Place Theory: A theory of hearing which states that pitch perception is determined by the place on the basilar membrane that is most strongly stimulated.

Frequency Theory: A theory of hearing which states that hearing receptors on the organ of Corti on the basilar membrane fire at the same rate or frequency of the sound wave that stimulates them.

Volley Theory: A theory of hearing used to explain perception of high-frequency (high-pitched) sounds. According to the theory, groups of receptor cells fire in quick succession to achieve a faster-than-normal rate of firing.

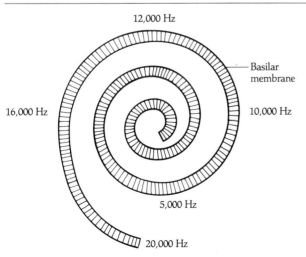

Figure 4.14 Place Theory of Perception. According to the place theory, the place on the basilar membrane that receives the maximum stimulation depends on the frequency of the sound.

Review Figure 4.13 until you can recall the three structures of the outer ear, the three bones (the ossicles) of the middle ear, and the three parts of the inner ear (the cochlea).

(Tallal, 1980, 1981). Consequently they develop speech and learning problems.

Today psychologists and other scientists are working with engineers, educators, and technicians in an effort to correct disabilities caused by failures in the basic process of sensation and perception. They are developing machines that can analyze and respond to the human voice or create musical patterns pleasing to the human ear. Again, research in the human senses has a number of practical applications. That is especially true in the case of vision.

VISUAL SENSATION AND PERCEPTION

Look at the picture of the archways in Figure 4.15. Without much effort you can imagine yourself inside the row of columns, looking down the path or up at the walls. Though the picture is printed on a flat surface, it almost looks as if you could walk down the path yourself. How is it that you can perceive depth on the flat surface of the page?

Figure 4.15 Depth Perception. *The archways of the collonade at the Vatican in Rome present a striking example of depth perception.*

According to traditional theory, not just this picture but everything you see is a two-dimensional representation of reality. The eye collects reflected light, focuses the rays with its lens, and casts a shadow-like picture on its rear wall. Like a photograph or a painting, this picture is two-dimensional. Yet most of the time you see a faithful picture of the object in three-dimensions—presumably because your brain is remarkably good at translating the two-dimensional sensation of light into a three-dimensional object. Although scientists have discovered feature detectors that respond directly to depth, without interpretation by the brain, traditional theory is still useful in explaining many otherwise unexplained phenomena.

For instance, some of the false perceptions, or illusions, you occasionally experience may be the result of the distortions that occur when a three-dimensional object is projected onto just two dimensions. The Necker cube, an illusion created by a Swiss scientist over a century ago, is a good example (see Figure 4.16). If you stare at the cube for a short while, the tinted area will appear to flip back and forth between the outer and inner surfaces of the cube. If you stare at it for several minutes, you might even have a consciousness-altering experience, just as Necker did. Examine the drawing closely. Notice that the sides are of unequal length, even though in a real cube the sides are equal. The fact is, a three-dimensional object cannot be projected onto a two-dimensional surface without distortion. That is why the Necker cube gives the false impression of fluctuation. The drawing cannot capture the true reality of the cube; the distortion of reality leads to a distortion in perception.

Vision is perhaps the most important human sense; certainly it is the sense that psychologists know the most about. Starting with the nature of light itself, let's take a closer look at how the eye converts light energy into physical sensations. Then let's look at how we perceive color and depth. (We will return to the topic of illusions later in the chapter.)

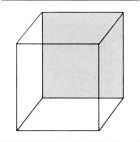

Figure 4.16 The Necker Cube. The tinted surface can appear as either in the front or the rear surface. If you stare at the cube, the tinted surface will appear to fluctuate between front and rear.

The Nature of Light

Light, the physical stimulus for vision, is a special kind of energy known as **electromagnetic radiation.** In simple terms, electromagnetic energy is produced when electrons, negatively charged particles that circle atoms, bounce out of their usual orbit. The disruption produces electromagnetic waves.

Different degrees of disruption produce waves of different lengths. At one extreme are radio waves, whose length from crest to crest can exceed thousands of meters. At the other extreme are tiny gamma rays, whose length is unimaginably small: ten trillionths of a meter. The entire range of electromagnetic wavelengths is known as the electromagnetic spectrum (see Color Plate 4C).

Of course you cannot see radio waves, nor can you see gamma rays. The human eye is sensitive to only a small part of the electromagnetic spectrum. Visible lightwaves vary from about 380 billionths of a meter, which is perceived as the color blue, to about 780 billionths of a meter, which is perceived as the color red. In fact, length of the visible spectrum is so short that scientists have had to develop a special measurement, called a **nanometer (Nm),** to distinguish among waves of various colors, or **hue.** One nanometer

Electromagnetic Radiation: Energy waves of different lengths ranging from radio waves to very tiny gamma rays, a small portion of which are visible as lightwaves.

Nanometer (Nm): A billionth of a meter.

Hue: The colors of the visible spectrum ranging from blue to red, measured in terms of the length of a lightwave.

(Nm) equals a billionth of a meter. As a lightwave is varied between 380 Nm and 780 Nm, its hue changes from blue to green, yellow, orange, and red (see Color Plate 4C). The purest lightwaves consist of just a single wavelength. Because they produce a pure hue—pure red, for instance—they are said to be **saturated** with color (see Color Plate 4D).

Saturation: The intensity or pureness of a color.

In addition to wavelength and purity, light can be described in terms of its physical intensity, or *amplitude*—the height of the wave. The higher the amplitude of a wave, the brighter it appears to be.

The Structure and Function of the Eye

Take a few moments to examine the drawing of an eye in Color Plate 4E. The first step in visual sensation occurs when light passes through the transparent, protective outer coating known as the *cornea*. In the process, the lightwaves are partially focused. Then they proceed through the dark circular opening known as the *pupil* into the eyeball. The *iris*, the colored part of the eyeball that surrounds the pupil, controls the amount of light entering the eyeball through its muscular contractions. It opens and closes automatically in response to varying levels of illumination.

Retina: The light-receptive surface at the back of the inside surface of the eye.

After passing through the pupil, light strikes the *lens*, which functions something like the lens of a camera, further resolving the incoming light and focusing it onto the **retina,** the light-receptive surface at the back of the eye. To focus light from objects at different distances, the lens adjusts its shape. This process of focusing is called **accommodation,** and it is controlled by the *ciliary muscles.*

Accommodation: Changes in the curvature of the lens of the eye to focus light from objects onto the retina at the back of the eye.

Between the lens and the retina, in the center of the eyeball, is a jellylike substance called the *vitreous humor.* This filler material maintains the pressure necessary to keep the eyeball in place in its socket. The resolved lightwave passes through the vitreous humor and falls on the retina in the form of a focused image. Figure 4.17 provides a schematic summary of the main structures of the eye.

The retinal image is an exact replica of its source, with three exceptions. First, it is inverted (upside down). Second, it is smaller; its size is inversely proportional to the distance of the source from the eye. That is, the shorter the distance, the larger the image; the longer the distance, the smaller the image. And third, it is two-dimensional, for the retina is like an artist's canvas. (See Figure 4.18 for a diagram of the projection process.)

The focusing of light on the retina is only the beginning of the visual process. Light on its way to the retina goes past two layers of cells to the

Figure 4.17 Schematic Summary of the Structure of the Eye.

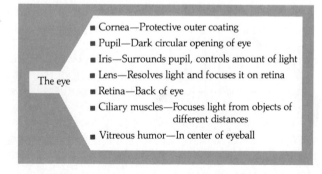

The eye

■ Cornea—Protective outer coating

■ Pupil—Dark circular opening of eye

■ Iris—Surrounds pupil, controls amount of light

■ Lens—Resolves light and focuses it on retina

■ Retina—Back of eye

■ Ciliary muscles—Focuses light from objects of different distances

■ Vitreous humor—In center of eyeball

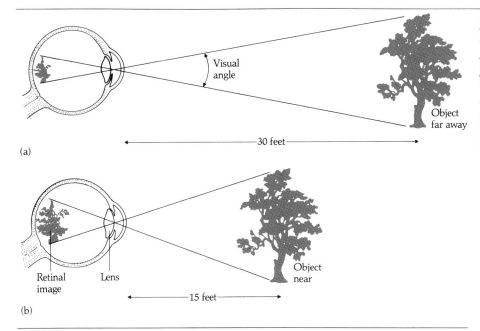

Figure 4.18 Retinal Image Illustrating Visual Angle. The further you are from an object, the smaller the size of the image on your retina (a); conversely, the closer you are to an object, the larger the size of the image (b).

photoreceptors—literally, "light receptors." There are two different kinds of photoreceptors, called rods and cones because of their shapes. The approximately 120 million **rods** in each eye are not sensitive to color, but are extremely sensitive to light and dark. Scientists believe that, when light strikes them, it causes the chemical breakdown of a substance called *rhodopsin.*

The **cones,** the second type of photoreceptor, are less sensitive to light and dark than the rods, but they play a critical role in color vision. Cones contain a pigment called *iodopsin,* which breaks down when struck by light. The eye has only about 6 to 8 million cones, of which there are three types, each primarily sensitive to a different wavelength.

You may recall that continuous stimulation of any receptor reduces its sensitivity, a process called sensory adaptation (see page 121). In the eye, continued stimulation of the rods and cones depletes the supply of rhodopsin and iodopsin. These chemicals need time to reconstitute after breakdown; in the meantime, the rods and cones cannot function fully. In short, the eye becomes less sensitive.

In darkness—or lack of stimulation—the process reverses itself. If you walk into a darkened theater, you will at first be able to see very little. After several minutes, however, your eyes will begin to adapt to (become more sensitive to) the decreased stimulation (light), a process known as **dark adaptation.** After about eight minutes the cones have adapted fully. The rods take roughly four times as long—about thirty minutes—to adjust (Cornsweet, 1970).

Such differences in adaptation reveal that reduced illumination does not affect all visual functions equally. When night falls, our ability to see drops dramatically and does not reach maximum capacity for some thirty minutes, due to the long time it takes for the rods to adjust. Even then, many night drivers tend to overestimate their ability to see what's ahead, which explains, in part, the inordinate number of night automobile accidents (Leibowitz & Owens, 1986).

Photoreceptors: Receptor cells for vision; rods and cones, which are the receptor cells that respond to light.

Rods: Rod-shaped receptor cells located in the eye that are sensitive to light and dark.

Cones: Receptor cells located in the eye that are sensitive to color.

Dark Adaptation: Becoming accustomed to dark; increased sensitivity to light caused by a decrease in stimulation of the photoreceptors (receptors for light).

Figure 4.19 Locating Your Blind Spot. *You can locate your blind spot, where the optic nerve connects to the eye, in the following manner. Holding the book about one foot from you, close your right eye and stare at the star in the upper right. Then slowly move the book back and forth until the (triangle) disappears and the bar appears unbroken. When this happens, the images of the triangle and break on the bar are falling on your blind spot.*

Optic Nerve: The bundle of fibers that join together in each eye and relay neural impulses to the brain.

Fovea: The most sensitive part of the retina, which contains only cones; the point of greatest visual acuity, where fine details can be seen.

Stimulation of the rods and cones culminates in a neural impulse in the **optic nerve** (see Color Plate 4E). The retina is completely blind where the optic nerve leaves it—a fact you can demonstrate to yourself by following the directions in Figure 4.19. Usually you are unaware of your *blind spots*, because whatever details you miss with one eye, you tend to pick up with the other (Hochberg, 1978). The point of greatest visual acuity, where fine detail is picked up, is called the **fovea.** This area contains only cones. From the optic nerve, the neural impulse is first relayed to the brain where it finally reaches the visual areas of the cerebral cortex. (For more on how visual inputs are relayed to the cortex, see Chapter 3.)

By now you should have a good idea of the nature of visual sensation. Physical energy is transduced in the retina to a neural impulse, which makes its way to the brain along the optic nerve. But the way in which we translate an impulse into a perception is more complicated. Color perception, for instance, involves a rather sophisticated analysis of incoming impulses by the brain.

Additive Color Mixing: The mixing of lights of two or more different wavelengths (colors) to form a new color.

Primary Colors: A set of three colors, which, when mixed, can produce all other colors.

Trichromatic Theory: A theory of color vision that states that the human eye has three types of color receptors, one for each of the additive color mixing primaries: red, green, and blue.

Color Perception

In the early 1800s the British scientist Thomas Young did an experiment with colored lights that suggested how humans might perceive color. He discovered that by mixing red, green, and blue lights, he could create any visible color. This phenomenon, in which two or more lights of different wavelengths (color) are projected onto a white screen to form a new color, is known as **additive color mixing** (see Color Plate 4F).

Red, green, and blue, the basic colors that, through additive color mixing, produce all the others, are known as **primary colors.** The fact that their mixture could produce any color suggested to thoughtful scientists that the human eye might have three kinds of color receptors. And that is, in fact, what the physiologist Hermann von Helmholtz proposed, about fifty years after Young made his discovery. His triple-receptor scheme is sometimes referred to as the **trichromatic theory** of color vision, or the Young-Helmholtz

■ Learning Check ■

Read the definition, then cover the right side and try to recite. Repeat.

Rods	Are photoreceptors sensitive to light and dark but not color.
Cones	Are photoreceptors sensitive to color.

theory. Three quarters of a century later, research confirmed the existence of three kinds of cones, each responsive to a wavelength roughly equal to one of the three primaries (MacNichol, 1964).

Despite this strong support, there are some phenomena that the trichromatic theory cannot fully explain. For one thing, if you look at a green surface for a while and then look away toward a white one, you will soon see red. To demonstrate this phenomenon, called a **negative afterimage,** to yourself, look at Color Plate 4G for about thirty seconds. Then look at a white piece of paper.

A similar effect will occur with any color. Look at the color wheel in Color Plate 4H. The colors are arranged according to wavelengths, starting with red, which has the highest visible wavelength, and moving counterclockwise to red-purple, which has the lowest visible wavelength. Any two colors that are directly opposite each other on the wheel are **complementary:** if lightwaves of these colors are blended together, they will cancel each other out, producing a neutral gray or white. If you stare at any of these colors, you will experience a negative afterimage that is the color of its complement on the opposite side of the wheel.

It was this phenomenon of the negative afterimage, in part, that led researchers to suspect that color vision involved more than three kinds of cones. If color vision were that simple, why would anyone see red while looking at a white piece of paper? In fact, stimulation of one of the three kinds of cones appears to be only the first stage of processing in color perception (Hurvich & Jameson, 1957, 1974). After the cones have been activated, they relay their information to a brain structure called the thalamus, which analyzes it in what is called the *"opponent process mechanism,"* pitting red against green, blue against yellow. Apparently, cells that respond to one color in a pair of complements inhibit cells that respond to the other color (DeValois, 1965a, 1965b). For example, cells that are activated by an impulse for red inhibit cells that are activated by an impulse for green, and vice versa. The result is that for a short time the viewer perceives the color of the activated cells but cannot see the opposite color. After the activated cells cease to fire, the cells for the opposite color burst into activity (Hurvich, 1978).

Research on color blindness supports the opponent process theory. There are three major kinds of color vision. The rarest is an inability to perceive color at all. People who are totally color-blind are called **monochromats:** their rods function, so they can see brightness, but they have no cone vision at all. A more common kind of color blindness occurs in the **dichromat,** a person who is insensitive to one of two color pairs, red-green or blue-yellow. Most dichromats are unable to discriminate between red and green (see Color Plate 4I). Persons with normal color vision, or **trichromats,** are sensitive to all visible color as well as to light and dark.

The tendency of the color-blind to be blind to pairs of opposing colors squares with the theory that colors are perceived according to an opponent process. Today most psychologists accept a two-stage theory of color vision. In the first stage, one or more of the three kinds of retinal cones is stimulated. In the second, the resulting impulses are recorded, opponent process fashion, in the lateral geniculate body of the thalamus before being sent on to the cortex (Hurvich, 1978). (See Box 4.2.)

Negative Afterimage: A sensory image following the termination of stimulus input, where the new image is the opposite of the initial image. For colors, the afterimage is the complement of the original stimulus (e.g., red is the complement of green. After looking at green, a red afterimage can be experienced by looking at a white surface).

Complementary Colors: Any two colors that are directly opposite to each other on the color wheel. If blended together as lightwaves they will cancel each other out, producing neutral gray or white.

Monochromat: An individual who is totally color-blind.

Dichromat: An individual who is partially color-blind, being insensitive to one of the two primary color pairs (red-green or blue-yellow).

Trichromat: An individual with normal color vision.

Box 4.2 PSYCHOLOGY IN ACTION: The Meaning of Color

Imagine yourself in a psychological investigation of the role of color in human behavior. You sit comfortably at a desk while the experimenter places 3 × 5 colored cards in front of you: first blue, then green, yellow, red, brown, and black in turn. You are asked to select your favorite. Then you complete a personality questionnaire. Do your color preferences in fact reveal anything about your personality—relatively enduring characteristics such as the tendency to be dependent or to be aggressive across a variety of different situations?

Psychologists have found that people do have definite color preferences and that, in some cases, these are in fact related to their personalities. People who prefer red tend to be extroverted—outgoing and sociable. Those who prefer blue have more of a tendency toward introversion. They tend to be less outgoing and less confident in social situations (Stimpson & Stimpson, 1979; Walters et al., 1982).

There is also good evidence that different colors convey specific meanings. In one study, for instance, people from twenty major world cities in North and South America, Europe, and the Middle and Far East were asked to rate the colors black, gray, red, yellow, blue, green, and white on a number of dimensions such as good-bad and strong-weak. The findings revealed cross-cultural similarities in feelings about colors. In general, black was evaluated as bad but strong, gray both bad and weak. White was rated good but weak; red, strong and active. Yellow was just plain weak, while blue and green were both simply rated as good (Adams & Osgood, 1973).

Do these results explain why bruise-em-up football teams such as the Los Angeles Raiders and Chicago Bears wear black? The fact is, the colors we wear do communicate a message, and it's one that seems to be understood the world over.

Depth Perception: The ability to see the world in three dimensions; the ability to perceive depth.

Binocular Cues: Cues to depth perception that come from the use of both eyes.

Retinal (Binocular) Disparity: A binocular cue to depth perception in which viewing with two eyes produces two slightly different projected retinal images because of the distance between the eyes.

Convergence: A binocular cue to depth perception caused when the eyes rotate inward to maintain focus.

Monocular Cues: Cues to depth perception that require the use of only one eye.

Linear Perspective: A cue to depth perception based on the fact that two parallel lines will appear to come together as they recede in the distance.

Depth Perception

Like color perception, **depth perception**—the ability to see the world in three dimensions—is more than a matter of the reception of snapshot impulses by the brain. Without realizing it, viewers use certain cues to determine the depth of their field of vision and the relative position of objects in it. Some of these cues require the use of both eyes, some only one.

Cues that come from the use of both eyes are called **binocular cues.** When you focus on an object, its retinal image differs slightly from one eye to the other. This difference, called **retinal (binocular) disparity,** occurs because each eye is viewing the object from a slightly different vantage point (Julesz, 1964).

Another binocular cue to depth, called **convergence,** is based on the movement of your eyes inward as they focus on closer objects. Try holding your thumb in front of you at arm's distance and gradually moving it toward your face. As your thumb gets closer, you will feel your eyes moving inward toward your nose. Though you are normally unaware of this feeling, it does provide a subtle cue to an object's depth.

Yet another cue to depth, one that occurs within the eye rather than between the two eyes, is the movement of the ciliary muscles that occurs in accommodation, the process in which the lens adjusts in order to focus an image on the retina (see page 138). Information about this muscular activity is relayed to the brain, where it is used as a cue to depth.

Most cues that require the use of only one eye, called **monocular cues,** are more noticeable than accommodation. Artists make extensive use of them in painting and drawing, to convey an illusion of depth; photographs, too, provide monocular cues. Perhaps the best known of such devices is **linear perspective,** a cue that is based on the fact that two parallel lines will appear to come together as they recede into the distance. If you stand on a perfectly straight railroad track, for instance, the two rails will appear to

Color Plate 4A   The Total Impression is More than the Sum of its Parts. *This painting, which is composed of separate daubs of paint, illustrates the Gestalt view that the total impression is more than the sum of its parts. (Untitled. Philip C. Lanza. Appears courtesy of the artist.)*

In understanding how the senses gather information and the brain translates these sensations into meaningful perceptions, it is crucial to recognize the unique qualities of each of the senses and the intricate interactions that exist among them.

For example, the motion senses allow us to encounter such diverse experiences as the thrill of a swiftly falling rollercoaster or the gentle rocking of a sailboat on choppy seas.

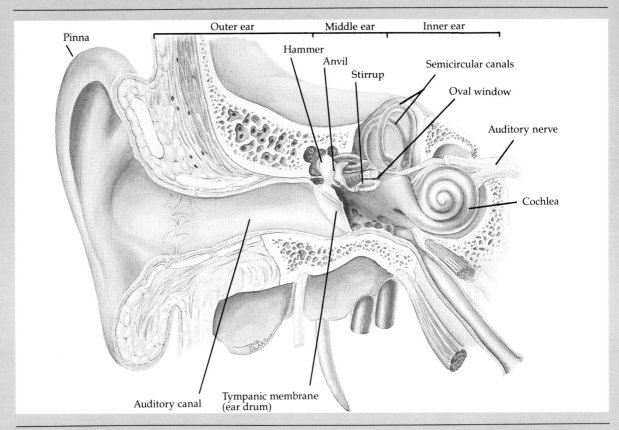

Pinna

Outer ear | Middle ear | Inner ear

Hammer

Anvil

Stirrup

Semicircular canals

Oval window

Auditory nerve

Cochlea

Auditory canal

Tympanic membrane
(ear drum)

Color Plate 4B **The Structure of the Human Ear.** *The outer, middle, and inner ear. (Compliments of Burroughs Wellcome Co. ®)*

The workings of the inner ear are crucial to our sense of motion. The ear also allows us to hear a complexity of sounds. Because of the ear's ability to detect different frequencies, we are able to experience the varying notes and rich overtones of organ music.

Our senses of touch, smell, and taste are also crucial to our enjoyment of our environment. To the artist, the feel of soft clay is pleasurable, and most of us are delighted by the fragrance of fresh-cut flowers.

When we snack on pastries and hot chocolate, our sense of smell combines with that of taste and we experience not only the dessert's rich, sweet flavor, but its enticing aroma as well.

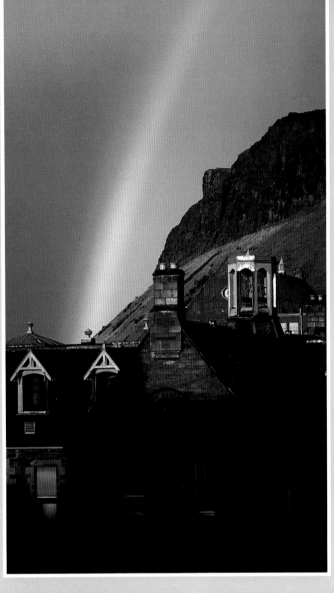

Vision perhaps contributes more than any other sense to our accurate perceptions of the world. With our ability to detect light of different wavelengths, we can see colors of various hues and perceive the brilliance of a rainbow.

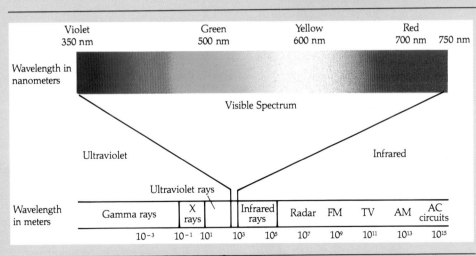

Color Plate 4C
The Electromagnetic
Spectrum.

Color Plate 4D
Saturation and
Brightness.

Color Plate 4E   The
Structure of the Eye.
A look at the inside of
the human eye.
(Compliments of
Burroughs Wellcome
Co.®)

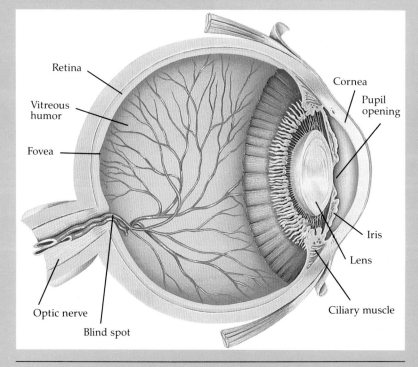

Retina

Vitreous
humor

Fovea

Cornea

Pupil
opening

Iris

Lens

Ciliary muscle

Optic nerve

Blind spot

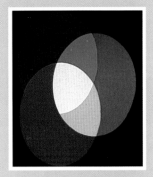

Color Plate 4F
Additive Color Mixing.

Our eye's intricate structure can also provide us with some interesting illusions and is crucial to our perception of depth. We accurately interpret such cues as linear perspective, texture gradient, and interposition, and therefore see the world in three dimensions.

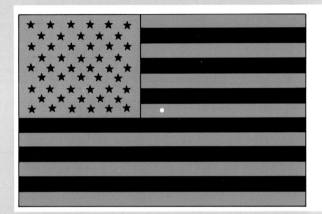

Color Plate 4G Negative Afterimage.   *Stare at the white dot at the center of the green, black, and yellow flag for about 20 or 30 seconds. Then look at the blank white space. The negative afterimage you see looks red, white, and blue, the way we usually see the American flag.*

Color Plate 4H   The Color Wheel. *Any two colors that are directly opposite each other are complementary.*

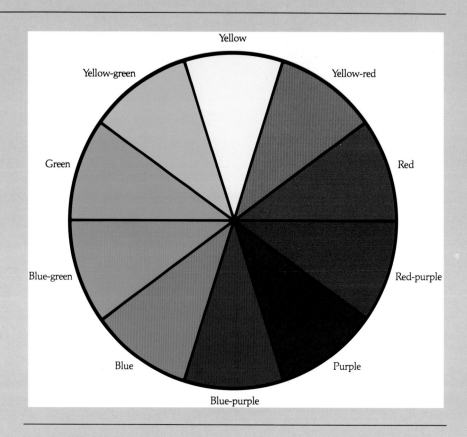

Yellow

Yellow-green

Yellow-red

Green

Red

Blue-green

Red-purple

Blue

Purple

Blue-purple

Color Plate 4I   Are You Color Blind? *A test for color blindness. (Courtesy of American Optical Corporation)*

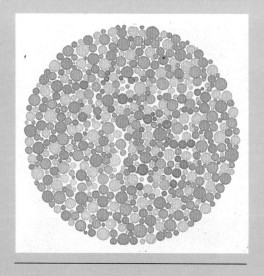

All of our senses interact in providing us with information, which our minds organize and evaluate. Via complex, active processes, we develop accurate perceptions of our world.

Figure 4.20 Linear Perspective. *The parallel cables in this photograph appear to converge, illustrating the monocular cue known as linear perspective.*

converge toward the horizon. Thus, an artist will draw a railroad track using converging rather than parallel lines. (See Figure 4.20 for an example of linear perspective.)

Size also provides a cue to depth: the farther away an object is, the smaller it appears to be. Artists use this cue when they paint two objects of the same size—horses, for example—one twice as large as the other. The smaller object will appear to be farther away, even though both are the same distance from the viewer (see Figure 4.21).

Figure 4.21 Relative Size. *These two horses are exactly the same distances from your retina. But because relative size provides a cue to depth perception, the smaller one appears to be farther away.*

Figure 4.22 Texture Gradient. *Due to texture gradient, the far tower in this photograph appears fuzzy; thus we accurately perceive its distance.*

Texture Gradient: A cue to depth perception based on the fact that, as objects recede into the distance, they appear to lose clarity and detail; a monocular cue for depth created by reducing clarity and detail.

Interposition: A monocular cue for depth in which two objects are drawn such that one partially blocks out the other.

A third monocular cue, **texture gradient,** is based on the fact that, as objects recede into the distance, they appear to lose clarity and detail. A tree on a distant hilltop will appear fuzzy compared to a tree a block away, which produces a much sharper image. Thus, by gradually reducing the clarity and detail of objects, a painter can create an impression of increasing depth (see Figure 4.22).

The partial overlap of objects provides still another monocular cue to depth. When one object stands in front of another, the closer object blocks part of the distant one. By overlapping two objects, then—a technique known as **interposition**—an artist can create the illusion of depth.

Finally, the speed with which objects seem to pass as you walk or ride by them tells you something about their depth, or distance. When you are riding in a car, objects that are close to you appear to pass by more rapidly than objects that are far away. Nearby telephone poles zoom past, but trees

Figure 4.23 Schematic Summary of Cues to Depth Perception.

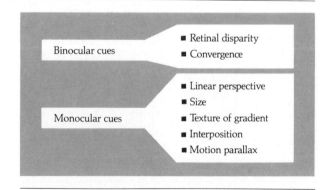

Binocular cues
■ Retinal disparity
■ Convergence

Monocular cues
■ Linear perspective
■ Size
■ Texture of gradient
■ Interposition
■ Motion parallax

in the distance do not seem to change position much in relation to your car. This phenomenon is known as **motion parallax** (Gibson, 1966). (Figure 4.23 provides a schematic summary of cues to depth perception.)

Motion Parallax: A monocular cue to depth based on the fact that, in motion, nearer objects appear to move by faster than objects in the distance.

THE INTERPRETATION AND ORGANIZATION OF VISUAL INFORMATION

Depth perception and color perception are two very specific examples of the way visual sensations are interpreted. In numerous other ways the brain organizes visual information and adjusts for distortions. Some of the general principles by which it works follow.

Constancy of Size, Shape, and Brightness

Recall that the farther away an object is, the smaller its retinal image (see Figure 4.18). When you look at two objects of equal size placed at different distances, their retinal images will differ: the one that is closer will be larger. Yet, in most situations, the two objects will *appear* to be about the same size.

Try this experiment. Sit at the back of your classroom or lecture hall. Notice that all the chairs appear to be the same size—which in fact they are. But again, your retinal image of the distant chairs is smaller than the image of the ones in front of you. Why can't you notice any real difference?

This phenomenon, in which your mental perception of the size of objects remains relatively constant regardless of distance and in spite of the projected retinal image is known as **size constancy.** Your mind maintains perceptual constancy for other visual properties besides size. Because of **shape constancy,** you perceive an object to be the same shape, regardless of the angle or position from which you view it (see Figure 4.24). For example, you see a deck of cards as a deck of cards whether you view it from the top, the side, or some other angle. Because of **brightness constancy,** an object appears to be of the same color and brightness, despite changes in lighting. Your house appears to be the same color at noon as it does at dusk. The physical conditions change, but your perception does not.

Size Constancy: The phenomenon in which objects of the same size appear to be the same size regardless of distance and in spite of differences in the size of the projected retinal image.

Shape Constancy: The phenomenon in which objects of the same shape appear to be the same shape regardless of the angle or position from which they are viewed.

Brightness Constancy: The phenomenon in which objects appear to maintain their appropriate color and brightness, despite physical changes in illumination.

Figure 4.24 Shape Constancy. Due to shape constancy, the door appears to be rectangular in all positions even though the retinal image changes to trapezoidal as the door swings open.

Constancy may be learned. Research has shown that children do not possess it to the same degree as adults (Zeigler & Leibowitz, 1957). What is more, the phenomenon of constancy does not occur in all cultures (Leibowitz & Pick, 1972). Pygmies, who live in dense forests and see few objects at a distance, tend to underestimate the size of a distant object when they view it in a flat, open area. In one study, pygmies who saw buffalo in the distance apparently thought they were insects (Turnbull, 1961). Their perceptual processes could not adjust to the reduced retinal images of the beasts. In the same way, you lose your sense of constancy when you take an airplane trip: high in the sky, you see the people and cars below as tiny ants. Your lack of experience viewing things from the air prevents you from adjusting to a reduced retinal image.

Such experiences are, fortunately, the exception. Most of the time, thanks to perceptual constancies, we view the world as stable, despite changes in the nature of the information we receive from our senses. We learn to see chairs as having a constant size or our houses as having a constant color, despite changes in distance or lighting, because the chairs are in fact the same size, and the color of our houses does not change from day to day. Constancies, then, allow us to see the world as it really is.

Illusions

Sometimes our perceptual process distorts the images we receive rather than correcting for superficial changes in appearance. The result is an illusion, a discrepancy between what a person perceives and reality. Illusions

Though the size of the moon stays the same, it appears much larger near the horizon than it does later in the night when it is directly overhead.

don't seem to be learned, nor can they be unlearned: knowing that the illusion isn't what it appears to be doesn't make it go away. Being told that a movie is actually a rapidly exposed sequence of still photos, for example, does not eliminate the illusion of movement that it creates, a phenomenon psychologists call **stroboscopic motion.**

Another everyday example is the moon illusion. Have you ever seen the moon on the horizon, just before dusk? You probably noticed that it appears larger near the horizon than it does later in the night, when it is directly overhead. Of course the moon doesn't shrink as the night wears on; your perception of it changes. And it changes in spite of the fact that your distance from the moon—and the image projected on your retina—stays about the same (Rock & Kaufman, 1962).

One explanation of the moon illusion depends on visual constancy. According to this theory, when the moon is close to the horizon, interposed objects in the environment serve as cues to its distance. Because of size constancy, you expect the image of a distant object to be small in comparison to objects in the foreground. But the moon isn't—it dwarfs the trees and houses on the horizon in front of it. Thus your brain automatically causes you to perceive it as very large (Gregory, 1968; Restle, 1970). No cues to distance exist when the moon is overhead, so your perception of its size is not so exaggerated.

Another well-known illusion, the railroad, or Ponzo illusion, has yet to be satisfactorily explained. In its simplest form, the Ponzo illusion consists of two gradually converging lines that give the impression of increasing depth, and in between, two crosswise parallel lines (see Figure 4.25). Note that the top crosswise line appears to be bigger. Both lines are in fact the same size, however, as you can prove to yourself with a ruler. Somehow the converging lines trick you into believing that the top line is farther away. If you cover the converging lines with your hand, the parallel lines will suddenly appear to be the same size.

Illusions have fascinated artists for centuries. Just as monocular cues can be used realistically to create the appearance of a third dimension, illusions can be used to suggest unreality (see Figure 4.26). Whether they occur in real life or in pictures, these phenomena remind us that we cannot always rely on our perceptions. But illusions do more than demonstrate our perceptual shortcomings. They indicate, as the Gestalt psychologists argued, that perception depends on the form or context within which something is viewed. And they provide clues to the principles that actually govern sensory perception.

Stroboscopic Motion: The perception of movement from a series of rapidly presented still photos.

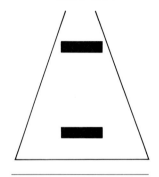

Figure 4.25 The Ponzo Illusion. *The two parallel lines are identical, yet the upper line appears longer.*

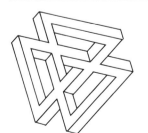 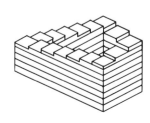

Figure 4.26 Impossible Figures.

Principles of Perceptual Organization

Perceptual Organization:
The automatic inclination to organize sensory elements into meaningful patterns.

Figure-Ground Relationship: The relationship between a pattern or figure and the surrounding background.

Figure-Ground Reversal: A reversal in the relationship between a pattern (figure) and surrounding background (ground). The figure becomes ground and the ground becomes figure, resulting in a scene or picture that can be seen in two distinct ways.

The human inclination to organize sensory data into meaningful patterns, called **perceptual organization,** was a topic that fascinated the Gestalt psychologists. Their work suggested that perception is governed by a number of inborn tendencies, most of which are further developed through experience. Among the most important of these tendencies is the inclination to distinguish an object from its background.

Look up from your book for a moment. Your field of vision can be divided into two categories: objects *in* your visual field, called figures; and the space *between* the figures, called the ground. Experiments with people who were born blind but were later cured indicate that the ability to distinguish figures from the space that contains them is inborn (von Senden, 1960). Newly sighted people can identify such **figure-ground relationships** immediately (Gregory & Wallace, 1963).

When the boundaries between figure and ground are unclear, the viewer's perception fluctuates between the two. What first appears to be ground suddenly appears to be figure, and vice versa. Because of this phenomenon, known as **figure-ground reversal,** some pictures can be seen in two different ways, depending on which part is perceived as figure and which ground. M. C. Escher's "Heaven and Hell" (see Figure 4.27) is a good illustration of a reversible figure and ground. The angels are light colored,

Figure 4.27 Figure-Ground Relationships. Escher's paintings make good use of figure-ground reversals. (© M. C. Escher Heirs c/o Cordon Art—Baarn-Holland).

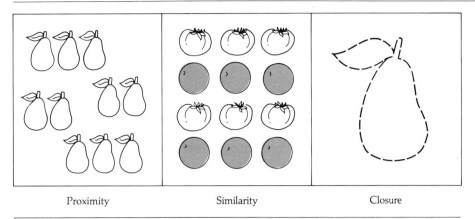

Proximity	Similarity	Closure

Figure 4.28 Law of Proximity, Similarity, and Closure.

the demons dark. But, since the boundaries between figure and ground are unclear, the viewer's perception fluctuates between angels seen against a dark background and demons seen against a light background.

A number of other laws govern the way you organize your visual world (see Figure 4.28). According to the **law of proximity,** you tend to group items that are close together. And, according to the **law of similarity,** you tend to see items that are similar in groups. The **law of closure** states that you will mentally fill in the missing parts of a figure.

Some psychologists have attempted to combine these laws of perceptual organization into a single overall principle. According to one theory, called the **principle of simplicity,** the Gestalt laws of proximity, similarity, and closure all illustrate the human tendency to group visual elements into their simplest form. And there is evidence that simple patterns are perceived more easily than complex ones (Attneave, 1954; Hatfield & Epstein, 1985).

Whatever principle you might choose to explain the way in which humans organize their field of vision, it is clear that what you see isn't always exactly what exists. When you examine a visual field, what you perceive is a function not only of what is there, but of the way you are disposed to see it.

Perceptual Set

Besides the Gestalt principles of organization, other more general tendencies affect the way in which you interpret your visual sensations. Your physical and emotional needs and expectations, for example, strongly influence your perceptions. If you need water, you are more likely to find it

Law of Proximity: The Gestalt Law of Organization that states that items that are near (close) to each other tend to be grouped together.

Law of Similarity: The Gestalt Law Of Organization that states that items that are similar tend to be seen in groups.

Law of Closure: The Gestalt Law of Organization, that states that there is a tendency to fill in or close missing gaps in a figure and see it as complete.

Principle of Simplicity: An explanation of the Gestalt Laws of Organization which states that humans group elements into their simplest form. Also referred to as the minimum principle (that we will perceive the simplest organization that will fit the stimulus).

■ **Learning Check** ■

Read the definition, then cover the right side and try to recite. Repeat.

Law of Proximity	Tendency to group items that are close together.
Law of Similarity	Tendency to see items that are similar in groups.
Law of Closure	Tendency to fill in the missing parts of a figure.

than if you do not need it. If you expect to like a person, you are more likely to do so than if you expect to dislike him. Also, because your needs and expectations become the focus of your attention, they tend to block out your perception of other things. You cannot attend to everything at once, so inevitably you miss things that to other people might seem highly important. (Figure 4.29 illustrates how perceptual set can influence the interpretation of ambiguous stimuli.)

Consider how perceptual set might affect a person's happiness or success in life. If what a person perceives is influenced by what she needs and expects, then two people in the same circumstances might respond to an opportunity in entirely different ways. If one person is looking for an opportunity and expects to find it, she is more likely to be successful than one who is pessimistic about her chances. Perhaps that is why some people seem to find opportunities wherever they look, while others miss even blatantly obvious chances.

In the same way, many scientific discoveries are made by accident—but not just because the scientists who make them are lucky. These people are searching for truth; when it reveals itself, they are able to seize on it. Their perceptual set, in effect, allows them to recognize clues to the solution of the mystery they are investigating, and eventually to solve it.

To conclude, perception is an extremely complex process. One thing, however, is clear: the process is an active one. You do not sit back and passively observe the world. Instead, you select from among the thousands of sensory experiences you have each day, and organize them into a mental perception that has meaning for you. In the next chapter we will look beyond the perceptual processes as we consider the topic of consciousness.

12　13　14

A　13　C

Figure 4.29 Effect of Context and Set. *The context of an item influences the way it is perceived. When seen in the context of numbers, the middle figure appears to be 13. But when seen in the context of letters it looks like a B.*

LEARNING FRAMEWORK

I. Theories of sensation and perception try to explain how sensory input becomes a meaningful perceptual experience.
   A. Traditional theorists said there was a point-to-point correspondence between sensory input and the neural message sent to the brain. (Review: *Receptor Cells; Transduction*)
   B. Gestalt psychologists said perception depended on the context in which a stimulus is viewed. (Review: *Figure 4.5 and Color Plate 4A*)
   C. According to J. J. Gibson's theory, we have receptor cells in the eye that respond to specific features of the environment. (Review: *Feature Detectors*)
   D. Modern theories emphasize that people actively interpret and try to make sense of sensory stimulation.
II. Attempts to describe the senses have led to discoveries concerning their general characteristics and their measurement.
   A. Sensory receptors respond to change. (Review: *Sensory Adaptation; Habituation*)
   B. Sensory capabilities are measured in terms of the least amount of energy and the least amount of change in energy that they can detect. (Review: *Absolute Threshold; Signal Detection Analysis; Difference Threshold; Tables 4.1 and 4.2*)

III. Our senses allow us to detect many different kinds of physical energy.

    A. Motion senses allow us to detect mechanical energy—active and passive movements. (Review: *Kinesthesis; Vestibular Sense and Figure 4.6*)

    B. Through taste and smell, we detect chemicals in the air and in our food. (Review: *Figures 4.7, 4.8, and 4.9*)

    C. There are different receptors scattered throughout the skin that detect heat and pressure. (Review: *Free Nerve Endings; Basket Cells and Figure 4.10*)

IV. Our sense of hearing can best be viewed in terms of the nature of sounds, the structure of the ear, and theories of how sounds are perceived.

    A. Sound waves vary in height, number of cycles per second, and complexity. (Review: *Amplitude; Frequency; Overtones; Figures 4.11 and 4.12*)

    B. Sound waves enter the outer ear where the tympanic membrane responds to their pressure by moving in and out and converts air pressure into physical vibrations. These vibrations ultimately cause movements in the organ of Corti. These movements, in turn, create a neural impulse that is sent to the brain along the auditory nerve. (Review: *Figure 4.13 and Color Plate 4B*)

    C. According to theory, pitch perception involves a combination of the characteristics of the sound energy and those of the structures that convert them to neural impulses. (Review: *Place Theory; Frequency Theory; Volley Theory and Figure 4.14*)

V. Our sense of vision can best be viewed in terms of the nature of light, the structure of the eye, and the way colors and depth are perceived.

    A. Lightwaves vary in length, purity, and height. (Review: *Hue; Saturation; Amplitude; Color Plates 4C and 4D*)

    B. Lightwaves enter the eye at the cornea and are focused on the retina where the receptors for light are located. Stimulation of these receptors creates a neural impulse that is sent to the brain along the optic nerve. (Review: *Accommodation; Rods; Cones; Figure 4.17 and Color Plate 4E*)

    C. According to theory, color perception is a two-stage process. (Review: *Trichromatic Theory; Negative Afterimage; Opponent Process Mechanism and Color Plates 4F, 4G, 4H*)

    D. Depth perception depends on the brain's use of information that comes in the form of binocular and monocular cues. (Review: *Retinal Disparity; Convergence; Linear Perspective; Texture Gradient; Interposition; Motion Parallax; Figures 4.20, 4.21, 4.22, 4.23*)

VI. Visual perception also depends on the brain's ability to organize visual inputs and adjust for distortions.

    A. The brain adjusts for changes of an object in position, shape, and brightness. (Review: *Size Constancy; Shape Constancy; Brightness Constancy and Figure 4.24*)

    B. Automatic adjustments for distortions help explain discrepancies between what a person sees and what exists in reality. (Review: *Illusion; Stroboscopic Motion and Figure 4.25*)

    C. We have a natural inclination to organize sensory inputs into meaningful patterns. (Review: *Figure-Ground Reversal; Principle of Simplicity; Figure 4.28*)

    D. What we perceive also depends, in part, on our needs and expectations. (Review: *Perceptual Set and Figure 4.29*)

5

Consciousness and Behavior

At about 4:00 AM on a windy March morning, one of the most serious nuclear accidents ever to happen in the United States was underway. Though warning lights were flashing in the control area of the nuclear power station at Three Mile Island, they went unnoticed. The plant operators also failed to notice that a valve that should have been closed was open. In fact, for more than two hours the operators failed to respond to warnings of impending disaster, and why? The operators weren't irresponsible, nor were they unqualified to perform their duties. But they had been placed on the night shift after a six-week period of constant shift rotation (Moore-Ede et al., 1982). And, due to internal rhythms that regulate the ebb and flow of human consciousness, the operators confronted the crisis at a time when, for most people, efficiency and alertness are at their lowest point. Fluctuations in consciousness apparently played a critical role in the "human failures" that jeopardized the lives of so many people and shocked the nation (Restak, 1984, p. 117). With their consciousness numbed by the shift change and early morning hour, the operators failed to sense the danger.

WHAT IS CONSCIOUSNESS?

Indian gurus pose a riddle to their pupils that goes like this: What is it that is constantly changing, yet always the same? There are, of course, many possible answers to the riddle, among them a river, an ocean, the sky. But the guru will accept only one answer: the soul, or what those of us in the West might prefer to call mind or consciousness.

Consciousness is indeed one of the great riddles, perhaps the greatest of all mysteries in the universe. No one has yet managed to solve it, nor is anyone likely to do so soon. Yet we must attempt to come to grips with consciousness, for it is the very essence of human experience.

In this chapter we examine both normal waking consciousness and altered states of consciousness such as sleep. In the process we will take up some of the most intriguing topics psychology has to offer, among them dreams, hypnosis, meditation, and mind-altering drugs. Let us proceed by confronting the answer to the question, What is consciousness?

Because little is known about consciousness, there are as yet no universally agreed on definitions, no comprehensive theories. One expert has identified at least seven different definitions of consciousness ranging from "direct awareness" through "a general state or condition of the person" (Natsoulas, 1978, 1983). As a working definition, **consciousness** refers to the process of knowing and of being aware. It includes your awareness of yourself as an individual—your sense of personal identity. Consciousness also includes your current cognitions—your thoughts, memories, feelings, concerns, ideas, and your awareness of these cognitions. Thus, you not only have an awareness of your thoughts, but you also know what you are thinking. This is the essence of the modern view of consciousness: the subjective experience of being aware, self-awareness, and knowing (Hunt, 1985).

Consciousness: The process of knowing and of being aware.

States of Consciousness

One way of viewing consciousness is in terms of its various states—quantitative and qualitative differences that occur during the course of the day and night. Just as water exists in different states, liquid, gas, or solid, so too does consciousness. The shift from one state of consciousness to another occurs automatically—a state of focused alertness about the problem of paying this month's rent melts into a hazy daydream of greath wealth; and the fantasy of wealth evaporates into a badly needed afternoon snooze.

Everyone spends at least part of the day in the state of consciousness called daydreaming, which is characterized by being absorbed in one's own thoughts and images. In daydreams people think about future plans and desires, create, plan, think through problems, relive past events, or just let the mind drift. Daydreams seem to fulfill many different functions—wishful thinking, relief from everyday reality or boredom, temporary escape, and so on. However, just why people daydream, and the relationship between daydreams and other aspects of consciousness, are still open questions.

Researchers still attempt to isolate the fundamental states of consciousness. According to one, there are two basic states, the typical waking state, and deviations from it called **altered states** (Tart, 1972, 1975). The waking state includes awareness of one's self and of one's surroundings during the day. Altered states include sleep, dreams, hypnosis, drug intoxication, and meditation.

Altered States of Consciousness: States of consciousness other than those that normally occur during normal waking (for example, drug-induced states, hypnosis, and meditation).

Others argue for more than two states of consciousness. Sleep could well be thought of as more than one state, dream sleep and non-dream sleep. And drug-induced states of consciousness too might be seen as divisible: your state of consciousness after drinking one glass of wine is quite different from your state after drinking an entire bottle (Wallace & Fisher, 1987). Some researchers have proposed a continuum ranging from alertness to daydreaming to drowsiness to light sleep and deep sleep (Bradshaw &

Nettleton, 1981; Weil, 1972). All these views are highly tentative. They are useful as working models, as frameworks for organizing existing knowledge and generating new ideas. But they are theories, not established facts. Most can agree, however, that the fluctuations in consciousness that occur naturally during normal waking consciousness are the result of biological rhythms.

Biological Rhythms and Consciousness

The sun rises, arcs across the sky, then falls below the horizon. There follows the darkness of night, and a new daily cycle at dawn. The rhythm of day and night is so much a part of the planet that it appears to be woven into the fabric of all living things. Body temperature, blood pressure, urine flow, bowel movements, stomach contractions, sugar and hormone levels all swing up and down in a physiological ebb and flow that is tied to the rotation of the planet. Whether a person sleeps late and stays up till all hours, or rises with the sun and retires early, the body settles into a pattern of regular daily fluctuations, called **circadian rhythms** (Latin for "around the day").

Circadian Rhythms: Biological rhythms that occur over a 24-hour cycle.

These daily rhythms have a profound effect on consciousness. For example, changes in mental alertness are correlated with rhythmic fluctuations in body temperature. Body temperature gradually rises from the early morning hours through midmorning. It reaches its peak in the afternoon and then begins to decline again. It is at its lowest point between 2 and 5 AM (Aschoff, 1981). Thus, we are usually less alert in the early morning hours than at midafternoon. Disruptions of one's normal rhythm can lead to some rather uncomfortable side effects, as those of you who have ever experienced jet lag, or a lack of efficiency due to a change in work shift, know.

Jet lag is a common experience for many people. It refers to the tiredness and irritability, sleeping difficulties, and digestive problems that people experience when their normal schedules are disrupted by an airflight that takes them over several time zones, like flying from San Diego to Boston, or from Boston to England. Jet lag is explainable, at least in part, as the result of a disruption of normal circadian rhythms. Whereas our body temperature may be falling and our mental alertness declining, the time on the clock in the new location and bright sunshine may tell us that it's too early to go to bed. So we fight our fatigue. Then, when our body temperature begins to rise, we try to go to sleep, and are frustrated when we can't.

Psychologists Timothy Monk and Curtis Graeber of NASA's Ames Research Center in Mountain View, California are attempting to determine how people are affected by jet lag by a careful study of pilots and their crews. Their findings have confirmed that jet lag negatively affects mood (people become uptight) and reduces motivation. And it seems to take at least three days, often longer, for the person to recover. One important personal lesson for people who travel is, if you are going to make important decisions, give yourself time to recover. Another is, realize that your efficiency will be temporarily reduced, and don't blame yourself for not performing up to par, a problem also dealt with by workers required to change shifts.

Along with our modern, fast-paced, everyday living are a number of special jobs that require people to work across all hours of the day and night. In addition to flight personnel, hospital employees and many factory workers are often called upon to work on any number of shifts. Because the graveyard shift, 11 PM to 7 AM, is undesirable, people are asked to rotate through the shifts, just as did the former operators at the Three Mile Island nuclear plant. A number of studies have revealed that such shift changes lower productivity and efficiency, and they have been linked to many near accidents by pilots and air controllers who had not adapted to their new shift. As Czeisler and colleagues (1980, 1981) have observed, shift work disrupts the body's timing system which controls the release of hormones and the timing of when we sleep and when we wake. Shift workers typically report feeling "lousy" most of the time and have trouble functioning at work and problems staying awake on the job. They go home feeling exhausted but can't sleep. Home problems, irritability, and depression are common. Although the majority (about 10 percent) seem to adjust after two to four days, some never do. To help such workers, Czeisler and colleagues have suggested that the time between shift rotations should be lengthened from, for example, one to three weeks. The researchers also believe that it's better to shift forward than backward—say, from the 11 PM–7 AM shift to the 7 AM–3 PM shift, as opposed to a shift from the 7 AM–3 PM backward to the 11 PM–7 AM shift.

Some natural cycles are longer than twenty-four hours, such as a woman's menstrual cycle. Other cycles are much shorter than a day. Have you ever noticed that at certain times during the day you seem to be in top form, while at other times you can't do anything right? These peaks and valleys are the result of biological rhythms of less than twenty-four hours, or **ultradian rhythms**—90-minute cycles of alertness that may explain the normal fluctuations of normal waking consciousness. In the next section, we will see how these 90-minute cycles continue while we sleep and examine the processes that underlie them.

Ultradian Rhythms: Biological rhythms that occur in less than twenty-four hours, usually over 90-minute cycles.

■ Learning Clue ■

As you read about sleep and dreams, remember that there are two main stages of sleep—one associated with rapid eye movements and one in which such eye movements do not occur.

SLEEP AND DREAMS

It was not quite 6 AM on a quiet morning in the 1950s. The renowned sleep researcher Nathaniel Kleitman and his young assistant, Eugene Aserinsky, had been awake all night. They did not know it, but they were on the threshold of a major scientific achievement—a discovery that would usher in the modern era of sleep research and open new doors to the study of human consciousness.

The volunteer subjects, most of them undergraduates at the University of Chicago, had been slumbering since about 11:30 PM. Each was attached to an **electroencephalograph,** an instrument that amplifies (enhances) and

Electroencephalograph: An instrument that enhances and records brain waves.

records brain waves, fluctuations in the electrical activity of the brain. As the pen on one of the machines began to quicken, and the pattern it was tracing shifted from large to small waves, the inquisitive Aserinsky observed something he had noticed once before while studying infants: a burst of movement behind the sleeping subjects' eyelids.

Kleitman was busy inspecting the graphic recordings of the subjects' brain waves, called **electroencephalograms,** or **EEGs** (see Figure 5.1). This was the third time that night that subjects' brain waves had shifted from slow to fast. Kleitman pored over the alternating peaks and valleys on the graph paper, looking for clues to their meaning. Meanwhile, Aserinsky was

Electroencephalogram (EEG): The actual graphic recordings of brain waves.

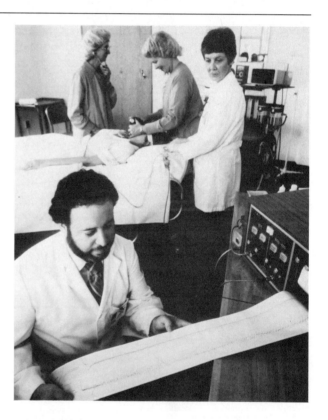

Figure 5.1   The Electroencephalogram.   *The long white sheet that this researcher is studying is the electroencephalogram (EEG)—the graphic recordings of a subject's brain waves.*

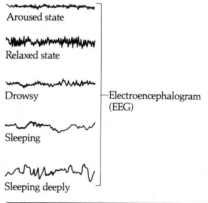

Aroused state

Relaxed state

Drowsy

Sleeping

Sleeping deeply

Electroencephalogram (EEG)

irresistibly drawn to the subjects' jerking eye movements. Why, he wondered, did these darting eye movements recur through the night?

Aserinsky hesitated to bother Kleitman with questions. If this periodic jerking of the eyeballs meant anything at all, he reasoned, then surely someone would have investigated it by now. Yet he had to solve the riddle. Risking embarrassment, he queried his distinguished mentor. To his surprise, the experienced researcher knew of not one scientific investigation of the nightly eye-dance ritual.

The researchers quickly made plans to subject these curious **rapid eye movements** (see Figure 5.2), or **REM** episodes, to the rigors of the scientific method. They soon verified that REM episodes were a regular part of the sleeping subjects behavior: most sleepers went through about four or five REM episodes during the course of seven or eight hours of sleep. Moreover, the rapid eye movements almost always appeared with a specific brain wave pattern, the small, fast waves that were essentially indistinguishable from those of a relaxed wakeful subject.

But the most exciting results came when the researchers began to awaken subjects before, during, and after REM episodes, to discover what was going through their minds. Subjects whose sleep was interrupted during or immediately following a REM episode usually reported vivid visual dreams. Subjects who were awakened forty minutes after their eye-dance had ended, however, generally had nothing to report but grogginess. In fact, no matter what the EEG looked like, subjects rarely reported dreams except when they were experiencing rapid eye movements (Aserinsky & Kleitman, 1953).

Later investigations revealed that people do sometimes dream during **nonrapid eye movement** sleep, or **NREM.** But that was a minor point compared to the profoundly significant discovery that there were distinguishable

Rapid Eye Movements (REM): Rapid darting of the eyes under closed eyelids which occurs during sleep, usually associated with dreaming.

Nonrapid Eye Movement Sleep (NREM): Periods of sleep during which rapid eye movements are not occurring. There are four stages of NREM that vary from light to very deep sleep.

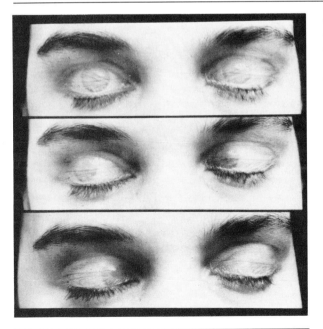

Figure 5.2 Rapid Eye Movements. The discovery of rapid eye movements ushered in the modern era of sleep research.

types of sleep. Once scientists realized that all sleep was not alike, they could begin to study it in smaller, more manageable units. If they could not determine the function of an entire night of sleep, they might still discover the function of one part of it. And today, Aserinsky, now a senior scientist, is building from his early discovery in a never-ending quest to solve sleep's mysteries (Aserinsky et al., 1985).

The discovery of REM freed scientists from dependence on subjects' self-reports. Now there was a way to verify claims such as "I never dream" or "I dream all night." With the discovery of REMs, the modern era of sleep research had arrived, and with it, a key to the mystery of human consciousness. For much of what is known about consciousness has come through the backdoor, so to speak—from the study of sleep and dreams and mental states other than normal waking consciousness.

The Sleep Cycle

With the discovery of REM, scientists could distinguish between two main types of sleep—one associated with rapid eye movements (REM) and nonrapid eye movement sleep (NREM), which was not associated with rapid eye movements. NREM, in turn, could be divided into four subtypes or stages based on measurable physiological changes (see Figure 5.3). REM sleep, which is commonly referred to as paradoxical sleep because the EEG pattern during this type of sleep resembles that of the waking person (Bowker, 1985), could not be further subdivided, however.

During waking consciousness, the typical EEG shows a variety of sizes and frequencies. Most of the waves are short, fast **beta waves** (see Figure 5.4). The individual's brain waves show no rhythmic pattern and are said to be **desynchronized.** In a desynchronized pattern, some waves are at their peak while others are at their low point. This is in contrast to a **synchronized** pattern where the same pattern of tracings occurs in all brain regions sampled by the electrodes, with peaks and troughs occurring simultaneously (see Figure 5.5).

If a waking subject closes his or her eyes, a number of slightly larger and more rhythmic waves, called **alpha waves,** typically begin to run through the betas, but the pattern remains desynchronized. The alpha waves usually become more prominent during relaxation or when subjects are asked to visualize a simple object (for example, a piece of ice) (Osaka, 1984).

Beta Waves: Small fast brain waves that dominate the EEG of an alert, awake subject.

Desynchronized EEG: Brain waves that show no clear pattern.

Synchronized EEG: A brain wave pattern in which the majority of the waves are coordinated in frequency and peak—going up and down at about the same time.

Alpha Waves: Brain waves that appear in the EEG of a relaxed subject with eyes closed. (These waves are larger and slower than beta waves.)

Figure 5.3   Schematic Overview of the Stages of Sleep.   There are two main stages of sleep, NREM and REM. NREM sleep is further divided into four subtypes: Stage 1 NREM; Stage 2 NREM; Stage 3 NREM; Stage 4 NREM.

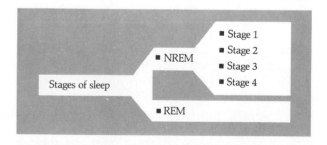

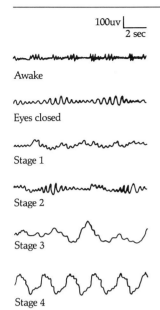

Figure 5.4 Brain Wave Stages of Sleep. *These EEG patterns illustrate the beta waves that are typical of wakefulness and those during the four stages of sleep.*

100uv

2 sec

Awake

Eyes closed

Stage 1

Stage 2

Stage 3

Stage 4

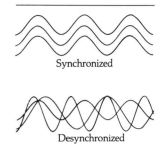

Synchronized

Desynchronized

Figure 5.5 Synchronized and Desynchronized Brain Waves.

When a person falls asleep, he or she enters the first subtype of NREM sleep, or stage 1 NREM. This is the lightest stage of sleep, a transition from waking to sleeping. Because the EEG pattern of stage 1 NREM is desynchronized, being practically indistinguishable from the waking pattern, its verification depends on the measurement of other behaviors. The slowing of eye movements is monitored by electrodes placed at the outer edge of each eye and recorded on what is called the **electroculogram** (EOG). A reduction in muscular tensions is monitored by electrodes on the chin and recorded on the **electromyogram** (EMG).

A few minutes after the onset of stage 1 NREM, the EEG begins to show brief bursts of waves that do not normally occur in waking subjects. One of these, distinctly larger and slower than beta or alpha waves, is called a **sleep spindle;** its appearance against the background of desynchronized EEG activity marks the onset of stage 2 NREM (see Figure 5.6). In stage 2, which makes up about half the total sleep time and is deeper than stage 1, the sleeper continues to relax and eye movement decreases further (Webb, 1975). Although sleepers in this stage still awaken relatively easily, they usually are pretty sure that they have been asleep. As in stage 1, dreams are uncommon.

About twenty or thirty minutes following the initial onset of sleep, the EEG, still desynchronized, is gradually punctuated by still larger and slower waves called **delta waves.** Like sleep spindles, delta waves usually occur only during sleep. When roughly two out of every ten waves on the EEG are deltas, the sleeper is said to be in stage 3 NREM. In another ten minutes, regular bursts of delta waves begin dominating the EEG, producing a pattern that is increasingly synchronized, or coordinated in frequency and peak with the waves rising and falling at the same time. A rapid transition to the deepest stage of sleep, stage 4 NREM, follows.

Electrocalogram EOG: The graphic recording of eye movement.

Electromyogram (EMG): The graphic recordings of changes in muscular tension.

Sleep Spindle: A type of brain wave pattern that occurs during sleep, generally associated with the onset of stage 2 NREM sleep.

Delta Waves: Very large, slow brain waves usually associated with the deepest stages (3 and 4) of NREM sleep.

Figure 5.6 Sleep Spindles and the Stages of Sleep.

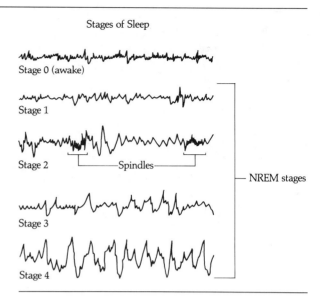

Stages of Sleep

Stage 0 (awake)

Stage 1

Stage 2 — Spindles —

Stage 3

Stage 4

NREM stages

Slow Wave Sleep (SWS): The regular pattern of large slow delta waves that occurs during the deepest stage of sleep also known as stage 4 NREM.

In stage 4 NREM, half or more of the brain waves are deltas, and their pattern is well synchronized. The regular pattern of synchronized deltas is sometimes referred to as **slow wave sleep (SWS).** The sleeper spends about thirty to forty minutes in this restful state, relaxed but able to shift position (see Figure 5.7). Though dreams sometimes occur in this stage, they usually are difficult to remember, and are not as vivid as those that occur in REM sleep. The exception to this rule—a particularly horrifying nightmare that is difficult to distinguish from reality—is produced by a rare sleep disorder called night terrors. The individual may awaken in panic, screaming and swinging wildly at the fading image of a terrifying nightmare. Their cause unknown, night terrors are most common in children and generally disappear as the person matures.

After a little more than an hour after the onset of sleep, the sleeper starts moving back through the four stages of NREM sleep in reverse order. Delta

Figure 5.7 Postural Movements During Sleep. The postural shifts of this subject, whose movements and brain waves are being recorded in a sleep lab, signal the transition from NREM to REM sleep.

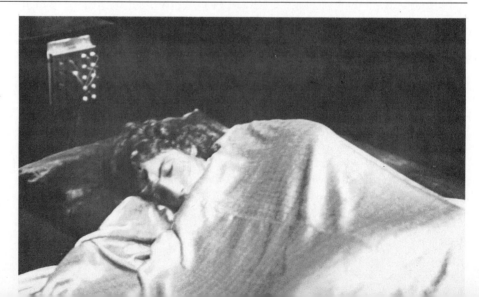

activity decreases, dropping to less than 50 percent, which defines stage 3. The EEG becomes increasingly desynchronized. When the percentage of delta waves drops below 20, the sleeper is back in stage 2. Within about ten minutes after the beginning of the ascent from stage 4, the EEG pattern is indistinguishable from waking.

With the ascent up NREM stages, the sleeper is ready for the night's first visual dream. The beginning of rapid eye movements (REMs) marks the beginning of the REM stage of sleep. Caught now in the world of dreams, the sleeper becomes physiologically aroused, as if awake—but curiously, for most people, the muscles are more relaxed than at any stage of NREM sleep. Apparently the ability to move about is switched off during REM sleep, perhaps to prevent the sleeper from acting on the images flashed before the mind's eye (Cartwright, 1978).

The first dream of the night usually does not last very long. The sleeper seems to have difficulty getting into the dream, and has trouble holding onto it. After about ten minutes (and perhaps a brief awakening), the sleeper begins another descent down the NREM stages to stage 4 NREM. The first 90-minute cycle is complete. (Table 5.1 summarizes the measurable activities that occur during this first 90-minute cycle.)

Table 5.1 Measurable Activities That Occur During the First 90 Minutes of Sleep

Stage	Behavior
Stage 1 NREM	Eye movement slows. Reduction in muscular tension. EEG desynchronized. Lasts about 5 minutes or less.
Stage 2 NREM	Appearance of sleep spindles. EEG desynchronized. Continued relaxation. Decreased eye movements. Lasts about 25 minutes.
Stage 3 NREM	Appearance of delta waves. EEG desynchronized. Lasts about 10 minutes.
Stage 4 NREM	Half or more waves are delta waves. EEG synchronized. Lasts about 30 minutes. Person relaxed but able to shift positions. If awakened, subject rarely reports visual dreaming.
REM	Rapid eye movements occur. EEG desynchronized. Subject physiologically aroused but relaxed. Person unable to shift positions. If awakened, subject usually reports visual dreaming. Lasts about 10 minutes.

Figure 5.8 Summary of Sleep Cycle. *The sleep cycle is characterized by three to five cycles down through NREM and back up again to REM. Each cycle is a bit different. Slow wave (stage 4) NREM dominates the first half of the night; REM sleep dominates the second half.*

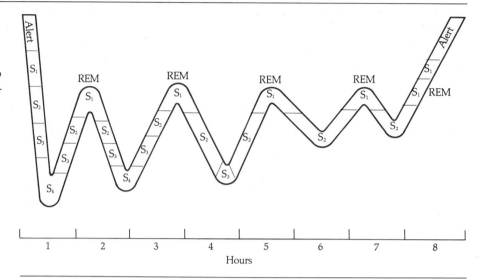

Another three to five cycles down through NREM and back up again to the vivid dream world of REM sleep follow. Each cycle is a little different from the last. As the night wears on, the sleeper spends progressively less time in stage 4 and more time in REM sleep, stopping in the last cycle for only ten minutes or less in stage 4, and tarrying thirty to forty minutes in the dream stage. Thus, the first half of the night is dominated by slow wave sleep, the second half by REM. The longest dreams are the last to occur before the sleeper awakes (see Figure 5.8).

The systematic study of the sleep cycle has helped to dispel a number of myths. First, except when under the influence of certain drugs, everyone dreams. You probably have about four to five dreams a night, whether or not you can recall them. Second, a person does not dream all night, as some people claim. Third, an entire dream does not happen in a flash, as sometimes seems to be the case; the last dream of the night, in fact, may last as long as a feature movie. Fourth, sleep is not a passive state; it is an active one characterized by fluctuating brain activity. Finally, as evidenced by changes in EEG patterns and the presence of rapid eye movements, there is

■ **Learning Check** ■

For each question: read, cover, try to recite, repeat.

Which stages of sleep are associated with a desynchronized EEG and which with a synchronized EEG?

Answer: Three stages of NREM (NREM 1, NREM 2, NREM 3) and the entire REM stage are associated with a desynchronized pattern. Only NREM 4 is synchronized.

What two types of brain waves are associated with waking or relaxing and what two are associated with NREM?

Answer: Beta and alpha waves are associated with waking or relaxing; sleep spindles and delta waves with NREM.

good evidence that human infants do in fact dream (Barlow, 1985), though the nature of these dreams remains a mystery.

The sleep cycle seems to parallel the 90-minute rest-activity cycle of the waking state. Just as we shift from alert to drowsy during the day, so too do we jump from light sleep to deep sleep. Just as we can skip from a quiet, relaxed state to one of keen concentration in our waking hours, so too can we jump from the depths of slow wave sleep to the busy REM stage. Clear documentation of the sleep cycle has been an important first step toward uncovering the secrets of both wakeful consciousness and sleep. But a whole new set of questions remains to be answered. What is the function of REM sleep? What are the physiological mechanisms that govern each stage of sleep? In the sections ahead we will examine these and other questions.

The Function of Sleep

All humans need sleep. It restores the body. But the precise function of sleep is not fully understood. In an effort to determine the purpose of sleep, researchers first tried depriving subjects of a certain amount of sleep and recording the behavioral effects.

Sleep Deprivation Studies. Researchers reasoned that, if sleep deprivation were to cause some kind of impairment, such as memory loss, then it might be hypothesized that sleep plays a role in the maintenance of normal memory functions. They found that, when deprived of sleep, people generally become irritable and less alert, and perform poorly on tasks involving memory, learning, and concentration. But these effects are generally no worse after two or three days of deprivation than after five or six hours. The major effect of sleep loss, it seemed, is that it makes people sleepy. The longer they are awake, the more they want to sleep.

In the 1960s, a disc jockey named Peter Tripp vowed to stay awake for 200 hours to raise money for the March of Dimes. Sleep researchers gathered to watch. For his protection, Tripp was given medical examinations, including a number of psychological tests, before and during the stunt.

After about 100 sleepless hours, Tripp experienced a substantial decrease in his ability to remember, attend to a task, or solve simple problems in mental arithmetic. After 170 hours he was manifesting some of the symptoms of severe mental disorders. He began to have visual hallucinations—that is, to see things that didn't exist—and became convinced that the doctors were conspiring to have him sent to jail. During one medical examination he somehow got the idea he was about to be buried alive. Strangely, during this severe mental disturbance, Tripp's brain wave pattern resembled that of a sleeping subject during NREM sleep, even though he appeared to be awake.

After 200 sleepless hours, Tripp slept for thirteen hours. He was mildly REM Rebound depressed for about three months, but otherwise showed no ill effects from the experience (Luce, 1965).

As a case study, Tripp's experience did not prove that sleep deprivation causes mental disturbances. However, it did provide a wealth of information and hypotheses. It opened up the possibility that sleep deprivation could lead to symptoms of severe mental disorder in some people, for instance.

A few years later, when a seventeen-year-old high school student named Randy Gardner attempted to break Tripp's record, the sleep researcher William Dement was there. Dement noted some memory lapses, irritability, and poor concentration in Randy long before he broke the 200-hour goal. Eventually Randy's EEG pattern, like Tripp's, began to resemble that of a sleeping subject, though he was awake. Unlike Tripp, however, Randy showed no symptoms of severe mental disorder. After 260 sleepless hours, he slept for fourteen solid hours, predominantly in stage 4 NREM and REM, and awoke with no apparent ill effects (Johnson et al., 1965).

Gardner's ordeal revealed that the development of severe mental disturbances was not a necessary outcome of prolonged sleep deprivation. But his case study confirmed the memory lapses, irritability, and poor concentration that follow sleep deprivation found in the case study of Tripp.

REM Deprivation Studies. One of the problems of both case studies of sleep deprivation was that they did not take into account the different stages of sleep. Researchers could not determine whether the effects they were observing were due to REM deprivation, slow wave sleep deprivation, or some more complicated loss. In an effort to be more precise, Dement began to concentrate exclusively on REM deprivation.

Dement deprived people of REM sleep by waking them up every time their eyes began to move rapidly. He quickly discovered that the more a person was deprived of REM sleep, the harder it was to keep him or her out of REM sleep. After a few nights he had difficulty continuing the experiment: no sooner had he disrupted one subject's REM sleep than another one would fall into it. Some REM-deprived subjects returned to REM immediately on going back to sleep; and, when REM-deprived subjects were allowed to sleep normally again, they spent more than twice as much time in REM than they ordinarily would. This **REM rebound** effect, as it came to be called, suggested that deprived subjects were trying to make up for their lost REM sleep.

REM Rebound: An increase in the amount of time an individual spends in the REM stage of sleep, which follows REM deprivation.

Based on these and other observations of REM-deprived subjects, Dement hypothesized that REM sleep must fulfill some essential need not met by NREM sleep. He speculated that long-term REM deprivation would almost certainly have disastrous consequences. However, no such disastrous effects of REM deprivation were documented, even in cats that were deprived for as long as three months. Though the failure to observe adverse long-term effects of REM deprivation does not necessarily preclude their existence, Dement's failure to find them led him to question the validity of his own hypothesis. Thus, the issue remains unresolved, though a case study of a thirty-three-year-old man with a sleep disorder may someday provide some important clues to the mystery.

Y. H. volunteered himself for study at the Technion Sleep Laboratory in Haifa, Israel. Routine testing revealed that he demonstrated almost no REM sleep. Subsequent examination of his brain through a procedure known as a CAT scan, which provides a visual image of the brain, revealed the presence of a shrapnel splinter that had passed through the region of the brain known as the pons (see Chapter 3) and became embedded nearby. The splinter, apparently the result of a wound suffered in 1971, blocked signals from the pons, which some scientists believe may be the brain structure from which dreams originate. In any case, Y. H. is the only known case of someone who lacks REM and still leads a normal life (Blakeslee, 1984).

Other Approaches to REM. Dement's REM deprivation approach to sleep is just one of many. Another links REM to learning. Researchers have observed an increase in REM sleep after intense learning. They have also shown that REM deprivation impairs learning. REM-deprived animals take more trials to learn their way through a maze than nondeprived animals do, and they seem to have more difficulty the next day remembering what they have learned (Pearlman & Becker, 1973, 1974), a finding that shows that, while not necessarily disastrous, REM deprivation can have harmful side effects.

Another promising hypothesis is based on developmental studies. In human subjects, researchers have found clear-cut age differences in the proportion of sleep time spent in the REM stage. Infants spend as much as 50 percent of their sleep time in the REM stage, and most sleep about twice as long as adults (sixteen hours). Some researchers believe that newborns need this extra REM sleep to assimilate all their new experiences in the world outside the womb. Other researchers have suggested that REM may foster the development of the infant's brain circuitry or speed its genetic programming (Jouvet et al., 1981). In any case, the percentage of time spent in REM sleep declines sharply as the child matures. The average two-year-old spends only about 30 percent of her sleep time in REM; the average ten-year-old, 20 to 25 percent, the same proportion as adults.

In addition to changes in our apparent need for REM sleep over the life span, there are many changes in our total need for sleep. The older we get, for instance, the less sleep we seem to need. Thus, as we develop from young adults to older maturity, we have fewer dreams, sleep less deeply, and need less sleep. Worrying about these changes, or trying to fight them by demanding of ourselves that we sleep like we did as a baby or a child, is often a cause of great concern, as discussed in Box 5.1.

Just as fascinating as sleep itself are the dreams that punctuate the night. In the next section we will discuss various theories of dreams.

Dreams

Throughout history, dreams have been a source of fascination and mystery. They have been called a window to the future, a journey of the soul to another dimension, a plane of reality as real as the waking world. In this section we discuss some important theories of dreams. Let's begin with Freud's.

Freud's View. Sigmund Freud, founder of psychoanalysis (see Chapter 1), saw dreams as a stage on which one's hidden conflicts and desires are played out. According to Freud, we dream in symbols that hide the real meaning of our dreams from us. A wish for sexual intercourse may be disguised as an elevator ride with a stranger; an impulse to kill might be disguised as a can of red paint on an old carpet. The symbolic meaning of the dream is called its **latent content.** What the dreamer experiences and recalls is called the dream's **manifest content.** The unacceptable impulse is fulfilled

Latent Content: In Freudian theory, the symbolic meaning of a dream.

Manifest Content: In Freudian theory, the actual content of a dream; what the dreamer actually experiences or recalls.

Box 5.1 PSYCHOLOGY IN ACTION: Understanding Insomnia

You haven't slept a wink all night. Gazing at your alarm clock you feel a sense of desperation and think, "I've got to get up in just three hours. I simply must get some sleep. I'm going to be tired all day." Unfortunately, your concern has made you even more wide awake than before. So the minutes keep on ticking by as you resign yourself to another night without sleep. If all this sounds familiar, it's not too surprising.

It has been estimated that as many as 75,000,000 people in the United States feel that their sleep is not what it should be, in either quantity or quality. Many seek relief by way of the 40,000,000 prescriptions that are written each year for sleeping medication; others turn to more natural remedies, such as exercise (Horne & Moore, 1985; Ware, 1979). Insomnia, or the inability to fall asleep, afflicts many of us. Sometimes it's a symptom of a more severe problem such as impendent depression or other serious emotional disturbances (Spielman, 1986). If you think you have a sleeping problem, consult a physician or clinical psychologist.

The reasons some people have difficulty sleeping can be summed up as follows: alcohol, caffeine, naps, lack of exercise (Pressman, 1986). Alcohol disrupts the normal sleep cycle. Though it may reduce the time it takes a person to fall asleep, as soon as its effects wear off, usually in about an hour or two, the person wakes up and then faces a long period of wakefulness followed by unsatisfyingly light sleep. Caffeine, which is found in coffee, tea, and many colas, is a stimulant. Taking it in the late evening can keep one awake. Naps reduce one's need for sleep and thus cause a person to feel too awake to sleep at bedtime. Lack of exercise also tends to keep people awake. The retired sixty-eight-year-old who sleeps in late (to make up for last night's loss of sleep), naps an hour after lunch, gets little exercise, has a mixed drink after dinner, and finishes off a cup of coffee or two just before a 9:30 bedtime shouldn't be surprised if he or she has trouble falling asleep, or if he or she wakes up at 3:30 AM every morning and cannot go back to sleep.

Going to bed at different hours each night can disrupt our normal circadian rhythm and delay or disrupt our sleep. A heavy meal, or any activity that gets the blood pumping—heavy exercise, intensive cramming for an exam, a hot argument with a spouse or roommate, a thrilling and provocative mystery movie—all can lengthen the time it takes to fall asleep. Considering the factors that keep us awake, Ware (1979, p. 43) provides a number of tips for better sleeping:

1. "Don't stay in bed too long. Closely regulate the time you spend in bed each night."

After a good night's sleep, many people feel rested enough to exercise. But for the insomniac, just getting to work can be a struggle.

2. "Go to bed and get up at the same time each day."
3. "A light snack before bedtime is a good idea; avoid heavy meals."
4. "Exercise—but avoid heavy exercise just before bedtime."
5. "Don't drink alcohol after supper."
6. "If you have trouble sleeping, cut down on coffee, cola drinks, and cigarettes—consider not using them at all."
7. "Engage in quiet activities before bedtime—relaxing in a hot tub, reading, meditating, praying."
8. "Never take a nap."

If you try these tips and still have trouble falling to sleep, or if your sleeping pattern suddenly changes without any known reason (for example, you suddenly start waking up at 4 AM every morning though there has been no change in your schedule, personal habits, living conditions, family situation, etc.), you have a very compelling reason to seek professional help. Keep in mind, however, that one of the most serious complications or causes of insomnia may be a person's attitude. If you go to bed worrying that you will not get enough sleep, your fears may prevent you from sleeping. If you go through the next day worrying that you didn't get enough sleep, your worries may be your only problem.

symbolically, but the manifest content spares the individual the anxiety and embarrassment of the dream's true meaning.

Freud believed that, for disturbed individuals, dreams provide an important link to deep-seated conflicts that cause emotional suffering. Through dream analysis, he attempted to bring deeply buried memories to the surface so that they could be understood, faced, and disposed of. (See Chapter 15 for more on Freud's approach to treatment.)

Jung's View. Carl Jung, a one-time associate of Freud who eventually developed his own theory, believed not only that dreams brought deeply buried memories to consciousness through analogies and parables but that the dream state was a fertile ground for sending and receiving extrasensory messages. "Dreams may express illusions, wild fantasies, telepathic visions, and heaven knows what else," he wrote. Although speculative, Jung's theory provides an interesting perspective. He called the dream a theater in which the dreamer was all at once the scene, actor, audience, author, and critic. He believed that in dreams the dreamer searches for and finds the person within; the other side of one's personality. Thus, dreams provide balance in our lives. Those who deny themselves in life are gratified in dreams; those who are excessively gratified in life are denied in dreams. People who receive kindness from others give to others in dreams. Though Jung claimed that dream interpretation could not be learned from books, one of his own, *Memories, Dreams, Reflections* (1963), presents one of the

According to Carl Jung, the dreamer searches for and finds the person within. Thus, in the story, "Wizard of Oz," the main character, Dorothy, discovers during a dream the importance of her family and friends, and that, "There is no place like home." As in Jung's theory, Dorothy's dream is really a journey to another dimension.

most readily understood discussions of the subject in print. (For more on Jung, see Chapter 12.)

Dreams as Adaptive. Many contemporary researchers agree with Freud and Jung that dreams help the individual to cope. For example, most believe that dreams might provide a safe way of solving problems or preparing for future events. Consider the dream of a little girl about to visit her father and his new wife, described by Cartwright.

Not having seen her father for some time, the girl was apprehensive. The night before the visit, she dreamed she was walking through a tall, black gate of a palace. There she encountered a cruel king who chased her— but just as she ran under a tree, a strange bird magically shrank the threatening king to the size of a baby. Looking back on the dream, the girl identified the king as her father and the bird as his new wife. In the dream she was able to conquer her fear of her father, which apparently helped her to cope, for afterwards she was less fearful of the situation she was facing (Cartwright, 1978).

Physiological Activation Theory. According to another school of thought, called physiological activation theory, dreams originate in the electrochemical impulses that bombard the brain's thought centers during REM episodes. The dream is the sleeper's attempt to impose meaning on these impulses, and the meaning imposed depends on the dreamer's personality and recent waking events (Epstein, 1985). An insecure person who recently hid in the bathroom trying to avoid his boss might dream of being chased or followed in a cold, empty place; a high-striving person, of achieving great deeds or, following a recent failure, of running furiously without getting anywhere (Hobson & McCarley, 1977). Thus, according to this theory, personality interacts with physiological processes to produce dreams.

■ Learning Clue ■

As you read, remember that serotonin is associated with NREM sleep; norepinephrine with REM and arousal.

The Biochemistry of Sleep

Chemical neurotransmitters, which transmit messages from one brain cell to another (see Chapter 3), also seem to be connected with the recurring cycle of dream and nondream episodes throughout the night. Prominent among these neurotransmitters are two called norepinephrine and serotonin. Serotonin has an inhibiting effect, which means its action on the brain slows down bodily functions, lowers arousal, suppresses emotions, and facilitates sleep. In general, the action of serotonin is associated with the nondreaming episodes of sleep—that is, the four stages of NREM sleep, especially stage 4 NREM. If the brain cells that control the release of serotonin are destroyed, an animal will suffer prolonged insomnia. In both animals and humans, drugs that prevent the formation of serotonin or block its action cause insomnia. On the other hand, L-Tryptophan, an amino acid from which serotonin is made, quickens the rate at which insomniacs fall asleep (Snyder, 1974; Ungerstedt, 1971). One of the reasons a glass of milk before bedtime can help a person fall asleep is that milk contains relatively high concentrations of L-Tryptophan.

The brain's more active states—waking alertness and the dreaming associated with REM sleep—are associated with the action of norepinephrine. Though its effects are actually quite complex, norepinephrine can be thought of as having an excitatory effect, which means its action in the brain speeds up bodily functions, increases arousal, accelerates thoughts, and augments emotions. In laboratory animals, destruction of the brain cells that control the release of norepinephrine completely abolishes REM sleep. And in humans as well as animals, drugs that block the formation of norepinephrine also abolish REM. A REM rebound follows withdrawal from such drugs (Pujol et al., 1968).

The actions of norepinephrine and serotonin complement each other to produce the cycles of NREM sleep and the REM sleep associated with dreams. In one classic study, a researcher injected a cat with *reserpine,* a drug which reduces brain levels of both serotonin and norepinephrine. Both REM and stage 4 NREM sleep were reduced. An injection of L-Tryptophan immediately restored stage 4 NREM. And an injection of a chemical from which norepinephrine is made produced REM sleep (Jouvet, 1967). Thus, underlying our dreams there appears to be a delicate balance of an ebb and flow of chemical neurotransmitters that first slow down our physiological processes and then speed them up.

Although the role of neurotransmitters in sleep has yet to be fully understood, one thing is certain: chemical substances have a profound effect on consciousness. This point will become especially clear when we consider the effects of drugs on consciousness in the next section, for consciousness-altering drugs frequently mimic the effects of the brain's neurotransmitters. (For more on neurotransmitters, see Chapter 3.)

CONSCIOUSNESS-ALTERING DRUGS

Consciousness-altering or **psychoactive** drugs produce changes in mood, thought, memory, attention, concentration, sense of time, perception, and other subjective experiences. They disrupt normal brain activity in a variety of ways. Some enhance or reduce the effectiveness of a neurotransmitter. Others may block or facilitate the chemical formation, reabsorption, or breakdown of a neurotransmitter. Drugs that are chemically similar to neurotransmitters may even substitute for them, producing the same effects. Indeed, virtually every drug that alters mental function does so by interacting with neurotransmitters in the brain (Snyder, 1984).

Psychoactive drugs affect the entire nervous system as well as the rest of the body. In general, they fall into three main categories: **depressants,** which inhibit or slow down (depress) normal functioning; **stimulants,** which excite or increase (stimulate) normal functioning; and **hallucinogens,** which both depress and excite and thus disrupt normal functioning. Figure 5.9 provides

Psychoactive Drugs: Drugs that alter consciousness by producing subjective changes in mood, perceptions, or experience, by virtue of their effect on the chemistry of the brain.

Depressants: Drugs that depress or reduce brain activity.

Stimulants: Drugs that stimulate or increase brain activity.

Hallucinogens: Drugs that disrupt normal brain activity.

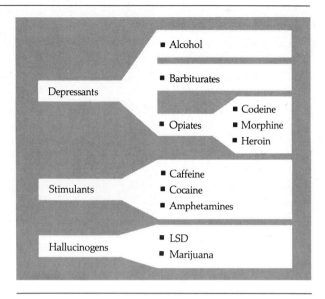

Figure 5.9 Schematic Overview of Categories of Drugs.

Depressants
- Alcohol
- Barbiturates
- Opiates
  - Codeine
  - Morphine
  - Heroin

Stimulants
- Caffeine
- Cocaine
- Amphetamines

Hallucinogens
- LSD
- Marijuana

Tolerance: An increase in the amount of a drug needed to obtain the same effect as when one first started using the drug.

Physical Dependence: An acquired physiological need for a drug.

Withdrawal Symptoms: Physical illness (e.g., vomiting, the shakes) that occur when an individual stops taking a drug that he or she is physically dependent on.

Psychological Dependence: A compelling need to take a drug even though the individual has no physical need to do so; a belief that normal functioning is not possible without regular use of a drug.

Alcohol: A depressant drug found in alcoholic beverages such as beer and wine or in more concentrated forms in whiskey, rum, vodka, gin, scotch, and brandy.

a schematic overview of these categories and the specific drugs within each category that we will discuss in this section.

Depressants

All depressants cause a reduction in the speed or efficiency of normal functioning, and with it, consciousness. In low doses they produce euphoria but reduce alertness and cause drowsiness. They do this by either interfering with those parts of the brain whose function is to activate or by enhancing those that inhibit. In large doses they can induce stupor or coma.

With repeated use of a depressant, the body develops a **tolerance** for it so that larger doses are required to produce the same consciousness-altering experience. Eventually the user may acquire a physiological need for the drug, called a **physical dependence,** which can be as compelling as the need for food or water. The person experiences a strong craving for the drug and suffers **withdrawal symptoms**—nausea, violent convulsions, even, in some instances, death—if deprived of it.

Long before the development of physical dependence on a drug, however, repeated use in small doses can cause **psychological dependence:** the belief that the drug is necessary to normal functioning. Psychological dependence often leads, eventually, to physical dependence. (For more on drug and alcohol dependence, see Chapter 14.)

Despite the well-known dangers, millions of people use depressants regularly. Probably the most freely used, and abused, is alcohol.

Alcohol. Alcoholic beverages are widely used for a variety of reasons. Because it relaxes them, reduces their anxiety, enhances their enjoyment at social gatherings, helps them to forget, and makes them feel better, people use **alcohol.** It accomplishes all these feats by suppressing the activity of the higher brain centers that normally inhibit us and cause us to act in a rea-

Some people use alcohol to dim their consciousness—to drown their sorrows.

soned, well-considered manner. Thus, though alcohol causes people to become less inhibited, it does so in a roundabout way: by depressing the brain centers that instruct us to inhibit our less sociable thoughts and actions. The depressing effects of alcohol also disrupt the brain's normal rest-activity cycle which naturally ebbs and flows throughout the day and night. In place of the natural rhythm of consciousness, it imposes a one-way decline that continues for some time after the substance is consumed.

For a person weighing 150 pounds, two ounces of vodka or its equivalent (two cans of beer, two glasses of wine) is enough to impair the highest brain functions, making the user less self-aware and less careful. Driving ability is impaired even before there are any clear signs of intoxication. With three or four ounces the user becomes self-centered, less aware of internal messages or environmental cues to hold back or ease up. A usually conservative individual may brag to excess or tell an off-color joke.

If the user continues to drink, the lower brain centers become affected as well. Basic emotions, usually held in check, begin to surface. Some drinkers become uncharacteristically aggressive. The person may argue more intensely than usual, or start a fight (Steele, 1986).

Coordination also suffers. The drinker sways, stumbles, or slurs words. Sexual performance is also impaired, though one's appetite for sex may actually increase. Behind the wheel of an automobile, the drinker is a hazard to self and others.

Regular heavy use of alcohol may induce one of the drug's most dramatic consciousness-altering effects, a **blackout**. Typically the drinker awakes and is unable to recall the events of the night before. It is as if the person has been functioning without the ability to form new memories. Whatever happens during the blackout cannot be recalled the next day.

Barbiturates. Like alcohol, a **barbiturate** is a depressant drug that depresses normal functioning (see Figure 5.10). In fact, the effect of a barbitu-

Blackout: An episode that occurs after large amounts of alcohol have been consumed, in which the individual is unable to recall any of his or her actions during the episode.

Barbiturates: Depressant drugs chemically related to alcohol that are used to induce sleep.

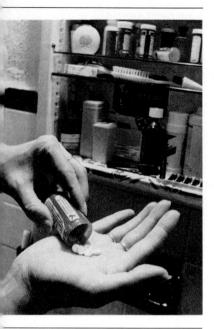

Figure 5.10 Barbiturates.
Regardless of their size and
shape, barbiturates depress
the central nervous system.

Cross-Tolerance: An effect in which one drug can take the place of another. Taking one increases tolerance for the other, and taking one can usually satisfy the need for the other.

Opiates: Depressant drugs that reduce or eliminate pain such as codeine, morphine, and the illegal drug heroin.

rate is very similar to that of alcohol. Inhibitions are reduced, coordination is impaired (due to a decrease in the normal brain processes that inhibit unnecessary movements), and thinking becomes more difficult. At low doses barbiturates reduce anxiety and cause euphoria. What was once a troubled consciousness becomes carefree and unconcerned. However, self- and social- awareness are reduced so that the individual may do things he or she normally wouldn't when not under the influence of the drug.

There is a relatively fine line between the size of the dose that produces euphoria and that which induces an irresistible urge to sleep. But, when that line is crossed, the depressing barbiturate drug thrusts the individual into a state of sleep deeper than NREM stage 4. The user's consciousness is so reduced, his or her brain wave pattern resembles that of a patient in surgical anaesthesia (Warburton, 1975). Like alcohol, barbiturates also suppress the REM stage of sleep, delaying its onset and reducing its length (Oswald, 1968). A REM rebound effect follows discontinuance of the drug. For up to two weeks following just a single dose of a barbiturate, the percentage of REM sleep climbs far beyond normal. Dreams and nightmares become more vivid. The increased brain activity that occurs with the rebound may keep the user from falling asleep the next night. Thus, there is a temptation to resume using the drug, and later to increase the dose to counteract a growing tolerance (Scharf & Brown, 1986).

Scientists suspect that barbiturates may work by stimulating the brain to release serotonin, the neurotransmitter that plays a role in NREM sleep. These drugs do increase brain levels of serotonin in animals (Anderson & Bonnycastle, 1960). The theory is that barbiturates cause the brain cells that normally store the neurotransmitter to release larger quantities than normal. The usual effects—the slowing of brain activity—are then increased and prolonged, until all at once the drug and the neurotransmitter are spent, producing the opposite effect: a rebound.

The barbiturates are so much like alcohol in terms of effects on the body and consciousness that taking one increases the body's tolerance for the other. Because of this **cross-tolerance,** regular users of alcohol require a larger first-time dose of barbiturates to achieve the same effect as does an individual who has never used either drug or uses alcohol in moderation. What is more, if a regular user of alcohol takes barbiturates, his or her tolerance for both drugs may be greatly increased.

Opiates. The **opiates,** which are derived from the poppy plant, include codeine, morphine, and heroin. Like alcohol and barbiturates, opiates, as depressants, slow down normal functioning. There are, however, a number of important differences between opiates and other depressants. Opiates do not cross-tolerate with alcohol or barbiturates, and their effects are somewhat different. Instead of gradually dimming consciousness, opiates induce a dreamlike state, as if the user is having a waking dream. And, though all depressants reduce pain, none does so as effectively as the opiates. Opiates also are far more likely than other depressants to create physical dependence. Heroin users, for example, are about eight times more likely to become dependent than are those who use alcohol or barbiturates.

The different effects of opiates can be attributed to differences in the way they suppress certain functions. Opiates mimic a special group of neu-

■ **Learning Check** ■

For each question: read, cover, try to recite, repeat.

What do opiates have in common with alcohol and barbiturates?	All Three: 1. Are depressant drugs. 2. Slow down normal functioning. 3. Lead to physical dependence and withdrawal symptoms.
How do the opiates differ from alcohol and the barbiturates?	They Differ in That: 1. Opiates do not cross-tolerate with alcohol and the barbiturates. 2. Opiates induce a dreamlike state rather than a dimming of consciousness. 3. Opiates are more effective painkillers and more likely to lead to physical dependence.

rotransmitters called *endorphins* (Hughes et al., 1975). Endorphins, as we've learned (see Chapter 3), are the body's natural painkillers.

In effect, an opiate increases the brain's supply of endorphins. The brain cells that normally manufacture endorphins respond to the increased supply by cutting back on production. When the drug is discontinued, the user is left with a lower-than-normal endorphin level and is temporarily more susceptible to pain (Snyder, 1974).

Regardless of exactly how they work, the net effect of all depressants is a plunge in normal consciousness and a rebound effect of increased arousal when their use is discontinued. To experience the desired effects, the user must either submit to its negative aftereffects or take the drug again. The longer the aftereffects are postponed, the worse they will be when the drug is finally discontinued.

Stimulants

Like depressants, stimulants disrupt the brain's normal rest-activity cycle, but in the opposite direction; they speed up normal functioning.

The two most powerful types of stimulants are cocaine and the amphetamines. Caffeine, which is found in coffee, tea, and soft drinks, is a mild stimulant. We will first discuss caffeine and then move on to the two more powerful stimulants.

Caffeine. Caffeine is so widely used that few people think of it as a drug. In small doses caffeine can increase alertness and concentration. In large doses it can cause insomnia, nervousness, rapid heartbeat, and anxiety.

When the effects of caffeine wear off, a rebound follows in which the user finds concentration more difficult than usual. The rebound is especially apparent the next day, when the person has difficulty waking up in the morning. To remedy the situation, the user takes another cup of coffee or tea. With repeated use a person may become psychologically dependent on the substance, convinced that normal functioning is not possible without the drug.

Unlike depressants, caffeine does not create a physical dependence in the user. The effects of discontinuing its use are largely psychological—irritability, fatigue, depression, and a desire to use the drug again. The psychological effects of a stimulant, however, can sometimes exert as much power over a user as the physical effects.

Cocaine. Cocaine produces a brief but intense alteration in consciousness. Within moments after inhaling or smoking a small quantity of the drug, the user begins to feel a sense of well-being and energy. Fatigue and unhappiness are replaced by alertness and euphoria; the user feels smarter, more competent.

These stimulating effects last about fifteen to thirty minutes. There follows an unpleasant rebound—depression, fatigue, self-doubts—almost as intense as the initial high (Resnick et al., 1977). This combination of exceptionally pleasant effects and exceptionally unpleasant aftereffects seems to create an irresistible psychological urge for the drug in some people. To avoid the rebound, the user takes another dose.

As with other drugs, the longer one continues to use cocaine and postpone the negative effects of the rebound, the more devastating those effects are. With repeated use a person eventually develops the feeling that normal functioning is not possible without the drug. The fatigue and depression that accompany the rebound reinforce this feeling, for the user is in fact less capable than usual, until the body's normal biological rhythms are restored.

With prolonged use, a person may develop hallucinations (seeing or hearing things that aren't there), delusions (false beliefs, such as the idea that people are trying to kill you), and other symptoms of the severe mental disorder known as paranoid schizophrenia (see Chapter 14). The user may lose touch with reality, in part because her overactivated brain begins to hallucinate, in part because his consciousness becomes so selective that he perceives only a fraction of reality.

Amphetamines. Amphetamines are extremely powerful stimulants. Until recently they were widely prescribed as diet pills. But today they are considered so dangerous, the number of prescriptions a physician writes for them is closely monitored. Amphetamines also produce symptoms of paranoid schizophrenia if used over a long period or in high doses—so consistently, in fact, that the condition has received a special name, amphetamine psychosis. In one study, normal subjects who had been carefully screened for mental disorders were given progressively higher doses of amphetamines. Within one to four days, all lost touch with reality and displayed symptoms of paranoid schizophrenia (Angrist & Gershon, 1970). This finding has since been replicated several times. Fortunately, the effects can be reversed by discontinuing the drug, rest, and medication.

The immediate effects of amphetamines are similar to those of cocaine, but less intense (unless large amounts are injected) and more long lasting. Instead of a 20- to 30-minute roller-coaster trip, amphetamines produce a high that may last for several hours. The user experiences a sense of competence, well-being, energy, and confidence. Because of the drug's relatively prolonged effects, the amphetamine user often suffers from insomnia. As the drug's effects begin to wane, the user experiences a rebound, and must either take another dose or suffer the negative aftereffects: irritability, depression, anxiety, fatigue, and an increased desire for sleep.

The exact way in which amphetamines and cocaine work has yet to be discovered. Scientists suspect that these stimulants increase the amount of norepinephrine and related neurotransmitters released by brain cells, causing them to send a stronger message than usual. In short, these drugs make the brain overactive. The schizophrenic-like symptoms of these drugs may be due to their causing the higher brain centers to be flooded with thoughts and feelings that would otherwise remain out of awareness (Matthysse, 1974). The drug user may even experience a **flight of ideas,** a train of thought that occurs so quickly, the logical relationship among ideas is lost. Because the user has no time to evaluate his thoughts against reality, he easily misreads small gestures that would usually go unnoticed—a twitch of the nose, a glance to the right—as secret messages or signals. Before long, the user is behaving abnormally.

Significantly, some schizophrenics report a similar experience. Their minds, they complain, are flooded with information; they can't shut it out. What is more, the drugs that are used to alleviate schizophrenics' symptoms, such as thorazine, will bring a person with an amphetamine psychosis back to normal. (For more on schizophrenia and drugs used to treat it, see Chapters 14 and 15.)

Flight of Ideas: A symptom in which the individual's ideas race so quickly that the logical relationship among thoughts break down and ideas are not evaluated against reality.

Hallucinogens

Hallucinogens are drugs that induce hallucinations—sensory experiences for which there is no appropriate stimulus—or distort sensory experience. Hallucinogens such as marijuana distort sensory experiences. For example, music seems to sound better. The more powerful hallucinogens such as LSD actually produce sensory images. The person may actually see or hear things that are not real.

Hallucinogenic drugs can produce a disruption of normal consciousness far more dramatic than the alterations associated with other kinds of drugs. They alter the usual waking experience—the sights, sounds, sense of time, and even body image—of the person who takes them.

Hallucinogens vary greatly in their strength. LSD (d-Lysergic Acid Diethylamide) is by far the most powerful. Marijuana, by contrast, is much milder. If its main active ingredient, tetrahydrocannabinol (THC), is taken in massive doses, the effects are similar to those of LSD. But, when consumed in small quantities, as it usually is, marijuana is as different from LSD as two cups of coffee are from a large dose of amphetamines or cocaine.

The effects of any drug depend in part on the user's expectations and past experience with the drug, along with the setting in which it is taken. Those factors are especially important with the hallucinogens, however. Inexperienced users who expect to experience anxiety or panic often do. And it's easy to confuse the pleasantness of the company of good friends with the effects of the drug.

Marijuana. Marijuana comes from the flowering tops and leaves of the mature female hemp plant. Users generally take the drug by smoking dried leaves in a pipe or hand-rolled cigarette. Specific reactions to the drug vary widely. Some users appear to experience stimulant-like effects: increased awareness, clearer thinking, and excitement (Satinder & Black, 1984). Others claim the drug impairs concentration, slows thinking, and induces sleep. Some of these differences no doubt stem from nondrug-related factors—expectation, setting, and experience with the drug. The quantity and strength of the dose that is taken also may account for various reactions. Even in the same person, however, the drug's effects can vary depending upon how long it has been in the body (Jones, 1971).

Marijuana has some notable differences from the depressants and stimulants. It does not lead to physical dependence, as do depressants, nor does it lead to increases in tolerance, as do stimulants. In fact, the drug produces a **reverse tolerance** effect: with repeated use, less of the drug is needed to produce the same effects. It produces neither the frenzy of the stimulants nor the stupor that comes from the depressants. It seems to produce fluctuations between rest and activity that approximate the usual one-and-a-half to two-hour rhythm of normal waking consciousness: the peak and rebound occur within about two hours. It can, however, create a strong psychological dependence, and abrupt withdrawal from it may cause insomnia and depression. And, when the drug is taken in larger doses, it can mimic the effects of the more powerful hallucinogen, LSD.

LSD. In the spring of 1943, the Swiss chemist Dr. Albert Hofmann developed a substance called LSD. He had been attempting to isolate a chemical that could be used to control bleeding when, by accident, he absorbed an extremely small amount of the drug through his skin. In less than an hour he experienced dramatic changes in consciousness: objects appeared to flutter back and forth or disintegrate into colorful cobwebs or spirals. Time went completely haywire—minutes seemed like hours—and he feared the experience would never end. Hofmann's sense of his body also changed. If he shut his eyes he couldn't tell whether he was standing, sitting, or floating upside down. His body seemed to drift away from his mind and dissolve into the walls (Hofmann, 1980).

LSD brutally thrusts consciousness to an extreme from which there is no return for six to eight hours. Its effects are highly subjective and range widely from person to person. Some people find the illusions it creates—of profound insights, great mental power, omnipotence, a merging with the creator—most pleasurable and exciting. For others, the feeling that time is standing still, that normal consciousness might never return, produces an almost unbearable terror. For a few, the experience returns months or even years later in the form of **flashback attacks.** Even experienced users report "bad trips," filled with panic, guilt, the illusion that something is wrong with their bodies, or the thought that they are about to die. Whether experienced as pleasant or unpleasant, the effects of the drug are always intense.

Like amphetamines, the hallucinogens seem to stimulate the release of greater-than-normal quantities of norepinephrine and related neurotransmitters that have a net activating effect. However, it also appears to interfere with the action of serotonin, whose normal function is to inhibit emotions, slow down brain activity, and lower arousal. The result is a dramatic and unchecked disruption of normal brain activity and a short-circuiting of normal consciousness. Sleep is almost impossible.

Reverse Tolerance: An effect in which, after repeated regular use of a drug, less of the drug is needed to produce the same effects as when the drug was first taken.

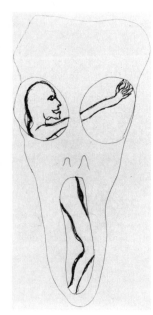

A person's perceptions become distorted under the influence of LSD.

Flashback Attacks: The recurrence of the experiences that one had while under the influence of LSD long after the drug is no longer present in the body.

The rebound from LSD can be just as distressing as a bad trip. The user may become despondent. Unable to face dull reality, she enters again the illusionary world.

The use of substances to alter consciousness is not a new phenomenon. People all over the world have been using depressants, stimulants, and hallucinogens from before the beginning of recorded history, not only for recreation and escape but also for religious purposes and generating insights (Weil, 1972). The drug experience may help an individual view a problem from a different perspective, enhance thinking temporarily, or facilitate a mystical experience—a sense of empathy with nature and the creator. However, because of the toll extracted by drugs—the risk of addiction, negative health consequences, and even imprisonment when illegal drugs are used—many people have sought other ways of altering consciousness. In the next section we will examine such techniques along with what they have taught us about normal waking consciousness.

ALTERING CONSCIOUSNESS WITHOUT DRUGS

In our final section, we will discuss three different ways of altering consciousness without drugs: meditation, biofeedback, and hypnosis. Each gives us some insight into the nature of consciousness.

Meditation

Meditation is a process involving sustained focused concentration, which produces a state of consciousness characterized by alert relaxation and calm. Unlike drugs, meditation produces a natural change in consciousness and body rhythms through certain exercises or rituals (Rigby, 1977). The whole procedure can be reduced to three simple steps (Benson et al., 1977).

Meditation: Conscious-altering techniques in which the individual uses a repetitive set of exercises or rituals (such as mentally repeating a sound over and over again) to achieve an altered state of consciousness.

In meditation, one abandons the logical, analytical mode of thinking.

First, find a comfortable chair, sit down, and close your eyes. Second, relax all the muscles in your body. Concentrate on one group of muscles at a time, beginning with your feet and moving up to the top of your head. Say to yourself, "My toes are relaxing; my legs are relaxing; my stomach is relaxing; my back is relaxing." As you do so, imagine that your muscles are actually relaxing—visualize them becoming limp. Third, breathe through your nose and concentrate on your breathing. Every time you breathe out, repeat some word. Any word will do, such as "landscape" or "one." Continue for about 15 to 20 minutes.

In meditation, one abandons the logical, analytical mode of thinking that characterizes much of normal waking consciousness. The limits of time and space, and the small details of daily life, seem to fade away. For some, this experience of "pure awareness," as it is sometimes called, can be one of ecstasy or rebirth (Maharishi Yogi, 1968). But for some people, too much meditation can cause unpleasant effects. After sessions of forty minutes or more, hallucinations, sorrow, disorientation, or intense fear can result (Earle, 1981). As one meditator put it, "Meditation could drive one crazy. I felt like a baby bird who couldn't fly . . . I didn't know where I was . . . It was very dangerous" (Amodeo, 1981, p. 149). Meditation, in other words, appears to be similar to hallucinogens and stimulants in its subjective effects: in small doses it can heighten awareness; in large doses it can produce either intense joy or panic.

Meditation seems to have an effect on brain activity and physiological functioning (Shapiro, 1983, 1985). The meditator's EEG shows more alpha waves than the EEG of the awake, relaxed person (Wallace & Benson, 1972). Generally, these waves, which are associated with drowsy, floating, or daydream experiences, appear only in the EEGs of calm, relaxed subjects whose eyes are closed. But meditators can produce alpha waves with their eyes open (Kasamatsu & Hirai, 1963). Experienced meditators produce an even slower wave that usually occurs only during the deeper stages of sleep (Kasamatsu & Hirai, 1969). Meditation, in fact, is so restful that, according to some researchers, when practiced regularly for about twenty to thirty minutes per day, it can reduce the need for sleep by as much as two or three hours (Walsh, 1978).

It should be emphasized, however, that much of the evidence supporting the effects of meditation is based on case studies of experienced meditators. When inexperienced meditators are used, or in studies in which a group of meditators is compared to a group of nonmeditators, results are much less clear cut. Consider, for example, studies on the effects of meditation on **somatic arousal**—the body's state of activation as measured by heart rate, respiration rate, blood pressure, skin temperature, and oxygen consumption.

Early studies of the physiological effects of meditation were based on the *own-control technique,* in which a subject is used as his own control (Holmes, 1984; 1985a). First the subject is asked to sit quietly without meditating. Then the subject is asked to meditate. Finally, the same subject is asked to again simply sit quietly. In the two quiet periods before and after meditation, the subject provides his own control against which the effects of meditation can be compared.

Using the own-control technique, researchers found that meditators experienced a rapid reduction in somatic arousal compared to simply sitting

Somatic Arousal: The body's state of activation as measured by indicators such as heart rate, respiration, blood pressure, skin temperature, and oxygen consumption.

quietly before and after meditation. Oxygen consumption was lower during meditation, as was blood pressure, heart rate, and other indicators of somatic arousal (Herbert, 1977; Wallace & Benson, 1972).

Studies involving comparisons of inexperienced meditators and nonmeditators, however, indicate that the arousal-reducing effects of meditation were no greater than simply resting (Holmes, 1984, 1985b). This is not to say that meditation is no different from simply resting (Benson & Friedman, 1985). Meditation produces subjective effects on consciousness that do differ from resting. It is a state of heightened awareness and alertness while relaxing. People who simply rest do not report the same subjective effects as the meditating subject. The history of the effects of meditation on somatic arousal parallels that of another technique that is used to alter consciousness without drugs, biofeedback.

Biofeedback

Biofeedback is a consciousness-altering technique in which feedback from instruments that monitor biological processes—heart rate, blood pressure, skin temperature, blood flow, brain wave activity—is used to help a person learn to modify those processes. Thus the term **biofeedback.** By modifying one's biological processes, especially brain activity, consciousness is presumably altered.

Biofeedback: A consciousness-altering technique in which feedback from instruments that monitor biological processes including brain wave activity is used to help a person learn to modify these processes.

Until recently, most scientists believed that heart rate and other automatic life-sustaining activities were beyond conscious control. They knew that meditation masters in India, Japan, and other Eastern countries could perform feats such as stopping their hearts, but few believed that such control was within the reach of the average person. Then, in the late 1960s, a handful of scientists published reports that indicated animals could learn to control heart rate and other automatic responses, and that humans could learn to control brain wave patterns (Kamiya, 1968; Miller, 1969).

One of the most exciting reports came from a small laboratory in San Francisco. There, a researcher named Joe Kamiya attached people to an EEG machine and fed the EEG data into a computer that was programmed to translate the data into sound. When the EEG showed increased alpha activity, the computer emitted a tone. Kamiya told subjects to try to make the computer emit the tone. By trial and error, most subjects learned how to do

Biofeedback provides an individual with information (feedback) about physiological processes (such as brain waves) that normally are not under voluntary control.

it—how to increase the percentage of alpha waves their brains were emitting and thus cause the computer to emit the tone. Experienced subjects could produce the tones in a few seconds.

Shortly after Kamiya published his findings on brain wave control through biofeedback, researchers began developing devices to provide feedback on heart rate, blood pressure, blood flow, muscle tension, and the like. People who suffered from migraine headaches learned to relax their neck muscles and direct the flow of blood from their heads to their hands, which brought relief from the headache (Sargent et al., 1973; Schultz & Luthe, 1969). Researchers tried the technique on everything from high blood pressure to learning disabilities, but results were mixed. Positive results found by one researcher often could not be consistently repeated in other laboratories. Moreover, not all patients could control their physiological activities; others could control them, but only for a short time. For example, some people with high blood pressure could lower it only while attached to a feedback machine; when they left the laboratory their blood pressure soon returned to elevated levels. Thus, the technique could help some people but not others.

As with meditation, however, it is necessary to distinguish between subjective effects and physiological effects. If biofeedback produces positive subjective alterations in consciousness for some people (e.g., a dreamy relaxed state), then it would seem to be of value for those people, despite inconsistent findings concerning its physiological effects. Moreover, the failure to find consistent physiological effects may be due to limitations in the sensitivity of the devices used to measure such effects, rather than in the technique itself. With more sensitive equipment, perhaps consistent effects would be observed.

Today, scientists continue in their attempt to apply biofeedback to practical problems, particularly stress-related disorders such as hypertension. (For more information, see Chapter 11.) However, they are more cautious in their conclusion concerning the willful control of physiological processes. Though such control is possible, it may be more limited than scientists once suspected. But, of all the techniques for altering consciousness without drugs, perhaps none is as controversial as our next topic, hypnosis.

Hypnosis

Hypnosis is a technique of producing an altered state of consciousness in which an individual is susceptible to suggestions. Unlike biofeedback, it has a long history. Yet hypnosis remains shrouded in mystery and myth. Some researchers believe the hypnotic state is an altered consciousness as different from the normal waking state as sleep. Others, frustrated by inconclusive or contradictory findings, are skeptical.

The hypnotic state can be induced in a number of ways. In one time-honored technique, people are asked to concentrate on a repetitive stimulus, such as a small crystal swung gently before the subject's eyes like a pendulum. In more modern procedures, the hypnotist speaks to the subject slowly and rhythmically, repeating the same words over and over again or encouraging the subject to visualize a particularly relaxing scene. For example, the hypnotist might say something like:

Imagine yourself in a peaceful old country mansion. The downstairs
fireplace is lit, and you can see it from the top of the old spiral staircase.
Now imagine yourself at the top of the staircase going down. The staircase
has 20 steps. Each and every time you take a step down the staircase, you
allow yourself to go deeper and deeper into a calm, peaceful, relaxed state.
When you reach the bottom, you become completely relaxed. Twenty, 19,
every muscle in your body is relaxing; 18, 17, going deeper and deeper; 16,
15, deeper still; 14, 13, relaxing more and more; 12, 11, 10, halfway down
the staircase and relaxing still more with every step you take. Nine, 8, 7, 6,
5, 4, 3, almost all the way down, relaxing still more with every step you
take. Two, 1, zero; deep asleep.

Actually, the subject does not go to sleep. The hypnotic state is more
akin to meditation than sleep—a relaxed awareness. Some subjects report a
feeling of oneness with the universe similar to the meditator's pure awareness (Tart, 1979). Though subjects usually feel in control and can get up and
walk away at will, most seem to prefer to remain relaxed and motionless,
absorbed by the soothing voice of the hypnotist.

They may become highly susceptible to the suggestions of the hypnotist.
If told that their arms are getting lighter, hypnotized subjects may raise their
arms, as if they were lighter than air. At the suggestion of the hypnotist,
they may say that they see something that isn't there, such as an extra finger
on the hypnotist's hand. Whether these are actual hallucinations, however,
is unclear. It may be that the person doesn't actually "see" the extra finger,
but merely says that she does to please the hypnotist (Barber, 1979).

If instructed to forget something that happened during the hypnotic session, susceptible subjects seem to do so, a phenomenon known as **posthypnotic amnesia.** For example, the hypnotist might instruct the subject to open
a window the next time the telephone rings, but to forget being told to do
so. If the telephone rings after the subject is counted out of the trance, she
will immediately get up to open the window. If asked to explain her behavior, she will invent some excuse, such as "I was getting hot." Again, however, the subject may only be saying she can't remember and then act
accordingly to please the hypnotist.

Despite the controversy concerning their validity, hypnotic hallucinations and posthypnotic amnesia can be remarkably effective in controlling
pain for some people during dentistry or surgery. Certain subjects can be
told not to see or be aware of the dentist's drill or the surgeon's knife, and to
forget the experience after it's over. Under such conditions, some people
show no evidence of pain during surgery; others show evidence of experienced pain (frowns, tight muscles, etc.), but deny feeling pain (Fredericks,
1980; Kroger, 1977).

Despite a number of impressive case studies, many scientists question
whether hypnosis is a separate state from normal waking consciousness.
The controversy began with the first published report of a hypnotic-like procedure by the Viennese physician Franz Mesmer (1734–1815). Mesmer
claimed he could perform miraculous cures, such as restoring sight to the
blind or hearing to the deaf. He did apparently perform such cures, but
whether a patient's ailments were due to psychological or actual physical
damage was never clarified. A committee appointed by the French Academy
of Medicine rejected the idea that any of Mesmer's cures were due to the in-

Posthypnotic Amnesia:
Specific memory loss
caused by a suggestion
given to a person while
under hypnosis to forget
the specific information.

duction of a trance-like state in his patients. Ever since then, both the trance theory and the state itself have been questioned.

One modern opponent of the trance theory has argued that all hypnotic phenomena can be attributed to the attitudes, motivation, and expectations of the subject (Barber, 1979). Indeed, years of intensive study have produced no noticeable differences in EEG or any other physiological measure between hypnotized and nonhypnotized subjects (Evans, 1979). And, if people pretend that they are hypnotized, even experienced hypnotists often cannot tell them from hypnotized subjects (Orne, 1979; also see Wilkes, 1986). One supporter of the trance theory, psychologist Ernest Hilgard, has argued that the fact that an objective measure of the hypnotic state has not yet been found does not mean that none exists. After all, it was only recently that REM episodes were discovered in the study of sleep. Similarly, reliable measures of hypnosis may yet be discovered.

Hilgard has conducted many experiments on hypnosis, especially on its effects on pain. He has observed that a subject oblivious to pain on one level may nevertheless be aware of it on another. For example, a hypnotized subject whose hand is suddenly thrust into painfully cold water may show no evidence of pain, and later insist that none was felt. But the same subject may describe the pain of the experience in vivid detail, if allowed to write about it during the experiment with his free hand.

To account for such results, Hilgard has proposed that hypnosis can induce a split in consciousness. He believes some mental structure—a kind of "hidden observer"—monitors everything that happens to a person. If that monitor can be separated from other aspects of consciousness, such as the experience of pain, a person might know of pain on one level without actually experiencing it (Hilgard, 1979).

Hilgard's theory of hypnosis as a division of consciousness provides yet another illustration of the various states of consciousness. Just as opiates and endorphins prevent pain messages from reaching the higher brain centers, hypnosis may somehow temporarily block the transmission of messages from one part of the brain to another.

In conclusion, the study of consciousness, though controversial, has numerous applications to everyday life and matters of practical significance. Its study helps us to understand how behavior can be affected by temporary influences such as circadian rhythms, drugs, and conscious-altering procedures like meditation and hypnosis. Such influences underlie the continual fluctuations in one's current state of consciousness, and that state, in turn, affects behavior for a short time. In the next chapter we will examine an influence on behavior that does not come and go, but rather leads to relatively permanent changes—learning.

LEARNING FRAMEWORK

I. Consciousness—the process of knowing and being aware—is constantly changing, yet always the same.
    A. Consciousness changes normally throughout the typical waking day. There are also a number of important deviations from this normal waking state. (Review: *Altered States of Consciousness*)

B. Normal biological rhythms underlie the fluctuations in consciousness during the day. (Review: *Circadian Rhythms; Ultradian Rhythms*)

II. Normal biological rhythms underlie changes from light to deep sleep and from dreaming to a non-dreaming state. (Review: *Electroencephalogram (EEG); Rapid Eye Movements (REM); Nonrapid Eve Movement Sleep (NREM)*

  A. The normal sleeping pattern consists of a number of cycles alternating between an aroused dream state and a nonaroused restful state. (Review: *Desynchronized EEG; Sleep Spindle; Slow Wave Sleep (SWS); Figures 5.3, 5.4, 5.5, 5.8, and Table 5.1.*)

  B. When the body's normal rhythms are interrupted through REM sleep deprivation, the individual appears to make up for it through a subsequent increase in REM sleep time. (Review: *REM Rebound*)

  C. According to physiological activation theory, a dream represents a sleeper's attempt to impose meaning on the impulses that bombard the brain during REM sleep. (Review: *Latent Content; Manifest Content; Physiological Activation Theory*)

  D. The ebb and flow of neurotransmitter substances in the brain parallel sleep's alternating cycles of arousal and rest.

III. Drugs alter consciousness by depressing, stimulating, or disrupting normal processes. (Review: *Psychoactive Drugs; Figure 5.9*)

  A. Depressants depress normal functioning. (Review: *Alcohol; Barbiturates; Cross-Tolerance; Opiates*)

  B. Stimulants speed up normal functioning. (Review: *Cocaine; Amphetamines; Amphetamine Psychosis; Flight of Ideas*)

  C. Hallucinogens speed up certain functions and depress others, causing a distortion of normal consciousness. (Review: *Marijuana; LSD; Flashback Attacks*)

IV. Consciousness can be altered without drugs.

  A. Through techniques that involve exercises or rituals to produce focused concentration, it is possible to induce an alert but relaxed state of consciousness. (Review: *Meditation; Somatic Arousal*)

  B. Through physiological feedback a person can control brain wave activity and hence state of consciousness. (Review: *Biofeedback*)

  C. Hypnotic techniques, in which people are asked to concentrate on a hypnotist's instructions, seem to produce a division of consciousness. (Review: *Posthypnotic Amnesia; Hilgard's Theory*)

P A R T

III

Cognitive Processes

6

Learning and Behavior

Chapter Outline

Long ago I learned that trying to keep a room tidy is a lost cause. You see, as a child I shared my room with my younger brother. Each of us was responsible for cleaning up our own belongings, but if either failed to clean up, both of us were punished. I used to try really hard to keep the room clean, but my brother kept on messing up. So night after night we both were punished. One day I just quit trying, and eventually, so did my mother! Believing that she was stuck with two hopelessly messy boys, she stopped the punishments and did the cleaning herself. Much later I came across an experiment conducted by a psychologist named Martin Seligman (Seligman & Maier, 1967; Overmier & Seligman, 1967) that helped me to understand how, in spite of my efforts and my mother's, I might have learned not to clean my room.

In Seligman's experiments, two groups of dogs received shocks, but one of them could terminate the shocks, both for themselves and also for the other group, by pressing a panel with their paws. While only one group could control the shocks, both groups received exactly the same number of shocks for the same length of time. At first the dogs that had no control over the shocks tried to get away, but there was nothing they could do. Most of them eventually gave up trying and just lay on the floor, whining quietly. Later, when Seligman placed them in a new situation from which they could escape by jumping over a barrier, they failed to take the opportunity. Seligman referred to the dogs' failure to learn to escape as **learned helplessness.** Apparently, through continual frustration of their early efforts, they had learned not to try. The group that had control over the shocks from the beginning, however, had no difficulty learning to avoid the shocks.

Learned Helplessness: Learning that trying is of no use when exposed to inescapable pain.

Seligman's results have been shown to be of relevance for humans as well as dogs (Miller & Norman, 1981). In one experiment people who had no control over receiving shocks subsequently had difficulty learning to avoid a shock. Apparently exposure to unavoidable pain reduces the motivation to control one's environment (Seligman, 1975). The conditions in Seligman's experiment are something like the situation I found myself in as a child; since my punishment depended on my brother's behavior, not mine, I had learned not to make an effort at cleaning up.

From this kind of experience we can see some of the dimensions of the learning process: **learning** is a relatively permanent change in behavior, and it involves the capacity to engage in a new pattern of behavior as a result of experience. Acquiring reading, writing, and arithmetic skills through study—all are examples of learning, as are the acquisition of social and job skills as we interact with others. But how exactly do these newly changed or learned behaviors develop? The story of how psychologists pursued this question is in large part the story of how the science of behavior grew. In this chapter we examine how psychologists have come to understand and conceptualize the learning process, starting with fundamentals of classical conditioning and moving to the more complex processes of operant conditioning and social and cognitive learning.

Learning: Any relatively permanent change in behavior (or behavior potential) that stems from experience.

CLASSICAL CONDITIONING: THEORY AND PROCESS

In the doctor's office the mere sight of a needle makes you become tense or faint. Certain stimuli—dentist's chair, for instance—cause gut reactions of fear or disgust. Such phenomena are due to a type of learning discovered by a Russian physiologist named Ivan Pavlov (1849–1936).

Pavlov was an internationally known scientist before he made his groundbreaking discoveries in learning. Indeed, he was primarily interested in **reflex responses**—involuntary behavioral reactions to stimulation of some kind that occur without previous learning or experience. Pavlov, in fact, had little interest in psychology; he made his discoveries in learning by accident, while studying the relationship between salivation and digestion in dogs.

Reflex: An inborn, automatic, involuntary, unlearned behavioral response to some event or condition.

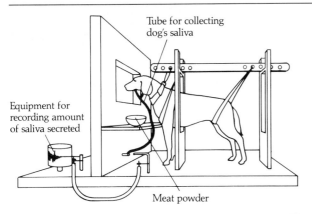

Tube for collecting dog's saliva

Equipment for recording amount of saliva secreted

Meat powder

Figure 6.1 Pavlov's Conditioning Apparatus.

Dogs salivate reflexively as soon as food reaches their tongues. The reflex can be experimentally induced simply by placing meat powder on the animal's tongue. In the course of his work, however, Pavlov found that salivation could also be set off by a wide variety of neutral stimuli that would not normally set off reflex reactions. At first the dogs salivated only when the meat powder was placed on their tongues. After a few days, however, they salivated at the sight of the meat dish; at the sound of the approaching experimenter's footsteps; and even at the mere sight of the experimenter, just as some people become frightened at the mere sight of a dentist or dentist's chair. Pavlov became aggravated. How was he to study salivation if the dogs salivated when they weren't supposed to? But eventually he became intrigued by the snag in his work, and began a systematic investigation to which he would devote himself for the rest of his career.

For his first experiment in learning, Pavlov selected a dog that had no previous experience with his procedures and trained the animal to stand still in a harness (see Figure 6.1). To eliminate the effects of confounding variables like the sound of his footsteps, he devised a way to deliver the meat powder to the dog by remote control and moved his experiment into a soundproof room.

Basic Terminology

Unconditioned Stimulus (US): A stimulus that dependably produces (elicits) a response without the subject's prior experience.

Unconditioned Response (UR): The unlearned response to an unconditioned stimulus.

Conditioned Stimulus (CS): A neutral stimulus that, when paired with an unconditioned stimulus, acquires the property to elicit a similar response.

Conditioned Response (CR): The learned response to a conditioned stimulus, which has previously been paired with a US. The CR is similar, but not identical, to the UR.

Classical Conditioning: The process in which a neutral stimulus comes to elicit a conditioned response through repeated pairings with an unconditioned stimulus.

Pavlov's typical procedure began with the presentation of a neutral stimulus like a light. Pavlov would turn the light on for several seconds to demonstrate that by itself it did not produce salivation. Then he would turn it on again and give the dog some meat powder. Naturally the dog would salivate. After a specific number of trials, in which the light and the meat powder were presented in close temporal succession, Pavlov found that the dog would salivate in the presence of the light alone, even if meat powder did not follow. His results were the same whether the neutral stimulus he used was a light, a bell, or a buzzer (Pavlov, 1927, 1928).

To describe his findings, Pavlov developed special terms for the stimuli and responses in his experiments. The stimulus that elicited the reflexive response (the meat powder) came to be called the **unconditioned stimulus (US)**, which was formally defined as any stimulus that dependably produces a response without the subject having any prior experience of it. The response to the unconditioned stimulus—in this case, salivation—was called the **unconditioned response (UR)**.

The neutral stimulus (the light) was dubbed **conditioned stimulus (CS)**, which referred to any neutral stimulus that, when paired with an unconditioned stimulus, acquires the property to elicit a similar response. And the response to the conditioned stimulus alone was termed the **conditioned response (CR)**.

The formal name for the process in which a neutral stimulus comes to elicit a previously reflexive response through repeated pairings with an unconditioned stimulus, is **classical conditioning** (see Figure 6.2). Classical conditioning makes it possible for an unconditioned, or reflex-action, response to be produced by a whole range of new and more indirect stimuli. The response itself changes little if at all, but through learning new stimuli come to elicit it. Thus, by pairing a light or buzzer with meat powder, the

Before conditioning

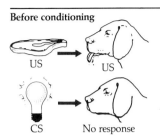

- *Unconditioned Stimulus* (US) Stimulus that dependably sets off response without learning (meat powder)

- *Unconditioned response* (UR) Response to the unconditioned stimulus (salivation)

During conditioning

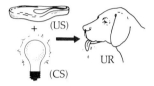

- *Conditioned stimulus* (CS) Neutral stimulus that, when paired with the conditioned stimulus, acquires the property to elicit a similar response (light paired with meat)

After conditioning

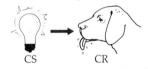

- *Conditioned Response* (CR) The learned response to a conditioned stimulus (salivation)

Figure 6.2 The Process of Classical Conditioning. *Before conditioning, the meat elicits salivation, but the bell does not. During conditioning, the bell and meat are paired. After several such pairings, presentation of the bell alone elicits salivation.*

Through classical conditioning, this cat has come to associate the sight of fish on the hook with the dinner that is soon to follow.

new stimuli come to elicit the same salivation that the meat did. Classical conditioning builds upon the inherent behavioral responses of the organism by allowing new stimuli to elicit similar responses.

In simple terms, before the procedure the unconditioned stimulus elicits salivation, but the conditioned stimulus does not. When the conditioned stimulus and unconditioned stimulus are first paired, the unconditioned response occurs as usual in response to the unconditioned stimulus. After several pairings, however, the conditioned stimulus comes to elicit salivation all by itself, and the response is then called a conditioned response. A dentist's chair can become a conditioned stimulus for fear, for example, after several pairings with the drill.

What is it that gives the conditioned stimulus the ability to elicit a response? Clearly it is the unconditioned stimulus. Through repeated pairings, the unconditioned stimulus breathes life into the conditioned stimulus. The conditioned stimulus becomes, in a sense, an extension of the unconditioned stimulus and acquires its power to elicit a response. But what would happen if the unconditioned stimulus, source of the conditioned stimulus's ability to elicit the conditioned response, were permanently removed? Would the conditioned stimulus continue to elicit the conditioned response indefinitely?

To find out, Pavlov conducted another experiment. After conditioning a dog to salivate to a light alone, he continued to present only the light to the dog. He found that the ability of the light to elicit salivation was only temporary. In just a few sessions without meat powder the amount of saliva elicited by the light began to decrease. Noticeably soon it diminished to nothing (see Figure 6.3). Pavlov called this reduction and gradual elimination of the

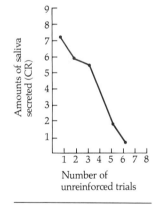

Figure 6.3 Extinction. *This figure illustrates the extinction of a classically conditioned response as a function of the number of unreinforced trials in which the CS is presented alone, without the US. As the figure shows, the strength of the response goes down as the number of unreinforced trials increases (After Pavlov, 1927).*

People who have learned to respond to a stimulus with fear can often learn not to respond this way if given the chance to experience the stimulus without negative consequences. Thus, though this child is fearful of water, eventually she will learn to associate water with the safe, encouraging words of mother and later with fun and recreation.

Extinction: In classical conditioning, the strength of a conditioned response, measured in terms of the number of unpaired presentations needed to extinguish it. The stronger the response, the greater is its resistance to extinction.

Inhibition: The process in which an organism learns to withhold a response to a conditioned stimulus when it is not followed by an unconditioned stimulus. In inhibition, the CS becomes a signal that the US will not follow.

Resistance to Extinction: In operant conditioning, the strength of a conditioned response measured in terms of the endurance of a response beyond the withdrawal of reinforcement.

conditioned response, through unpaired presentations of the conditioned stimulus, **extinction.**

To account for extinction, Pavlov theorized that, after a number of trials in which presentation of the conditioned stimulus is not followed by the unconditioned stimulus, a subject learns to withhold a response—a process he called **inhibition.** Pavlov saw extinction *not* as a passive process involving a gradual weakening of association of the CS and US, but rather as an active process in which a subject learns not to respond. Thus, the conditioned stimulus does not return to being a neutral stimulus through extinction. Instead, it becomes a signal not to respond. People who, through classical conditioning, learn to respond to the dentist's chair with fear can learn not to respond that way if they are given several opportunities to sit in the chair without having any dental work done. But the success of such efforts depends on many factors, one of the most important being the strength of the original conditioning.

The Strength of a Conditioned Response

With the discovery of extinction, Pavlov learned that some conditioned responses are stronger than others. That is, some were more resistant to extinction. Whereas one animal's conditioned salivary response might be extinguished after twenty presentations of the light alone (unpaired trials), another's might extinguish after only ten. Subsequent experimentation revealed that the strength of a conditioned response, measured in terms of the number of unpaired presentations needed to extinguish it—that is, its **resistance to extinction**—depends primarily on three factors (Kimble, 1961). These are: (1) the frequency of CS–US pairings during conditioning; (2) the time interval between presentation of the conditioned stimulus and presentation of the unconditioned stimulus; and (3) the order in which the two stimuli are presented.

In general, the more pairings, the stronger the response. All else being equal, a child with five bad experiences in the dentist's chair would require far more painless experiences in the dentist's chair to feel at ease than the child with only one or two unpleasant experiences. Small variations in the time interval between presentation of the conditioned and unconditioned stimuli have a dramatic effect on the strength of the conditioned response. An interval of half a second produces the strongest response in most laboratory situations. Shorter intervals, simultaneous presentations, or longer intervals all produce a weaker response. Pairings at intervals longer than two seconds usually prove ineffective in establishing a conditioned response. Thus, presenting meat powder several seconds after the light has been turned off will not establish a conditioned salivary response to the light. Finally, presenting the conditioned stimulus after rather than before the unconditioned stimulus can produce conditioning, but the response is generally weak and easily extinguished. Thus, to produce the strongest responses—those with the greatest resistance to extinction—the conditioned stimulus should be presented about half a second before the unconditioned stimulus many times.

Other Aspects of Classical Conditioning

With resistance to extinction being the major yardstick for measuring the strength of conditioning, Pavlov always insisted on exact counts of the number of unpaired trials needed for extinction, as he was a very careful scientist (Jenkins, 1979). Imagine what Pavlov's reaction would have been, then, if he found his assistant, assigned to study the course of extinction in a newly trained animal, taking a nap. "But I finished my assignment, Dr. Pavlov," said the assistant. "The animal acquired a conditioned salivary response to a bell after only eighty trials. The response reached its peak after 100 more trials and completely extinguished after twenty-six presentations of the bell alone." "Completely extinguished?" questioned Pavlov. "Let's go see." Pavlov rings the bell and the dog salivates. The nervous assistant cannot believe his eyes. "The response was extinguished—at least I think it was," he squealed.

Was the assistant incompetent, a victim of circumstances, or just plain lazy? Actually, his unfortunate experience was the first step in the discovery that an extinguished response will temporarily reappear with rest, a phenomenon Pavlov called **spontaneous recovery.** The supposedly extinguished conditioned response comes to life again the first time a conditioned stimulus is presented following a resting period of no stimulation (see Figure 6.4).

Spontaneous Recovery: In classical conditioning, the temporary reappearance of an extinguished conditioned response with rest.

■ **Learning Check** ■

Read the right side, then cover and try to recite. Repeat.

Three ways to increase resistance to extinction.

1. Use many CS–US pairings.
2. Use short ($\frac{1}{2}$ second) intervals between pairings.
3. Present the CS before the US.

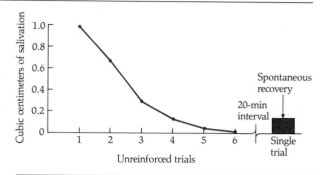

Figure 6.4   Spontaneous Recovery. *After six unreinforced trials, the conditioned stimulus elicited almost no salivation. But after a twenty minute rest, the next presentation of the conditioned stimulus elicited a strong response (After Pavlov, 1927).*

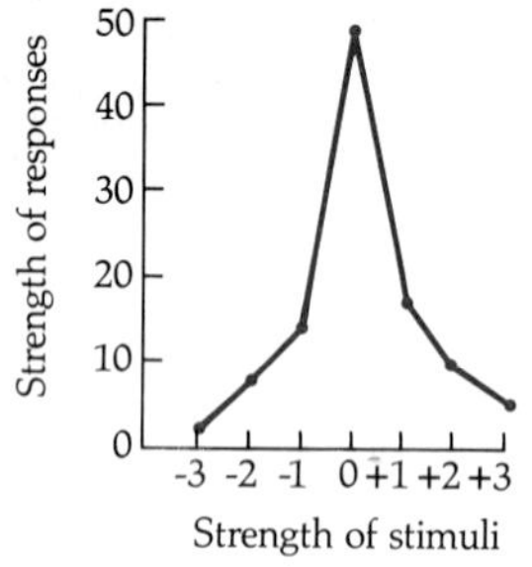

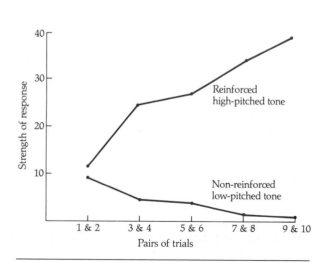

Figure 6.5   Stimulus Generalization. *The strength of the conditioned response is shown on the vertical axis. The strength of the stimuli (in terms of similarity) relative to the original conditioned stimulus appears on the horizontal axis. The original conditioned stimulus falls at the center of the horizontal axis; stimuli of decreasing and increasing strength fall to the left and right side.*

Thus, a conditioned response that has been extinguished on Thursday evening might reappear Friday morning in response to the conditioned stimulus.

Let's say, for instance, that a motorist looks into her rear-view mirror, spots a police car, and gets pulled over. An officer delivers a nasty tongue-lashing and a $50 ticket, and her blood pressure rises. As a result of this sequence of experiences she develops a conditioned fear of police cars. Every time she notices one in the rear-view mirror, her heart begins to pound as her blood pressure rises. But, as the months roll on, her conditioned fear begins to lessen, because the appearance of the police car is not followed by being pulled over and so extinction is taking place. Then one day, driving along and minding her own business, she spots a police car on her tail and her heart pounds wildly. The reappearance of her fear response is probably due to spontaneous recovery.

If the appearance of a blue and white patrol car causes your heart to shift into high gear, perhaps you've noticed a similar reaction to vehicles that merely look like the real thing. It turns out that, once a CS–US relationship has been learned, stimuli that resemble the conditioned stimulus will elicit a similar, though weaker, response. If a particular tone has become a conditioned stimulus for salivation, a higher or lower tone will also elicit

Figure 6.6   Stimulus Discrimination. *In this figure, presentation of the high pitched tone was reinforced (that is, followed by an unconditioned stimulus). Presentation of a low pitched tone was not reinforced. The strength of response for the reinforced high pitched tone increases, but the strength of response for the nonreinforced low pitched tone decreases. Eventually the organism responded only to the high pitched tone and thus learned to discriminate between the two tones.*

salivation. This phenomenon, in which stimuli similar to a conditioned stimulus elicit a similar conditioned response, is known as **stimulus generalization.** The look-alike stimulus elicits a response without even a single CS–US pairing—as if some automatic transfer of learning from the original stimulus to the new stimulus had occurred. The closer the new stimulus to the original conditioned stimulus, the stronger the response (see Figure 6.5).

Fortunately there is an opposite process, called **stimulus discrimination,** in which a subject comes to respond only to the original conditioned stimulus and not to similar stimuli. Thus, you soon learn the difference between look-alikes and the real McCoy and respond only to the latter. The typical procedure for establishing stimulus discrimination in the laboratory is to present two or more neutral stimuli, such as two tones of different pitch, but to follow only one of them with an unconditioned stimulus. The experimenter might give a dog meat powder after a high-pitched tone but not after a low-pitched one. At first, the dog fails to respond to either tone. Then, due to stimulus generalization, the animal salivates in response to both. But after a few more trials the dog will respond more to the high-pitched tone than to the low-pitched tone, and eventually *only* to the high-pitched tone (see Figure 6.6).

COMPLEX LEARNING THROUGH CONDITIONING

Basic classical conditioning, as we have seen, involves associating a new stimulus with an unconditioned stimulus that elicits such reflex reactions as pain and other physiological responses. How can this limited range of reactions develop into a pattern of learning for more complex new behaviors? The answer lies in some of the aspects of classical conditioning just examined, especially stimulus generalization and discrimination.

Through stimulus generalization, stimuli that are similar to the original conditioned stimulus can also come to elicit fear. Thus, a child's fear of bees could generalize to other things that buzz—flies, mosquitoes, and hummingbirds. Through further experience, however, the child will probably learn to discriminate between those stimuli that pose a real threat, such as bees, and those that are more or less harmless.

Sometimes stimuli that don't even resemble the original conditioned stimulus can elicit a similar emotional response. A child who has been stung by a bee may come to fear a garden that attracts a lot of bees, because every time she walks past the garden she hears the buzzing sound she fears. Apparently once a neutral stimulus has become a conditioned stimulus, it may be capable of transferring its properties to yet another stimulus. Just as the power to run a company is handed down from president to vice-president to supervisor, the power to elicit a response is sometimes transferred from unconditioned stimulus to conditioned stimulus to new conditioned stimulus.

This process, in which a conditioned stimulus is paired with a neutral stimulus in the formation of a new conditioned response, is known as **higher-order conditioning.** Pavlov demonstrated higher-order conditioning by pairing a bell with a light that had previously been paired with meat pow-

Stimulus Generalization: In classical conditioning, the phenomenon in which stimuli similar to a conditioned stimulus elicit a similar response without prior learning, though to a lesser degree.

Stimulus Discrimination: In classical conditioning, the process in which the organism comes to respond only to the original conditioned stimulus and not to similar stimuli. It is the opposite of stimulus generalization.

Higher-Order Conditioning: The process in which a conditioned stimulus is paired with a neutral stimulus in the formation of a new conditioned response.

Table 6.1   Higher-Order Conditioning

Stimulus	Response
1. Pair meat powder (US) + light (CS)	Elicits salivation (UR)
2. Repeat step 1 several times	
3. Present light alone (CS)	Elicits salivation (CR)
4. Pair light (CS) with second neutral stimulus, bell (CS_1)	Elicits salivation (CR)
5. Repeat step 4	
6. Present bell alone (CS_1)	Elicits salivation (CR_1)

der (see Table 6.1). At first glance, one might think that, through higher-order conditioning, just about any stimulus could gain emotional significance. As a general rule, however, higher-order conditioning is much weaker and shorter-lived than basic classical conditioning. The most common way in which it affects our everyday lives is in the attachment of feelings to certain words in our language, a process called semantic conditioning.

The process by which a previously neutral stimulus, like the buzzing of a bee or mosquito, comes to elicit an emotional response through association with an unconditioned stimulus like pain is known as **emotional conditioning.** Emotional conditioning is not limited to fear. It can produce hate and disgust, love and pride as well. To the sailor who has been at sea for eleven months, the sight of home elicits all the positive feelings associated with the presence of family and friends. The raising of the flag or playing of the national anthem elicits the positive emotion of love of country. But note that the objects, sounds, and symbols that produce these emotions have no inherent positive or negative meaning. They acquire their power through association with painful or pleasant stimuli.

Some psychologists suspect that severe and unrealistic fearfulness may be acquired during childhood through classical conditioning. A mother's warning scream, for example, stimulates fear in a child. If every time a child goes near the edge of a swimming pool the mother screams, the child may become extremely fearful of the water. Such fears might persist into adulthood, causing the grown person to avoid swimming, boating, or any activity involving water.

Classical conditioning provides just one perspective on the practical significance and role of learning in everyday behavior. A second perspective can be found in a form of learning, first studied in the United States, known as operant conditioning.

Emotional Conditioning: The process in which a previously neutral stimulus comes to elicit an emotional response by virtue of being paired with an unconditioned stimulus.

■ **Learning Clue** ■

As you read what follows, be alert to the differences between Pavlov and Thorndike and Skinner. Pavlov emphasized what happens before a response, stimulus–stimulus connections, and elicited (reflexive) responses. Thorndike and Skinner, by contrast, emphasized what happens after a response, stimulus–response connections, and freely emitted responses.

OPERANT CONDITIONING: THEORY AND PROCESS

Several years before Pavlov began his work on classical conditioning, the American psychologist Edward Lee Thorndike (1874–1949) was making observations that led him to quite different conclusions about conditioning. Thorndike (1898) found that, in some situations, what happened *after* a response could be just as important as what happened before it. The critical link, moreover, did not appear to be the connection between two stimuli (CS and US), but between a stimulus and a response.

In his experiments Thorndike used a "puzzle box," a cage with a door that could be unlatched from inside by pulling on a string or pressing a lever. Thorndike would place hungry kittens in the box and a dish of food just outside. Then he would record how quickly the kittens learned to release themselves and get to the food. He found, among other things, that each time a kitten escaped it took less time to do so than in past trials. The first time it might take forty minutes to find the solution through trial and error. It would claw at the bars, meow, skirt back and forth, and make other useless responses. Finally it would stumble on the correct response by accident. But, with repeated trials, the same kitten would make the appropriate response in a matter of seconds. The useless behaviors gradually dropped out of the kitten's repertoire. In effect, the kitten repeated behaviors that had useful consequences and eliminated those that did not. Such learning Thorndike called **instrumental conditioning.**

From his experiments, Thorndike (1905) eventually postulated what he believed to be two general laws of learning. According to his first, the **law of effect,** if a response to a stimulus is accompanied or followed by "satisfaction," the association between the response and the stimulus will be strengthened, so that, when the stimulus recurs, so will the response. Conversely, stimulus–response connections that are accompanied or closely followed by discomfort are weakened. Thus, in a city new to you, several of your attempts to ask directions from strangers might be unsuccessful before you finally get reliable help, perhaps from a friendly-looking person. At the next step you might look for friendly types, avoiding people with angry or vague expressions, and so get a higher rate of favorable reinforcement.

According to Thorndike's second law, the **law of exercise,** under the same conditions stimulus–response connections are strengthened by repetition. Thus, all else being equal, the more often you successfully get directions from friendly people, the stronger will be your tendency to ask similar people again.

Because of its emphasis on the bond between stimulus and response, Thorndike's work became the basis for what came to be known as S–R theory. Probably the biggest difference between S–R theory and Pavlov's theory, classical conditioning, is S–R theory's emphasis on the consequences of a response as the main ingredient of learning. Thorndike could have built his puzzle box so that the cat had to walk around the cage, meow three times, or claw at the floor to escape. As long as those responses led to food, they would have been strengthened. In Pavlov's classical conditioning, the consequences of a response are irrelevant to learning. The subject learns as a

Instrumental Conditioning: The term used by Thorndike to describe learning due to consequences. Responses that are instrumental in a given situation, that serve some purpose, become strengthened and are more likely to recur in that situation than responses that serve no purpose.

Law of Effect: Thorndike's first law of learning, which states that stimulus–response connections are strengthened when accompanied or followed by satisfaction and weakened if accompanied by discomfort.

Law of Exercise: Thorndike's second law of learning, which states that, other things being equal, stimulus–response connections are strengthened by repetition.

*B. F. Skinner, the psycholo-
gist who developed the idea
of operant conditioning.*

result of one stimulus becoming associated with another, and the response is predetermined.

The two viewpoints also differ in the role they assign to the learner. In classical conditioning, the subject plays very little, if any, active role in the learning process. No matter what the subject does or does not do, the unconditioned stimulus becomes associated with a conditioned stimulus by virtue of its ability to elicit a reflex reaction. In S–R theory, learning depends on the subject doing something that has satisfying consequences.

Despite these differences, Thorndike saw no contradiction between his work and that of Pavlov (Hull, 1937). Each, he believed, simply emphasized a different aspect of learning—stimulus–stimulus connections in the case of Pavlov; and stimulus–response connections in the case of Thorndike. In both cases, learning results from the formation of associations due to the close time intervals for two events. Not until the psychologist B.F. Skinner published *The Behavior of Organisms* (1938) did a majority of learning theorists begin to believe that the two viewpoints represented two different kinds of conditioning.

Skinner agreed with Thorndike in his emphasis on the consequences of behavior. However, Skinner saw classical conditioning as very limited to a narrow range of responses—those that are "elicited" by a stimulus originating outside of us and producing reflex reactions. Skinner showed that most responses originate from within the organism and are not really automatic reflex reactions. For instance, if you hear a distant car horn in traffic, you don't necessarily expect a traffic crisis automatically; your response to the horn is not always the same and is not a reflex directly elicited by the horn. Similarly, the presence of your instructor in class does not automatically cause you to pay attention to what he or she is saying. You select those behaviors from a repertoire of possible responses. Similarly, though the buzz of a bee may elicit fear in you, it does not elicit whatever behavior follows. Some people run; some freeze; others continue to approach the bee despite their fear.

Skinner used the term **emitted response** for behavior that organisms originate for themselves without obvious outside causes. Some emitted responses, such as tossing a pebble into a pond, may seem random in that they have no known relevance to an individual's obvious purpose. Those that become associated with a specific motivation, however, are called **operants,** because they operate on the environment to produce a desired consequence for an individual. Thus, when the tossed pebble makes a noise that wakes a friend we want to see, it becomes an operant for a specific purpose. Skinner's viewpoint became known as **operant conditioning,** a term that Skinner preferred to "instrumental" conditioning. Like instrumental (S–R) theory, operant conditioning explains behavior in terms of its consequences. An organism emits a response; if the response has consequences, those consequences influence the chance that the behavior will occur again. For example, if you turn right instead of left on your way to the supermarket and find a shortcut that gets you there much faster, the consequences of turning right will influence the chances that you will do so in the future. Like instrumental conditioning and unlike classical conditioning, the critical factor is not what precedes the response, but what follows it.

Skinner spent a great deal of time studying the various types of consequences that might follow an emitted response. He found that both the nature of the consequences and the manner in which it occurred had definite effects on the strengths of learning.

Basic Terminology

To designate an event that follows a response and strengthens it, in the sense that the response will be more likely to recur under similar circumstances, Skinner used the term **reinforcer.** The chief defining characteristics of a reinforcer are its relationship to the response (it follows it) and its function (it strengthens it). Any stimulus can be a reinforcer. Worms can be a reinforcer for the person who likes to fish. And, though food can be, and usually is, a reinforcer, it isn't for the person who has just finished a heavy meal. A stimulus is a reinforcer if and only if it increases the frequency of the behavior that preceded it.

A reinforcer may affect behavior by its appearance or by its disappearance. A stimulus that strengthens a behavior by its appearance following a response is called a **positive reinforcer.** Consider the politician who makes a statement on gun control and for the first time hears the audience cheer. Subsequently she talks more and more about this issue. In that case, cheering is a positive reinforcer for her statements on gun control.

A **negative reinforcer,** on the other hand, strengthens behavior by its disappearance. When we kill a biting fly after swatting at it, our accurate fly-swatting behavior is linked to the permanent disappearance of the biting, and our fly-swatting is more likely to be repeated. Thus, the biting fly, with our desire to swat it, has become a negative reinforcer, strengthening our re-

Emitted Response: A behavior that occurs spontaneously and originates from forces within the organism without obvious outside causes.

Operants: Emitted behaviors (those that occur spontaneously) that operate on the environment to produce consequences.

Operant Conditioning: The term Skinner used, in place of instrumental conditioning, which refers to the process in which the frequency of occurrence of any given emitted behavior is influenced by the consequences of the behavior.

Reinforcer: In operant conditioning, any stimulus that occurs as a consequence of an operant and increases its probability of recurrence.

Positive Reinforcer: A stimulus that strengthens a behavior by its appearance. Its presentation or appearance as a consequence of behavior is called positive reinforcement.

Negative Reinforcer: A stimulus that strengthens a behavior by its disappearance; an aversive stimulus that has positive consequences by its removal. The removal or disappearance of an aversive stimulus (negative reinforcer) as a consequence of behavior is known as negative reinforcement.

Aversive Stimulus: A stimulus that is harmful, painful, noxious, or very unpleasant. Electric shock, extremes of hot and cold, bee stings, and snake bites are examples of aversive stimuli.

Escape: Behavior in which the organism terminates (escapes from) an aversive stimulus by making an appropriate response after experiencing it.

Avoidance: Behavior in which an organism terminates (avoids) an aversive stimulus by making an appropriate response before experiencing it.

Primary Reinforcer: A stimulus that acts as a reinforcer without any previous experience; a stimulus that has the power to reinforce the first time it is used.

Conditioned Reinforcer: A stimulus that acquires reinforcing properties through conditioning. A stimulus that gains its power to reinforce because of its association with a stimulus already having that effect.

Punishment: The presentation of an aversive stimulus as a consequence of a response.

sponse aimed at killing it. This negative reinforcer is also called an **aversive stimulus,** one that is harmful, painful, noxious or very unpleasant. Anything we might try to avoid, such as electric shocks or loud noises, are aversive stimuli; behaviors that lead to their removal are strengthened. Technically, if a subject gets away from an aversive stimulus only after its delivery, this shows **escape** behavior; if the subject is conditioned to get away before experiencing it, this shows **avoidance** behavior.

The power of some stimuli to act as a reinforcer is inherent; they have the ability to reinforce the first time they are used. Others acquire their powers as a positive or negative reinforcer through association with another reinforcer. A stimulus that acts as a reinforcer immediately, without any previous experience on the subject's part, is referred to as a **primary reinforcer.** Primary reinforcers usually have biological significance: that is, they affect the subject's well-being. Food, water, and electric shock are among the most powerful of primary reinforcers.

A stimulus that acts as a reinforcer only by association with a primary reinforcer is called a **conditioned reinforcer.** Money is a conditioned reinforcer. It has no special meaning to the newborn child; only through repeated experiences in exchanging it for peanuts or ice cream or other satisfying treats does the child come to see it as a reward for good behavior. The peanuts and ice cream, primary reinforcers, lend their power to reinforce to an object (in this case, money) that is, in and of itself, biologically unsatisfying.

It is important to note that reinforcers—whether they are positive ones that we seek, or negative ones we avoid—strengthen the behaviors associated with them. By contrast, **punishment** is the presentation of something we wish to avoid *after* we have made a certain response. Rather than strengthen a response, punishment tends to suppress it. If the politician makes an antiabortion statement and then hears the crowd jeer, this is punishment and will discourage similar statements later in the speech.

Punishment is often confused with negative reinforcement. This is because punishment does involve an aversive stimulus that we wish to avoid—such as a slap, or a severe scolding. But, in negative reinforcement, the aversive stimulus is *removed* immediately following a response, and its removal thus leads to a strengthening or reinforcement of that response. In punishment, the aversive stimulus presented *following* a response punishes what we just did, and so, rather than increasing its probability of recurrence, *decreases* the probability that the response will be repeated under similar circumstances.

Punishment, then, would appear to be the exact opposite of negative reinforcement. But it does not lead to exactly the opposite effect. Negative reinforcement strengthens a response. Punishment does not necessarily weaken a response; it merely suppresses it temporarily, for as long as punishment is delivered. Once the punishment is terminated, the response can occur without being penalized, and is likely to return to its normal strength. A father who punishes a child for cursing at home does not weaken the strength of the behavior, but merely suppresses it in the situation in which it has been punished. The child will probably continue to curse in situations in which cursing is not punished—for example, when playing with friends. And, if punishment is completely withdrawn, the behavior returns to its

■ Learning Check ■

For each of the following pairs of terms on the left, read the information on the right, then cover and try to recite. Repeat.

Positive Reinforcer vs. Negative Reinforcer	Both strengthen behavior; positive reinforcer by its appearance, negative reinforcer by its disappearance.
Escape vs. Avoidance	Both involve getting away from an aversive stimulus; escape *after* the stimulus has been delivered, avoidance *before* it has been delivered.
Negative Reinforcement vs. Punishment	Both involve an aversive stimulus; in negative reinforcement its removal strengthens behavior, in punishment its presentation suppresses behavior.

Box 6.1 PSYCHOLOGY IN ACTION: How—and How Not—to Use Punishment

Experimental findings have led researchers to conclude that, besides being inefficient, punishment can have a number of undesirable consequences (Parke & Walters, 1967; Azrin & Holz, 1966). First, people who have been punished tend to use punishment themselves in dealing with others. Thus, a child who has been punished is likely to use punishment in dealing with peers. Likewise, adults who were abused as children are likely to abuse their children. Second, to be effective, punishment must be intense. Yet intense punishment can be physically harmful. It is all too easy for adults to underestimate the intensity of punishment; they forget that the person being punished is much younger and weaker than the punisher. Third, punishment must be delivered based on carefully monitored and specific undesirable behaviors. Any exceptions either in monitoring or delivery will weaken the effect of punishment.

Fourth, the effects of punishment may become generalized. The punisher may become as distasteful to the child as the punishment, so that the child reacts with fear or hate. A child who is punished by a teacher, for instance, may develop a negative attitude toward the teacher, the school, and, in extreme cases, public institutions and authority figures in general. The punished response may also generalize to other similar responses. A child who is punished for cursing might simply talk less. The parents then wonder why their children never tell them anything. Finally, punishment may result in a general negative self-evaluation. Punished children may come to feel that it is they, not the responses that they make, that are bad.

If punishment is used, it is important to be very clear about what is being punished. "Punish the response, not the person" is good advice. That is, avoid calling the child lazy, stupid, or bad; label the *response* with those words. (Instead of "You are bad because you cursed," say, "Cursing is bad.") Moreover, the punishment should be administered as quickly as possible after the unwanted response occurs, with the maximum reasonable intensity, and then terminated quickly. Then provide some alternative response, so the child knows how to behave in an acceptable manner. When the child makes the appropriate response, reward it. A reward for good behavior following punishment reduces the negative effect of punishment on the personal relationship. Finally, if you use punishment, use it each time the unwanted behavior occurs. Otherwise the behavior might quickly return to previous levels.

Punishment, when used, should be administered as quickly as possible after the undesired response occurs, with the maximum reasonable intensity, and then terminated quickly.

Figure 6.7 Reinforcement and Punishment.

	Stimulus	
	Positive	Negative
Apply	Positive reinforcement (↑) increases likelihood of response	Punishment (↓) decreases likelihood of response
Withdraw	Response cost (↓) decreases likelihood of response	Negative reinforcement (↑) increases likelihood of response

previous frequency in the original situation. If the father stops punishing the child for cursing, the child quite likely will begin to curse again in his presence. The ineffectiveness of physical punishment in weakening a response has led many researchers to disavow it as a means of disciplining children. Box 6.1 presents the case for the uses—and uselessness—of punishment.

Another form of punishment that does not involve the infliction of pain is called **response cost**—the removal of a positive reinforcer following a behavior. When a parent takes away the keys to the family car because a daughter came home too late the night before, they are using response cost to discourage this behavior. (Figure 6.7 summarizes the distinction between the two types of reinforcement and the two types of punishment.)

People use reinforcement and punishment every day in an effort to influence each other. Your best friend praises you for being on time, using positive reinforcement to encourage you to be prompt. Your parents nag and nag until you clean your room, using negative reinforcement to encourage you to be neat. Your lover rebukes you for dancing too closely with another, punishing the behavior. You retort with response cost and refuse to have the next dance as you originally had promised.

Thus, Skinner developed a working vocabulary for his formulations of operant conditioning. The next step was to devise a way to examine the conditioning process in the laboratory.

Response Cost: The removal of a positive reinforcer following a behavior. In response cost, a form of punishment, we take something desirable away following a response in order to discourage that response (for example, we get charged a fine for parking illegally to discourage such behavior).

The Conditioning Process

To study the operant conditioning process under rigorous experimental conditions, Skinner developed a special cage ideal for studying learning in rats and pigeons. It is now known as the **Skinner box** (see Figure 6.8). Sound-insulated and electronically equipped to record responses and deliver reinforcers, the box houses one animal. The box allows the animal to operate on its environment in an observable and measurable way—by pressing a lever or by pecking at a light. Hooked up to the lever or the light is a mechanism that delivers food pellets or water to the animal through a little chute, much as vending machines deliver candy and soft drinks. The device can be adjusted to provide reinforcers in specific quantities according to a specific time interval or a specific number of responses. Outside the box a recording device (often linked to a computer) monitors the animal's responses.

Skinner Box: A specially designed cubicle that gives an experimenter precise control over the environment in order to study operant behavior.

In the typical operant conditioning experiment, the experimenter's first task is to get the animal to make the desired response. For, unlike classical conditioning, in which the experimenter has only to present an unconditioned stimulus to elicit a response, operant conditioning procedure depends on the subject responding voluntarily. The process is the same as that used in Thorndike's experiment with cats (page 199). In the course of exploring its new environment, the animal emits a variety of responses. Eventually it makes the desired one and is reinforced by the appearance of food or water. If the animal has been deprived of food or water for several hours, it will soon make the response with increasing frequency.

Or so the theory goes. Actually, getting an animal to emit a specific response isn't always that easy. Suppose you want to get a pigeon to peck at a light. You place the pigeon in a Skinner box fitted out with a light and wait patiently with your finger on the button that delivers food pellets to the box. The pigeon walks around, bops its head, pecks at the walls of the box—does everything but peck at the light. After about half an hour you begin to wonder if the pigeon is ever going to peck at the light. Is there anything you can do but continue to wait?

Fortunately, the experimenter doesn't have to sit back, passively waiting for a subject to emit a response. In a technique known as **shaping,** the technician first reinforces any response that approximates the desired response, then gradually limits reinforcement to those responses close to the desired one. To shape your pigeon's behavior, you would wait for the first response that even remotely resembles pecking at the light. Say the pigeon turns in the direction of the light. Immediately you press the button to deliver a food pellet to the pigeon. Next, you wait for a response that is even closer to light pecking than the last. Rather than rewarding the pigeon simply for turning toward the light, you wait until the pigeon turns toward the light *and* steps up to it as well. When the pigeon turns toward the light and steps up to it, you again push the button. Eventually the bird starts to peck at the wall around the light, and you reinforce that behavior. You keep limiting the range of responses that will earn the pigeon a food pellet until finally it pecks at the light.

Figure 6.8 A Skinner Box. A Skinner box, used for studying learning by consequences.

Shaping: The gradual reinforcement of responses that are similar to (approximate) the one you are interested in and the nonreinforcement of all other responses.

Animal circus acts are developed through long painstaking hours of shaping, in which the animal's behavior is reinforced as it approximates the desired response.

Acquisition: In operant conditioning, an increase in the frequency of an emitted response or the appearance of a new (i.e., previously unobserved) response.

Once the animal has made the desired response, the experimenter simply reinforces it when it occurs again. In a short time the animal will learn to repeat the response. Technically speaking, the animal is said to have **acquired** a response when it emits the response more frequently than it did prior to the introduction of reinforcement.

But who has conditioned whom? Has the experimenter conditioned the pigeon to peck at the light, or has the pigeon conditioned the experimenter to reward it for pecking? Operant conditioning, especially in the real world, can be a two-way street. For example, if you regularly frequent a particular coffee shop, you may think that by your generous tips you are reinforcing your waiter's prompt service. From his standpoint, however, his efficient service is reinforcement for your good tipping behavior. And what do you suppose might happen if you stopped leaving tips?

In the laboratory situation, the outcome of withholding reinforcement for a previously reinforced response results in a decrease in its frequency, or its **extinction.** Failure to provide a food pellet for pecking at a light for a pigeon that has previously been so reinforced results in a rapid decrease in the frequency of the response.

Extinction: In operant conditioning, the procedure in which reinforcement is withheld for a previously reinforced response, which results in a decrease in the rate of the response.

Note that, in operant conditioning, extinction is accomplished by withholding a stimulus (the reinforcer) that *followed* the response. This differs from extinction in classical conditioning, which is accomplished by withholding a stimulus (the unconditioned stimulus) that *preceded* the response. However, as in classical conditioning, an extinguished response may **spontaneously recover.** That is, after decreasing in frequency due to lack of reinforcement, it may suddenly increase.

Spontaneous Recovery: In operant conditioning, a temporarily higher rate of responding observed at the beginning of a subsequent experimental session following a session in which extinction has occurred.

For example, a fisherman may be angling in one spot, getting a bite every three casts, and a catch every twenty, when all at once the fish stop biting. After twenty or thirty more casts getting nothing, the fisherman quits; his casting behavior at that spot is now extinguished. Yet two hours later, if he is a practiced fisherman, he is likely to be back in the same spot casting; his behavior pattern has spontaneously recovered.

Spontaneous recovery of a response can be especially disconcerting when the response in question is of significance to the individual's emotional or physical health, as in the spontaneous recovery of headbanging behavior in a severely disturbed child. In clinical situations, to enhance its effectiveness, extinction is often combined with a program of positive reinforcement. In this way, desirable behaviors are strengthened, while at the same time the frequency of undesirable behavior is reduced.

FACTORS THAT INFLUENCE ACQUISITION AND EXTINCTION

Given the relevance of operant conditioning to clinical situations as well as to everyday behavior, scientists have devoted considerable energy to understanding the factors that influence the acquisition and extinction of a response. One of the most important, they have discovered, is the schedule on which a response is reinforced.

Schedules of Reinforcement

The term **schedule of reinforcement** is used to describe both the pattern and the frequency of reinforcements that occur to strengthen a response. Schedules may be divided into several categories. (See Figure 6.9 for a schematic overview.) On the most basic level, they may be distinguished according to whether or not reinforcers are delivered unfailingly, following every occurrence of a given response. On a **continuous schedule** of reinforcement, every occurrence of a given response is followed by a reinforcer. On an **intermittent schedule** of reinforcement, only selected occurrences of a given response are followed by a reinforcer.

Intermittent reinforcement more closely resembles real life than continuous reinforcement. Seldom if ever does a person receive reinforcement for every instance of a response. No matter how hard you study, sometimes you get a good grade, sometimes you don't. Or you ask someone for the time; sometimes you get it, sometimes you don't.

As a general rule, responses are acquired more quickly on a continuous schedule of reinforcement than on an intermittent schedule. It stands to reason that your dog will learn to sit faster if you give it a biscuit every time it obeys. But responses also extinguish more quickly on a continuous schedule than on an intermittent schedule. Again, this stands to reason. If your dog gets a biscuit every time it obeys and then suddenly gets nothing, the shift to nonreinforcement will be much more distinguishable to your dog than if it is accustomed to getting a biscuit only once in a while. One of the great advantages of an intermittent schedule of reinforcement, then, is that it develops resistance to **extinction,** which in operant conditioning is measured in terms of the endurance of a response beyond the withdrawal of reinforcement. One way to combine the advantages of the two schedules is to use a continuous schedule during the acquisition of a response, then shift to an intermittent schedule before withdrawing reinforcement altogether.

Little was known about intermittent schedules until Skinner made an accidental discovery in his laboratory (Skinner, 1938, 1956). He was running an experiment with rats when he discovered he didn't have enough food pellets to last through the afternoon. At first he thought he would have to quit early. Then he got an idea. Instead of giving the rats a pellet each time they responded, he would ration the pellets at the rate of one per minute. In this way, Skinner had devised a special kind of intermittent schedule, called an **interval schedule,** based on the passage of time. On an interval schedule,

Schedule of Reinforcement: The pattern and frequency of reinforcements that occur to strengthen a response.

Continuous Reinforcement: Reinforcement of every response.

Intermittent Reinforcement: Noncontinuous reinforcement in which some, but not all, occurrences of a response are followed by a reinforcer.

Extinction: In classical conditioning, the reduction and gradual elimination of the conditioned response through unpaired presentations of the conditioned stimulus.

Interval Schedules: Intermittent schedules of reinforcement based on the time.

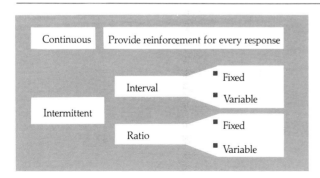

Figure 6.9 Schematic Overview of Schedules of Reinforcement.

Ratio Schedules: Intermittent schedules of reinforcement based on the number of responses emitted by an organism.

Fixed Schedule: A consistent schedule of reinforcement in which each reinforcement is based on the same numbers of responses or the same interval of time.

Variable Schedule: An inconsistent or irregular schedule of reinforcement in which each reinforcement is based on a different number of responses or on a different interval of time.

Fixed Ratio (FR): A schedule of intermittent reinforcement in which a response is reinforced after a fixed number of responses. (Ratio refers to the ratio of responses per reinforcement.)

the first response to occur after the interval has passed is reinforced, no matter how many responses are made during the interval. Another kind of intermittent schedule, the **ratio schedule,** is based on the number of responses made by the organism. On a ratio schedule, a subject must make a certain number of responses before getting a reinforcer.

Skinner tried numerous versions of both ratio and interval schedules to see what their effects would be. He found that results differed depending not only on whether he used ratio or interval schedules, but on whether or not he varied the pattern of reinforcement. In a **fixed schedule,** reinforcers are provided following either a specific number of responses or a specific amount of time. In a **variable schedule,** reinforcement is inconsistent: the number of responses or the amount of time between reinforcers varies.

Schedules in which a fixed number of responses must be made for each reinforcer are called **fixed ratio (FR) schedules.** The fixed ratio schedule generally produces high response rates. Since reinforcement is based on the number of responses, the subject makes a lot of responses. Because reinforcement does not usually occur twice in a row, however, the subject who wants a rest can afford to pause after each reinforcement—and quickly learns to do so. Typically the subject makes the prescribed number of responses, is reinforced at the rate fixed, and then pauses briefly. The pause is followed by a burst of activity that lasts until the next reinforcement. Witness the factory worker who is paid a dollar for every six items assembled. A worker keeping count of her production assembles six items, takes a short breather, hurries to assemble six more, and so on. During extinction the breaks, or pauses between reinforcers, grow longer and longer, until finally the response rate approaches zero.

The behavior of this slot machine player is maintained on a variable ratio schedule of reinforcement. Hitting the jackpot depends on the number of responses, but the number varies unpredictably.

In the **variable ratio (VR) schedule,** reinforcement again depends on the number of responses made, but the number varies unpredictably. First three responses might be required, then two, then five, six, and four. The variable ratio schedule produces a high response rate with no pause following reinforcement. Because subjects can never tell how many responses to make for the next reinforcer, they respond at a steady high rate. People who gamble are on a variable ratio schedule. The craps player may throw the dice and get three winning sevens in a row, or he may throw twenty times without getting a seven; he never knows. People who work on commission are also on a variable ratio schedule. Responses established on this kind of schedule are extremely difficult to extinguish; they continue steady and high long after reinforcement has been withdrawn. Eventually pauses do occur; they lengthen and increase in frequency until the response finally ceases.

Interval schedules produce noticeably different results from ratio schedules. In a **fixed interval (FI) schedule,** a specific amount of time must pass before reinforcement is made available. Timing begins from the last reinforced response, but the interval is held constant for each reinforcement. Responses that occur before the interval has elapsed are ignored. The fixed interval schedule produces a pause immediately after reinforcement, followed by a gradual increase in the rate of response as the end of the interval draws near. (Note the difference from response to the fixed ratio schedule, in which the initial pause is followed almost immediately by a high rate of response.) Students in a large lecture course, as opposed to a small discussion group, are on a fixed interval schedule. No matter how much they study, their only opportunity to show their knowledge is on exams, say once every three weeks. If you are like most students in such a course, you probably won't study much the first week or second. As the end of the three-week period comes closer, however, you will begin to study with increasing frequency. Cramming for an exam at the last minute is an especially good example of the effect of a fixed interval schedule. Responding is low until just before the interval elapses, when it becomes high. Following the exam is the characteristic pause and low levels of responding of the fixed interval schedule until the deadline for the next exam grows near.

On a **variable interval (VI) schedule,** reinforcement occurs after varying amounts of time. A typical cycle might contain intervals of one minute, five minutes, three minutes, and seven minutes. Reinforcement occurs for the first response following the prescribed interval. All others are ignored. The variable interval schedule produces a steady rate of response with no pause following reinforcement. The response rate is not as high as on a variable ratio schedule, however. Extinction occurs gradually and steadily, with no pauses or rapid change in response rate as in the other three schedules. Police and firefighters are on a variable interval schedule. They never know how much time will pass before they will again be called for duty. Thus, they remain ready to respond to an emergency even during relatively long intervals of no action. Table 6.2 summarizes the four basic types of intermittent schedules of reinforcement.

The effects of the various schedules of reinforcement can be seen when the rates of response they produce are graphed. Fixed ratio and variable ratio schedules yield the steep curves characteristic of high rates of response (see Figure 6.10). The short pauses that occur after reinforcement in the

Variable Ratio (VR): A schedule of intermittent reinforcement in which the number of responses necessary for each reinforcement varies after each reinforcement.

Fixed Interval (FI): A schedule of intermittent reinforcement in which the first response occurring after a fixed time interval, measured from the preceding response, is reinforced.

Variable Interval (VI): A schedule of intermittent reinforcement in which reinforcements are provided at irregular intervals.

Table 6.2 Schedules of Reinforcement—A Summary

	Fixed Ratio (FR)	Variable Ratio (VR)	Fixed Interval (FI)	Variable Interval (VI)
Reinforcement Occurs...	...after fixed number of responses	...after varied, unpredictable number of responses	...after passage of fixed amount of time	...after passage of varied unpredictable amounts of time
Rate and Pattern of Response	● High	● High	● Pause after each reinforcement	● High
	● Pause after each reinforcement	● Steady with no pause	● Gradual increase in response	● Steady with no pause
Pattern of Extinction	● Increasingly long pauses approaching zero	● Difficult	● Increasingly long pauses approaching zero	● Gradual steady
		● Eventual long pauses approaching zero		

Scallop-Shaped Curve:
A fan-like response curve that reflects an accelerated rate of performance as the end of an interval grows near in a fixed interval schedule of reinforcement.

fixed ratio schedule are reflected in small horizontal steps, which makes the fixed ratio curve look like a steep staircase. Interval schedules produce flatter curves. The long pauses and accelerating response in the fixed interval schedule is reflected in a **scallop-shaped curve.**

Of course, nothing is ever as neat in real life as it is in the laboratory. Most life situations involve a combination of two or more of the basic schedules (Ferster & Skinner, 1957). For the person who enjoys fishing, reinforcement is based both on the number of responses (casting the line) and amount of time spent. Specifically, fish usually bite at irregular intervals following an irregular number of casts. Thus, fishermen are on a combined VI–VR schedule.

Schedules of reinforcement help to explain much that is exasperating or puzzling about human behavior: procrastination and sudden flurries of activity, and the persistence of a behavior long after it has ceased to be rewarding. You might want to look at your own behavior with an eye toward the schedules on which it is reinforced and the reinforcers that are maintain-

Figure 6.10 Typical cumulative curves for four different schedules of reinforcement. In obtaining these curves, a device records the total number of responses an organism emits within a given amount of time. The recorder releases paper at a fixed time and a pen traces the subject's record of responding. Each time a subject emits a response, the pen moves upward a notch. Otherwise the pen doesn't move. With little or no responding, the pen records a straight, horizontal line. High rates of responding cause the pen to move upward again and again, producing a steep curve.

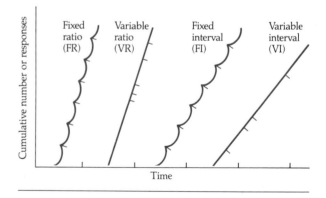

ing it. Have you felt annoyed by someone continually asking for a favor and said yes once or twice just to avoid hurting his or her feelings? If so, that person's approaches may prove difficult to extinguish. Consistency is essential in extinguishing a previously reinforced response.

Similarly, you can use the knowledge that response rates increase as deadlines draw near by setting a goal and a deadline for its achievement. Try finishing a chapter in two hours, for example. Make sure that you can't obtain reinforcers (food, cigarettes, telephone, or television) before you finish. You are more likely to succeed under those conditions than if you set no time limit for yourself (Huber, 1985).

Nature and Timing of Reinforcement

We have seen how schedules of reinforcement can have a powerful effect on the strength of a learned response. Two additional factors that affect the acquisition of a response are the nature of reinforcement—its quality and quantity—and the timing of its delivery.

All else being equal, high-quality reinforcers produce faster acquisition, greater resistance to extinction, and more rapid response rates. That is, a highly desirable or attractive reinforcer, like a piece of meat for a hungry dog, will usually produce better results than a run-of-the-mill reinforcer like a dog biscuit. A high-quality negative reinforcer—one that is extremely unpleasant or harmful—is more effective than a less aversive stimulus. You learn more quickly to put on your coat in below-zero weather than you do when it is cold but not freezing. The more aversive the stimulus, the stronger the learning.

Likewise, many reinforcers are more effective than a few. Two food pellets generally produce stronger conditioning than one. A $4,000 commission for the sale of a house is more effective than a $400 commission for the rental of the same house. Other things being equal, a real estate agent will learn to try for a sale before settling for a rental of the same property.

The idealized curve in Figure 6.11 expresses the relationship between the quality and quantity of reinforcement and a subject's performance. Performance goes up as the quality and quantity of the reinforcer rises.

The timing or **immediacy of reinforcement**—how quickly a reinforcer follows a response—is among the most important influences on the strength of learning. To be effective, reinforcement must be delivered as soon as possible after a response. The longer reinforcement is delayed, the weaker the learning (see Figure 6.12). In animals, delays of just a few seconds can reduce the effectiveness of a reinforcer to zero. Humans are not so easily affected, perhaps because of previous experience with long delays. Nevertheless, Skinner and others have argued that employers and educators might use reinforcers more effectively by delivering them more quickly. Instead of waiting days or weeks to give students the results of an exam, teachers might find a way to return the scores within twenty-four hours.

The effectiveness of immediate reinforcement can help explain a number of common, but peculiar, everyday happenings. A gambler who strikes a jackpot on a slot machine after rubbing the winning coin subsequently may rub all coins destined for the slot machine. In such cases reinforcement oc-

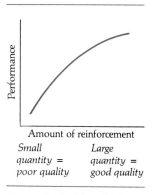

Figure 6.11 The relationship between performance (vertical axis) and quantity (quality) of reinforcement (horizontal axis).

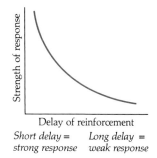

Figure 6.12 The relationship between performance (vertical axis) and delay of reinforcement (horizontal axis).

Immediacy of Reinforcement: The speed with which reinforcement follows a response.

curred immediately following a response, but only as a coincidence. Skinner has argued that such superstitious behaviors might be explainable in terms of operant conditioning.

Skinner (1948) noted that pigeons would perform all sorts of unreinforced behaviors—circling the box, bowing, walking back and forth—before making a learned pecking response. If pecking was the only response that had been reinforced, why did the pigeon bother to perform the other responses? Skinner's explanation: pigeons tend to repeat any behavior that they happen to be doing at the time of reinforcement. If by coincidence they are bobbing their heads when a food pellet appears, they will bob their heads more often in the future.

Conditions for Reinforcement

So far, our discussion of operant conditioning has focused on the reinforcers that follow a response. But the conditions that precede a response also have an effect on the strength of learning. As a rule, the strength of an operant response is greatest under conditions that existed when the response was reinforced. The gambler who hits the jackpot on a slot machine after rubbing the winning coin will tend to repeat the coin rubbing, but only when gambling—not when receiving change from a store clerk or when leaving a tip at a lunch counter. And the child who is reinforced with praise for raising her hand in the classroom will raise her hand more often, but only in the classroom. At home, the conditions that accompanied the reinforcer don't exist.

At first glance, these conditions may resemble the role of unconditioned stimuli in classical conditioning. But note that in this case the conditions do not *elicit* the response, as in classical conditioning. They merely indicate or signal that a reinforcer is likely to be available.

Discriminative Stimuli: The conditions that signal the availability of reinforcement or set the occasion for responding.

Stimulus Control: The tendency for the probability or rate of responding to vary with the presence and absence of a signal.

Stimulus Generalization: In operant conditioning, the phenomenon in which an organism that has been reinforced to emit a response to one stimulus emits the same response to similar stimuli, though to a lesser degree.

The conditions that signal the availability of a reinforcer are called **discriminative stimuli.** Discriminative stimuli are all around you. McDonald's golden arches, vacancy signs outside motels, twenty-four-hour liquor stores with lights flashing on and off, and so on. Responses that occur with greatest frequency under certain circumstances, such as going to the grocery store during business hours or showing up for class at the scheduled times, are said to be under **stimulus control.** That is, they occur almost exclusively in the presence of the discriminative stimulus, which signals the availability of reinforcement, and occur infrequently, if at all, in its absence.

Stimulus generalization occurs in operant conditioning when a response is under the stimulus control of a stimulus that only resembles a discriminative stimulus. A pigeon that has been reinforced to peck at a yellow light, for instance, will peck more at any colored light than a pigeon that has never been so reinforced (see Figure 6.13). Stimulus generalization explains why we sometimes mistakenly ask for assistance from another shopper wearing clothing that resembles that of the clerks in a hardware or department store. Stimulus generalization also occurs when we respond with contempt to all members of a religious or ethnic group on the basis of an experience with only one individual from the group. As in classical conditioning, stimulus generalization occurs when a new stimulus shares some physical property, such as light, with the original stimulus. In fact, the stimulus gen-

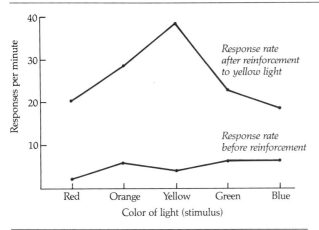

Figure 6.13 Stimulus Generalization in Operant Conditioning. *The bottom line of the figure shows the average pecks per minute a pigeon made for variously colored lights before reinforcement. As the line indicates, before reinforcement responding was low and approximately equal for all colors. The top line shows the average number of pecks to variously colored lights after the pigeon had been reinforced for pecking at a yellow light. (After Reynolds, 1968).*

eralization curve produced in operant conditioning is remarkably similar to the stimulus generalization curve produced in classical conditioning. Compare Figure 6.5 with Figure 6.13.

In a reverse process, subjects can learn to respond differently to similar stimuli. If a pigeon is reinforced for pecking at two lights of different color, and reinforcement is then withheld for one color, the pigeon will learn to tell the difference between the two. The curve in Figure 6.14 illustrates the rapid decline in response to the unreinforced light that occurs under these conditions. This difference in the rate of response to two stimuli that share some properties but not others—a red light versus a green light, soft tone versus loud tone—is called **stimulus discrimination.** Humans are adept at stimulus discrimination. A high school student who asks a lot of questions of one teacher and few of a second is displaying stimulus discrimination. Perhaps

Stimulus Discrimination: In operant conditioning, a different rate of responding to two stimuli produced by a different rate of reinforcement for the two (for example, reinforce for pecking at a red key, don't reinforce for pecking at a green key).

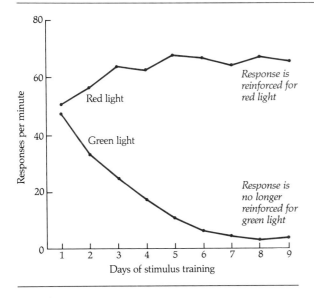

Figure 6.14 Stimulus Discrimination in Operant Conditioning. *During acquisition the pigeon had been reinforced for pecking at either a red light or a green light and had come to respond to the two with a similar frequency of responses. To form the discrimination, the experimenter withheld reinforcement for pecks at the green light, but continued to reinforce pecks at the red light. With each day of the experiment the pigeon's response to the two lights became increasingly different. By the ninth day the pigeon was making less than five responses per minute to the green light and more than 60 per minute to the red light. (After Reynolds, 1968).*

■ Learning Check ■

Read the right side, then cover and try to recite. Repeat.

Five phenomena that can be observed in both classical and operant conditioning.

1. Extinction
2. Spontaneous Recovery
3. Resistance to Extinction
4. Stimulus Generalization
5. Stimulus Discrimination

the first teacher reinforced the student for asking questions by giving good answers, while the second rejected questions.

Like stimulus generalization, stimulus discrimination occurs in both operant and classical conditioning, and the curves produced by the two bear a remarkable resemblance to each other. Compare the curve shown in Figure 6.6 with the curve in Figure 6.14.

The fact is, classical and operant conditioning have so much in common it is often difficult to determine where one leaves off and the other begins (Hearst, 1979). If a young child touches a hot stove, she may associate the pain of being burned with the stove and consequently may come to fear the stove. On the other hand, since touching the stove resulted in a negative consequence, the child will be hesitant to repeat the behavior. Through classical conditioning the child learned to associate two stimuli (the stove and heat). Through operant conditioning the child learned to associate a response (touching the stove) with a stimulus (heat). In such learning situations, particularly those involving avoidance and punishment, both classical and operant conditioning occur at the same time.

CHALLENGES TO THE BEHAVIORIST VIEW OF LEARNING

The strong influence of the American psychologists Thorndike, Watson, and Skinner produced a "behaviorist" school of learning theory based on the learning principles discussed above. Behaviorists maintained that all learning can be explained on the basis of classical and operant conditioning originating from the environment. This idea has been challenged by researchers who suggest that the learning process can be strongly influenced by the characteristics that learners bring to the situation. We will see that the behavior of learners can be shaped by more than the environment; it is shaped by biologically determined patterns of behavior, as well as by the cognitive or thinking capacities of the organisms.

When Conditioning Doesn't Work

One of the reasons scientists first questioned conditioning as an explanation for all learning was that animals and humans don't always behave as conditioning theory dictates. According to behaviorist principles, one emitted response should be just as easy to condition as another. Pigeons will increase whatever response they happen to be emitting when they receive a reinforcer, from circling the cage to flapping their wings (Skinner, 1948). But researchers noticed some exceptions. Two psychologists who were conditioning animals to perform tricks as an advertising stunt found that the animals preferred innate behaviors to reinforcement. A raccoon they had taught to drop a token into a slot in order to start a music box insisted on treating the token as if it were a food object. Instead of dropping it into the slot, the raccoon went through the motions of washing it, as raccoons do with all their food. The raccoon did what was natural to it, not what it had been reinforced to do according to conditioning theory (Breland & Breland, 1961).

Chickens proved even more uncooperative. They had been repeatedly reinforced for standing still while a music box played, but that behavior was almost impossible for them, even for fifteen seconds. Instead, they scratched at the platform, as if they were scratching for feed in a barnyard. Audiences found the chickens' behavior rather amusing, for they appeared to be dancing to the music. But, though the stunt was a success from an advertising standpoint, it was most unsettling to the behaviorists.

Like animals, humans do not always behave according to simple "laws" or principles of learning. In fact, humans are especially apt to produce surprises in the laboratory; they sometimes do the exact reverse of what is expected according to conditioning theory (Davison, 1973; Mahoney, 1974). Suppose you were placed in a desert-hot chamber (about 110° F.) and asked to indicate the louder of two tones by pressing one of two buttons. Depending on your response, you would receive either a blast of still hotter air or a refreshingly cool breeze. Which result would you work for? Believe it or not, college students placed in such a situation worked to produce a blast of hot air after they were told that it indicated a correct answer (Dulany, 1968). Their desire to get the right answer overcame the effects of the aversive blast of hot air.

All these phenomena call into question the formula of learning purely by environmental conditioning. Animals don't learn to associate just any two stimuli that occur together, or to repeat just any behavior that is followed by a reinforcer. Through inherited dispositions they somehow screen out stimuli and reinforcers that are irrelevant or unimportant to them. In other words, learning is often best viewed in terms of a product of an interaction between heredity (inborn qualities) and environment (life experience).

During the past two decades further evidence for biological predispositions toward learning has accumulated. We now know, for humans as well as animals, certain associations are more easily formed than others. Have you ever thought about the fact that many people learn to fear spiders, but few quake at the sight of a tree? To describe such apparent differences in ease of learning, psychologists use the term **preparedness,** meaning an inborn predisposition toward specific kinds of learning. The idea of preparedness runs counter to Pavlov's belief that any neutral stimulus—light, tone, footsteps—can become an effective conditioned stimulus by being paired with an unconditioned stimulus like meat powder.

Research with animals and humans has supported the idea of preparedness. In one study, volunteers were shown pictures of various objects and

Preparedness: An inherited predisposition to learn certain things. Prepared behaviors are behaviors that are learned rapidly due to an inherited predisposition.

Galvanic Skin Response (GSR): A drop in the electrical resistance of the skin associated with sweating.

organisms before receiving a mild shock. Some saw spiders or snakes, others flowers, fruits, or houses. The experimenters knew that a shock elicits a **galvanic skin response (GSR),** a drop in the electrical resistance of the skin. They found that the group that saw spiders or snakes developed an emotionally conditioned reaction to the animals, as shown by their GSR. After several shocks the pictures alone produced the GSR. The groups that saw flowers, fruits, or houses showed no special reaction to those stimuli when the shock was omitted (Öhman et al., 1975).

Similar predispositions can be seen in animals. Birds will learn to avoid certain foods they associate with illness. But, unlike humans and rats, they seem to blame their discomfort on sight rather than taste. For example, quail were given a sour, blue-colored water before they were given a dose of radiation that made them nauseous. Later, some of the birds were offered clear, sour-tasting water, others unflavored, blue-colored water. The birds drank the sour-tasting water freely but refused to drink the blue-colored water (Revusky, 1968). Thus, they seemed to associate their nausea with the color, but not the taste, of the water.

The implication of these preparedness experiments is that findings about learning in animals cannot always be applied to humans. Lever pressing in rats and pecking in pigeons may have little relevance to humans. Ultimately only human experiments can answer all of the questions of how humans learn.

Vicarious Conditioning

Imagine you are participating in an experiment on conditioning. You are told that half a second following the flash of a light, you will receive an electric shock that will produce a galvanic skin response in you. The aim of the experiment is to pair the light, a neutral stimulus, with the shock until the light alone elicits a change in GSR. How many times would you estimate you would need to be shocked before the light alone would elicit a GSR? The answer might surprise you: it's zero. A human being can acquire a classically conditioned response without a single direct exposure to an unconditioned stimulus.

In numerous studies, experimenters have found that simply telling subjects about an expected CS–US relationship could produce conditioning. In the typical demonstration of this phenomenon, subjects are hooked up to electrical equipment and told that a shock would follow the presentation of some neutral stimulus such as a light. As a rule the neutral stimulus elicits a GSR immediately, before delivery of a single shock. Indeed, some of these subjects show a stronger GSR than others who actually experienced light–shock pairings. Other studies have shown that a conditioned response formed by CS–US pairings can be extinguished in one trial—far fewer than usual—if subjects are *told* that the shock will no longer follow (Brewer, 1974).

Confederate: An assistant of the experimenter who pretends to be a subject in an experiment.

Subjects can also learn to react to a light just by observation. In one study, subjects observed **confederates,** or secret assistants of the experimenter, reacting as if they were being shocked half a second after a light was turned on. Tested later, the observers showed a GSR to the light. Neither group was shocked, yet conditioning occurred (Bandura & Rosenthal,

1966). This phenomenon, in which learning occurs through observation alone, without direct experience, is known as **vicarious learning.**

Vicarious learning occurs in animals as well as humans (Bandura, 1969). Pigeons that watch another pigeon being rewarded for pecking at a light will learn to peck at the light more quickly than usual. In the same way, humans will learn to solve problems or perform a task more quickly if allowed to watch others doing so. You've probably had the experience of becoming frustrated with the written directions for doing something, then mastered the process immediately after watching someone else do it.

Vicarious learning perhaps explains how a child can learn to be embarrassed by sex long before engaging in it. Watching a parent blush or become uncomfortable when the topic is mentioned teaches the child the parent's attitudes. It's as if the parent's attitudes are contagious. Vicarious conditioning might also explain how seeing one child punished for a behavior teaches many other children to suppress that behavior.

Vicarious learning cannot be explained by traditional S–R models of learning, which include only the stimuli (S) that precede or follow a response and the response (R) itself. The internal processes in learning—what goes on inside the learner—are not addressed. Yet learning that occurs by observation, without direct experience, must somehow involve processing within the organism. To account for phenomena such as vicarious learning, many psychologists have turned to what has been called S–O–R theory. The O in between the S and the R stands for *organism,* or the processing that occurs within the organism: mental representations, reasoning, imagining, remembering, and so forth (see Figure 6.15). Two new theories of learning have sprung from this approach, social learning theory and cognitive learning theory.

Vicarious Learning: Learning through observation alone, without direct experience.

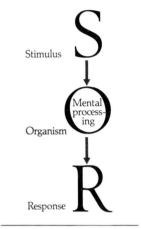

Figure 6.15 S—O—R Theory of Learning.

SOCIAL AND COGNITIVE LEARNING THEORIES

Cognitive and social learning theories emphasize the active role played by a learner. They focus on the mental representation that a person may create during the learning process, and also on how this internal picture is manipulated in the mind of a person who is learning by observing. According to these theories, the mere association of a response and reinforcement is not considered sufficient for learning; the learner must also be alert and aware, and paying conscious attention to the association in order to form a mental image of it (Carlson & Dulany, 1985).

Social Learning Theory

Social learning theory emphasizes the role of observation and imitation, especially for learning in a social context. Social learning theorists reject the view that we learn to act like our parents, family, and friends—acquire good table manners, for instance—by a slow process of the formation of stimulus–response associations through reinforcement. Instead, as vicarious con-

These students are learning ballet by watching their teacher demonstrate the proper behaviors. Such learning is a primary focus of the social learning theorists.

ditioning shows, people can show a newly learned behavior without having to go through the process of first emitting the new response and then receiving the reinforcer that is associated with it. Instead, the association of the response and reinforcer is observed by the learner, who forms a mental image or representation of it in his or her mind.

Support for the role of observation in human learning comes from a variety of studies (Bandura, 1969, 1977). In general, children will imitate an adult's behavior, especially if the results are rewarding. For example, preschool children who observed an adult choose between two compartments in a wooden box later made the same choice that the adult made. They also imitated other behaviors displayed by the adult that had nothing to do with the task; when the adult scratched his head, so did the child who was observing him. A child observes her parents being polite to guests and the positive response of the guests. The connection between politeness and a positive response is made as a mental image. Thus, the child displays new polite behavior toward guests without ever having emitted that response previously. She learns through observation and imitation (Ohnogi, 1985).

Because much learning takes place as a result of mental representations of events, as opposed to direct experience, the way events are interpreted plays an important role in the learning process. Thus, a major notion of social learning theory is that expectations and beliefs have an important bearing on what an individual learns and on what his or her response will be to any given stimulus (Bandura, 1986). For example, if you expect caring and kindness from a new instructor, then you might construe her correcting the assertions of another student during class discussion as constructive criticism. You might learn, then, that it's good to express your ideas in class, to clarify possible misunderstandings on your part. On the other hand, if you have been led to believe that the teacher is unsympathetic to students struggling to learn, then her same actions might be construed by you as harsh and critical. In this case, you would learn not to express your ideas.

The critical role of mental processes in learning, advocated by the social learning theorists, is the starting point for the newest, and one of the most popular, learning theories to gain acceptance among scientists—cognitive learning theory (White, 1985).

Cognitive Learning Theory

According to cognitive learning theory, all learning involves the acquisition of information in the form of **cognitions**—thoughts, memories, symbols—and the manipulation of that information by the mind. Cognitivists do not necessarily deny the existence of the kind of association-based learning observed by Pavlov and Skinner. Their point is that conditioning produces learning because it provides information—not because it strengthens a bond between stimulus and response. A conditioned stimulus works by telling a subject what is about to happen.

Suppose, for example, that you are participating in an avoidance experiment in which a bell signals that you are about to be shocked through an electrode resting beneath your finger. You quickly learn to withdraw your finger when the bell sounds. The question is, Why do you learn to do so? Cognitivists would say that the bell provides you with information about what is to come. You raise your finger because the bell informs you of the impending shock, not because of some automatic bond between the bell, the shock, and your response. To give another example, a mother praises her daughter for doing her homework. The praise informs the girl not only that mother is pleased, but that she can gain her praise in the future through similar behavior.

Cognitivists support their emphasis on information with experiments that show that, if a conditioned stimulus provides no new information, learning will not occur. Such an experiment typically follows the procedure for higher-order conditioning (see page 197), with one exception. After subjects have been exposed to a CS–US pairing such as a light and shock and a conditioned response has been established, the second neutral stimulus—say, a tone—is presented *at the same time as the light.* Under these conditions, subjects show little or no response to the tone when it is presented alone (Kamin, 1969). In other words, higher-order conditioning fails to occur. Cognitivists say that, because the tone occurs at precisely the same time as the conditioned stimulus, it provides no new information to the subject. These experiments are called **blocking experiments,** because the presentation of one conditioned stimulus at the same time as another is said to block the acquisition of a new conditioned response.

Other experiments have explored learning that seems to depend on the forming of mental images and expectations. Dawson and Schell (see Carpenter, 1985) measured the GSR of subjects who were shocked according to a specific pattern, following five different tones. Only certain tones in the pattern were followed by a shock. Some subjects figured out the pattern—that is, they showed a conditioned GSR response to the tones that had been paired with shock—while others showed no pattern of response to the tones.

Such evidence would seem to suggest that mental awareness—or lack of it—plays an important role in learning. If learning requires the acquisition of information and the formation of expectations, then the learner must necessarily be conscious of the process (see Box 6.2).

Cognitions: Thoughts, memories, symbols, mental representations, and all the processes and products involved in knowing.

Blocking Experiments: Experiments in which the signal value of a CS is blocked or masked due to an already established CS–US relationship.

Box 6.2 PSYCHOLOGY IN ACTION: Controlling Your Thoughts

From the cognitivists' stress on the role of awareness and thought in learning there have sprung a number of therapeutic tools. Among the most popular of these is a family of techniques known as *cognitive behavior modification,* a method of treating problem behaviors by modifying a person's thoughts (Meichenbaum & Genest, 1980). Cognitive behavior modification has shifted clinical applications of learning theory from overt behavior to cognitions.

The basic idea behind cognitive behavior modification is to control one's actions by controlling one's thoughts—in particular, the things a person mentally tells himself or herself. With the patient's cooperation, the therapist attempts to correct destructive patterns in the person's inner speech, on the assumption that what a person thinks has a powerful impact on what he or she does. The idea is that thoughts can be modified through reinforcement just as readily as observable actions can (Meichenbaum, 1977).

Suppose, for instance, that you are on a diet. On your way out to the library you notice a big piece of your favorite dessert sitting on the kitchen counter. Will you eat it? According to cognitivists, that depends on what you say to yourself. If you think something like, "I always blow my diet," "I won't be able to study if I don't eat," or "It's no use, I've starved myself all day and I haven't lost a pound," you will probably eat the dessert. You stand a better chance of resisting temptation if you tell yourself: "I'm not hungry," "I can live without that dessert," or "I'll study better if I'm not worrying that I blew my diet." In cognitive behavior modification therapy you would be made aware of your self-instructions and taught to adjust them to encourage self-control.

The modification process involves three phases. In the first phase, the patient identifies the problem behavior and observes related thoughts, feelings, and actions as well as any stimuli, internal or external, that precede or follow the problem behavior. In the second phase, the patient learns to develop a new inner dialogue by adopting cognitions and actions that interfere with the problem behavior. If the thought "Dieting is useless" is the first step on an eating binge, the person can be taught to think something contradictory as soon as that thought emerges: "If I have patience I can lose weight." The idea is to inhibit the harmful impulse as early as possible. In the third and final phase, the person learns how to apply the cognitive behavior modification technique to new behavior problems (Meichenbaum, 1977).

The impact of self-instructions on behavior has been demonstrated in a number of studies. In one experiment, nursery school children were asked to concentrate on fitting assorted pegs into a pegboard. While they were working, the experimenters attempted to distract the children with Mr. Clown, a dummy that emitted tape-recorded messages. "Hi, I have big ears and love it when children fill them with all those things they think and feel, no matter what," Mr. Clown would say. Some of the children had been warned that Mr. Clown would try to interfere with their work and had been given help in resisting. Children who were encouraged to resist by using temptation-inhibiting thoughts exclusively proved better able to resist Mr. Clown than others. By concentrating on telling themselves, "I'm not going to look at Mr. Clown," they generally succeeded in concentrating on the pegboard. Children who received only task-facilitating instructions—"I'm going to look at my work"—did no better than a control group that received no instructions. A group encouraged to use both temptation-inhibiting and task-facilitating statements did as well as, but no better than, the youngsters who received just the temptation-inhibiting instructions. (For more on cognitive behavior modification, see Chapter 15.)

The debate about the nature of learning is still ongoing. Reacting against cognitive theories of learning based on associations partly conditioned by mental images, B. F. Skinner replied sharply. Basing his arguments on his belief that behavior changes only because of changes in the environmental stimuli that surround us, he asserted:

> We need to change our behavior and we can do so only by changing our physical and social environments. We choose the wrong path at the very outset when we suppose that our goal is to change the minds and hearts of men and women rather than the world in which they live. (Skinner, 1978, p. 112)

Figure 6.16 Schematic Summary of Learning Theories.

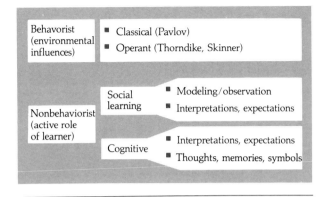

Figure 6.16 presents a schematic summary of behaviorist and non-behaviorist learning theories.

LEARNING FRAMEWORK

I. In classical conditioning, stimuli that are associated with those that set off reflex responses come to set off similar responses.
   A. In Pavlov's experiments, the meat powder elicited the reflex response, salivation. By pairing a light with the presentation of meat powder, the light came to set off salivation. (Review: *Figure 6.2*)
   B. The strength of a conditioned response depends on the frequency and order of pairings of a conditioned and an unconditioned stimulus, as well as on the time interval between presentations. (Review: *Resistance to Extinction*)
   C. Through experimentation Pavlov learned of the subtleties of classical conditioning. (Review: *Spontaneous Recovery; Stimulus Generalization; Stimulus Discrimination*)
II. Classical conditioning can be used to explain how we acquire irrational fears. (Review: *Higher-Order Conditioning; Emotional Conditioning; Table 6.1*)
III. Operant (and instrumental) conditioning emphasizes the consequences that follow behavior. (Review: *Thorndike's Laws of Effect and Exercise; Emitted Response; Operants*)
   A. Responses that lead to positive consequences or the removal of negative consequences are strengthened. Responses that lead to negative consequences become suppressed. (Review: *Escape; Avoidance; Figure 6.7*)
   B. Once a response has been acquired by reinforcement, it can be extinguished through lack of reinforcement. (Review: *Shaping; Acquisition; Extinction*)
IV. A number of factors influence the acquisition and strength of a response acquired by reinforcement.
   A. Response acquisition and resistance to extinction depend on the timing and pattern of reinforcement. (Review: *Figure 6.9; Table 6.2*)
   B. How quickly a subject acquires a response also depends on the quality, quantity, and timing of reinforcement. (Review: *Immediacy of Reinforcement; Figure 6.11; Figure 6.12*)

        C. Operant conditioning is also influenced by the antecedent conditions—those that precede a response. (Review: *Discriminative Stimuli; Stimulus Control; Figure 6.13; Figure 6.14*)

V. A number of phenomena challenge the behaviorist notion that all learning can be explained on the basis of classical and operant conditioning.

        A. Humans and animals don't always behave according to conditioning theory. (Review: *Preparedness*)

        B. Humans can acquire a classically conditioned response indirectly by observation. (Review: *Vicarious Learning; Figure 6.15*)

VI. Recent formulations go beyond the idea of stimulus–stimulus and stimulus–response associations in learning.

        A. Social learning theory argues that responses are learned indirectly through observation and mental representations of events.

        B. Cognitive learning theory stresses the informational value of direct experience and observations. (Review: *Cognitions; Blocking Experiments*)

CHAPTER

7

Memory

Chapter Outline

There is good evidence that one's ability to remember decreases slightly in later life (Jackson & Schneider, 1985). But at the 1985 United States senior chess championship, eighty-one-year-old international chessmaster, George Koltanowski, demonstrated an incredible feat of memory. On the stage sat a large chessboard. People in the audience were asked to provide some information that Koltanowski could not have known beforehand. The first person provided a phone number, which Koltanowski promptly wrote in one of the sixty-four squares of the chessboard. The next person gave her street address, which Koltanowski recorded in a second square. This continued until all sixty-four squares had been filled with people's birthdates, birthplaces, phone numbers, favorite movie stars, and anything else they could think of. There was a heavy silence as Koltanowski examined the chessboard for about three to four minutes. Finally, he turned his back to the board and faced the audience. A volunteer was asked to point to any square, which one of the judges of the event identified to Koltanowski as the "b6" square. "Let's see," said Koltanowski, "in the b6 square is a phone number, 693–9436." Then the volunteer was asked to place a knight, a chess piece that moves in the shape of an L, on the b6 square. His back still turned, Koltanowski directed the knight's path through the rest of the squares on the board, identifying them by their contents, without ever entering the same square twice or making so much as one small error.

Koltanowski's memory is indeed remarkable. In 1937 he set the world record for blindfold chess by taking on thirty-four players at the same time. Facing away from the boards, he told the referee (teller) his thirty-four moves, one for each board. The teller then went to the players one at a time, told them Koltanowski's moves, recorded their moves, and returned to tell Koltanowski. Koltanowski replied with thirty-four new moves—and so on until the end of the game. The result, after twelve and a half hours of play: twenty-four wins for Koltanowski, and ten draws (Koltanowski, 1985). More recently, in Marin County, California on March 5, 1986, Koltanowski, at the age of eighty-two and a half, played five games of simultaneous blindfold chess, winning four, drawing one.

I was fortunate to have met up with Koltanowski about twenty-five years ago, when I was still in high school. I and several others started following Koltanowski to his exhibitions and chess tournaments. Eventually he began teaching us the secrets of his phenomenal memory. No, I never became a blindfold chess expert. But what I did learn has put me forever in Koltanowski's debt, for it has helped me in so many ways in meeting the challenges of everyday life. In this chapter I will try to help you with the practical problem of developing more effective ways of using your memory. To accomplish this, we will examine how psychologists have attempted to understand its mysteries.

WHAT MEMORY IS

The term memory comes from the Latin word *memoric*, meaning "to be mindful of" or "to serve as a reminder." And often people do think of memory in the limited sense of remembering, of retrieval of information once learned. People who claim to have a poor memory for names don't mean that they cannot learn a new name and use it in the course of a conversation. They mean that on some future occasion they will probably have trouble recalling the name. Given the right cues, like a photograph or a fragment of a conversation, such people may suddenly retrieve the forgotten name from its place in memory. They don't really have poor memories, just poor retrieval skills.

If we take a closer look at Koltanowski's feats, we can get a better idea of the various aspects of memory. First, he must take the information in, as when he examines the sixty-four squares containing people's birthdates, telephone numbers, and other bits of information. In other words, he must transform external information into a code or internal representation—a process psychologists call **encoding.** Then, after he encodes the information he

Encode (Encoding): Getting information into memory by transforming it into a code or internal representation; transforming input information into a form the memory system can use.

At the age of 82, chessplayer George Koltanowski still exhibits remarkable feats of memory.

■ **Learning Check** ■

Read the right side, then cover and try to recite. Repeat.

Three important aspects of memory:

1. Encoding—transforming input into a usable internal code

2. Retention—holding information in storage

3. Retrieval—recalling stored experiences

Retention: Storage of information. Holding information in storage for later use.

Retrieve (Retrieval): Recovering or extracting previously encoded information; to call back or recall; the act of bringing stored experiences into a conscious, activated state.

Memory: The process of encoding, retaining, and retrieving information and experience; the capacity that permits organisms to benefit from past experience.

must concern himself with its storage or **retention**—holding information in storage for later use. But the mere ability to store information does not account for Koltanowski's memory feats; he also must be able to call back or recall stored information in order to use it. This process of recovering previously encoded material psychologists call **retrieval.**

Memory can be defined in terms of these three processes—encoding, retention, and retrieving information and experience. Memory is the capacity that permits us to benefit from past experience (Tulving, 1985). Because of it we are able to transform input information into a form that we can hold and retrieve for later use.

In this chapter we will consider how psychologists have attempted to understand and study memory. First we will consider the question of how and why we forget, which was a major focus of early approaches to memory. Next we will consider a major viewpoint that divides memory into different storage compartments. We will then contrast the compartments theory to an alternative theory which emphasizes different types of memory processes. Then we will consider the question of how our memories are organized and structured. Finally, we will focus on the issue of how we get things in and out of memory—the encoding and retrieval of memories. In so doing, we will consider some strategies for memory improvement. Throughout we will see how psychologists' attempts to understand memory have led to information of practical, everyday relevance.

EARLY APPROACHES TO MEMORY: HOW AND WHY WE FORGET

Like people who think of memory in terms of their ability to retrieve names, the first psychologists to study memory tended to concentrate their efforts on the question of how and why we forget. Such was the thrust of a series of studies by Herman Ebbinghaus (1850–1909), who developed some of the earliest procedures for the experimental study of memory.

Ebbinghaus's Curve of Forgetting

Ebbinghaus's goal was to study memory by the scientific method. To accomplish this task he had to find a standard unit of measure, free of meaning or prior associations that could bias his results. He rejected words, sentences, and prose paragraphs as unsuitable for that purpose. Eventually he hit on the **nonsense syllable,** a meaningless combination of consonant, vowel, and consonant—for instance, *zeg, bok,* or *xac.* Ebbinghaus constructed a pool of over two thousand such syllables, from which he selected up to forty items at a time for use in his experiments. Using himself as a subject, Ebbinghaus tried to measure the rate of **forgetting**—the inability to make use of or retrieve information previously experienced.

Ebbinghaus used a technique known as **savings method,** in which he calculated how much time he saved in relearning. First he would learn a list of nonsense syllables through **rote rehearsal**—reading the list again and again, without regard to its meaning or organization, until he could reproduce it perfectly. Then he would wait a certain amount of time. Finally he would attempt to relearn the list through rote rehearsal. The difference between the time it took him to learn the list the first time and the time it took him to relearn it was his savings, which he expressed as a percentage. For example, if he took ten minutes to learn a new list and five minutes to relearn it, his savings score would be 50 percent; his relearning time was only half as long as his original learning time.

In one marathon study Ebbinghaus learned and relearned over 1,200 lists, each of which contained thirteen nonsense syllables—a "heroic effort," as James (1890) put it. Each day he learned eight different lists of thirteen syllables each. Following a lapse of time from twenty minutes to thirty-one days long, he then relearned the lists. His goal was to determine how much information is forgotten (and how much retained) as a function of the time lapse between learning and relearning.

Figure 7.1, known as the **curve of forgetting,** shows Ebbinghaus's results (1885). After a twenty-minute interval, he saved almost 60 percent of his original learning time. Or, put another way, he sustained a 40-percent loss in learning after only twenty minutes! After an hour's lapse, Ebbinghaus's savings dropped to less than 50 percent. Thereafter his losses tapered off; savings went down only slightly between six days and thirty-one days.

Such findings reveal the futility of Ebbinghaus's rote rehearsal approach for students who attempt to study for an exam simply by repeating a list again and again without thinking. Indeed, the rapid forgetting Ebbinghaus reported using rote rehearsal is not an individual phenomenon. It has been

Nonsense Syllable: A meaningless three-letter combination of a consonant, a vowel, and another consonant (e.g., *zeg, bok, xac*).

Forgetting: The inability to make use of or retrieve information previously experienced.

Savings Method: A method for measuring forgetting by comparing the time it originally took to learn to the amount of time for relearning.

Rote Rehearsal: Memorizing without regard to meaning or organization.

Curve of Forgetting: Ebbinghaus's curve, which plots the decline in savings (or percentage of retention) as a function of the lapse of time since original learning.

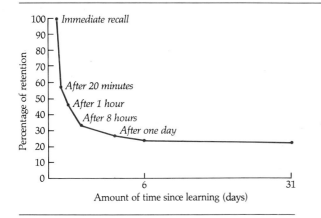

Figure 7.1 Ebbinghaus's curve of forgetting shows how much is retained (measured by relearning) as a function of elapsed time since the original learning. (After Ebbinghaus, 1885).

demonstrated several times in experiments involving groups of subjects (Woodworth & Schlosberg, 1954). Thus, we know that memorizing by rote, as in Ebbinghaus's approach, leads to rapid forgetting. But why is the forgetting so rapid? Why, indeed, does it occur at all?

Decay and Interference Theories of Forgetting

Decay Theory: A theory of forgetting that states that traces (hypothetical changes in the brain that result from experience) automatically fade away or "decay" with time.

Trace: The hypothetical physical changes in the brain that are the neurological correlates of learning and memory.

Amnesia: Loss of memory due to brain injury, surgery, or trauma.

Early theorists believed that the major cause of forgetting was **decay**—the fading away of a memory trace with the passage of time. According to this decay theory of forgetting, experience creates a memory **trace**—a physical change in the brain. With the passage of time, the trace wears out.

Though the decay theory seems sensible at first glance, it fails to explain a number of irregularities in the process of forgetting. How is it that a thing forgotten one day can be remembered the next? Undoubtedly you have had the experience of struggling in vain to remember a name or a fact, only to have the information pop into awareness a day or two later. This common personal experience has been noted by writers, philosophers, and scientists of many ages. The implication is that the information you cannot recall is not lost, but simply unavailable at the moment.

The most dramatic examples of rediscovered memories come from case histories of **amnesiacs,** people who have lost their memories because of head injuries (selective memory loss due to psychological causes will be discussed in Chapter 14). Shortly after an accident, victims may have trouble remembering their names, addresses, or even the appearance of close relatives. Fortunately, most amnesiacs gradually regain their memories within a few minutes or hours (Squire et al., 1985). They never actually lose their memories; they simply cannot retrieve them for a time.

Discoveries made by researchers eventually challenged the old decay theory. In a classic experiment, scientists asked two groups of college students to learn a list of ten nonsense syllables. One group then went to sleep; the second continued with its daily activities. Both groups were tested after one, two, four, and eight hours. The results were striking. Sleep consistently produced less forgetting than a comparable amount of time spent on waking activities (see Figure 7.2). The implication seemed to be that we forget not because of some passive decay process, but because new information interferes with old information (Jenkins & Dallenbach, 1924). This explanation of forgetting, which has some interesting implications for studying, became known as the **interference theory.**

Interference Theory: A theory of forgetting that states that a trace (hypothetical changes in the brain that result from experience) will persist unless or until something occurs that interferes with it.

Researchers soon devised new ways of testing the interference theory. In a typical experiment subjects would first learn a list of paired nonsense syllables—for instance, XAB–AOY, NOQ–TIX, and so on. Then they would be divided into two groups. One, the experimental group, would learn a new list; the other, the control group, would engage in some unrelated activity, such as piecing together a puzzle. Finally, both groups would be tested on the original list. Given the first item of a pair, subjects would be asked to supply the second. As researchers predicted, the control group consistently outperformed the experimental group. Apparently the information in the new list studied by the experimental group interfered with memories of the old list.

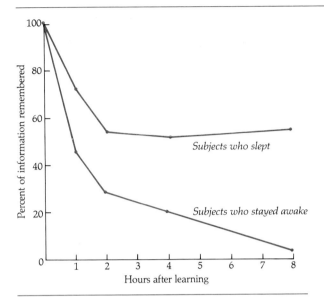

Figure 7.2 *This graph shows the amount of material remembered for subjects who slept immediately after learning and for subjects who continued normal waking activities after learning. As the graph shows, the subjects who slept remembered considerably more material (After Jenkins & Dallenbach, 1924).*

Thus, in their attempt to understand why people forget, psychologists gained information of practical everyday relevance: namely, that after having memorized something it is usually best to perform some unrelated activity (watch television, go for a drive, go to the movies) or go to bed. If at all possible, after cramming for an exam, one should not study another subject.

The interference of new learning on previous learning is called **retroactive interference** (retro means after). But new learning isn't the only source of interference. Old learning can also interfere with the formation of new memories. For example, if a company you do business with changes telephone numbers, you would probably have more trouble remembering the new telephone number than you would if you never knew the old one. Such interference, in which previous learning interferes with the formation of new memories, is called **proactive interference** (Underwood, 1957). Table 7.1 summarizes the two types of interference.

Retroactive Interference: The phenomenon in which new learning can interfere with previous learning.

Proactive Interference: The phenomenon in which previous learning can interfere with new learning.

Table 7.1 Retroactive and Proactive Interference

	Stage 1	*Stage 2*	*Stage 3 (Recall Task)*
RETROACTIVE Experimental Group	Learn List A	Learn List B	Recall List A
Control Group	Learn List A	Solve Puzzles (non-learning activity)	Recall List A
PROACTIVE Experimental Group	Learn List A	Learn List B	Recall List B
Control Group	Solve Puzzles (non-learning activity)	Learn List B	Recall List B

Although interference is still generally viewed as one possible source of forgetting (Nelson et al., 1985), and it can be demonstrated when meaningful materials (prose passages, for example) are used instead of nonsense syllables (Dempster, 1985), many researchers have complained that such procedures are too far removed from real life experiences to provide a complete understanding of forgetting (Bruce, 1985). Indeed, certain kinds of real life forgetting—the pain of a rejection or loss of a loved one—occur, not because of interference or decay, but because people want to forget (Geiselman & Bagheri, 1985). In the next section we will see why some psychologists attribute recall failures to a failure to transfer information from one memory compartment to another.

■ Learning Clue ■

As you read, keep in mind that the compartments theory views memory in terms of separate compartments that differ in terms of how much information they can hold (capacity) and how long they can hold it (duration).

THE COMPARTMENTS THEORY OF MEMORY

While Ebbinghaus was concentrating on how fast a person could memorize and forget, his contemporary William James (1890) was hypothesizing the notion of a distinction between different *types* of memory. James had observed that, when the mind receives a small amount of information—a street address, the time and date of a future appointment, or a specific fact—it remains readily available only for about twenty or thirty seconds. During this brief time one can recite it with ease; it does not have to be retrieved, for it has not yet been forgotten. James referred to this fleeting state of accessibility as "primary memory." Memories that had been stored away for later use, that had to be "fished up," so to speak, belonged to what he called "secondary memory."

To give a practical example of James's distinction, if someone tells you, "Okay, see you tomorrow at 10 a.m. in the library," that information will persist for a short time in your primary memory. You might even repeat it out loud just to show your friend that you got the message. Suppose, however, that moments later you are diverted by a chance encounter with someone you think you recognize. Immediately you delve into what James called your secondary memory in an effort to place the person. As you do, the contents of your primary memory may change. Instead of your planned meeting at the library, it is now filled with an awareness of the person you are trying to identify. When the person leaves, you find that the information about your upcoming meeting is no longer readily accessible. "Let's see," you ponder, "was that 9 or 10 a.m., and are we meeting at the cafeteria or the library?" The distinction between these two types of memory helps to il-

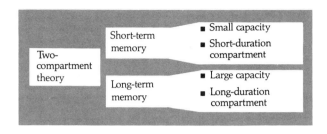

Figure 7.3 Schematic Summary of the Two–Compartments Theory.

lustrate that, if we do not make a special effort to record new information while it is still readily available, it can easily be lost.

Although James never suggested that his primary and secondary memory types were physically separate from each other, his distinction between the two set the stage for the development of just such an idea. In the **compartments theory,** memory is viewed as a system of interlocking storage compartments, each of which performs a different kind of information analysis. After information has been operated on by one compartment, it is transferred to another for further processing and storage.

At first theorists tended to think in terms of just two compartments, a short-term compartment, which corresponded to James's primary memory, and a long-term compartment that corresponded to secondary memory. More specifically, **short-term memory** was defined as a small-capacity and short-duration compartment in which information remains briefly available (for about thirty seconds) while being transferred to a much larger storage bin, long-term memory. **Long-term memory** was thought of as a very large capacity and long duration compartment—the permanent storage place for information (Atkinson & Shiffrin, 1968). (See Figure 7.3 for a schematic summary.) It was not long, however, before psychologists found evidence for a still more "primary" compartment called **sensory memory,** where first impressions are registered in our consciousness for a fleeting moment. In this section we will discuss each of these compartments in detail.

Sensory Memory: Forgetting in Less Than a Second

In an effort to explore the limits of short-term memory, psychologist George Sperling (1960) discovered evidence for a different memory compartment that held incoming information for less than a moment. How many letters or digits, Sperling wondered, could an individual remember after a

Compartments Theory: A theory of memory, which holds that memory is made of a series of separate, distinguishable storage compartments.

Short-Term Memory: Memory for short intervals, generally less than thirty seconds; a hypothetical small capacity and short duration compartment in which information is briefly held until it can be transferred to long-term memory.

Long-Term Memory: Memory for long retention intervals; a hypothetical large capacity and long duration storage compartment, in which permanent memories are held.

Sensory Memory: The initial representation of an external stimulus in the nervous system; the hypothetical storage compartment in which information is very briefly retained in an unprocessed state while being transferred to short-term memory.

■ Learning Check ■

Read the right side, then cover and try to recite. Repeat.

Three hypothetical memory compartments:

1. Sensory Memory
2. Short-Term Memory
3. Long-Term Memory

single brief presentation? To find out, he devised a way to expose subjects to matrices of letters and numbers for just a split-second.

A typical matrix looked like the one shown in Figure 7.4. Printed on a card, it was placed in a machine called a **tachistoscope,** a kind of rapid-fire viewer. The tachistoscope illuminated the screen on which the image of the card is projected with a carefully timed light flash.

In general, a human takes about two-tenths of a second to make a voluntary eye movement. Sperling presented his matrices for only one-twentieth of a second, a period long enough for subjects to see them but much too fast to permit eye movement. Thus, subjects got no more than a fleeting glance at the matrix. After exposing a matrix, Sperling would ask subjects to report as many letters or numbers as they could. Using this **whole report technique,** he found that, no matter how many rows of letters or numbers were printed on a matrix, subjects could, on the average, recall only about five items (Sperling, 1960). This low rate of recall bothered the subjects, for they were sure they had seen the entire matrix. In fact, a few reported that they could still see the matrix for a brief time even after the light went out.

If subjects had seen the entire matrix, why couldn't they recall every item? Even more curious, how could they have seen the matrix after the light went out? To answer these questions, Sperling proposed the existence of a *sensory memory compartment*, which briefly retained incoming information in raw form while it was being transferred to short-term memory. It was as if the eye took a picture of the outside world, a fleeting image which one researcher (Neisser, 1967) called an **icon** (the Greek word for image). The icon contained far more information than could be held in short-term memory; for a single brief exposure, a subject might see everything. But, if the amount of information in the icon exceeded the capacity of short-term memory, some of it would be lost through decay. The icon was the reason subjects could see a matrix even after the light had gone out. They didn't see the card; they saw the picture in their sensory memory.

Sperling used an ingenious method to demonstrate the existence of the icon. He presented the matrices to subjects again, but instead of requesting them to report as many letters as they could, he asked for only a **partial report.** After the letters had disappeared, he indicated which row of a matrix a subject should report by sounding tones of varying pitches—high for the first row, lower for the second, and so on (see Figure 7.4). Sperling found that even though the letters had disappeared *before* the tone sounded, sub-

Tachistoscope: An instrument used to present items for very brief durations (usually less than 200 milliseconds or two-tenths of a second).

Whole Report Technique: A technique in which subjects are asked to recall as much as they can from a briefly presented stimulus.

Icon: A hypothetical image or replica of an external stimulus, which was believed to be briefly retained in sensory memory while awaiting additional processing.

Partial Report Technique: A technique in which subjects are asked to report only a portion of a briefly presented stimulus, rather than the entire stimulus.

Figure 7.4 Sperling's Partial and Whole Report Techniques (*After Sperling, 1960*).

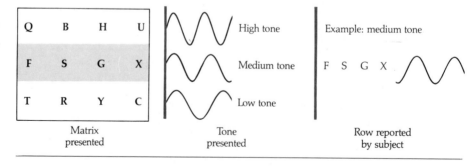

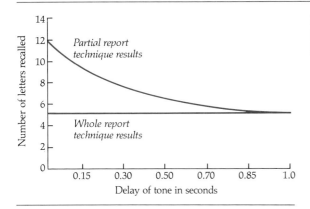

Figure 7.5 *This graph shows the difference in performance between the whole and partial report techniques. (After Sperling, 1960).*

jects could almost always report the designated row with perfect accuracy. It was as if they could see the letters even after they were gone—just as they had told him.

To measure the duration of sensory memory, Sperling varied the interval between the disappearance of the letters and the sounding of the tone. He found that, if the tone was sounded immediately after blackout of the letters, subjects had no difficulty reporting the designated row. As the interval between blackout and tone increased, however, subjects became less and less accurate in their recall. After an interval of just one second, performance dropped to a level no better than that achieved with the whole report technique (see Figure 7.5). Sperling concluded that the icon of sensory memory lasts only about a second.

Sperling's results have been replicated by other researchers, using both visual and auditory input (Crowder, 1976). Sensory memory for sounds is called *echoic memory* and may last up to four seconds. Presumably, our sensory systems are able to maintain an impression just long enough to allow us to experience a continuous stream of events, like a movie camera, rather than a sequence of discrete snapshots. Sensory memory is like a short-lived photographic memory, as discussed in Box 7.1.

In sum, Sperling's work had provided evidence for a sensory memory compartment where incoming information is first represented before being transferred to short-term memory. In the next section we will look at some of the experimental evidence that supported the existence of separate short-term and long-term memory compartments.

Eidetic Imagery (see Box 7.1): A visual image replica of an external stimulus that is no longer physically present; the ability to maintain a clear, vivid, and identical mental image of a stimulus after it has been experienced.

■ Learning Check ■

Read the right side, then cover and try to recite. Repeat.

Characteristics of sensory memory:

1. It holds information before it is transferred to short-term memory.

2. It is of very short duration.

3. It is of relatively large capacity—representing information much like a photograph (icon).

Box 7.1 PSYCHOLOGY IN ACTION: Photographic Memory

Too bad that sensory memory is so short, you say? Wouldn't studying be much easier if your mind could retain its fleeting snapshots? A few lucky individuals do actually have a photographic-like memory, called **eidetic imagery.** They report that they can "see" a visual replica of an external stimulus up to several minutes after it is no longer present.

The procedure for studying this skill is to show a subject a picture for about thirty seconds, remove it, and ask for a description of it. Subjects with eidetic imagery will describe even the most minute details of the picture, almost as if they were still looking at it. In one study, a boy was able to describe the complicated picture of Alice and the cat (see below) in striking detail, right down to the number of stripes on the cat's tail (Haber, 1969).

Investigations of eidetic imagery show that it is rare. It occurs mostly in children, but even the majority of children who are shown pictures such as this one either report seeing nothing following its removal or can provide only a vague description. Only about 5 percent of children under age twelve show evidence of eidetic imagery that lasts longer than thirty seconds. Most of them cannot retain exact replicas, as evidenced by omissions, additions, and distortions in their reports. Except in a very few cases, children with this skill lose it by adolescence or early adulthood.

The chessmaster George Koltanowski is one of the exceedingly rare adults with highly developed eidetic imagery skills. Koltanowski uses his imagery to good advantage in executing his memory feats, but he maintains that such imagery is only a very minor aspect of his memory skills (Koltanowski, 1985). Moreover, psychologists know of at least one case in which eidetic imagery worked to someone's disadvantage (Luria, 1968). "S" remembered only in images, not words. After looking at a picture for three or four seconds, the minimum amount of time he needed to imprint it in his memory, S could describe it in precise detail. If shown a large matrix of randomly arranged numbers, he could report them forwards, backwards, up and down, diagonally, or just about any other way desired. But S often found it difficult to remove an image

Look at this figure for 30 seconds, then try to describe it without looking. In one study a boy was able to describe a picture similar to this in striking detail, down to the number of stripes on the cat's tail.

from his mind. Sometimes one image would merge with another, as in a double exposure photograph. At other times sensations from different senses would merge, and S would hear "cold sounds" or see a "salty fence." And what was perhaps worse, S reported that he could not forget; his mind, he complained, was cluttered with useless trivia. He often had difficulty concentrating—simple conversations confused him to the point that those who did not know him well thought him slow-witted. Think about it. Would you really want your sensory memory to last longer than a second or two?

Experimental Evidence for Short-Term and Long-Term Compartments

According to the compartments theory, after information gets transferred to short-term memory (from sensory memory), it still must be transferred to the long-term memory compartment before it can become a relatively permanent part of our memory. In this section we will discuss three types of experimental evidence that supported the distinction between a short-term and long-term memory compartment.

Dichotic Listening. Among the earliest studies used in support of the compartments theory were **dichotic listening** experiments, studies in which subjects wearing headphones heard two different messages simultaneously, one in each ear. In a typical experiment, the right ear might hear the names of four different colors—red, blue, black, and green. The left ear might hear the names of four common objects—chair, pencil, bed, and book. The subject's task would be to repeat both messages. If you were participating in such an experiment, in what order would you repeat the items? Would you alternate between the two lists—"red, chair, blue, pencil"—or would you first repeat the entire message from one ear and then go on to the other?

Results showed that subjects consistently reported the entire message from one ear, then the message from the other (see Figure 7.6). How, scientists wondered, did subjects maintain the second message while reporting the first? The second one must have been held in a short-term storage compartment while the first was being reported, they reasoned (Broadbent, 1958).

The scientist who conducted these experiments, D. E. Broadbent, also found that if the messages heard by subjects contained seven items or more, most subjects could report only one message or the other. Presumably the second message decayed while the listener was attending to the first. You can probably think of a time when you were absorbed in your studies or in the conclusion of an exciting mystery novel and someone tried to interrupt you with a message. You may have heard the person's words and even acknowledged them, but later you insisted you never received the message. Broadbent (1958) would have argued that you received the message and held it temporarily in short-term memory. But, by the time you put down your book and started attending to other things, the message had decayed. You would not be able to remember the information because it was not transferred to long-term memory. Thus, one cause of forgetting is a failure to transfer information from one compartment to another.

Recall Studies. Support for short-term and long-term memory compartments also came from studies of subjects' ability to recall information after a brief interval. Consider, for example, the **serial learning method,** in which subjects were read a string of digits, letters, or words and then asked to recall them in the order they were presented. Subjects almost always make more errors for the items from the middle of the lists than for those presented first or last. Psychologists dubbed this phenomenon the **serial position effect.**

A variation of the serial method produced similar results. In the **free recall method,** subjects were asked to recall items in any order they wished (Murdock, 1962). Figure 7.7 shows the typical finding of such experiments. As the curve shows, recall was greatest for items presented last, a phenomenon known as the **recency effect.** Recall for items presented early,

Dichotic Listening: Listening to two different messages presented at the same time, one to each ear.

Figure 7.6 In the dichotic listening procedure, different messages are presented to the right and left ears at the same time.

Serial Learning: A technique of memory research in which items are presented in a specific order and must then be recalled in the same order.

Serial Position Effect: The phenomenon in which the percentage of errors is greater for items presented in the middle of a list than for those presented first or last.

Free Recall: Recalling, without the aid of notes or external cues, in any order of one's choosing.

Recency Effect: The phenomenon in which items presented at the end of the list are more easily recalled than those in the middle.

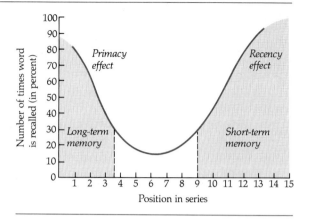

Figure 7.7 This graph illustrates both primacy (better recall for items presented at the beginning of a list) and recency (better recall for items presented at the end of a list) effects. Items presented first or last are more readily recalled than items presented in the middle of the list. (After Murdock, 1962).

though not as good as for those presented last, was far better than for those in the middle of the list. This phenomenon is known as the **primacy effect.**

Why were items in the middle of the list more difficult to recall? To many, the compartments theory provided the perfect explanation. By the time of recall, the items presented early would have been transferred to long-term memory. The items presented last would still be available in short-term memory. The items in the middle, however, would be in limbo. On their way out of short-term memory but not quite into long-term memory, these items, lacking a secure resting place, would be easy to lose.

Primacy Effect: The phenomenon in which items presented first in a list are more accurately recalled than those in the middle.

Auditory Confusion. Later experiments brought support for the two-compartment theory in the form of differences in errors made by subjects. In one study involving recall after a very short time lapse (thirty seconds or less), many of the errors proved due to auditory confusion—a mix-up based on the sound of an item. Subjects who had read a printed list of letters confused letters by sound rather than by shape. They mistakenly confused V with B or S with X, for instance. Rarely did they confuse letters that looked alike, such as T and F (Conrad, 1964).

To scientists, these findings suggested that items contained in short-term memory were represented in an **acoustic code** (a code based on sound). Presumably, before a visually presented item can enter short-term memory, it must be transformed into a sound. Thus, a V is represented not as the visual image V, but as the sound *vee.*

Acoustic Code: Coding in terms of sounds or transforming visual information into words, as when the sight of a book is coded mentally in terms of the word "book."

Curiously, errors made after fairly long time lapses—twenty minutes or more—tended to be based on meaning rather than sound. Subjects asked to recall the word *tire* would often report a similar word, like *wheel*, instead; asked to recall *cart*, they would substitute *wagon*. Thus, long-term memory seemed to rely on an entirely different method of representation, which scientists called a **semantic code.** Once again, experimental evidence seemed to confirm the theory of two separate compartments of memory.

Semantic Code: Coding in terms of meaning.

In sum, three types of experimental evidence supported the compartments theory: (1) dichotic listening experiments; (2) recency and primacy effects in serial learning and free recall experiments; and (3) studies of auditory confusion for visually presented material. Such evidence had an important implication: briefly presented information in short-term memory will be lost unless it is transferred to long-term memory. Thus, when you hear a person's name, you cannot expect to remember it later unless you make an effort to get that information into long-term memory.

Neurological Evidence for Short-Term and Long-Term Compartments

Not just experiments, but case histories of brain-damaged patients lent support to the notion of separate short-term and long-term memory compartments (Scoville & Milner, 1957; Graf et al., 1985). For example, following brain surgery for severe, uncontrollable epileptic seizures, an individual referred to as "HM" emerged intact in all ways except one. He was unable to retain new information for much longer than a few seconds. Reduced to a moment-to-moment existence, he might ask the same question five times in as many minutes, each time as if it were the first. He reworked the same puzzles again and again, as if he had never seen them before. And, though the same nurses treated him day in and day out, he never got to know them. He even had to be reminded to eat (Milner et al., 1968). Yet he showed a good memory for events that had taken place before his operation.

HM suffered from an interesting type of amnesia known as **anterograde amnesia,** or an inability to learn or remember new information. Such amnesia is one of the most prominent symptoms in the crippling memory disorder of old age known as Alzheimer's disease (Ober et al., 1985). In the case of HM, an extensive study of his memory disorder led to the conclusion that HM's major problem lay in an inability to transfer information from short-term memory to long-term memory (Milner, 1966). HM's short-term memory was intact; he could repeat up to six or seven digits, letters, or words after a single reading. His long-term memory was also intact; he could recall events that happened before the operation. His problem, it seemed, was getting new information into permanent storage.

Other neurological evidence supported such an interpretation of HM's problem. Psychologists had long known that *electroconvulsive shock (ECS)*—an electric shock strong enough to produce a convulsion—causes a loss of

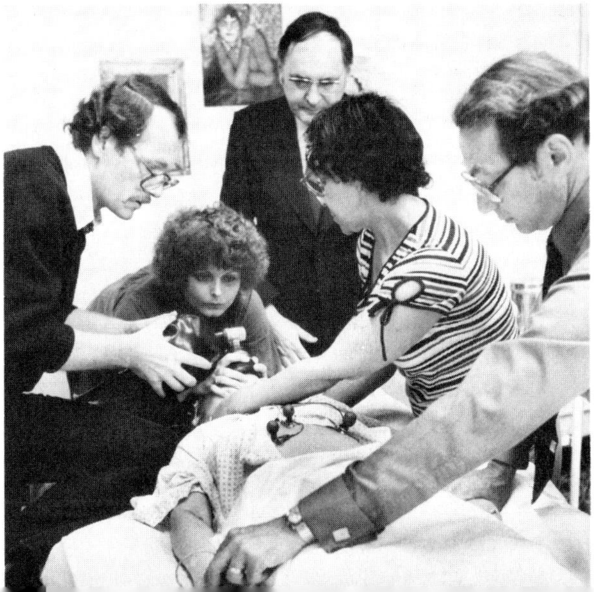

Anterograde Amnesia: An inability to learn or remember new information following brain injury or surgery.

Figure 7.8 Electroconvulsive Therapy. In electroconvulsive therapy (ECT) an electric current is passed through the brain, causing a convulsion. The memory losses that patients experience for events just prior to the treatment support the idea that short-term memories must be "consolidated" before becoming permanent.

Figure 7.9 Schematic Summary of Evidence for Separate Short-term and Long-term Compartments.

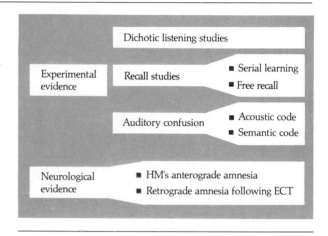

Retrograde Amnesia: The inability to recall the events that preceded some injury or traumatic event.

memory for events that occurred just before the shock. This **retrograde amnesia** is a common experience of patients undergoing *electroconvulsive therapy (ECT)* (see Figure 7.8) for severe depression (see Chapter 15). "What's happening?," "How did I get here?," "Where am I?" the confused patient demands. Some psychologists proposed that the shock these patients receive interrupts the passage of information from short-term to long-term memory, producing their memory loss.

Consolidation Theory: A theory that states experience sets up a trace, which requires a certain amount of time to become permanent. Forgetting is viewed as a failure in consolidation.

According to their theory, called the **consolidation theory** (originally formulated by Hebb, 1949), each new experience creates a trace—a chemical or structural change in the brain. Initially the trace is unstable, like a sand castle built at the edge of the beach at low tide. Presumably, if it is left undisturbed, it solidifies and becomes part of one's established memory. If something happens to prevent its consolidation, however, the trace decays and is lost forever, just as a sand castle crumbles and washes away with the tide. Electroconvulsive shocks and other traumatic events, such as head injuries, could conceivably disrupt the consolidation of a new trace. Thus, patients' memories of the events immediately preceding shock therapy are lost, while older memories are unaffected. Figure 7.9 provides a schematic summary of the evidence in support of a distinction between short-term and long-term memory.

Chunking and Rehearsal in Short-Term Memory

Another line of evidence for the existence of separate short-term and long-term compartments in memory came from studies of the capacity and duration of short-term memory. Numerous studies, dating from the early work of Ebbinghaus, had shown that, following a single brief presentation of letters, digits, or nonsense syllables, humans could only repeat about seven, give or take two. But, for well-learned information, people can recall far more than seven items. The discrepancy between our limited recall following a single brief presentation and our almost unlimited recall for well-learned facts, figures, names, dates, and so on, again was consistent with the idea of two distinct memory systems: one of very limited capacity and a

The use of a seven digit telephone number is no accident. Seven digits is the number that most humans can retain in short-term memory and repeat accurately after just a single presentation.

second of practically unlimited capacity. Work conducted by psychologist George Miller supported such a distinction, even though he demonstrated that the amount of information that could be maintained in a highly accessible form could be greatly increased if one used the right strategy.

Like others, Miller (1956) found that, if subjects were shown or read lists of isolated **bits of information**—a random sequence of numbers or letters, for instance—they could repeat only about seven immediately after a single reading. He also discovered, however, that, if subjects were trained to reorganize the items into meaningful groups, they could repeat much more. For example, if each letter in the sequence REDBATAIM were treated as an isolated bit of information, most subjects would be unable to repeat all of them following a single reading. But, if subjects were trained to organize the items into three groups (RED, BAT, AIM), each of which could be viewed as a single unit of information, they would be able to repeat the entire list with ease.

Miller used the term **chunking** to refer to the process of translating two or more isolated bits of information into one large chunk. It is a time-tested technique of memory improvement (Frankish, 1985). Miller (1956) found that a considerable amount of information could be held in a chunk, as long as it represented something that could be dealt with as a whole. As an example he cited Morse code, which has only two basic units, a long and a short click. At first the apprentice telegraph operator hears each "dit" and "dah" separately, as a single unit (bit) of information. But, as the operator becomes more experienced, the individual clicking sounds blend into words, phrases, and even whole sentences. An operator capable of chunking a message into phrases or sentences would write it as such, rather than as a stream of isolated clicks.

Bit: A single piece of isolated information; a unit of information.

Chunking: Translating two or more isolated bits of information into some larger unit through grouping, organizing, or coding them into something that can be treated as a whole.

The same rule applies to information in a textbook. A first-grader learning to read might view CAPACITY as a sequence of eight letters, while the more experienced reader codes it as a word. Likewise, "short-term memory is of limited capacity" can be seen as seven words or as one idea. Even a paragraph of several sentences—dozens of words and scores of letters—can be treated as a single unit of information and coded as such. In this way, a whole string of paragraphs might be boiled down to a single idea.

Miller's concept of chunking reveals that one's technique for handling incoming information can make a vast difference in how much information can be maintained in a highly accessible state. By grouping information into meaningful units, the amount of information that can be held in an immediately accessible form can be greatly increased. Thus, in preparing for an exam where information must be recalled rather than simply recognized, one should attempt to organize the information into about five or six major units and concentrate on memorizing these units.

Though there seemed to be almost no limit to the number of individual bits of information that could be stored in a chunk, Miller found that there was a limit to the number of chunks that could be handled in a single presentation: seven plus or minus two. So again, research seemed to support the idea of two separate memory compartments, distinguishable on the basis of capacity. And related work added support to this view.

About the same time Miller was studying chunking, researchers in Britain and the United States achieved a major breakthrough in the study of short-term memory by testing the effects of *rehearsal,* or practice, on recall. In one classic study (Peterson & Peterson, 1959), college students were shown three-consonant **trigrams** (meaningless letter combinations, like TBL) followed by a number (for example, 355). Their task was to recall the trigram after intervals of zero, three, six, nine, twelve, or eighteen seconds. Surely, one would think, a college student could recall one small trigram after just eighteen seconds. But there was one catch. To prevent subjects from repeating the item to themselves or studying it in any way, the experimenters required them to count backward by threes (355, 352, 349) after learning the trigram, until the interval was over (see Figure 7.10).

The results were so unexpected, scientists' reactions varied from surprise to near disbelief. For immediate recall (zero seconds), the subjects' performance was almost perfect. The few errors they did make were due to minor misperceptions, like mistaking an H for an A. But after only three seconds, subjects' recall dropped to about 80 percent. Thereafter performance fell like a lead weight from the leaning tower of Pisa. For the fifteen-second interval, recall actually dropped below 20 percent (see Figure 7.11).

Trigram: A meaningless three-consonant stimulus (e.g., DBL, DPS, LSH).

Figure 7.10 Peterson and Peterson Trigram Experiment (After Peterson & Peterson, 1959).

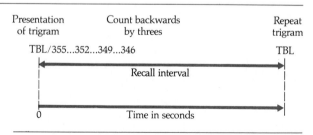

Presentation of trigram   Count backwards by threes   Repeat trigram

TBL/355...352...349...346   TBL

Recall interval

0   Time in seconds

Few researchers would have guessed that information could be lost so quickly. True, Ebbinghaus had found a dramatic fall in his curve of forgetting (see page 229), but the shortest period he tested was twenty minutes. Other researchers confirmed the findings; short-term recall dropped off quickly in all cases (Brown, 1958; Murdock, 1961).

Experiments on the effects of rehearsal in short-term memory vividly illustrate the need for rehearsal if new information is to be retained. Effective rehearsal is the key to remembering a person's name or preparing for exams. In terms of short- and long-term memory, rehearsal is the means by which information is transferred from short-term memory to long-term memory. Failure to rehearse is thus one reason information is not transferred from short-term to long-term memory and is hence forgotten.

Atkinson and Shiffrin (1968) combined the evidence for sensory memory with that for short- and long-term memory in their three-compartment model of memory (see Figure 7.12). According to their model, the processing of incoming information began with the representation of environmental information in brief sensory memory. Presumably this image-like information might then be transferred to the limited-capacity short-term memory. Because not all incoming information could fit into short-term memory, some of it would be lost through decay. Information that did reach short-term memory could be maintained indefinitely by rehearsal, however. But information that is not rehearsed also would be lost.

The researchers theorized that rehearsal of items in short-term memory led to a back-and-forth exchange of information with long-term memory. If rehearsal was sufficient, the information would become part of long-term

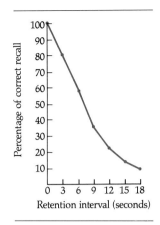

Figure 7.11 This figure shows the percentage of items correctly recalled (vertical axis) as a function of the retention interval (horizontal axis) in the Peterson and Peterson experiment. (After Peterson & Peterson, 1959).

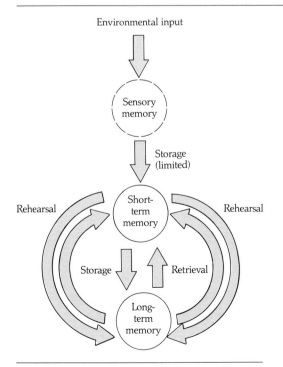

Figure 7.12 **The Three-compartment Model.** (*After Atkinson & Shiffrin, 1968*).

The memories we have of our friends and relatives are stored in long-term memory. Though we may not have these relatives on our minds all the time, our memories of them stay with us and we can, for the most part, recall their faces and names when we see photos of them, even after a very long time.

memory, a storage place of virtually limitless capacity and duration. There memories of a lifetime were stored and would remain available for as long as the person lived.

The compartments theory provides an important perspective for understanding memory and organizing the methods of memory research. Indeed, terms such as short-term memory and long-term memory, as well as primary and secondary memory, are still in common use (List et al., 1985; Wickens et al., 1985). However, another important perspective views memory, not in terms of separate compartments, but in terms of different processes carried out by a single memory system. In the next section, we will discuss this levels of processing theory of memory.

■ Learning Check ■

Read, try to recite, repeat.

Memory Compartment	Capacity	Duration
Sensory Memory	Large	Very Short (1–4 seconds)
Short-Term Memory	Small	Short (about 30 seconds)
Long-Term Memory	Very large	Very long (indefinitely)

■ **Learning Clue** ■

As you study the levels of processing theory, remember that it's not that the compartments theory is wrong and the levels theory is right, but that both theories provide an important perspective for understanding memory and organizing research.

THE LEVELS OF PROCESSING THEORY OF MEMORY

In the mid to late 1970s, when the compartments model was finding widespread acceptance, a small but important minority of researchers proposed an alternative view: that memory was but one unified system capable of operating on a variety of levels (Craik, 1979; Kintsch, 1977; Nilsson, 1979; Spear, 1978). These "levels of processing" theorists questioned the compartments theory for a number of reasons, one of which was difficulties with notion of rehearsal. According to the Atkinson-Shiffrin three-compartment model (Figure 7.12), rehearsal—viewed as the process of mentally repeating an item, as in Ebbinghaus's rote repetition method—would maintain an item in short-term memory until it could be transferred to long-term memory. As we have learned from Ebbinghaus's work, however, rote rehearsal is an *ineffective* technique for long-term recall, as it produces very substantial and rapid forgetting. Indeed, most people know from personal experience that merely repeating an item (for example, a telephone number) over and over again, either mentally or out loud, usually does not produce long-term retention. So critics of the compartments view began to closely examine the role of rehearsal in memory.

Elaborative Rehearsal and Shallow vs. Deep Processing

To achieve long-term recall, this dissenting group of scientists argued, more meaningful rehearsal is needed. An item must somehow be related to what one already knows. This process of thinking about new information they called **elaborative rehearsal,** to distinguish it from simply repeating an item, which they referred to as **maintenance rehearsal.** To give an example, if you simply repeat the zip code 02108 ten or fifteen times (maintenance rehearsal) and then study your textbook for an hour, the odds are you will not be able to recall the zip code soon after you finish studying. If you *think* as you rehearse, however, concentrating on the numbers, their position, the fact that there are two zeros, and the difference between this zip code and your own, your chances of recalling it will go up considerably.

You can prove this to yourself. Select two unfamiliar zip codes. Take the first and simply repeat it, either mentally or out loud, about a dozen times. An hour later try to write it down. Do not check your work or rehearse in any way. Then wait until the next day and try again. After writing down

Elaborative Rehearsal:
Elaborating upon an item by relating it to what one already knows.

Maintenance Rehearsal:
Repeating an item out loud or mentally to keep it in an activated state.

your answer, study the second zip code using elaborative rehearsal. Write it down an hour later and again the next day, without checking or rehearsing in between. You should find you are more successful using elaborative rehearsal.

The levels of processing theory reveals that there is more than one type of rehearsal and that some are better than others. For long-term recall, elaborative rehearsal is more effective than rote (maintenance) rehearsal. Thus, when studying, think about the material.

Comparisons of the results of elaborative and maintenance rehearsal prompted many memory theorists to look at their subject in an entirely new way. Instead of different kinds of memory compartments, theorists now emphasized different degrees of elaboration and different levels of processing or encoding. **Deep processing** they defined as analysis and encoding of an item in terms of its meaning. **Shallow processing,** by contrast, involved only analysis and encoding in terms of physical features. The difference between shallow and deep processing might be likened to the difference between memorizing the lines of a poem based on the sounds of the rhyming words, without understanding them, and learning the meaning of the lines. The deeper and more elaborative the processing, the better the retrieval (Craik & Lockhart, 1972; Craik & Tulving, 1975).

Likewise, the shallower the processing, the worse the retrieval. According to this theory, forgetting occurs not because of interferences in the consolidation of a trace, as brain experts had proposed (page 240), but because information is not encoded properly in the first place. This explanation of forgetting became known as the *depth of processing theory of forgetting*. The depth of processing theory of forgetting reveals that, if you don't learn something well to begin with, you can't expect to recall it later on. And the way to learn it well to begin with is to process in terms of meaning and relate the new information to what you already know through elaborative rehearsal.

Support for the new theory came from a study in which subjects were asked different kinds of questions about a list of words (Craik & Tulving, 1975). Some were asked whether the words would fit into a sentence—for

Deep Processing: Encoding in terms of the meaning of an item.

Shallow Processing: Encoding in terms of physical features such as sound or appearance rather than meaning.

When learning their lines, these Shakespearean performers will do best if they engage in deep processing; if the actors understand the meaning of the lines, they are more likely to remember them.

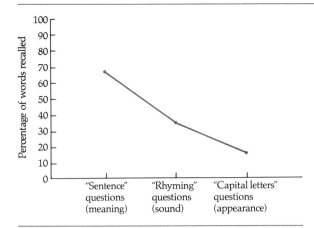

Figure 7.13 *This graph shows the percentage of words recalled (vertical axis) as a function of the task requirement at the time of encoding (horizontal axis). Recall was best when subjects were required to process in terms of meaning. (After Craik and Tulving, 1975).*

example, whether the word *stamps* would be used in the sentence, "The price of _____ keeps going up." Such questions forced subjects to process the words in terms of their meaning. Other subjects were asked if the words rhymed with other words ("Does *stamp* rhyme with *lamp*?"). Those subjects had to process the words only in terms of sound. Still other subjects were asked questions like, "Is the word STAMP written in capital letters?" This third group of subjects had to process the words only in terms of their appearance (see Figure 7.13).

Subjects had no idea they would later be asked to recall the lists, so all learning was **incidental,** or unintentional. The findings were clear. Subjects who were required to process at a deeper level recalled significantly more words. In simple terms, the more you think about something, the better you know it.

The chessmaster George Koltanowski processes information both deeply and elaboratively. First he attempts to determine the meaning of a player's move—What is the threat? What does it accomplish? How good is the player? Then he attempts to relate the move to his previous experiences. How does this position compare to others he has seen before? Has it ever occurred in master practice? What is the best way to counter it? With each question, Koltanowski breathes additional life into the information he holds in his head, thus making it harder to forget. Indeed, except for his first attempt at blindfold chess when he was just eighteen, Koltanowski has never lost because he failed to retrieve the positions of the pieces in a game. In fact, he usually displays better comprehension of a game than players who spend all their time looking at the board.

Memory as a Single Unified System

With the distinction between maintenance vs. elaborative rehearsal and shallow vs. deep processing came the notion that what theorists had called short-term memory might be better thought of as the conscious or active part of a single unified system. Instead of being a separate compartment, short-term memory might be no more than the small slice of memory that is

Incidental Learning: Learning without the intention to learn.

available to consciousness at any given moment—the activated portion of memory.

Consider this analogy. Imagine yourself alone at night in a dark library, with only a small flashlight to guide you. Around you are thousands of books, newspapers, and journals. Some are arranged on the shelves by category; others are scattered around, waiting to be put into place. You can shine your flashlight on only a few things at a time—on a nearby newspaper, to read of recent events; or on the scattered books, where you might find something of interest by accident. Or you can shine the light on the books on the shelf and systematically search for a specific book or topic.

So it may be with memory and consciousness. Just as you can direct the flashlight here or there, so too can you direct your consciousness according to your needs and intentions. You can attempt to activate an old experience, think about the happenings of the day, or mull over your psychology assignment. But you cannot call to mind all your memories at once. Like the flashlight, your consciousness at any given moment is limited to but one smidgen of the spectrum of memories to which it can be directed.

The interesting thing is that this concept of short-term memory as the conscious or activated part of a much larger system is exactly what James (1890) meant by primary memory (see page 232). Seen from this viewpoint, memory is a constant process of extracting, reducing, using, discarding, and refining information. At some point information from a briefly exposed stimulus (as in Sperling's sensory memory experiments, page 234) reaches consciousness. But, with only shallow processing, it will soon be lost in the background. If selected for more elaborative processing, it will become more memorable. Such information need not necessarily be seen as hopping from one compartment to another—from sensory memory to short-term memory to long-term memory. Only one compartment or system, which selects some items for additional processing and neglects others, so argue the levels of processing theorists, is needed to account for the fact that some memories are more memorable than others.

The levels of processing theory provided an alternative framework from which to view memory. Today, some psychologists believe that there are different types of memory systems, as argued by the compartments view; others, by contrast, believe that memory involves different kinds of processes carried out by a single unified system, as in the levels view. Both views have merit because they provide us with important insights into how we can best use our memories to acquire information and later recall it. But our story does not end here, because there are some important questions that neither the compartments nor the levels theory adequately addresses. What is the organization of our stored knowledge? Do we put everything we know about psychology in one place, and everything we know about history in another? How is our knowledge represented? Do we store it in the form

■ **Learning Check** ■

Read the right side, then cover and try to recite. Repeat.

| Two dimensions of encoding: | 1. Maintenance rehearsal vs. elaborative rehearsal |
| | 2. Shallow processing vs. deep processing |

of words, or images? These are just some of the questions that we will examine in the pages ahead.

THE STRUCTURE OF MEMORY

You have in your mind certain kinds of information: you know what a car is; you know what a dog is; and so on. Many psychologists believe that what you know—the information you can recall or recognize because of previous encodings—is stored in some systematic way, rather than as just a random hodgepodge of facts and figures. This system by which your knowledge is filed away is your **memory structure.** For example, all of your knowledge of animals—dogs, cats, cows, horses, pets, farms, and other related ideas—might be seen as being stored in one place. When you go to a museum or a zoo and come across a totally unfamiliar animal—say, an aardvark—you can place what you learn about it in this existing memory structure.

Memory Structure: The organization of memory—the system by which memories are coded and stored.

Many everyday experiences are explainable in terms of memory structure. Have you ever noticed that the more you know about something, the easier it is to acquire and recall new information about that topic? The more you know about football, the easier it is to remember the plays in a game or the names of the teams. The more you know about clothes, the easier it is to keep up on the latest fashions. And the more you know about math or psychology, the easier it is to acquire new information about these subjects. Conversely, it is difficult to acquire and recall even simple facts if you know little about a topic. If you move to a new neighborhood, at first you'll have difficulty remembering the street names. But after a while, as you start to acquire a base of knowledge about the area, new information will fall into place more quickly. When you encounter a strange street, you will be able to relate it to the streets you already know.

Notice that early in the learning process prior knowledge may actually interfere with new learning. If your old neighborhood was arranged in square blocks and the new one has lots of cul-de-sacs, you may find yourself making many turns down dead-end streets, thinking that the new area is mapped out like the old. Such errors are probably due to proactive interference (see page 231) and illustrate how prior memories can make the formation of new memories more difficult. However, once your knowledge of the new area starts to become more organized and distinct from the old, your prior memories actually enhance new ones. For example, you might note that, whereas you always used to turn right in a particular situation, you now turn left. Thus, prior memories can enhance or interfere with the formation of new ones, depending on how they are organized.

The importance of memory structure has been demonstrated in a number of studies. In these experiments, the performance of subjects who are already familiar with a topic is compared to the performance of subjects who are not. Both groups are required to learn something new about a topic. They are given the same amount of time and the same instructions. The result: the high-knowledge groups invariably learn and retain much more than the low-knowledge groups (Reiser et al., 1985; Voss, 1979). In one study, for example, a group of baseball fans were compared to a group that knew little about baseball. Both groups read an account of half an inning. The high-knowledge group not only recalled more, but was far more accurate than the low-knowledge group (Spilich et al., 1979).

The difficult task in the acquisition of knowledge, then, is to build the framework on which to hang later learning. Once that structure has been built, what at first seems confusing or overwhelming becomes clear and manageable, and related information can be added easily.

Semantic Memory and Episodic Memory

Semantic Memory: Memory in terms of language and words. The organization and structure of information stored in terms of language.

When researchers began to probe the question of how memories are organized, they learned that the answer depends in part on the way in which particular memories are encoded. Much of what a person knows appears to be encoded and stored in the form of language, and organized in terms of its meaning. This body of knowledge, called **semantic memory,** appears to have a *hierarchical structure.* That is, it is arranged in top-down rank order, with the most general category at the top. For instance, an animal hierarchy would include the term *animal* at the top, along with a number of specific facts associated with animals (see Figure 7.14). Nested under animal in the figure are two more specific categories, birds and fish, and each of those is directly associated with specific facts. Further down the hierarchy are still more specific categories, canary and ostrich (two kinds of birds), and the specific facts associated with them.

Figure 7.14 An Example of Hierarchical Structure. (*Adapted from Collins, A. M., & Quillian, M. R. (1969). Retrieval time from semantic memory.* Journal of Verbal Learning and Verbal Behavior, 8, *240–247. Figure 1. p. 241).*

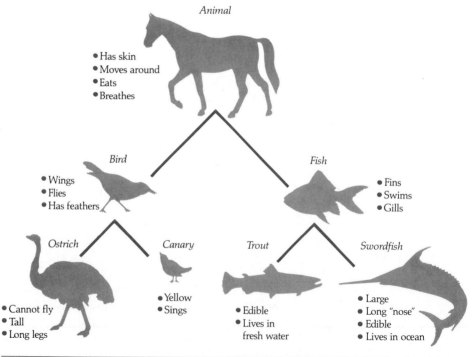

Critics have argued that the hierarchy model of semantic memory is an oversimplification. Although most concede that there is probably some truth to the theory, they argue that no one's memory is organized as neatly as the model suggests. Be that as it may, other research has shown that using hierarchies in studying can greatly facilitate recall.

Not all information that is stored in the form of words is hierarchically organized (Tulving, 1972). **Episodic memory,** or the memory of specific events—the time, place, or date—is not so arranged. In fact, given the poor memory most people have for episodic information, there may be no system to its organization at all. For instance, you are reading this book and learning about memory at a specific time and place. Later you may recall what you have learned (semantic memory), but you may not remember when and where you acquired your knowledge (episodic memory). Perhaps episodic details are difficult to remember precisely because they so often represent

Episodic Memory: Memory for information pertaining to specific episodes or events—the time, place, or date of an experience (as opposed to semantic information). Episodic memory deals with one's personal experiences.

Box 7.2 PSYCHOLOGY IN ACTION: Eyewitness Testimony

The unreliability of eyewitness testimony stems in part from the difficulty people have in recalling episodic memories as compared to semantic memories. A witness who has observed a crime clearly and who has been greatly affected by it will nevertheless have difficulty retrieving the details of the episode later on. What is worse, the witness may tend to fill in missing details, or reconstruct them in a slightly different form.

The tendency of people to fill in memory gaps with reconstructed details has been vividly demonstrated. In one study subjects were shown a film of an automobile accident. It was only a minor fender-bender—no glass was broken—but the film clearly showed an accident happening. Later the subjects were divided into groups and asked to estimate how fast the cars were going at the time of the accident. One group was asked, "How fast were the cars going when they *smashed*?" Another was asked, "How fast were the cars going when they *contacted*?" The answers revealed that subjects' estimates had been influenced by the way the question was worded. When the word *smashed* was used, subjects estimated an average speed of 40.8 miles an hour. When the word *contacted* was used, they estimated an average speed of only 31.8 miles an hour—almost a ten-mile-an-hour difference in response to a change in just one word (Loftus & Palmer, 1974).

Why would a slight change in the wording of a question make so much difference? The finding is explainable if we assume that subjects retained only semantic information, and filled in the details when they reconstructed the experience in order to answer the question. Subjects who were asked how fast the cars

were going when they smashed were led to believe that the impact had been more powerful than it was. Not knowing the exact details, they reconstructed a more serious accident than they had witnessed, as illustrated here by the photo. If the cars "smashed," the subjects probably reasoned, they must have been going fast.

A week later subjects were asked if they had seen any broken glass in the film. Though most subjects correctly answered no, more than twice as many subjects in the "smashed" group (16 out of 50) as in the "contacted" group (7 out of 50) reported that they had seen broken glass. It's a bit frightening to realize that calculated questioning can so easily produce distortions in the testimony of an eyewitness. (For more on eyewitness testimony and juries, see Chapter 13.)

Subjects' recall of a scene similar to this was strongly influenced by the type of questions they were asked.

very specific information that is rarely repeated (Salasoo et al., 1985). Semantic information is gained through so many different experiences that the contexts in which it is encoded tend to drop out, leaving only the general information. You know what a chair is, but you have experienced chairs in so many different contexts you cannot recall when and where you first learned what a chair is—nor would you have much reason to.

The poor reliability of episodic memory becomes crucial only when a person really needs to remember what happened at a particular time and place—to testify at a trial, for instance. Imagine yourself accused of a serious crime you did not commit. How, you wonder, could someone accuse you when you know you are innocent? The question is not an idle one. Many innocent people have gone to jail on the basis of false eyewitness testimony (see Box 7.2).

Verbal and Nonverbal Coding

So far we have considered only the structure of verbal (language-related) memory. But memory contains much nonverbal information as well. The chessmaster George Koltanowski uses the technique of visualization in blindfold chess. When the teller reports a player's move, Koltanowski first places it in an acoustic code by repeating the teller's words, out loud and then mentally. If he stopped there, however, he might not remember the move later. To enhance his recall, he encodes the information in a second way by visualizing the position.

Recall can be enhanced by the use of two codes instead of one: a word plus a picture of the item represented by the word. When studying, it's often helpful to visualize the concepts you learn or study the artwork and photographs that accompany the material.

Many techniques memory experts use on stage are in fact not the magic tricks they appear to be but practical ways of exploiting the natural workings of the mind. If the memory is organized in certain codes or structures, then coding or structuring incoming information in those ways should make that information easier to store and retrieve. And that is exactly what psychologists' attempts to understand encoding and retrieval have shown.

ENCODING AND RETRIEVAL OF MEMORIES

Suppose you have volunteered to participate in an experiment. You are given sixty seconds to study a list of fourteen words; your task will be to recall the list after a two-minute wait. Immediately you begin to think, "Sixty seconds isn't very long; how should I approach this task?" Then the experimenter presents the list (see Figure 7.15).

Is there any way you can make the best use of the short time you have to study the list? Probably the least effective approach would be rote rehearsal—mentally repeating the list without regard to meaning. Processing the words in terms of their meaning and rehearsing them mentally or out loud would be better. But can you do anything else? Yes! You can organize the list.

Look at the list again. (Even better, try mastering it.) You'll notice that some of the items on the list can be related to each other. *Horse, dog,* and *wolf* are all animals; *boat, bicycle,* and *train* are all means of transportation. In fact, every item on the list can be organized into one of those two categories. If you study all the related items together, then, you can make your task far more manageable. You can encode all animals together and then all the means of transportation, and you can use the category names—animals and transportation—as a retrieval cue. By organizing information into categories, you will ensure that you store the items in a logical manner, so they will be easier to locate and retrieve later on.

Strategies for Encoding

Bousfield (1953) conducted a classic demonstration of the human tendency to organize incoming information. Subjects were presented with lists similar to the fourteen-item list you were just asked to study. The items, which were drawn from four main categories, were presented in random order, without category headings. Nevertheless, Bousfield found that, if subjects were allowed to recall the items in any order, they tended to retrieve them by category membership. For example, if the list were presented as *chocolate, milk, Hershey, butter, pen, eggs, paper, Life Savers, bar, desk,* subjects would recall in an order like this: *chocolate, Hershey bar, Life Savers; milk, butter, eggs; pen, paper, desk.*

Bousfield's findings were extended when another researcher began testing subjects on a list of totally unrelated items (for example, *window, bottle, table, Bible, wallet*). Subjects saw the list sixteen times, each time in a different order, and were asked to recall it after each presentation. With no consistent order of input and no relationship among the items, what do you think happened? The researcher found that subjects' output order became more alike on each successive trial, despite the constantly varying order of presentation (Tulving, 1962). Apparently, in the absence of any obvious relatedness among items, subjects created their own, a phenomenon the experimenter referred to as **subjective organization.**

Different subjects will organize the same list of unrelated items differently. One might begin with *table* and end with *bottle;* another might prefer to begin with *bottle,* followed immediately by *table.* Any systematic way of grouping items seems to work. Approaching a task with this kind of strategy in mind to begin with is of even more help. Thus, when studying, you should attempt to impose some type of organization on the material, as is done in the schematic overviews and summaries that appear throughout this book.

Why does organizing at the time of encoding aid in retrieval? A number of explanations can be advanced. Organized information is, for one thing, more compact. When items are grouped, they can be dealt with as a single unit or chunk rather than as so many bits of isolated information (see page 241). An organized list is also more meaningful, and hence easier to process at a deeper level. Creating your own organization requires effort, attention, and thought, all of which make for more effective encoding and retrieval

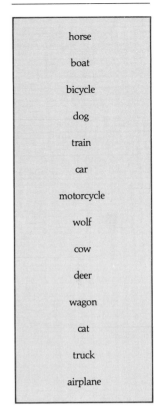

Figure 7.15 Study this list for 60 seconds. Then wait two minutes and try recalling the items.

Subjective Organization: Specific output order effects for unrelated information presented in a different input order for each presentation; recalling a list in an increasingly similar order, following each presentation of a randomly presented list.

Figure 7.16 Schematic Summary of Memory Theories. *The schematic summaries and overviews presented throughout this book are actually hierarchical organizations. This figure shows a hierarchical organization of memory theories. Studying the material in such an organization has been shown to markedly enhance recall, when compared to studying the items as an unorganized list.*

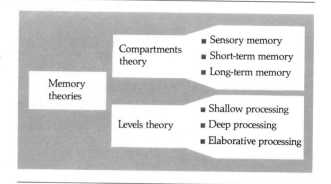

(Glisky & Rabinowitz, 1985). And the organization itself can be used as a system of cues, or reminders. In Figure 7.16, for example, *levels theory* can be used as a cue for retrieval of shallow, deep, and elaborative processing.

Cues and the Learning Context

Just as organization can aid in the process of encoding, so can the use of cues at the time of encoding prove helpful at the time of recall (Winograd & Soloway, 1985). In one study, subjects were shown lists of related items, each of which was headed by a category name (for example, FRUIT: *apple, peach, pear, plum, grape, orange, lemon, apricot, banana*). The experimenter read the category names with the lists, but told the subjects that they needed to memorize only the items on the lists, not the categories. The subjects were then divided into two groups. Half were given sheets of paper with the category names; the other half received blank sheets. Both groups were asked to recall as many items from the lists as they could.

Did having the category names make any difference in a subject's performance? There was no question about it: subjects who were given the category names greatly outperformed the ones who were given blank sheets. What was even more striking, when subjects in the second group were later given the category names, their recall improved dramatically. Apparently the category names served as cues, helping to jog the subjects' memories (Tulving & Pearlstone, 1966).

Such findings led scientists to propose that successful recall depends on the use of the cues that were present at the time of encoding (Tulving & Thompson, 1973). According to this principle, known as the **encoding specificity principle,** retrieval is a two-part process. Effective encoding is the first step in that process; retrieving the cue used in encoding is the second. To the extent that the circumstances of encoding match those of retrieval, recall will be enhanced (Watkins, 1979). To the extent that they do not, we forget. Thus, retrieval failure is an important cause of forgetting. If cues that were present at the time of encoding are not present at the time of retrieval, or if competing cues block the original cues, even a carefully processed fact may remain out of reach. This explanation of forgetting is known as the **cue-dependent theory** of forgetting.

The cue-dependent theory of forgetting reveals two important applied concepts: First, after you have organized your knowledge, attach a category

Encoding Specificity Principle: A principle that states that retrieval depends on the availability of the cues that were present at the time of encoding; something will be remembered only if the cues available during encoding are also available at the time of recall.

Cue-Dependent Theory: A theory of forgetting, which states that forgetting is due to a failure to retrieve the cues that were present at the time of encoding.

name to each major category. Second, you must make a special effort to overlearn your category names so that you can recall them at will and thus have ready access to the information these names represent.

The discovery that cues used during encoding will increase recall if presented at the time of recall has led to interest in the *context* in which encoding and retrieval take place (Cech & Shoben, 1985; Kintsch & Mross, 1985). Context includes both external factors—the place and time of day, background material, order of presentation—and internal factors—fatigue or alertness, hunger, emotional state. All else being equal, retrieval is enhanced if the context at the time of recall is similar to the context at the time of encoding. Students do better, for example, if they take their final exams in the same room in which their class was held. Even the environment in which a person studies can affect recall. Students who attempt to study at a hot, noisy beach often have difficulty retrieving information in a cool, quiet classroom. In effect, the environmental conditions at the time of encoding become cues in themselves.

The same can be said for one's internal state or context. If encoding occurred during a physiological state of hunger, or arousal, retrieval may be impaired unless the student is in a similar state at the time of recall. Even the mood we are in at the time of encoding can influence recall (Ellis et al., 1985). If we are in a good mood at the time of encoding, memory will be impaired if we are not also in a good mood at the time of retrieval (Bower, 1981). Psychologists use the term **state-dependent learning** to refer to the effects of the internal state of a learner during encoding and retrieval.

The phenomenon of state-dependence is especially evident in studies of the effects of drugs and alcohol on recall. A good argument against studying while using drugs is that you may find recall difficult when the effects of the drug wear off. Likewise, alcoholics have been known to hide a bottle of liquor while intoxicated, only to forget where it is when they sober up. Only after becoming intoxicated again do they recall its hiding place. Marijuana users have observed similar effects. An experience or event that occurred while they were under the influence of the drug suddenly pops into mind the next time they smoke.

Thus far we have seen that there are a number of things a person can do—rehearse elaboratively and deeply, organize input, encode category names as cues, and so on—to enhance recall. (Figure 7.17 presents a sche-

State-Dependent Learning: The physiological state of the organism at the time of learning (for example, fatigued, on a drug, angry, etc.). Retrieval is impaired if the physiological state of an individual at the time of recall does not match that at the time of encoding.

■ Learning Check ■

For each theory listed on the left, read the associated explanation of forgetting on the right. Then cover the right side and try to recite. Repeat.

Interference Theory	Forgetting due to retroactive and proactive interference
Compartments Theory	Forgetting due to a failure to transfer information from one compartment to another
Levels Theory	Forgetting due to a failure to process deeply and elaboratively
Cue-Dependent Theory	Forgetting due to a failure to retrieve the cues that were present at the time of encoding

Figure 7.17 Schematic Summary of Techniques for Enhancing Recall.

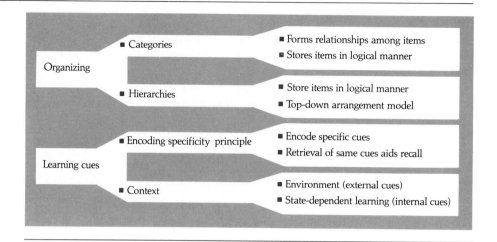

matic summary of encoding and retrieval devices.) But are there any ways to train your memory in general, as a runner trains the body to run, so that with time you will find it easier and easier to remember?

MEMORY TRAINING

George Koltanowski (1985) claims that he developed his memory, and he believes others can do the same. What is more, his position is supported by a rapidly accumulating body of research. Countless studies point to the conclusion that memory can be improved. You *can* learn to make better use of your time—reduce the hours and minutes you now spend studying, or make them more fruitful.

In fact, since the time of the ancient Greeks, and perhaps earlier, students have been searching for techniques to help them cope with the task of recalling large amounts of material. And, indeed, the Greeks did develop a method of encoding that allowed students of rhetoric, or speechmaking, to deliver long speeches without referring to notes. Such techniques are known as **mnemonic devices,** after the Greek word for memory.

Mnemonic Device: Technique for improving memory; rules for encoding that enhance retrieval.

Mnemonic Devices

The mnemonic device used by the Greek and Roman orators, a device that is still used today, was the **method of loci** (*loci* in Latin means "places"). In this method, a familiar sequence of places or events is used as a vehicle for new material. The student forms a mental image for each of the new facts and attaches it visually to the familiar series of places. Imagine yourself walking through each of the rooms in your home in a specific order; for example, beginning at the entrance. In each room you place a visual image of something you wish to remember. Take the items on your shopping list: the oranges can go in the kitchen, the bananas in the living room, the butter in the bedroom, and the milk in the bathroom. The livelier the images you in-

Method of Loci: A mnemonic device in which information to be remembered is placed within a very familiar sequence of events or locations. Items to be remembered are visualized in the familiar locations.

vent, the easier they will be to remember. So you might visualize a gigantic orange in the kitchen, then imagine yourself slipping on a banana peel in the living room. Then, when the time arrives to retrieve the items on your shopping list, you simply imagine yourself walking through your house and recovering the items you placed there.

Any familiar series of locations will work in this method. Many memory experts prefer to use places along some well-traveled path, such as the way to school or to work. George Koltanowski uses the sixty-four squares of the chessboard as his familiar path. To him, each of those squares is as distinctive as the different rooms in a house. The important point is to arrive at the places in a specific order or sequence to reduce the risk that you will overlook an item because you skipped that location.

Though the method of loci has been used successfully for centuries, the reasons for its effectiveness are not fully understood. Clearly the locations in which the items are stored provide cues that are useful in both encoding and retrieval. The act of inventing a visual image provides an additional code for the information. And the technique provides a convenient means for rehearsal.

Each time you review a series of items, you will enhance your retrieval. In one classic study, for example, students who spent 80 percent of their time recalling and 20 percent reading learned better than students who spent 80 percent of their time reading and 20 percent recalling (Gates, 1917). In another experiment, students who studied for only one session and then spent four additional sessions attempting to recall their knowledge performed just as well as a second group that spent all five sessions studying from the book (Hogan & Kintsch, 1971). Recalling what you have studied without notes, then, is one of the most powerful techniques you can use to fix the information in your mind.

Five Suggestions for Memory Improvement

There are no magic tricks in memorizing, in other words; only superior ways of encoding and processing information. In closing, let's summarize some of the ways you can enhance your ability to encode and retrieve information.

First, organize information. Group incoming information in categories, or clusters of interrelated facts. Organizing it in this way will help you to reduce it to a small number of manageable units. The category names may also serve as retrieval cues.

Second, process deeply and elaboratively. Analyze incoming information in terms of its meaning and its relationship to what you already know. Ask yourself questions about it; try to look at it from as many different angles as possible. Thinking about new information will make it more memorable. It will also create a structure to which you can easily add new, related information.

Third, use familiar cues to encode and retrieve information. Attach a new fact to a familiar cue, like a room in your house. When you need to retrieve it, retrieve the cue.

Fourth, use more than one coding system when possible. Supplement your verbal codes with vivid visual images of the terms. The distinctiveness of the image and the elaborative processing it requires can greatly enhance recall.

Finally, practice recalling. Attempt to recall what you have learned. Try using time you would otherwise waste for this purpose—waiting time at the supermarket, for instance. Active recitation is one of the most powerful techniques for enhancing your ability to retrieve information. Practice in recalling will also space your study time, so you will avoid cramming at the last minute. Just before an exam, make one final effort to recall; then check your accuracy. This last bit of overlearning will help to keep the information fresh in your mind during the exam. (For more hints on how to study, consult the box on studying in Chapter 1.)

In the next chapter, we will elaborate on some of the topics we've covered in relation to memory. We will explore further the idea of verbal versus nonverbal information and get into the structure and acquisition of language. Then we will consider how we use our memories and other cognitive abilities to solve problems. Finally, we will consider the issue of intelligence and its measurement.

LEARNING FRAMEWORK

I. Memory—taking in, storing, and calling back information and experience. (Review: *Encoding; Retention; Retrieval*)

II. Forgetting—the inability to make use of or retrieve information previously experienced.
   A. Ebbinghaus found rapid and substantial forgetting following rote memorization of meaningless material. (Review: *Nonsense Syllable; Savings Method; Rote Rehearsal; Curve of Forgetting*)
   B. Forgetting is not simply a passive process in which what we have learned gradually fades away. (Review: *Decay Theory; Interference Theory; Retroactive Interference; Proactive Interference; Table 7.1*)

III. The compartments theory of memory, which proposed the existence of separate memory compartments that differ in duration and capacity, was supported by several lines of investigation. (Review: *Figure 7.3; Figure 7.9*)
   A. Sensory memory receives input information as a very brief image or internal sound. (Review: *Whole Report Technique; Partial Report Technique; Figures 7.4* and *7.5; Icon; Echoic Memory*)
   B. Three lines of experimental evidence supported the idea of separate short-term and long-term memory compartments. (Review: *Dichotic Listening; Figure 7.6; Acoustic Code; Semantic Code*)
   C. Neurological evidence also supported the notion of a distinction between a short-duration, small-capacity, short-term memory and a long-duration, large-capacity, long-term memory. (Review: *Anterograde Amnesia; Retrograde Amnesia; Consolidation Theory*)
   D. Research on chunking revealed that the capacity of short-term memory was limited to seven chunks of information; research on rehearsal showed that short-term memory was of limited duration. (Review: *Chunking*)

IV. The levels of processing theory provided an important alternative to the compartments theory.
   A. According to the levels view, information can be encoded in different

degrees of elaboration and in terms of meaningfulness. (Review: *Elaborative Rehearsal; Shallow Processing; Deep Processing*)

   B. According to levels theory, different degrees or levels of encoding occur within a single memory system.

V. Memory structure—the system by which memories are stored—depends on the nature of encoding.

   A. Information may be encoded in the form of language and organized in terms of its semantic meaning or it may be encoded as a specific event. (Review: *Semantic Memory; Figure 7.14; Episodic Memory*)

   B. Encoding can be verbal or nonverbal.

VI. There is a strong relationship between the way we encode information and our ability to retrieve it.

   A. All else being equal, organized input is easier to retrieve than unorganized input. (Review: *Subjective Organization; Figure 7.16*)

   B. All else being equal, retrieval is best when the cues that were present at the time of encoding are present at the time of retrieval. (Review: *Encoding Specificity Principle; Cue-Dependent Theory; State-Dependent Learning; Figure 7.17*)

VII. Memory can be improved.

   A. Mnemonic devices provide rules for encoding. (Review: *Method of Loci*)

   B. To improve memory: organize, use deep and elaborative processing, use familiar cues, use verbal and nonverbal codes, and practice recall. (Review: *Five Suggestions for Memory Improvement*)

8

Language, Thought, and Intelligence

Chapter Outline

In Berlin, during the early 1900s, there lived the most intelligent animal of all time—or so many people thought. Clever Hans was indeed no ordinary horse. Ask him to solve a complex arithmetic problem, like 80 divided by 8, and he would paw the ground with his hoof ten times. Say to him, "At six cents each, what would three cigars costs?" and his hoof would strike the ground exactly eighteen times. A trick, you say? Then how else would you explain Hans's ability to solve these and other problems that had been written on a large blackboard, with not a word of help from his trainer or the audience? Even some of Germany's most distinguished scientists became convinced that this horse could calculate, read, and spell.

According to Hans's trainer, a high school teacher, Hans learned the same way any other student might—from blackboard demonstrations, flash cards, and so on. The horse could spell by converting each letter of the alphabet to a number—for example, *a* equaled 1, *b*, 2, and so on. Asked to spell *able*, Hans would tap once, then twice, and twelve times, and then five times, with a brief pause after each letter. To a question requiring only a simple yes or no—any question—Hans would reply by moving his head up and down or side to side. "Do bees sting?" a skeptic would cry from the audience. "Yes," Hans would reply by shaking his head up and down. "Is it false that you're not going to leave tonight?" someone else would ask, trying to fool Hans with a double negative. But Hans could not be fooled. Since this would be his last night in town, and he *was* going to leave, it was false to say he was *not* going to leave. So, to everyone's amazement, Hans would shake his head yes. This animal was nobody's fool.

Scientists began to ask, "Are all horses this intelligent, or just some? Is this a special horse with unique abilities?" If Hans's accomplishments were merely of training, then, given the proper experiences, all horses might someday learn to read, spell, calculate, and communicate with humans. But if Hans had inherited some special traits from his parents, then only horses with a similar genetic blueprint would be able to achieve these feats, no matter how carefully they were trained.

Finally a German psychologist put an end to speculation on the question of whether Hans's intelligence was due to heredity or environment. The psychologist solved the mystery of Hans's apparent genius by demonstrating that, if no one in the horse's presence knew the answer, the horse could not answer the question (Pfungst, 1904). Hans's performance, in other words, depended on his ability to read extremely subtle cues from his trainer and the audience. If an answer required fifteen stomps, everyone might remain tense until Hans pounded out the fifteenth stomp. Then they would relax—and so would Hans. Without even realizing it, the trainer and the audience gave Hans the cues that told him when to stomp, or which way to shake his head. Hans could not read, calculate, or understand the words spoken to him; he merely responded on cue.

It is easy to attribute complex cognitive processes—the ability to communicate through language; the capacity to think in words or symbols; and the intelligence needed to solve complicated problems—to horses, dogs, and other favorite animals. What happier explanation for the amazing feats of a pet or a circus animal than to believe that the animal thinks and understands language as humans do? But, following the embarrassing lesson of Clever Hans, most scientists remain skeptical about claims of talking apes or thinking horses. The illusion of intelligence in animals like Hans helps to illustrate the interrelatedness among language, problem solving, and thought. In this chapter we will discuss each of these cognitive processes in turn. Beginning with a brief discussion of language in animals, we will examine the reasons why most experts consider human language a uniquely human skill. Then we will look at the role that language plays in thought—especially the kind of thought involved in problem solving. Finally, we will touch on the delicate and often misunderstood concept of intelligence. Most definitions of intelligence include the ability to think effectively and to solve problems. If you have those skills, does that mean you are intelligent? Does intelligence guarantee you success in the real world?

These questions have led to some fiercely fought battles among scientists and the general public alike. For the basic question—the extent to which cognitive processes are the result of inborn factors (nature) and environment and learning (nurture)—is relevant, not only to the field of psychology, but to the way people are educated and advanced in everyday life.

■ Learning Clue ■

As you read what follows, be alert to differences between human and animal language. Human language has a basic structure and set of rules that permit the creation of new meaning through the application of these rules.

LANGUAGE

Language is something that must be learned. Support for this statement can be found in the fact that infants always speak the language of their parents and the country or regional area in which they are raised—and with the same accent at that. Children born in the United States and raised by English-speaking parents always learn English, regardless of their national heritage. Take these infants and raise them in Japan with Japanese-speaking people, and they will learn Japanese. To acquire language requires exposure to it.

But if language is learned, why do humans master it so quickly and animals so slowly, if at all? Many scientists believe that the capacity for language is inborn (inherited) and, specifically, that the human brain is predisposed to acquire language. This natural aptitude for language, they argue, explains why human infants readily learn the language of their parents. By contrast, even with patient teaching, animals have been able to produce only a poor imitation of human language.

Language in Animals

Early attempts to teach language to chimpanzees—the animal closest to humans in body and brain structure—failed. Psychologists brought up chimps in their homes, treating them as their own children. Some even went so far as to raise an infant chimp along with their own infant, exposing the two to nearly identical environments (Kellogg & Kellogg, 1933). In all cases the human child acquired language; the chimp uttered not a word. Critics argued that these experiments were an unfair test of a chimp's abilities, however. The chimp's vocal structure prevented it from imitating the sounds of human speech.

Later, two psychologists appeared to break through the animal language barrier by teaching a chimpanzee named Washoe some of the gestures of American Sign Language (ASL), a system of communication used by the deaf (Gardner & Gardner, 1975). In ASL, each gesture stands for a word (see Figure 8.1). By rewarding Washoe for imitating the various gestures, the psychologists eventually accomplished something no one had ever done before; they had a conversation with an animal.

Other scientists soon devised new symbolic languages for animals to use. One researcher taught the chimp Sarah to use plastic chips of different colors and shapes to convey meaning (Premack, 1976). Sarah learned to arrange the chips on a magnetized board to form sentences such as "Give Sarah apple," meaning "Please give me that apple, as you always do when I arrange these symbols like this." (See Figure 8.2.)

Figure 8.1 Language in Animals. Washoe the chimp was able to learn to use some of the gestures of American Sign Language.

But critics argued that the chimps were simply engaging in behaviors that they had acquired through imitation and reinforcement. Did they really know what their gestures and symbols meant, or were they engaging in a modern version of the story of Clever Hans? Scientists could not be sure. For, despite numerous demonstrations that chimps, gorillas, and even orangutans can learn to imitate signs, arrange symbols, or even type words on a computer keyboard, researchers have not been able to show that animals possess language abilities comparable to humans' (Limber, 1977).

The case of Koko, a gorilla, illustrates the point. Koko could carry on a conversation of sorts by using signs she had already learned and been rewarded for using. The day after she bit a companion, her teacher, Penny Patterson (1979), had the following talk with her.

Figure 8.2 Sarah's Language Chips.

Patterson: What did you do yesterday?
Koko: (in sign language) Wrong, wrong.
Patterson: What wrong?
Koko: Bite.

When Koko was asked, "Are you an animal or a person?" she replied, "Fine animal gorilla." But Koko's "speech" lacked one of the most basic properties of human language: the creation of new meaning through the application of grammatical rules. Humans can generate meaningful sentences they have never been exposed to; animals, so far, have not. And humans develop their language skills as they grow older, imitating others less and less; animals, if anything, have the opposite tendency (Terrace, 1981). Thus, current evidence, though not the final word, reveals that animals cannot produce language that is comparable to human language.

What is it that humans do with language that animals cannot? The answer lies in the structure of language and the way in which it can be used to create new meaning.

The Basic Structure of Language

Human language is made up of sounds, which, when combined according to certain rules, have meaning. Every language has a specific set of basic sounds, called **phonemes**—the smallest units of speech that serve to distinguish one utterance from another in a language. Phonemes include both vowel sounds, such as *e* and *u*, and consonant sounds, such as *b*, *c*, and *t*. The number of sounds that a human can utter and still tell the difference between them is actually quite small. In fact, no language has more than a hundred phonemes, and most have far fewer. English has forty to forty-six, depending on dialect and interpretation. Most are represented by a single letter, such as the long *a* sound in *ate* or the short *a* sound in *at*. A few are signified by letter combinations, including *th*, as in *the*, *oi*, as in *oil*, and *ng*, as in *sing*.

Perhaps, when you were learning to read, your teacher asked you to "sound out" the individual phonemes in a word. If so, you learned by the phonetic method, so called because of its emphasis on the phonemes that combine to form meaningful words. In support of this method, a considerable body of literature indicates that an important aspect of skilled reading is the ability to rapidly generate the pronunciations of both known and novel

Phoneme: The simplest sound (smallest unit of speech) that serves to distinguish one utterance from another in a language; the basic unit of sound.

By the time he is six, this child will have a vocabulary of about 2,000 words, which he will use according to the rules of grammar.

Morpheme: The basic unit of meaning in a language.

Prefix: A meaningful unit of language (morpheme) that can be put at the beginning of a word to modify its meaning (e.g., *pre* as in *pre*determine or *pre*digest).

Suffix: A meaningful unit of language (morpheme) that can be put at the end of a word to modify its meaning (e.g., *ing* as in work*ing* or mov*ing*).

Denotative Meaning: The dictionary definition of a word; what the word stands for.

Connotative Meaning: The ideas or evaluations associated with a word.

words (Rosson, 1985). Thus, mastery of the forty-six basic sounds of English, the phonemes, appears to be one important key to the development of good reading as well as good pronunciation skills.

Phonemes, the basic units of sound, convey information by allowing us to discriminate between different utterances, as in *pit–bit* or *bit–but*. But, when combined, phonemes produce a bigger unit of language, the **morpheme**—the basic unit of meaning in a language. *She* is a morpheme formed by two basic phonemes, *sh* and *e*. Unlike the phonemes of which it is made, *she* conveys a specific meaning. All told, the English language contains about 100,000 morphemes, all made from just forty to forty-six phonemes.

Not all morphemes are whole words. **Prefixes,** like *un-* in *unhappy,* and **suffixes,** like *-ed* in *studied,* are also morphemes, for they too convey meaning. *Un* means "not," as in "not happy." *Ed* means that something happened in the past, as opposed to the present or the future.

Just as phonemes can be combined to form sounds with meaning, so too can morphemes be combined to form sounds with complex meaning. For instance, the morpheme *determine* can be combined with the morphemes *pre-* and *-ed* to form *predetermined.* In this way the 100,000 English morphemes can be combined to make more than a million words, each of which has its own meaning. Thus, despite the limited ability to produce distinguishable sounds, there is virtually no limit to the number of words that can be produced. And, in many cases, there is more meaning to a word than meets the eye.

Words can have at least two kinds of meaning: a **denotative** meaning, or strict dictionary definition; and a **connotative** meaning, which includes all the implications and feelings associated with a word. *Smell, breathe,* and *sniff* all have roughly the same denotative meaning, "to take in air." But, because each has a different connotative meaning, one can convey an entirely different meaning from another. Compare the phrases "breathe the air," "sniff the air," and "smell the air," for example. Each conveys a slightly different

Though words alone provide a rich source of information, there's more to language than words. Our facial expressions, body postures, and hand gestures are all part of language and communication.

meaning. *Breathe* suggests a passive taking in of air; *sniff* an active inhaling. And *smell* suggests the perception of a specific odor. The study of these differences in the meaning of words and languages is called **semantics.**

Because words with similar denotative meanings can have quite different connotative meanings, it is possible to slant or distort the meaning of a message without changing the essential facts. Suppose you are viewing a TV newsreel that shows a few hundred soldiers setting up camp. The announcer reports, "Peacekeeping troops arrived today." You switch stations and find exactly the same scene, but this time the announcer's message is, "Foreign troops landed today." What would your reaction be? Soldiers from another country can be described in many ways: "liberating army," "military advisers," "invading forces," "mercenaries," "allies," "conquerors," and so on. The message each term conveys, however, is quite different. The way one interprets a message often depends heavily on connotative meaning. By choosing their words carefully, speakers, political hopefuls, government leaders, even reporters and newscasters, can sway listeners toward a biased viewpoint while still providing an accurate account of the facts.

Though words alone, with their connotative and denotative meanings, provide a rich source of information (e.g., Danger), there is far more to language than words. When combined into sentences—that is, complete thoughts—words can express an almost endless variety of ideas. To be understood, however, they have to be combined in some standard way, according to generally accepted rules.

Semantics: The study of the meaning of language.

The Ground Rules of Language

Every language has its own **grammar,** or rules for combining words into sentences. Probably the most basic rule is that a sentence must form a complete thought. "The boy threw the ball" is a combination of words that conveys a whole idea, a meaning beyond that of each individual word. As such

Grammar: The rules of a language for combining words into sentences.

Figure 8.3 Schematic Summary of the Basic Levels of Language.

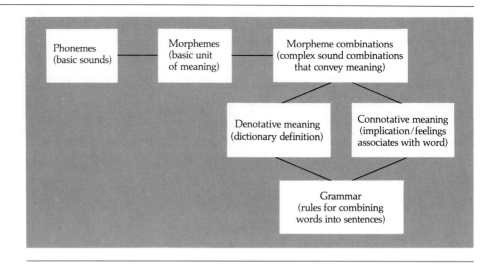

it qualifies as a sentence. The same cannot be said for other combinations—for instance, "The apple mailbox of the with book town." (See Figure 8.3 for a schematic summary of the basic levels of language.)

Although the rules of grammar restrict the ways in which words can be combined, they actually multiply the meaning that can be conveyed. Consider, for example, the rules that govern the order of words in sentences, or **syntax.** Depending on their order, the same words can be used to convey different meanings. "Hurt that" does not mean the same as "That hurt." Not only the words but the order in which we use them tells the listener what is meant.

Using the rules of grammar to forge new meaning out of words and sounds, humans can create sentences that they have never seen or heard. Herein lies the basic distinction between human language and the gestures and symbols chimps have learned to use. So far, the language produced by animals has been highly specific and limited to their previous experience. No animal has ever been able to apply general grammatical principles to a set of meaningful symbols—sounds, gestures, or chips of different shapes and colors—to create original ideas. In contrast, by the age of six, most normal children have a vocabulary of about two thousand words, which they use according to the rules of grammar to express an almost endless variety of thoughts. (See Chapter 2 for a discussion of language development.)

Researchers have been surprised to find that animals can pass on signs they have learned from humans. For example, a group of experimenters in-

Syntax: The set of rules pertaining to the order of words in sentences and phrases.

■ **Learning Check** ■

Read the definitions for each of the following aspects of language, then cover the right side and try to recite it. Repeat.

Morpheme	Basic unit of meaning
Syntax	Rules of word order
Phoneme	Basic unit of sound

troduced Washoe to a ten-month-old male chimp shortly after her own infant died (Fouts et al., 1979). Within a few months, Washoe had taught Louis eleven signs. By the time he was eighteen months old, Louis was using a number of double-sign combinations ("Come eat," "Me food") that Washoe had learned from her trainers (Chevalier-Skolnikoff, 1981). Perhaps someday chimps will develop an ability to use signs in a more creative way than they now do. If so, we may gain important insights about their thoughts.

THOUGHT

Thought—The mental representation and manipulation of symbols, images, and ideas—is often based on language. Though we can think nonverbally, words provide such a convenient and efficient way of referring to events and experiences, we would be seriously handicapped without them. In this section we will examine the relationship between language and thought. We will also explore some special techniques of thinking that are especially helpful in problem solving.

Thought: All the mental operations or processes that go on in a person's head as the person attempts to solve problems, master the environment, or synthesize information.

■ Learning Clue ■

As you read, take note of how language influences thought and of how thought influences language.

Language and Thought

A new invention—the product of thought—can lead to the creation of a whole new set of words. Videogames, for example, began with the idea of combining computers with television to create a new kind of game. The thought came before the word. But soon a whole new vocabulary had sprung up: "Video-Olympics," "Pac-Man Fever," "Video-Dungeons and Dragons," and the like.

But, just as thoughts influence language, so too language influences thought. Imagine if English had only one word to describe where people lived, *dwelling*. Both a dorm and a mansion would be described as dwellings, and both college students and millionaires would be said to live in dwellings. But of course a dorm is more than just a dwelling, and the word *dorm* conveys that extra information. Thus, a language that has many different words for dwelling—*dorm, mansion, apartment, house, home, condominium, townhouse, shack, room, tent, cave, bomb shelter, mobile home, trailer*—allows speakers to think about dwellings in very precise terms.

Or consider the Eskimo language, which has at least thirty different words to describe snow (Whorf, 1940). Snow for making igloos, falling snow, melting snow, snow covering the ground—the Eskimos have a different term for each. The availability of these different words helps the Eskimo speakers to think about snow in a more exact way than people born and raised in Los Angeles or Miami, who rarely encounter snow.

Linguistic Relativity Hypothesis: The theory that language shapes the way people think—that people who speak different languages think differently because of differences in their language.

The idea that language actually shapes the way we think is called the **linguistic relativity hypothesis** (Whorf, 1956). According to this theory, since language is the primary tool of thought, the words that are available in any given language will determine how precisely people think, the way they view things, even what they think. It's an interesting idea, but the fact is, not all thinking requires language. The theory also underestimates the influence of culture and environment on language and thought. Snow is a critical aspect of the culture and environment of the Eskimos. They encounter it all the time, and their very lives depend on having a clear idea of the distinction between melting ice on a lake and igloo blocks. Consequently, Eskimos think about snow more than most people—a fact that may explain why they have so many words for it. Today most scientists would agree that language can predispose or influence people's thinking or actions, but they reject the view that one is a prisoner of one's own language (Patterson et al., 1986).

Concepts

Concept: A symbol that represents a particular class of objects, words, or ideas that have something in common.

The interdependence between language and thought becomes especially evident when one considers **concepts**—symbols that stand for groups of related ideas, objects, or events. For instance, the word *chair* expresses a concept that includes large chairs, soft chairs, modern chairs, and folding chairs—any seat with a back that is meant for one person. With the exception of proper nouns that name some place or person—Boston, John Smith, and the like—most words stand for concepts. *Tree, pen, book, automobile, bus, school, teacher*—these words do not stand for something in particular. Each is a general term encompassing a large number of related items.

Think of how difficult it would be to think, learn, or deal with your environment without concepts. Every object, event, or experience would have to be described separately. How, for example, would you explain that you were late for dinner because of a traffic jam, if you didn't have a general concept for motor vehicles? You couldn't just say the road was jammed. You would have to say there was a big yellow car with a bent bumper, a small foreign car going too fast, a dump truck, and so on. And you couldn't possibly remember and store your experiences with all the cars and trucks on the road, let alone communicate them to your family. Your mind would be so cluttered with specific details that you would probably find it hard to think at all. Concepts provide an efficient and flexible tool for organizing, storing, and thinking about information and problems.

Problem Solving

Concepts provide the basis for another critically important aspect of thought, problem solving. "Solving a problem," one mathematician put it, "means finding a way out of a difficulty, a way around an obstacle, attaining an aim that was not immediately understandable" (Polya, 1962). If you wish to achieve something but have no clear or immediate way of proceeding, you have a problem. Life is full of them. How do you prepare for three exams in just a week, when all three fall on the same day? How do you get the money to support yourself while you're going to college? How do you get a date for the football game when you don't know anyone well enough to feel comfortable asking? What do you do if both your parents and your closest friend are expecting to see you Sunday afternoon?

As in concept formation, the solution to a problem often involves language—but not necessarily. Helen Keller, who was both deaf and blind, solved the problem of communicating with others despite her handicaps. But language can be a tremendous aid in problem solving, because it helps us to conceptualize a problem. It is also the medium we use to store past experiences in problem solving and guidelines for future attempts.

Once a general approach to solving a problem has been learned, it can be applied to new problems. Such general strategies or guidelines for prob-

Analogy: A heuristic in which one attempts to solve a problem using the ideas behind a previous solution to a similar problem.

Subgoals: A heuristic in which a problem is broken down into smaller, more manageable units.

Box 8.1 PSYCHOLOGY IN ACTION: Some Practical Heuristics

It's easy to see the value of heuristics in war, sports and games. But can general strategies for problem solving be applied to real-life situations? Let's go back to the problems mentioned on page 270: having only a week to prepare for three exams, supporting yourself through school, getting a date, and being expected to be in two places at the same time. Let's assume that you have not one, but all these problems at the same time (things could be worse). How would you proceed?

First, start with the idea that you *can* solve your problems. This heuristic of maintaining a positive attitude will help you to persist in the face of setbacks. If you believe you can handle your problems—knowing you have handled difficult situations before—at least you are off to a good start.

Of course, you can't rely on hope alone, as genuine as it might be. You must next analyze your problems and identify your priorities. After all, why worry about supporting yourself through college if finals are next week, and you must pass them just to stay in school? A useful method of setting priorities is to write down all your problems and the deadlines for solving them. Given your four hypothetical problems, your list might look something like this:

1. Figure out what to do on Sunday, when both my friend and my parents are expecting me (3 days left).
2. Prepare for 3 exams (7 days left).
3. Obtain $2,400. (As soon as possible. I have enough money to last 2 more weeks, until the end of the school term, but I need money for the next term.)
4. Get a date (10 days before the dance).

Next comes perhaps the most important step, con-

centrating as much energy as possible on your top priority before going on to the second. This was Napoleon's master strategy. By concentrating all his forces at a single point, he achieved victory against much larger armies. The alternative—dividing your efforts evenly—tends to scatter your energy.

Suppose you decided to concentrate first on the problem of whom to spend Sunday afternoon with; you would then need to figure out a technique for solving it. You might try the heuristic technique called **analogy:** comparing your problem to a similar problem you've experienced in the past, to see if it might have a similar solution. Were you ever expected to be in two places at once before? If so, what did you do?

After you have done everything possible to solve your top-priority problem, solved or not, you must temporarily forget it and concentrate as much as possible on your second priority. To deal with the task of studying for three exams in one week, you might use the heuristic technique of breaking the problem down into smaller, more manageable goals, or **subgoals.** For example, you might divide your task into three parts, studying for the psychology exam, for the history exam, and for the business exam. Each of these, in turn, can be divided into chapters or units to be studied. Next, you can create a schedule by assigning each subgoal a deadline. (For example, Friday read one chapter in psychology, one in business; Saturday read two chapters in history, etc.)

Creating a schedule frees you from worrying about how you are going to get the job done. You need only concentrate your effort on each day's assigned task, taking first things first, and modifying your schedule as necessary.

Heuristics: Strategies for solving a problem that provide general guidelines but do not necessarily guarantee success.

lem solving, or **heuristics,** can provide a very powerful tool for approaching a variety of new problems (Reed et al., 1985).

Problem solving is often as much a matter of taking the right approach as it is of one's intelligence, determination, or strength. The person who masters heuristics is like the general who works according to plan to overcome great odds. Consider Napoleon. Though his armies were often outnumbered, sometimes by as much as 5 to 1, he overcame brute force with carefully planned strategy. Heuristics can also be a valuable aid in solving real-life problems, as Box 8.1 discusses.

Box 8.1 illustrates how heuristics can be applied to the solution of everyday problems. In the next section we will consider heuristic techniques for finding a part-time job, and in future chapters we will look at techniques for dealing with other real-world problems. Of course, heuristics can also be used to solve puzzles, math problems, riddles, and the like (Kintsch & Greeno, 1985; Lederman et al., 1985). In each case the general idea is to approach a problem systematically, divide it into smaller units if possible, take first things first, and rely on any past experiences that might apply. Although following such a plan takes time and effort, and doesn't guarantee success, any reasonable plan is almost always better than no plan at all. You might say it's the intelligent thing to do.

INTELLIGENCE

Intelligence—one of the most publicized and emotionally charged concepts in psychology—is a topic of interest to college students, parents, educators, employers, politicians, and journalists. If you have ever wondered how intelligent you are or how fair intelligence tests are, you are not alone. Interest in these topics runs about as high as the feelings about them.

Of all the concepts in psychology, intelligence is also one of the hardest to define. One major approach is to define it in terms of a broad set of behaviors.

■ **Learning Clue** ■

A central concept concerning intelligence is the notion of a single general factor called "g." As you read, play close attention to the notion of "g" and take note of the evidence for and against it.

Intelligent Behavior

More of human behavior can be classified as intelligent than you might at first think. Supporting a family, getting the most for your money, finding a way to spend time with friends and loved ones in spite of tremendous pressures—cannot all these be considered examples of intelligent behavior? No doubt you can think of other examples. Intelligent behavior, in fact, can involve anything from surviving in an inner-city ghetto to discovering the atom. Alfred Binet, the psychologist who developed the first intelligence

 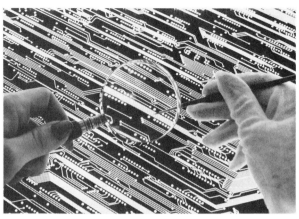

Intelligence can involve anything that involves goal-directed behavior and flexibility to make adjustments. The behavior of the river rafter, like that of the engineer, both involve goal-directed behaviors and require the ability to solve problems and make adjustments. Though quite different, are not both intelligent behavior?

test, proposed that intelligence was "the tendency to take and maintain a definite direction [goal-directed behavior]; the capacity to make adaptations for the purpose of attaining a desired end; and the power of auto-[self] criticism" (cited in Terman, 1916).

Assume, for example, that you need a part-time job to support yourself while going to college. What would be the intelligent way to get one? Goal-directed behavior, in this case, might begin with a realistic assessment of the type of job you could qualify for and the number of hours you could work. Then you could search the newspapers for an opening that suits you. If you don't succeed in finding a job this way, you may have to alter your behavior. Making adaptations requires an ability to criticize your approach in order to discover what adjustments you need to make. Perhaps you need help in preparing a resume, or hints on how to present yourself effectively in an interview. Finally, you must make the necessary adjustments—ask your friends for help, consult an expert, or read a book on the subject. You might volunteer your services at first to gain experience or make contacts. Or you might take a special course to strengthen your qualifications for the job.

This tendency to follow a definite course of action, in conjunction with the flexibility to make adjustments as necessary in the solution of a problem, is a key part of Binet's definition. Thus, intelligent behavior is far more than blind determination, for determination alone can't turn a poor plan into a good one.

A definition similar to Binet's was subsequently offered by psychologist David Wechsler, author of a major intelligence scale for children and adults still in use today. According to Wechsler (1958), intelligence is the "capacity of the individual to act purposefully, to think rationally and to deal effectively with the environment." (See Table 8.1 for a comparison of the two definitions of intelligence.)

What is it that enables one to follow a definite course and to deal effectively with an ever-changing environment? Wechsler believed that a complex of interrelated mental processes contributed to intelligent behavior. Ef-

Table 8.1   Comparison of Binet's and Wechsler's Definitions of Intelligence

Binet	Wechsler
1. Tendency to take and maintain a definite direction	1. Capacity to act purposefully
2. Capacity to make adaptations	2. Capacity to think rationally
3. Power of self-criticism	3. Capacity to deal effectively with the environment

fective thinking, concept formation, and problem solving were three processes that he cited.

But are these mental processes independent of each other, or are they all just aspects of one overriding characteristic called intelligence? The question is a crucial one. If all of one's intelligence springs from the same root, then a person who is good at one mental process will be good at them all. If, on the other hand, one's intelligence originates from many different roots, then a person who is good at one kind of mental operation—say, math—won't necessarily be good at another.

Until recently, most theories of intelligence tended to emphasize a single general factor. The apple falls from the tree, the rock from the cliff, and the rain from the sky because of a common force, the pull of gravity. Like gravity, intelligence was thought to be a single general force that underlay a broad range of very different behaviors.

General Intelligence ("g")

"g": The symbol used by Spearman to denote general intelligence.

The idea of a single, all-around factor that plays a role in all intelligent behavior is supported by the work of psychologist Charles Spearman (1863–1945), who referred to this factor as "**g**," or general intelligence (Spearman, 1927). General intelligence can be thought of as being similar to the central power station that lights an entire city. Although there are many different kinds of lighting equipment—large fluorescent tubes to light office buildings, small lamps for study desks, and so on—the same source breathes life into all of them. If the power source is weak or undependable, all the lights are negatively affected—as sometimes happens in a brownout. So too, theorists have argued, the many different kinds of intelligent behavior—planning, reasoning, conceptualizing—draw strength from the central source of general intelligence.

Support for the existence of "g" comes from statistical analyses of the scores that people receive on a broad variety of tests of complex mental processes: vocabulary development, concept formation, numerical reasoning, problem solving, and the like. There is a high correlation among the scores on these tests. (Correlation, you may recall, is a statistical expression of the relationship between two variables (see Chapter 1)). That is, people who score high on vocabulary tests also tend to score high on concept formation, problem solving, and numerical reasoning tests. Though positive, however, the corrrelation among these tests isn't perfect. The best problem solvers have good vocabularies, but not necessarily the best vocabularies.

These results suggest that intelligence involves two components, general intelligence ("g") plus a number of highly specific abilities for the more particular mental processes. Solving math problems, for instance, would require general intelligence plus numerical ability. Fixing diesel trucks would require general intelligence plus mechanical ability. But, while "g" could be thought of as being present in all intelligent behaviors, the specific factors would be totally independent of each other. Having a high degree of mechanical ability wouldn't necessarily help in solving numerical tasks.

Consider, for example, the reading lamp in your bedroom and the light in your bathroom. Both receive power from the same source. If the source is efficient, both can function at their maximum efficiency. But the amount of light that comes from the bedroom lamp has nothing to do with the bathroom light; that depends on the fixture itself and its light bulb. Similarly, your ability to fix a car has nothing to do with your ability to solve word problems, though presumably "g" affects both. Figure 8.4 illustrates this theory of intelligence—one general factor plus a number of highly specific factors (s), each related to a particular task.

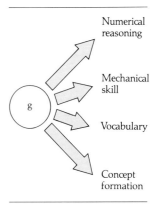

Figure 8.4 Spearman's Model of Intelligence.
The model holds that intelligence involves one general factor (g), plus a large number of specific factors (s).

Primary Mental Abilities and Multiple Intelligences

But is it really necessary to assume that one single factor is common to all intelligent behavior? Couldn't intelligence be due to a number of specific abilities that operate independently of each other? The operation of a city depends on many factors that have little to do with each other. The quality of the school system has little to do with the quality of the fire department or the health care system. A city with poor street lighting might have an excellent fire department. Similarly, must the ability to work with numbers and the ability to understand the meaning of words depend on a single core characteristic like "g"?

In contrast to Spearman's notion of intelligence as a single process, psychologist Louis L. Thurstone (1887–1955) attempted to demonstrate that intelligence was actually due to a number of independent factors, or *primary mental abilities*, of equal weight (Thurstone, 1938). Years of painstaking work revealed, however, that tests of verbal skills, numerical reasoning, memory, perceptual speed, and other suspected primary mental abilities were, in fact, correlated. Thus, the existence of "g" could not be completely ruled out. But some theorists argued that "g" was not as important as had first been thought, because each primary mental ability could also be shown to play a role in a variety of tasks. For example, verbal skills are important in reading, writing, and speaking. Numerical skills are important in doing simple arithmetic, balancing the checkbook, and creating a budget. One need not suppose that each of these talents is due to "g" plus one very specific ability, say for reading or balancing checkbooks. One overall factor and a number of primary abilities might play a role in several specific skills (see Figure 8.5).

More recently, some psychologists have taken a somewhat different tack in pursuit of independent components of intelligence. Drawing on knowledge concerning how the brain develops and relationships between brain and behavior, psychologist Howard Gardner (1983) has proposed a theory of multiple intelligences. According to Gardner, there are at least seven dis-

Is this girl's musical ability the product of a pervasive general ability factor plus a specific musical ability factor, or is her musical ability distinct and independent? Psychologists continue to debate such questions.

Figure 8.5 Schematic Summary of Primary Mental Abilities in Relation to g *and Specific Abilities.*

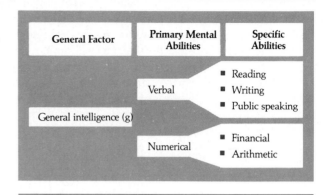

General Factor	Primary Mental Abilities	Specific Abilities
General intelligence (g)	Verbal	■ Reading ■ Writing ■ Public speaking
	Numerical	■ Financial ■ Arithmetic

tinct and independent "intelligences": (1) linguistic, (2) body-kinesthetic, (3) spatial, (4) logical-mathematical, (5) musical, (6) intrapersonal, (7) interpersonal.

Although Gardner's ideas have yet to be put to an adequate test, they represent another phase in the continuing controversy concerning a general factor in intelligence. Indeed, the existence of "g" and its relative importance continue to be major topics among experts (Cordes, 1986; Detterman, 1982). And a central question is this: does the high correlation among intelligence tests demonstrate the existence of "g"? Let's consider the relatively simple example of a ball-throwing contest.

Contestants will compete to see who can throw five different balls—a tennis ball, a baseball, a golfball, a basketball, and a football—the farthest. In all likelihood, those who are good at throwing the tennis ball will also be good at throwing the other balls, since many of the same factors—arm and body strength, arm size, muscular coordination—are involved in all five tasks. The correlation won't be perfect; one person might have a special talent for throwing a football, another a flair for pitching a baseball. Yet certainly the correlation among all five tests should be high. But what would that prove? Certainly not necessarily the existence of a general factor that underlies all physical activity. It would only demonstrate that the same talent or ability plays a role in all five tests. Nor would the correlation tell us

■ Learning Check ■

For each question: read, cover, try to recite, repeat.

Q. Why was Louis Thurstone unable to rule out the existence of "g" through his concept of primary mental abilities?

A. Tests of his so-called primary mental abilities were found to correlate. Thus, Thurstone could not demonstrate that these abilities were independent of each other.

Q. On what basis did Howard Gardner reintroduce the concept of independent sources of intelligence?

A. Gardner has argued that the correlations among tests of mental abilities does not prove the existence of "g." To back his theory of multiple intelligences, Gardner uses findings relating to the brain and its development.

what underlying talent—strength, coordination—is being measured by each test.

In the same way, the positive correlation among various tests of cognitive ability does not tell us what is being measured. To answer that question, we must know more about intelligence tests.

EVALUATING INTELLIGENCE TESTS

Intelligence tests measure behavior. Defining words, repeating digits, selecting the symbol that completes a pattern—all are behavior. Intelligence tests measure individual differences in performing those behaviors with accuracy and speed. That people differ in their ability to perform such tasks is clearly documented; on that point there is no dispute. What those differences in ability mean, however, is a matter of dispute.

In an effort to better understand intelligence tests, we will first look at the standards psychologists use to evaluate them. Then we will consider some of the strengths and limitations of intelligence tests.

■ Learning Clue ■

In reading this section try to answer the question, "What do intelligence tests measure"? The answer may surprise you.

Testing Standards

In evaluating tests, psychologists look for many things. Prominent among these are reliability and validity.

Reliability. An intelligence test must produce scores that are dependable and consistent, a quality psychologists refer to as **reliability.** In technical terms, reliability refers to the extent to which a test result is free of errors due to measurement. A yardstick is a reliable measure of the length of this page if you get the same result every time you use it. An intelligence test would be considered reliable if it produced about the same results each time it was given to the same person. But suppose you had a rubber yardstick that stretched out of shape every time you picked it up. It would not give you an accurate measurement and would be useless as a measure of length. Similarly, an intelligence test whose results vary at every administration cannot be an accurate measure and is useless. If a test gives you an IQ (Intelligence Quotient, see page 283) of 100 on Monday, of 60 on Tuesday, and of 140 on Wednesday, what could its results possibly mean? Certainly they would tell you little that would be of use to you about your intelligence.

Psychologists must therefore show that a test is reliable. Two major methods for determining a test's reliability are the test-retest method, which evaluates the stability of test scores over time, and the internal consistency method, which evaluates the degree to which each test item measures the

Reliability: The dependability or consistency of a test. The extent to which a test is free of errors due to measurement.

Test-Retest Reliability:
The consistency of test results over time, based on two administrations of the same test to the same people.

same thing. In the **test-retest method,** psychologists give a test to a group of people, wait a certain period of time, and then give the same test to the same group. The degree of correlation between individual scores for the two sittings tells how reliable the test is. If individuals maintain a similar relative position on both testings—that is, those who obtained high scores the first time also get high scores the second, and individuals who obtained relatively low scores the first time get low scores the second—the test is considered reliable over time. The higher the correlation, the more reliable the test.

Internal Consistency Reliability: The extent to which the items of a test correlate with each other.

In the **internal consistency method,** psychologists give a test to a group of people and then correlate the scores for half of the items with the scores for the other half. If there are 50 items, psychologists might correlate the scores for the first 25 items with the scores for the last 25; or the scores for the odd items with the scores for the even ones. The degree of correlation between the two sets of scores tells how consistent the test is in terms of what it measures. If the people who received high scores on the first 25 items also received high scores on the last 25, and the people who scored low on the first 25 scored low on the last 25, the test would be considered internally consistent. Whatever the items measure, they are probably measuring the same thing. Reliability is essential in an intelligence test, because a test that does not correlate with itself cannot correlate with anything else.

An unreliable test would be like a clock whose minute hand moved at a different speed each time it circles around the dial—sometimes faster, sometimes slower. But unlike such a clock, standard intelligence tests have proved to be highly reliable. For example, test-retest reliability coefficients for intervals between two and seven weeks for the IQ score obtained from the Wechsler Adult Intelligence Scale, Revised, average about .95, which is very close to a perfect correlation of 1. Estimates of the internal consistency of the IQ score are even higher, with an average reliability coefficient of .97 (Wechsler, 1981). Other major intelligence tests, such as the Stanford-Binet, enjoy equally impressive reliabilities. (For more on the Wechsler Adult Intelligence Scale and Stanford-Binet, see pages 282–285.)

High reliability itself, however, is no guarantee that a test measures intelligence. Knowing that intelligence tests are highly reliable tells us nothing about what those tests measure. For that information we must turn to measures of validity.

Validity: The meaning of a test. The extent to which a test measures what it claims to measure.

Validity. Validity is a technical term for the extent to which a test measures what it purports to measure. Simply put, a valid test measures what it claims to measure. If a history exam is supposed to measure your knowledge of history and does, then it is valid. If you feel a test didn't really measure your knowledge, what you are really saying is that it wasn't valid. It didn't measure what it was supposed to measure.

Some support for the validity of intelligence tests comes from an examination of their content. The items on intelligence tests are clearly related to abilities that are included in most theories and definitions of intelligence: concept formation, problem solving, language, and thinking skills. Because the content of the items sample the skills that theoretically define intelligence, these tests are said to have **content validity.**

Content Validity: The extent to which the content of a test is consistent with the definition or theory of what it is supposed to measure.

Psychologists usually do not rely on content validity alone in evaluating a test, however. Simply to say that intelligence involves problem solving, concept formation, and the like, and then to maintain that we are measuring intelligence because a test includes those tasks, is a bit circular. It is a step away from saying intelligence is what intelligence tests measure. The argument may sound logical, but there is no evidence to prove it.

To be considered truly valid, a test must be related to something beyond itself—school grades, for instance. Tests that correlate well with some external measure of performance are said to have **criterion validity.** If a test correlates well with the criterion of school grades, and if grades do in fact reflect intelligence, then we have some outside support for the test's validity. And indeed, besides the scores on other intelligence tests, the single most important correlate of an intelligence test score is scholastic achievement (Cronbach, 1970; Sattler, 1982). People who do well on intelligence tests get good grades in school; they also stay in school longer. This last fact may help to explain why intelligence test scores also correlate with the profession or occupation a person is likely to enter. You can't get into medical school with a high school education. And, since people with the highest IQ scores tend to stay in school longer than others, we might expect them to dominate the professions that require many years of education. Thus, intelligence tests predict future behavior in learning situations, namely, academic performance and academic achievement. (See Figure 8.6 for a summary of the standards used to evaluate intelligence tests.)

We cannot say, however, that having a high IQ causes a person to become a doctor or lawyer. Nor can we say that, because members of certain professions have high IQs, they must be highly intelligent. You may recall from Chapter 1 that correlation does not indicate cause-and-effect relationships. Some third variable—an encouraging parent, a high need for prestige and status, a love of problem solving—might explain the relationship between IQ score and occupation.

In fact, intelligence test scores correlate with a whole cluster of interrelated factors: academic success, occupation, and socioeconomic status. People who obtain high IQ scores also tend to do well in school, are more likely

Criterion Validity: A type of validity that tells what test scores mean by determining what criteria a test relates to or what kinds of behaviors it can predict.

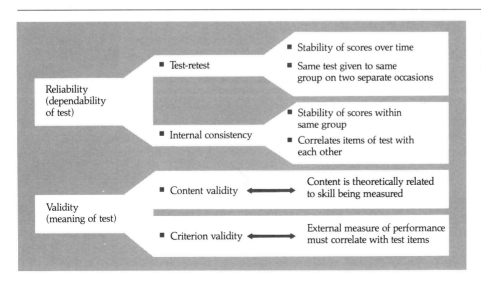

Figure 8.6 Schematic Summary of the Testing Standards Used to Evaluate Intelligence Tests.

to enter a profession such as law or medicine, and tend to earn more money (Matarazzo, 1979).

The strong relationship between IQ and school success can be traced back to the beginnings of intelligence testing. There was a high correlation between performance on the very first intelligence test, the Binet-Simon Intelligence Scale (see page 282), and teachers' judgments about children's intelligence. Since then, the relationship between IQ and school performance has increased, for, in later revisions of the Binet Scale, items that correlated poorly with academic success were eliminated. With time, the Binet Scale, as the first and most established IQ test, became the standard by which other intelligence tests were judged. Tests that didn't correlate well with the Binet Scale were usually discarded as invalid. Thus, it is partly by design that scores on intelligence tests can be related to each other and to scholastic achievement.

Though intelligence tests do predict who will do well in school and who won't, they should not be thought of as absolute measures of a person's potential. In the next section we will consider some of their shortcomings.

Shortcomings of Intelligence Tests

All intelligence tests contain at least some degree of cultural bias. A second shortcoming of such tests is that they do not appear to relate to creativity. And a third shortcoming concerns the relatively poor relationship between intelligence tests and criteria other than those related to school achievement and academic success. Let's briefly consider each of these three shortcomings.

Cultural Biases. Consider the bias contained in vocabulary items like *skyscraper, expressway,* and *personal computer.* Faced with the problem of defining these items on an intelligence test, a person born and raised in a large metropolitan area would have a distinct advantage over a person of equal intelligence who was born and raised in a small, isolated, rural area. Theoretically, if two people come from identical environments and they take an intelligence test that is reliable and valid, the differences between them on the test should reflect differences in their intellectual functioning.

But the crucial words in this statement are "identical environments." If people with fewer opportunities than others to acquire knowledge are given a test that depends heavily on knowledge or specific experiences, they are likely to score lower than people of the same or even lower intelligence but greater opportunities. Thus, intelligence tests that include only vocabulary and other language-related items can be biased. But no test, including those that use only symbols (see page 286) can completely eliminate cultural bias. Indeed, no test can eliminate the effects of past learning and experience.

Intelligence and Creativity. Attempts to correlate intelligence test scores and **creativity**—the ability to be original, to combine known facts in new ways, or to find a new relationship between known facts—have failed (Horn, 1979; Nelson & Crutchfield, 1970). At any given IQ level, some people are more creative than others. And those with the highest intelligence aren't necessarily the most creative.

The absence of a relationship between IQ and creativity is a bit curious,

Creativity: The ability to be original, to combine known facts in new ways, or to find a new relationship between known facts.

for creativity often plays a role in problem solving and is linked to effective thinking. One of the techniques used in problem solving is to think of as many solutions as possible, an aspect of creativity known as **fluency.** Another technique is to think of new or unusual solutions, an aspect of creativity known as **originality. Flexibility,** the ability to shift direction or change one's approach, to try again in a different way or to apply an old idea in a new way, is also a creative talent. But a creative solution is not something that is different, new, or original. It also must be effective.

The absence of a correlation between intelligence and creativity may be explained in part by the finding that creativity is greatly enhanced by training (Glover, 1980). Given two people of equal intelligence, the one who has learned creative skills, either by deliberate effort or by chance, will fare better.

Intelligence and Real-Life Success. Like creativity, real-life success is not necessarily correlated with intelligence test scores. Running a successful business, making a scientific breakthrough, becoming a great leader—none of these accomplishments is reserved for people with IQs of a certain value. Researchers who compared the intelligence test scores that established scientists had obtained in school with ratings of their later accomplishments in the real world found no relationship between the two (Harmon, 1963). Another study found no correlation between real-world achievement and scores on the Scholastic Aptitude Test (SAT), a college entrance exam that correlates well with standard IQ tests. Students who got low SAT scores generally achieved just as much as those who got high scores; some did better (Wallach, 1976).

Such studies can be criticized on the grounds that the actual differences between the people tested were quite small: People with very low SAT scores are unlikely to be admitted into college. What is more, high correlations usually emerge only when the people being tested are considerably different. Otherwise, the similarities between people outweigh the differ-

Fluency: An aspect of creativity based on the total number of solutions one can generate for a given problem.

Originality: An aspect of creativity referring to how new (novel) or unusual a person's solutions to a problem are.

Flexibility: An aspect of creativity involving the ability to shift direction or change one's approach.

■ Learning Check ■

For each question: read, cover, try to recite, repeat.

Q. What are some of the strengths of intelligence tests?

Answer:
1. They predict future behavior in learning situations.

2. They are highly reliable.

3. They are related to occupational and socioeconomic status.

Q. What are some of the limitations of intelligence tests?

Answer:
1. All intelligence tests contain some degree of cultural bias.

2. Intelligence test scores do not relate to creativity.

3. Real-life success depends on much more than one's score on an intelligence test.

ences. Nevertheless, once a person has a certain level of intelligence—say, that sufficient to graduate from a rigorous high school or two-year college—other factors may determine who will excel and who will not.

Suppose, for instance, that you had to select one of two people to manage a bank. Assume that past experience has shown that an average IQ score is more than sufficient to meet the demands of the job. Of the two candidates, one has an IQ of 100, which is average; the second an IQ of 135, which is very superior (see page 283). Why wouldn't the one with the higher IQ automatically be the better candidate? The answer is fairly obvious. If both candidates have more than a sufficient IQ for the job, then having a higher IQ is probably not as important as other factors. Honesty, past experience, an ability to get along with others and motivate them to do their best—all would have to be considered.

Most experts recognize the limitations of the intelligence test and acknowledge the importance of nonintellective factors—energy, social skills, attitudes, and emotional stability—in real-world achievement. And certainly nonintellective factors such as persistence and positive self-concept do contribute to one's ability to "act purposefully" and "deal effectively" with the environment (Matarazzo, 1972; Howe, 1982).

The critical factor may be not how much potential one has, but how one uses it. Intelligence in the broad sense, as opposed to the IQ score on an intelligence test, may perhaps be best viewed as a power that must be harnessed, developed, disciplined, and directed.

INTELLIGENCE TESTING

Now that we have considered some of the standards for evaluating intelligence tests and have identified some of their strengths and limitations, let's examine the characteristics of specific intelligence tests and look more closely at the meaning of the IQ score. In this section we will consider traditional approaches to intelligence testing as well as some of the newer approaches.

Development of the Intelligence Test

Binet-Simon Scale: The original version of the first modern measure of human intelligence. (In the United States, this scale has been revised into a test called the Stanford-Binet.)

The **Binet-Simon Scale,** the first major test of intelligence, relied on the fact that older children have greater capabilities than younger children. The typical four-year-old knows the meaning of more words, can identify more objects, and can communicate more effectively than the typical three-year-old. The typical five-year-old, in turn, has greater capabilities than the typical four-year-old.

To determine the abilities of the average child of various ages, Binet and Simon first developed a number of tasks, such as pointing to parts of the face, repeating digits, copying symbols, and defining words. Then they administered the items to large numbers of children of different ages and analyzed the results statistically. They found, to give an example, that at least two out of three four-year-olds could repeat three digits. Fewer three-year-olds could accomplish that task, but even more five-year-olds could do it.

That item, along with others that were of comparable difficulty, they se-lected as a measure of the intelligence of the typical four-year-old. The abil-ity to name familiar objects, such as a nickel, also proved a good test of the average four-year-old's capabilities. Copying a square proved a good mea-sure for five-year-olds; copying a diamond and repeating five digits, good tests for seven-year-olds.

Binet and Simon threw out items that did not discriminate among chil-dren of various ages. By selecting only those items that separated children by age, they were able to estimate a child's **mental age,** or mental capabili-ties, independently of his or her actual, or **chronological,** age. That is, if Marie could pass items at the five-year level but not those at the six-year level, then Marie could be assumed to have the mental capabilities of the typical five-year-old, no matter what her real age might be. Her mental age would be expressed as five. If she were actually five, her mental ability would be about average for children her age. If she were three, she would be far ahead of her age group; if she were ten, far behind.

The relationship of a child's mental age to his or her chronological age can be expressed as an **intelligence quotient,** or **IQ.** This technique, first suggested by Stern (1914), was used by Lewis Terman of Stanford Univer-sity in his initial American version of the Binet-Simon Scale.

An IQ is simply the ratio of mental to chronological age—MA divided by CA—multiplied by 100 to eliminate decimals. That is, IQ = MA/CA × 100. If Peter's chronological age is 5 and his mental age 10, for instance, then Pe-ter's IQ = 10/5 × 100, or 200. If his chronological age is 10 and his mental age 5, then his IQ = 5/10 × 100, or 50. (The highest chronological age that is used to divide by is 18 years.)

Children with average IQs have a mental age about equal to their chronological age. For example, a ten-year-old who can complete the tasks of the average ten-year-old has both a mental and a chronological age of 10. In that case, the IQ is 10/10 × 100, or 100. In fact, the average IQ for any-one, child or adult, is 100.

Ultimately the IQ concept was abandoned in favor of a more statistically precise index called the deviation IQ. For the most part, such deviation IQs varied from the intelligence quotient by no more than a few points.

Figure 8.7 shows the relative frequency of IQ scores among the general population. The majority of IQs fall between 90 and 110; a smaller percent-

Mental Age: A child's age-equivalent perfor-mance on a test. A child who can perform at the level of the average five-year-old, for example, has a mental age of five.

Chronological Age: An individual's actual age—the number of years and months since an individ-ual was born.

Intelligence Quotient (IQ): The ratio of mental age to chronological age. IQ = mental age divided by chronological age times 100 (IQ = MA/CA × 100).

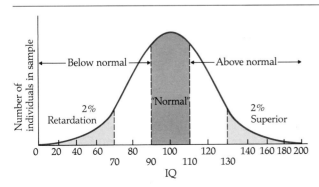

Figure 8.7 *Examination of this frequency distribution of IQ scores reveals that most scores are average, and fall within a range of 90–110. Further examination reveals that scores below 70 or above 130 are rare, with only about 2 percent of the popu-lation falling within these extreme limits.*

Stanford-Binet Intelligence Scale: The United States version of the Binet-Simon Scale, first published by Lewis Terman of Stanford University in 1916.

age of scores fall equally on either side of that range. The further a score is from the average of 100, the rarer it is. Only about 2 percent of all IQs fall below 70. Another 2 percent fall above 130, a score that indicates very superior intelligence.

Terman's revision of the Binet-Simon Scale, called the **Stanford-Binet Intelligence Scale,** has been revised and updated regularly since its publication and continues to be widely used. It has been criticized, however, on the grounds that it yields only one score, the IQ, and that this is primarily a measure of verbal ability (see Kaplan & Saccuzzo, 1982).

Performance Tests

Performance Tests: Tests that require the subject to perform in some activity (e.g., copy symbols, put blocks together, point to a missing object.)

In an effort to help counteract bias toward the measurement of verbal ability on the Stanford-Binet, Wechsler (1939) developed an intelligence test that included a separate scale consisting only of **performance tests.** Such tests require a person to complete some activity, like copying symbols, putting blocks together in a certain design, or pointing to the missing part of an object.

The Wechsler Intelligence Scale has two parts, verbal and performance. Both parts are divided into subtests, each of which attempts to measure a specific aspect of intelligence. Table 8.2 lists the six verbal tests and five performance tests of the Wechsler Adult Intelligence Scale–Revised (WAIS–R), which is designed for people sixteen and older. A parallel version, the Wechsler Intelligence Scale for Children–Revised (WISC–R), is for children five to sixteen years of age. The Wechsler Preschool and Primary Scale of Intelligence (WPPSI) is made for children four to six and a half.

The Information Subtest of all three versions of the Wechsler Intelligence Scale contains items that test a person's range of knowledge, like "What is the capital of Spain?" The Comprehension Subtest measures practical judgment with questions such as, "Why do we need a sewer system?" The Digit

Table 8.2   The Subtests of the Wechsler Adult Intelligence Scale–Revised (WAIS–R)

	Major Function Measured
Verbal Scales	Range of knowledge
Information	Judgment
Comprehension	Concentration
Arithmetic	Abstract thinking
Similarities	Immediate memory,
Digit span	anxiety
Vocabulary	Vocabulary level
Performance Scales	
Digit symbol	Visual-motor functioning
Picture completion	Alertness to details
Picture arrangement	Planning ability
Block design	Nonverbal reasoning
Object assembly	Analysis of part-whole relationships

Source: R. M. Kaplan, and D. P. Saccuzzo, *Psychological testing: Principles, applications, and issues* (Monterey, Calif. Brooks/Cole, 1982.)

Symbol Subtest asks the individual to copy symbols as fast as possible, which provides a measure of visual-motor speed and persistence. The Object Assembly Subtest contains puzzles that the person must put together as fast as possible. It measures a person's ability to see part–whole relationships (Matarazzo, 1979).

In contrast to the single IQ score of the Stanford-Binet, the Wechsler yields separate IQ scores for the Verbal and Performance Scales, a composite score called the *Full Scale IQ,* and separate scores for each of the subtests. The Full Scale IQ presumably reflects "g," or the general factor underlying all the specific abilities measured by the scale. The Verbal and Performance IQs are analogous to the primary mental abilities as depicted in Figure 8.5. The specific subtests, in turn, are analogous to the specific abilities.

In yielding several scores, the Wechsler often provides more information about a person than can be communicated in the single score of the Stanford-Binet. The Stanford-Binet, by contrast, is more sensitive to extreme scores—those above IQs of 130 or below 40. In addition, for individuals in the lower IQ ranges, the Stanford-Binet usually takes less time to administer.

Regardless of which test is used, however, only one person can be tested at a time. Such tests are referred to as **individual tests.** Individual tests are particularly useful in clinical situations, which require a thorough and detailed evaluation of an individual. Where such detail is not necessary or is impractical, **group tests**—tests that can be administered to large numbers of people in a single session by one examiner—are used.

Individual Test: A test that can only be administered to one person at a time: a single examiner for a single (individual) subject.

Group Test: A test that can be administered to many people at the same time: a single examiner for many (a group of) subjects.

Group Tests of Intelligence

The first group tests of mental ability were the Army Alpha and the Army Beta, developed by the U.S. military during the First World War for use in assigning recruits according to their abilities. The Army Alpha was exclusively **verbal,** which means its items required subjects to read or make verbal responses. The Army Beta, by contrast, was a **nonverbal test;** though it did not require subjects to complete some activity as in a performance test, its questions were posed in symbols rather than words. A typical nonverbal item might look like the one shown in Figure 8.8.

Intelligence tests that rely on nonverbal items like the one in Figure 8.8 can be used to test people who might not be able to understand oral or written instructions, such as deaf persons or speakers of a foreign language.

Verbal Test: Tests that involve language, requiring reading ability or a verbal response.

Nonverbal Test: Tests that do not involve language or reading ability.

■ **Learning Check** ■

For each type of test, read the information on the right, then cover the right side and try to recite. Repeat.

Individual Test	One subject, one examiner
Group Test	Two or more subjects, one examiner
Verbal Test	Items require reading ability or verbal response
Nonverbal Test	Items use symbols rather than words
Performance Test	Nonverbal tasks that require the person to perform some activity

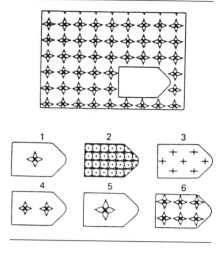

Figure 8.8   Item from A Nonverbal Intelligence Test.   *Pick the item that best fits the missing part of the larger figure.* (Figure A5 from the Raven Standard Progressive Matrices. Used with permission of J. C. Raven Limited.)

Such tests begin with simple items that can be answered by the average five-year-old, just to give examinees an idea of how the test works. More difficult items are then introduced.

Recent Developments in Intelligence Testing

In an effort to improve the technology of intelligence testing, many contemporary researchers are looking for new ways of conceptualizing and measuring intelligence. One of the more promising of these newer approaches emphasizes the processes that constitute intelligent performance (Sternberg, 1985). One such process, for instance, may be the speed with which one is able to acquire, analyze, and make use of information. That is, the faster and more efficient one's brain is at processing information, the higher one's intelligence. To measure intelligence, these investigators test subjects on some relatively simple tasks and note their reaction time (Jensen, 1980, 1986).

In such procedures, the subject sits in front of a panel containing a number of lights, each with a button underneath. When one of the lights goes on, the subject presses the button below it as fast as possible, and an electronic device records the reaction time. It can be fun, trying to predict which light will come on next so as to be ready for it. Jensen (1986) has argued that this reaction time task measures mental speed as well as intelligence. As with all new approaches, however, results are far from conclusive.

Other researchers have used a different method of measuring processing speed (Brand, 1980; Saccuzzo et al., 1986). Imagine yourself sitting alone in front of a personal computer. The instructions tell you to look at the center of the screen. Two lines will appear briefly, one just to the left of center, the other just to the right. Your job will be to determine which of the two is longer. If you think the one on the right is longer, you are to push the button marked → . If you think the one on the left is longer, you are to push the button marked ← . Accuracy, not reaction time, is what counts.

Following a brief warning signal (a tone), two lines appear for about a tenth of a second. The one on the right looks longer, so you press → .

"That's very good," the computer replies. Soon you hear the warning signal again, and this time the lines are flashed on and off still faster. You press ← and get another compliment on your response. "Now keep going," you are told. The lines appear faster and faster, and it gets harder to tell which line is longer. The computer seems to sense your frustration and slows down a bit, then speeds up again. After about thirty minutes, you are done.

Some researchers think this technique may prove to be one of the purest measures of human intelligence ever devised (Brand, 1980). Others, including some of the researchers who first introduced the procedures, remain skeptical (Nettelbeck, 1982). While these new tests of processing speed may discriminate between retarded persons and those of normal intelligence (Saccuzzo & Michael, 1984), so far they have been of little value in distinguishing differences in intelligence within the normal ranges (Sternberg, 1981; Mackintosh, 1981). Currently, researchers are attempting to refine their measures of processing speed in an effort to make them more accurate and predictive of individual differences in intelligence. They also hope that such new measures will provide some insights into the nature of intelligence and its determinants (Saccuzzo et al., 1986).

DETERMINANTS OF INTELLIGENCE

The issue of what determines intelligence—heredity, environment, or some combination of the two—is part of one of the most hotly disputed issues in psychology, the nature–nurture controversy. The case for **nature,** or heredity, can be illustrated by the experience of a farmer who has two plots of land, one rich and fertile, the other barren and depleted; and two sacks of seed, one corn and the other nightshade, a deadly poison. Suppose the farmer takes one of each kind of seed and plants it in the good soil. He waters, fertilizes, and tends each seedling with equal care. Soon two plants, one corn and one nightshade, develop. But no matter how hard the farmer tries to treat the two plants equally, they will never be the same. The differences between the two plants are determined by differences in their inherited genetic make-up.

In like manner, a human is different from an ape or a chimpanzee. No matter how hard someone might try to treat a newborn human and a newborn ape equally, the two will not turn out the same. The human will learn to talk and the ape won't; the human will have a larger brain, a different bone structure, and a higher intelligence than the ape. So human intelligence is due to inherited factors, not to environment; on that point there is no dispute. Rather, the question is *to what extent* the differences between one human or group of humans and another are due to inherited characteristics; *to what extent* to environment; or to what extent to some combination of the two.

Let's go back to our farmer again. Suppose he takes two handfuls of corn and plants the first in the fertile plot, the second in the barren plot. Further suppose that he gives the best of care to the seeds planted in the fer-

Nature: That side of the nature–nurture issue that represents the influence of heredity.

tile soil, and the bare minimum of care to the others. Which plants would be more likely to grow tall and produce an abundant, sweet-tasting crop of corn?

The answer is that, on the average, the seeds planted in the fertile soil will do better. Not every plant in the fertile plot will be bigger or sweeter than the plants growing in the barren soil. A few plants in the barren soil—the hardiest of the bunch—might easily grow to be as large and sweet as the best in the other plot. But, if we measured each plant in each plot and figured the average height, we would no doubt find the plants in the fertile plot to be superior. We would attribute this difference to environmental factors (nurture). Each handful of seeds, we would assume, contained about an equal number of good seeds and bad seeds—some with a genetic blueprint to be tall and sweet, others with a genetic blueprint to be short and bland tasting.

Nurture: That side of the nature–nurture issue that represents the influence of environment.

This is the reasoning of psychologists who take the **nurture** side of the nature–nurture argument. They assume that differences in IQ between one group of individuals and another—such as differences in IQ between upper-class whites and lower-class whites—are due to environment. Those who take the nature side of the argument assume that the group differences are due largely to genetic factors. Why is it, they ask, that even in the good plot some plants will grow taller and sweeter than others? Since the environment is the same, the differences between the plants must be due to differences in genetic make-up.

Heritability: The extent to which differences between one group and another are due to genetic factors; the percentage of variability in a trait associated with differences in genetic composition of the individuals in the group.

The extent to which differences between one group and another are due to genetic factors is referred to as **heritability.** Some psychologists have argued that the heritability of human intelligence is 50 to 80 percent (Bouchard & McGue, 1981; Herrnstein, 1982). Others maintain that it is zero; that all variation in IQ between one group and another is due to environment (Kamin, 1978). Yet a third group believes that group variation in IQ scores is due to the *interaction* between heredity and environment. Consider again the farmer and his corn. Suppose that one strain of corn does best in dry soil, while another thrives only in damp soil. If both kinds of seed were placed in the same plot and given equal care, they would develop differently, because the two kinds respond differently to the environment. Thus, the differences in their growth would be due to the interaction between their inherited characteristics and their environment. According to the interactionists, the effects of nature and nurture are so intertwined, they cannot be separated. Let's look at the arguments for nature and nurture more closely.

Heredity (Nature)

Gene: The basic unit of heredity.

Heredity: Inborn or inherited—the transmission of a characteristic from parent to offspring.

The usual way of determining the heritability of a given characteristic is to compare its occurrence in families to its occurrence in unrelated individuals. The assumption is that members of a family share more **genes,** the basic unit of heredity, than unrelated individuals. (See Chapter 2 for more on the mechanics of **heredity.**) Therefore, if the characteristic is heritable, related individuals should share it to a greater degree than unrelated individuals. And, as a matter of fact, the IQs of family members are closer than the IQs of unrelated persons. Whereas the correlation between the IQs of unrelated children reared apart is zero, that between the IQs of parents and their chil-

Table 8.3 Correlation of IQ's in Twins and Siblings[1]

Relationship	Average Correlation
Monozygotic twins reared together	.86
Monozygotic twins reared apart	.67
Dizygotic twins reared together	.58
Siblings reared together	.45
Siblings reared apart	.24

[1] Adapted from Bouchard & McGue (1981).

dren, or brothers and sisters reared together, is .5 or higher (Bouchard & McGue, 1981; Erlenmeyer-Kimling & Jarvik, 1963).

But because families share not only genes but the same environment, these studies provide no absolutely conclusive evidence that intelligence is a heritable characteristic. Consequently, researchers have had to develop more sophisticated techniques, the most popular of which is to compare the IQs of identical or **monozygotic twins.** Monozygotic twins develop from a single *ovum,* or egg, and are therefore genetically identical. If the nature viewpoint is correct, monozygotic twins should have highly similar IQs, regardless of whether they are reared apart or together.

Researchers have also compared the IQs of fraternal or **dizygotic twins** reared together. Since dizygotic twins develop from two separate ova, they are no more genetically alike than two brothers or sisters. But, if they are reared together, their environments are about as similar as the environments of monozygotic twins reared together. If environment is the critical factor in IQ, then the IQs of monozygotic twins and dizygotic twins reared together should be about the same. If heredity is more important, however, the IQs of the monozygotic twins should be closer than the IQs of the dizygotic twins. Table 8.3 shows the average correlation of IQs among monozygotic twins, dizygotic twins, and siblings reared together and apart, drawn from over a hundred studies. Keep in mind that the highest possible *positive* correlation is 1. The correlation of .86 for monozygotic twins reared together is thus remarkable. In fact, because it is about as high as the correlation between any two intelligence tests, this less-than-perfect correlation for

Monozygotic (MZ) Twins: Identical twins, developed from one ovum and one sperm.

Dizygotic (DZ) Twins: Fraternal twins, developed from two ova fertilized by two sperm. They may be of the same or opposite sex.

Are the similar IQ's of these twins due to their identical genetic make-up, or to their life's experiences? It is difficult to separate the role of genetic factors from the role of environmental factors in evaluating the determinants of intelligence.

monozygotic twins can be attributed to errors of measurement in the test. As might be predicted from the genetic hypothesis, the correlation for dizygotic twins is much lower, though significant; and the correlation for siblings lower still.

When the correlations in Table 8.3 are compared to the correlations for unrelated individuals, the evidence looks even more striking (Loehlin et al., 1975). Studies have shown a zero correlation among unrelated individuals reared apart, and a correlation of only .17 for unrelated individuals reared together.

These data do not rule out the effect of environment, however. As you can see, the correlation for monozygotic twins reared *together* is higher than the correlation for monozygotic twins reared *apart*. Similarly, the correlation for siblings reared together is higher than that for siblings reared apart. And, though there is zero correlation among unrelated individuals reared apart, the correlation goes up to .17 when unrelated individuals are reared in the same environment. Supporters of the genetic hypothesis have taken these findings as evidence that intelligence is about 80 percent heritable, 20 percent nurturable—that is, due to environment.

Environment (Nurture)

Despite all the evidence pointing to the heritability of intelligence, the issue is far from settled. First, all heritability estimates are based on intelligence tests, which, as we have seen, relate primarily to academic achievement. IQ scores may be heritable, but to say that intelligence is heritable would be to stretch the evidence.

Furthermore, the IQ scores of monozygotic twins reared apart have been known to vary widely. In one study, the difference in IQ was 28 points, a spread so broad that it could make the difference between retarded and average intelligence, or between average and superior (Skeels, 1966). The environmental theory is also supported by a number of studies that show that, when disadvantaged children are placed in enriched environments, their IQ scores increase by an average of 15 to 20 points (Pines, 1979; Ramey et al., 1976). In one study, researchers randomly assigned newborn infants from forty disadvantaged families into one of two groups (Heber et al., 1972). One group was exposed to an extensive educational program that stressed language development, problem solving, reading, and mathematics. Their mothers, whose IQs were 75 or less, also received educational assistance through adult education classes in reading and arithmetic. The other group, the control group, was simply given IQ tests at various intervals. The results were dramatic. By the age of four, the children in the experimental group had IQs that averaged about 30 points higher than those in the control group.

Critics have questioned the validity of this study (Sommer & Sommer, 1983). However, a comparable study done in France produced similar, though not as dramatic, improvements in IQ (Schiff et al., 1982). And other studies have supported the influence of specialized training and experience on intelligence test scores. In one study, fifth- and sixth-graders were taught how to think more effectively. They practiced finding the similarities and differences in pairs of items such as *sad–happy, dog–lion,* and *math–science.*

Two years later the researchers noted a significant increase in the students' IQ scores (Helcomb & Thomas, 1981).

Supporters of the genetic hypothesis have countered that a 20- to 30-point rise in IQ as a result of improved environment is exactly what one would expect if the heritability of intelligence is 80 percent (Eysenck, 1982). So supporters of the environmental theory have taken another tack: they have found minor but undeniable flaws in every study that supports the genetic hypothesis (Kamin, 1976, 1982). One of their criticisms has to do with the sampling procedure used in these studies. Human beings are not corn seed, and scientists can't simply separate twins and siblings just to prove a theory. Consequently, not a single study of the heritability of intelligence is based on a random sample. People who adopt children are certainly not a random sample of all parents; they may constitute a biased sample. The same can be said for monozygotic twins, who certainly do not represent a random sample of the general population. Another major problem is that many of the monozygotic twins in these studies were not separated until six months of age or older. Thus, they shared the same environment during the critical early months of their development. Even after separation, the environments they knew were often quite similar, for adoption agencies usually try to match foster parents and children as closely as possible.

The obstacles to conducting a flawless study on the heritability of intelligence are so great as to make the attempt all but futile, at least for the foreseeable future. So the debate over nature versus nurture with respect to intelligence is likely to go on indefinitely. For the time being, then, intelligence, like so many other characteristics, is perhaps best viewed as the result of the interaction between heredity and environment.

Having considered cognitive processes, we will now turn our attention to motivational and emotional determinants of behavior. In Chapter 9 we will consider basic concepts of motivation and emotion. Then, in Chapters 10 and 11, we will apply some of these basic concepts as we study human sexuality and coping with problems of life-style.

LEARNING FRAMEWORK

I. Language must be learned, but humans appear to be predisposed to acquire it.
   A. Evidence to date indicates animals cannot learn to produce language comparable to humans'. (Review: *Figure 8.2*)
   B. A distinguishing feature of human language is that it has a basic structure and set of rules for combining sounds into meaning. (Review: *Phoneme; Morpheme; Semantics*)
   C. Human language also has a set of rules for combining smaller units of meaning into more complex units. By the age of six most normal children automatically apply these rules in their own speech. (Review: *Grammar; Syntax; Figure 8.3*)
II. Thought is intimately linked to language and our ability to solve problems.
   A. The relationship between language and thought is a two-way street. (Review: *Linguistic Relativity Hypothesis*)

B. Through words we also represent groups of related ideas, objects, or events, which facilitate our thinking. (Review: *Concept*)

C. Language helps us to conceptualize and think about solutions to problems. (Review: *Heuristics*)

III. The nature of human intelligence remains a matter of controversy and debate.

A. Alfred Binet and David Wechsler both included the idea of acting with a purpose and the ability to accomplish that purpose by rational thinking or self-criticism in their definitions of intelligence. (Review: *Table 8.1*)

B. Spearman defined intelligence in terms of a general factor called "g" that presumably is the underlying source of all intelligent behavior. (Review: *Figure 8.4*)

C. Thurstone and Gardner proposed the existence of several independent abilities or different types of intelligence. (Review: *Figure 8.5*)

IV. Psychologists use specific standards to evaluate tests.

A. Tests can be evaluated in terms of their dependability as well as in terms of their meaning. (Review: *Reliability; Validity; Figure 8.6*)

B. Though they are reliable and predictive of future behavior in learning situations, intelligence tests are limited in important ways. (Review: *Shortcomings of Intelligence Tests*)

V. Psychologists have used a number of approaches to measure intelligence.

A. The intelligence quotient, or IQ, compares an individual's mental age to his or her chronological age. (Review: *Mental Age*)

B. The Wechsler Intelligence Scale attempts to measure verbal and nonverbal intelligence. (Review: *Figure 8.7; Performance Tests; Individual Test*)

C. Intelligence tests may be individually or group administered; verbal or nonverbal. (Review: *Group Test; Nonverbal Test; Figure 8.8*)

D. Newer approaches to intelligence testing measure speed of information processing through relatively simple tasks.

VI. A major debate in psychology concerns the extent to which intelligence is due to inborn versus environmental factors. (Review: *Nature; Nurture; Heritability*)

A. In support of the nature side of the argument, there is a well-documented relationship between similarity of genes and similarity of IQ. (Review: *Monozygotic Twins; Dizygotic Twins; Table 8.3*)

B. In support of the nurture side are the differences that have been found in the IQs of identical twins and the positive effect of enriched environments on the IQs of some impoverished individuals.

P A R T

IV

Motivational and Emotional Processes

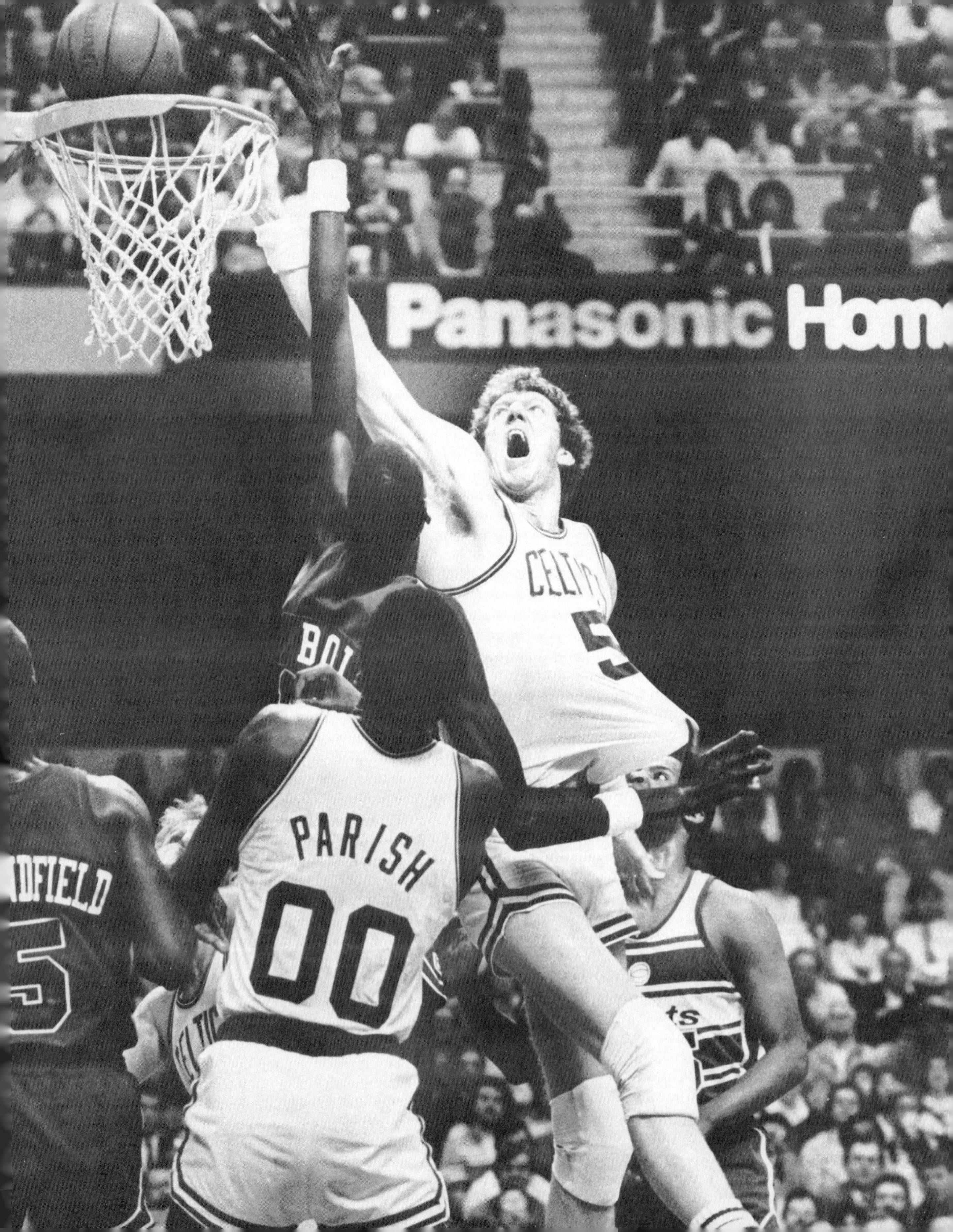
Panasonic
PARISH
00

CHAPTER

9

Motivation and Emotion

Chapter Outline

The Concept of Motivation
Biological Theories of Motivation
    Motivation as Instinct
    Drive Reduction Theory
    Arousal Theory
Theories of Social and Personal Motivation
    Murray's Theory of Learned Need
    Maslow's Theory of Motivation
The Role of Cognition in Motivation
    Expectation × Valence = Motivation
    Locus of Control
    Intrinsic vs. Extrinsic Motivation
The Physiology of Motivation
    Study of Hunger

Homeostasis in Hunger
The Concept of Emotion
    The Components of Emotion
    Distinguishing Emotion from Motivation
Theories of Emotion
    Darwin's Evolutionary Theory
    Early Theories: The Sequence of Emotion's Components
    Biological Theories
    Cognitive Theories
    Box 9.1 How to Maximize Performance
    Box 9.2 How to Read Emotion

295

As you watch athletes training and competing, can you say what it is that makes one or two push themselves harder than the others? Why is it that some players seem to try harder when behind while others seem to lose their spirit when the score is against them? What is it inside that tells an athlete to stop training and go get something to drink? Why a person does one thing instead of another has been a subject psychologists have studied for over a hundred years. They have also tried to understand why a person acts at all. In this chapter we will look at motivation to see what it is that energizes and directs people's behavior. We will look in detail at the physiological side of motivation by studying hunger.

If you continue to watch athletes compete, you will find that, even though you may be too far away to hear exactly what they say, you can still tell how they feel. If two football players get angry at each other, it's not hard to tell from the expressions on their faces. If a player is discouraged, surprised, or joyful, that emotion is visible, too. In this chapter we also look at psychologists' attempts to understand emotion. What are the elements that make up such a powerful part of our lives?

THE CONCEPT OF MOTIVATION

Motivation: The forces that energize and direct behavior.

Psychologists use the term motivation to describe the forces that move people. They define **motivation** (from the Latin word *movere*, "to move") as the forces that energize and direct behavior. Notice that there are two components to motivation, energy and direction. Also note that the idea of motivation is used to account for the whys of behavior, as opposed to the hows. Motivation describes not how a pitcher throws a baseball, but why.

Motivation itself cannot be directly observed; only the behavior it incites can be seen. One cannot see the forces that energize and direct the athlete to

What are the forces that energize this thirty-year-old athlete to train several hours a day in order to lift this 344 pound weight in the New England Regional Powerlifting Championship?

train several hours a day. Instead, we observe the athlete's actions and infer what his or her motivation is. Motivation is always inferred from behavior.

To explain motivation, psychologists have proposed a number of theories and investigated several topics. They have examined inborn traits and biological needs such as those for food, water, and air. They have tried to determine what role thinking and expectation play in motivation; and they have looked at motivation that seems learned and uniquely human, such as the desire to achieve. No single area of investigation has been able to explain all that motivation is. In the sections that follow we will examine several theories of motivation and note the strengths and weaknesses of each.

BIOLOGICAL THEORIES OF MOTIVATION

In this section we consider three major theories, each of which is based on a biological view of motivation. We will begin with an early theory of motivation, which looked for the basis of motivation in inborn (inherited) characteristics of the organism, and then a theory based on the regulation of biological needs and another on the need for sensation and stimulation.

Motivation as Instinct

Early notions of motivation relied heavily on the notion of **instincts**—inborn inclinations to behave in a particular way when circumstances are

Instincts: Inborn inclinations to behave in a particular way under appropriate circumstances. Instinct requires no learning; it is transmitted genetically from parent to offspring.

■ Learning Check ■

Read the right side, then cover and try to recite. Repeat.

Three important facts
about motivation:

1. It energizes and directs behavior.

2. It cannot be directly observed.

3. It expresses the whys of behavior, not the hows.

---

right. Instinct requires no learning; it is transmitted genetically from parent to offspring. According to the instinct theory, all energized and directed behavior originates from instinct. James (1884), for instance, once argued that no woman could resist the charm of a small, naked baby, which he believed involved "maternal instinct." Presumably, we care for our children due to a maternal (paternal) instinct; we hunt, gather food, and plant crops due to a feeding instinct; we fight and wage war due to an aggressive instinct. Instinct theory emphasizes a hereditary-based view of motivation; however, it also provides a role for learning in determining how an instinct is expressed in behavior.

The concept of motivation as instinct is based on Charles Darwin's (1859) theory of evolution, which holds that species of human beings descended from species of animals. According to Darwin, animals' behavior is determined by instincts. From this assumption it follows that human behavior is also due to instincts, since humans and animals are related in origin.

McDougall's Instinct Theory. By 1908 British psychologist William McDougall had proposed that instincts, as the "driving power" of behavior, were the basis of all human activity. According to McDougall (1908), without instincts, an organism would "be inert and motionless like a wonderful clockwork whose mainspring had been removed or a steam engine whose fires had been drawn."

McDougall defined instincts as "compelling sources of conduct" and proposed that there were eighteen in all, including the tendencies to court and mate; to flee from threatening stimuli; to explore; to build shelters; to care for the young; to obey; to dominate others; and to cry for help (McDougall, 1933). Each instinct provides the driving force for a particular class of behavior, the actual expression of which can be modified by learning and experience. For instance, though the urge to seek food stems from the food-gathering instinct, learning and experience influence the kind of food a person seeks. People born near the sea learn to fish; those born inland learn to farm or hunt. Thus, the underlying urge to gather food comes from a specific inborn tendency, the instinct, but the manner in which the urge is expressed depends both on the specific instinct and on environmental experiences (learning).

Instinct and Environment. In the 1950s, instinct became an important conception of **ethology**—that part of biological science concerned with the behavior of animals. Ethology developed in Europe separately from American psychology. Consistent with Darwin, ethologists emphasize both evolutionary explanations of behavior and the continuity between human beings

Ethology: That part of biological science concerned with the behavior of animals.

and lower animals (Lorenz, 1950, 1966). Ethologists also emphasize the relationship between instincts and environment. In their studies European ethologists found that environment awakens instincts through specific cues. These environmental cues that trigger instinctual behavior they refer to as **releasing stimuli.** When an animal encounters a releasing stimulus, it instinctively engages in a genetically programmed behavioral pattern. When a male stickleback fish, for example, encounters the red underside of another male stickleback, it begins fighting movements, making threatening advances to defend its territory (see Figure 9.1). The red underside of another male is the releasing stimulus for fighting behavior in sticklebacks (Tinbergen, 1951). Direct, face-to-face, eye-to-eye contact with an angry facial expression is a releasing stimulus for instinctive anger in human beings, according to this theory (Lorenz, 1966).

Releasing Stimuli: Environmental cues that trigger instinctive behaviors. When an animal encounters a releasing stimulus, it instinctively engages in a genetically programmed behavioral pattern.

Strengths and Limits of Instinct Theory. In providing a role for learning and experience in motivation, instinct theory contributed to the modern view that any behavior is the joint product of genetic and environmental effects. The instinct theory itself, however, is subject to a number of limitations. One of its biggest flaws is its circularity. Reasoning is circular when a phenomenon that needs to be explained is used as an explanation of itself. McDougall proposed that humans must have an instinct to build shelters; his evidence for that instinct was shelter building. Similarly, it's circular to claim aggressive behavior proves that there is an instinct of aggression. Second, cross-cultural observations do not support the existence of human instincts. If humans have instincts, then all humans should have the same instincts. Cross-cultural variations do not square with the idea of universal human instincts. Third, instinct alone is insufficient to explain motivation (Eibl-Eibesfeldt, 1975). The red underside of a male stickleback acts as a releasing stimulus for fighting behavior in another male only when certain hormones are active (Tinbergen, 1951), for example. If behavior depends in part on certain physiological states, such as the activity of hormones, instinct alone is insufficient to account for motivation. Finally, predictions from instinct theory do not always conform to the observable evidence. For example, critics of James's idea of a maternal instinct have noted that some new mothers are actually awkward with their first child and do not always do those tender, loving things that supposedly characterize the "maternal instinct" (Watson, 1924).

Figure 9.1 *According to ethologists, specific environmental stimuli trigger instinctive behaviors. Such stimuli are called releasing stimuli. In this illustration, the red underside of another male stickleback fish is a releasing stimulus for fighting behavior. Upon encountering the releasing stimulus, the stickleback engages in a genetically preprogrammed behavior pattern of territorial defense.*

In an effort to deal with the limitations of instinct theory, psychologists developed the drive reduction theory, which views motivation in terms of the interaction of biological needs and learning.

■ Learning Clue ■

Keep in mind that need creates drive, then drive creates action.

Drive Reduction Theory

Need: An excess or deficiency in some product related to survival, such as air, food, or water.

Drive: An unpleasant state that results from need and that arouses and energizes the organism to satisfy the need.

Arousal: A general state of the organism involving excitation, or a feeling of being stimulated.

Drive reduction theorists such as Clark L. Hull (1943) explained motivation in terms of biological **need**—an excess or deficiency in some product related to survival, such as air, food, or water—and **drive**—an unpleasant state that results from need and that arouses and energizes the organism to satisfy the need. According to drive reduction theory, need creates drive, which in turn energizes the organism. The energized organism is then more likely to engage in behaviors that lead to the satisfaction of the need. With the need satisfied, drive is reduced and the individual becomes less active.

Note that needs themselves do not affect behavior directly, according to this theory. Instead, they create drive. A drive is thus the consequence of a need. Drive energizes behavior by increasing **arousal,** which is a general state of the organism involving excitation, or a feeling of being excited. But a feeling of excitement does not cause any specific behavior; it merely increases activity. Thus, drive only energizes behavior; it does not direct it.

The stronger the need, the more powerful the drive as well as the urge to reduce it. But, regardless of the need that caused it or its strength, drive always has the same effect; it moves the organism to act. The direction for behavior comes from past experience.

Consider a tennis player who has just stepped onto the court for an important match. As she begins to play, she has no need for water or rest. As the match progresses and becomes more intense, however, she begins to use up her body's supply of water and minerals, soon creating a need to replenish them. Her needs create a drive. She experiences a heightened state of arousal. And, as her need becomes greater, the drive becomes more intense. But this drive state does not cause her to stop playing and seek water and minerals. Instead, it activates all of her responses. She runs faster; hits the ball harder; serves more vigorously. Through past experience, she has

Drive reduction theory attempts to explain motivation in terms of biological need, such as our need for water, and drive—an unpleasant state that results from need and that energizes the individual to satisfy the need.

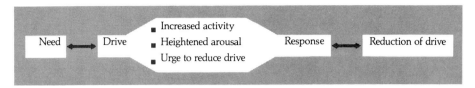

Figure 9.2   Schematic Summary of Drive Reduction Theory.   According to drive reduction theory, need incites drive. Drive causes increased activity, heightened arousal, *and an urge to reduce drive. Guided by previous experiences and goals, the organism engages in behaviors that reduce drive.*

learned to play on, though her mouth is dry and her body yearns for water. She may even play on to the point of exhaustion. As her need increases and her drive mounts, however, her urge to reduce the drive also becomes more intense. Playing harder won't reduce her need for water, but drinking will. So, when she drinks between sets, it will reduce her drive.

According to drive reduction theory, the direction for behavior stems from past experience. Behaviors that result in the reduction of drive are reinforcing, that is, rewarding, and hence more likely to be repeated under similar circumstances. Since the tennis player cannot stop to drink while the ball is in play, she learns to drink between sets.

The product that will reduce drive is referred to as a **goal.** In the case of a thirsty tennis player, water is the goal that will reduce the drive. The more attractive the goal, moreover, the greater its **incentive value,** meaning the greater the motivation to get it. Cold, clear water has more incentive value as a goal than warm, stale water.

To sum up, according to drive reduction theory, need induces a drive, which causes heightened arousal and increased activity, urging the individual to action (see Figure 9.2). Behaviors that lead to goals that reduce the drive tend to be repeated under similar circumstances.

Goal: A product that will reduce drive; water is the product that will reduce the drive of a thirsty person.

Incentive Value: The attractiveness or desirability of a goal. The greater the incentive value of a goal, the greater the motivation to get it.

Homeostasis and Drive Reduction. The drive reduction theory is based on the importance of **homeostasis**—the body's tendency to maintain a relatively constant internal state and to maintain its physiological balances. The word root *homeo* means "similar" or "equal"; *stasis* refers to "standing" or "static." Our bodies maintain a relatively constant internal state in terms of such factors as temperature, blood volume, and concentrations of minerals, nutrients, and oxygen in the blood. Deviations from an internal steady state set into motion a complex chain of events that work to restore the balance. For example, when the body temperature rises above normal levels, we sweat to cool off. We also become more activated and hence more likely to take a cold shower and restore the body to its normal temperature.

Homeostasis: The body's tendency to maintain a relatively constant internal state and to maintain its physiological balances.

Strengths and Limits of Drive Reduction Theory. One of the major advantages of drive reduction theory was that it defined motivation in terms of specific, observable behaviors. A drive was defined in terms of how long an organism had been deprived of some physiological necessity like food or water. The longer the deprivation, the stronger the drive. Learning was defined in terms of the number of times an organism had reduced a drive with a specific behavior. The more experience an animal had had in pressing

Figure 9.3 In a study by Heron (1957), the experimenters covered subjects' arms, hands, and eyes and shut them in a soundproof room. Subjects who tolerated such sensory deprivation for several hours experienced hallucinations, apparently producing their own sensations to reach a comfortable level of arousal.

Sensory Deprivation: Eliminating or greatly reducing input to the senses.

a bar to get food, for example, the greater would be its tendency to repeat the behavior following food deprivation. By defining motivation in terms of specific operations and observable events, drive reduction theory avoided the problem of circularity. Moreover, the theory did much to explain motivated behaviors whose goal is survival. The theory has some important limitations, however, and today it is generally viewed as incomplete.

Drive reduction theory presumes that, as long as all of its physiological needs have been met, an animal's excitation—and, consequently, its motivation—remains at zero. The goal of motivated behavior is to meet a need and reduce activity to a minimum. Although such a view works well for survival behaviors, it does not explain what motivates people to struggle with a Rubik's Cube, to run a mile in less than four minutes, to sky-dive, or to go to the World Series. It cannot account for the higher motivations, such as curiosity and exploration, or why a person will climb a mountain, risking life and limb. The goal of many behaviors, in fact, is not to return to some ground level of stimulation, but to increase it.

Arousal Theory

One explanation for behaviors that clearly are not aimed at correcting physiological imbalances is that there must be more to motivation than drive reduction. That is the premise of the arousal theory of motivation, originally developed by psychologist Hebb (1955). According to this theory, just as organisms have an optimal internal state based on air, water, and other biological necessities, they also have an ideal state of excitation or physical stimulation. That ideal is not zero, but rather some mid-point between too much and too little stimulation. When the level of arousal becomes too high, the organism is motivated to reduce it. When the level becomes too low, the organism is motivated to increase it. For example, after being alone for awhile in a quiet house, you may seek stimulation by turning on the radio or television. But, after a three-hour rock concert, you will probably seek peace and quiet.

Sensation Seeking. Stimulus-seeking behaviors that do not make sense from a drive reduction viewpoint, such as mountain climbing and hang-gliding, are logical if one assumes that they spring from a need to maintain an optimal level of arousal. Experiments also support the need for a certain level of arousal. In a classic study, college students were paid handsomely to do nothing and to feel nothing. To keep stimulation to a minimum, the experimenters covered the subjects' arms, hands, and eyes (see Figure 9.3) and shut them up in a soundproof room. Subjects found such **sensory deprivation,** that is, eliminating or greatly reducing input to the senses, almost impossible to tolerate. Those who endured it for several hours experienced hallucinations—seeing or hearing things that don't exist—and other side effects such as difficulty concentrating. Deprived of sensation, the subjects apparently began to create their own in order to reach a comfortable level of arousal (Heron, 1957).

Arousal theory is more an extension of than a contradiction to drive reduction theory. It simply raises the ideal level of excitation from zero to a point somewhere above. Drive reduction is still reinforcing at high levels of

Motivation and emotion are two of the most powerful determinants of our behavior. Yet the forces that direct us to achieve, or move us to tears, are still somewhat of a mystery, and many theories exist to explain these uniquely human characteristics.

Some suggest that inborn tendencies are the driving force of our behavior; thus a bird of prey will instinctively seek food in order to survive.

Yet, human motivation goes beyond the fulfillment of basic biological needs. We seem to be meeting higher motivational desires when we risk our lives to experience the thrill of flying...or practice diligently to develop our talents to their fullest potential. Sometimes, our thoughts alone are the driving force of our behavior; we build castles in the sand simply because the act itself is rewarding.

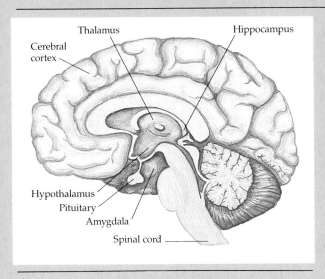

Color Plate 9A *The limbic system and hypothalamus of the brain play an important role in emotions.*

Cerebral cortex

Thalamus

Hippocampus

Hypothalamus

Pituitary

Amygdala

Spinal cord

Our emotions, too, are regulated by our biology and our cognitions. While our brain activity and facial expressions provide us with outward emotional responses, our thoughts also control our feelings.

Color Plate 9B *These naturally occurring pictures of infant faces illustrate what Izard and colleagues believe to be basic and universal expressions of emotion.*

Though we may cry at a wedding and at the loss of a loved one, our emotions are clearly quite different.

Whether controlled by our internal body states, or our thoughts and beliefs, our motivation and our emotions strongly influence our reactions to the world, and allow each of us to express our own unique personalities.

Box 9.1 PSYCHOLOGY IN ACTION: Maximizing Performance

Job applicants often conduct themselves more competently in job interviews when they are only moderately interested in a job than when they are very interested in the job. Similarly, have you ever noticed a sports team play below its ability during championship games? How can greater motivation lead to poorer performance or lesser motivation to better performance?

The answer was first revealed in a classic experiment by Yerkes and Dodson in 1908. The experimenters were interested in determining how efficiently a mouse could learn to tell the difference between different levels of brightness. They studied three levels of discrimination: easy, in which there was a large or obvious difference between degrees of brightness; moderately difficult; and extremely difficult. They also used three levels of shock, from mild to strong to intense, to motivate the animals to learn. Following each mistake, the animals received one of three levels of shock.

The experimenters found that the strongest shock produced the quickest learning for the easy discrimination only. For the more difficult discriminations, the mildest shock produced the most rapid learning. For

the most difficult tasks, the highest shock actually impaired performance rather than improved it (Yerkes & Dodson, 1908). This relationship, illustrated in the figure, is known as the Yerkes-Dodson Law. According to this law, for difficult tasks, a low level of motivation produces better performance than higher levels. It's only when the task is very simple that increases in motivation also lead to increases in performance. Thus, for simple tasks, the optimal level of arousal is higher than for difficult tasks. A person's performance can actually go down when motivation is very high and the demands great.

To maximize performance, then, we would try to increase a person's arousal when it's below optimum, and try to reduce it when it is extremely high. For example, if a person's desire to do well on an exam or job interview is already high, urgings from well-meaning friends might do more harm than good by increasing arousal beyond optimal levels. Similarly, the efforts of a coach to motivate a team can improve the performance of players whose motivation is below the optimum; but it can actually impair the performance of those who are already extremely motivated.

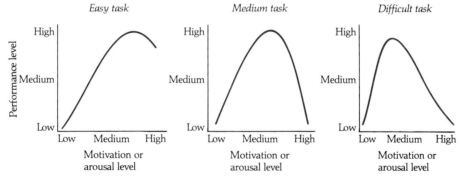

According to the Yerkes-Dodson Law, there is a complex relationship between performance, task difficulty, and level of arousal. For difficult tasks, a low level of arousal or motivation produces better performance than a high level. For simple tasks, by contrast, high levels of arousal produce better performance. Thus, the optimal level of motivation is different for hard tasks than for easy ones.

excitation. But, at low levels of excitation, drive increase is reinforcing. The actual direction of behavior is still determined by learning; that is, those behaviors that have led to optimal arousal in the past tend to be repeated.

Like drive reduction theory, arousal theory is based on the importance of homeostasis. Deviations above or below the optimal state set off a complex chain of events aimed at correcting the imbalance. When you've eaten more than you need, your discomfort can be just as motivating in driving you to stop as the discomfort of an empty stomach is in driving you to eat.

Table 9.1 Comparison of Biological Theories

Theory	Proponent	Energizing Force	Directing Force
Instinct	McDougall Lorenz	Inborn instinct	Instinct plus learning and environmental stimuli
Drive Reduction	Hull	Drive caused by biological need	Past experience; incentive value of goal
Arousal	Hebb	Deviations from optimal physiological arousal	Past experience

Besides explaining stimulus-seeking behaviors, arousal theory accounts for some unexpected phenomena—such as the tendency for performance to get worse as motivation increases (see Box 9.1).

Strengths and Limits of Arousal Theory. Arousal theory extends the drive reduction view and helps us to understand paradoxes such as the adverse effect of extreme levels of motivation. But, like the instinct and drive reduction theories, arousal theory is based on a biological view of motivation. (See Table 9.1 for a summary and comparison of these theories.) Arousal theory states that, in addition to basic survival needs, there is also a need for an optimal internal state of physiological arousal, but it does not account for social needs such as the need to be with others and the need to form personal relationships. In the next section, we consider theories that attempt to account for such social needs.

THEORIES OF SOCIAL AND PERSONAL MOTIVATION

In this section we will examine motivation from the perspective of needs that are not based in one's biological requirements. Striving for competency and excellence, for example, does not depend on biological need or the maintenance of homeostasis. As we examine these so-called higher needs, we will take a close look at two viewpoints. The first states that the higher human needs are acquired through learning; the second that such needs are no less inborn than those based on biological requirements.

Murray's Theory of Learned Need

Henry Murray (1938) was primarily interested in needs that he believed were acquired through experience, as opposed to the physiological needs for

■ **Learning Check** ■

Review Table 9.1 until you can recite the energy and directing force for each theory.

Table 9.2 Partial List and Description of Murray's Psychogenic Needs

Need	Abbreviation	Description
Achievement	n. Ach.	The need to accomplish something difficult; to surpass others
Affiliation	n. Aff.	The need to be near and cooperate with others; to please others and win their affection
Autonomy	n. Auto.	The need to be independent and free to act; to resist coercion; to defy convention
Defendance	n. Def.	The need to defend oneself against assault or criticism; to protect oneself and one's honor
Dominance	n. Dom.	The need to control one's environment; to influence, persuade, or command others
Harm Avoidance	n. Harm.	The need to avoid pain, physical injury, death; to escape danger
Nurturance	n. Nur.	The need to give sympathy and gratify the needs of someone helpless; to support or comfort others
Order	n. Ord.	The need to put things in order; to be neat, organized, tidy
Sex	n. Sex	The need to form and further an erotic relationship; to have sexual intercourse

Source: Adapted from H. A. Murray, *Explorations in personality* (New York: Oxford University Press, 1938).

oxygen, water, and food. He called such learned needs **psychogenic needs.** He proposed the existence of twenty psychogenic needs, which he believed each of us learns to one degree or another by interacting with others and with the environment. Table 9.2 provides a partial list and brief description of needs described by Murray (1938).

Murray believed that psychogenic needs were structured in a hierarchy and that, for each person, the hierarchy was different. Each of us may, for example, possess the need for achievement (to excel), the need for affiliation (to be with others and to form interpersonal relations), and the need for dominance (to influence or control others). For each individual, however, the needs will be in a different order of importance. For one, achievement might be strongest, followed by affiliation and dominance. For another, the need for affiliation might be strongest, with little need for achievement or dominance. If, for instance, you must choose between spending a relaxing evening with some friends and spending those same hours alone improving a term paper you've drafted, you'll choose the former if your need to be with others is stronger than your need to excel. According to Murray, if two incompatible needs arise, the stronger (that is, the higher on the hierarchy) would be satisfied first, even at the expense of the other.

Need for Achievement (n. Ach.). An examination of the need for achievement, or n. Ach., illustrates how Murray's psychogenic needs are studied. The need is measured by interpreting the stories subjects are asked to make up about ambiguous pictures. Subjects are shown, for example, a

Psychogenic Needs: According to Murray, needs acquired through experience; psychological or learned needs as opposed to physiological needs.

picture of a boy sitting at a desk and asked to make up a story about what led up to the scene, about what the character is thinking and feeling, and about what will happen next (McClelland et al., 1953). Consider the following two hypothetical responses to the picture of a boy at his desk (see Figure 9.4).

> This boy has been working on a special school project all day. It's after school and all the other kids have gone home but he's staying after to put in a few extra hours. He's thinking that this is going to be really good and will probably win first prize in the upcoming science exhibit. He's feeling pleased with himself. Suddenly he realizes he's been daydreaming and that he'd better get to work. As he works he dreams of becoming a famous inventor. He finishes the project and wins first prize.

> This boy is staying after school for disturbing the class. He's the class clown, always trying to be funny. He's thinking how funny he was and how everyone seemed to enjoy the little prank he played on the teacher. He feels lonely though, and wishes he could go and play with his friends. He apologizes to his teacher and she lets him go home.

In interpreting these stories, researchers would note that the first contains several references to high achievement (working all day; putting in extra hours; becoming a famous inventor); the second, none. Thus, the first storyteller would be placed in a high n. Ach. group; the second in a low n. Ach. group.

How do some people acquire a strong need for achievement while others acquire a weak need? Studies of individuals who score high and low on measures of n. Ach. point to the importance of early learning experiences in explaining how differences in n. Ach. are acquired. Examination of subjects' backgrounds reveal that a high n. Ach. is associated with being rewarded with praise and affection for accomplishments as a child. But, in conjunction with these rewards, parents of high n. Ach. individuals also demanded more of them. Mothers of boys high in the need for achievement had required them to show signs of independence—putting themselves to bed, making their own beds, staying home alone—at a much earlier age than had mothers of low n. Ach. boys. For example, they had made about as many demands on their sons at age five as had the mothers of the low n. Ach. boys at age seven (McClelland, 1961).

In addition to rewards and parental expectation, high n. Ach. children also seemed to learn to strive for their goals through modeling. That is, they

Figure 9.4 Examination of Need for Achievement: This is a picture similar to a scene depicted in the Thematic Apperception Test (TAT), which attempts to evaluate a person's needs. Subjects are shown pictures such as this one and asked to make up a story that includes what led up to the situation, what the individual is thinking and feeling, and what the outcome will be.

imitated their parents, who demonstrated achievement-oriented behaviors. The fathers of high n. Ach. children, for instance, tended to have supervisory or management positions, or jobs requiring independence and decision making. The fathers of low n. Ach. children, by contrast, tended to report to supervisors (Bandura, 1982; Turner, 1970).

If a behavior is learned, then presumably it can be unlearned. And, with respect to achievement, research suggests just that. In one study, business owners were taught to establish moderate goals rather than impossible or overly easy ones. They were encouraged to take responsibility for getting things done, and to attribute their successes to their own efforts rather than to chance. Two years later, the trained group had started more new businesses, invested more money in expansion, and employed more people than a control group that received no training (McClelland, 1978). Such results show the value of training people to set challenging but realistic goals and to take responsibility for increasing productivity.

Strengths and Limits of Murray's Theory. While studies of achievement motivation and other psychogenic needs have yielded important insights into human motivation, the theory that higher needs are acquired remains controversial. The data relating parental child-rearing practices and n. Ach. are correlational; they do not demonstrate cause and effect. There are many other correlates—income, education level of parents, social class, and ethnic background—that might also account for the relationship (Castenell, 1983). For example, highly educated parents who demand independence earlier tend to raise high n. Ach. children, have more money, might have a certain genetic background, and so on. Any number of such factors might cause or contribute to a high score on a picture-interpretation test of need achievement.

Thus, like other theories, that of learned need might best be viewed as possibly one piece of the puzzle, or an important perspective from which to view motivation, rather than a complete explanation.

Maslow's Theory of Motivation

According to Maslow (1970), a need to develop our potentials to the fullest is innate. It is this inborn need for the fulfillment of one's potential, according to Maslow, that motivates each person to develop and use unique talents that might otherwise remain dormant. Maslow gave this need the name **self-actualization.** The highest of human needs, self-actualization moves the individual to attempt goals beyond mere survival. It is self-actualization that urges the artistically talented person to paint and develop artistic skill despite poverty and severe critics.

Self-Actualization: According to Maslow, the inborn need for personal growth or for the fulfillment of one's potential. The highest of human needs, self-actualization, moves the individual to attempt goals beyond mere survival.

Maslow's Hierarchy of Needs. Before the energy to achieve self-actualization can be released, however, it is necessary to fulfill, at least in part, other, more basic needs. Like Murray, Maslow theorized that human needs could be arranged in a hierarchy, according to their relative urgency (see Figure 9.5). But whereas Murray said that each individual has a different hierarchy of needs, Maslow proposed just one hierarchy of needs that applied to all. For Maslow, it is only after the crucial survival needs are satisfied that

Figure 9.5 Maslow's Hierarchy of Needs.

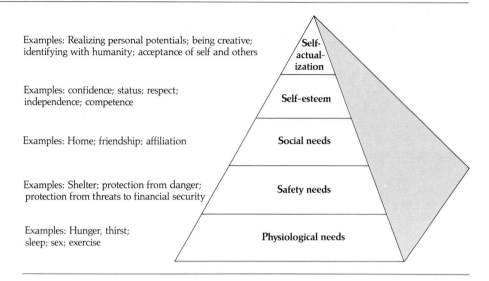

Examples: Realizing personal potentials; being creative; identifying with humanity; acceptance of self and others — Self-actualization

Examples: confidence; status; respect; independence; competence — Self-esteem

Examples: Home; friendship; affiliation — Social needs

Examples: Shelter; protection from danger; protection from threats to financial security — Safety needs

Examples: Hunger, thirst; sleep; sex; exercise — Physiological needs

the higher needs become dominant. Thus, when the needs for hunger and thirst are satisfied, safety becomes more important. When safety needs are met, those for belongingness and love become prominent. Consequently, as in Murray's theory, the direction for behavior is guided by the relative strength or urgency of a need. But, for Maslow, humans are not simply slaves of unmet lower needs. Often a higher need will override a lower one and provide the direction for behavior.

Maslow (1970) recognized that a lower need did not have to be completely satisfied for a person to be motivated by a higher one. People risk their lives to save their loved ones from fire and flood. Artists paint while hungry and ill clad; scientists and inventors endure scorn and social rejection to achieve their goals. But the idea of a need hierarchy does underscore how preoccupation with a lower need can keep a person from ever reaching the goal of self-actualization. Overconcern with being accepted by others (affiliation), for instance, can prevent a creative individual from expressing original but unpopular ideas.

Strengths and Limits of Maslow's Theory. Maslow's theory addresses the issue of how needs based on biological requirements and the higher needs such as those for self-esteem and self-actualization might be related. The theory has applications in business and industry. It suggests that, to unleash the creative forces and full potential of employees, organizations might take steps to insure that all of their lower needs are met by providing adequate pay, insurance, even memberships in a country club to meet the need for belongingness. The theory has been criticized, however, on the grounds that it is difficult to prove, excessively complex, and too closely tied to middle class cultural experience (Locke, 1976; Steers & Porter, 1975). In the next section we will consider a somewhat different perspective on sources of motivation that are not based on biological requirements. We will consider the role of cognition in motivation.

THE ROLE OF COGNITION IN MOTIVATION

One of the more recent developments in motivation theory is the view that cognitions—thoughts, beliefs, expectations, and other mental processes—play a critical role in both energizing and directing behavior (Bandura, 1982; Deci, 1980). What you think, the way you evaluate situations, your beliefs and expectations—all forms of cognition—can influence motivation. Consider the power of expectations. **Expectation** can be defined as a person's estimate of what is likely to happen in any given circumstance. Do you think, for example, that saving $20 each week will enable you to buy a reliable used car next summer? How strongly do you think so, on a scale of 0 to 5? (0 equals "don't think so"; 5 equals "absolutely certain") The power of expectation can be seen in its influence on one's determination and effort in the pursuit of a particular goal. If you rate your chances as zero, then you probably won't see much use in putting $20 aside each week. Nor will you be inclined to look for a suitable used car that fits your needs as well as your budget. By the same token, a recent college graduate who expects that finding a personally rewarding and highly paid job is impossible won't have much energy to comb the help-wanted ads and follow up every lead. Such an individual might even consider applying for desirable jobs advertised in the newspaper as a waste of time.

Expectation won't change one's ability or the job market. It can, however, influence the amount of effort one expends in seeking a job. Optimistic expectation generally produces greater effort, and greater effort can, in turn, increase one's chances of finding a suitable job. Pessimistic thinking, by contrast, reduces motivation.

Expectation, however, is only one of two variables that determine one's motivation to pursue a goal. The second is the value of the goal.

Expectation: A person's estimate of what is likely to happen in a given circumstance.

Expectation × Valence = Motivation

Like beauty, the value of a goal is in the eye of the beholder. Recognizing this, psychologists have devised a special term, **valence,** to signify the value of a goal to the individual. How badly would you like a reliable used car, on a scale of 0 to 5? (0 meaning "not at all" and 5 meaning "a whole lot")

According to one viewpoint, if we know both a person's expectations of achieving a goal and its valence (value to that person), we can determine the strength of the person's motivation. To do so, we multiply the expectation that the behavior will be successful by the valence (Atkinson, 1964). Thus, the energy and direction for behavior is a joint product of expectation times the value of a goal. One of the most significant results of this formula is that, if either expectation or valence is zero, then motivation will be zero, too. That is, if the goal—a reliable used car—has no value to the individual, motivation to save will be zero no matter how high the expectation for success. Similarly, if the expectation for success is zero, motivation will be zero no matter what the value of the goal.

Valence: The value a goal has to a particular individual.

This candidate's motivation to seek political office stems from both his desire to win and his belief that he can.

This point is well illustrated by the multimillion-dollar giveaways some companies stage to promote their products. To enter, contestants need only fill out a form and send it in. Some companies even go so far as to print the contestants' names on a form, followed by an announcement like, "You may have already won $1,000,000, or any one of thousands of other prizes." Yet only a small percentage of the people who receive these offers in the mail respond to them. A million dollars is an extremely high valence for most people, but it can't overcome the widespread expectation that there's no chance of winning. Zero expectation of success times extremely high valence equals zero motivation. There is no energy for behavior; no direction. The influence of cognitions on motivation is apparent also in the expectations people have regarding their control over events.

Locus of Control

Some people believe that the pleasures and pain of life depend mostly on forces beyond their control—luck, circumstance, or powerful others. To them, getting a good job is a matter of being in the right place at the right time. Such people may be said to have an **external locus of control,** or the belief that the outcomes one obtains—rewards and punishments—come from powerful others or are the result of luck and circumstances. They see little if any relationship between their behavior and the outcomes they experience (Rotter, 1954, 1966).

Other people believe that the rewards of life are mostly dependent on their own behavior. They see themselves as the causal agent in what they achieve, good or bad. If they get a good job, it is because of their skill, persistence, and preparation. If they fail to get a job, it is because they didn't

External Locus of Control: The belief that the outcomes one obtains—rewards and punishments—come from powerful others or are the result of luck and circumstance.

prepare well enough to make a good enough impression on the interviewer. Such people can be said to have an **internal locus of control,** or the belief that the outcomes one obtains—rewards and punishments—are the result of one's own effort.

Locus of control is an expectation concerning the likelihood that one's behavior will lead to a desired outcome. People with an internal locus of control believe that, through personal efforts, they can influence the outcomes they experience; they have a high expectation that their behavior will lead to the outcomes they seek. This higher expectation, in turn, leads to a higher level of motivation. People with an external locus of control see little relationship between their behavior and their outcomes. Hence, their expectation for success is generally lower, along with their motivation to achieve those things that are of value to them.

An internal locus of control is associated with higher motivation than an external locus—a fact that shouldn't surprise anyone. People who see themselves as the main cause of whether or not the rent is paid or whether an assignment is done on time are more likely to set high goals, persist at a task, and achieve better results than those who don't (Lefcourt, 1976; Betts, 1982). But one's expectations can also depend on the way rewards are perceived.

Intrinsic vs. Extrinsic Motivation

Something that you willingly do for its own sake or because you like to, such as solving a crossword puzzle, has intrinsic value. It is its own reward and therefore provides **intrinsic motivation**—motivation to perform a task or activity when no apparent reward is received except that directly involved with the task itself. A job that you don't want to do, such as painting a fence, you may do for pay. Since the reward of money is outside the nature of the task—painting—it provides **extrinsic motivation**—motivation inspired by the desire for some external reward or the avoidance of punishment. But what happens when you are paid for something that you willingly do for its own sake? Numerous experiments have shown that an extrinsic reward for an intrinsically rewarding task actually reduces motivation to perform the task (Harackiewicz et al., 1985).

In a typical experiment, a group of subjects is paid to perform an intrinsically rewarding activity, such as playing a game, and a second group is not. Both groups play the games just as long. After the paid subjects have

Internal Locus of Control: The belief that the outcomes one obtains—rewards and punishments—are the result of one's own effort.

Locus of Control: An expectation concerning the likelihood that one's behavior will lead to a desired outcome.

Intrinsic Motivation: Motivation to perform a task or activity when no apparent reward is received except that directly involved with the task itself; doing something because you like to.

Extrinsic Motivation: Motivation inspired by the desire for some external reward or avoidance of punishment.

■ Learning Check ■

Read the definitions, then cover the right side and recite. Repeat. (Do each word separately.)

Expectation	is a person's estimate of what is likely to happen in a given circumstance.
Valence	is the value of a goal.
Locus of control	is an expectation concerning the likelihood that one's behavior will lead to a desired outcome.

Figure 9.6   Schematic Summary of the Role of Cognition in Motivation.

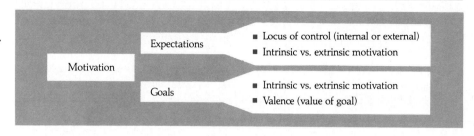

received their rewards, both groups are given the opportunity to play some more. Those who have been paid are told that they will no longer receive pay. Typically, the paid subjects show less interest in resuming play than the nonpaid ones (Deci & Ryan, 1980). Children who were given money for working puzzles subsequently spent less time on similar puzzles during a free period than children who had not received money (Deci, 1972).

In contrast, other studies have shown that providing an extrinsic reward for an intrinsically motivated activity can increase motivation. The motivation of workers who enjoy their jobs and get periodic bonuses is usually increased by the bonus, not decreased by it. How can the discrepancy be explained?

According to Deci (1980), the effect of a reward on intrinsic motivation depends on cognition. In other words, the effect depends on how the reward is interpreted. He argues that, when a reward changes the perceived locus of control from internal to external, intrinsic motivation will be lowered. Suppose, for example, you volunteer to campaign for a political candidate. You work hard because you believe in the candidate and feel you are doing what you want to do. If the candidate begins to pay you, you might come to feel that the reason you are working is for the money. If so, your perception of the situation has changed from internal control (you're doing this because you want to) to external control (you're doing it to get the money). On the other hand, if you perceive the pay as token appreciation for your work (and you evaluate the reward as confirming your belief that the candidate is generous and kind), you might work even harder. (Figure 9.6 presents a schematic summary of the role of cognition in motivation.)

Having considered the role of cognition, as well as theories of social and personal motivation, we will now return to the biological side of motivation by taking an in-depth look at the physiology of hunger.

THE PHYSIOLOGY OF MOTIVATION

Scientists have long known that a hungry person or animal tends to be more aroused and active than one that is not (Dashiell, 1925). And the hungry person or animal tends to use this energy to find food rather than to achieve some other goal (Baumeister et al., 1964). Hunger, therefore, nicely fits our definition of motivation: it energizes and directs behavior.

Though the mechanisms of hunger are not yet fully understood, it is clear that both physiological and psychological processes are involved. In this chapter we focus on the physiological, to provide an in-depth account of the physiological activities that occur during motivation. In Chapter 11 on life-style and coping, we will present the psychological aspects of hunger as we describe research on obesity.

■ **Learning Clue** ■

As you read this section, note that there are five physiological mechanisms—(1) brain structures, (2) specialized receptors, (3) internal organs, (4) blood composition, and (5) neurotransmitter substances—that are believed to play a role in hunger.

Study of Hunger

In this section, we trace the major developments in the study of hunger and describe some of the procedures that have led researchers to their current views about hunger. First, we consider whether the stomach regulates eating, then whether sections of the brain or chemicals in the brain do.

Cannon's Theory. Early investigators of hunger supposed that the need for food is regulated in the stomach. Presumably, stomach contractions—what we experience as hunger pangs—provide the signal that energizes and directs eating. Eating was presumed to quiet the contractions, thus terminating the signal regulating the sensation of hunger.

At first research seemed to confirm this hypothesis. A scientist named Cannon persuaded human subjects to swallow a balloon, which he inflated once it was in the stomach. Then he attached the balloon to a pressure-measuring device, which recorded the subject's stomach contractions by recording pressure in the balloon, and asked the subjects to push a telegraph key whenever they felt hungry. His results showed that stomach contractions and hunger pains were in fact related. Subjects were more likely to press the telegraph key when they were experiencing stomach contractions than when they were not. Because his data showed a correlation between the two factors, Cannon concluded that stomach contractions caused hunger (Cannon, 1929).

What was wrong with Cannon's reasoning? He made the common error of confusing correlation with causation. Just because stomach contractions and feelings of hunger occur together, that does not mean that the contractions cause the hunger. The reverse could just as easily be true; or both variables could be controlled by some third factor, like signals from the brain. Nor could Cannon's theory account for the fact that ulcer and cancer victims who have had their stomachs removed surgically still feel hunger. Eventually, Cannon's theory gave way to the idea that hunger was regulated in the brain.

Start-Stop Eating Centers in the Brain. Striking evidence for the new theory came when two researchers reported a dramatic change in the eating behavior of a laboratory rat following damage to one part of its hypothala-

Hyperphagia: Continuous overeating; eating to excess.

Ventromedial Hypothalamus (VMH): An area of the hypothalamus from which signals to stop eating are believed to originate; the satiety or "stop" center for eating.

mus, called the ventromedial hypothalamus (VMH) (Hetherington & Ranson, 1939). It ate continuously and excessively (see Figure 9.7), a condition known as **hyperphagia** ((*hyper* means "over"; *phagia* means "eating"). Not until the animal had more than tripled its original weight did it stop its overeating. Then it restricted itself just enough to maintain its new high weight. Researchers concluded that the **ventromedial hypothalamus (VMH)** is the area of the hypothalamus from which signals to stop eating originate. It became known as the satiety or "stop" center for eating.

Subsequent work showed that hyperphagia could be routinely induced in rats by surgical damage to the VMH. The animals would eat ravenously for several weeks, become obese, and then eat just enough to maintain their new weight. Curiously, however, once they became obese, these animals were very particular about what they ate. If their food didn't taste good—for example, if it was laced with quinine—they wouldn't eat it, although nonobese rats would (Teitelbaum, 1955). What was more, these obese rats were not only more finicky than their normal cousins, they were less willing to put forth effort in order to obtain their food. In order to receive food, they would not pull as much weight as a normal rat, when attached to carts like a mule, for example (Teitelbaum & Epstein, 1962). Although researchers couldn't fully explain the VMH-damaged rats' finickiness and laziness, they agreed that the VMH must somehow have provided the signals that instructed the animals to stop eating.

If there was a stop-eating center in the brain, researchers reasoned, then perhaps there was a start-eating center as well. And, indeed, when they tried destroying another part of the hypothalamus, called the lateral hypo-

Figure 9.7 Hyperphagia.
Destruction of this animal's ventromedial hypothalamus (VMH) led to continuous and excessive eating, a condition known as hyperphagia.

thalamus (LH), the rats and cats they had operated on refused to eat. Unless force-fed, these animals soon died of starvation. Presumably the destruction of their start-eating mechanism had caused their condition of not eating, called **aphagia** (*a* means "without"; *phagia* means "eating"). They simply never received a signal to begin eating (Anand & Brobeck, 1951). Researchers concluded that the **lateral hypothalamus (LH)** is the area of the hypothalamus from which the signals to start eating originate. It became known as the "start" center for eating.

Further support for the existence of start-stop eating centers in the hypothalamus came when researchers discovered that electrical stimulation of the VMH, the Stop center, inhibited eating behavior, even in animals that had been deprived of food. Conversely, electrical stimulation of the LH, the Start center, caused rats that had just eaten their fill to begin eating again (Hoebel & Teitelbaum, 1962). Nevertheless, the notion of start-stop centers has not gone unchallenged. Some critics have pointed out that it is difficult to destroy the VMH or LH without damaging other areas of the brain as well. Thus, the VMH and LH may not be the only seat of control for eating (Stricker & Zigmond, 1976).

Neurotransmitters as START-STOP Hunger Switches. While the debate about a Start-Stop eating center in the brain continues, other scientists have been pursuing a new theory. According to this line of thinking, neurotransmitters, the chemicals that transmit messages from one part of the brain to another, may be just as important as the hypothalamus in signaling when to start and stop eating. One study revealed that destruction of the cells that manufacture norepinephrine will cause hyperphagia, even if the VMH is left completely intact. Apparently norepinephrine can act independently as a stop-eating mechanism (Ahlskog & Hoebel, 1973).

Two other neurotransmitters, serotonin and dopamine, also seem to be involved in the control of hunger. A number of findings suggest that serotonin may act as a stop-eating mechanism. When serotonin stores are depleted by chemical injection, for example, rats become hyperphagic, as if their stop-eating mechanism had been destroyed (Ahlskog et al., 1975). Dopamine, on the other hand, seems to serve as a general activator that stimulates eating behavior when food is available. In the absence of food, it encourages other well-esablished behaviors, such as grooming (Rowland & Antelman, 1976). The implication is that dopamine acts as a general energizer rather than as a specific motivational signal to start eating. The more scientists learn, the more complicated the hunger system appears to be.

Homeostasis in Hunger

In fact, research shows that hunger involves a delicate interplay of events throughout the entire body—not just in the brain. The hypothalamus is merely the central mechanism in that interplay, which, like other homeostatic processes, helps to maintain a steady internal state. The hypothalamus's power to detect the need for food rests on its wide-ranging connections with other parts of the body. It receives messages indicating body temperature and the contents of digestive organs like the stomach, liver, and intestines. And it responds to information on the blood levels of sugar, hormones, and enzymes, all chemical by-products of the digestion and use

Aphagia: Cessation of eating; refusal to eat.

Lateral Hypothalamus (LH): An area of the hypothalamus from which signals to start eating are believed to originate; the hunger or "start" center for eating.

Glucose: A sugar; the main source of energy for the brain.

of food. For example, information on blood levels of **glucose**—a sugar that is burned for energy and is the main source of energy for the brain—enables the hypothalamus to call for the release of either insulin (which lowers glucose levels) or sugar (which raises them) from the liver.

This model of hunger fits the concept of homeostasis nicely. The hypothalamus integrates information it receives on nutritive conditions throughout the body. When there are deviations from the optimal internal state, the hypothalamus attempts to reverse the condition by calling for corrective action, such as the release of sugar or insulin in the bloodstream. If those actions fail, the hypothalamus signals for the start or stop of eating.

Two separate homeostatic hunger systems seem to exist. One regulates short-term food intake—the hour-to-hour eating behaviors that determine how much you eat during any given meal, or over the course of the day. The second regulates long-term food intake, enabling you to maintain a relatively stable weight over time—weeks and months—to avoid dangerously wide fluctuations in weight. We will examine each of these.

Short-Term Control of Eating. What is it that regulates the fluctuations of hunger and satiation during the day? We have already seen that it is not the stomach as Cannon had thought. And we have seen that research shows that start-stop centers in the brain and neurotransmitters have independent roles in regulating hunger. More recent research suggests that short-term homeostasis centers on the availability of nutrients in the blood, and that it is a set of detectors in the liver that tells the brain whether enough glucose and other nutrients are available in the blood (Russek, 1971). When blood levels of essential nutrients (primarily glucose, or blood sugar) become low, cells in the liver detect it and send a message to the brain. As a result, we experience feelings of hunger. Once we begin eating, there is apparently no mechanism to tell us to stop until the stomach becomes full. Its distension causes discomfort and signals the brain that enough has been received.

Liporeceptors: Specialized cells in the hypothalamus that respond to the level of fats (fatty acids) stored in the body.

Free Fatty Acids: The products of the breakdown of fat substances that build up in the blood when one has not eaten recently and that quickly diminish shortly after eating has begun.

Set Point Theory: The theory that the body will tend to stay within certain maximum and minimum weights, due to an internal mechanism that maintains a relatively constant weight over the years.

Long-Term Control of Eating and the Set Point Theory. Long-term weight control appears to be influenced by special cells in the hypothalamus called **liporeceptors** that respond to the level of fats stored in the body (Liebelt et al., 1973). Theoretically, liporeceptors monitor the level of **free fatty acids**—the products of the breakdown of fat substances that build up in the blood when one has not eaten recently and that quickly diminish shortly after eating has begun—in the blood as it passes through the hypothalamus. If the acids indicate that body weight has fallen below a set level, the liporeceptors cause an adjustment in the sensitivity of the VMH downward. Thus, the person eats more. If body weight rises above a set level, the liporeceptors cause an adjustment in the VHM's sensitivity upward, producing the opposite effect (Oomura et al., 1969).

The idea that the body weight will tend to stay within certain maximum and minimum limits is called the **set point theory** (Keesey, 1980). According to the set point theory, the body has an internal mechanism that maintains a relatively constant weight over the years. It states that there is a homeostatic mechanism for weight control, which, according to some experts, is based on the number of fat cells a person has (Nisbett, 1972). The more fat cells a person has, the higher the set point. When an individual's weight drops below the set point, there is a tendency to eat more; when weight gets above the set point, there is a tendency to eat less. The set point theory is supported by experiments similar to those with hyperphagic rats. As you may recall, VMH-damaged rats eat continuously to a certain point and then stop; thereafter they will eat only enough to maintain their new, higher weight. Experimenters have found that, if these obese animals are placed on a forced diet, they will lose weight. But they will gain it back again once they are given free access to food. Apparently the damage to their VMH somehow alters their set point from normal to obese. Similar results have been obtained with LH-damaged rats. If force-fed, these near-starving animals will eventually start eating again, but they will not eat enough to return to a normal weight. Presumably the damage to their LH somehow drops their set point below normal (Mitchel & Keesey, 1974).

The idea of a set point mechanism in weight control is supported, too, by observations of animals in the wild, which maintain a relatively constant normal weight over their adult lives (Brownell, 1982). Even if wild animals are force-fed until they become obese, or put on a semi-starvation diet, they will usually return to their normal weight when allowed to eat freely again (Bennett & Gurin, 1982). Humans who were put on such diets during a three- to six-month experiment returned to their normal weight shortly after the experiment (Sims et al., 1973). There are many unanswered questions, however. Hunger involves such a complex interplay among organs throughout the body that current physiological theories at best provide a simplified or incomplete view of the numerous checks and balances that are involved in determining when a person eats or stops eating.

In spite of all that researchers have learned about motivation, there is still more to be learned. The only safe thing to say at this point is that moti-

■ Learning Check ■

Read the questions and answers, then try answering the questions with the answers covered.

1. Question: How did Cannon confuse correlation with causation in his hunger experiment?

1. Answer: He thought that, just because stomach contractions and feelings of hunger occurred together, the first caused the second; but correlation (being related) doesn't equal cause (making something happen).

2. Question: What parts of the brain appear to be stop-start centers for eating?

2. Answer: Ventromedial hypothalamus (VMH): stop-eating center; lateral hypothalamus (LH): start-eating center. (Remember: L comes before V, start comes before stop)

3. Question: What is the homeostatic mechanism for long-term weight control according to set point theory?

3. Answer: Set point theory states that the body will tend to stay within certain maximum and minimum limits, due to an internal mechanism that maintains a relatively constant weight over the years.

In discussing motivation, we first considered instinct theory, drive reduction theory, and arousal theory. Looking at social and personal motivation, we examined Murray's and Maslow's theories. Which theory appealed most to you? Why?

vation is complex and multi-determined. Instincts, biological needs, sensation-seeking, and cognitions all play a role in motivation. In future chapters we will explore further many of the topics of motivation. In Chapter 10 we will discuss a motivational system that humans share with lower organisms but which has uniquely human aspects, sexuality. In Chapter 11 we will discuss the psychological sides of hunger. In Chapter 12 we will discuss Maslow's theory as it pertains to human personality. For now, let us turn to a topic that is very closely related to motivation—emotion.

THE CONCEPT OF EMOTION

The central importance of emotion in human behavior can be seen when we try to imagine what life would be without it. Without emotion, the world would be a dull place. We would know that events were taking place but would have little investment in them. There would be no happiness; no sadness; just moment-to-moment change. In this section we will discuss the various components of emotion and try to distinguish motivation from emotion.

The Components of Emotion

In everyday life we recognize in ourselves and others emotions such as joy, anger, surprise, disgust, interest, fear, and sadness. Yet to date psychologists disagree on an exact definition. Basically, the psychologists studying emotion are working with four components in their attempt to formulate a scientific definition of emotion. These components are: (1) reaction to a stimulus; (2) physiological activity; (3) personal or subjective feelings; (4) expression. To start our discussion of emotion, we will examine each of these components.

Reaction to a Stimulus. The first essential component of emotion is that it is a reaction. One doesn't suddenly experience anger, joy, or fear, without some cause. One reacts with anger to frustration, with joy to reunion with old friends, or with fear to a threat. The stimulus may be real or imagined. If late at night you imagine you hear the sound of footsteps in the attic, you may experience fear although there are no real footsteps and no real threat. Emotion occurs in response to a stimulus whether real or imagined.

Physiological Activity. Another aspect of emotion is that it involves physiological activity. With emotion comes activity in areas of the brain such as the limbic system and hypothalamus, which in turn activate the autonomic system (see Color Plate 9A), causing **autonomic arousal**—a heightened state of the autonomic nervous system usually characterized by such physiological changes as rise in heart rate, blood pressure, skin temperature, and blood circulation. As you may recall, the sympathetic branch of the autonomic nervous system generally acts to mobilize the individual and prepare the body for action: it arouses and activates. With anger, for instance, comes an acceleration of the heart. With shame and fear comes an increase in the volume of blood being pumped to the face. The pupils dilate in surprise; the palms sweat in fear.

Activity in the brain and autonomic nervous system may continue for several minutes after an emotional stimulus, which helps explain why, once activated, emotions are difficult to control. Thus, an angry person needs time to "cool down." Emotional states also involve altered activity of the endocrine system (see Chapter 3). Anger and fear are associated with the release of norepinephrine and epinephrine by the adrenal glands, for example. Once released, these hormones have a pervasive effect on the body that can last for some time, which again shows that, when an emotion is activated, it takes time to run its course.

Personal or Subjective Feelings. A personal, or subjective, feeling is associated with every emotion. Someone may speak of the warm glow of joy, for example. While the subjective experience may be pleasant or unpleasant, it is never neutral. It may be intense or slight. The subjective feeling may be fused to a thought, memory, image, or evaluation. The thought that "this is great" may be fused with the feeling of joy. The thought "I shouldn't have done this" may be fused with shame. Thus, the subjective component of emotion may in part be cognitive.

Expressive Quality. Emotions are more than reactions to stimuli, physiological changes, and subjective experiences. Accompanying such internal components of emotion is external expression. People "show," or communicate, their emotions in their posture, tone of voice, and facial expressions.

Several investigators have found that congenitally blind children express emotion in the same way as do seeing children (Eibl-Eibesfeldt, 1972). Although they have never seen the expressions of happiness or sadness, children blind from birth smile when happy and frown when hurt or sad. Moreover, a number of studies have revealed that certain emotions have the same basic expressive and experiential qualities in widely different cultures from all over the world (Plutchik, 1980b).

Autonomic Arousal: A heightened state of the autonomic nervous system, usually characterized by such physiological changes as a rise in heart rate, blood pressure, and skin temperature and an increased blood circulation.

■ Learning Check ■

Read, recite, and try to repeat.

The four components of emotion:

1. *Reaction* to a stimulus
2. *Physiological* activity
3. *Subjective* feeling
4. *Expressive* quality

Often we try to control or disguise our emotional expressions. The defeated athlete struggles to wear a smile to hide a frown of disappointment, for instance. Despite our best efforts, however, it is exceptionally difficult if not impossible to inhibit at least some expressive aspect of an emotion. Thus, we communicate with others through our emotional expressions and can better understand others by reading theirs.

Interplay Among Components. In considering the components of emotion, it is important to keep in mind that they operate as a unit—a whole that is more than the sum of its individual parts. Physiological arousal, for example, is just arousal when it occurs in the absence of other components that form the circuit of emotion. If arousal is not accompanied by a subjective feeling and an expression, it is not an emotion. Stressors such as noise or crowding can create a physiological state comparable to an emotion but without an expressive or subjective component. (We will look at stress more closely in Chapter 11.)

Distinguishing Emotion from Motivation

You have seen in the sports pages the emotion of joy expressed in the photograph of a winning team's faces. And you can imagine the intensity of the motivation that led up to that victory. The need to affiliate and to excel no doubt energized and directed the team to play hard and to play well. After the victory, the emotion of joy energized and directed the team to celebrate. It is common to think of motivation and emotion going together. Nevertheless, there are important differences, and understanding these will help clarify the nature of both motivation and emotion.

One way of distinguishing motivation and emotion concerns how each is activated. Although there is some overlap between the two, emotion is always a reaction to a stimulus, while motivation does not need to be. Motivation is based on a relatively stable need structure that becomes regularly activated regardless of environmental stimuli or cognition. Motivated behavior can occur in the absence of any real or imagined stimulus. One need not necessarily see or think about food to become hungry. Another distinction is that emotion always involves a subjective feeling, whereas motivation need not. Normally, we breathe without experiencing any emotional feeling. Finally, whereas emotional behavior serves a communication function, motivated behavior need not. If a person sitting next to you in the bleachers looks angry, the expression of emotion tells you to be on guard. On the other hand, a track star motivated to practice the 50-yard dash in order to excel is not communicating with others.

THEORIES OF EMOTION

Theories of emotion provide important insights into the nature of emotion as well as important perspectives from which to view emotion. As with motivation, initial attempts to understand emotion were influenced by Darwin's theory of evolution. Within this context, two major early theories, the

James-Lange theory and the Cannon-Bard theory, were developed. These theories differed in their view of the sequence in which the various components of emotion unfold. Both of these theories became a focal point for two modern approaches: one emphasizing the role of biologically determined factors in emotion as in Darwin's theory; the second, the view that emotion depends on how we appraise or evaluate a situation. We will discuss each of these positions, beginning with the early theories and concluding with the two major modern views.

Darwin's Evolutionary Theory

Charles Darwin (1872) believed that the concept of evolution applied to behavior and mental life as well as to anatomy. Emotion, he proposed, is something we inherited from our earliest ancestors to prepare us to deal with an ever-changing environment. Fear, for example, helped early human beings to avoid danger; anger helped them to conquer enemies and a hostile environment; interest helped them to discover better ways to satisfy their needs. Without emotion, the individual would not be as physically or mentally prepared to respond to the environment. Darwin believed that emotions in this way increased the chances of survival for early human beings, who were particularly vulnerable to conditions of their environment.

Darwin believed that the value of emotion was in part due to its communicative quality. We know a person is afraid by observing the trembling of hands and the paleness of skin. The fear is expressed in the body and written on the face. Because of such expressions, emotions help us to predict behavior: an individual in fear is likely to seek help or protection; a sad individual is likely to seek comfort and reassurance; an angry individual could be a threat. Knowing what to expect improves chances to adapt and survive.

The way people express fear, anger, and other emotions is, according to Darwin, inherited and the same the world over. Certain facial expressions, he believed, had a universal meaning. And he argued that the face was the primary vehicle through which emotions were expressed.

Darwin emphasized the inherited, or biologically determined, nature of emotions. He supported his theory by pointing to the universality of emotional expression. Shortly after Darwin, psychologists began to debate whether physiological changes or subjective feelings occur first in the experience of emotion.

■ Learning Clue ■

As you read the next two theories, notice that one (the James-Lange theory) states that bodily changes occur *before* the subjective experience of emotion, and that the other (the Cannon-Bard theory) states that bodily changes *accompany* the subjective experience.

Early Theories: The Sequence of Emotion's Components

Darwin's evolutionary theory of emotion provided the context from which later theorists worked. The survival value of emotions, the importance of their communicative properties, their biological determination, and their universality were the Darwinian ideas these theorists started with. The James-Lange and Cannon-Bard theories extended Darwin's views by attempting to specify the sequence in which an emotion's components are activated and experienced.

The James-Lange Theory. William James (1884, 1890) was particularly interested in the physiological component of emotion. He believed that emotion was the feeling or perception of those bodily changes that occur when one responds to a stimulus. For instance, you see an automobile heading directly toward you as you drive down a one-way street. In response to the threatening stimulus, you blast your horn, swerve to the side, and miss hitting the car by inches. As you take evasive action, your heart beats faster, your blood pressure increases, and your body trembles. According to James, it is your awareness of these bodily changes that is the emotion. You see something that causes your heart to beat faster and your body to tremble. Your recognition of a rapid heartbeat and trembling body is fear. This concept of emotion—as the perception of one's bodily changes that occur in response to an event—was also formulated independently of James by Carl Lange (1885) and is known as the James-Lange theory.

The James-Lange theory contradicts the popular notion that emotion precedes action. Most people assume that bodily changes occur because of the emotion—that you tremble because of your fear. But James and Lange argued that first you see a threat and then your body reflexively responds to it. Finally, you experience fear, which is your awareness of these bodily responses.

The James-Lange theory attempted to address the question of how the various components of emotion interrelate. To this end, it used the concept of feedback—one component providing information to another. According to the James-Lange theory, the subjective experience of emotion results from the feedback one receives from the body, particularly the autonomic nervous system. Although few modern theorists agree with the specifics of the James-Lange theory, most continue to rely on the concept of feedback to explain the experience of emotion.

Figure 9.8 Schematic Summary of the James-Lange Theory.

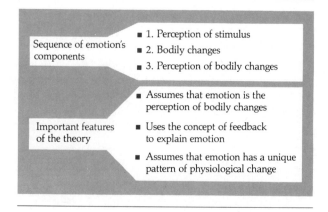

Sequence of emotion's components
- 1. Perception of stimulus
- 2. Bodily changes
- 3. Perception of bodily changes

Important features of the theory
- Assumes that emotion is the perception of bodily changes
- Uses the concept of feedback to explain emotion
- Assumes that emotion has a unique pattern of physiological change

Another important feature of the James-Lange theory is its assumption that each emotion has a unique pattern of physiological change. Although all bodily changes provide feedback for the subjective experience, those of the autonomic nervous system play the major role. The changes in heart rate, blood temperature, skin temperature, and other aspects of autonomic nervous system activity, according to the James-Lange theory, are different for anger, fear, joy, and the other emotions. (Figure 9.8 summarizes the James-Lange theory.)

The assumption that a unique pattern of physiological activity exists for each emotion provided a pivotal point for emotion researchers. Some agreed; others took the opposite view, arguing that, physiologically, all emotions are similar.

The Cannon-Bard Theory. The first serious challenge to the James-Lange theory came in a series of critiques by Walter Cannon (1927, 1929) and later Philip Bard (1934). A new view, called the Cannon-Bard theory, emerged.

Cannon was the first to challenge the position that each emotion has a unique pattern of autonomic arousal. He maintained that all emotion involves the same pattern of change; namely, increased activity of the autonomic nervous system. This increased autonomic activity, or arousal, includes increases in heart rate, blood pressure, blood circulation, and skin temperature and a decrease in the rate of digestion. The heart rate can only go up or down; and, in emotion, it always goes up, Cannon said.

Cannon also noted that there are situations in which bodily changes are not perceived as emotion. If emotion is the perception of bodily changes, as James and Lange say, why doesn't one experience emotion during vigorous exercise? Emotion, he argued, has to be more than an awareness of an aroused bodily state, since arousal can occur in the absence of emotion, as it does in exercise. Cannon and Bard proposed, instead, that bodily changes and the feeling of an emotion result from the activation of two separate brain structures at the same moment. According to the Cannon-Bard theory, information from a stimulus event is relayed as a neural impulse to two

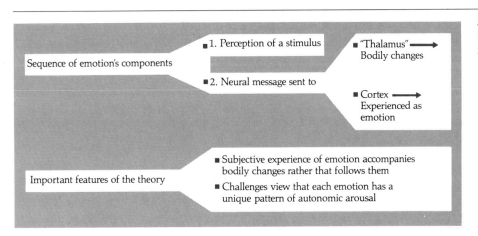

Figure 9.9 Schematic Summary of the Cannon-Bard Theory.

Sequence of emotion's components

- 1. Perception of a stimulus
- "Thalamus" → Bodily changes
- 2. Neural message sent to
- Cortex → Experienced as emotion

Important features of the theory

- Subjective experience of emotion accompanies bodily changes rather that follows them
- Challenges view that each emotion has a unique pattern of autonomic arousal

parts of the brain at the same time—the "thalamus," where the impulse results in autonomic nervous system activity and therefore causes bodily changes; and the cortex, the seat of higher cognitive processes in the brain, where the impulse is experienced as emotion. In Cannon's day, scientists had yet to make a clear distinction between the thalamus and the hypothalamus. It is the latter that actually governs endocrine and autonomic nervous system activity (see Chapter 3). The important point is, however, that, according to the theory, the subjective experience of emotion accompanies bodily changes rather than follows them, as James and Lange had claimed. And, in locating the experience of emotion not in feedback from the body but in stimulation of the cortex, Cannon and Bard anticipated the development of cognitive theory. (Figure 9.9 summarizes the Cannon-Bard theory.)

■ Learning Clue ■

As you read what follows, be alert to the differences between modern biological theories and modern cognitive theories. They have different views on how emotions are activated and experienced. The dividing line between the two seems to concern one question: Can emotion be activated and experienced without cognition?

Biological Theories

Modern biological theories, such as those of Izard (1977), Tomkins (1981), and Plutchik (1980a), are based on Darwin's view that emotions are inborn and universal, on the concept of feedback, and on the position that each emotion is associated with a unique pattern of physiological activity. According to such theories, emotion is the result of a biologically programmed sequence of responses that occur throughout the body when activated by a stimulus. These theories hold that an emotion can be activated and experienced without cognition.

Izard's Position. According to Izard, there are ten fundamental emotions: interest, joy, fear-surprise, sadness, anger, disgust, contempt, shame, shyness, and guilt (Izard, 1971). These fundamental emotions can combine, he says, to create more complex states such as embarrassment, a combination of shame and guilt. Izard states that each fundamental emotion must have three main components: a unique physiological response, a unique facial expression, and a subjective experience.

According to Izard's theory, emotion begins with an internal event (a memory, image, thought, or another emotion) or an external stimulus (an old song, the arrival of a loved one, and the like) which causes a change in nervous system activity. The change, in turn, triggers a specific genetically programmed facial expression. The nervous system's response to the sight of a loved one may trigger a smile; the memory of past defeats, a frown. The idea is that the facial expression is appropriate to the stimulus and that it occurs automatically in response to it according to a predetermined genetic program. The theory holds that sensory feedback from the face generates the subjective experience of emotion, an aspect of the theory known as the **facial feedback hypothesis.** Physiological changes such as changes in heart

Facial Feedback Hypothesis: The theory that sensory feedback from the face generates the subjective experience of emotion.

rate, hormone secretion, and respiration then follow to regulate or accompany the emotion.

Izard's theory is like the James-Lange theory in that it associates each emotion with a unique pattern of physiological activity. Izard's theory and the James-Lange theory also both state that emotion involves a reflexive reaction to a stimulus. But, according to Izard, it is the innately determined facial expression, rather than the autonomic nervous system, that is responding reflexively to the stimulus. Furthermore, like the James-Lange theory, the subjective experience of emotion is attributed to feedback; but, in Izard's theory, the feedback comes from the face rather than from the organs that respond to the autonomic nervous system (heart, liver, stomach, salivary glands, sweat glands, and so on). (Figure 9.10 summarizes Izard's theory.) In localizing the subjective experience of emotion in the face, Izard's theory suggests that such experience might be controllable, at least in part. By inhibiting facial expressions, one can theoretically blunt, alter, or reduce the intensity of an emotional experience.

Izard has studied the facial expressions of infants in order to determine whether there is a unique facial expression for each emotion and to describe, in an objective way, any facial expression of emotion. He works with infants on the assumption that they are too young to have learned the emotions they have or the emotional expressions they use. His research begins with the videotaping of babies' faces as they experience emotion-producing stimuli such as the feel of an ice cube, separation and reunion with mother, a balloon popping in front of their face, the taste of lemon rind, receiving a favorite toy, and so on. Researchers then view the tapes and record the differences in facial movement. The top, middle, and lower parts of the face are screened separately for the researchers. In this way, the researchers cannot know the stimulus or emotion the child was experiencing; they can therefore concentrate on objectively describing the physical changes they see. Coding

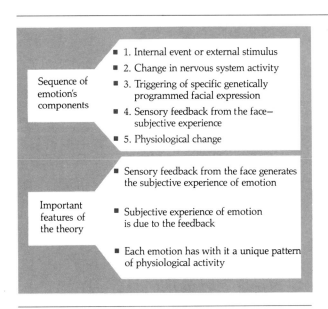

Figure 9.10 Schematic Summary of Izard's Theory.

Sequence of emotion's components

- 1. Internal event or external stimulus
- 2. Change in nervous system activity
- 3. Triggering of specific genetically programmed facial expression
- 4. Sensory feedback from the face— subjective experience
- 5. Physiological change

Important features of the theory

- Sensory feedback from the face generates the subjective experience of emotion
- Subjective experience of emotion is due to the feedback
- Each emotion has with it a unique pattern of physiological activity

one minute of videotape can take these researchers up to one hour of precise observation and description (Izard et al., 1983).

Izard's research has revealed that all babies express the same emotion in the same way. (See Color Plate 9B.) For surprise, for example, the pattern consists of raised eyebrows, widened eyes, and an oval-shaped mouth. For anger, it consists of eyebrows drawn down and together, eyes narrowed, and the mouth opened in a squarish shape. The importance of the face in emotion, originally suspected by Darwin, has also been confirmed by the work of Ekman and his colleagues.

Ekman's Work. Ekman, Levenson, and Friesen (1983) found that voluntary changes in facial expression, changes that corresponded to specific emotions, produced significant changes in heart rate and skin temperature. Researchers asked professional actors to move their facial muscles, section by section, into patterns that only the researchers knew were associated with particular emotions (see Figure 9.11). As the actors followed instructions, the researchers monitored the actor's heart rate and skin temperature, both indicators of autonomic arousal. To produce the expression of fear, for example, the actors were asked first to raise their brows and pull them together, then to raise their upper eyelids, and finally to stretch their eyes horizontally back toward their ears. They were not told to produce a specific expression or emotion, only to move their faces as instructed. The list of movements was derived from cross-cultural studies of universal facial expressions (see Box 9.2).

Ekman found that, as the actors expressions changed, so did their heartbeats and skin temperature. When they took on the expression of anger, the

Figure 9.11 Ekman's Actors' Expressions.
Actor Tom Harrison moves his facial muscles according to commands provided by psychologist Paul Ekman, in order to match the facial expressions Ekman has evidence to believe are associated with basic universal emotions.

Box 9.2 PSYCHOLOGY IN ACTION: Interpreting Facial Expressions

The illustration shows pictures of faces used by Ekman, Sorenson, and Friesen (1969) to study the universality of emotional expression. Individuals from all over the world, even those from very isolated and nonindustrialized societies, agreed on the meaning of each expression. Members of the Fore tribe of New Guinea were told little stories to describe fear, happiness, and anger. They were then asked to match the three pictures of Caucasians, whose faces expressed these emotions, to the stories. People of the tribe identified the emotions depicted in the faces in the photographs with at least 80 percent accuracy. And American college students were just as accurate when asked to identify the emotions of Fore natives, based on photographs of the natives' facial expressions when asked to make the same kind of face they thought people would make if they were experiencing the events described in the same little stories.

In another study, Izard (1971) showed photographs of faces expressing nine different emotions to people from twelve different countries in North America, South America, Europe, and Asia. For each expression, 60 percent or more of the individuals from each country agreed on its meaning, and agreement was much higher (80 percent or better) for the three emotional expressions (fear, happiness, and anger)

studied by Ekman and colleagues. Such studies indicate that the language of emotion, as expressed on the face, is indeed universal. The friendly expression of a smile is understood the world over.

Support for the universality of emotional expression does not rule out, of course, the influence of learning and culture. People learn to hide or disguise their emotions. Moreover, people of different social backgrounds and different cultures learn facial movements that modify innate expressions. For example, the Chinese stick out their tongues to show surprise—not contempt, as in the United States.

Under most circumstances, it is possible to read emotion from the expression on a person's face. Consider, for instance, what we pick up when there is a discrepancy between a speaker's facial expression and the message of the words that accompany it. If the speaker's face looks angry, but her words, or even her tone of voice, sound conciliatory, we still know that she is angry. Similarly, when the face of a person whose dinner invitation we've just turned down looks sad, it's hard to believe the words of the message, "Oh, that's okay; no problem." Often facial expressions are far more powerful than words in reading emotions.

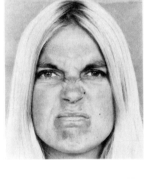

The faces above are similar to those that Paul Ekman showed to tribespeople in isolated New Guinea. The tribespeople had no difficulty matching the pictures to short stories depicting happiness, anger, and disgust. The pictures below show the expressions of one tribesman when asked to make the same kind of face he thought the tribespeople would make if they were experiencing the events depicted in the same stories.

■ **Learning Check** ■

For each question: read, cover, try to recite, repeat.

1. *Question:* What do modern biological theorists of emotion (Izard and Ekman) have in common with Darwin?

Answer: All say: (a) Emotions are inherited and biologically programmed. (b) Emotions are universal. (c) Faces are the main expressions of emotion.

2. *Question:* What do modern biological theorists of emotion (Izard and Ekman) have in common with early biological theorists (James and Lange)?

Answer: All say: (a) Each emotion has a unique pattern of physiological activity. (b) Feedback from the body triggers the subjective feeling component.

heart rate jumped an average of six beats a minute and skin temperature rose by an average of 0.1 degrees centigrade. (It is not surprising that we associate anger with being hot.) Happiness is a cool emotion. Ekman and colleagues found that, with happy expressions, temperature fell about 0.05 degrees centigrade and heart rate increased only about two and a half beats per minute.

The findings of Ekman and colleagues (1983) indicate that specific facial expressions trigger the changes in autonomic arousal associated with emotion. Moreover, the finding of different patterns of arousal for different expressions supports the James-Lange hypothesis of a specific pattern of bodily change for each emotion.

Cognitive Theories

The relationship between emotion and cognition is reciprocal—each influences the other. On this point, nearly all modern theories of emotion agree. What one thinks influences what one feels and vice versa. But is it possible to have an emotion without cognition? It is on this point that modern theories do not agree. In fact, it is the dividing line between all major modern theories of emotion—that is, whether or not an emotion can be activated and experienced without cognition.

Zajonc (1984) believes that certain patterns of sensory stimulation, such as might be caused by a putrid odor or the sudden appearance of an unfamiliar animal in the immediate environment, are capable of activating an emotional circuit involving bodily changes, expressive behavior, and subjective feeling. Cognitive activity, he believes, can follow or be completely bypassed. Izard and others who support biological theories would agree. Cognitive theorists would not.

Cognitive theorists hold that emotion depends on how we appraise or evaluate a situation. According to the cognitive theorists, a stimulus cannot cause you fear unless you judge it to be potentially harmful. Thus, they would ask, how can something frighten you unless you think it's dangerous. The role of cognitive appraisal in emotion is exemplified by the Schachter-Singer two-factor theory.

The Schachter-Singer Two-Factor Theory. According to this theory, whether or not physiological arousal becomes emotion depends on a cognitive evaluation of the situation that caused the arousal. The theory holds that emotion depends on two factors: an internal state of arousal and an appropriate cognition with which to label that state. According to Schachter and Singer, stimulus events produce general arousal, which the person then labels as happiness, fear, anger, or whatever seems appropriate to the situation.

To test their view, Schachter and Singer (1962) devised an experiment. Subjects were told that the experiment concerned the effects of a new vitamin compound on vision. The compound actually was epinephrine, a hormone that, in actual emotion, induces arousal of the autonomic nervous system. Though all subjects thought they were being injected with a vitamin, an informed group was told what bodily changes to expect as a result of the injection. An uninformed group was given no information. A misinformed group was told that the injection might cause some numbness and itching. A control group was injected with a placebo, a saline solution, rather than epinephrine and given no information.

After the injections, each group of subjects was seated in a waiting room and told to relax while the injections took effect. In the waiting room the subjects encountered a confederate of the experimenters, who pretended to be another subject. For half of the subjects in each of the four groups, the confederate acted happy; for the other half, the confederate acted angry and irritated. The results of the experiment indicated that the uninformed and misinformed subjects were emotionally influenced by the confederate's behavior. Those who were uninformed or misinformed and who observed the happy behavior reported later a greater degree of happiness than informed and placebo control subjects who observed the same behavior. Uninformed and misinformed subjects who observed angry behavior reported feeling angrier than the informed and placebo control subjects reported feeling.

In interpreting the results, Schachter and Singer proposed that the informed group had logically attributed their increased heart rate and blood pressure to the drug. Their experience was simply that of arousal without emotion. The misinformed and uninformed subjects, by contrast, didn't have a logical way to explain their arousal. The environmental cue provided by the confederate suggested to them that their arousal was due to happiness or due to anger, depending on the cue. They labeled their arousal as such and attributed it to an emotion.

According to the Schachter-Singer two-factor theory, cognition provides the framework within which one interprets and understands bodily feelings. Without this framework, arousal is nothing more than a state of heightened physiological activity. Within the framework, arousal becomes emotion—anger, sadness, or joy, depending on the circumstances.

The Schachter-Singer experiment seemed to support the assumption that the physiological aspects of emotion are roughly the same for all emotions, as Cannon and Bard had believed. There is, however, a difference between the arousal one experiences in real life and that which was artificially produced by injections of epinephrine in the Schachter-Singer experiment. In real situations, epinephrine is released into the bloodstream at the end of a sequence of events that begins with activities in the brain. Although the release of epinephrine into the blood augments all the bodily aspects of arousal, it is in real life a product of arousal, not its cause, as in the experiments. It is possible that anger and happiness both result in the release of epinephrine yet differ in other physiological respects.

Schachter and Singer were also incorrect in concluding that all emotions involve the same pattern of physiological activity (i.e., heightened arousal). The importance of the Schachter-Singer experiment rests with the role their theory suggests for cognition. The notion that appraisals are a source of emotion rather than a result, as in the James-Lange theory, remains a central premise in modern cognitive theories of emotion.

■ Learning Clue ■

Does a person's interpretation of an event (cognitive appraisal) have to be conscious, or could it occur without conscious awareness? The research you are about to read tries to answer this question.

Cognitive Appraisal: Interpreting an event in terms of its effect on well-being.

Lazarus's Theory. Modern cognitive theories are best exemplified by the views of Lazarus (1984) and colleagues. According to these theorists, to respond to an event with emotion, people must first interpret the event in terms of its effect on well-being; that is, they must come to a **cognitive appraisal** of the event (for example, is it good or bad; beneficial or dangerous, etc.?). Cognitive activity, therefore, is considered to be a necessary precondition for emotion. In fact, the subjective feeling of emotion stems directly from the appraisal. The person feels fear from an appraisal of danger; sadness from an appraisal of loss; and so on.

The appraisal process takes place continuously, shaping the emotional response as the process is occurring. Physiological changes follow the appraisal. For example, you're crossing a busy street when suddenly you hear the screeching tires of a speeding car. You appraise the situation; if you don't hurry you might get run down. Perceiving the situation as a life-threatening danger, you experience fear. Your heart beats faster and you hasten to the other side as the car approaches the intersection and begins to slow down. Although you're now quite safe, you think that you might have been hurt because of a reckless driver and your fear boils into anger. Then the car comes to a complete stop. The person inside motions you to come. It's someone you recognize, your neighbor, but you've never seen that car before. Did she just buy a new car? Your new appraisal arouses interest. Thus, your emotion changes in line with your cognitive appraisal (Figure 9.12 summarizes Lazarus's theory.)

According to Lazarus, cognitive appraisals need not involve conscious thought. When confronting a speeding car coming at you, you may realize without thinking that you are in danger; you experience fear; and you get out of the way. Conscious deliberations don't come until later. Since there is little doubt that people do at times respond emotionally without conscious thought, the theory that cognition is a necessary precondition for emotion can only be correct if cognitions need not be conscious.

Lazarus's theory grew, in part, from the results of an experiment that suggested to him that subjects are able to evaluate threat without conscious awareness (Lazarus & McCleary, 1951). In the first half of one experiment, subjects were asked to identify nonsense syllables such as XOV, BIX, and IAG. The syllables were flashed very rapidly on a screen—so rapidly that subjects frequently could not accurately report what had been shown. Fol-

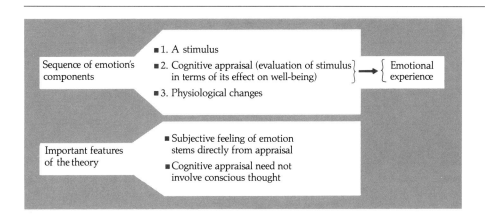

Figure 9.12 Schematic Summary of Lazarus's Cognitive Theory.

Sequence of emotion's components
■ 1. A stimulus
■ 2. Cognitive appraisal (evaluation of stimulus in terms of its effect on well-being) → Emotional experience
■ 3. Physiological changes

Important features of the theory
■ Subjective feeling of emotion stems directly from appraisal
■ Cognitive appraisal need not involve conscious thought

lowing certain syllables, whether or not they had been correctly identified, subjects were given a painful electric shock. In the second half of the experiment, the syllables were again briefly presented, and the subjects' **galvanic skin response (GSR)**—a lowering of the resistance of the skin to the passage of electric current—was measured. GSR is an indicator of autonomic arousal—as arousal goes up, skin resistance goes down. Through the GSR, the researchers could evaluate the strength of a subject's reaction to syllables that were associated with shock and to those that were not. As predicted, subjects' GSR increased when syllables that had been followed by shock were shown, indicating that shock and the syllables had become associated. Subjects' GSR did not increase when syllables not associated with shock were shown. To the surprise of the researchers, however, subjects' GSR increased for the shock-related syllables that had been misperceived and misreported. To explain this finding, Lazarus and colleagues reasoned that subjects must have perceived the syllables, though not consciously, and learned their association to the shock without awareness. To Lazarus and colleagues, these findings suggested that subjects could somehow discriminate between threatening and nonthreatening stimuli without awareness. The possibility of nonconscious evaluation was later to become an essential aspect of Lazarus's cognitive theory of emotion (Lazarus, 1984).

Another line of support for the cognitive view has come from a number of studies on the relationship between appraisal and emotion (Lazarus et al., 1970). In a typical experiment, people are subjected to a stressful event, such as a film showing gruesome woodshop accidents. Some subjects are instructed to detach themselves from the stressful event; others to involve themselves more fully. Subjects told to be detached are asked to remind themselves that what they are seeing isn't real, that the "victims" of the accidents are acting. Subjects told to be involved are instructed to remind themselves that such accidents could happen to them. Results showed that detached subjects experience less emotion, as indicated by heart rate and self-report, than involved subjects.

Such findings indicate that the way a person appraises and copes with a situation can have an important bearing on an emotional response. Subjects that detach themselves are able to dampen their emotional response, reducing the impact of the event.

Galvanic Skin Response (GSR): A lowering of the resistance of the skin to the passage of electric current; an indicator of autonomic arousal.

■ **Learning Check** ■

The next time you observe someone happy or angry or whatever emotion, see if you can answer these questions: (1) What stimulus is this person reacting to? (2) Can I see any evidence of physiological arousal in this person? (3) What subjective feeling does this person seem to be experiencing? (4) In what physical ways is this person communicating the feeling?

In sum, support for the cognitive view comes from a variety of sources. The assumption of cognitive theory that cognition is a necessary precondition of emotion, however, is no more proven than is the assumption of biologically determined theories that emotion can occur before, and even in the absence of, cognition (Lazarus, 1984; Zajonc, 1984). Both cognitive and biological theories provide an important perspective from which to view emotion, and both offer applications of everyday personal relevance.

LEARNING FRAMEWORK

  I. Motivation—unobservable forces that energize and direct people's behavior.
 II. Three theories try to explain motivation in biological terms. (Review: *Table 9.1*)
      A. Instinct theory describes motivation in terms of inborn (biologically determined) inclinations to behave in a particular way under particular circumstances. (Review: *McDougall's Instinct Theory; Ethology*)
      B. Drive reduction theory describes motivation in terms of drives that help regulate biological (or survival) needs such as the needs for food, air, sleep, and so on. (Review: *Figure 9.2; Homeostasis*)
      C. Arousal theory describes motivation in terms of the need for an ideal level of stimulation. (Review: *Yerkes-Dodson Law*)
III. Two theories try to explain social and personal motivation.
      A. Murray's theory describes social motivation in terms of needs acquired through learning (such as the need to affiliate or the need to excel). (Review: *Psychogenic Needs; n. Ach.*)
      B. Maslow's theory describes personal motivation in terms of an inborn urge for fulfillment. (Review: *Self-Actualization; Figure 9.5*)
 IV. What role does cognition (thoughts, beliefs, desires, expectations) play in motivation?
      A. Both *desire* for a goal and *belief* that the goal will be reached strengthen motivation. (Review: *Expectation; Valence; Figure 9.6*)
      B. Belief in personal control increases motivation. (Review: *Locus of Control*)
      C. Rewards can strengthen motivation or weaken it, depending on how rewards are interpreted and evaluated. (Review: *Intrinsic Motivation; Extrinsic Motivation*)
  V. How the body regulates hunger and eating shows the complexity of physiological activity in motivation.
      A. Cannon believed (incorrectly) that stomach contractions were the hunger signal that energized and directed the behavior of eating.
      B. Experiments with rats have indicated that there is a stop-eating center

(VMH) in the brain and also a start-eating center (LH). (Review: *Ventromedial Hypothalamus (VMH); Lateral Hypothalamus (LH)*)

C. Experiments with rats have suggested that the chemicals that transmit messages from one part of the brain to another may also signal when to start and stop eating. (Review: *Neurotransmitters as Start-Stop Hunger Switches*)

D. There are two homeostatic systems for hunger, one that regulates eating hour by hour and another that regulates it over weeks and months. (Review: *Liporeceptors; Set Point Theory*)

VI. Although psychologists have not yet defined emotion, they have described its four main components: (1) reaction to a stimulus; (2) physiological activity; (3) personal or subjective feeling; (4) expression.

VII. So far no theory has been able to explain the nature of emotion entirely.

A. Darwin's evolutionary theory stated that emotions, in part because of their ability to communicate, increased the chances of survival of early human beings.

B. Early theories of emotion disagreed on the sequence of components: Does the subjective experience of emotion follow its physiological activity or do they occur at the same time? (Review: *James-Lange Theory; Figure 9.8; Cannon-Bard Theory; Figure 9.9*)

C. Modern biological theories state that emotion is a programmed physiological response to a stimulus—a different response for each emotion, but the same response in all people. (Review: *Izard's Position; Ekman's Work*)

D. Is it possible to have an emotion without cognition? Cognitive theorists say that emotion depends on how we appraise or evaluate an event in terms of its effect on our well-being. (Review: *Schachter-Singer Theory; Lazarus's Theory; Figure 9.12; Cognitive Appraisal*)

10

Human Sexuality

Chapter Outline

People have a natural curiosity about sex. It is a subject that catches most people's interest immediately, and it is a subject that most people do not easily tire of. In addition to curiosity, most people seem to have strong emotional and symbolic associations with sex. People associate the physical expression of sexuality with emotional intimacy, being male or female with personal identity, and sexual union with religious and aesthetic meanings (Carroll et al., 1985; Reis et al., 1985).

We have such a regular and profound interest in sex that we learn about it almost everywhere. Our ideas about sexual behavior and our associations with it come to us from friends and parents, church and school, entertainment and advertising, our own sexual experiences, and the era in which we live. The knowledge of sex that we acquire in these ways can vary a great deal from one source to another and even from the same source. If we look at this fluctuation from an historical and cultural point of view, we can see it more clearly. In China, for example, for centuries people thought of sexual pleasure as a valuable means of finding spiritual harmony with the universe. In current and recent times, however, Chinese culture tells the individual that the opposite is true—abstinence from sexual pleasure brings spiritual harmony (Philip Rawson, *Oriental Erotic Art*, New York: Gallery Books, 1981, p. 12). In the Western world, different eras also spread different ideas about sex. For example, many children might learn today that masturbation will not hurt you, if you don't do it "too much" (a matter of degree that tends to emerge according to individual choice). Our parents and grandparents, however, learned that masturbation was absolutely wrong and would drain energy while causing severe mental and physical illness (Bullough & Bullough, 1977).

Is there a way to reach beyond this historical and cultural fluctuation in order to learn something more objective about human sexual behavior? Is it possible to understand the source of our interest in sex? Yes. Psychology can provide us with the scientific knowledge accumulated so far on human sexual behavior. In this chapter we will discuss sex as motivation, sex as an emotion, psychological influences on the sexual response, and nature vs. nurture in human sexual behavior. In addition, we will describe the sexual anatomy, the cycle of human sexual response, and common sexual problems and disorders.

WHAT SEX IS

Sex can be compared to hunger and other biologically based motivations in that it energizes and directs behavior. Like hunger, sex is associated with a delicate interplay among physiological processes, such as the interaction of hormones and brain activity. Yet sex differs from hunger in a number of important ways. First, there are no needs based on tissue deficits. Thus, sex is not essential for individual survival; it preserves the species, not the individual. Second, there are no Start-Stop sex centers, as there are in the short- and long-term control of hunger (Whalen, 1976). Among humans, there is no direct relationship between hormonal state and sexual responsiveness (Beach, 1977a; Masters et al., 1982). Both male and female humans can have the desire and ability to engage in sexual activity at any time, regardless of concentrations of sex hormones in the bloodstream. They may also turn down a sexual opportunity when levels of hormones are at their highest peak. Though sex has much in common with motivation, the concept of motivation alone does not fully capture its essence.

Sex is also related to emotion. It involves reaction to a stimulus, physiological activity, subjective feelings (in particular, those associated with love), and expression. Yet sex is different from emotion in important ways. It is possible to have sex without love or any other feeling typically associated with emotion; people can engage in casual sex whose goal is simply physical pleasure. Further, the emotion of love need not be associated with sex, as in parent–child or sibling relationships and close platonic friendships.

Sex has both motivational and emotional properties, yet it does not fit neatly into either. It is unique—grounded in biological need and physiological processes, associated with strong subjective feeling, yet not dependent on any single list of components or processes. It is influenced by our personalities and preferences, our experience and culture, and our values and standards. Sex is also highly personal and individual; the range of individual differences in sexual appetite, capacity, and preference is great.

Because sexual behavior can be so dependent on complex and individual circumstances, it is difficult to talk about beyond the level of subjective experience. In order to conduct a credible discussion on sex, we need to look

---

■ Learning Check ■

Read, try to recite, repeat.

Two differences between sex and hunger:

In sex
1. there are no needs based on tissue deficits.
2. there are no Start-Stop sex centers.

very early at what kind of scientific study is possible on this kind of human behavior.

SCIENTIFIC APPROACHES TO HUMAN SEXUALITY

Scientific approaches to human sexuality have relied heavily on three major research methods: survey techniques, case studies, and laboratory methods. (These were described briefly in Chapter 1.) Survey techniques use questioning by telephone, mail, or face-to-face interviews to study people's sexual attitudes, opinions, preferences, and beliefs. In the case study method, a scientist makes extensive recordings of the behavior and responses to detailed questioning of a single individual or some well-defined group of individuals (e.g., a specific group of prostitutes). In the laboratory method, subjects are studied under laboratory conditions. The laboratory method may involve direct observation of the sexual behavior of volunteer subjects in the scientist's laboratory. Alternatively, the scientist may conduct an experiment in which certain variables are manipulated in order to determine their effects on other variables. For example, a researcher may change the number of times a group of individuals is shown a particular sexually stimulating picture, in order to determine how repeated exposure of such pictures affect sexual arousal (O'Donohue & Geer, 1985). (Figure 10.1 summarizes the major methods of research).

■ Learning Clue ■

As you read, you will see that each of the three scientific approaches—survey, case study, and laboratory—has unique strengths and limitations.

Survey Techniques

Suppose that you received a questionnaire in the mail inviting you to participate in a sex survey—to respond to questions such as, "How old were you when you had your first sexual encounter?", "Have you ever experienced orgasm?", and so on. Would you respond? And, if you did choose to respond, could you be entirely honest? Whether you could answer yes to

Figure 10.1 Schematic Summary of Methods of Research.

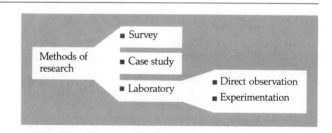

both questions, or answered the survey at all, the results of the survey would be subject to important limitations. In fact, the results of all sex surveys are biased because they include responses from volunteers—those who agree to respond. There is no way of knowing whether the results of the survey apply to those who did not respond; in fact, the results would very likely be quite different if the non-respondents were to participate in the same questions under different circumstances. Thus, in conducting a sex survey, it is virtually impossible to obtain a scientifically representative or random sample of the general population. Moreover, many surveys suffer from a demographic bias. Typically, the sample used in sex surveys contains a larger proportion of Caucasian, middle class, and college- or high school-educated persons than the general population.

In a widely publicized survey conducted by *Redbook* magazine, for example, readers were asked to answer a 60-item, multiple choice questionnaire. Over 100,000 women replied; about 99,000 of them reported having experienced sexual intercourse (**coitus**) as well as **oral-genital contact** (Tavris & Sadd, 1977). Such findings can be very misleading because they are based on a sample of *Redbook* readers, most of whom are married, between twenty and forty years of age, Caucasian, and middle or upper middle class. In short, the sample in the *Redbook* survey is not representative of the general population and thus not accurate when applied to the population as a whole. It does, however, tell us something about the segment of the population from which the sample was drawn. Nevertheless, as with any survey, *Redbook's* results must be interpreted with caution, because there is always room for doubt in any study that relies on self-report. When people respond to a question, whether multiple choice, essay, or interview, their memories may not be accurate. Or they may report what they think the experimenter wants to hear rather than what really happened—like the proverbial fisherman telling of "the one that got away." The way a question is phrased may also influence the subject's response.

When evaluating a survey, it is necessary to examine the nature of the sample and the limits of the findings in terms of its application to the general population, as well as possible biases in the types of questions asked and the way they are phrased. For example, in the highly publicized Hite (1981) report on male sexuality, 119,000 questionnaires were distributed to males throughout the United States. Only 7,239 men chose to respond to such questions as, "Do you like manual stimulation of your penis by a partner?" "Do you often orgasm this way?" (p. 540). Results pertaining to the limited sample of volunteers who responded clearly would not pertain to the general population.

Because of their limitations, sex surveys might best be viewed as general guides that apply to a certain segment of the population, not necessarily to everyone. So viewed, surveys, when carefully conducted and interpreted with caution, can provide a wealth of information and insights into human sexuality. Such was the case for the sex surveys conducted by Alfred C. Kinsey and colleagues.

Kinsey's sex surveys, administered to large samples of volunteers in the late 1940s and early 1950s, were among the most solid and carefully conducted sex surveys to date. The findings from Kinsey's surveys, though limited in certain respects, opened a new era of understanding of the varieties

Coitus: Penile-vaginal intercourse.

Oral-Genital Contact: Mouth to genital sexual stimulation.

of human sexual behavior and provided a basis of comparison for modern trends.

In obtaining a sample, Kinsey and colleagues began with a variety of social groups and organizations such as college classes, professional organizations, and residents of rooming houses. In an effort to obtain data from people who ordinarily would not volunteer for sex survey research, Kinsey encouraged initial volunteers to persuade their friends to participate. In the end, more than 12,000 married and unmarried men and women from across the country, representing a wide range of ages, occupations, educational levels, and religion, were personally interviewed and responded, in confidence, to a carefully worded set of questions concerning their sexual behavior.

Kinsey and his colleagues presented the first of two reports on their findings in a book called *Sexual Behavior in the Human Male* (Kinsey et al., 1948). In spite of its scholarly nature, the work achieved best seller status, generating intense reactions, both positive and negative, in the process. For some readers, the finding that 40 percent of the married men admitted to being unfaithful to their wives was shocking. Others were surprised to learn that more than eight out of ten adolescent males had masturbated to orgasm by age fifteen, that nine out of ten men had masturbated at least once in their lives, and that **masturbation** was a regular practice among a significant percentage of men of all ages, according to the self-reports of the respondents. Many readers were also disturbed by Kinsey's report that more than one out of three men had admitted to having a homosexual experience after **puberty.**

Masturbation: Self-stimulation of the genitals to orgasm.

Puberty: The stage of life during which the reproductive organs mature.

Premarital Sex: Coitus before marriage.

Critics of Kinsey's report called it everything from "primitive," "oversimplified," and "illogical" (Trilling, 1948) to an "assault on the family as a basic unit of society" (Wickware, 1948). But even many of those who accepted Kinsey's first report as valid refused to believe the results of his second. In 1953, *Sexual Behavior in the Human Female* (Kinsey et al., 1953) shattered the popular belief that all "nice girls" were virgins until their wedding night and thereafter faithful to their husbands. Half the married women in Kinsey's sample of 5,940 reported experiencing **premarital sex** (intercourse before marriage), and more than one in five reported having extramarital affairs. Sixty-two percent of the women revealed that they had experimented with masturbation, and most agreed that the act was "a desirable and often necessary sexual outlet."

Kinsey's reports stirred up more controversy than he could have ever imagined. He became a target for severe criticism and ridicule (Christenson, 1971). Today the value of Kinsey's pioneer studies is widely recognized. Though his results were not based on a representative sample, Kinsey's data revealed a number of previously unrecognized trends. For example, it exploded a widely held myth concerning female sexuality: it revealed that sex was just as important and pleasurable to women as to men. Most of all, Kinsey's data brought to light the wide range of variability in human sexual behavior.

Case Studies

Whereas surveys obtain information on relatively large samples, case studies examine the sexual behavior of a single individual or well-defined group. Because fewer numbers of persons are involved, case studies can provide more depth and greater detail than surveys. Their applicability to the general population, or even some well-defined segment of the population, is, on the other hand, more limited. Case studies are often used to describe the atypical or the unusual. They also can be used to illustrate a point, or to demonstrate exceptions to the rule. For example, an interesting dimension of transsexualism—the desire to change one's gender to that of the opposite sex—was revealed in the case of Marty/Mary Ann, a man who waited until he was widowed and aged seventy-four before carrying out a life-long transsexual desire (Docter, 1985).

A case study like this can have much value beyond its built-in curiosity value. In this instance, it provides a contradiction to the theory that early upbringing or a parental role model always plays a significant role in the desire for a sex change operation, as had been found in the case histories of other transsexuals. By comparing the case histories of transsexuals, contemporary researchers are able to look for similarities and differences. It must be kept in mind, however, that the information obtained about Marty depended on the questions asked by the interviewer, who no doubt had a particular interest in some of Marty's unusual behaviors. In addition, as in all case studies, it is difficult to find an appropriate standard or control by which to compare the subject's behavior. Finally, as with surveys and case studies in general, data for the case are based on self-report. As such, it is limited by the memory and ability of the respondent to provide an objective, unbiased report.

Laboratory Studies of the Sexual Response

Masters and Johnson's (1966) laboratory studies of human sexual behavior overcame the drawbacks of self-report data, substituting direct observation and objective measurement techniques for subjective reports. In some studies, Masters and Johnson observed volunteers perform the sex act while monitoring physiological changes in heart rate, muscle tension, and so on with sensitive electronic devices. In other cases they experimentally manipulated some variable—for instance, alcohol—to determine its effect on the sexual response. Subjects would drink different amounts of alcohol, and a control group would drink a nonalcoholic beverage. Then their response to sexually arousing pictures would be measured in terms of change in penis size or amount of vaginal lubrication.

Experimental studies such as this alcohol study allow scientists to specify cause-and-effect relationships (see Chapter 1). For example, it can be said that, contrary to popular belief, alcohol *reduces* the strength of the sexual response. Moreover, the more you drink, the less responsive you become (Athanasiou et al., 1970; Briddel & Wilson, 1976; Wilson & Lawson, 1976). Because only volunteers can be studied, however, the results cannot be considered representative of the general population. We cannot be certain that the responses of volunteers are the same as those of people who are unwilling to participate. Furthermore, the laboratory situation is artificial; though the effects of observation on the behaviors observed are difficult to gauge, scientists do know that people behave differently when they think they are being watched.

The limitations of laboratory studies of sexual behavior are the same as

William H. Masters and Virginia E. Johnson.

those encountered in laboratory studies of other human behaviors. But sex studies are hampered more than others by ethical considerations, due to the highly personal nature of the behavior. In addition, the field of sex research is relatively new. The myths and misconceptions of the past serve as a powerful reminder to scientists to exercise caution in interpreting new findings. Nevertheless, taken together, these studies have told psychologists much about the human sexual response.

RECENT TRENDS IN SEXUAL BEHAVIOR

Masters and Johnson's laboratory studies and Kinsey's myth-shattering surveys were important landmarks in the so-called sexual revolution underway in the 1950s and continued to be reported through the 1970s. One reflection of increased sexual freedom could be seen in the increase in the reported premarital sexual intercourse among adolescents, especially teenage girls. Whereas Kinsey et al. (1953) found 17 percent of the unmarried American teenage females (between thirteen and nineteen years of age) reported having sexual intercourse, independent surveys by Sorenson (1973) and Zelnik & Kantner (1977) found that the figure had increased to 45 and 46 percent, respectively. And, by the end of the 1970s, the percentage had increased to about 70 percent (Zelnik & Kantner, 1980; Katz & Cronin, 1980). Other studies showed a trend of increasing extramarital sex, homosexual en-

Sex education in the schools is one result of the sexual revolution.

counters (male–male and female–female), and masturbation (Hunt, 1974). Women became more concerned with issues such as control of their bodies, sexual exploitation by men, and equal work opportunity (Usher & Fels, 1985).

But along with increased sexual freedom came unexpected developments. Unwanted pregnancies skyrocketed, as did cases of sexually transmitted diseases. Researchers began to question whether sex education efforts in the schools were having the effects intended (Dignan et al., 1985); it has proved difficult to explain why so many unmarried teenagers who do not want to become pregnant fail to use contraceptives (Sack et al., 1985).

In the early 1980s, surveys showed people taking a second look at the attitudes spawned by the sexual revolution. Desire for sex without love was apparently being replaced by a greater emphasis, for both males and females, on the importance of a serious relationship and feeling loved and needed (Carroll et al., 1985). Casual sex seemed to be undergoing reexamination in the light of fear of sexually transmitted diseases (e.g., see Manne & Sandler, 1984).

In the pages ahead we will discuss these and other trends in greater detail. In particular, we will see why, when it comes to human sexuality, psychological factors—in particular, a person's cognitions (body image, expectations, and attitudes toward oneself or one's partner)—are as important or even more important than physical factors. The human sexual response is far more than anatomy and physiology. Before going on to the psychological aspects, however, we must first consider the biological and physiological aspects of sex.

SEXUAL ANATOMY AND PHYSIOLOGY

From early childhood we are taught to keep our sex organs hidden and our mouths closed on the subject of sex. Consequently many people are misinformed about sexual anatomy and physiological processes—that is, about the sexual parts of the body and the way they function. Unfortunately, inaccurate or incomplete knowledge of these matters can cause guilt, anxiety, and feelings of personal inadequacy. Information on sexual anatomy and physiology can dispel many common worries.

The Basic Parts and Their Function

Figure 10.2 shows the sex organs of the pelvic region, called the **genitals.** The female genitals include the outer structures of the pelvis, collectively called the **vulva,** and the inner space called the **vagina,** which is a muscular canal that leads to the uterus and forms a channel for the penis to place sperm near an egg. Among the parts of the vulva are the area over the pubic bone (the **mons veneris**); the outer and inner lips (the **labia majora** and **labia minora**); the area inside the inner lips, called the **vestibule;** and, within the vestibule, the tiny **clitoris,** an organ whose function is to focus

Genitals: Sex organs in the pelvic region; in males, the penis, testes, and scrotum; in females, the vulva and vagina.

Vulva: The external sex organs of the female including the mons veneris, labia, clitoris, vestibule, and opening to the vagina.

Vagina: An expandable muscular organ in the female that receives the penis during intercourse.

Mons veneris: A sensitive triangular area over the pubic bone in females consisting of a cushion of fatty tissue and covered by skin and pubic hair.

Labia Majora: The outer lips of the vulva.

Labia Minora: The inner lips of the vulva.

Vestibule: The area of the vulva inside the labia minora and outside the vagina.

Clitoris: A highly sensitive part of the female external genitals whose function is to focus and accumulate sexual pleasure.

Figure 10.2 Female and Male Genitals.

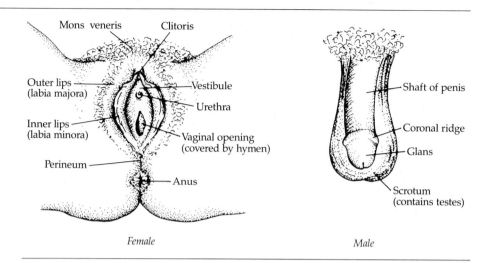

Female *Male*

Perineum: An area of hairless skin between the vagina and anus in females and between the scrotum and anus in males.

Hymen: A thin tissue that partially covers the opening of the vagina.

Scrotum: The sac of skin that contains the testes.

Glans: The tip or head of the penis (glans of penis) or clitoris (clitoral glans).

Coronal Ridge: A sensitive rim of tissue that separates the glans of the penis from the shaft.

Frenulum: A highly sensitive triangular fold of skin on the underside of the penis that connects glans and foreskin.

Homologous Organs: The corresponding parts of the female and male sexual anatomy.

Clitoral Glans: The tip or head of the clitoris.

and accumulate sexual sensations. The **perineum,** an area of smooth skin between the entrance to the vagina and the anus (the opening through which bowel movements pass) is also considered part of the vulva, along with the **hymen,** a fold of tissue that partially covers the vaginal opening. Though the hymen is typically broken during the first intercourse, an intact hymen is not an indicator of virginity. Some women accidentally tear it during vigorous exercise; others are born without one. Moreover, intercourse can occur without tearing a very flexible hymen. (The female sexual anatomy also includes the breasts and a number of other organs involved more in reproduction than in sexual arousal.)

The male genitals include the penis and the **scrotum** containing the testes where sperm is manufactured (see Figure 10.2). At the tip of the penis is the head, or **glans,** which is separated from the rod-shaped shaft by a rim of tissue called the **coronal ridge.** In a triangular space on the underside of the penis, a thin strip of skin called the **frenulum** attaches to the glans.

Up to about six weeks after conception, the male and female genitals are essentially identical. Thereafter preprogrammed genetic instructions and hormones act to shape the genitals into male or female form (see Chapter 2, Figure 2.16). Because the genitals of both sexes originate from the same structures, each sex has organs corresponding to those of the other. These **homologous,** or corresponding, parts are far from identical, but they do share much in common. Rather than discuss them separately, we will, when possible, treat them together, for many of their functions are similar.

The Clitoris and Corresponding Parts of the Penis. Though they may not look it, the clitoris and penis are homologous. As the center of erotic pleasure, each is exquisitely sensitive to touch, pressure, temperature, and other forms of stimulation. The clitoris, however, is not a miniature penis. Although it has erectile tissue and does enlarge during sexual arousal, it has no reproductive or urinary function. In fact, the clitoris is the one sexual organ in either sex whose only known function is to focus and accumulate sexual sensations (Masters & Johnson, 1970).

The tip of the clitoris, the **glans,** corresponds to the glans of the penis (see Table 10.1). Each is exceptionally sensitive. Under the right circum-

Table 10.1 Homologous Sex Organs

Male	Female	General Function
Glans of Penis	Glans of Clitoris	Sensitive area, stimulation of which can lead to orgasm
Shaft of Penis	Shaft of Clitoris	Main part of penis or clitoris; in males, it is the primary reproductive structure
Foreskin of Penis	Hood of Clitoris	Protective skin covering the glans in males; the glans and shaft in females
Underside of Penile Shaft	Labia Minora	Plays an important role in sexual arousal and pleasure
Scrotal Sac	Labia Majora	In males, the sac contains the testes; in females, the labia majora surround the vaginal opening
Testes	Ovaries	Manufacture hormones that govern sexual development and influence sexual interest

stances, direct stimulation of the glans can lead to orgasm, the sudden, highly pleasurable discharge of accumulated sexual tension. Under most conditions, however, most men and women find direct stimulation of the glans irritating or even painful—especially when arousal is low or mild or stimulation is prolonged. Thus, in masturbating, women and men usually stimulate the glans indirectly by gently manipulating the shaft of the clitoris or penis (Masters & Johnson, 1966).

The glans is covered by a protective skin called the **hood** in females, the **foreskin** in males. The hood of the clitoris covers the **shaft** as well as the glans, in such a way that the shaft cannot be directly exposed. The glans can be exposed by gently pushing up the hood. The foreskin of the penis is absent in many American men, for often it is surgically removed shortly after birth in a procedure called **circumcision.** The operation completely exposes the glans, including its sensitive coronal ridge.

The Labia and Corresponding Male Parts. The female labia minora, or inner lips, are homologous to the underside of the penile shaft. Both structures are loaded with sensitive nerve endings, and both play an important role in sexual arousal and pleasure. In the male, the area called the frenulum is particularly sensitive. For the female, the outer lips, or labia majora, correspond to the male scrotum, the sac that contains the testes. When the clitoris and labia minora become engorged with blood during sexual arousal, they push the labia majora apart, exposing the opening to the vagina.

The Ovaries and Testes. The **testes,** the pair of male sex glands in the scrotum, and their female counterpart, a pair of internal organs called the **ovaries,** manufacture hormones that govern sexual development and influence sexual interest. Both produce **testosterone,** which is sometimes called the male hormone because it is produced in far greater quantities in males than in females. Testosterone affects the sexual desire of both sexes.

Clitoral Hood: A fold of skin that covers the clitoral shaft.

Foreskin: The skin that covers the glans of the penis.

Clitoral Shaft: That part of the clitoris is covered by the clitoral hood and ending in the clitoral glans.

Circumcision: Surgical removal of the foreskin of the penis.

Testes: The pair of male sex glands contained in the scrotum that produce hormones (such as testosterone) and sperm (the male's sex cells).

Ovaries: The pair of female sex glands that produce hormones such as estrogen.

Testosterone: A hormone found in both sexes but generally referred to as the male sex hormone.

Estrogen: A hormone present in both females and males; but usually considered a female hormone because it controls the development of female secondary sex characteristics and plays an important role in governing the menstrual cycle. In men, its function is unclear.

Progesterone: A hormone present in both males and females but primarily known as a female sex hormone. It is present in high levels during pregnancy.

When it falls below normal levels, desire may decrease; excessively high levels may enhance desire (Bancroft, 1978). Testosterone does not *control* sexual behavior and responsiveness, however, as in rats and other lower organisms. Psychological factors—the thought of having an intimate, exciting sexual experience, or the desire to please and satisfy a loved one—are far more important in determining sexual behavior than hormone levels. Even the lowest levels of testosterone would not cool the passion of two infatuated lovers; nor would the highest levels drive a person to make love to an unattractive partner. This hormone might best be viewed as an agent that interacts with psychological factors to increase or decrease alertness to sexual opportunities.

Another hormone produced by both the ovaries and testes is **estrogen,** sometimes called the female hormone because it is produced in much greater quantities in females than in males. Together with another hormone produced by the ovaries, **progesterone,** estrogen plays an important role in the woman's menstrual cycle. Unlike testosterone, however, estrogen is unrelated to sexual interest. It has no clearly established function in males, though excessive amounts can reduce sexual appetite in males and contribute to breast enlargement.

Noncorresponding Parts of the Female Anatomy. Some parts of the female sexual anatomy have no corresponding part in the male. Of these, the mons veneris (literally "mound of Venus," after the Greek goddess of love) is probably the most important. A triangular pad of fatty tissue covered by pubic hair, the mons is concentrated with sensitive nerve endings that can produce pleasurable sensations when stimulated by touch and pressure.

Females are generally more responsive to stimulation of their breasts than males—though here the difference between the sexes may not be as great as is generally believed. Among women reactions vary; some women find breast stimulation extremely arousing and pleasurable, while others hardly feel it. The same is true for men. Individual responsiveness may also vary, depending on the circumstances.

The vagina, of course, has no counterpart in the male. This canal adjusts readily in shape and size. If a finger is inserted, the vaginal walls expand just enough to fit snugly around it. Yet it can dilate enough to allow the passage of a baby. During coitus, the walls of the vagina expand just enough to fit the penis. Although the outer third of the vagina is far more sensitive than the rest, even that has relatively few nerve endings. Many men seem to be unaware of the relative insensitivity of the organ; they overestimate the effects of an inserted finger. According to Masters and Johnson (1966) and others, only a small percentage of women insert a finger in their vagina during masturbation. Women may value coitus as much for the psychological feeling of closeness it produces as for the actual physical sensations—which illustrates the point that psychological factors interact with the physical in human sexual behavior.

The Human Sexual Response

The most comprehensive study of the human sexual response to date is Masters and Johnson's (1966) investigation, in which over ten thousand sex-

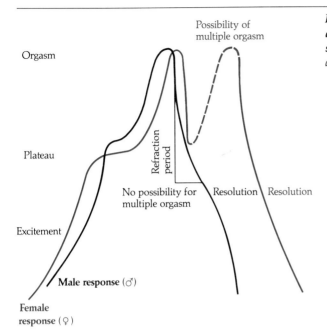

Orgasm

Plateau

Excitement

Refraction period

Possibility of multiple orgasm

No possibility for multiple orgasm

Resolution \ Resolution

Male response (♂)

Female response (♀)

Figure 10.3 The Male and Female Sexual Response. (*After Masters and Johnson, 1966*).

ual experiences were observed and recorded, from arousal through the return to a nonaroused state. Based on their findings, Masters and Johnson proposed that the sexual response, male or female, could be divided into four stages: excitement, plateau, orgasm, and resolution. They defined these stages somewhat arbitrarily; the transition from one stage to another is not always as sharp and clear as described in the definition. There is also considerable variation in the duration, intensity, and subjective experience of the various stages, not only among different people but within the same individual, for the human sexual response is not a mechanical one, akin to a push-button reflex. As Masters and Johnson have more recently pointed out, it is a richly complex response involving not just the body but the person's thoughts, feelings, images, beliefs, values, and expectations—in short, the whole person (Masters et al., 1982).

Masters and Johnson's four-stage model has been criticized for its arbitrary definitions and its strictly objective approach to a highly subjective experience. Despite its limitations, however, the model provides a good framework for discussion. Among other things, it reveals that, from the beginning, the sexual responses of men and women are quite similar (see Figure 10.3).

Excitement. The first stage of the sexual response, **excitement,** begins when a man or woman becomes sexually aroused by some kind of stimulation: a thought or fantasy; an intention to have a sexual experience; a visual cue (nudity, provocative clothing or pictures); an invitation, verbal or nonverbal, to make love; or direct physical contact (dancing or touch, for instance). The arousal can occur in just about any circumstance at just about any time. It may be welcomed, or it may be unexpected and unwanted.

Excitement: According to Masters and Johnson, the first of four stages of the human sexual response cycle, characterized by the vasocongestion (flow of blood to the pelvic region) that follows sexual arousal.

Erection: An increase in the size of and hardening of the penis.

Vasocongestion: A rush of blood to the pelvic region that occurs during sexual arousal and results in penile erection in the male and vaginal lubrication in the female.

Plateau: According to Masters and Johnson, the second stage of the human sexual response cycle in which continued vasocongestion causes the tissues of the vagina and the testes to swell.

In the male, the first physical sign of arousal is penile **erection;** in the female, it is vaginal lubrication. Both responses occur because of a rush of blood to the pelvic region, a process called **vasocongestion.** Other physiological changes (increased heart rate, deeper breathing, and so on) occur as well, and, if arousal is welcome, the response will intensify until the second stage is reached.

Plateau. During the second phase, called the **plateau stage,** increased stimulation leads to increased sexual tension. The tissues of the vagina begin to swell due to continued vasocongestion. In males the diameter of the head of the penis increases. Vasocongestion causes the testes to swell. High levels of arousal are maintained and intensified through fantasy, touch, or any of the other stimuli that can initiate arousal in stage 1.

The duration of the plateau stage varies widely, depending on desire, intent, the relative effectiveness of stimulation, and—in the male—the ability to control ejaculation. (If the man ejaculates prematurely, the experience may be disappointing; therapy can help correct the problem—see page 362). The length of the plateau stage does not necessarily affect the quality and strength of the orgasm that follows, however. Sometimes a short plateau stage is followed by a very intense orgasm; on other occasions, by a mild one.

Masters and Johnson define the plateau stage in terms of the many physiological changes that occur at this time. In women, the clitoris pulls back and disappears beneath its hood. Its apparent disappearance can be alarming to a man who has been taught that clitoral stimulation is the way to bring a woman to orgasm. The change is perfectly natural, however, and stimulation of the labia minora can be substituted for clitoral stimulation, with the same results for most women. In males, the size of the testes increases, nearly doubling in some cases. Both men and women experience a measurable increase in muscular tension in the buttocks and thighs, as well as an increase in heart rate and blood pressure.

Orgasm: The sudden, highly pleasurable discharge of accumulated sexual tension characterized by muscular contractions in the pelvis; according to Masters and Johnson, the third stage of the human sexual response cycle.

Ejaculation: The release of semen from the penis.

Orgasm. In the third stage of the cycle, sexual arousal and pleasure peaks in a sudden discharge of accumulated sexual tension called **orgasm.** An orgasm may be an intense and all-consuming experience, or a relatively mild one, depending on dozens of factors: fatigue, length of time since the last orgasm, feelings, depth of emotional involvement, type of stimulation, and so on. Strong or relatively weak, however, an orgasm involves more than the genitals; it is a total body response. Even the person's brain wave pattern changes during orgasm (Cohen et al., 1976).

Sexual release is one of the few aspects of the sexual response that seem to differ in men and women. Both men and women experience sudden, rhythmic muscular contractions in the pelvic region and elsewhere. But in men these contractions are followed by a second release, **ejaculation**—the spurting of semen from the tip of the penis. Females also experience more variation in duration and intensity of the orgasm than males. Nevertheless, the subjective experience of orgasm is remarkably similar for men and women. When judges were asked to identify whether descriptions of orgasm were written by males or females, they could not do so (Proctor et al., 1974).

According to Masters and Johnson, only women can experience **multiple orgasms**—that is, one or more additional orgasms shortly after the first—without dropping back to a state of nonarousal. Men, however, must enter a **refractory period** immediately following the orgasm—a time of recovery in which additional orgasms are impossible. Self-reports of male multiple orgasm can be found in some surveys, such as the Hite report discussed on page 339, but, as of yet, such reports have yet to be documented by laboratory research.

Resolution. After orgasm comes the final stage of the sexual cycle, **resolution.** During this stage, which includes the refractory period in men, the physiological changes that occurred during arousal are reversed, returning the person to a nonaroused state. In females the vagina begins to shorten in both width and length, the clitoris returns to its usual size and position. In males erection diminishes and the penis returns to its usual flaccid state.

Masters and Johnson's study of the human sexual response has added much to our knowledge not only of normal sexual behavior but of sexual difficulties and their treatment. We will refer to their work again in the pages ahead.

Multiple Orgasms: A series of two or more orgasms without dropping below the plateau level of arousal.

Refractory Period: According to Masters and Johnson, a period of time following orgasm during which the male is physiologically incapable of having another orgasm.

Resolution: According to Masters and Johnson, the final stage of the human sexual response cycle during which the individual returns to a sexually unaroused state.

PSYCHOLOGICAL INFLUENCES ON THE SEXUAL RESPONSE

Masters and Johnson's investigation emphasized the physiological side of the sexual response. But, as we have seen, psychological influences are probably as important as physical factors, both in stimulating arousal and in coloring the subjective experience of the response. One example of the power of psychological factors is the importance of trust and communication in a sexual relationship.

Trust and Communication

Effective stimulation throughout the human sexual response is far more than a matter of rubbing or stroking the right spots. In a sexual relationship,

---

■ Learning Check ■

Read the definition, then cover the right side and try to recite. Repeat.

Excitement	Stage 1 of the human sexual response cycle characterized by arousal and vasocongestion
Plateau	Stage 2, in which continued vasocongestion causes the tissues of the vagina and testes to swell
Orgasm	Stage 3, in which there is a sudden discharge of accumulated sexual tension
Resolution	Stage 4, in which the physiological changes that occurred during arousal are reversed

trust and communication play an integral part in each partner's responsiveness. In fact, as we have seen, a trend in contemporary sexual attitudes has been a renewed emphasis on sex in the context of a close, caring relationship (Carroll et al., 1985). For many people today, being aroused and being responsive to another means far more than physical pleasure. It is an opportunity to share, to communicate, and to be close in a relationship.

Communication is particularly important in a sexual relationship. Unfortunately, many people find it difficult to communicate with their partners about their sexual feelings. The way many of us were reared—taught to cover our genitals and to hide signs of sexual pleasure—contributes to a feeling of shame and discomfort with sexual functioning for many people. Second, many home social environments have discouraged open discussion of sex or recognition of sexual feeling. Consequently, children have limited exposure to adult models for handling mature discussions of sexual matters and little opportunity to acquire a comfortable vocabulary for talking about sex. Many of us, who will have learned very little about what to say to our lover when we want to have sex, may come up with either a very blunt "Let's do it," or "Let's sleep together," or a stilted movie dialogue like "My place or yours?" (For information on how to communicate with your partner, see *Our Sexuality* by Robert Crooks and Karla Baur (1983), which devotes an entire chapter to the subject.)

The role of communication in a sexual relationship helps to illustrate the importance of psychological factors in human sexuality. A similar illustration is provided when we consider the effects of psychologically suggestive materials and thoughts, such as erotic art and fantasy.

Erotica and Fantasy

Erotica: Inanimate stimuli (literature, photos, art, etc.) that are sexually arousing.

Scientists have raised a number of questions about the effects of **erotica**—inanimate stimuli (literature, photos, art, etc.) that are sexually arousing—on human sexual response and behavior. Studies of the effects of erotica use objective measures of arousal as well as subjective ratings. In men, arousal is defined as a change in the size of the penis, as recorded by a sensitive ring-like device placed around the subject's penis. In women, it is defined as a change in vaginal lubrication, as measured by a tampon-like device inserted in her vagina. Studies of this sort have shown that the idea that females are less responsive to erotica than males is a myth. While women may prefer different types of erotica than men—a detailed description of a passionate love affair versus close-up photos of nudes—they respond just as frequently and powerfully to erotica as males (Athanasiou, 1980).

Other studies have shown that people do not go wild or turn into sex maniacs when exposed to erotica, no matter how arousing. Such materials do not incite men to rape or women to become sexually impulsive (Money, 1980). In fact, sex offenders like rapists and child molesters generally receive less exposure to erotic materials during adolescence than nonoffenders (Goldstein, 1973). And, when such materials were legalized in Denmark in 1965, the incidence of many sex crimes decreased sharply (Kutchinsky, 1970).

Erotic materials can provoke anxiety, however (Morokoff, 1985). Some people find sexually explicit materials disgusting rather than arousing. And

Though preferences vary, females are just as responsive to erotica as males.

indeed, the more bizarre materials, like those that depict torture, would revolt almost anyone. But the major objections to sexually explicit materials seem to be moral rather than psychological. The moral case is especially strong when human beings, many of them youths, are exploited in sexually explicit photographs.

If erotica can have a powerful psychological effect on the human sexual response, sexual fantasy and imagination can be just as powerful, if not more so. In one study, subjects of both sexes were first asked to rate their level of response to pictures and verbal descriptions of various erotic acts, such as heterosexual intercourse, oral-genital contact, and masturbation. Then they were asked to simply imagine such acts. The results: the mean ratings for the imagined scenes were nearly twice as high as the mean ratings for pictures and verbal descriptions (Byrne & Lamberth, 1971). The mind, as someone has suggested, may indeed be the ultimate **erogenous zone** (sexually sensitive area). Fantasies about sexual behaviors one has never experienced—oral-genital contact, for example—can provide excitement or help to prepare a person for future experience. And fantasies involving new partners, group encounters, or exchanging partners can provide vicarious gratification minus the difficulties such behaviors might create in real life.

Erogenous Zone: Areas of the body that are responsive to sexual stimulation.

Some fantasies can be disturbing. It is not uncommon for a man to fantasize about being conquered or tortured, or for a woman to fantasize about being raped (Crooks & Baur, 1983). Such thoughts do not necessarily indicate that a person desires the imagined acts, however. What people fantasize and what they actually do or want to do are two different things. Such fantasies may simply be a way of working out fears or coping with forbidden desires.

While the effects of fantasy and erotica seem limited to the sexual responses they contribute to, other psychological influences are longer lasting. The behavior of parental role models, for instance, has a great deal to do with the sex roles assumed by their children. Just how much of human sexuality results from learned behaviors is, in fact, a subject of controversy. In the next section we will explore two major questions in the nature-nurture debate: how a person develops a sense of maleness or femaleness, and what determines a person's sexual preferences, heterosexual or homosexual.

NATURE VERSUS NURTURE IN HUMAN SEXUAL BEHAVIOR

Gender Role and Identity

What determines maleness or femaleness—anatomy, behavior, a personal sense of being male or female, or some combination of these? Earlier in the chapter we briefly considered the example of Marty/Mary Ann, an individual whose anatomy was transformed from male to female through surgery and hormones. Did this change of sexual anatomy transform a male named Marty to a female, Mary Ann? Or was Marty really a female all along, trapped in a male's body for 74 years?

Genetic Sex: A biological aspect of sex that is determined at conception by the presence of an XY chromosome pair (male), or an XX chromosome pair (female).

Anatomical Sex: A biological aspect of sex determined by the presence of male or female genitals.

Gender: Maleness or femaleness in a psychological or social sense.

■ Learning Clue ■

It's important to keep in mind the distinctions between genetic sex, anatomical sex, gender identity, and gender role. That will be easier if you take a look at Figure 10.4 before you read the following pages.

In grappling with such questions, scientists have had to make some distinctions in terms (see Figure 10.4 for a schematic overview). Biological sex has two aspects: **genetic sex,** which is determined at conception by the presence of an XY (male) or an XX (female) chromosome pair; and **anatomical sex,** which is determined by the presence of male or female genitals. Maleness or femaleness in a psychological or social sense is referred to as **gender.**

Figure 10.4 Schematic Overview of Terms Related to Maleness and Femaleness.

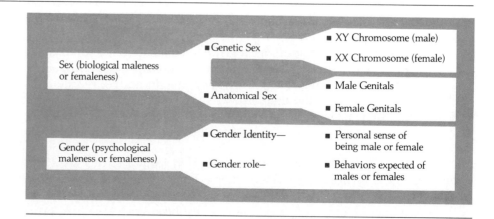

Like sex, gender can be thought of as having two aspects. **Gender identity** refers to an individual's personal sense of being male or female; **gender role** refers to a person's behavior, male or female. In assuming a gender role, an individual engages in the typical behaviors expected of males or females in a given society. In American society, men are supposed to be assertive, aggressive, and strong; women nurturant, passive, and emotional. Boys learn to be masculine and girls feminine by adopting the socially prescribed gender roles, and they are under strong pressure to do so.

As we learned in Chapter 2, males and females typically are treated differently from birth (Condry & Ross, 1985). Boys are expected to be active, girls to be quiet and passive. Boys receive rougher physical treatment from parents; girls are talked to more (Lewis, 1972). In one study, adult subjects were asked to play with a group of six-month-old babies. Some subjects were told the babies were boys; others believed they were playing with girls. Subjects who thought the infants were boys played with the tots longer and more vigorously than the other subjects, who smiled at the infants and tried to give them dolls (Walum, 1977).

Differences in the way boys and girls are treated continue throughout life. Teachers commonly assign "male" tasks, like cleaning the blackboard, to boys, and "female" tasks, like secretarial tasks, to girls (Sedker & Sedker, 1985). Television commercials portray men as authoritative, decisive, and competitive; women as passive, unintelligent, and submissive (Atkin, 1982). Because of cultural pressures and expectations, individuals with the appropriate chromosomes and anatomy usually learn to engage in either male or female gender role behaviors, which in turn contributes to a corresponding gender identity. But this is not the entire story.

Some studies have explored the role of biological differences in the formation of gender role behavior and identity. In one study, undergraduate female students completed a set of questionnaires designed to measure the extent to which they identify with traditional male or female role behaviors. Meanwhile, levels of testosterone concentrations, the so-called male hormone (see page 345), were also determined from saliva samples the women provided. Results revealed that the females with the higher testosterone concentrations tended to be the same ones who identified more with traditional male gender role behaviors. Those in the high testosterone group perceived themselves as self-directed, action-oriented, and resourceful. Those in the low testosterone group viewed themselves as conventional, socialized, nurturant, and anxious (Baucom et al., 1985). A study of **transsexuals,** by contrast, failed to find any differences between male-to-female transsexuals and normal male controls in their response to male or female hormones, throwing doubt on the theory that the development of a female gender identity in transsexuals is due to some difference or defect in the way these males respond to hormones (Goodman et al., 1985).

In all, it would appear that the formation of one's sense of being male or female and the adoption of prescribed gender role behaviors is the result of a complex interaction of biological heritage, experience, and culture. Regardless of how we adopt them, however, gender roles can be a source of considerable anguish and discomfort.

Gender roles place a heavy burden on both women and men. Women were traditionally supposed to have been delicate and cooperative. They

Gender Identity: One's personal sense of being male or female.

Gender Role: All behavior socially expected of males or females in a given culture.

Transsexualism: A strong desire to possess the genitals of the other sex which often leads the person to have a sex change operation.

were supposed to wait for a man to invite them out or initiate a sexual encounter. If they did not, they might have been labeled "easy" or "promiscuous." With the opening of new job opportunities for women, especially those in management and the professions, many women found that, in order to succeed, they had to abandon traditional female stereotype role behaviors and become aggressive and competitive. But when they did this, they opened themselves to the scorn and ridicule of their male counterparts (Wine, 1985). Indeed, the opening of new opportunities and attitudes toward the female gender role has created a dilemma for women no matter what direction they choose.

The woman who wishes to pursue a career and enter an arena that was once considered a man's world may feel a dilemma in balancing career and family goals. As a psychologist, I have heard many expressions of such conflicted feelings. Recently, a former female student told me she felt guilty and perhaps a bit selfish in her successful business career because she hadn't yet started a family. She worried that if she should decide not to have children she might regret it later in life. Another married woman student expressed the fear that, if she had children now, she might never complete her degree, but if she waited, she might never find a good time to have children. Still another woman student feels she has to be a superwoman—pursue her career, compete with men, and be the perfect mother all at the same time. She, like most other women in her predicament, does not receive equal help from her husband in performing household duties (see Greenglass, 1985). She fears that she will run out of energy or collapse from exhaustion. Women who are full-time homemakers also feel some conflicts. If they are continually exposed to the feminist view that a housewife's role may not be enough, they are plagued by personal doubt and low self-esteem (Usher & Fels, 1985).

Gender roles also place a burden on men, though the issues may not be as well defined or as widespread as for today's women. Men are supposed to be strong decision makers, steeled against fear, failure, and other emotionally taxing experiences. In sexual encounters they are expected to be the initiators as well as the experts on sex. Some men simply cannot live up to this role. Others are uncomfortable with it.

Gender role expectations create a great deal of social pressure, and they limit the freedom of both men and women to express their individuality. Fortunately, as the problems of gender roles begin to surface, recent social trends are producing a gradual but unmistakable softening of gender roles. The distinctions between the female and male behaviors are becoming less and less obvious. The popularity of the unisex look—clothes and haircuts appropriate for both sexes—illustrates, for instance, the modern trend of a blending of traditional male and female roles.

Sexual Preference

Why do so many people prefer partners of the opposite sex, while many seek partners of the same sex? Like gender identity, sexual preference probably results from the interaction of biological, psychological, social, and cultural factors.

Homosexual: A preference for sexual partners of the same sex.

As far as is known, heterosexual behavior is preferred by most people (Beach, 1977b). Nevertheless, **homosexual** encounters are known to have oc-

During the past decade or two, homosexuals have been "coming out" and openly expressing their preference for same-sex partners.

curred throughout history. At different times and places, such behavior has been accepted, condoned, or even encouraged; at other times and places, strongly discouraged or forbidden. The Kinsey reports and other surveys of sexual behavior revealed that sexual experimentation between members of the same sex is quite common, especially during adolescence. At the time Kinsey's report revealed an unsuspected prevalence of homosexual activity; a great many people were shocked. But, over the last decade or two, homosexuals have been "coming out"—announcing to family and friends their preference for partners of the same sex. Nevertheless, a survey based on a relatively large nationwide sample revealed that, as of the early 1980s, more than two-thirds of the respondents said that homosexual relations are "always wrong" (Schneider & Lewis, 1984).

Though prejudice paints homosexuals as fundamentally different from other people, the truth is that researchers have not been able to find any specific differences between heterosexuals and homosexuals, either biologi-

■ Learning Check ■

Read the definition, then cover the right side and try to recite. Repeat.

Genetic Sex	Biological; determined at conception by the presence of XY or XX chromosome pair
Anatomical Sex	Biological; determined by the presence of male or female genitals
Gender Identity	Psychological; referring to an individual's personal sense of being male or female
Gender Role	Psychological; the typical behaviors expected of males or females in a given society

Figure 10.5 Continuum of Sexual Orientation.
(After Kinsey et al., 1948).

Exclusively heterosexual	Predominantly heterosexual	Equally heterosexual and homosexual (bisexual)	Predominantly homosexual	Exclusively homosexual

cal or psychological. An early study suggesting a genetic determinant for sexual preference (Kallman, 1952) was later shown to be inconclusive; the sample was small and biased, and the results were not replicated (Heston & Shields, 1968). Speculation that hormones might account for sexual preference also were not supported. Early studies reported testosterone deficiencies and high levels of the so-called female hormones in male homosexuals. Lesbians were also reported to have relatively high levels of testosterone and relatively low levels of the female hormones (Kolodny, 1971). However, subsequent studies revealed that hormone levels vary just as much in heterosexuals as in homosexuals (Meyer-Bahlburg, 1977, 1979).

Nor have psychological tests produced any differences in personality or emotional stability between people of different sexual preference (Saghir & Robins, 1973; Reiss, 1980). No consistent differences have been found in these groups' childrearing or in their social learning experiences (Newcomb, 1985). Just as many heterosexual males had poor relationships with their fathers as homosexual males, for instance (Siegelman, 1974). And exposure to homosexual role models appears to be just as common in both groups (Marmor, 1980; Tripp, 1975).

Like any of the relatively common patterns of sexual behavior, including masturbation, premarital sex, extramarital sex, sexual fantasies, and oral-genital sex, homosexuality appears to be a normal expression of human sexuality. No single factor accounts for sexual preference; it is multiply determined. And the dividing line between people of different sexual preference is not as clear-cut as many seem to think. Sexual preference is perhaps best viewed in terms of a continuum (Kinsey et al., 1948). At one end are the exclusively heterosexual individuals—those who have never had a same-sex experience and never intend to. Somewhere in the middle of that scale are those who have enjoyed partners of either sex—**bisexuals.** And at the other end are those who are exclusively homosexual (see Figure 10.5).

Bisexual: An individual who is sexually attracted to and has sexual contact with both male and female partners.

SEXUAL PROBLEMS, DYSFUNCTIONS, AND DISORDERS

Sex is inseparable from our emotions, our physical condition, and our problems, both social and psychological. Sex-related difficulties run the gamut, from communicable diseases that are transmitted sexually to mental disorders that manifest themselves in abnormal sexual behavior. Even normal sexual behaviors can be disrupted by negative emotions, like anxiety or guilt. In this section we look first at sex-related health and social problems. Then we will consider the sexual dysfunctions, or difficulties in functioning sexually. Finally, we will touch on abnormal sexual behaviors.

Sex-Related Health and Social Problems

Today, at a time when people have greater access than ever before to contraceptives, medical care, and information about sex, an epidemic of sexually transmitted diseases and unwanted pregnancies is sweeping the nation. Why? No simple explanation can be given. But the issues are of more than academic interest to most of us.

Sexually Transmitted Diseases. Sexually transmitted diseases are communicable diseases that are passed from one person to another during sexual interaction. Some are relatively harmless, and some, though deadly, are easily identified and cured. Others are vicious and untreatable.

Gonorrhea is a sexually transmitted disease caused by a bacterium that is spread through genital, oral-genital, or anal-genital contact. The first sign of **syphilis,** another sexually transmitted disease caused by a bacterium, is a painless sore called a "**chancre**" (pronounced shanker). In its final stages, after twenty years or more of dormancy in the tissues of the infected person, the disease can cause blindness, paralysis, severe mental disturbances, and even death. Fortunately, both gonorrhea and syphilis are treatable by antibiotics.

Genital **herpes** is a contagious disease which causes painful blisters on the genitals, blisters that may go away after a few weeks, but can erupt again at any time. It is caused by a virus closely related to those that cause cold sores around the mouth. The disease is transmitted through genital, anal-genital, or oral-genital contact. An estimated 10 to 20 million Americans are affected, and about half a million new cases are diagnosed each year (Holmes, 1982). There is no known cure for genital herpes, and those who suffer from it often suffer psychological side effects such as depression and lowered self-esteem.

A sexually transmitted disease that has caused a state of near national panic is **acquired immune deficiency syndrome (AIDS).** This viral disease is a condition of dangerously lowered resistance in which the body cannot defend itself from numerous infections that can normally be avoided. Both males and females, whether heterosexual, bisexual, or homosexual, may be at risk of contracting the disease if the AIDS virus enters the bloodstream or body by direct contact or by intimate sexual contact. Those most at risk of having the virus enter the bloodstream are in these categories: (1) sexually active homosexual and bisexual males, especially those with many previous sexual contacts, with a preference for anal intercourse, and a history of sexually transmitted disease; (2) those who receive blood transfusions with blood containing the virus; (3) intravenous drug abusers who share hypodermic needles; and (4) any sex partners of the above groups, male or female. Also, any female from the above categories who is pregnant is at risk of giving birth to an infant with AIDS. For those in the risk groups, an initial condition of poor health and nutrition, with low disease resistance, may be associ-

Sexually Transmitted Diseases: Diseases spread through sexual contact.

Gonorrhea: A sexually transmitted disease that is caused by a bacterium that is spread through genital, oral-genital, or anal-genital contact.

Syphilis: A sexually transmitted disease that causes a chancre during the early stages and can lead to severe symptoms, such as blindness, and even death in later stages, if left untreated.

Chancre: A red, painless sore that appears on the genitals or in the vagina in the early stages of syphilis.

Herpes: A sexually transmitted disease characterized by painful blisters on the genitals.

Acquired Immune Deficiency Syndrome (AIDS): A sexually transmitted viral disease that drastically lowers the body's resistance to ward off infections.

AIDS, a sexually transmitted disease that affects the body's ability to defend itself from infection, has caused national concern, and is currently the target of extensive research efforts in hopes of finding a cure.

ated with greater likelihood of contracting the virus. Infection with the virus is not easy to trace, especially because the incubation period is from one month to as long as eight years. Symptoms include swelling glands, unexplained bleeding or weight loss, persistent fatigue, and recurring infections of various kinds. A person can be tested for the presence of the virus, but, as of 1986, there was no known cure (Gordon & Snyder, 1986).

Chlamydia Trachomatis: A sexually transmitted disease that is transmitted through sexual contact of infected mucous membrane from either male or female.

Another fast-growing sexually transmitted disease, **Chlamydia trachomatis** (kla-mid'-i-a), has been responsible for sterility in approximately 11,000 women per year during the 1980s. Transmitted by intimate sexual contact of infected mucous membrane from either male or female, its effects on males may be similar to those of gonorrhea; for women it creates a severe cervical or vaginal infection which may lead to pelvic inflammatory disease (PID) and sterility. Most women will display no symptoms until it is too late to stop the infection, which unfortunately threatens their fetuses and newborns with lung and eye infections. If detected, the disease must be treated in both sex partners to prevent reinfection (Gordon & Snyder, 1986).

Researchers in behavioral medicine—a relatively new field of psychology concerned with the modification of behaviors and life-styles associated with medically related problems—are attempting to find ways of helping people to cope with such problems as the psychological stress of genital herpes and fear of AIDS. These researchers are also trying to find ways of helping people to modify their behavior or life-styles in order to reduce the spread of such diseases. For example, washing the genital area before and after sexual contact and urinating after sexual contact are simple behaviors that can reduce the risk of contracting gonorrhea or syphilis, if people would only do them (Brecher, 1975).

Unwanted Teenage Pregnancy. Also of interest to researchers in behavioral medicine are unwanted pregnancies, especially among adolescents. As

Along with the increase in the number of sexually active teenagers has come a dramatic rise in the number of unwanted teenage pregnancies—children with children.

we have seen, since Kinsey's surveys in the late 1940s and early 1950s, the percentage of youths reporting premarital intercourse has been rising steadily. Each year about 700,000 unmarried adolescents become pregnant, and about half of those pregnancies are terminated in abortion (Byrne, 1977; The National Center for Health Statistics, 1985).

Not long ago, **contraceptives**—devices for preventing pregnancy—were illegal in the United States. Even to provide information about contraceptives was a crime. Today, however, contraceptives and the information on how to use them are widely available. Yet, many young people do not use them.

In a large-scale survey of women aged fifteen to nineteen, Zelnik and Kantner (1979) found that, of those women who had intercourse more than once without contraception, only about 4 percent of white and 9 percent of black females were actually trying to become pregnant. The researchers also found that more than half of these women believed they could not become pregnant. Actually, the overwhelming majority of women over fifteen can become pregnant—and it takes only one sexual experience to do it. Thus, many adolescents base their behavior on misconceptions or lack of information.

Of those young women who thought they could become pregnant, a large segment (20.3 percent of the entire sample) had not expected to have intercourse. Whether or not their partners had similar expectations cannot be determined. The failure of young men to take responsibility for contraception must be counted as another major cause of unwanted pregnancies, however. Moreover, communication among the young men and women appears to be important; couples with good communication patterns were more likely to practice effective contraception (Polit-O'Hara & Kahn, 1985).

Contraceptives: Devices for preventing pregnancy.

Sexual Dysfunctions

Anyone can experience isolated difficulty in performing the sex act. Inability to have an erection or an orgasm due to anxiety, guilt, overexcitement, fatigue, or too much alcohol, for example, is a common occurrence. Sometimes, however, the problem is much more severe and enduring and

Sexual Dysfunction: Difficulties or inability at any stage of the normal sexual response cycle.

involves a **sexual dysfunction**. Some individuals may never have been able to respond sexually as most people do. Others suddenly lose their sexual capability and cannot regain it. When sexual difficulties become this persistent, they can affect every part of a person's life—relationships, self-image, even the ability to function normally at work. In such cases, consultation with a specialist in sexual dysfunctions is advisable. Fortunately, most can be successfully overcome with the aid of an appropriately trained therapist.

There are three main kinds of sexual dysfunction: those involving an avoidance of sex and difficulty in becoming sexually aroused; those involving difficulty in obtaining or maintaining penile-vaginal contact; and those involving difficulty in having orgasm. All three types affect both men and women alike.

Sexual Aversion: An extreme or irrational fear and avoidance of sexual activity.

Sexual Aversions. A **sexual aversion** is an avoidance of sexual activity due to extreme or irrational fears or negative feelings like disgust. A number of therapies are available for treating sexual aversions. The effectiveness of such therapies depends on many factors such as the severity and duration of the problem, the individual's motivation for treatment, and the availability of social support. As with the psychological therapies in general (see Chapter 15), success rates vary between roughly 67 and 90 percent of those treated (Zilbergeld & Kilmann, 1984). Having an understanding and caring partner participating in the treatment process is particularly helpful in treating the aversion.

Sensate Focus: A technique used in the treatment of sexual dysfunctions. It involves touching and communication to enhance sexual pleasure and reduce sexual inhibitions and performance pressures.

Sensate focus exercises, a therapeutic technique devised by Masters and Johnson, aid in the treatment of sexual aversions and other sexual problems. In the early sessions, the couple is instructed not to have sexual intercourse or even to touch each other's genitals. Nor are they to worry about goals, but to take turns giving and receiving sensual pleasure for its own sake. One partner touches and strokes the other, giving pleasure, communicating closeness, and learning what the other enjoys. The receiver relaxes and experiences the pleasure and closeness, communicating what feels good and what doesn't. Later, when they are more relaxed and less fearful of failure, the couple moves gradually toward intercourse.

Erectile Dysfunction: An inability to obtain and/or maintain an erection firm enough for coitus; impotence.

Vaginismus: A sexual dysfunction characterized by involuntary spastic contractions of the outer third of the vagina whenever penile insertion is attempted.

Maintaining Penile-Vaginal Contact. Difficulties in obtaining or maintaining penile-vaginal contact include inability to have an erection, **erectile dysfunction,** formerly known as impotence, and strong involuntary contractions of the outer third of the vagina when intercourse is attempted, known as **vaginismus.** We will discuss both types of sexual dysfunction.

One relatively easy way to tell whether a man's erectile dysfunction is physical or psychological is to observe him during sleep. Normal males, from infancy through old age, experience erections periodically throughout the sleep cycle. If a man has erections during his sleep but not when attempting coitus, the problem is most likely psychological.

One common psychological cause of erectile dysfunction is performance anxiety. The man may be so worried about whether he will be able to perform—to please his partner or to have an erection—that he is unable to do so. In treatment, the pressures to perform are removed by instructing the couple to enjoy each other's bodies without goals, as in the sensate focus exercises. In fact, the couple is forbidden to have any kind of penile-vaginal contact during the early sessions. With the pressure removed, the man often achieves a good hard erection (Zilbergeld & Kilmann, 1984).

In a related approach, the couple is instructed to gradually increase their level of intimacy. During the first session the couple may simply talk or touch each other while partly dressed. During later sessions they may gently stimulate each other's genitals. The couple is allowed to become increasingly intimate, but always sexual intercourse is forbidden. The treatment is complete when the couple is unable to abide by the therapist's restriction.

Vaginismus, an automatic, involuntary spasm of the vaginal walls, either prevents penetration by the man's penis or makes it extremely painful for the woman. Sometimes the woman's partner erroneously believes she is faking the spasm or doing it on purpose. The first step in treating vaginismus is to clarify that the spasms are indeed real and involuntary. Then specific treatments can be implemented. In Masters and Johnson's approach, the woman is given a set of penis-shaped plastic dilators of graduated width. She begins by inserting the smallest, and gradually works up to the larger ones. Sensate focus exercises and other techniques can also be used with the dilators.

Difficulties in Having Orgasm. It is a common experience for a woman not to have an orgasm during a sexual encounter (Tavris & Sadd, 1977). But an estimated 10 to 15 percent of American females have never had an orgasm, despite the fact that all normal women are physiologically capable of it (Masters & Johnson, 1970). Many other women report not having their first orgasm until they were in their late twenties or thirties. While a woman need not experience orgasm to gain immense pleasure and enjoyment from coitus, an inability to do so, or **orgasmic dysfunction,** can be extremely distressing to her and her partner. Both may view their lovemaking experiences as a failure.

Orgasmic Dysfunction: An inability for a woman to have orgasm.

In the usual treatment for orgasmic dysfunction, the woman is encouraged to masturbate. The therapist gives her the necessary information about her body and how to stimulate it, and encourages her to express any negative feelings she may have about sex. Then, by a gradual, step-by-step approach, which removes the pressure to perform, she learns how to arouse her body. Sometimes a vibrator is used. The success rate is generally high, especially when a partner is involved (Adkins & Jehu, 1985).

In the man, orgasmic dysfunction can take the form of premature or delayed ejaculation. A man with **ejaculatory incompetence** is unable to ejaculate during coital sex play. He can continue to have sexual intercourse until both he and his partner are completely exhausted, but without release. Fear of impregnating one's partner and strong dislike or rejection of a partner are among the most common causes of ejaculatory incompetence (Masters & Johnson, 1970).

Ejaculatory Incompetence: A sexual dysfunction in which the male is unable to ejaculate in the vagina.

While men with ejaculatory incompetence are overcontrolled, men with **premature ejaculation** suffer a lack of control; they ejaculate too soon, disappointing both their partner and themselves. Premature ejaculation has been defined in terms of how long a man can withhold ejaculation after penetration of the woman's vagina—thirty seconds, one minute, ninety seconds. Masters and Johnson (1970) are opposed to such stopwatch definitions; in-

Premature Ejaculation: According to Masters and Johnson, the inability of a male to withhold ejaculation long enough to satisfy his partner in half or more of their sexual encounters.

Figure 10.6   Schematic Summary of Sexual Dysfunctions and Their Common Treatments.

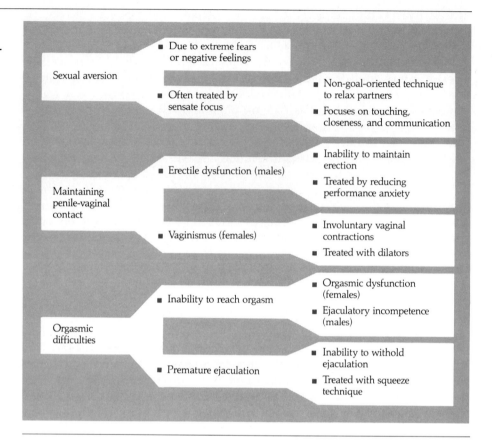

stead, they define the dysfunction as an inability to withhold ejaculation long enough to satisfy one's partner during at least 50 percent of coital encounters.

A number of techniques can be used along with sensate focus and communication exercises to deal with premature ejaculation. The most effective is the so-called **squeeze technique,** in which a woman delays her partner's ejaculation by squeezing the frenulum and coronal ridge of his penis for about four seconds whenever the man signals to her that ejaculation is imminent. Eventually, most men then learn how to delay ejaculation themselves. (See Figure 10.6 for a schematic summary of sexual dysfunctions and their treatment.)

Squeeze Technique:
Method for preventing premature ejaculation in which the penis is firmly squeezed with the hand at the glans (or at the base of the shaft).

■ Learning Check ■

For each term, read the information on the right side and try to recite it. Repeat.

Sexual Aversion	Avoidance of sexual activity
Erectile Dysfunction	An inability to have an erection
Orgasmic Dysfunction	An inability for a woman to have orgasm
Premature Ejaculation	An inability for a man to withhold ejaculation

Many of the techniques developed by Masters and Johnson for treating sexual dysfunctions have been incorporated into a wide variety of psychotherapeutic treatments. Their value has been strongly supported by the majority of studies (Zilbergeld & Kilmann, 1984). With the aid of a trained specialist, most people suffering from a sexual dysfunction have an excellent chance of obtaining relief. Persons with a sexual dysfunction should look for a therapist with at least three to four hundred hours of special training and supervised experience and who devotes a major portion of his or her practice to the treatment of sexual dysfunctions. (Most qualified practitioners will be willing to discuss their qualifications.)

Abnormal Sexual Behaviors (Paraphilia)

While many people have difficulty engaging in normal sexual behavior because of simple anxiety or fear, some are all too active in an abnormal way. Their sexual behavior may be bizarre, cruel, or antisocial and is considered deviant or perverted by the average person. Such behaviors are referred to as **paraphilia**—literally, "beyond love." There are two main kinds of paraphilia; those that involve a nonhuman source of sexual arousal (an object or an animal) and do not victimize others; and those that, in one way or another, do victimize other people. With only two exceptions (sadism and masochism), virtually all reported cases of paraphilia have been males (APA, 1980).

Paraphilia: Sexual behaviors in which the individual's primary source of sexual gratification and arousal is a nonhuman or an inappropriate human partner.

Paraphilia That Do Not Victimize Others. Fetishism is a preference for sexual excitement by a nonliving object—a shoe, for instance. Another paraphilia, **transvestism,** involves a preference or desire for the clothing of the other sex. A transvestite repeatedly and persistently dresses in women's clothing in order to become sexually aroused. Such men are usually heterosexual or bisexual, and many are married. Despite their preference for female sexual partners, however, they must cross-dress to experience sexual excitement or orgasm.

Fetishism: A condition in which an individual's preferred source of sexual arousal and gratification is from masturbation with, or in the presence of, an inanimate object.

Zoophilia is a preference for sex with animals instead of humans. The man may have intercourse with an animal, or may train it to sexually excite him by licking or rubbing. The zoophiliac actually prefers animals for obtaining sexual gratification, even when appropriate human partners are available.

Transvestism: A preference or desire to dress in the clothing of females (cross-dressing).

Zoophilia: A preference for sex with animals instead of humans.

Masochism is the preference for gaining sexual excitement through one's own suffering. Masochists may inflict injury on themselves, but, more typically, they are someone else's willing victims. A man may pay a prostitute to whip, bind, or humiliate him; a woman may submit to spankings or even brutal beatings.

Masochism: A preference for gaining sexual excitement through one's own suffering.

Paraphilia That Victimize Others. The need to obtain sexual gratification from a shoe, a woman's dress, or even one's own pain may strike the average person as pitiable, but such behaviors do not harm others. Paraphilia that victimize other human beings are in quite another category.

Voyeurism is the preference for sexual excitement by spying on unwilling women as they undress or engage in sexual activity. The voyeur, or Peeping Tom, usually reaches orgasm by masturbating while spying. Even if

Voyeurism: A preference for sexual excitement by spying on unwilling women as they undress or engage in sexual activity.

voyeurs do not injure their victims, they invade their privacy. The experience of discovering a voyeur in the act can be most unsettling to the victim.

Sadism: The infliction of physical or psychological suffering on another person in order to obtain sexual excitement.

Pedophilia: A preference for sex with children to sex with adults (child molester).

Rape: Sex by force or the threat of force with an unwilling partner.

Sadism is the infliction of physical or psychological suffering on another person in order to obtain sexual excitement. The sadist may be satisfied with forcing a partner to submit to being spanked or whipped, but some are not content unless the victim is brutally tortured.

Pedophilia is a preference for sex with children to sex with adults. The pedophiliac tends to be an immature person, incompetent in normal sexual situations. Finding children less threatening than adults, the pedophiliac may encourage a child to engage in mutual genital manipulation, or may force the child to submit to oral-genital or anal-genital contact. The experience may leave deep psychological scars on the child and is frequently associated with the development of a psychosexual dysfunction when the child reaches adulthood (McCary, 1978).

Rape is a brutal paraphilia which is focused on inflicting humiliation and pain more than on sex as such; it can cause severe physical as well as psychological harm to the victim. In a rape, one or more individuals force another to have sexual intercourse, oral-genital or anal-genital contact, or any combination of these sex acts. Though males are frequently gang-raped in prisons and sometimes on city streets, the usual victim of a rape is female.

Rape is a problem on many college campuses. In addition to being attacked by a stranger when alone after dark, many women are victimized by date rapists. Typically, a date rapist forces himself on the woman after one or two dates. Though the woman may resist, he convinces himself that she really wants to have sex with him. Many cases go unreported. Studies of date rapists have revealed that such individuals have exaggerated aspiration levels, desiring a higher degree of success than is realistic for them (Kanin, 1985).

In addition to physical harm, rape can leave emotional scars long after the attack. The reaction involves both acute short-term shock effects and long-term effects of phobia and sexual dysfunction. Fortunately, most women eventually recover, as indicated by a study in which 70 percent of a sample of rape victims felt that they had recovered when contacted four to six years after the rape (about half of these reported being recovered within a few months; the other half within several years). About 25 percent of these women, however, reported that they had still not recovered (Burgess & Holmstrom, 1979).

Regardless of whether or not they recover, most rape victims take action to ensure their future safety (for example, changing telephone numbers, moving in with a friend, taking self-defense classes). Others become involved in educational programs to help other women protect themselves. Box 10.1 discusses the importance of alertness and responsibility in rape prevention.

Like all sexual behavior, the subject of rape is heavily laden with emotional sentiments, personal values, and moral attitudes. In future chapters we will touch upon some of the issues raised by the study of human sexuality. In Chapter 11 we will discuss stress, coping, and adjustment from a more general perspective, rather than from the standpoint of specific prob-

Box 10.1 PSYCHOLOGY IN ACTION: Preventing Rape

In an effort to prevent students from being raped, the Public Safety Department of San Diego State University, in conjunction with University Police, the Department of Women's Studies, and other concerned members of the campus community, have issued a report (1983) that faculty are encouraged to discuss with their classes at the beginning of each new term. To prevent rape on campus, the report lists five suggestions:

1. *Be alert.* Being alert includes looking around to see if anyone is following you and looking ahead (especially at night) when going to your car. If you feel you are in danger, make as much noise as possible; run if necessary.
2. *Go in groups.* There is safety in numbers. Students who attend night classes can arrange to return to their cars or dorms in groups.
3. *Stay in the light.* Well-traveled and well-lighted routes are relatively safe. Poorly lighted shortcuts can spell danger.
4. *Check your car.* Before entering your car, make sure no one is in it. Always lock your car and, when returning to it, have your keys in hand.
5. *Be responsible.* Preventing rape is a responsibility shared by everyone. If you see someone in danger, ask if you can help or report it to the police. Being responsible also involves taking steps not to inadvertently threaten others (for example, don't stare, follow too close, or make unwelcome comments).

To prevent rape at home, the report lists four additional suggestions:

1. *Lock up.* Take responsibility to make sure your house is safe and secure.

Women who walk alone at night and take poorly-lit shortcuts are prime targets for rape.

2. *Check out visitors.* Don't open your door (especially at night) without first checking to see who it is. If a salesman calls on you after dark, ask him to return during the day.
3. *Keep areas well lighted.* Hallways, garages, and entrances should be well lighted. Electric timers can be used to conserve electricity and give the appearance that someone is home.
4. *Attend workshops.* By attending workshop, self-defense classes, discussions, or lectures on rape, you can obtain valuable information and maintain a high level of awareness of the dangers.

---

lems such as gender role behavior or dealing with rape. In Chapter 14 we will discuss abnormal behavior from a more general perspective; and, in Chapter 15, general approaches to the treatment of abnormal behaviors.

LEARNING FRAMEWORK

I. Sex has both motivational and emotional properties, but does not fit neatly into either category.
II. Each of the three major approaches to studying human sexuality has unique strengths and limitations. (Review: *Figure 10.1*)
   A. Surveys provide useful information about the individuals who re-

spond to them, but their results may not apply (generalize) to the general population.

B. Case studies provide more depth and greater detail than surveys, but their applicability to the general population is more limited.

C. Masters and Johnson's laboratory studies of human sexual behavior overcame the drawbacks of self-report data, substituting direct observation and objective measurement techniques for subjective reports. These studies did not overcome the problem of sample bias, however.

III. Today people seem to be taking a second look at the attitudes spawned by the sexual revolution. Sex without love is being replaced by a greater emphasis, for both males and females, on the importance of a serious relationship and feeling loved and needed.

IV. There are a number of striking similarities in the male and female sexual anatomy and sexual response.

A. Because the genitals of both sexes originate from the same structures, each sex has organs corresponding to those of the other. (Review: *Figure 10.2; Table 10.1; Homologous Organs*)

B. Masters and Johnson observed that the sexual response of both males and females could be divided into four stages: excitement, plateau, orgasm, and resolution. (Review: *Figure 10.3; Vasocongestion*)

V. Psychological influences are as important as physical ones on the human sexual response.

A. Trust and communication play an important role in the sexual responsiveness of both men and women.

B. Men and women alike respond to erotic materials.

VI. Maleness and femaleness are determined by both biological (nature) and psychological (nurture) factors.

A. Biological sex is based on one's genetic inheritance and sexual anatomy; psychological sex is based on one's personal sense of being male or female and a set of male or female behaviors. (Review: *Figure 10.4*)

B. No single factor accounts for sexual preference; nor is the line between people of different sexual preferences clear-cut. Sexual preference is perhaps best viewed on a continuum. (Review: *Figure 10.5*)

VII. Sex-related difficulties run the gamut from communicable diseases, problems in having sex, and mental disorders that manifest themselves in abnormal sexual behavior.

A. An epidemic of sexually transmitted diseases is sweeping the nation. (Review: *Gonorrhea; Syphilis; AIDS; Chlamydia Trachomatis*)

B. There are three main kinds of sexual dysfunctions: those involving an avoidance of sex; those involving difficulty in obtaining or maintaining penile-vaginal contact; and those involving difficulty in having orgasm. (Review: *Sexual Aversion; Vaginismus; Orgasmic Dysfunction; Premature Ejaculation; Figure 10.6*)

C. There are two major categories of abnormal sexual behavior—those that victimize others and those that don't. (Review: *Paraphilia*)

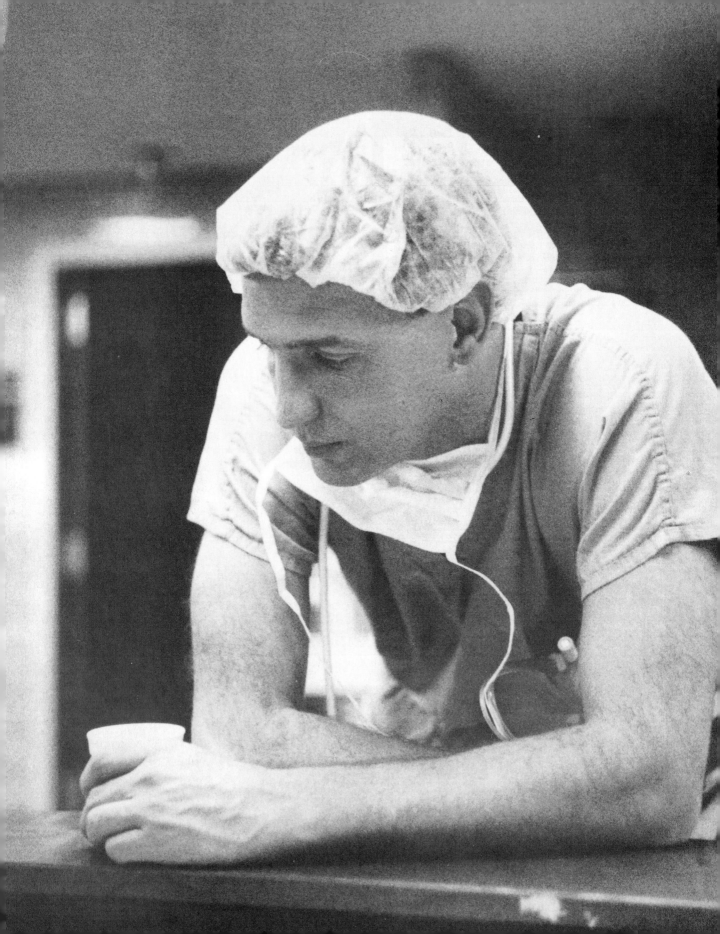

Life-Style and Coping

Chapter Outline

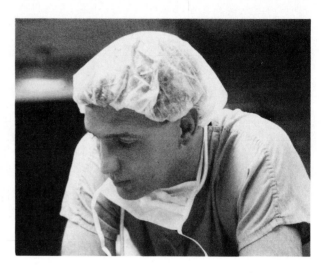

There should be a law against Monday mornings. At least that's what Sheila thought as she slammed her hand down hard on the alarm clock and slowly forced herself up out of bed—more tired than when she went to sleep five or six hours ago. There was no time to cook breakfast, so Sheila gulped down her coffee along with a couple of half-stale jelly donuts. Tomorrow I'm going to have to get back on my diet, she thought, as she lit up a cigarette and dashed out to her car. Sleeping in to the last minute had made her late, so she tried to beat the traffic, dangerously darting in and out of the fast lane. Unfortunately, she had trouble finding a place to park, so she was late for work anyway. When she arrived at her desk, she found a whole stack of new work piled up on top of the mountain of old work she didn't finish last week.

After another cigarette and a few more cups of coffee, Sheila was ready to go. She worked right through lunch to meet an important deadline. She was up for promotion and badly needed the salary increase it would bring, for she always seemed to be short of cash. Nevertheless, when 5 o'clock rolled around, she rushed out of the office and into the crowded shopping mall to buy a birthday present for her mother. For dinner she managed to pick up a rather good-tasting hot dog smothered with onions, an order of greasy french fries, and a diet cola, finishing the whole thing off with another cigarette. One of these days I'm going to reform, she assured herself.

Sheila knew that her life-style was not doing her health any good. Her striving to succeed while having to meet all of her family and other social obligations, her poor eating habits and use of tobacco, not to mention the stresses and strains of everyday living, were all beginning to take their toll.

Today there is a growing consensus among health professionals that a person's health depends heavily on long-term patterns of behavior. Good health is not necessarily a matter of luck; nor disease a matter of random misfortune. There is, in fact, increasing evidence that individuals who have acquired a health-promoting life-style—good eating habits, regular exercise, and skills for coping with stress—increase their chances of remaining healthy. The evidence also shows that some life-style patterns have the opposite effect and are associated with increased risk for disease and premature death.

Although certain health determinants—factors such as age, gender, heredity, and unusual accidents—cannot be controlled, eating and exercise habits, the way one deals with stress, and other behaviors can be. **Self-control** refers to the ability of a person to maintain or alter the course of his or her behavior independently of obvious external influence (Pomerleau & Brady, 1979). In this chapter we examine some examples of how behavioral patterns of life-style and health are related; we also look at some major techniques of self-control that psychologists have developed to help people cope with the problems of their life-style.

We will begin our discussion by considering the concept of stress. After examining the numerous sources of stress in our lives, we will see how stress affects the body. The consequences of stressful events are not predetermined but depend heavily on one's attitudes and behavior. This important point will become particularly apparent as we look at the various techniques of coping with stress. Later in the chapter we will consider obesity as an example of a problem that psychologists attempt to help people cope with through self-control techniques. In our discussion, we will examine the limits of self-control—physiological and genetic factors beyond a person's control—as well as its promise.

Self-Control: The ability of a person to maintain or alter the course of his or her behavior independently of obvious external influences.

WHAT STRESS IS

Stress is a part of everyday living. Pressures to perform, difficult decisions, and unexpected setbacks are normal in most people's lives. The machines we use, and depend on, break down at the worst times. And, after fighting traffic, following a long hard day on the job, many people face family demands, marital discord, unpaid bills, and other pressures. We call all these things stressful, but what exactly is stress?

Stress is a complicated phenomenon which has been defined in many different ways. The concept, as suggested by one psychologist, encompasses three interrelated notions (Justice, 1985). First, there is a demand of some kind placed on the individual, a **stressor.** Though a stressor typically is noxious or aversive, it need not be. Any demand on the person, whether unpleasant—for instance, sitting in a dentist's chair—or pleasant—for instance, exchanging a passionate kiss with a lover—is a stressor (Selye, 1985). **Stress** refers to the exposure to a stressor. The body's response to a stressor, the physiological changes induced by stress, in turn, refers to the **stress response** (Justice, 1985).

Stress is something that each of us has experienced at one time or another; it is an inevitable part of normal, everyday living. Just for a minute consider how many different demands you face each day and in the course of the year. These demands force you to change, to adapt, or to cope with the situation facing you. The way you change or cope, in turn, can have an important bearing on how the stress affects you.

Stressor: Any demand placed on the individual.

Stress: Exposure to a stressor.

Stress Response: The body's response to a stressor; the physiological changes induced by stress.

■ **Learning Check** ■

Read the definition, then cover the right side and try to recite it. Repeat.

Stressor	Any demand placed on the individual
Stress	Exposure to a stressor
Stress Response	The body's response to a stressor; the physiological changes induced by stress

---

STRESSORS IN EVERYDAY LIFE

There are many sources of stress. Some of these come in the form of the day-to-day decisions we must make. Others involve the inevitable but often unexpected major life events we face throughout the life cycle. Some, like the job duties we must perform to make a living, are external. Others, the duties and tasks we take upon ourselves because of our personal standards and aspirations, are internal.

Conflict

Do you do something purely for fun at least once a week? The pressures of daily living—studying for exams, maintaining family and social relationships, earning a sufficient income—often force us to choose between what we would rather do and what we believe we should or must do. Such decisions involve **conflict**—a situation in which a choice must be made between two or more important goals.

Many of the stressors we encounter in everyday living stem from conflict (Roth & Cohen, 1986). Having to choose between mutually exclusive alternatives—a career in business versus one in engineering, or completing one's education versus taking a relatively good job now—can be extremely demanding. And doing nothing can be just as bad, or worse. Even having to choose between two equally pleasant but mutually exclusive alternatives, like going to a movie or to a football game, can be sufficiently demanding to trigger a stress response.

Conflicts in which one must choose between two equally desirable but mutually exclusive alternatives are called **approach-approach conflicts** (Dollard & Miller, 1950). An example of an approach-approach conflict in everyday living is deciding where to spend your vacation. You can go to the mountains for peace and quiet or to a big city for excitement. Both are equally desirable, but your time and money are limited. You must choose one or the other. Moreover, you can't procrastinate and not do anything, because you must make plans and reservations no matter what you choose to do. The longer you delay your decision, the more urgent the situation becomes.

A somewhat different situation occurs in an **approach-avoidance conflict,** in which you must decide whether or not to pursue a goal that has both positive and negative qualities. The challenges of growing up often fit

Stressors are everywhere, and sometimes, they seem to come out of nowhere.

Conflict: A situation in which a choice must be made between two or more important goals.

Approach-Approach Conflict: Having to choose between two equally desirable but mutually exclusive alternatives.

Approach-Avoidance Conflict: Having to choose whether to pursue a goal that has both positive and negative qualities.

in this category, as when a young person is attracted to the opposite sex but must overcome embarrassments and self-doubts that are painful to face in order to reach an attractive partner. In the approach-avoidance conflict, getting closer to a desirable situation also brings you closer to a negative one. You must take the bad to have the good.

Another type of conflict involves choosing between evils. In an **avoidance-avoidance conflict,** you must choose between two equally undesirable options. The choice may be between working four hours per evening Monday through Thursday or working eight hours per day over the weekend. Or an individual convicted of speeding might be forced to choose between a large fine or a weekend in the county jail. In addition to the conflict, the individual must also face the additional stressor of an undesirable event.

Some conflicts are even more complicated than a choice between evils. In the **double approach-avoidance conflict,** the choice is between two alternatives, each of which possesses both positive and negative attributes. Your job may be secure but boring or low-paying. Should an opportunity arise to take on a risky but more exciting or higher-paying job with another company, you could be facing a double approach-avoidance conflict. Double approach-avoidance conflicts are often difficult to sort out. It isn't easy to cal-

Avoidance-Avoidance Conflict: Having to choose one of two equally undesirable options.

Double Approach-Avoidance Conflict: Having to choose between two alternatives, each of which possesses both positive and negative attributes.

Approach-Approach

Approach-Avoidance

Avoidance-Avoidance

Double Approach-Avoidance

Figure 11.1 Types of Conflict.

culate the relative importance of the positive and negative features in each alternative (see Figure 11.1).

Stressful Life Events

Stressful Life Events: Situations that necessitate significant change in a person's life-style (marriage, divorce, graduation, changing jobs, etc.).

In addition to conflict, we periodically face situations that necessitate significant change in our life-styles. Such situations, or **stressful life events**—for example, marriage, divorce, graduation, changing jobs—have long been known to place strong demands on an individual.

Table 11.1 shows a number of common stressful life events and the relative value of each as a stressor. This scale, known as the Holmes and Rahe social readjustment scale, is based on the subjective ratings of about 5,000 people. As the scale indicates, getting married is a more potent stressor than experiencing trouble with the boss. Thus, different events have different relative values as stressors, and, as the scale indicates, any situation that necessitates change, positive or negative, can be a stressor.

Life Cycle Crises. An adult's experiences of stress have sometimes been described in terms of crisis stages that accompany change at key points in the life cycle. As the process of maturing forces us to cope with new challenges, our reaction to these stressors may involve us in a complex replay of earlier unresolved conflicts in our lives—as outlined by Freud, Erikson, and other stage theorists whom we discussed in Chapter 2. An internal conflict that has not been fully resolved—as in a person's uncertain acceptance of a sexual role during adolescence or early adulthood—may reappear in new form when he or she faces a new stressor. In this situation, coping with the stressful events listed in the Holmes and Rahe scale can become harder and more complex as someone moves into a new developmental stage; for anyone in doubt about "who I am," coping with one stressful event might involve him or her in a series of new ones on the list.

Sometimes the occurrence of a series of such events can be a danger signal that a person may be approaching a crisis stage in life that calls for personal reevaluation and renewed self-awareness. While several life cycle crises were identified in connection with the discussion of Freud and Erikson in Chapter 2, it is worthwhile examining one of the better-known examples, to see how a turning point in a person's life can become the center of difficult and stressful events. The phrase "mid-life crisis" is usually applied to people between forty to forty-five who have come to a transition point of agonizing self-appraisal and disenchantment with their life (Levinson, 1978). At this stage, many people experience varying degrees of turmoil and tension—and a number of stressful events—in the process of trying to work out a way to face the inevitability of aging. This is a time when people have in some way established themselves in life and have realized they now may face twenty or thirty more years in that same situation. Is this where they want to be for the rest of their lives? The self-doubts of a mid-life crisis come alive in contemporary lyrics, such as those by David Byrne (from "Talking Heads") that give us the voice of a man bewildered, for "Once in a lifetime," with his big car, big house, and beautiful wife, he asks himself, "Well . . . How did I get here?"

People at this point are likely to realize that they have not achieved all they set out to do as young adults, and that time is running out. For the first

Table 11.1 Social Readjustment Rating Scale

Rank	Life Event	Mean Value*
1	Death of spouse	100
2	Divorce	73
3	Marital separation	65
4	Jail term	63
5	Death of close family member	63
6	Personal injury or illness	53
7	Marriage	50
8	Fired at work	47
9	Marital reconciliation	45
10	Retirement	45
11	Change in health of family member	44
12	Pregnancy	40
13	Sex difficulties	39
14	Gain of new family member	39
15	Business readjustment	39
16	Change in financial state	38
17	Death of close friend	37
18	Change to different line of work	36
19	Change in number of arguments with spouse	35
20	Large home mortgage	31
21	Foreclosure of mortgage or loan	30
22	Change in responsibilities at work	29
23	Son or daughter leaving home	29
24	Trouble with in-laws	29
25	Outstanding personal achievement	28
26	Wife begins or stops work	26
27	Begin or end school	26
28	Change in living conditions	25
29	Revision of personal habits	24
30	Trouble with boss	23
31	Change in work hours or conditions	20
32	Change in residence	20
33	Change in schools	20
34	Change in recreation	19
35	Change in church activities	19
36	Change in social activities	18
37	Small home mortgage	17
38	Change in sleeping habits	16
39	Change in number of family get-togethers	15
40	Change in eating habits	15
41	Vacation	13
42	Christmas	12
43	Minor violations of the law	11

Source: Reprinted with permission from *Journal of Psychosomatic Research,* 2, 1967, 213–218, Pergamon Press, Ltd. T. H. Holmes & R. H. Rahe, The social readjustment rating scale.

*Numbers indicate the relative stressfulness of each event on a scale from 1 to 100. The higher the number, the more stressful the event.

time, they may doubt their ability to reach the goal, or they may doubt the value of the goal, without knowing how to proceed. Life has become a very complex series of double approach-avoidance conflicts, and a normal amount of self-doubt may turn a troubled person to desperation and dissat-

The mid-life crisis involves a stressor that some people respond to with a renewed sense of purpose.

isfaction with all aspects of life—marriage, job, family responsibilities, values, and commitments. This is a time of life that can produce a change of career, a divorce, a separation; it can also produce a struggle to achieve a renewed sense of purpose, new and more realistic goals, and a better appreciation of life. Not everyone will have a mid-life crisis experience (Neugarten & Datan, 1974); those who do may achieve a successful transition that helps them face the normal stress situations of later years.

The Holmes and Rahe "point" approach may be a useful way to view the overall effects of stress on a large population; however, for an individual, the stressfulness of an event often depends on how a person evaluates and appraises that event (Lazarus, 1982, 1984). One person might construe a divorce as a devastating loss; the same event would be far less stressful for the person who views the divorce as an opportunity to be free from the grips of an abusive, stifling relationship. Thus, the effect of a stressor on the individual depends on the person's attitude toward it. An important technique of self-control, as we will see later (page 388), involves an attempt to interpret events from the most constructive viewpoint that we can.

Stressors in the Workplace

The demands of life events, like those of conflict, are generally episodic. Some stressors, by contrast, occur on a regular basis. One's work, for example, can make dealings with stressors a daily event.

All else being equal, which job do you think would provide the greatest amount of stress: family physician, corporation president, secretary, or chicken inspector? According to a report released by the National Institute of Occupational Safety and Health (NIOSH), after laborers, no other occupation is associated with more stress-related illness, such as ulcers and hyper-

Table 11.2   Top 40 Jobs Associated with Stress-Related Illness

1. Laborers	21. Bank Teller
2. Secretary	22. Teacher's Aide
3. Inspector	23. Telephone Operator
4. Lab Technician	24. Sales Manager
5. Office Manager	25. Sales Representative
6. Foreman*	26. Public Relations Person
7. Administrator	27. Policeman*
8. Waiter and Waitress	28. Fireman*
9. Machine Operator	29. Electrician
10. Farm Owner	30. Plumber
11. Mine Worker	31. Machinist
12. House Painter	32. Mechanic
13. Health Technologist	33. Structural Metal Craftsman*
14. Licensed Practical Nurse	34. Railroad Switchman*
15. Nurse's Aide	35. Warehouseman*
16. Registered Nurse	36. Clergyman
17. Dental Assistant	37. Musician
18. Social Worker	38. Hairdresser
19. Health Aide	39. Guard
20. Computer Programmer	40. Watchman*

*Or, of course, a woman in the same job.

Source: National Institute of Occupational Safety and Health (NIOSH). Occupational Stress. Proceedings of the Conference on Occupational Stress, Los Angeles, Nov. 3, 1977. U.S. Dept. of Health, Education, and Welfare, 1978.

tension (high blood pressure), than secretary and inspectors (NIOSH, 1978). Table 11.2 shows NIOSH's list of the top forty jobs associated with stress-related illness. Notice that family physician and corporation president aren't even on the list.

What makes a job like secretary so stressful? First, secretaries have little sense of control over their job activities. They must type what the boss wants typed, file what the boss says to file. What is more, they often can't control when they will perform their duties. If the boss says stop filing and type, what are their choices (see Pfeiffer, 1986)?

Not experiencing a sense of control is a major source of stress in many jobs. Consider the plight of the chicken inspector. The inspector stands for eight hours in a small corner as chickens pass by on a conveyor belt. Each must be inspected for some twenty different diseases. Every hour 1,200 chickens pass by; each day, the inspector must accept or reject 9,600 chickens. The machine allows roughly three seconds per decision, no more, no less. Hopefully the inspector has good health benefits, for the risk of a stress-related illness under those conditions is high.

Several other health-related occupations, such as nursing jobs, have high responsibility but few options (nurses must follow doctors' orders), relatively low pay, and far less status than the doctor. These are the people whose jobs make dealing with stress an everyday event.

Psychologists who work in business and industry, such as the industrial psychologist (see Chapter 1), attempt to deal with the problems of stressors in the workplace. Such psychologists might help managers develop techniques to reduce the amount of stress employees experience by enhancing

For these assembly line workers, experiencing a lack of control in their jobs can be a major source of stress.

their sense of control. The idea of flexible working hours—allowing employees to decide for themselves when they will begin or end their workday—is just one possible way to improve a person's perceived sense of control. Other psychologists might be more concerned with how the employees behave in relation to stress, focusing on patterns of living that may be even more important than the stressors themselves.

LIFE-STYLE AND STRESS

As we have seen, the value of a stressor cannot be measured in absolute terms. Though the actual demands on a physician may be greater than those on a secretary or chicken inspector, the physician may experience less stress. Thus, stressors must be viewed in the total context of a person's stage of life, one's attitudes and interpretations of events, and the pattern of one's life-style. In this section we will look more closely at the relationship between life-style, stress, and illness.

■ Learning Clue ■

Keep in mind that it's one's life-style, and not stress per se, that can be hazardous to one's health.

A number of studies have revealed a relationship between stressful life events and physical problems (Greene et al., 1985). In such studies, subjects are asked to indicate the stressful life events they've experienced during the past year. They are then assigned stress scores based on the sum of all reported events. A person who reports having had a marital separation (valued at 65 on the Holmes and Rahe readjustment scale), sex difficulties (valued at 39), and vacation (valued at 13), would have a total score of 117. Typically, high scores are associated in research studies with health-related problems. In one study of ninety young physicians, for example, 70 percent of those subjects who obtained scores over 300 suffered from ulcers (sores on the lining of the stomach) or a similar problem within two years. Only 37 percent of those who scored less than 200 suffered similar ailments (Holmes & Rahe, 1967). Holmes and Rahe believe that accumulating over 150 points of stressful life events within a year definitely increases one's risk of illness or accidents. While critics have charged that the claim is oversimplified (Fergusson et al., 1985), there seems little doubt that a strong relationship exists between stress-filled living and health problems.

Epidemiology is the study of the health and disease of people in relation to their environment and way of living. Epidemiological studies have, in fact, demonstrated a relationship between behavior and disease. In one classic study, every other man and woman between thirty and sixty years of age in the New England town of Framingham, Massachusetts, were studied over a twenty-year period. Each was healthy and had no significant disease. Every two years, subjects were given a thorough physical examination and a detailed interview about their life-style. Over the course of the study, many of these individuals developed heart disease, the most common cause of death in the United States (National Center for Health Statistics, 1980). The findings revealed that the development of the disease was not a matter of pure chance: some people were far more prone to develop the disease than others. Older males were much more likely to suffer a heart attack or stroke than women or young males. Nevertheless, a number of behavioral factors—smoking, obesity, high cholesterol level (associated with a high animal fat diet), physical inactivity, and excess tension and stress were found to be among the best predictors of heart disease (Kannel et al., 1968).

As an example of a strong relationship between behavior and health problems, we will look at Type A behavior pattern, which has been associated with an increased risk for heart disease. We will also look at its counterpart, the Type B pattern. Then we will consider a more refined view of the Type A pattern and see the importance of looking at one's total life-style pattern, rather than just certain aspects of it. Finally, we will look more closely at how and why certain diseases are related to life-style.

The Type A Behavior Pattern

A number of studies have been directed toward one particularly stressful life-style. The **Type A behavior pattern** represents a life-style characterized by competitiveness, achievement striving, time urgency, and impatience. According to Meyer Friedman and Ray Rosenman in their book, *Type A Behavior and Your Heart* (1974), people who exhibit the Type A pattern are involved in an incessant struggle to achieve more and more in less and less time and, if required to do so, act against the opposing efforts of other persons. Such individuals are aggressive, hard-driving, competitive, and almost always in a hurry. The relative absence of Type A characteristics defines its opposite, the **Type B behavior pattern** (Kelly & Houston, 1985). People who exhibit the Type B pattern tend to be easygoing, relaxed, noncompetitive,

Epidemiology: The study of the health and disease of people in relation to their environment and way of living.

Type A Behavior Pattern: A life-style characterized by competitiveness, achievement striving, time urgency, and impatience.

Type B Behavior Pattern: A life-style characterized by the absence of Type A characteristics. People who exhibit the Type B pattern tend to be easygoing, relaxed, noncompetitive, and nonstriving.

Figure 11.2 Do You Have a Type A Behavior Pattern? (*After M. Friedman and R. H. Rosenman.* Type A Behavior and Your Heart. *New York: Knopf, 1974, p. 82–84*).

Answer Yes or No to Each of the Following

_____ I almost always do everything very rapidly? (For example, I eat, walk, talk, and move quickly.)

_____ I am usually impatient, especially when it comes to the speed at which things are accomplished? (For example, people talk too slowly for me, and when I read, I skim the material as quickly as possible.)

_____ I often find myself trying to get two things done at the same time. (For example, I read while I eat or groom myself while driving.)

_____ I find it difficult to goof off and do nothing. I even feel guilty when I take a vacation or just relax for a few hours.

_____ I do not take time to be aware of beautiful things (for example, admiring a sunset or the new flowers of spring).

_____ I frequently schedule more activities than I can possibly accomplish.

_____ I evaluate my worth in quantitative terms such as salary, grades, number of papers written, amount of money in the bank, or number of accomplishments.

and nonstriving. Figure 11.2 provides examples of the type of statements used to evaluate the Type A pattern.

Do you have a Type A life-style? There is a good chance you do if you said yes to all of the items in Figure 11.2. Overt manifestations of the Type A pattern include a heightened pace of living, impatience with slowness, and self-preoccupation (Glass, 1977). It also includes a general tendency to become angry at the slightest provocation.

Actually, the Type A–Type B distinction is not a matter of either/or, but rather is best seen as a continuum ranging from frequent and persistent to occasional manifestation of behaviors of the Type A variety (see Figure 11.3). Those who fall at the one extreme are without question in the Type A category and those at the opposite extreme are Type B; most people fall in between (Friedman et al., 1985). As one's Type A-like behavior becomes more persistent, intense, and characteristic, one falls higher on the Type A end of the Type A–Type B continuum (Matthews, 1982).

In general, people who fall on the Type A end of the continuum are more successful in school, attain higher occupational status, and gain greater distinction in their careers than people who fall on the Type B end

Figure 11.3 The Type A–Type B Continuum.

Always competitive	Often competitive	Sometimes competitive	Rarely competitive	Never competitive
1	2	3	4	5

Type A   Type B

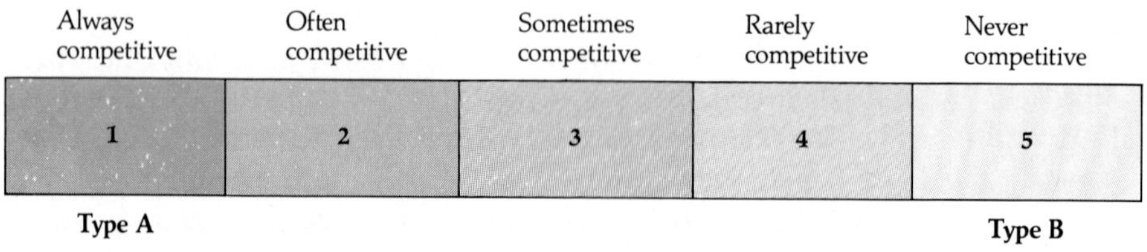

(Strube et al., 1985). With these benefits, however, come certain risks. Rosenman and colleagues (1970), for example, reported that people who exhibit the Type A life-style are twice as likely to develop coronary heart disease as those in the Type B category. The Type A life-style has also been associated with a greater risk for stroke and arteriosclerosis (hardening of the arteries) (Zyzanski et al., 1976) as well as for infectious disease (Barton & Hicks, 1985). But recent investigations of Type A behavior have found that its relation to illness is not as simple as was once believed.

Beyond the Type A–Type B Distinction

Soon after the dangers of the Type A pattern became apparent, a number of popular books were published which contained prescriptions for living to reduce the chance of dying of heart disease and other ailments associated with a stressful life-style (Fisher, 1981). More recent studies have indicated, however, that dealing with the problems of a stressful life-style are far more complicated than following a set of rules for living. First, research demonstrates that people have a great deal of difficulty implementing health-enhancing behavior changes (DiMatteo & DiNicola, 1982; Hopeful-Harris, 1980). It's not enough to tell people to relax or to exercise on a regular basis; they must be taught how to do these things by learning to use the techniques of self-control we will discuss a bit later. Second, it is an oversimplification to look at a specific pattern of behavior without considering other aspects of the individual.

Type A behavior becomes increasingly dangerous as a person grows older. A group of researchers found that young adults (approximately twenty to forty years of age) who scored high on a measure of Type A behavior actually scored higher on a measure of psychological well-being than a comparable group of Type Bs. For older subjects, however, the pattern reversed itself, with the Type Bs showing greater well-being than the Type As (Strube et al., 1985). According to the researchers, the hard-driving, achievement-oriented Type A life-style may be adaptive in younger age groups, but leads to lower well-being in later life, while the easy-going Type B life-style seems particularly adaptive in later maturity. Thus, the Type A pattern becomes maladaptive if one cannot change to the Type B pattern in his late 30's or early 40's.

In addition to one's age, our view of the Type A pattern also depends on a person's sex. The ambitious, driven, impatient, angry life-style descriptive of Type A behavior applies much more to males than to females. A number of researchers have argued that the daily social roles of women—being a mother, wife, and paid worker all in one, for instance—create a unique set of demands (Barnett & Baruch, 1985; Kandel et al., 1985). Braiker (1984), for instance, has argued that the life-style comparable to the Type A pattern (in men) is really quite different in women. A **Type E pattern,** she argues, is a female life-style in which a woman spreads herself too thin and tries to be everything to everybody. Type E women are not necessarily aggressive and angry, but their life-style is nevertheless quite stressful. Type E women are constantly juggling one demand against another: the needs of her family versus her job commitments; her recreational needs versus her need for rest, and so on. The Type A pattern is not the only life-style that is stressful; in

Type E Behavior Pattern: A female life-style in which a woman spreads herself too thin and tries to be everything to everybody.

considering only Type A behavior, we may be inadvertently ignoring other potentially hazardous patterns, such as Braiker's Type E woman.

More recently, Friedman and colleagues (1985) have criticized the Type A–Type B distinction and proposed a more *refined view* of it. Sixty men classified as Type A or Type B were asked to complete a questionnaire that measured the extent to which they expressed themselves nonverbally. Trained judges also evaluated the subjects' use of gestures, facial expressions, and other nonverbal expressions by observing them. The findings revealed two categories of Type A individuals. Those in the illness-prone category were tense and nonexpressive. A healthy category of Type As who were expressive, charismatic, talkative, and in control was also found. In addition, Type B men who were nonexpressive, submissive, and tense were

Figure 11.4 How Vulnerable Are You to Stress? ("*Vulnerability Scale*" *from the* Stress Audit, *developed by Lyle H. Miller and Alma Dell Smith, Boston University Medical Center. Copyright 1983, Biobehavioral Associates, reprinted with permission.*)

How Vulnerable Are You To Stress?

The following test was developed by Psychologists Lyle H. Miller and Alma Dell Smith at a Boston University Medical Center. Score each item from 1 (almost always) to 5 (never), according to how much of the time each statement applies to you.

_____ 1. I eat at least one hot, balanced meal a day.

_____ 2. I get seven to eight hours sleep at least four nights a week.

_____ 3. I give and receive affection regularly.

_____ 4. I have at least one relative within 50 miles on whom I can rely.

_____ 5. I exercise to the point of perspiration at least twice a week.

_____ 6. I smoke less than half a pack of cigarettes a day.

_____ 7. I take fewer than five alcoholic drinks a week.

_____ 8. I am the appropriate weight for my height.

_____ 9. I have an income adequate to meet basic expenses.

_____ 10. I get strength from my religious beliefs.

_____ 11. I regularly attend club or social activities.

_____ 12. I have a network of friends and acquaintances.

_____ 13. I have one or more friends to confide in about personal matters.

_____ 14. I am in good health (including eyesight, hearing, teeth).

_____ 15. I am able to speak openly about my feelings when angry or worried.

_____ 16. I have regular conversations with the people I live with about domestic problems, (e.g., chores, money and daily living issues).

_____ 17. I do something fun at least once a week.

_____ 18. I am able to organize my time effectively.

_____ 19. I drink fewer than three cups of coffee (or tea or cola drinks) a day.

_____ 20. I take quiet time for myself during the day.

_____ TOTAL

To get your score, add up the figures and subtract 20. Any number over 30 indicates a vulnerability to stress. You are seriously vulnerable if your score is between 50 and 75, and extremely vulnerable if it is over 75.

found to be illness-prone when compared to the more expressive Type B individuals. Such findings again illustrate the importance of looking beyond the Type A–Type B distinction and considering the entire life-style, rather than only a relatively narrow range of behaviors, when evaluating the healthfulness of the way we live.

Stress and the Total Life-Style

Stress can add up. Stress from financial worries combines with stress from time and schedule pressures, and these sources of stress combine with others. Figuratively, all sources of stress fuel the same engine and can have a cumulative effect on the individual's ability to cope (Rosenthal & Rosenthal, 1985). In evaluating the stressfulness of any particular life-style, then, it is necessary to consider all the sources of stress to which a person is exposed. These alone, however, do not provide a complete picture.

Take a minute and respond to the 20-item stress questionnaire reproduced in Figure 11.4. As you respond to the items, notice that your vulnerability to stress depends not on how much stress is in your life, but on the things you do either to add to or to counterbalance the everyday stressors and life events to which you are exposed. A life-style that includes behaviors such as eating balanced meals, getting a good night's sleep, vigorous exercise, and doing things for fun tends to keep your overall vulnerability to stress down. An important point here is that, while stress is inevitable, we can do things to counterbalance its effects. It's not the stressors of modern living that are the problem; it's the person's total life-style. Later on in the chapter we will consider positive behaviors that a person might want to acquire in order to cope better with stress and other life-style problems. But first, let's consider how stress affects the body and its relationship to disease.

THE STRESS RESPONSE

Now that we've examined the various sources of stress and the relationship between stress and life-style, it's time to take a closer look at the stress response. In this section we consider what actually happens to the body when the stress response is triggered. We will then consider what happens under conditions of prolonged and chronic stress—long-term exposure to a stressor. Finally, we will take a closer look at the relationship between stress and health or disease.

The Physiology of Stress

The body responds to stress with a specific pattern of changes. Regardless of the nature of the stressor, the physiological changes that occur are essentially the same: a heightened state of arousal that prepares the body for action.

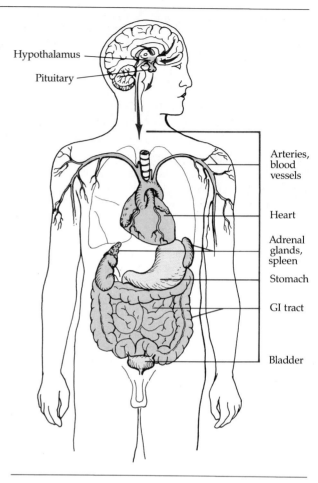

Figure 11.5 *This figure shows the major brain structures and internal organs associated with the stress response.*

Hypothalamus

Pituitary

Arteries, blood vessels

Heart

Adrenal glands, spleen

Stomach

GI tract

Bladder

Sympathetic Arousal: A heightened state of sympathetic nervous system activity characterized by such physiological changes as rises in heart rate, increased blood pressure and blood circulation, and inhibition of digestion.

Figure 11.5 shows some of the major brain structures, internal organs, and other parts of the body that are involved in the stress response. The brain, via control centers in the hypothalamus, activates the sympathetic branch of the autonomic nervous system (see Color Plate 3A in Chapter 3) and triggers the release of hormones from the inner core of the adrenal glands, the adrenal medulla. The heightened state of the sympathetic nervous system activity, or **sympathetic arousal,** that follows is characterized by such physiological changes as rise in heart rate, increased blood pressure and blood circulation, and inhibition of digestion. The adrenal glands release the activating hormones, epinephrine and norepinephrine. These hormones further increase arousal. The blood pressure accelerates even more, for instance.

At the same time, the brain sends a second message, the effects of which are felt throughout the entire body by means of an intricate chemical messenger system. This second message stimulates the hypothalamus to release a chemical messenger called corticotropin. Corticotropin, in turn, stimulates the pituitary gland to release still another chemical messenger called adrenocorticotropin (ACTH). The ACTH circulates through the bloodstream until it reaches the outer shell of the adrenal glands, the adrenal cortex.

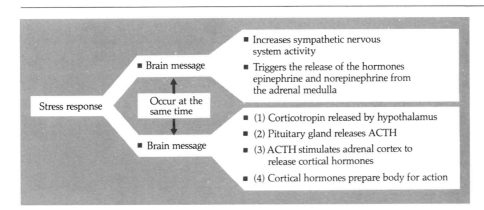

Figure 11.6   Schematic Overview of the Stress Response.

Stimulated by ACTH, the adrenal cortex releases some thirty different corti-cal hormones (Elliott & Eisdorfer, 1982). Cortical hormones, such as cortisol and cortisone, have a wide range of functions that prepare the body for ac-tion (see Figure 11.6).

Scientists have yet to learn how the numerous cortical hormones interact and affect the body. Needless to say, they increase the body's state of pre-paredness for action. Cortisol and cortisone, for instance, cause stored fats to be released into the bloodstream for energy and help reduce inflammation in case the stressor results in injury.

The complex chain of events involved in the stress response can perhaps best be summarized by the phrase, "all systems go." The body kicks into high gear and is ready for action, or as Cannon (1929) put it, for fight or flight. In this state, the body is prepared to meet the demands posed by the stressor.

The Consequences of Prolonged Stress: The General Adaptation Syndrome

The physiological chain reaction that occurs in response to stress serves the individual well in genuinely dangerous, life-threatening, or extraordi-nary situations. The body is prepared to cope. Think what might happen, however, if the body remained in its hyper-prepared state for an extended period? Vital resources would soon be depleted. The body would be con-stantly working at maximum capacity. Blood pressure would remain chroni-cally high. The heart would be overworked.

The consequences of chronic stress were the subject of a long-term study by a physician, Hans Selye (1936). As a medical student in the 1920s, Selye

■ Learning Check ■

As Figure 11.6 shows, two brain messages take place simultaneously in stress re-sponse. One activates the body by increasing sympathetic nervous system activity and triggering the release of the hormones epinephrine and norepinephrine. Review Figure 11.6 until you can remember the four steps that follow the other brain mes-sage.

Figure 11.7 Schematic Summary of the General Adaptation Syndrome.

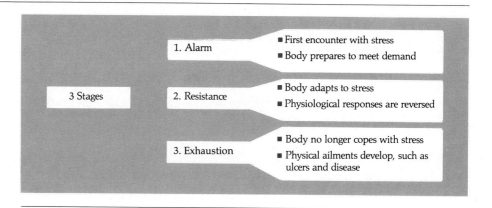

General Adaptation Syndrome: A three-stage sequence in response to prolonged stress, identified by Selye: the alarm stage, the resistance stage, and exhaustion.

Alarm Stage: The first of the three stages of the general adaptation syndrome in which the body goes into a state of activation (alarm) and prepares to meet a demand.

Resistance Stage: The second of three stages of the general adaptation syndrome in which the body resists the effects of a prolonged stressor and temporarily adapts to it.

Exhaustion Stage: The third and final stage of the general adaptation syndrome in which the body is no longer able to cope with prolonged stress.

Hypertension: Chronically high blood pressure; medically defined as a blood pressure above some given level, such as 160/95.

Biofeedback: The use of conditioning techniques to help people learn to control responses traditionally regarded as involuntary.

observed that many diverse illnesses seem to produce a number of common symptoms: fever, loss of weight and appetite, general weakness, and so on. In his quest to understand these common symptoms, Selye discovered that when an organism was subjected to stress for a prolonged period, regardless of the nature of the stressor, a number of common consequences could be observed. These consequences, he believed, occurred in a three-stage sequence, which he referred to as the **general adaptation syndrome:** alarm, resistance, and exhaustion (see Figure 11.7).

The first of the three stages of the general adaptation syndrome, according to Selye, occurs when the stressor is first encountered. He called this the **alarm stage;** the body goes into a state of activation (alarm) and prepares to meet the demand. Under normal conditions, the demand is then met and the body returns to normal. If, however, the stress continues, there is no chance to rest or recover. The body then enters the second stage called **resistance**—in which the body resists the effects of prolonged stress and temporarily adapts to it. In the resistance stage, the body learns to live with stress. Although still taxed, the body manages to reverse the physiological responses of the alarm stage. For a while, the body is able to function normally in spite of stress. Coping with stress is draining, however, and continued exposure ultimately leads to the third and final stage, **exhaustion**—in which the body is no longer able to cope with prolonged stress. The stomach becomes covered with bleeding ulcers, the adrenal glands enlarge, and the body's defense against disease becomes impaired. If the stress continues unabated, death is the end result.

More recently, Selye (1985) has emphasized the importance of psychological factors in stress. According to Selye, the effects of a stressor depend not on its quality or intensity, but on the person's ability to handle it. As he states, "what matters is not so much things that happen to us, but the way we take them."

In his book, *Stress Without Distress*, Selye (1974) makes the argument that whether we perceive an experience as good or bad is largely a matter of attitude. Being fired from a job, for example, could be viewed as an opportunity to grow and to develop one's talents in new directions. Converting a negative event into a positive one by adopting the right attitude is what Selye

Box 11.1 PSYCHOLOGY IN ACTION: Understanding and Controlling Hypertension

Hypertension, or chronically high blood pressure, is a good example of a physical problem associated with stress. Blood pressure, roughly speaking, is an indicator of how hard the heart works. When your doctor tells you your blood pressure is 110/70, the top number reflects how hard the heart works during contractions, or systolic pressure; the bottom number reflects how much rest your heart gets between contractions, or diastolic pressure. Medically defined, hypertension refers to a blood pressure that is above some given level, such as 160/95 (Smith, 1977). Blood pressure that is 140–159/90–94 is considered borderline hypertension (Julius, 1977).

In determining what blood pressure is ideal for any given individual, it is necessary to consider such factors as age and sex. Blood pressure tends to increase with aging, for instance. In addition, between the ages of about twenty and forty-five, men have higher blood pressures than women. Then, due to hormonal changes after menopause, this sex difference reverses itself so that the average blood pressure of women exceeds that of men. At ages twenty to twenty-four, for instance, the average blood pressure is 122/76 in men and 116/72 in women. At ages seventy to seventy-four, it is 146/81 in men and 159/85 in women (Epstein & Eckoff, 1967; Moser & Goldman, 1967).

Regardless of how it's defined, hypertension has been related to a variety of health-related problems, including heart attack, stroke, and kidney damage (Eyer, 1979; Kannel et al., 1970). According to the American Institute for Preventative Medicine (1985), high blood pressure increases the risk of illness and death for some 65 million Americans.

In fighting hypertension, behavior change plays a key role. Learning to relax is a major tool for combating the physiological changes associated with the stress response. Deep muscle relaxation procedures, as discussed in Table 11.3, for example, have been shown to be of value in reducing hypertension in several studies (Agras & Jacob, 1979).

Another behavioral approach to hypertension is **biofeedback,** in which conditioning techniques are used to help people learn to control responses traditionally regarded as involuntary. Special instruments keep track of a person's blood pressure and emit sounds to indicate increases in blood pressure above a certain level. The sound provides feedback that the individual then uses to gradually gain some control over his or her blood pressure. Hearing the sound fade away provides the reward that strengthens the person's control. Although the procedure doesn't work for everyone, some people are able to use biofeedback to achieve modest but important decreases in their average blood pressure reading (Shapiro et al., 1972; Brady, 1979).

Life-style changes such as reducing salt intake, decreasing weight, and a regular program of exercise also help in many cases (Freis, 1976). Even so, when medication is prescribed for treatment, the individual must take it. And this may require certain life-style adjustments (Agras & Jacob, 1979).

Hypertension, a physical problem associated with stress, can often be corrected with life-style changes such as developing a regular exercise program.

Eustress: Positive stress; converting a negative event into a positive one by adopting the right attitude.

calls **eustress** (eu = good), or positive stress. The idea of eustress again illustrates how the effects of stressors are not predetermined, but depend to a large degree on how the person reacts to them.

Stress, Behavior, and Disease

Selye's work helped to illuminate the connection between disease and behavior. Simply put, a person's pattern of behavior can cause physical diseases such as ulcers and chronic high blood pressure (hypertension). Such physical diseases, traceable to psychological rather than physical factors like a virus or bacteria, are called **psychosomatic disorders** (psycho = of the mind; somatic = of the body). Prolonged stress, the result of a person's lifestyle, causes ulcers, because a normal part of the stress response is an increase in the secretion of powerful stomach acids. The stomach cannot tolerate elevated levels of such acids indefinitely, and eventually they eat away at its lining. (See Box 11.1 for an in-depth look at the relationship between behavior and high blood pressure.)

Psychosomatic Disorders: Physical diseases, such as ulcers and hypertension, that are traceable to psychological rather than physical factors.

Today it is widely recognized that many problems of physical health are linked to behavior (Maler & Laudenslager, 1985). Certain types of cancer, lung disease, and heart disease are linked to a life-style that includes smoking, lack of exercise, overeating, a high fat diet, excessive alcohol consumption, and other behavioral patterns (Institute of Medicine, 1982; American Cancer Society, 1979).

Behavioral Medicine: A field of psychology that focuses on the application of behavioral knowledge to problems of physical health (e.g., coping with stress).

If behavior causes physical problems, then developing strategies for changing disease-causing life-styles requires a science of behavior. **Behavioral medicine** is a field of psychology that focuses on the application of behavioral knowledge to problems of physical health. Topics in behavioral medicine include approaches to coping with stress, to which we will now turn.

COPING WITH STRESS

Different people respond differently to the same degree of stress. Holahan and Moos (1985) asked men and women to complete two questionnaires. One, similar to the Holmes and Rahe social readjustment scale (see page 375 and/or Table 11.1), measured the amount of stress each was being subjected to. The other, which asked them to indicate if they were experiencing physical and other stress-related symptoms, measured their reaction to stress—the amount of distress they were experiencing. The researchers found that these subjects could be divided roughly into two groups. One, called the distressed group, seemed to be suffering considerable distress, as evidenced by their reports of physical complaints, tension and other problems. A second group, which Holahan and Moos referred to as the stress-resistant group, was relatively free of distress. Yet both groups, as indicated by their stress scores, were experiencing comparable levels of external stress.

Holahan and Moos (1985) found that, when compared to the distressed group, men and women in the stress-resistant group were more easygoing. They took things in stride and did not overreact to stressful life events. In addition, stress-resistant men exhibited greater self-confidence; stress-resistant women had closer and more secure family relationships. Most important, the researchers identified a major difference in the way the two groups coped with stress.

Stress-resistant individuals of both sexes dealt with stressful life events through what Holahan and Moos described as an *approach coping strategy*—taking positive action, stepping back to take an objective look at stressful situations, gathering more information about the problem. They confronted their problems directly and took steps to solve them. The distressed group, on the other hand, relied on an avoidance coping strategy—keeping their feelings "bottled up" and taking their negative feelings out on others. Holahan and Moos suggest that to cope better with stress, people should be helped to identify, and then eliminate, their use of avoidance coping strategies and finally taught to use more positive strategies, as in the stress-resistant group.

Though we can't eliminate stressors from our lives, we can control the way we react to them. Such is the idea behind positive approaches to coping with stress. In this section we will consider two such approaches: cognitive and physical.

Cognitive Approaches

Cognitive approaches are based on the idea that the way we interpret events and evaluate our coping resources shapes the personal impact of an event. By finding a positive way of looking at events and believing in our abilities to cope with them, we can reduce or minimize their potentially negative impact on us.

A major premise of the cognitive approaches is that, rather than being passive spectators of the environment and life's events, people play an active role in processing environmental information and influencing their environment. A stressful encounter is viewed as a dynamic, unfolding process in which the individual makes a series of appraisals; these appraisals, in turn, determine the impact of the stressor on the individual (Folkman & Lazarus, 1985). According to cognitive theorists, the initial evaluation a person makes, or **primary appraisal,** is an evaluation of the event in terms of its significance to personal well-being (Lazarus, 1982). Is the event potentially harmful or potentially beneficial? If your boss informs you that a work slowdown has forced him to lay you off for the rest of the week, you might view this event in more than one way. It might be a good opportunity to catch up on your studies or take a badly needed vacation. Alternatively, you might appraise the event as potentially harmful—a threat to your ability to earn money. The way you view the event is your primary appraisal.

Following the primary appraisal, the individual makes what is called a **secondary appraisal**—an evaluation of one's resources for handling a stressful encounter. In making a secondary appraisal, the individual estimates his or her ability to meet the demands posed by the stressor. For example, you

Primary Appraisal: The initial evaluation of an event for its significance to personal well-being.

Secondary Appraisal: An evaluation of one's available options and resources for handling a stressful encounter that follows a primary appraisal.

might evaluate your current financial situation and your ability to find a new source of income.

Secondary appraisals, according to cognitive theory, are critical in determining how much distress you might experience from an event. If your secondary appraisal indicates your financial situation is so bad that you can't afford to lose even one day's income, then the boss's call could be extremely distressing for you. Thinking back to previous stressful encounters that you have experienced, perhaps you can recall a time when your initial appraisal made things look very bad; then, upon reexamination, perhaps you found that you had more resources than you first realized. If your appraisal changed, so did the amount of distress you experienced. The essence of using the cognitive approach is to find a way of looking at a situation and your resources for dealing with it in the least stressful way possible. By reappraising an event, its negative, distressing impact can be reduced, minimized, or even turned into a blessing in disguise.

Cognitive Restructuring:
A cognitive approach to coping in which people learn to handle a stressful event by changing (restructuring) their interpretation of the event or by viewing it from a broader or different perspective.

In using a cognitive technique called **cognitive restructuring,** people can learn to handle a stressful event by changing (restructuring) their interpretation of it or by viewing it from a broader or different perspective. For example, flunking a driving test can be quite stressful. The extent of the distress, however, depends, at least in part, on how it is interpreted. Interpreting it as simply a bad performance on that particular test, rather than as a reflection of personal inadequacy or an irreversible setback, helps to restrict the damage. People sometimes multiply negative situations by interpreting the consequences as being far greater than they are. Further, by taking a broader view, people can see some value in responding positively to a stressful experience. For instance, the driving test may show need to practice further, to be better assured of passing next time, and to become more confident of one's life-long ability to handle all traffic conditions, police officers, and driving stresses. Whether the failed test was a minor, a major, or an overwhelming stressor, or perhaps a challenge, depends on how it is interpreted.

One of the benefits of cognitive restructuring is that it helps the person gain a sense of control over stressful events (Sadowski & Blackwell, 1985). Instead of being a totally passive victim to unavoidable events such as illness and job loss, the individual can at least feel like there is something he or she can do to influence the personal impact of the event. You can't wish the event away, but you can try to look at it in a way that will reduce its stressful effect and that will benefit you—that is, by looking at some constructive aspects of the event.

To use cognitive restructuring to handle stressful events in your life, you need to take charge of the way you appraise events and your coping resources. Specifically, you'll want to focus on your strengths and capacities to deal with the situation to your benefit, rather than on your possible weaknesses or limitations.

Figure 11.8 contains a number of situations along with both negative and more positive ways of viewing them. As these examples indicate, though the situation does not change, one's reactions to it can be altered. There are limits to this strategy, of course; when a close relative or friend dies, no amount of positive thinking can make things right. Nevertheless, there are some ways of viewing loss situations that are more constructive

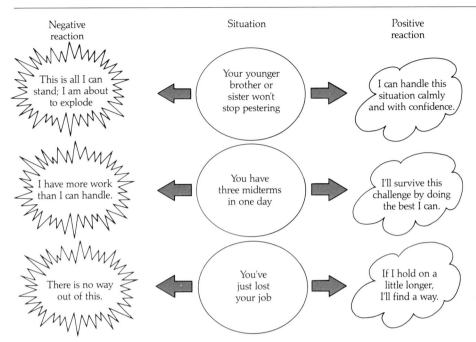

| Negative reaction | Situation | Positive reaction |

Figure 11.8 Positive and Negative Reactions to the Same Situation.

than others. For example, instead of dwelling on a feeling of helplessness and disorganization from the loss, one can try to ease the pain by thinking about how the lost person had a significant role in one's own life and that of others, and how that may influence everyone in the future. In addition, one might try to relax better by using a physical approach.

Physical Approaches

Physical approaches involve physical activity and a variety of relaxation procedures designed to counteract the overaroused state associated with the stress response. Following physical activity such as swimming, cycling, biking, jogging, and brisk walking, there is a rebound, or opposite, effect. The muscles relax and the body rests. Overarousal due to stress melts into a calmer state of low arousal. There is an opportunity to recuperate from the ravages of stress (Folkins & Sime, 1981).

A second way to counteract overarousal is through meditation, self-hypnosis, and other techniques that produce a state of deep relaxation. Some of these stress management techniques were discussed in Chapter 5 in the context of their consciousness-altering effects. Here we consider a major physical approach to managing stress—**deep muscle relaxation**—a procedure in which a person systematically tenses then relaxes each of the major muscle groups.

To use deep muscle relaxation, find a quiet place and systematically tense and relax your muscles. It doesn't matter whether you begin with your toes or your forehead, nor does it matter exactly how long you tense each muscle—anything between ten and twenty seconds will do. It is extremely

Deep Muscle Relaxation: A physical approach to coping with stress in which the individual systematically tenses then relaxes each of the major muscle groups.

important to relax all the muscles, however, including those of the face. Table 11.3 shows some guidelines to follow when you first try the technique. You might find it helpful to concentrate on the sensations you experience as you tense and relax.

Self-hypnosis is similar to deep muscle relaxation, except that, instead of actually tensing and relaxing your muscles, you just concentrate for a few moments on each of your major muscle groups. Tell yourself something like, "My forehead is relaxing; my nose is relaxing; my mouth is relaxing," and so on until you get to your toes. As you concentrate, try to visualize your muscles relaxing. Don't worry about thoughts or other distractions. Nor ought you worry about how well the procedure is working. Just keep returning to your muscles, and occasionally tell yourself something like, "Each time I breathe out I become more relaxed" or "Every muscle in my body is becoming loose and lazy." (For more on hypnosis and meditation, see Chapter 5.)

Many people who begin with deep muscle relaxation turn to self-hypnosis within a few weeks. After a few months of practice, merely concentrating on one's muscles can, for many people, be as effective as tensing and relaxing them. Whichever method you use, after you are finished you might want to take a few more minutes to concentrate on thinking positively. For

Table 11.3   Deep Muscle Relaxation Procedures

1. Find a comfortable spot, take a deep breath, exhale, and totally relax.
2. Tense your forehead (about 15 seconds). Now relax. Notice the cool feelings of relaxation (10 to 20 seconds).
3. Wrinkle your nose. Relax.
4. Tense the muscles of your mouth by smiling broadly. Notice the feelings of tension. For the rest of the day, every time you become aware of tension, automatically relax. Now relax, letting all the muscles in your face go limp.
5. Tense your chin. Now relax.
6. Tense your neck. Relax.
7. Make a fist with your left hand. Notice the tension. Now relax and notice the pleasant feelings. Every muscle in your body is relaxing more and more every time you exhale.
8. Tense your left arm. Now relax. Maybe you are thinking about something else, it doesn't matter. Just concentrate on the feelings in your body and they will help you to relax.
9. Make a fist with your right hand. Now relax.
10. Tense your right arm. Now relax. All the muscles in your body are relaxing more and more with every breath you take.
11. Tense your back by moving your shoulder blades together. Now relax.
12. Tense your abdominal muscles. (If you have trouble, imagine someone is about to punch you in the stomach.) Now relax.
13. Tense your left leg. Relax.
14. Tense your right leg. Relax.
15. Tense your left foot by curling your toes. Relax.
16. Curl your right toes. Relax.
17. Every muscle in your body is relaxing more and more with every breath you take.

The entire procedure should take about 15 minutes. The more you practice, the easier it should get.

example, you can say something like, "I feel calm, confident, and relaxed. I can study effectively and remember what I study." In doing so, you will be combining a cognitive technique with a physical one. When you are finished, mentally count to five and open your eyes—that is, if you haven't fallen asleep, as people sometimes do.

In using cognitive or physical approaches to coping, you will be adding positive behavioral patterns to your life-style. But coping with stress is only one of many life-style problems. In the next section, using obesity as an example, we will look at coping strategies for other life-style problems that involve both a physical and a behavioral dimension.

COPING WITH OTHER LIFE-STYLE PROBLEMS: THE EXAMPLE OF OBESITY

Obesity is not a minor problem in people's lives. Approximately 30 percent of American women and 15 percent of American men are **obese,** which means they weigh 20 percent above their ideal body weight (Abraham & Johnson, 1979; Bray, 1976). What is more, beginning in their mid thirties, most people have a strong tendency to add excess padding to their hips and thighs and midsections, despite their best efforts to stay trim. Both men and women tend to grow heavier as they pass from young adulthood to middle age (Parizkova, 1977; Scala, 1978).

Obese: Weighing 20 percent above one's ideal body weight.

The fattening of the American people is not easily explained. Obese people are subject to strong cultural and social pressures to try becoming or remaining slim. Employers hesitate to hire them, and people of normal weight tend to exclude them from their social groups. When children were asked to rate pictures of other children in terms of likability, a picture of an obese child got the lowest rating of all. Even obese children in the study ranked the obese child last—less likable than children of normal weight, including many with serious physical disabilities (Staffieri, 1967).

Doctors constantly warn the obese about health hazards associated with excess weight: increased risk of hypertension, gallbladder disease, heart disease, and diabetes. Health spas, health food stores, and weight reduction clinics woo them, too. The fact is, people aren't overweight because they don't want or try to be trim; every year Americans spend millions of dollars on dieting aids and diet plans. Many obese people do not like the way they look and perceive their bodies as detestable, unattractive, even repulsive to others (Brownell & Foreyt, 1985). And they are not overweight because of their affluence, for obesity is far more common among those of low socio-economic standing than among the wealthy (Stunkard, 1975).

Perhaps most baffling is the discouraging success rate for weight loss. Very few people—less than 5 percent—succeed in losing weight for more than six months. As one researcher has noted, the cure rate for obesity is lower than the cure rate for many forms of cancer (Brownell, 1982). If they lose weight at all, most gain it back. What could be the reasons for the great difficulty people experience in losing weight?

Obesity involves genetic, physiological, and behavioral factors. For the factors that are inborn or due to normal bodily processes, there is little an individual can do to influence the process directly. Psychological approaches to obesity concentrate on those things a person can do something about—namely, on those behaviors that contribute to weight gain or facilitate weight loss.

Hereditary and Physiological Factors in Obesity

Some researchers suspect that heredity is behind the seemingly permanent nature of obesity. The children of obese parents are more likely to become overweight than the children of normal-weight parents (Abraham et al., 1971). According to one researcher, some people are "biologically programmed" to be fat—endowed at birth, in effect, with a higher set point for fat storage than others (Nisbett, 1972).

The idea of being programmed for obesity is supported by animal studies. Some rat families tend to be fatter than others. If a rat from an obese strain is overfed, it quickly gains weight and keeps it on. Rats from normal-weight strains, by contrast, seem to be resistant to weight gain. Even if forced-fed for weeks, they gain weight very slowly, and lose it quickly after the experiment is over (Rothwell & Stock, 1979). If you have a weight problem, you probably recognize this phenomenon. Many weight watchers complain that all they have to do is walk by a bakery to gain five pounds, while their skinny friends seem to gorge themselves all day without gaining an ounce.

The fact is, normal-weight people can eat more and still weigh less than obese people. One study found, for example, that the children of obese parents actually ate less than the children of normal-weight parents but weighed more (Griffiths & Payne, 1976). What's more, numerous studies have found that most obese people eat no more than their nonobese counterparts (Garrow, 1978; Thompson et al., 1982). One possible reason obese people can gain weight while eating the same as, or even less than, individuals of normal weight is that they require fewer calories, either because they expend less energy or because they burn calories more efficiently (James & Trayhurn, 1981). Indeed, the **basal metabolism**—the amount of energy expended while at rest—is lower in obese adults and their children, which means they burn calories more slowly (Griffiths & Payne, 1976).

Basal Metabolism: A measure of the amount of energy expended while at rest.

Inherited disposition is only one possible way a person may become biologically programmed for obesity. Studies have shown that, when humans or animals are undernourished during the fetal stage of development, they are twice as likely to become obese later in life (Ravelli et al., 1976; Jones & Friedman, 1982). Apparently, being deprived of adequate nutrition while still in the mother's womb can predispose an individual to become obese later in life.

Early feeding patterns may also provide the basis for obesity later in life (Knittle & Hirsch, 1968). Obese children are often overfed as infants. As a result, although most infants start out with roughly the same number of fat cells, by age two, obese toddlers have up to two or three times as many fat cells as toddlers of normal weight. Unfortunately, it is during the first few years of life that the majority of one's fat cells are formed. And, once formed, fat cells don't go away. Dieting may cause the cells to shrink in size, but will not reduce their number (Knittle & Hirsch, 1968).

Theory holds that, because the number of fat cells a person has remains essentially fixed from early adulthood on, there is a limit to how much weight our overfed toddler can lose as an adult. Weight loss can only occur until the fat cells have reached normal size. Thus, a person with three or four times more fat cells than others can lose as much weight as possible and still remain relatively fat. The implication is that, for some obese people, no amount of behavior change will make them the ideally thin person they would like to become.

It is important to recognize the difficulty of overcoming physiological factors operating against an obese person. As adults, we put on extra pounds by consuming more calories than we burn. What we don't use for energy gets stored in fat cells and causes them to enlarge. Unfortunately, when a fat cell enlarges, its capacity to store additional fat increases (Salans et al., 1968). The extra fat also slows down basal metabolism. To add to the problem, if the person begins to cut back on the number of calories consumed, the body responds by a further slowing down of the basal metabolism (Garrow, 1978). The less an obese person eats, the less he or she needs, because the body adjusts by reducing the amount of calories it burns during rest (Rodin, 1981). Obesity can also make physical activity more difficult and exercise less pleasurable than for those of normal weight. Ironically, the decreased activity can lead to an even further decrease in metabolism (Garrow, 1978).

For some people, then, obesity is far more complicated than a lack of appetite control. Nevertheless, whether a person is only ten or twenty pounds overweight or severely obese (more than 100 percent above ideal body weight), any attempts to deal with the problem must involve behavior change. (Even if a person has fat removed surgically, he or she most certainly must make some changes in eating habits to avoid gaining it back.) Fortunately, there is considerable evidence that, for many obese people, behavior change programs can help them to control their weight despite their physiological dispositions (Stunkard, 1979). In the sections ahead we will discuss such behavior change programs. But first, let's look at some of the studies upon which these programs are based—studies that point to the role of behavioral factors in obesity.

Behavioral Factors in Obesity

Besides the genetic and physiological factors in obesity, there are mental and emotional complications. Psychological factors can cause people to ignore physiological signals to start or stop eating. Environmental stimuli—a freshly cooked ear of sweet corn basted in melted butter, for instance—can tempt even a satisfied diner to eat more. Some people may be much more responsive to such external signals than others. Cognitive factors may also cause a person to ignore start or stop signals. The belief that one is being a good guest by finishing everything that was served for dinner might cause a person to continue eating long after feeling satisfied, for instance.

The power of environmental cues over the eating behavior of certain people was vividly illustrated in an ingenious series of studies by the psychologist Stanley Schachter. In one set-up, Schachter led subjects to believe

Along with heredity and physiological factors, there are many psychological complications in obesity. Environmental cues, such as the sight and smell of tempting high calorie foods, often lead to unnecessary eating.

External Theory: A theory of obesity proposed by Schachter, which states that obese people are more responsive to external cues for eating and less responsive to internal cues than people of normal weight.

that mealtime was drawing near by rigging the clock on the wall. Obese subjects responded differently from subjects of normal weight. Unaware that their eating behavior was being recorded, they began to nibble on the snacks that were made available to them. Normal-weight subjects refused the snacks (Schachter & Gross, 1968). Schachter concluded that obese people respond to external rather than internal eating cues. According to his **external theory,** obese people are more responsive to external cues for eating and less responsive to internal cues than people of normal weight. A number of studies seemed to support his theory.

Follow-up experiments showed that obese subjects were more finicky in their tastes for food than nonobese subjects. When offered ice cream laced with bitter-tasting quinine, they ate less than normal-weight subjects. Without the quinine, they ate more than the others (Nisbett, 1968). Obese subjects also responded more to the sight of food than people of normal weight; they ate about twice as many cashew nuts when the snack was brightly lit as when it was offered in a dim light. Normal-weight subjects ate approximately the same amount under both conditions (Ross, 1974).

Finally, obese subjects wouldn't work as hard to get food as their normal-weight counterparts. If they had to shell nuts to eat them, they would eat fewer than the normal-weight subjects. They ate more than the normal-weight subjects, however, when the nuts were already shelled (Schachter, 1971).

Though it sounds plausible, Schachter's interpretation of these results has been criticized on a number of grounds (Rodin, 1981). First, the relationship between the subjects' eating behavior and their obesity is correlational. Obese subjects may indeed be more externally controlled than normal-

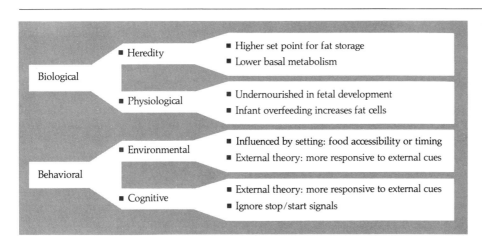

Figure 11.9 Schematic Summary of Possible Factors Involved in Obesity.

weight subjects, but that does not prove that their eating behavior causes their obesity. Both may be the result of some third variable. Second, the obese may only seem to respond more to external cues than normal-weight subjects. In the presence of a rigged clock, for example, normal-weight subjects may not eat so as not to spoil their dinner. In that case, their eating behavior is governed by the clock just as surely as the obese subjects. Third, obese people might actually be more sensitive to internal cues than normal-weight subjects; faced with the necessity of continuously disregarding them, they come to rely heavily on external cues like clocks.

Although critics have shot holes in his external theory, Schachter's work supported two important notions. First, it indicated how eating behavior might be influenced by nonphysiological cues such as the accessibility of food (shelled nuts versus unshelled nuts) and the apparent time of day. In addition, it suggested that there might be some important differences in the eating behavior of obese and normal-weight individuals. These two notions figure heavily in behavioral approaches to the treatment of obesity. Figure 11.9 summarizes the factors involved in obesity.

Behavioral Approaches to Weight Control

Behavioral approaches to weight control are based on the theory that one's eating behaviors are acquired and maintained (learned) according to the same principles that govern any learned behavior (see Chapter 6). According to these principles, overweight individuals can presumably learn to modify those behaviors that cause them to gain weight or that prevent them from losing it. Behavioral approaches define behavior in terms of observable actions and assume that our behavior is controlled by the stimuli that both precede and occur as a consequence of what we do. Behavioral techniques attempt to bring about behavior change—not only for eating but for other life-style behavior patterns—by manipulating an individual's environment.

Behavioral theorists reason that, if certain environmental cues increase the probability that a person will eat, then obese people should try and limit the cues associated with their overeating. To accomplish this, it is necessary

Stimulus Control Analysis: Identifying, through careful observation, the environmental stimuli that precede an undesired behavior.

to conduct what is called a **stimulus control analysis,** in which the environmental stimuli that precede an undesired behavior are identified through careful observation. Typically, the individual is asked to keep a diary of everything he or she eats and drinks, as well as the time, place, and circumstances in which the behavior occurred.

In conducting a stimulus control analysis, a person trying to lose weight attempts to identify what environmental cues act as a signal to start eating. Once identified, efforts are made to change the response to them or at least restrict the person's exposure to them as much as possible. For example, the person may learn that he or she is most likely to begin eating in the evening when watching television and when a commercial comes on. If so, there are a number of possible ways to change the TV-watching environment to reduce temptation. Behavioral programs also call for a person to eat only at specific times and specific places. The goal is to restrict the cues that signal eating. And, because tempting foods are kept out of sight (better still, out of the house), the person is less likely to be lured into eating unnecessarily.

Another objective of the behavioral approach is to teach obese individuals new eating behaviors. Specifically, the goal is to help them to acquire a style of eating more like that of nonobese persons. It is commonly assumed, for example, that obese individuals eat more rapidly than individuals of normal weight (Stunkard, 1979; Overholser & Beck, 1985). Thus, behavioral programs attempt to help the person acquire such behaviors as laying down utensils between bites, chewing more slowly, or drinking water to interrupt eating during meals.

To effect changes in eating behavior, it is necessary to change the consequences of eating. Things are arranged so that the individual is rewarded for engaging in the desired behavior. A spouse, friend, or trained therapist can observe the person eating and provide a reward in the form of a compliment when the person puts his or her fork down between bites, for instance. Sometimes the person is asked to put up two or three hundred dollars, which can be earned back by engaging in the desired behavior.

Contingency Management: Attempting to change behavior by altering its consequences.

Attempting to change behavior by altering its consequences is called **contingency management.** In contingency management, the person tries to control his or her behavior by deliberately building in a system of rewards. Contingency management is based on the assumption that behavior is shaped by its consequences (Skinner, 1953). Behaviors that have rewarding consequences become strengthened. By controlling the consequences of one's own behavior—by making slower eating contingent on getting a re-

Figure 11.10 Schematic Summary of Behavioral Approaches to Weight Control.

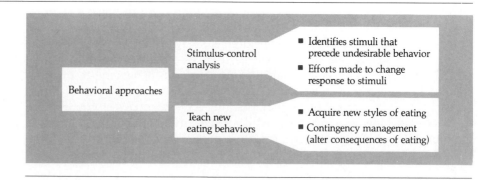

ward, for instance—a person can control his or her own behavior. Figure 11.10 summarizes the behavioral approaches to weight control.

Table 11.4 outlines the four basic steps used in most behavioral approaches to obesity. First, it is necessary to specify what behavior is to be controlled. It is not enough to say, "I'm going to lose fifteen pounds." Instead, it is necessary to state those behaviors (specific eating habits) that one wishes to change in order to lose the weight. Next, behavioral programs attempt to identify environmental stimuli that influence one's eating behavior so that they too can be controlled. Gradually the person restricts the cues associated with eating. He or she may, for instance, be encouraged not only to eat in the kitchen and at 8 a.m., 12 p.m., and 6 p.m., but to use an unusually colored place mat and napkin.

As the third step, the individual employs specific techniques to control eating. Among these techniques are those designed to help a person eat more slowly. Another is to count each mouthful of food eaten during a meal to increase one's control over the eating process. The individual may also be encouraged to avoid pairing any unrelated activity (reading, watching television) with eating. Finally, to establish the desired behaviors—eating more slowly or whatever—the consequences of eating are modified through contingency management.

Early studies of the behavioral approach revealed some rather dramatic results. Stuart (1967) attempted to treat ten obese women using the four-step approach described above. Two dropped out. Eight others followed the program and showed substantial weight loss in the course of a twelve-month period. Six of them lost thirty pounds or more. The pattern of weight loss

Table 11.4 Steps in the Behavioral Approach to Weight Reduction*

Step	Example
Describe the behavior to be controlled	Ask client to keep records of what they eat, under what circumstances they eat, who they were with, how they felt before and after eating.
Identify the stimuli that precede eating	Focus attention on characteristics of situations associated with eating. For example, does the client eat while cooking, does he or she eat at a particular location in the house, is the setting of the table a cue for food consumption?
Employ behavior methods for eating control	There are many behavior methods for regulating food intake. Examples include asking clients to count each mouthful of food, putting down their eating utensils after each third mouthful of food, and avoiding "distracting" activities such as watching TV while eating.
Change the consequences of eating	Develop methods whereby clients are rewarded for complying with the program. Points can be awarded for accurate record-keeping, counting chews, etc. The client might agree to wait until he has accumulated a certain number of points before he treats himself to a desired activity such as going to a movie.

*Based upon the University of Pennsylvania program described by Stunkard (1979).

for four of the women is illustrated in Figure 11.11. As the figure shows, weight loss was gradual and steady. Presumably, these women had learned more effective eating habits and thus were able to lose weight without going on a special diet.

The apparent effectiveness of the behavioral approach and its relatively simple four steps (outlined in Table 11.4) led to its becoming one of the most widely used methods of weight control (Brownell & Foreyt, 1985). Despite its continued widespread use, more recent studies have found the behavioral approach less effective than was originally thought (Brownell, 1982; Jeffery et al., 1985). Apparently, for many people, controlling environmental cues and the consequences of their eating behavior simply is not enough.

Hereditary and physiological factors in obesity probably account for some of the failures of the behavioral approach. If an obese person can eat less than a normal-weight person and still gain weight, how is counting mouthfuls of food and eating more slowly going to help? Realizing that obesity is complex and multiply-determined, a number of psychologists are recommending a more extensive approach based on social learning theory (Brownell & Foreyt, 1985). Building on the basic ideas of the behavioral approach, this newer one includes **cognitions**—beliefs, thoughts, expectations, and other mental processes—among the targets of behavior change. In addition, techniques of behavior change may be used to change not only eating patterns but any behavior (including cognitions) that might play a role in the person's weight problem. For example, if learning to eat less or differently won't do the job, then perhaps changing the person's activity level through walking, jogging, and other exercise might.

Cognitions: Beliefs, thoughts, expectations, and other mental processes.

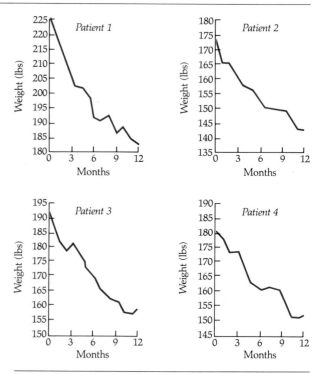

Figure 11.11 Profiles of Four Women Following Behavioral Treatment of Obesity. (*Reprinted with permission from* Behavior Research and Therapy, 5, R. B. Stuart, *Behavioral Control of Overeating,* 1967, Pergamon Press, Ltd.)

Social Learning Approaches to Weight Control

Social learning theory refers to the viewpoint that much learning occurs in the social context, through observation of others (Bandura, 1977). A basic assumption of social learning theory is that people can acquire a new behavior without direct experience. For instance, a child may learn to eat more quickly by observing his or her parents do the same. The theory holds that the child is able to mentally represent the parents' behavior and anticipate the consequences for acting similarly.

A major difference between social learning theory and the behavioral approach is its emphasis on cognition. Rather than restricting themselves to the modification of overt behavior through manipulation of the individual's environment, social learning approaches also attempt to identify and manipulate cognitive factors that may be implicated in the person's weight problem.

Self-monitoring, for instance, refers to the social learning technique of observing one's own behavior including cognitions. The purposes of self-monitoring include increasing a person's self-awareness and providing information that can be used to help a person change. Self-monitoring goes beyond the stimulus control analysis used in behavioral approaches in that the person takes note of cognitive as well as environmental cues that may be linked to his or her obesity. Do certain thoughts trigger eating? What does the person say before, during, and after eating? Like environmental cues, cognitions can provide signals to eat unnecessarily. And, if self-monitoring reveals that the belief that one cannot lose weight is the main cause of one's failure to stick to a sensible diet and program of exercise, then that belief can be challenged. At the same time, a new belief, such as that small but noticeable weight losses are attainable, can be cultivated in its place.

In using social learning theory, researchers have also reexamined the targets of behavior change. One reason many people fail is that their goals are unrealistic (Mahoney, 1974). One person might want to lose forty pounds in fifty days. Another may demand a perfectionistic adherence to an all-but-impossible program of self-denial and torturous exercise. And, when their unreasonable program fails, they give up and splurge—a phenomenon that Mahoney and Arnkoff (1979) call the "saint or sinner" syndrome.

People who fall prey to the "saint-or-sinner" syndrome assume that self-control is an either/or phenomenon; that is, all or nothing. Either they are following a program to the letter or they are completely failing. If they make just one small mistake, they figure that they might as well splurge. Their reasoning is that, if you've committed one forbidden act, you might as well go ahead and do them all. Such thinking is sometimes associated with repeated cycles of restrictive diets and uncontrollable binge eating (Marus et al., 1985). Learning to be realistic, and realizing that self-control is not a matter of being on or off some rigid program, can be important targets of change (Mahoney & Arnkoff, 1979).

Another aspect of the social learning approach can be found in its use of **self-reinforcement**—presenting rewards or punishments to oneself based on behavior. Rather than rely on environmental manipulation (points, compliments, etc.) to alter the consequences of eating, individuals are taught to reward themselves with mental praise following desired behaviors. In one

Self-Monitoring: Observing one's own behavior, including cognitions.

Self-Reinforcement: Presenting rewards or punishments to oneself based on behavior.

study of such reinforcement methods, a group of subjects were instructed to assign themselves a grade following each meal to indicate the extent to which they followed a behavioral program (for example, eating more slowly and at a particular time and place). Compared to a control group that attempted to follow the same program without grading themselves, the grade-assigning group lost roughly twice as much weight after seven weeks (Bellack, 1976). Apparently, knowing they were going to evaluate their own performance helped subjects in the graded group to stick to their program. And the good grades they gave themselves helped to strengthen the desired behavior.

Covert Rehearsal: Mentally practicing a desired behavior.

Still another use of cognition in helping people achieve better self-control is **covert rehearsal**—mentally practicing a desired behavior. For example, the individual may use imagery to practice behaviors such as turning down extra helpings, resisting temptation, and laying down eating utensils between bites. In using covert rehearsal, an individual attempts to strengthen a desired pattern of behavior without direct experience. Through imagination, the person can anticipate problems and the best way of handling them before they actually arise. Figure 11.12 summarizes the social learning approaches to weight control.

An interesting study provides some insights into the role of cognition in behavior change. Obese people followed one of three treatment programs for six months. The first, the behavior change group, used only behavioral and social learning techniques such as self-monitoring and self-reinforcement. Its members kept track of their eating and exercise patterns and eventually identified cues that were likely to lead to overeating. They avoided such cues, and rewarded themselves for sticking to their low-calorie diet plans and exercising. The second group was given only an appetite suppressant drug to help control its eating. The third group used a combination of the behavior change methods used by the first group plus diet pills as used by the second. One control group received no treatment at all, and another received advice and encouragement.

At the end of the six months, all three treatment groups had lost more weight than the two control groups. The group using a combination of behavior change and drugs lost the most, an average of 33.7 pounds per subject. The drug therapy group lost 31.9 pounds per subject, a close second. The first group, which used only behavior change methods, ran a poor third at 24 pounds per subject.

Figure 11.12 Schematic Summary of Social Learning Approaches to Weight Control.

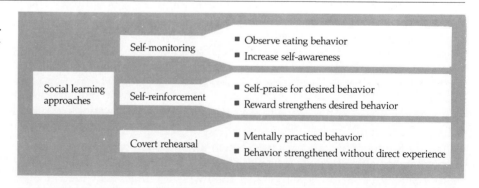

■ **Learning Check** ■

Social learning approaches extend behavioral approaches in at least four ways. Match the numbered terms with the letters for the appropriate behavior patterns below:

(1) *self-monitoring*

(2) *targets of change*

(3) *cognitions*

(4) *covert rehearsal*

(a) keeping track of thoughts that may signal undesired eating behavior

(b) mentally practicing desired behaviors

(c) keeping aware of thoughts that may signal undesired behavior

(d) new attitudes developed to reinforce desired behavior; e.g., being more realistic

(*Answers:* 1 = a; 2 = d; 3 = c; 4 = b)

At the end of twelve months, all groups showed an average increase in weight. A rather interesting reversal had occurred, however. The group that had used only behavioral change had become the most effective dieters: subjects in this group still weighed an average of 19.8 pounds less than they had originally. The diet pill group averaged a net loss of 13.8 pounds, and the group that used both methods, only 10.1 pounds (Craighead et al., 1981). To account for the success of the group that used only behavior change methods, the researchers proposed that their experiences, more than those of any other group, had taught them that they could master their eating habits. They had acquired a sense of **self-efficacy:** the belief or expectation that one can successfully perform the behavior demanded by a situation. Having faith in their ability to lose weight made a critical difference in their ability to actually do so. Subjects in the groups that were given drugs probably attributed their weight loss to the drugs rather than to their own efforts. Without the faith in their ability to control their weight that the behavior change group had developed, they gained back most of the weight they had lost earlier.

According to social learning theorists, it is this feeling of self-efficacy that underlies the success of all behavior change techniques (Bandura, 1977). In learning the methods of behavior change, people learn that it's within their power to lose weight. It's this knowledge and confidence in their ability to change that allows them to make the changes that are necessary to accomplish their goals.

Self-Efficacy: The belief or expectation that one can successfully perform the behavior demanded by a situation.

Social Support, Exercise, and Other Considerations

Social learning theory approaches to obesity emphasize its complexity and the importance of factors other than environmental cues and overt behavior. In addition to cognitive factors, other important considerations include the role of social and family supports and the value of exercise.

An important consideration in obesity and other life-style problems is the social context in which the behavior occurs. Family, friends, and other personal relationships influence us in many ways. The success of an obese person's attempts to lose weight often depends on the nature of this influence. When a married person makes an effort to lose weight, both spouses have to make adjustments. According to Brownell and Foreyt (1985), there are many important reasons why some spouses don't like it when their husband or wife loses weight. The couple may need some kind of outside assistance to help them work out the issues that they face when one goes on a diet; they may need professional therapy, or the dieter may have to find support outside the home. Overeaters Anonymous (OA) is a self-help group modeled after Alcoholics Anonymous. People with weight problems meet regularly to discuss their mutual concerns and problems and to support each other's efforts to change.

Another important issue in obesity concerns the dieter's physical activities. Exercise is a behavior and, as such, can be modified using behavioral and social learning techniques. Exercise does not really burn off that many extra calories. A 150-pound person would have to jog something like six hours straight or swim for five hours just to burn off the equivalent of one pound of fat (Gwinup, 1975; Petrie, 1974). Nevertheless, for reasons not yet fully understood, exercise has been found to be one of the few factors associated with long-term weight loss (Dahlkoetter et al., 1979).

Some experts believe that exercise helps to offset the reduction in basal metabolism that occurs with dieting (Stern, 1984). Indeed, when an individual engages in sustained exercise, like brisk walking or swimming for twenty minutes or more, metabolism rate remains higher than normal well

---

Box 11.2 PSYCHOLOGY IN ACTION: The Smoking Habit

Smoking is one of the clearest examples of how behavior affects health. According to the American Institute for Preventative Medicine (1985), some 350,000 Americans die prematurely each year of smoking-related causes—heart disease, emphysema, chronic bronchitis, stroke, and many types of cancer. Pregnant women who smoke also take risks for their unborn children. Several substances in cigarette smoke, such as nicotine and hydrogen cyanide, can cross the placenta and have a direct impact upon the fetus. Babies of smoking mothers are smaller, have more respiratory infections, require more hospitalizations, and perform more poorly on a wide range of tasks than babies of nonsmoking mothers (U.S. Department of Health and Human Services, 1980).

The dangers of smoking have been known for some time. The problem is that most people who want to quit can't (Guilford, 1966; Hunt & Matarazzo, 1982). Like obesity, smoking is a complex problem that involves physiological as well as psychological factors.

Because smoking is such a persistent habit, many experts consider prevention to be the major hope for future generations (Evans, 1979; Hurd et al., 1980). But those who are already hooked might want to try applying some of the techniques of behavior change that

The first step in kicking the smoking habit is to study when and under what conditions the undesired behavior occurs.

were discussed in relation to obesity. All psychological approaches to smoking try to reduce the probability of smoking behavior and increase the probability of alternative responses. The accomplishment of these goals

■ Learning Check ■

Now that you have a better understanding of life-style and health, look at your own life-style and reflect for a moment on the kinds of behavior changes that you might want to make. For an exercise, try to apply a program of behavior change to some area of your life-style.

beyond the time the person stops the activity (McArdle et al., 1981). Other experts point to the psychological benefits of an exercise program (Brownell & Stunkard, 1980). Exercise may act as a cue to eat less or to help a person avoid falling prey to the "saint or sinner" syndrome (see page 401). Because he or she is exercising, the person may feel that self-improvement is occurring despite occasional overeating.

Exercise also has benefits beyond its role in weight control. Numerous studies have found that people who are more active live longer and are significantly less prone to heart disease than those who live a sedentary life (Parizkova, 1973, 1977). Even former varsity athletes who become inactive after retiring from sports show an increased risk for heart disease. Regular exercise is associated with a longer as well as an improved life-style (Crews & Aldinger, 1967; American Institute for Preventative Medicine, 1985). (Before beginning any new program of physical activity, consult your physician.)

Box 11.2 *(cont'd)*

can be reduced to three basic steps: (1) observation (self-monitoring), (2) stimulus control, and (3) contingency management.

The first step in any program of behavior change is to observe the behavior in question, taking note of when it occurs, the condition or cues that precede it, and the consequences that follow it. The smoker therefore keeps a diary of, and records the time, place, date, and circumstances surrounding, each cigarette smoked. After a few weeks, the individual should have a good idea of how often he or she smokes and the environmental or cognitive cues associated with smoking.

Next, the smoker attempts to bring the behavior under stimulus control by gradually reducing and restricting the cues associated with the smoking. For example, a person who smokes twenty cigarettes a day may identify four cues—say, after meals, while driving, while studying, and when at home alone and feeling bored—to circumstances in which most smoking occurs. As an initial attempt at stimulus control, the individual may limit his or her smoking to these four circumstances and no other. Gradually other cues can be eliminated until finally all smoking is limited to just one or two of them.

Finally, some systematic program is used to change the consequences of smoking. To accomplish this, you might mentally reward yourself each time you succeed in resisting the urge to smoke. If this self-reinforcement fails, you might want to enroll in a professional treatment program. Such programs alter the consequences of smoking by associating the behavior with unpleasant consequences. In the rapid smoking technique, for instance, the person keeps on puffing on a cigarette until the next puff produces a feeling of nausea. Another approach is to pair smoking with electric shock or some other unpleasant stimulus such as a room full of old cigarette butts and a foul stench.

If you are thinking about quitting, you might want to first consult with your doctor. Perhaps one of the newer medicines containing nicotine will help you to kick the habit. And don't forget that, though you may fail many times, you only have to succeed once. Enlist your friends and relatives to help you, unless of course they have a smoking habit themselves and might sabotage your efforts. Finally, don't fall prey to the saint or sinner syndrome. Just because you have one or two cigarettes doesn't mean you have to smoke the whole pack. If you can't quit, then cutting back may be the best thing you can do.

Though our discussion has focused on obesity, the issues we've considered apply to many other life-style problems as well. Box 11.2 illustrates how such techniques can be applied to the problem of smoking.

LEARNING FRAMEWORK

I. The concept of stress encompasses three interrelated notions: a demand placed on the individual (stressor); being exposed to this demand (stress); and the physiological response to this demand (stress response).

II. Three major sources of stress are conflict, stressful life events, and the workplace.
   A. Much everyday stress comes in the form of the decisions we must make. (Review: *Conflict; Figure 11.1*)
   B. In the course of life, we all must face a number of stressful situations. Dealing with such situations can be complicated by the different crises we face over the life span. (Review: *Stressful Life Events; Table 11.1*)
   C. Jobs that offer little status, provide little in the way of financial and personal rewards, and give a person few opportunities to exercise personal control are the most stressful.

III. Certain life-style patterns have been associated with a number of health-related problems. But, in considering the risks, it's necessary to look at the total life-style.
   A. A pattern of behavior characterized by achievement striving, time urgency, and aggressiveness has been associated with an increased risk for heart disease and related ailments. (Review: *Type A Behavior Pattern; Type B Behavior Pattern; Figure 11.2*)
   B. A hard-driving aggressive life-style is particularly dangerous for males past middle age who are submissive and have difficulty expressing their emotions. (Review: *Type E Behavior Pattern; The Refined View of the Type A–Type B Distinction*)
   C. In evaluating the stressfulness of a life-style, it is necessary to consider the cumulative effect of all sources of stress as well as the counterbalancing effects of positive behaviors. (Review: *Figure 11.4*)

IV. Studies of the body's responses to stress have led to a better understanding of the relationship between behavior and health.
   A. Through a complicated chain reaction that begins with messages from the brain, the body responds to stress with heightened arousal that prepares it for action. (Review: *Figure 11.5; Figure 11.6*)
   B. Prolonged stress results in a three-stage sequence of alarm, resistance, and exhaustion. (Review: *Figure 11.7; General Adaptation Syndrome; Eustress*)
   C. Many physical diseases are known to be linked to behavior. (Review: *Psychosomatic Disorders; Behavioral Medicine*)

V. We cope with stress mentally as well as physically.
   A. Mental, or cognitive approaches, focus on the importance of the way we view events and our capacity to cope with them. (Review: *Primary Appraisal; Secondary Appraisal; Cognitive Restructuring; Figure 11.8*)
   B. Physical approaches include exercise and techniques designed to produce a deep state of muscle relaxation. (Review: *Deep Muscle Relaxation*)

VI. Obesity is a complex problem that involves both physiological and psychological factors. Though there is little that one can do to change the physiological aspects, behavior change programs can help people to make significant life-style changes.

A. Several lines of evidence indicate that physiological factors play an important role in the development and maintenance of obesity. (Review: *Basal Metabolism*)

B. Experiments by psychologist Stanley Schachter suggested that the eating behavior of obese individuals was under the control of external cues rather than internal physiological signals. (Review: *External Theory; Figure 11.9*)

C. Behavioral approaches to weight control assume that obesity is the result of learned behaviors. (Review: *Stimulus Control Analysis; Contingency Management; Table 11.4; Figure 11.10*)

D. Social learning approaches consider factors in addition to eating behavior and environmental cues in treating obesity. (Review: *(Cognitions) Self-Monitoring; Self-Reinforcement; Covert Rehearsal; Figure 11.12*)

E. The role of social factors, such as spouse involvement, and behaviors other than eating, such as exercise, also reflect the complexity of obesity.

PART

V

Individual and Group Processes

CHAPTER 12

Personality and Its Assessment

Chapter Outline

A lthough John's classmates saw him only three times a week, during the 9 a.m. lecture-discussion philosophy class, most felt like they knew him. He was radical in his ideas and outspoken in voicing them. Just about every class period, he would vigorously spout some anti-conventional view. Whether they admired John or dismissed him as a joke, by the end of the term, just about everyone could predict how he might react to any given issue. The classroom situation is fairly structured and roles are well-defined, so individual students soon exhibit distinctive patterns of behavior. One is radical and outspoken; a second quiet and reserved; a third relaxed and self-assured. Still another might be described as apprehensive and tense, in contrast to the student who is serious and the one who is easygoing. Careful observation reveals that each can be described in terms of a number of behavioral characteristics that are as unique as tone of voice and facial features; for each has a unique personality.

WHAT PERSONALITY IS

Personality: Relatively stable and distinctive patterns of behavior that characterize an individual and his or her reactions to the environment.

In this chapter we examine the concept of **personality,** which can be defined as the relatively stable and distinctive patterns of behavior that characterize an individual and his or her reactions to the environment. In observing other students in the classroom, you soon find some consistency in their behavior. One expresses strong personal views several times throughout the term; this student you characterize as outspoken. Another disrupts the class almost regularly, by chatting with neighbors during lectures or talking out of turn. This student you characterize as discourteous.

These students' personalities are so characterized—that is, one as outspoken and one as discourteous—because the characteristics are relatively

■ Learning Check ■

Read the right side, then cover and try to recite. Repeat.

Three important facts about personality:	1. It is relatively stable.
	2. It is distinctive.
	3. It characterizes an individual and his or her reactions to the environment.

stable (the person is fairly consistent in exhibiting the characteristic) and distinctive (the characteristic distinguishes the individual from others). Sometimes, however, an individual may respond "out of character." During the week of finals the discourteous student may be as polite as can be; the outspoken student unusually agreeable. Thus, our definition of personality includes how an individual reacts to the environment. Because it includes both the relatively stable and distinctive behavioral patterns that characterize an individual and his or her reaction to the environment, our definition allows us to address two apparently conflicting issues. The first concerns why different people respond differently to the same event. The second concerns why the same person responds differently to different situations.

There are several major psychological theories of personality. Some (psychoanalytic and trait theories) emphasize the consistency of a person's behavior across various situations to explain why different people respond differently to the same event. Others (behavioral theories) emphasize the variability of a person's behavior across situations to explain why the same person responds differently in different situations. And for some (humanistic theories), consistency is in the eye of the beholder. In this chapter we will discuss each of these major approaches to personality. At the end of the chapter we discuss different kinds of personality tests and how they are used to assess or describe personality.

FREUD'S PSYCHOANALYTIC THEORY OF PERSONALITY

The first major theory of personality was proposed by Sigmund Freud (1856–1939), a Viennese physician who based his thinking on the case histories of his patients. The theory of personality developed by Freud is referred to as **psychoanalytic theory.** In his psychoanalytic theory, Freud focused on hidden forces and underlying mechanisms, which he believed motivate a person's actions. Such forces and mechanisms provide the foundation or structure of the personality. They govern behavior and account for its stability across different situations.

Psychoanalytic Theory: The theory of personality developed by Sigmund Freud.

According to Freud, personality can be conceptualized in terms of a three-part structure—the id, ego, and superego—which operates at any one or more of the three levels of awareness: conscious, preconscious, and unconscious (see Figure 12.1). He attempted to explain how personality emerges and is formed during what are called the *stages of psychosexual devel-*

Figure 12.1 Schematic Summary of Freud's Concept of Personality.

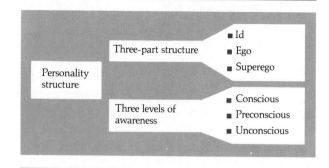

opment. And, through the concept of *defense mechanisms*, Freud revealed his views concerning the dynamics of personality—how the different aspects of personality interact. In this section we discuss each major aspect of Freudian theory. (It is important to keep in mind that Freud modified this theory during the course of his career and that all of his original work is in German. There is some disagreement among scholars regarding what Freud really meant. The definitions given here may differ somewhat from those you may encounter in other books.)

■ Learning Clue ■

The ego is an outgrowth of the id; the superego, an outgrowth of the ego.

Personality's Three-Part Structure

The personality, according to Freud, has a three-part structure, which blends together like the lenses of a telescope or the colors of a painting (Freud, 1933). The id, ego, and superego are not separate compartments, but three interrelated aspects of personality, each of which has distinctive properties.

According to Freudian theory, this little boy is learning that he cannot always satisfy his id urges and have whatever he wants. His ego and superego develop in order to help him control his urges and learn to deal with reality.

The **id** comprises all inherited biological needs and instincts and is the ultimate source of all the mental energy that drives the individual. Present at birth, the id demands instant gratification, regardless of reason, logic, or morals. Following its **pleasure principle**—the goal to obtain pleasure and avoid pain—it pushes the person to obtain food, water, or other bodily needs without concern for others. Like a spoiled child, the id demands what it wants when it wants it. Inevitably it suffers frustration, because the external world cannot tolerate a personality that does whatever he or she pleases. Thus, the id is ineffective in dealing with the realities of the outside world.

Beginning about six to eight months of age, a part of the id becomes specialized to deal with external reality. This part Freud referred to as the **ego,** an outgrowth of the id that is formed to provide direction for a person's impulses in accordance with reality. The ego operates according to the **reality principle**—the goal of delaying gratification of instinctual urges until a suitable object and method are found. The ego keeps the demands of the id in check until a socially appropriate outlet can be found.

At about three to five years of age there emerges the **superego,** an outgrowth of the ego that represents the ideals and values of parents and society. The superego provides an individual with a sense of right and wrong. Through a process called **internalization,** the child adopts as his or her own the rules, restrictions, and moral standards that were originally imposed by the parents. (See Figure 12.2 for a summary of the id, ego, and superego.)

With the development of the superego, the ego has the dual burden of directing the individual's impulses in accord with reality and in accord with the dictates of the superego. In fact, all three parts of the structure—id, ego, and superego—are in constant conflict. This conflict helps to define the individual's personality. In the healthy, mature personality, the ego is able to balance id demands against those of the superego. Impulses are gratified, but in a manner that is both realistic and consistent with the superego's internal standards. But, for some individuals, such balance is not achieved. The id may dominate, resulting in an impulsive, demanding, and selfish personality. Or the superego may dominate, resulting in a strict, rigid, and overconforming personality.

Id: All inherited biological needs and instincts; the ultimate source of all the mental energy that drives the individual.

Pleasure Principle: The goal to obtain pleasure and avoid pain.

Ego: According to Jung, the center of consciousness, a unifying force responsible for our feelings of identity and continuity as human beings.

Reality Principle: The goal of delaying gratification of instinctual urges until a suitable object and method are found.

Superego: An outgrowth of the ego that represents the ideals and values of parents and society.

Internalization: A process in which the child adopts as his or her own the rules, restrictions, and moral standards that were originally imposed by the parents.

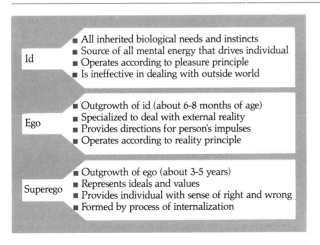

Figure 12.2 Schematic Summary of Id, Ego, and Superego.

Levels of Awareness

The interactions of the id, ego, and superego can be described in terms of three levels of awareness: **conscious,** or those mental activities and phenomena of which an individual is aware at any given moment; **preconscious,** or those mental activities and phenomena of which the individual is not immediately aware but which can be brought into awareness by attending to them; and **unconscious,** or those mental activities and phenomena of which the individual is unaware and cannot bring into awareness, except under special circumstances.

The id is entirely unconscious. The individual is not aware of the inborn instincts or of the basic processes that drive him or her to seek gratification of them. The superego operates at both a conscious and an unconscious level. At the conscious level, the superego represents the inner voice, or conscience, that warns the individual not to do this or that and the feelings of guilt that result if he or she does do it. The superego can also create unconscious guilt that causes the individual to act in certain ways without knowing why. Unconscious guilt, for example, may be a cause of self-destructive behaviors, such as continuing to smoke after one has suffered a heart attack. Because of the unconscious guilt, the person behaves in a way that is self-punishing, without knowing why.

The ego operates at all three levels of awareness. Some of its activities are inaccessible to awareness. Others are part of immediate awareness or

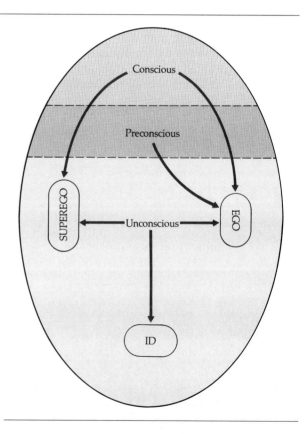

Figure 12.3 The Three-part Structure in Relation to Three Levels of Awareness. This model of Freud's three-part personality structure illustrates how the id is exclusively unconscious, the superego conscious and unconscious, and the ego conscious, preconscious, and unconscious. (Adapted from Freud, 1933).

can readily be brought into awareness. (Figure 12.3 illustrates the id, ego, and superego in relation to the three levels of awareness.)

Defense Mechanisms

The ego is best understood in terms of its **defense mechanisms**—mechanisms it uses to control anxiety as it deals with the conflicting demands of the id, superego, and external world. Through its defense mechanisms, the ego unconsciously distorts reality or excludes experiences from awareness (Freud, 1946). Though the person may be aware of his or her actions, the motives for them remain hidden. The particular defense mechanisms that an individual relies on further help to define the personality.

In **repression,** anxiety-provoking thoughts, desires, or memories are made unconscious and thus inaccessible to conscious awareness. Although removed from awareness, repressed material continues to affect one's behavior in irrational and sometimes bizarre ways (Freud, 1915). For instance, a child who is toilet-trained harshly must exert unusually strong control over her physical functions in order to gain her parent's love and support. To escape the painful memory of this conflict, the child may repress the experience. Later in life, however, she may exert unusually strong control over all of her behavior in an unconscious desire to gain acceptance. She may become compulsively neat and tidy, a perfectionist who spends hours fussing over every last detail on every task. At a conscious level, she does so because she wants to; the real cause of her behavior, an unconscious striving to gain acceptance, escapes her.

In another defense mechanism, **projection,** the individual attributes his or her own unacceptable impulses to another person. For example, you may have an aggressive impulse toward your brother, your boss, or your rival on the swimming team. But this primitive impulse from your id conflicts with your superego, causing you anxiety. To relieve the conflict, your ego distorts reality so that, as far as you're concerned, it is the other person—brother, boss, rival—who wants to hurt you. In short, you take your own impulse and attribute it to the other person.

Another defense mechanism is **rationalization,** in which the individual attempts to justify what otherwise would be unacceptable behavior. In rationalization, a behavior is reinterpreted to make it acceptable. Some college students use rationalization to justify cheating on their exams. They tell themselves something like, "Everybody cheats; if I don't I'll be at a disadvantage."

If you get caught doing something you aren't supposed to be doing, and deny any wrongdoing, you're using the defense mechanism called **denial,** in which an individual attempts to cope with threatening experiences by denying their existence. Denial is a typical early reaction to a loss or a tragedy. On being informed of the death of a loved one, the bereaved person often responds, "No, it isn't true."

In still another defense mechanism, **reaction formation,** the individual deals with unacceptable impulses by taking an extreme position against them. People who crusade against the sale of sexually arousing materials may be displaying a reaction formation against their impulse to read them. To counter the unacceptable impulse, they take the opposite point of view

Defense Mechanisms: Mechanisms used by the ego to control anxiety as it deals with the conflicting demands of the id, superego, and external world.

Repression: A defense mechanism in which anxiety-provoking thoughts, desires, or memories are made unconscious and thus inaccessible to conscious awareness.

Projection: Defense mechanism in which the individual attributes his or her own unacceptable impulses to another person.

Rationalization: Defense mechanism in which the individual attempts to justify what otherwise would be unacceptable behavior.

Denial: Defense mechanism in which the individual attempts to cope with threatening experiences by denying their existence.

Reaction Formation: Defense mechanism in which the individual deals with unacceptable impulses by taking an extreme position against them.

*Table 12.1 **Summary Table of Defense Mechanisms***

Repression	Anxiety-provoking thoughts, desires, or memories are made unconscious and thus inaccessible to awareness.
Projection	Individual attributes his or her unacceptable impulses to another person.
Rationalization	Individual attempts to justify what would otherwise be unacceptable behavior.
Denial	Individual attempts to cope with threatening experiences by denying their existence.
Reaction Formation	Individual deals with unacceptable impulses by taking an extreme position against them.
Sublimation	Sexual and aggressive impulses are channeled into socially acceptable outlets.

and attack pornography. Freud (1940) believed that anyone who takes a strong stand on matters involving sexuality or aggression may be using reaction formation as a defense. If someone suggests that you might have some aggressive feelings toward your father, and you protest violently, your protest would be viewed as a reaction formation against your feelings of aggression. The dilemma is, you can't win. If you agree that you have these feelings the matter is settled. If you disagree, you're displaying a reaction formation.

Sublimation: Defense mechanism in which sexual and aggressive impulses are channeled into socially acceptable outlets.

In still another defense mechanism, **sublimation**, sexual and aggressive impulses are channeled into socially acceptable outlets. The artist redirects his sexual impulses to painting; the surgeon redirects her hostile impulses to help people rather than hurt them (see Table 12.1).

According to Freud, reliance on defense mechanisms is a normal part of everyday behavior. Throughout the day people rationalize their actions, project their unacceptable impulses onto others, and sublimate their sexual and aggressive impulses into socially acceptable pursuits. When certain defenses, such as denial and repression, are used to an extreme, however, or when one's defenses fail to ward off anxiety, an abnormal behavioral pattern may develop. We will discuss these abnormal patterns and Freud's treatment of them in Chapters 14 and 15.

Stages of Development

Stages of Psychosexual Development: According to Freud, a fixed sequence of stages in which personality development proceeded.

Freud believed that the development of the personality proceeded in a fixed, biologically determined sequence of stages, which he referred to as the **stages of psychosexual development.** During each stage of psychosexual development, the energies of the id's pleasure-seeking sexual and life-preserving instincts, known as **libido,** focus on different regions of the body: first the mouth, second the anus, and third the genitals. These regions, or **erogenous zones**—areas of the body capable of producing pleasure when stimulated—become the major source of excitation and energy. Traumatic

Libido: The sexual and life-preserving instincts of the id.

Erogenous Zones: Areas of the body capable of producing pleasure when stimulated.

events at any given stage may result in **fixation,** in which the energies of the libido become attached to a specific stage of development. Fixation occurs due to excessive stimulation, unusual deprivation, or alternations between extremes during a particular stage of development; it results in long-term personality characteristics.

During the first eighteen months of life, the **oral stage** of psychosexual development, the energies of the libido focus on the mouth, tongue, and gums, and the child demands pleasure through sucking, swallowing, and biting. Harsh attempts to wean the infant, overindulgence, or alternation between these extremes may result in fixation at this stage and produce a number of oral personality characteristics. The individual may become sarcastic, symbolically biting at others. Or, the person may become highly gullible (willing to swallow anything). Because of the infant's extreme dependency, fixation during the oral stage may lead to lifelong patterns of overdependency.

From about ages two to three years, the **anal stage** of psychosexual development, the energies of the libido are redirected to the anal zone of the body. During this stage the infant becomes aware of the pleasure of bowel movements (Freud, 1925). But during this time too, the parents begin to toilet train the child, and the infant's desire for pleasure is thwarted. The pleasure of bowel movements becomes counterbalanced by the parent's insistence on the control of bowel movements.

Harsh or inconsistent attempts to toilet train may result in fixation at this stage and produce a number of anal personality characteristics. The individual may become withholding, or what is sometimes called anal-retentive. Anal-retentive individuals, in a symbolic attempt to withhold their feces, are excessively neat, orderly, stubborn, and miserly. By contrast, the individual may become anal-expulsive, sloppy, acquiescent, and overgenerous.

Fixation: The attachment of the energies of the libido to a specific stage of psychosexual development.

Oral Stage: The stage of psychosexual development that occurs during the first year of life, in which the energies of the libido focus on the mouth, tongue, and gums, and the child demands pleasure through sucking, swallowing, and biting.

Anal Stage: The stage of psychosexual development that occurs during the second year of life, in which the energies of the libido are redirected to the anal zone of the body.

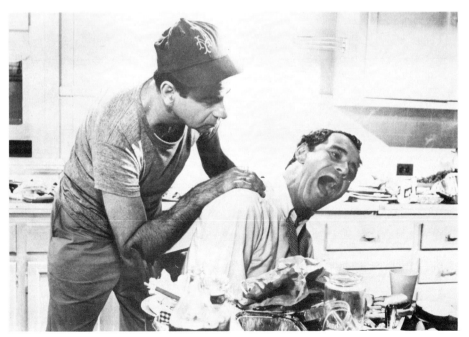

Felix Unger (Jack Lemmon) and Oscar Madison (Walter Matthau) from the movie "The Odd Couple" are perfect examples of individuals with "anal" personalities; the neat, precise Felix is anal-retentive, while the sloppy, relaxed Oscar is anal-expulsive.

Phallic Stage: In Freudian theory, the third stage of development, taking place in the third to fifth year of life, in which the child becomes aware of sex differences and develops sexual desires.

Castration Anxiety: A boy's fear that his father will retaliate against him for his sexual desire for his mother by cutting off his genitals.

Oedipus Conflict: A young boy's (age three to five years) sexual desire for his mother and desire to eliminate his father.

Electra Complex: A young girl's (age three to five) sexual desire for her father and desire to eliminate her mother.

Beginning at about age three and lasting until about age five or six, the energies of the libido are once again redirected, this time to the genital zone of the body. During this **phallic stage** of psychosexual development, the child becomes aware of the physical differences between the sexes and develops sexual desires. The boy becomes acutely aware of his penis and the girl of her lack of one. Freud (1933) believed that in this stage the child derived pleasure and gratification from physical contact with the parents, especially while being changed, bathed, or nursed.

Eventually the child's craving for parental contact develops into a preference for the parent of the opposite sex—and an envy of the parent of the same sex, who becomes the child's rival for the other parent's affection. Secretly the child wishes to eliminate the rival parent, a thought that causes the child intense fear or anxiety. A boy may fear that his father will retaliate by cutting off his genitals, a dread known as **castration anxiety.** The boy's sexual desire for his mother and desire to eliminate his father is known as the **Oedipus conflict,** after the mythical Greek king who unknowingly killed his father and married his mother. In the girl, sexual desire for her father and wish to eliminate her mother is known as the **Electra complex,** after Electra, who, in Greek mythology, induced her brother to murder their hated mother.

Freud believed that successful resolution of the Oedipus and Electra complexes is necessary to prevent fixation at the phallic stage. In the boy, this resolution occurs when he begins to identify with his father, taking on the father's characteristics and gaining some vicarious or indirect satisfaction of his sexual impulses toward his mother. In the girl, resolution of the Electra complex is less pressing, because she does not have to fear castration in pursuing her sexual desires for the father. Consequently, Freud believed that fixation was much more likely to occur for boys than for girls during the phallic stage (Freud, 1940). Fixation during this stage resulted in such characteristics as immaturity, an excessive concern for sexual activity, and self-love (vanity).

The phallic stage is followed by a *latency* period in which the child's erotic desires become deemphasized. Lasting between ages six to twelve years, the latency period is not a psychosexual stage of development. The libido is not focused on an erogenous zone; fixation cannot occur. The child concentrates on exploring and adjusting to the world outside the home. Friendships with peers of the same sex characterize the latency period.

Friendships with peers of the same sex characterize the latency period.

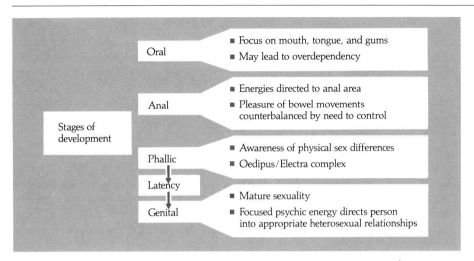

Figure 12.4 Schematic Summary of Freud's Psychosexual Stages of Development.

Stages of development

Oral
- Focus on mouth, tongue, and gums
- May lead to overdependency

Anal
- Energies directed to anal area
- Pleasure of bowel movements counterbalanced by need to control

Phallic
- Awareness of physical sex differences
- Oedipus/Electra complex

Latency

Genital
- Mature sexuality
- Focused psychic energy directs person into appropriate heterosexual relationships

At puberty the sexual energies of the libido reawaken and again focus on the genitals. This final stage, the **genital phase** of psychosexual development, is characterized by mature sexuality—a desire for sexual intercourse, reproduction, and interest in other people. Fixation is not a problem at this stage because this is where the libido should be focused in a psychologically healthy and mature adult. And Freud (1933) believed that, as long as the majority of libido successfully reaches this last stage, there will be sufficient psychic (mental) energy to direct the person to appropriate heterosexual relationships. Figure 12.4 summarizes Freud's stages of psychosexual development. For more on Freud's stages of development, see Chapter 2.

Genital Phase: The stage of psychosexual development, beginning at puberty, which is characterized by mature sexuality—a desire for sexual intercourse, reproduction, and interest in other people.

Evaluation of Freudian Theory

Freud's theory has been a matter of controversy throughout most of this century. His three-part structure of personality, hypothetical levels of awareness, concept of defense mechanisms, and stages of psychosexual development have all been subjects of intense debate among scholars.

On the positive side, the constructs that Freud used to describe personality—id, ego, superego, fixation, repression, and the like—continue to provide therapists with a useful framework in thinking about problem behaviors. Freud's system of psychoanalysis, as we see in Chapters 14 and 15, continues to be used to understand and to treat abnormal patterns of behavior. And many of Freud's ideas have been supported, at least in part, by research (Luborsky & Spence, 1978).

Support for Freud's notion of a three-part personality structure has come from psychological tests that are used to measure various aspects of the personality. For example, according to Freudian theory, the reality-oriented ego keeps the id's blatantly sexual and aggressive impulses out of awareness, where they might generate anxiety or provoke inappropriate behavior. Presumably, if the ego were to falter in its duties, the id's impulses would break into awareness. And that is what seems to happen to schizophrenics, who suffer from a loss of contact with reality (see Chapter 14). When tested, schizophrenics give more responses of a sexual and aggressive nature than do nonschizophrenic control subjects to the Rorschach inkblots (Exner, 1974, 1981; Hayden, 1981). (The Rorschach test is described on page 448.) Although indirect and far from conclusive, such evidence shows that Freud's view of personality is not entirely speculative.

But critics have argued that support for Freudian theory is weak and, at best, inconclusive (Fisher & Greenberg, 1977; Holmes, 1974). For instance, in Freudian theory, alcoholism is interpreted as the result of oral fixation—a lifelong quest for oral gratification. Investigations into the cause of alcoholism, however, have failed to support the idea that infant feeding patterns are related to alcoholism. And other research has shown that, contrary to Freud's notion of a period of sexual latency, sexual experimentation continues throughout childhood (Kolodny, 1980). Most experts, in fact, view such activity as a valuable developmental experience (Money, 1980).

While the debate over Freud's theory has been raging, many alternatives have been proposed, debated, and tested experimentally. Some are closely related to Freud's views; others, which we will discuss later, are much different in their approach to personality.

DEVIATIONS FROM PSYCHOANALYTIC THEORY

Soon after Freud published his psychosexual theory of the personality, other theorists began to propose modifications to it. Like Freud, these neo-Freudians (literally, "new Freudians") based their ideas on keen observation of patients in psychotherapy. Though none of their theories has generated as much attention as Freud's, they do help to round out Freud's theory and illuminate its meaning. We will discuss three of them briefly.

Jung's Theory of the Collective Unconscious

Carl Jung (1875–1961) was so impressed by Freud's early work that he journeyed to Vienna to work with him following three years of regular correspondence that began in 1906 (Jung, 1961). Jung agreed with Freud's emphasis on hidden forces and underlying mechanisms and, in particular, with the notion of unconscious mental activities. He supported the idea of inborn instincts as a driving force for behavior. Like Freud, he viewed the personality in terms of interrelated structures that interact in a struggle for dominance and balance.

During his association with Freud, however, Jung also found many significant points of disagreement. He had a broader view of the unconscious and found it necessary to posit two distinct types of unconscious (personal unconscious and collective unconscious). He believed that Freud overemphasized sexual instincts, arguing that people were driven by nonsexual instincts as well. Jung's view of the structure of personality and the nature of the struggle among its components was quite different from Freud's. Moreover, Jung objected to Freud's assumption that personality is shaped exclusively by past events, such as the way one was weaned or toilet trained. In addition to past determinants, Jung argued that behavior must also be understood in terms of its purpose; people, Jung said, are not only pushed by past experience, they are pulled by their goals and the direction they set for the future. Finally, Jung did not see a need to divide the development of personality into specific stages, as Freud had done. Instead, he saw personality development as a gradual, lifelong unfolding of one's unique characteristics and potentials, a process called **individuation.**

By 1912, the differences between Jung and Freud had become glaringly apparent to both men. According to Jung, in his book, *Memories, Dreams, Reflections* (1961), the more he matured and developed as a theorist, the more disturbed he became by what he saw as a lack of scientific rigor in Freud's approach and in Freud's refusal to even consider alternative views. The turning point in the relationship between the two men came when Freud insisted that they must protect Freud's psychoanalytic theory "at all costs" (Jung, 1961). By 1913, Jung and Freud had severed their professional ties to each other. Jung subsequently resigned from his post as president of the psychoanalytic society to establish his own approach called analytical psychology.

Individuation: According to Jung, a gradual, lifelong unfolding of one's unique chracteristics and potentials.

■ Learning Check ■

For each question: read, cover, try to recite, repeat.

1. *Question:* What did Freud and Jung have in common?

1. *Answer:* Both:

Emphasized hidden forces and underlying mechanisms.

Believed in the existence of unconscious mental activities of which the individual is unaware.

Viewed personality in terms of interrelated structures that interact in a struggle for balance and dominance.

2. *Question:* In what ways was Jung different from Freud?

2. *Answer:* Jung:

Believed that there were nonsexual instincts as well as sexual and objected to Freud's emphasis on the latter.

Took a broader view of unconscious and posited two distinct types of unconscious.

Had a different view of the specific components of personality and the nature of their interaction.

Believed that behavior is determined by future (goals) as well as by past events.

Ego: In Freudian theory, outgrowth of the id that is formed to provide direction for a person's impulses in accordance with reality.

Personal Unconscious: According to Jung, all personal experiences that are not in awareness, including those that can be brought into awareness by attending to them and those that are blocked from awareness.

Collective Unconscious: Inborn memories, instincts, and predispositions that the individual inherits.

Archetypes: According to Jung, universal thought forms and emotions which predispose the individual to perceive the world in particular ways.

Persona: An archetype consisting of the role a person plays to meet the demands of others and express innermost feelings in an acceptable way.

Jung maintained that there were three basic components to the personality: the ego, the personal unconscious, and the collective unconscious. Jung's concept of the ego was quite different from Freud's. For him, the **ego** was the center of consciousness, a unifying force responsible for our feelings of identity and continuity as human beings (Jung, 1917). It begins to develop at about the fourth year of life and results from experiences that led the person to distinguish "I" from "non-I." Unlike Freud's conceptualization of ego, Jung's operated only at a conscious level and did not act as an intermediary between instinctual (id) urges and internalized (superego) standards.

The **personal unconscious** refers to all personal experiences that are not in awareness, including those that can be brought into awareness by attending to them and those that are blocked from awareness. Jung's personal unconscious encompasses Freud's notions of both preconscious and unconscious. The personal unconscious is so called because its contents are those that the individual has personally experienced. It begins to form just after birth.

The **collective unconscious,** by contrast, is inborn and consists of memories, instincts, and predispositions that the individual inherits. The collective unconscious is formed by the experiences of generations past, transmitted from parent to offspring (Jung, 1917, 1943). From time immemorial, Jung argued, all humans have had certain common experiences. All are born; all have a mother; all experience the natural rhythm of day and night. Jung believed that the memory of these common experiences is passed from generation to generation in the genes. His conception of the collective unconscious thus added past generations, ancient ancestors, and even animal forebears to the list of theoretical influences on the human personality and behavior.

Jung believed that the collective unconscious exerts its influence through a number of specific structures he called **archetypes**—universal thought forms and emotions which predispose the individual to perceive the world in particular ways. The idea of mother, for instance, is common to all cultures. Jung would have said that you inherit an archetype of mother and instinctually seek to find in your own mother the universal qualities of this mother archetype. Thus, you are predisposed to see your mother as good and kind and nurturing. Your perception of your mother is influenced not only by archetypal images, however, but by your personal experience of her. If your real-life mother deviates markedly from your archetypal mother, you could develop psychological problems, according to Jung (1943).

Other archetypes include the young hero, the wise old man, God, good and evil, and the magic wand that can transform lead into gold, or humans into animals—all symbols that recur throughout the world's literature and legends and occult religions. Jung also noted fundamental similarities of theme in his patient's dreams: pursuit by a dark, mysterious figure; running as fast as possible but getting nowhere. Such similarities, he felt, stemmed from universal fears, the archetypal heritage of all people. And indeed, though magic is rarely practiced nowadays, and people pride themselves on their skepticism toward old-fashioned attitudes, the archetypes still seem to be with us. Jung would have recognized the appeal to archetypal symbols in contemporary movies that depict good against bad; the warrior who overcomes powerful evil forces in the pursuit of justice.

One important archetype is the **persona**—the role a person plays in order to meet the demands of others and express innermost feelings in an acceptable way. The persona is like the clown's painted smile that masks the pain inside. Another archetype, the **shadow,** represents the inferior, evil, or dark side of a person. The **self** is the archetype that represents the person's inner potential and strivings.

Jung viewed the interaction among the personality structures in terms of a struggle between opposite forces of equal strength. The persona opposes the feelings and attitudes it masks. These feelings and attitudes, in turn, struggle, with equal force, to manifest themselves. The outward expressions of behavior are thus compensated for by an equally strong opposing tendency in the person's subjective experiences. The waitress who wears a mask of cheer and enthusiasm all day is despondent when alone and pessimistic about her own life, for instance.

Another illustration of opposing opposite tendencies can be seen in the archetypes for femininity (**anima**) and masculinity (**animus**). If anima is outwardly expressed, the person will manifest characteristics associated with femininity, such as nurturance and sensitivity to the feelings of others. Its opposite, animus, will be manifest to an equal degree in the person's subjective life. Such a person, for example, might have fantasies or dreams of being assertive and dominant. Jung believed that the ideal is to strike a balance in the outward expression of one's opposing forces. The same person could be nurturant or dominant, sensitive or assertive, as circumstances demand.

Another important set of opposing tendencies are the attitudes of extroversion and introversion. **Extroversion** represents the outgoing, carefree, bold side of one's personality; **introversion,** the reserved, serious, introspective, shy side. Each person manifests a certain degree of extroversion and introversion in outward behavior. For Jung, the more extreme one's outward behavior in either of these qualities, the more extreme its opposite would be manifest in subjective life. The overly shy individual has fantasies dominated by themes of exhibitionism, for instance. Thus, there is an opposite side to every person: for everything that is manifest on the outside, an equally powerful, but hidden, force lurks within (see Figure 12.5).

The idea that an organism can inherit anything as a result of the experience of previous generations is contrary to widely held convention. If your mother plays the flute, you might become a good flute player yourself, but only because of inherited musical ability, encouragement, and the opportu-

Shadow: An archetype that represents the inferior, evil, or dark side of a person.

Self: An archetype that represents the person's inner potential and strivings.

Anima: In Jungian theory, the feminine archetype, which both males and females possess.

Animus: In Jungian theory, the masculine archetype, which both males and females possess.

Extroversion: According to Jung, the outgoing, carefree, bold side of one's personality.

Introversion: According to Jung, the reserved, serious, introspective, shy side of one's personality.

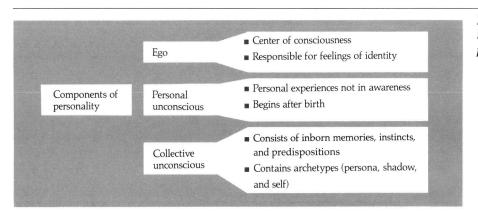

Figure 12.5 Schematic Summary of Jung's Components of Personality.

nity to practice, and a desire to learn. As far as modern science is concerned, none of your mother's experience with flute playing would be passed down to you through your genes. Because Jung's notion of the collective unconscious implies just such a genetic transmission of characteristics, his entire theory has been questioned by some. Others have criticized Jung's theory as overcomplex and lacking in empirical support (Stern, 1976).

On the positive side, Jung's views provided the basis for an approach to psychotherapy that is still in use today. Moreover, many of the ideas, such as his concept of the self and his distinction between introversion and extroversion, have been incorporated into the theories of others. And, when very specific predictions are made, for instance, that introverts and extroverts will differ in their responses to social situations, positive results have been found (Kilmann & Taylor, 1974). Additional efforts to support Jung's theory continue in the *Journal of Analytical Psychology*, published by the World Medical Association.

Adler's Theory of Social Interest

Another deviation from Freud's psychoanalytic theory came from Alfred Adler (1870–1937)—like Jung, an independent thinker who was more a collaborator than a student of Freud. Adler worked with Freud for several years before fundamental disagreements destroyed their relationship.

Adler could not reconcile himself to the idea of dividing the personality into parts. Instead, he regarded personality as an indivisible unity (Adler, 1927). Although he agreed with the notion of an unconscious—that much of the personality is beyond awareness—he didn't think that there was one part of the mind that was blocked from another. Instead, we remain unaware because of lack of self-understanding and self-knowledge. Like Jung, Adler believed that behavior is determined by goals and intentions as well as by past experience. Adler did not propose specific developmental stages. He rejected the idea that the person is primarily driven by animalistic (id) impulses, and he posited the existence of a nonsexual driving force—the impulse to relate to and be with others, and to adapt oneself to them—which he called **social interest.** Though Adler called his approach *individual psychology*—he wanted to underscore the uniqueness of each individual—his focus on social interest was his real contribution. It added a new dimension to the study of human personality, the influence of others on the acquisition and development of one's distinctive patterns of behavior.

Social Interest: The impulse to relate to and be with others, and to adapt oneself to them.

One example of the formative influence of others is the effect of the order of birth on children's personalities. Adler believed that birth order could have profound, lifelong consequences. Being born first, for example, would predispose a child to be dependent and anxious, because parents tend to be overprotective of firstborns. In an attempt to do everything just right, they hover over the child, giving help that isn't needed and praise that isn't deserved. Such actions tend to discourage independence and foster feelings of inadequacy in the child (Adler, 1933).

A middle-born child, less protected by parents and driven by the urge to compete with older brothers and sisters, tends to be independent. Unlike the firstborn, who, if circumstances permit, stays close to home as an adult and adopts the parents' values, middle-borns do best on their own, and

Adler believed that birth order could have a profound lifelong effect.

they fare well in society. Last-borns, Adler believed, are the most dependent of all. With older siblings around to watch and take care of them, they develop a passive life-style. Even in adulthood they prefer to have others do things for them.

Studies have confirmed that firstborns are more like each other in terms of their dependency, their need to be with others, and their response to painful stimuli than they are like their sisters and brothers. In one classic study, female subjects were led to believe they would be shocked. Some subjects were told that the shocks would be very painful, others that they would hardly feel it. All were told that they would have to wait ten minutes as part of the experiment, and all were given the option of waiting alone or with others. The result: significantly more firstborns chose to wait with others, regardless of whether or not they expected a painful experience. When asked to rate their fear, moreover, firstborns reported significantly more anxiety than later-borns (Schachter, 1959). Some scientists have wondered whether the firstborn's heightened fear of pain is connected to their comparatively low participation rate in dangerous sports like football (Nisbett, 1968).

Too many factors besides birth order can influence a child's development, however. What about the number of years separating the births? If two children are born many years apart, wouldn't the second-born be more like a firstborn? And if parents have only two children, is the second-born more like a middle-born or a last-born? The theory is less than precise on many such questions (Schooler, 1972).

Although the findings on birth order are not as clear as Adler would have predicted, the idea that the social environment can and does play an important role in the development of the personality is well documented.

Today, social interests are recognized as one of the key building blocks that shape personality. References to Adler's work can be found in many contemporary journals, and efforts to verify, elaborate, and modify his views continue in the *Journal of Individual Psychology*.

Horney's Theory of the Need for Security

Karen Horney (1885–1952) attempted to represent psychoanalytic theory from a female standpoint. Horney (pronounced "Horn-eye") was a second-generation theorist—schooled in Freud's psychoanalytic approach—who disagreed significantly with traditional Freudian views and went on to develop her own theory. Freud, she argued, had approached psychology from a traditionally male standpoint, the view that women are inferior to men. To describe the jealousy he believed young girls feel when they realize they lack a penis—an omission that, according to Freud, is symbolic of their inferiority—Freud had coined the term "penis envy." Horney contradicted such sexist teachings. If women achieve less than men, she suggested, they do so, not because of an inborn inferiority to men, but because of the unequal opportunities and negative attitudes imposed on them by a male-dominated society. Horney charged that, in reality, men are envious of women's ability to bear children (Horney, 1967).

For males as well as females, Horney believed, the need for safety and satisfaction is a major factor in the development of the personality. Healthy personalities, like healthy bodies, need a safe and secure environment to grow up in. Parents, by communicating a sense of love, warmth, and affection to the child, provided such an environment. Indifferent, inconsistent, or rejecting parents, by failing to provide the proper environment, create a deep sense of anxiety, which she called **basic anxiety,** in the child.

Basic Anxiety: A deep sense of anxiety in a child caused by a failure of the parents to provide a safe and secure environment.

The way a person deals with basic anxiety does much to determine his or her personality. Horney identified three major behavioral patterns that might emerge from a child's attempt to cope with basic anxiety; which she called moving-toward-people, moving-against-people, and moving-away-from-people (Horney, 1937). Whereas a healthy personality integrates these three patterns, an unhealthy personality rigidly relies on only one to an extreme.

Children who adopt the moving-toward-people strategy become passive and compliant. Declaring themselves helpless, they place their destiny in the hands of a more powerful figure on whom they rely for support, reassurance, and protection. To obtain this person's approval, they will give up their own needs, interests, and prerogatives, no matter how painful the sacrifice is. A person with a moving-against-people strategy, by contrast, becomes aggressively independent. Because such people view others as threats or enemies to be dominated and controlled, they are overly concerned with matters of position, power, status, and authority. Those who adopt the moving-away-from-people strategy, finally, deal with anxiety by detaching themselves from others. They attempt to build a psychological wall around themselves, so that no one can penetrate their defenses and hurt them.

Horney's characterization of unhealthy personality as excessively dependent, independent, or detached is consistent with modern thinking on abnormal personality patterns (Millon, 1981). We will explore these basic personality types further, in relation to mental and emotional disorders, in Chapter 14. For now, let us turn to another major approach to personality, one which views personality in terms of basic dispositional tendencies called traits.

■ **Learning Clue** ■

Trait theorists attempt to account for the consistency of behavior across different situations.

TRAIT THEORISTS

Trait theorists conceptualize personality in terms of **dispositions**—tendencies to act, think, or feel in a certain manner. Dispositions that are relatively enduring and that distinguish one individual from another are called **traits.** Traits account for individual differences in behavior—for why different people respond differently to the same stimulus—and for the consistency of behavior for any given individual across different situations. An easygoing person responds to an unintended insult with laughter; an aggressive person with a verbal counterattack. A person's traits are presumed to apply across different situations. When the easygoing person and the aggressive person are exposed to the same situation, each will respond according to their predominant traits.

According to trait theorists, traits represent the basic underlying mechanism of personality. They believe that personality can best be described in terms of different degrees of a given number of traits. The structure of personality is viewed in terms of a person's traits or clusters of related traits and their relative strength. The dynamics of personality are viewed in terms of how traits interact.

Dispositions: Tendencies to act, think, or feel in a certain manner.

Traits: Relatively enduring dispositions (tendencies to act, think, or feel in a certain manner in a given circumstance) that distingish one individual from another.

Trait theorists conceptualize personality in terms of dispositions—tendencies to act, think, and feel in a certain manner. Thus, it can be assumed that if a person is being helpful in one situation, she will act accordingly in other situations.

A major goal of trait theorists is to identify the most important human traits and to describe their interrelationships (Buss & Poley, 1977). Trait theorists also attempt to determine how traits are acquired—that is, whether they are inborn or learned—and how they become organized. Finally, trait theorists are concerned with finding dependable ways of measuring individual differences in traits through tests and other techniques. In this section we will briefly explore the ideas of three major trait theorists: Gordon Allport, Raymond B. Cattell, and Hans Eysenck.

Allport's Three Kinds of Traits

Gordon Allport (1897–1967) was the first researcher to base a theory of personality on the concept of traits. He struck out on his own as a theorist as the result of a rather unpleasant meeting with Freud, which he described in his autobiography (1967). Nervous and intimidated by the world-renowned psychoanalyst, Allport couldn't think of a thing to say. As he did with patients, Freud sat in silence waiting for Allport to speak. Seconds seemed like minutes. Finally, Allport told Freud about a little boy he had seen on the way to Freud's office, who seemed to have a fear of dirt. No wonder, observed, Allport, considering the boy's "well starched" mother. "And was that little boy you?" Freud replied.

Allport was flabbergasted. How dare Freud treat him like a patient? His brief encounter with the man convinced him that there was something fundamentally wrong with the psychoanalytic approach: an overemphasis on hidden, unconscious forces. He went back to school to obtain a Ph.D. in psychology and then devoted himself to developing a genuine alternative to psychoanalytic theory.

In sharp contrast to the Freudians, Allport organized his theory around the single concept of traits. He did distinguish among various kinds of traits, however. The most pervasive traits, those that influence practically every aspect of a person's life, he called **cardinal traits.** Cardinal traits can be seen (or identified) in nearly every aspect of a person's behavior. The external optimism that disposes some people to see everything through rose-colored glasses is a good example of a cardinal trait. Less pervasive traits that influence some but not all major aspects of a person's behavior he referred to as **central traits.** Much of Allport's work, in fact, was devoted to the identification of individuals' central traits. He believed that any personality could be described reasonably well in terms of six to ten central traits (Allport, 1937, 1961). One of Allport's subjects, for example, was described in terms of eight central traits: quarrelsome, self-centered, independent, dramatic, artistic, aggressive, cynical, and sentimental (Allport, 1965). Try to imagine what she was like. Because central traits are general and apply to many aspects of a person's behavior, they can be used to make predictions about future behavior. How would you predict Allport's subject (described above) to react if she didn't like the way a hairstylist had cut her hair? Would she passively accept the outcome, thank the stylist for a fine job to avoid hurting his feelings, and leave a big tip?

Traits that are highly specific and narrow were dubbed **secondary traits:** they apply only to a restricted segment of an individual's life. All of a person's preferences are secondary traits. A person may prefer chocolate ice

Cardinal Traits: Pervasive traits that influence nearly every aspect of a person's life.

Central Traits: Traits that influence major aspects of a person's life; less pervasive than cardinal traits.

Secondary Traits: Traits that are highly specific and narrow; traits that apply to a restricted segment of an individual's life.

■ Learning Check ■

For each type of trait, read the definition, then cover the right side and try to recite. Repeat.

Cardinal Traits	Traits that influence and that can be seen in nearly every aspect of a person's behavior.
Central Traits	Traits that influence major aspects of a person's life.
Secondary Traits	Highly specific and narrow traits that apply only to a restricted segment of an individual's life.

---

cream over butterscotch, for instance. Such traits are highly limited and tell us little about the person in general.

Allport (1961) believed that personality formation begins at birth and is based on a person's physiological endowments and unique experiences with others. Neural cells, present at birth, permit the formation of a number of conditional reflexes. Reflexes combine into habits; the integration of habits, in turn, becomes a trait. The organization and interaction of all of a person's traits are the total personality.

Although Allport built his theory around the trait concept, there were other important aspects to his theory. During the course of personality development, he believed, the person develops a basic sense of self-awareness. From this self-awareness the individual comes to distinguish between himself or herself and the environment, developing a sense of self, or what Allport referred to as the **proprium**—the unifying core of the personality. Included in the proprium are a number of distinctly personal aspects of existence such as one's sense of continuing self-identity, one's self-image, and one's conscience.

Proprium: According to Allport, a sense of self; the unifying core of the personality.

Cattell's Sixteen-Factor Theory

Allport was only the first of a group of trait theorists. His interest in identifying the most important human traits is shared by Raymond B. Cattell (1905–), who introduced the use of sophisticated statistical techniques in the study of personality.

Cattell used psychological tests like those described at the end of the chapter to measure the strength of subjects' traits. Then he searched for correlations, or statistical relationships, among specific traits. If people who scored high on measures of suspiciousness also scored high on measures of skepticism, then he concluded that suspiciousness and skepticism were related. The two traits are related, though scientists can't say why. But they can say that, because the two occur together in the same people, both may be related to some third, more basic, factor, such as a mistrust of others.

To single out such basic factors, Cattell used another statistical technique, called **factor analysis**—a mathematical procedure for sorting trait items or test responses into clusters of related groups. Factor analysis allows researchers to determine the interrelationships among dozens or even hundreds of variables. Once clusters of related variables have been identified, researchers can look for a single factor common to each cluster. In this way,

Factor Analysis: A mathematical procedure for sorting trait items or test responses into clusters or related groups.

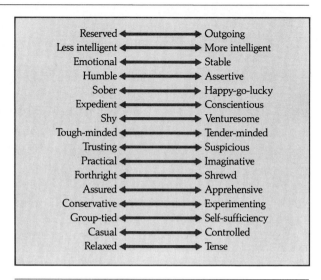

Figure 12.6 Each of Cattell's 16 dimensions or source traits applies in varying degrees to every person. For example, each person can be described in terms of some degree ranging from reserved to outgoing; each can also be described in terms of some degree of emotional to stable, etc. (After Cattell, 1965).

large numbers of related variables can be reduced to a smaller number of basic factors.

A summary of one of Cattell's studies will give some idea of the enormity of the task. Cattell began with a list of more than 4,500 traits compiled by Allport (Allport & Odbert, 1936). He reduced the list by eliminating all synonyms. If he had already included *confident*, he eliminated *self-assured*, *certain*, *sure*, and *self-reliant*. He was left with a list of about 170 traits, which he asked subjects to rate their friends and relatives on.

Cattell was able to reduce his list of 170 traits to sixteen independent factors, because most items on the list were correlated. Factor analysis revealed, for example, that people who were rated as submissive were also rated as dependent, considerate, diplomatic, obedient, docile, accommodating, humble, and conventional. Because people who exhibit any one of these characteristics also tend to exhibit the others, Cattell assumed that all nine have some fundamental property in common (Cattell, 1957, 1965). Thus, they could be reduced to one distinguishable underlying factor, or source trait, rather than nine separate characteristics. For Cattell, the sixteen **source traits** (see Figure 12.6) that he identified through factor analysis represent the basic elements of personality (Cattell, 1973, 1976; Cattell & Kline, 1976). Each applies in varying degrees to every person. (For a discussion of the personality questionnaire that Cattell developed to measure the sixteen source traits see page 447.)

Source Traits: According to R. B. Cattell, the basic elements of personality.

Eysenck's Theory of Personality Types

Whereas Cattell's massive factor analytic studies revealed sixteen independent elements of personality—distinguishable traits that each apply to people in varying degrees—work conducted by Hans Eysenck (1916–) has been geared toward the discovery of a smaller number of **personality types**—basic dimensions that underlie traits. The difference between Eysenck and Cattell lies at the level at which each looks for the basic dimensions of personality. Whereas Cattell looks for the elements of personality,

Personality Types: Basic dimensions that underlie traits.

Eysenck looks for broad general categories, or types, that presumably underlie these elements. Thus, Eysenck takes matters a step further and tries to determine if Cattell's sixteen source traits can, themselves, be further grouped into even more general categories.

From his studies, Eysenck (1967, 1970) has found evidence for two basic dimensions that presumably underlie all traits. One, called neuroticism, reflects the basic stability or unstability of the personality. The second, introversion–extroversion, is very much like the introversion–extroversion distinction made by Jung (see page 425).

According to Eysenck, those who are high on the **introversion** end of the introversion–extroversion dimension tend to be quiet, reserved people who enjoy contemplating themselves, their environment, the meaning of life, and other questions of philosophical or academic interest. Introverts dislike crowds; they would rather read a book or share an evening with an intimate friend than go to a big party. They characteristically avoid excitement, preferring to fish or row on a calm river rather than ride the white rapids. Emotionally, introverts tend to control their feelings and are rarely aggressive. They are cautious people who prefer to plan ahead and act on the basis of careful deliberation. They prefer occupations in which they do not have to interact much with others. Generally, they can be characterized as steady, reliable people (Eysenck, 1975). Thus, introversion underlies a large cluster of related traits.

People who are high on the **extroversion** end of the dimension, on the other hand, are described as sociable and outgoing, with many friends. They seem to need to be around other people, so much so that they hate doing anything—reading, studying, fixing their car—alone. Extroverts also have a strong need for excitement: they love to take risks, and they often act on impulse. They don't spend much time planning for the future, philosophizing, or worrying about how others view them. These are generally carefree, easygoing, happy-go-lucky, and likable people. They can become aggressive, however, and they lose their tempers easily (Eysenck, 1970, 1975).

Of course, few people fall at the extreme ends of the introversion–extroversion dimension. Most simply have some tendency toward one extreme or the other. But the importance of introversion–extroversion as an index of personality has been confirmed by numerous studies (Digman & Inouye, 1986; Larson & Saccuzzo, in press; Wilson, 1978). The correlations among the various characteristics associated with either introversion or extroversion are relatively high. And commonsense measures confirm the findings: researchers can usually distinguish people who score high on either characteristic simply by observing their behavior.

Eysenck believes that differences between introverts and extroverts can be traced to inherited differences in the nervous system. Introverts differ from extroverts in their level of physiological arousal and their response to various levels of stimulation (Eysenck & Eysenck, 1969). As one might predict, introverts are far more tolerant of sensory deprivation and isolation than extroverts. Extroverts, however, are more tolerant of physical pain. Perhaps because introverts experience a generally higher state of arousal than extroverts, their response to external stimulation is stronger. Eysenck theorizes that introverts have inherited a nervous system that keeps them in a high state of arousal; thus their avoidance of excitement, crowds, and other conditions that might overstimulate them. Extroverts, underaroused

Introversion: According to Eysenck, one end of a basic introversion–extroversion dimension of personality. People who score high on the introversion end of the dimension tend to be quiet, reserved, and contemplating.

Extroversion: According to Eysenck, one end of a basic introversion–extroversion dimension of personality. People who score high on the extroversion end tend to be sociable and outgoing, with many friends.

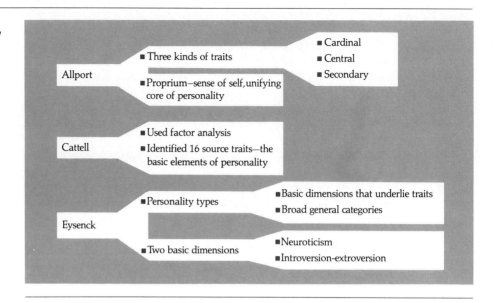

due to their inherited disposition, seek excitement and stimulation. (See Chapter 9 for more information on the theory of an optimal level of arousal.)

In support of the theory of an inherited physiological basis for traits, a number of studies have produced some remarkable similarities in the personalities of identical twins, even those reared apart. If one twin was hot-headed or easygoing or anxious, so was the other. This was true even for a pair of twins who were raised in different countries. One was brought up in Germany as a Catholic and a Nazi; the other on an Israeli kibbutz, as a Jew. Not only were the two remarkably similar in temperament; they also shared a number of unlikely habits, like flushing the toilet before using it, and dipping buttered toast in their coffee (Bouchard et al., 1981; Lykken, 1982).

Critics of trait theory have argued, however, that personality is not so stable from situation to situation as trait theorists suggest (Mischel, 1968). Indeed, trait theorists do acknowledge that the demands of an immediate situation can influence the manner in which a trait is expressed (Allport, 1961; Cattell, 1976). Nevertheless, the emphasis of trait theorists is on internal dispositions that an individual brings to a situation. Figure 12.7 summarizes trait theory and theorists. In the next section we will see how the behavioral theorists view personality from the standpoint of the external environment.

BEHAVIORAL THEORISTS

In contrast to the psychoanalytic and trait theories, which emphasize the role of internal mechanisms and dispositions, behavioral theories focus on behavior and its relation to the external environment. Through hypothetical

Table 12.2 Behavioral Theories vs. Trait and Psychoanalytic Theories

Behavioral Theories	*Trait and Psychoanalytic Theories*
Focus on behavior and its relation to external environment.	Focus on internal mechanisms and dispositions.
Attempt to account for variability of behavior in response to changing circumstances.	Attempt to account for stability of behavior in response to changing circumstances.
Emphasize conditions that affect acquisition, maintenance, and performance of behavior.	Emphasize structure and organization of personality.
Emphasize principles of learning.	Emphasize hypothetical internal mechanisms and processes.

internal mechanisms such as unconscious processes, instincts, and traits, psychoanalytic and trait theorists attempt to account for the stability of behavior in response to changing circumstances. Behavioral theorists, by contrast, attempt to account for the variability of behavior in response to changing circumstances. In so doing, they place less emphasis on the structure and organization of personality and instead focus on the conditions that affect the acquisition, maintenance, and performance of behavior. Behavioral theorists are also distinctive in their emphasis on principles of learning. (Table 12.2 summarizes some of the major distinctions between the behavioral theories and the trait and psychoanalytic theories.) In this section we consider two major types of behavioral theories—traditional behaviorist theory and social learning theory.

Traditional Behaviorist Theory

In Chapter 6 we discussed the theories of learning, including the basic behaviorist concepts of John B. Watson and B. F. Skinner. The behaviorist theory of learning is relevant to all of psychology, including personality. Since behaviorists believe that all behaviors, except the most basic reflexes such as sucking, are learned by direct experience with the environment, they would maintain that even the distinctive behavior patterns that define the personality are acquired through some kind of conditioning.

To be specific, behaviors that bring reinforcing consequences—a reward or an escape from pain, for instance—will tend to be repeated in similar situations. Eventually, if they are repeated often enough in a variety of situations, they may become enduring and distinctive. The twelve-year-old girl who argues with her mother and refuses to give in, for example, may learn to argue if her mother gives in. She is rewarded with getting her own way when she argues, so she continues to argue. If the girl receives other opportunities to argue and win—with her sisters and brothers, cousins, and friends, for instance—she may become a characteristically combative or aggressive person. And, according to behaviorist theory, her actual behavior, not some hypothetical internal mechanism, is her personality.

Behaviorist theory also allows for differences in behavior from one situation to another. If in school the twelve-year-old learns that resistance is of no use, she may become passive in that situation. She repeats the behavior she has been rewarded for only under similar circumstances.

Traditional behaviorist theorists see no need to speculate about hypothetical internal mechanisms such as unconscious processes and traits. Instead, they restrict their studies of personality to observable behavior. For the traditional behaviorist, you are what you do; and what you do is determined by the consequences of your actions as you interact with the environment. Personality, they argue, is learned behavior, acquired by the principles of learning and shaped by environmental consequences.

In studying observable behavior, the traditional behaviorists approach personality with the utmost objectivity. There is no debate concerning which instincts are more important; no assumptions to defend. Today, its important points have been incorporated into the broader, more flexible social learning theory.

Social Learning Theory

Cognition: Beliefs, thoughts, preferences, expectations, self-perceptions, and the like.

Social learning theory retains the behaviorist assumption that personality is learned behavior, but includes **cognition** (beliefs, thoughts, preferences, expectations, self-perceptions, and the like) in its definition of behavior and emphasizes the acquisition of behavior in a social context. In treating cognition as behavior, social learning theorists (sometimes known as cognitive social learning theorists or cognitive learning theorists) could again examine internal processes as well as environmental influences in the acquisition, performance, and maintenance of behavior. An explanation of personality, they argue, must include both the characteristics of the person (for example, traits and cognitions) and the person's environment or situation. They further argue that learning could occur in the absence of direct experience with the environment. A person does not have to receive an actual reward to learn, and behavior need not be performed to be reinforced, according to social learning theorists. Through **observational learning,** or learning by watching, people acquire complex behaviors by watching others. And the way an event is interpreted determines whether it is rewarding or punishing. Much of the theory is founded on the work of Julian Rotter (1916–), Walter Mischel (1930–), and Albert Bandura (1925–).

Observational Learning: Learning by watching; the acquisition of complex behavior by watching others.

Behavior Potential: The probability that a person will display a certain behavior in any given situation.

Expectancy: An anticipated outcome; an individual's estimate of the probability that a behavior will lead to a desired result.

Valence: The importance of a goal or particular outcome to an individual.

Rotter's Concept of Generalized Expectations. Rotter (1954) believed that personality must be studied in the context within which it is expressed—namely, situations. Based on his observations, he proposed that the probability that a person will display a certain behavior in any given situation—which he referred to as the **behavior potential**—depends mainly on two cognitive factors. One is the anticipated outcome, a person's estimation that the behavior will lead to the desired result; Rotter called it **expectancy.** The other is the importance of the outcome to the person, which he dubbed **valence.** (See Chapter 9 for a further discussion of expectancy and valence.)

Like the traditional behaviorists, Rotter recognized that the probability to act in a given situation depends on specific environmental conditions. But he also recognized the importance of internal processes like cognitions.

Rotter allowed, too, for the possibility that some behaviors might be consistent across various situations. He proposed that, through experience, a person may acquire **generalized expectations,** or expectations that apply in a variety of circumstances. One example of a generalized expectation is *locus of control*—a person's beliefs concerning the determinants of rewards and punishments. People with an external locus of control believe that the rewards and punishments they receive are determined by outside forces such as luck, chance, and circumstance. People with an internal locus of control believe that rewards and punishments are the result of their own efforts or choices.

Generalized Expectations: Expectations that apply to a variety of situations.

Generalized expectations such as locus of control underscore the social learning theorists' view concerning the role of cognition in behavior. Such expectations, Rotter believes, help to predict a person's response to any given social situation. Other social learning theorists, by contrast, focus more on the situation itself.

Mischel's Study of Situation-Specific Behaviors. One of Rotter's students, Walter Mischel, inquired into what extent people's behavior is consistent across various situations. He first searched the journals for evidence of such consistency but found very little. Then he examined the various tests that psychologists had devised to measure personality. Mischel (1968) found that, in general, people who score high on one test for a trait, such as extroversion, also tend to score high on most other tests for that trait. And he learned that people are quite consistent in the way they describe themselves. People who rate themselves honest, for example, do so consistently (Mischel, 1968).

Not satisfied to rest the case for consistency of behavior on what people say they do, Mischel tried testing their responses to specific situations. He found that just about every trait he tested varied across different situations. Aggression, dependency, self-control, sociability, response to authority, leadership—all differed in strength in the same person, depending on the circumstances (Mischel, 1968). A man who customarily exhibits aggression to his wife, children, and subordinates may be surprisingly passive when he is in the presence of his superiors, for example.

Mischel's findings indicated to him and other social learning theorists that the situation does in fact play a major role in personality and should not be minimized as it is in trait theory. By taking into account the role of the situation, social learning theorists hope to explain why the same person responds differently in different situations (Mischel, 1973, 1979).

Bandura's Concept of Reciprocal Determinism. Bandura's (1971, 1986) work integrated the social learning emphasis on cognition on the one hand and the role of the situation on the other. He stressed that the relationship between the individual and the external environment is one of **reciprocal determinism**—that the individual and the environment affect each other. Your next-door neighbors can make it difficult for you to study by playing their radio loudly every afternoon. You need not be a passive victim of their noisemaking, however. You can shut your windows, go to the library, or try to persuade your neighbors to lower the volume. By changing your environment, you change the way it affects you. Notice also, though, that the outcome depends heavily on cognitions; specifically how you evaluate and han-

Reciprocal Determinism: Bandura's term meaning that the individual and the environment affect each other in a mutual way.

dle the situation. If you evaluate the noise as a willful attempt to bother you, you might yell at your neighbors instead of tactfully suggesting a compromise, and they in turn might turn the volume even higher.

Bandura's concept of reciprocal determinism underscores the basic premise of social learning theory: that behavior is a result of a complex interplay between characteristics of the person and environmental influences (Bandura, 1977; 1986). And foremost among these characteristics are cognitions, the basic structure of personality in social learning theory.

Because of cognitions, what is reinforcing depends on what it means to the person and how it is evaluated. A dollar-per-hour increase in pay could be viewed as generous or insulting, depending on one's perspective. Moreover, a person need not directly experience an event for it to affect behavior. Observing another employee being reprimanded for being late, or even learning of the reprimand from others, can be enough to deter one from being late. We need not directly experience an event in order to learn; for, by observational learning, we come to anticipate consequences. These anticipated consequences, in turn, affect future behavior.

For Bandura and the social learning theorists, personality development is primarily the development of cognitive processes. One such process emphasized by Bandura, which he believed results from the continuous interaction between individual and environment, is **self-efficacy**—a generalized expectation that refers to one's perceived ability to cope with situations in the environment. As the child gradually masters new situations, his or her self-efficacy increases. The child gradually develops faith in his or her ability to cope with situations in the environment and so takes a more active role in dealing with new situations. A child who does not develop such faith, by contrast, becomes less active in dealing with new situations (Bandura, 1977).

To sum up, social learning theorists believe that people differ in their behavior because of the mutual influence of the person and the situation. Generalized expectations such as an internal locus of control or self-efficacy can produce consistency in behavior across situations. Such generalized expectations can be modified by experience, however—altering, in turn, one's behavior in specific situations. In short, personality reflects the interaction of characteristics of the person (in particular, cognitions) and environmental influences (see Figure 12.8).

Self-Efficacy: One's perceived ability to cope with situations in the environment.

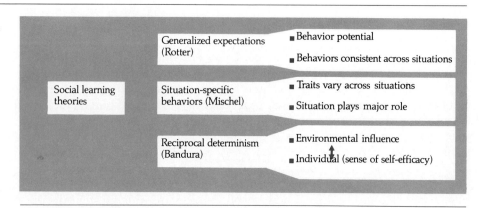

Figure 12.8 Schematic Summary of Social Learning Theories. The three major social learning theories emphasize expectations, situations, and the mutual interactions between the environment and the individual.

■ Learning Check ■

Read the questions and answers. Then try answering the questions with the answers covered.

How do traditional behaviorists and social learning theorists differ regarding:

1. *Question:* the role of experience in learning?

1. *Answer:* Traditional behaviorists believe direct experience is necessary for learning; social learning theorists believe learning can occur without direct experience.

2. *Question:* the existence of hypothetical inner processes?

2. *Answer:* Traditional behaviorists do not speculate about internal processes; social learning theorists give cognition, an internal process, a central role in their theory.

3. *Question:* the acquisition, performance, and maintenance of behavior?

3. *Answer:* Traditional behaviorists consider only environmental contingencies in the acquisition, performance, maintenance and behavior; social learning theorists add observational learning, expectations, and other cognitive processes.

Evaluation of Social Learning Theory. Like the psychoanalytic theories, social learning theory is useful to therapists in conceptualizing and treating psychological disorders, it is, in fact, the basis for a treatment approach known as cognitive behavior therapy (see Chapters 14 and 15). And it is scientifically based, with substantial evidence in support of learning by observation (Bandura & Rosenthal, 1966). Its interactional view is consistent with a broad array of experimental findings; the theory is far from proven. And critics argue that it is far from complete (Wachtel, 1977). In comparison to the psychoanalytic viewpoint, social learning theory covers a relatively limited range of phenomena and is incomplete in specifying how personality develops. The theory is current, however, and—with new research—findings may soon fill in the gaps (Bandura, 1986; White, 1985).

HUMANISTIC THEORIES

Humanistic theories focus on those qualities that distinguish humans from lower animals, hence the term *humanistic.* Humanistic theories focus on an internal mechanism toward growth and self-fulfillment, as opposed to the drive for pleasure and gratification advanced by Freud. According to humanistic theorists, external forces have meaning only insofar as they are given meaning by the individual. As in social learning theory, cognition plays an important role in the humanistic theories. But one's subjective experience is also noncognitive and therefore cannot be fully described in words alone. More than any other type of theory, humanistic theories focus on the role of self-awareness and personal experience in one's distinctive and unique patterns of behavior and reaction to the environment. In this section, we consider two major humanistic theorists, Carl Rogers (1902–) and Abraham Maslow (1908–1970).

Rogers's Theory of the Self

Carl Rogers's thinking, like Freud's, grew out of his clinical experience with his patients. In fact, Rogers was trained in the psychoanalytic tradition. But unlike other theorists from that school—Jung, Adler, Horney—Rogers developed a theory that in no way resembled Freud's.

Freud taught that the individual is driven by animalistic impulses for pleasure and life preservation; Rogers said that all behavior is governed by what he called the **actualizing tendency**—an inborn tendency of the individual toward growth and the development of his or her capacities. For Rogers, the actualizing tendency is a very positive force that fosters personal growth and self-development.

Freud had taught that the most important determinants of behavior are unconscious; Rogers said they are conscious. Of special significance, Rogers argued, are those conscious aspects of the individual's world associated with "I" or "me", which he called the **self**—an organized set of characteristics that the individual perceives as being peculiar to himself or herself. Included in the self are a person's sense of personal identity and self-awareness. A particularly important aspect of the self is the person's self-definition or **self-concept**—an organized and relatively consistent set of assumptions that a person has about himself or herself. All those things you believe about yourself form your self-concept, and those beliefs in turn exert a strong influence on how you feel, think, and ultimately act.

The self-concept provides the foundation for future learning and experience. Experiences that are consistent with the self-concept are accepted and integrated into it; experiences that are inconsistent are rejected. If your self-concept includes clumsiness, for example, you will accept as yours all clumsy behaviors, but dismiss those that are graceful. You may actually stumble no more than other people, but every time you do you tell yourself, "See, I'm clumsy." Even if others insist you are well coordinated, you won't believe them. Over time, your self-concept becomes increasingly consistent and resistant to change (Rogers, 1959).

Negative self-concepts can impose artificial limits on a person. You may have the talent to be an Olympic champion, but if you define yourself as clumsy and unathletic, then you will probably avoid athletic events and fail to develop your talents. A negative self-concept can also affect the way you relate to others. You might be quite attractive, but if you see yourself as unattractive you will tend to act in a way that confirms your belief. You might not search for the hairstyle and clothing that will make the most of your appearance, for example. But the scenario doesn't end there. When you act as if you are unattractive, people respond as if you are. You create a **self-fulfilling prophecy,** in which you cause the very outcome you expect.

Self-fulfilling prophecies can work both ways, of course. If you believe you are good at math, then you will not be discouraged by difficult problems. Your belief that you can solve them will keep you working at them un-

Actualizing Tendency: According to Rogers, an inborn tendency of the individual toward growth and the development of his or her capacities.

Self: According to Rogers, those conscious aspects of an individual's world associated with "I" or "me"; an organized set of characteristics that the individual perceives as being peculiar to himself or herself, including a person's sense of personal identity, self-awareness, and self-definition.

Self-Concept: A person's self-definition. In Rogers's theory, an organized and relatively consistent set of assumptions that a person has about himself or herself.

Self-Fulfilling Prophecy: A phenomenon in which an individual creates or causes the conditions or outcomes that he or she expects.

til you come up with the right answer—no matter how many tries it takes.

Thus, two people can have the same experience from an objective standpoint, yet, from a personal standpoint, experience something quite different. Two runners may tie for first in a long-distance race; from an objective standpoint, the experience is the same. But, from a subjective point of view, one runner may be elated, the other deflated, by the experience. Reality, according to Rogers, is what you experience—or what your self-definition allows you to experience.

Thus Rogers's answer to the question of why different people respond differently to the same event lies in the self-concept. Because people perceive things differently, based on their different self-concepts, they behave differently. Rogers believed that the self-concept is organized and consistent and that behavior is relatively consistent across various situations. Moreover, since people respond to the world according to their own unique view of it, what may seem consistent to the individual engaging in a behavior may seem inconsistent to an observer. For example, a person who sees himself as caring and nurturant and presents himself as such when with family and friends may nevertheless act hard and tough with subordinates, if he believes that he must to maintain their respect. Thus, the variability of behavior across situations is only in the eye of the beholder. In addition, people sometimes behave in a way that contradicts their self-concept in order to receive social acceptance and approval.

According to Rogers, with the actualizing tendency the person has a natural guide for living in a way that maximizes growth. But the individual also has a need for **positive regard**—to be valued, accepted, and cared for. In order to receive positive regard, a person may act according to **conditions of worth,** which are rules for living that other people impose as a condition for their approval (positive regard).

In conforming to conditions of worth to receive positive regard, the individual is forced to ignore his or her own natural guidance system toward growth. Experiences and behaviors that meet with disapproval from others may be denied or distorted. Eventually the person loses touch with his or her true feelings and the messages from the actualizing tendency. Divorced from the natural guidance system of the actualizing tendency, the person becomes confused, unable to judge which behaviors will lead to growth and which will not. (In Chapter 15 we will consider the technique of therapy developed by Rogers to help a person get back in touch with his or her actualizing tendency.)

Rogers does not specify any specific developmental stages. Personality development, he believes, begins with subjective experience. Gradually the individual begins to distinguish between those aspects of experience that are associated with "I" or "me" and those that are not; from this distinction the self develops. The ultimate ideal of adulthood is to be able to accept all of one's experiences without conditions of worth. Individuals who achieve this ideal are called fully functioning persons. Such individuals are open to experience, have a deep sense of trust in themselves and their inner guidance system, and are willing to take risks if they feel good about a new venture (Rogers, 1961).

Like other theories based on clinical observation, Rogers's theory is useful in conceptualizing and treating psychological problems. Some of

Positive Regard: According to Rogers, the need to be valued, accepted, and cared for.

Conditions of Worth: Rules for living that other people impose as a condition for their approval.

Q-Sort Technique: An experimental procedure in which individuals are asked to sort cards containing descriptive statements into piles ranging from those that are most characteristic to those that are least characteristic.

Ideal Self: The self-concept we would like to have or believe we should have; the way we think we should be.

Rogers's ideas, such as the actualizing tendency, are as difficult to prove as many Freudian assumptions, however. One of the more successful experimental tests of the theory involved the use of what is called the **Q-sort technique.** Subjects are given about fifty cards, each of which bears a personally descriptive statement such as "Most people like me," "I am basically honest," or "I feel good about myself." The subjects are asked to sort the cards into five to seven categories, from most characteristic to least characteristic. Then they are asked to re-sort the cards according to the way they think they ought to be. The first sort describes the real self, the second, the **ideal self.** Consistent with Rogers's hypothesis, large discrepancies between the two selves reflect adjustment problems and a lack of self-esteem (Rogers, 1961; Wylie, 1974, 1978).

Though Q-sort studies confirm the usefulness of Rogerian theory in treating psychological problems, they cannot actually verify Rogers's description of the self-concept and its effect on behavior. Nevertheless, attempts to support the theory continue to appear in periodicals such as the *Journal of Humanistic Psychology.*

Maslow's Theory of Self-Actualization

Self-Actualization: According to Maslow, an inborn tendency toward growth and fulfillment.

Abraham Maslow was another humanistic theorist who, like Rogers, concentrated on a hypothetical inborn tendency toward growth and fulfillment—a tendency that he called the need for **self-actualization.** Maslow saw this need for self-actualization as the capstone of an accumulating pyramid—the hierarchy of needs which were discussed in Chapter 9 on motivation. In Maslow's view, people work upward from a foundation of more basic needs for safety and social acceptance, striving for satisfaction in fulfillment—or "actualization"—of their life potential. To discover the components of this tendency to self-fulfillment, Maslow began by analyzing the personalities of friends and associates who he believed had achieved a high level of self-actualization. He also studied the careers of outstanding public figures, like Abraham Lincoln, Albert Einstein, and Eleanor Roosevelt. In this way he tried to identify any characteristics these self-actualized individuals might have in common.

Maslow found that self-actualized people are autonomous and independent. They can work on their own, without support, in the face of criticism and doubt from others. Self-actualizers are also spontaneous: they express themselves freely and don't bind themselves to a rigid schedule or set routine. Trusting and accepting of self and others, tolerant of different view-

Figure 12.9 Schematic Summary of Humanistic Theories of Personality.

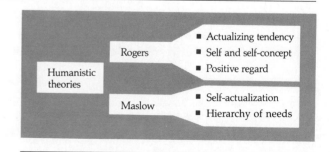

■ Learning Check ■

From your own personal perspective, which theory do you find most appealing? Considering the concepts of all the theorists we have covered, which do you find the most useful? Why? Which do you find the least useful? Why?

points, and nonconforming themselves, these people are free of prejudice and strongly supportive of democratic values. Perhaps because they are creative, they have a strong desire for solitude and privacy. Self-actualizers are accurate in their perception of reality and possess a philosophical sense of humor that allows them to laugh at frustrations and setbacks.

Maslow then tested a large sample of people, including over 3,000 college students, for the presence of these characteristics. He was not surprised to find that very few people (less than one in one hundred) possess all the characteristics he had identified (Maslow, 1970).

Like Q-sort studies, Maslow's surveys do not offer direct support for humanistic theory. They do not demonstrate the existence of a natural tendency in each of us to achieve our full potential. They do describe the characteristics of an especially mature and well-adjusted personality, however, which therefore can serve as a model for therapists in guiding their patients' growth. Partly because of the special attention it pays to the exceptional personality and to personal growth, Maslow's theory is influential despite the relatively limited experimental support for it. (For more on Maslow, see Chapter 9.)

Humanistic theory in general (summarized in Figure 12.9) provides the basis for one of the single most important methods of psychotherapy (see Chapter 15). The concept of a core of self-definitions that guides behavior is as useful a way of looking at personality as any other. It provides perspective on how the meaning of an event hinges on an individual's interpretation of it. But perhaps most important of all, humanistic theory, more than any other major theory, emphasizes the uniqueness and humanity of each person.

Each major theory of personality, in fact, offers important insights into why people behave as they do. Given the contribution each has to make, there is little to be gained—and perhaps much to be lost—in an argument over which theory is best. The human personality is complex enough to benefit from analysis from several perspectives.

Before going on, first to the subject of social psychology and then to abnormal behavior and methods of treating it, let us consider the various tests psychologists have developed to measure personality. Because of the many factors that contribute to personality—traits, learning, situations, cognitions—and their complex interaction, the measurement of personality is one of the more difficult tasks psychologists face.

PERSONALITY TESTS

Obviously, no test can cover all the factors that contribute to personality, no less predict how they will influence one another. Even the best personality tests have their limitations. Used wisely in conjunction with other sources of information such as case histories, however, personality tests can still be of real help to counselors and employers.

Depending on their use, personality tests can be either objective or projective. We will examine both kinds.

Objective Personality Tests

Objective Personality Test: A test of personality that provides a self-report statement (for example, "I like rock and roll music") and requires an individual to choose between two or more alternative responses such as "True" or "False."

Objective personality tests provide a self-report statement (for example, "I like rock and roll music") and require an individual to choose between two or more alternative responses such as "True" or "False." They are like the multiple-choice and true-false tests you take in school, except that there are no right and wrong answers. Instead, the examinee responds true or false, yes or no, or "most like me" to a list of descriptive statements such as "I am usually calm and relaxed." The goal of the test is to identify an individual's distinctive dispositions, or those traits that are relatively enduring across situations. Thus, these tests minimize the role of the situation in the personality.

The first objective personality test was developed during the First World War, when the army needed a fast and dependable way of evaluating recruits. The Woodworth Personal Data Sheet (Woodworth, 1920) required examinees to answer yes or no to statements such as "I wet the bed." The authors of the Woodworth had naively assumed that examinees' responses could be taken at face value. If, for example, an examinee marked "no" to "I wet the bed," the authors assumed that he didn't. That was not, in fact, always the case. Some recruits were no doubt embarrassed to admit to bedwetting; others couldn't read, so they simply filled in the yes and no boxes at random. Still others may have marked no because they did not want to be judged unfit for service. Experience quickly indicated that an examinee's response to an objective personality test item could not be taken at face value.

The fact is, even people who do their best to be sincere will sometimes endorse an item because it seems the appropriate or socially desirable way to respond—"I am courteous and helpful," for example. Some people have such a great need to please others by agreeing that they will answer yes to most items. Others have an equally strong need to disagree. Psychologists call the tendency to respond to test items in a particular way, regardless of their content, **response bias.** Needless to say, a test that does not in some way account for response bias is unlikely to give dependable results.

Response Bias: The tendency to respond to a test item in a particular way (e.g., agree or disagree) regardless of the content of the item.

In 1943 psychologists devised the Minnesota Multiphasic Personality Inventory (MMPI), the first objective personality test to deal successfully with the problems of the Woodworth. The authors made no assumptions about the meaning of any particular item; they took no answer at face value (Hathaway & McKinley, 1943). Instead, they assembled groups of people who manifested certain traits, as determined by trained judges such as psychiatrists, and tested their responses to all kinds of items, from "I like money" and "I eat a lot" to "I'm always tired." Then they selected those items that distinguished people with a particular trait from others in a control group. The approximately seventy items that measure depression, for instance, were selected because a group of hospitalized depressed patients tended to respond the same way to them. Most answered true to the statement "I am sad most of the time" and false to "My father is a hard worker." A control group responded the same way to only a few of those items. Thus, it is not the content of the items, but the way they are endorsed that discriminates between the depressed and the nondepressed.

The seventy items that form the depression scale of the MMPI are scattered throughout the 566 items on the test, as are the items for other characteristics. Examinees cannot easily tell what trait a given item measures. As a result, the MMPI is difficult to fake (see Figure 12.10).

The test even includes special scales, called **validity scales,** to detect faking, response biases, and random responses. If you responded at random, tried to exaggerate or minimize your problems, or didn't read or understand the items, the validity scales would probably detect it. The F scale, for example, contains sixty-four items that even extremely disturbed people rarely endorse. If you marked a significant number of those items in the scored direction (some are scored true, others false), the examiners would suspect that you are trying to appear disturbed, or that you didn't read or understand the questions.

The MMPI is widely used for everything from evaluating delinquency to screening nursing students (Lueger & Hoover, 1984; Noce & Whitmyre, 1981). The test is not without limitations, however. Its results do not hold

Validity Scales: Scales in the MMPI that evaluate the validity of a person's response to the test. The F scale, for example, can help determine if an individual exaggerated the extent of his or her problems.

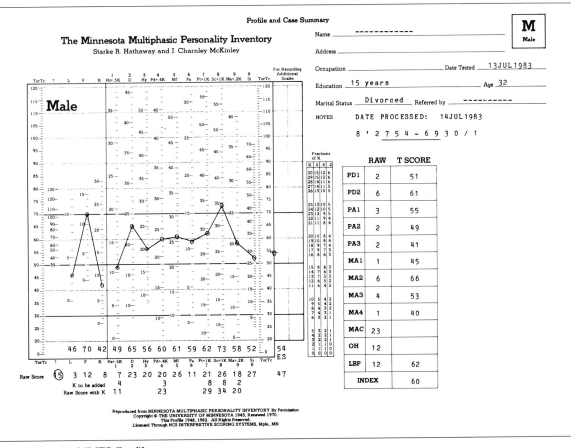

Figure 12.10 An MMPI Profile.

up well for more than about a year, and perhaps should not be expected to. Naturally, if a person with a psychological problem improves with treatment or is cured, test results will change. Scores on the MMPI must also be interpreted differently depending on the respondent's sex, race, socioeconomic status, and even place of residence (Gynther & Gynther, 1976). What is nor-

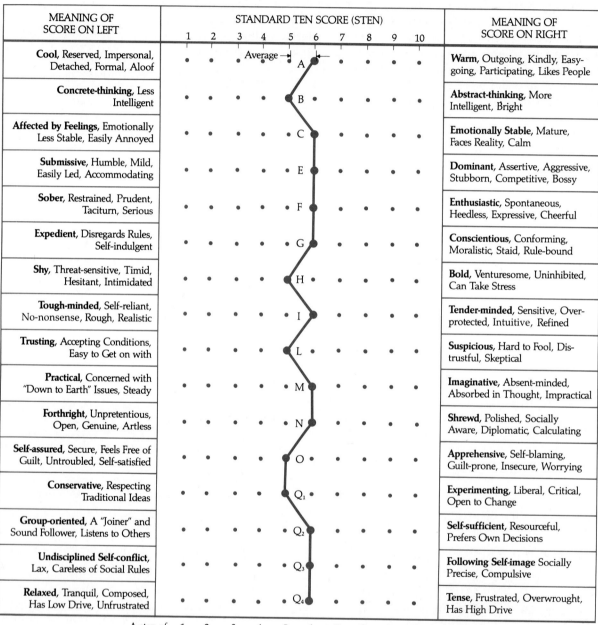

MEANING OF SCORE ON LEFT	STANDARD TEN SCORE (STEN)										MEANING OF SCORE ON RIGHT
	1	2	3	4	5	6	7	8	9	10	
Cool, Reserved, Impersonal, Detached, Formal, Aloof			Average →			A					**Warm,** Outgoing, Kindly, Easygoing, Participating, Likes People
Concrete-thinking, Less Intelligent						B					**Abstract-thinking,** More Intelligent, Bright
Affected by Feelings, Emotionally Less Stable, Easily Annoyed					C						**Emotionally Stable,** Mature, Faces Reality, Calm
Submissive, Humble, Mild, Easily Led, Accommodating					E						**Dominant,** Assertive, Aggressive, Stubborn, Competitive, Bossy
Sober, Restrained, Prudent, Taciturn, Serious					F						**Enthusiastic,** Spontaneous, Heedless, Expressive, Cheerful
Expedient, Disregards Rules, Self-indulgent					G						**Conscientious,** Conforming, Moralistic, Staid, Rule-bound
Shy, Threat-sensitive, Timid, Hesitant, Intimidated					H						**Bold,** Venturesome, Uninhibited, Can Take Stress
Tough-minded, Self-reliant, No-nonsense, Rough, Realistic					I						**Tender-minded,** Sensitive, Overprotected, Intuitive, Refined
Trusting, Accepting Conditions, Easy to Get on with					L						**Suspicious,** Hard to Fool, Distrustful, Skeptical
Practical, Concerned with "Down to Earth" Issues, Steady					M						**Imaginative,** Absent-minded, Absorbed in Thought, Impractical
Forthright, Unpretentious, Open, Genuine, Artless					N						**Shrewd,** Polished, Socially Aware, Diplomatic, Calculating
Self-assured, Secure, Feels Free of Guilt, Untroubled, Self-satisfied					O						**Apprehensive,** Self-blaming, Guilt-prone, Insecure, Worrying
Conservative, Respecting Traditional Ideas					Q_1						**Experimenting,** Liberal, Critical, Open to Change
Group-oriented, A "Joiner" and Sound Follower, Listens to Others					Q_2						**Self-sufficient,** Resourceful, Prefers Own Decisions
Undisciplined Self-conflict, Lax, Careless of Social Rules					Q_3						**Following Self-image** Socially Precise, Compulsive
Relaxed, Tranquil, Composed, Has Low Drive, Unfrustrated					Q_4						**Tense,** Frustrated, Overwrought, Has High Drive

A sten of 1 2 3 4 5 6 7 8 9 10 is obtained
by about 2.3% 4.4% 9.2% 15.0% 19.1% 19.1% 15.0% 9.2% 4.4% 2.3% of adults

Figure 12.11 A 16 PF Profile. (*Profile from* Tabular Supplement of Norms No. 1, *Copyright © 1970, IPAT. Reproduced by permission.*)

mal for a factory worker is not necessarily normal for a lawyer. To deal with these and other problems, supporters of the MMPI have updated it, adding over 200 items, and testing them on thousands of normals throughout the United States (Butcher, 1986).

The Cattell Sixteen Personality Factor questionnaire, which was discussed earlier (see pages 431–432), is also an objective personality test, but it was developed by a different strategy from the MMPI's. Instead of looking for items that discriminated between those who possessed a particular trait and those who did not, Cattell selected the items that correlated most closely with each of his sixteen factors. As with the MMPI, examinees cannot easily tell what an item is testing, for answers are not interpreted at face value. Items from each of the sixteen scales are scattered throughout the test. Individuals who endorse a relatively large or small number of items on a scale are presumed to possess a corresponding degree of the trait that scale measures (see Figure 12.11).

The main weakness of all objective personality tests, as stated previously, is their assumption that behavior is stable across situations. To the extent that behavior varies across situations, then, these tests are limited. But they can provide some indication of a person's general dispositions under most usual circumstances.

Projective Tests

The second kind of personality test, the **projective test,** requires a person to respond to an ambiguous stimulus. Such tests are based on the assumption that a person attempting to interpret an ambiguous stimulus will reveal his or her needs, feelings, and cognitions—in short, personality—in the effort. In other words, the response a person gives is a reflection of him or her. In exactly the same inkblot one person sees an evil mask, another a smiling face (see Figure 12.12).

Unlike objective personality tests, whose directions are clear and simple, projective personality tests give the examinee no clear idea of how to respond. The lack of direction permits a wider range of responses, but intro-

Projective Test: A test of personality that requires a person to respond to an ambiguous stimulus, thus projecting his or her feelings and needs.

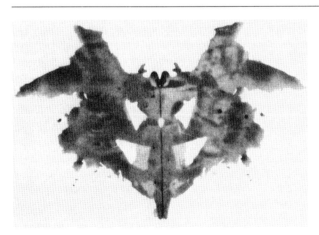

Figure 12.12   Card 1 from the Rorschach Inkblot Test.   An individual's description of what this card might be is assumed to reflect his or her own feelings, needs, and thought processes. (Card I from the Rorschach Inkblot Test by H. Rorschach, in Psychodiagnostik. Copyright 1921, renewed 1948, by Verlag Hans Huber Bern.)

Box 12.1 PSYCHOLOGY IN ACTION: Assessing Personality in an Employment Interview

Tests such as the MMPI and Rorschach are used to assess personality in clinical situations. In employment situations, personality is most commonly evaluated in an employment interview—a planned face-to-face interaction between a representative of a company or business and a prospective employee.

Suppose you have applied for a highly desirable, well-paying job. You get a call from a representative of the company informing you that, of 250 applicants, you have been ranked in the top five. Each of you are to be individually interviewed to determine who is to be offered the position. A little knowledge about the nature of how your personality is evaluated in the employment interview might just make the difference between almost getting the position and getting it.

One of the most important things to keep in mind is the importance of first impressions. It is no myth that the initial image one projects in an employment interview plays an extremely influential role in how one is ultimately evaluated. If you have to fumble through your desk to find your appointment book, then the interviewer may get the impression you are disorganized. If, by contrast, you convey a sense of enthusiasm and confidence, then the battle may be

half won. Right from the start, the inteviewer will be attempting to evaluate your personality.

One of the reasons first impressions are so important is that they influence the way the interviewer processes and interprets subsequent information. If the interviewer initially gets the idea you are disorganized, she subsequently tends to look for confirming information and actually overlooks or minimizes disconfirming evidence. First impressions establish the general personality categories or dispositional tendencies into which additional information about you will be organized. The interviewer subsequently tends to think about you in terms of these categories. For example, if, in your initial impression, you convey a strong interest in the position, discussing the working conditions or inquiring about the salary would be interpreted as additional signs of your interest. If, however, you initially convey a weak interest, even if unintentionally, then the interviewer might begin to wonder if you think the salary is too low when you inquire about it.

When you arrive for the interview, naturally you want to look your best. Studies of employment interviews have revealed that an applicant's appearance

---

duces a subjective element into the scoring and evaluation of responses, just as in essay examinations.

The two most widely used projective tests are the Rorschach inkblot test and the Thematic Apperception Test (TAT). The Rorschach was published in Switzerland in 1921 and has been used by clinical psychologists in the United States since just before the Second World War. The test contains ten cards bearing inkblots, some colored and some black and white (see Figure 12.12). The examiner gives the cards to the subject one at a time and asks "What is that?" or "What might this be?" Other than these brief questions, the examiner gives no clue to what is desired. In some cases the examiner will sit to the side of the subject to prevent the subject from picking up nonverbal cues that might indicate how to respond.

Drawing inferences about people from the Rorschach can be hazardous, for a variety of reasons. A person's responses to the test tend to vary considerably from one administration to the next. Thus, results generally are not **Reliability (of a test):** The consistency of a test result. consistent, or **reliable,** over time. Proponents of the Rorschach argue that, since its goal, like that of the MMPI, is to evaluate current functioning, the problem of poor reliability over time is not a serious one. There are other problems, however.

Studies of the meaning of specific responses are conflicting or inconclusive (Exner, 1974). Thus, there is always room for doubt in the interpretation of a response. And, as has been mentioned, an examiner can inadvertently influence an examinee's responses through nonverbal clues. If a normal person gives a response typically found in disturbed persons, for example, and

---

Box 12.1 *(cont'd)*

plays a role in the final outcome (Dipboye et al., 1975). Your appearance has an impact on the overall impression the interviewer will form of you, and from this impression he or she may generate a number of specific conclusions about your personality. For example, based on a positive overall impression, the interviewer may, without any specific evidence, conclude that you are honest or hardworking.

Numerous studies of the employment interview have revealed that a more qualified applicant who conveys an early negative impression has less chance of landing the job than a far less qualified applicant who manages to convey a good impression. An employment interview, more often than not, is a search for negative evidence. Moreover, interviewers make their decisions quickly and, once made, generally stick to them. Thus, the earlier in an interview that negative evidence is found, the more damaging its effect. Put yourself in the place of an interviewer. If you have to select among several good applicants, it's easier to justify why one should not be hired because of some negative attribute than it is to justify not hiring an applicant because he has less of a given positive attribute than another. For example, there is no problem reject-

ing John because he's disorganized. But how can we justify rejecting him if he's very organized but perhaps a little less so than Lynn? So, the next time someone is evaluating your personality, be sure to put your best foot forward.

Making a good first impression is more than half the battle in a successful job interview.

---

the examiner perks up and thinks "Ah ha," her reaction may encourage the examinee to think of similar responses.

Currently, the Rorschach is a controversial test. Some psychologists believe it is one of the most useful, if not the most useful device for detecting

Figure 12.13   Card 12F from the Thematic Apperception Test.   *The examinee is asked to make up a story about this picture. As with the Rorschach, it is assumed that the individual's response reflects his or her own feelings, needs, and thoughts. (Reprinted by permission of the publishers from THEMATIC APPERCEPTION TEST, by Henry A. Murray, Cambridge, Mass.: Harvard University Press, Copyright © 1943 by the President and Fellows of Harvard College; ©1971 by Henry A. Murray.)*

subtle emotional problems (Piotrowski, 1984). Just as many believe it is completely unreliable. So many studies of the test have been published that almost about any position can be supported (Kaplan & Saccuzzo, 1982).

The Rorschach is used primarily in clinical settings, as an aid in determining the nature and severity of patients' psychological problems. Another projective test, the Thematic Apperception Test (TAT), is used both in clinical settings and in studies of normal personalities—particularly motivational traits like the need for achievement (see Chapter 9). Like the Rorschach, the TAT uses cards which the examinee is asked to interpret (see Figure 12.13). But, instead of inkblots, the cards bear pictures of people in an unexplained situation. The subject is asked to make up a story describing what led up to the scene, what the characters are thinking and feeling, what is happening, and what the outcome will be.

Like the Rorschach, the TAT has been criticized because of poor reliability over time. In the hands of a competent examiner, and when used with other sources of information, however, the TAT can provide insights into a respondent's personality that can help in the treatment of problem behaviors (Shill, 1981).

Chapter 13 covers the area of social psychology. Following Chapter 13 we consider the types of abnormal patterns of behavior that psychologists attempt to evaluate using psychological tests. Then, in Chapter 15, we consider approaches to the treatment of such patterns.

LEARNING FRAMEWORK

I. Personality—relatively stable and distinctive patterns of behavior that characterize an individual and his or her reactions to the environment.

II. Freud's psychoanalytic theory of personality proposed a three-part structure, three levels of awareness, defense mechanisms against anxiety, and specific stages of development as the major determinants of personality. Freudian theory remains a matter of controversy to this day. (Review: *Figure 12.1*)

A. The id, ego, and superego form an interrelated three-part structure that is constantly in conflict. (Review: *Pleasure Principle; Reality Principle; Internalization; Figure 12.2*)

B. Mental activities take place at three different levels of awareness—conscious, preconscious, and unconscious. (Review: *Figure 12.3*)

C. Through its defense mechanisms, the ego attempts to cope with anxiety as it balances the demands from the id, superego, and external reality. (Review: *Table 12.1*)

D. Development of the personality proceeds through four biologically programmed stages of psychosexual development in which the energies of the libido focus on different erogenous zones. (Review: *Fixation; Oral Stage; Anal Stage; Phallic Stage; Genital Stage; Figure 12.4*)

E. There is some support for Freud's theory, but it is inconclusive and sometimes contradictory.

III. A number of theorists retained certain aspects of Freud's psychoanalytic approach while rejecting others.

A. Carl Jung retained Freud's emphasis on hidden forces and underlying mechanisms but rejected Freud's emphasis on sexual instincts. Jung's theory of the collective unconscious, which proposed the existence of universal thought forms, represented a significant deviation from Freud's psychoanalytic approach. (Review: *Personal Unconscious; Collective Unconscious; Archetypes; Figure 12.5*)

B. Alfred Adler contrasted his theory to Freud's. In contrast to Freud, Adler did not divide the personality into parts. He viewed the unconscious in terms of lack of self-understanding. And he proposed the existence of a nonsexual driving force. (Review: *Social Interest*)

C. Karen Horney provided a female perspective of psychoanalytic theory. She focused on the importance of safety and satisfaction in healthy personality development and identified three major types of unhealthy personality patterns. (Review: *Basic Anxiety*)

IV. Trait theorists are primarily concerned with discovering the dimensions of personality—enduring and distinctive dispositional tendencies that are believed to be the basis for behavioral consistency across different situations. (Review: *Figure 12.7*)

A. Gordon Allport distinguished among three types of traits, depending on their pervasiveness. (Review: *Cardinal Traits; Central Traits; Secondary Traits*)

B. Raymond B. Cattell used sophisticated statistical procedures to identify sixteen independent and distinguishable dimensions, each of which he believed applied in varying degrees to all people. (Review: *Factor Analysis; Source Traits; Figure 12.6*)

C. Hans Eysenck attempted to identify a small number of personality types—basic dimensions of personality that underlie clusters of related traits. (Review: *Introversion; Extroversion*)

V. Behavioral theories emphasize the situational determinants of behavior. They fall into two distinct groups, depending on their definition of behavior. (Review: *Table 12.2*)

A. Traditional behaviorist theory defines behavior only in terms of observable actions and environmental consequences.

B. According to social learning theory, cognitions are an integral aspect of behavior. (Review: *Observational Learning; Generalized Expectations; Mischel's Study of Situation-Specific Behaviors; Reciprocal Determinism; Figure 12.8*)

VI. Humanistic theories focus on the person and those qualities that are distinctly human. (Review: *Figure 12.9*)

A. Carl Rogers's theory attempted to show how a person's subjective experience determined how he or she behaved and reacted to events. (Review: *Actualizing Tendency; Self-Concept; Positive Regard; Conditions of Worth*)

B. Abraham Maslow's theory emphasized a hypothetical inborn tendency toward growth and fulfillment. (Review: *Self-Actualization*)

VII. Psychologists attempt to measure personality with two different types of tests.

A. Objective personality tests provide a list of items and ask an individual to indicate how the item applies to him or her. (Review: *Response Bias; MMPI; Cattell Sixteen Personality Factor Questionnaire*)

B. Projective tests attempt to measure personality by evaluating a person's reaction to an ambiguous stimulus such as an inkblot. (Review: *Rorschach Inkblot Test; Thematic Apperception Test; Reliability*)

CHAPTER

13

Social Psychology

Chapter Outline

- Social Knowledge
  - Social Perception
  - The Process of Attribution
  - Self-Perception
  - Social Cognition
- Attitudes
  - How Attitudes Are Formed and Measured
  - Attitude Change Through Persuasive Communication
  - Attitudes and Behavior
  - Changing Attitudes Through Behavior
  - Change and Cognitive Inconsistencies
  - Prejudice and Related Concepts
- Social Influence
  - Obedience
  - Compliance
  - Conformity
  - Groups and Group Influences
- Social Relations
  - Interpersonal Attraction
  - Aggression
  - Altruism
- Applications of Social Psychology
  - Environmental Psychology
  - The Legal System
- Box 13.1 Understanding Power
- Box 13.2 Groups and Real-World Problems: The Robber's Cave Study

Recently one of my colleagues informed me that some of his psychotherapy clients were being pressured to join a cult. They had been asked to attend an all-night get-acquainted meeting; their friends were welcome, too. My colleague and I decided to accompany one of the patients. We presented ourselves as sales representatives for the company the client worked for.

The cult began by using subtle pressures to influence potential members. They asked everyone for a small contribution—not much, just a dollar or some change from anyone who could spare it. They told us the money would be used as funds for their project to feed hungry children in the United States. One individual quickly stood up and said that she would give more than a token amount of money and tossed a handful of bills into the collection box. Two others quickly followed suit. The behavior of these contributors seemed rehearsed, which led me to suspect they were actually members of the cult. Nevertheless, I conformed and tossed in $2.00. Already the presence of others and pressures of the cult group were influencing my behavior.

We were then asked to break up into pairs and to reveal something secret about ourselves to each other. Before I could blink, a good-looking young woman touched my arm and escorted me to a corner. Her behavior seemed as smooth and rehearsed as the generous contributors I had encountered earlier, so I suspected she too was a cult member. She looked into my eyes and tried to get me to talk about myself. I guess I wasn't as cooperative as the typical prospective member. Finally she became angry at me for "putting on a front." I wasn't moved by her anger or her long silence. Before the end of this part of the experience, however, she attempted to resolve the conflict and make up.

After a while we were asked to circulate and get to know others. People who were members of the cult took turns coming to me. Some shook my hand; others hugged and embraced me, clearly attempting to create an atmosphere of warmth and acceptance. Finally, we heard about the various activities we could become involved in by joining the cult. Then one of the leaders asked us to gather around. He appealed for help. The city apparently had refused to grant the group a permit that would allow them to convert one of their properties into a drop-in crisis center. He was most persuasive, and by daylight several people had volunteered to help the group and attend future meetings. My colleague and I left about 6:30 a.m., exhausted and frustrated.

Cults provide a rather dramatic and extreme illustration of how the presence of others influences the behavior of an individual. Such influences are not restricted to organizations that purposefully attempt to control the lives and even the minds of individuals. In the home, our behavior depends, in part, on the actions of others in the family. On the job, our behavior depends, in part, on co-workers, supervisors, and the rules and regulations of the company. Most behavior takes place in a social context. Much of our behavior is **social behavior**—it takes place in the context of social situations.

The field of psychology that studies behavior within a social context is called **social psychology.** Social psychologists are concerned with how the social context, including the real, imagined, or anticipated presence of others, affects our actions, feelings, and thoughts. The power of a cult to shape a person's attitudes is just one example of how the behavior of an individual is influenced by other people and the social environment they create. Another is the ability of a group of jurors to persuade a single dissenter to vote guilty despite the dissenter's conviction of the defendant's innocence.

In this chapter we consider some of the many topics of interest to social psychologists. First of all, we consider how we acquire social knowledge. We will examine the specific ways in which we perceive and understand others and how we come to know ourselves in relation to them. Next, we examine attitudes. We will see how others influence the formation of our attitudes and how our attitudes, in turn, influence our behavior toward others. Third, we will look at the nature of social influence. We will see how social structure, groups, and other broad social contexts influence us. Then we discuss three types of social interaction—attraction, aggression, and helping. Finally, we will discuss the application of social psychology in the fields of law and environment.

Social Behavior: Behavior (overt actions, feelings, thoughts) of individuals in social situations.

Social Psychology: The study of behavior within a social context.

SOCIAL KNOWLEDGE

We come to know and understand others through our direct experiences with them and through our efforts to interpret the meaning of their actions. Our knowledge and interpretation of others, in turn, influence the way we perceive ourselves. In this section we will consider four major aspects of our social knowledge: social perception, the process of attribution, self-perception, and social cognition.

Social Perception

Suppose a stranger moves into the apartment next to yours. You notice that he's tall, trim, and athletic as he carries in his furniture. He briefly glances into your eyes and then looks away. On the way back to his moving truck he introduces himself. Already you might be thinking that he seems like a nice person.

Your brief encounter with him is an important first step in **social perception**—the process through which we come to know and understand others. First impressions, physical appearance, and nonverbal messages such as eye contact play a major role in social perception.

Social Perception: The process through which we come to know and understand others.

First Impressions. Of all the interactions and experiences you have with another, perhaps none is more important than your first impression. This is because, once you have formed an impression of another, it tends to stick. Information inconsistent with the impression tends to be ignored, whereas consistent information stands out and confirms your view. If you see your new neighbor getting into an argument after you've decided he's a nice person, you'll probably think he's just tired and frustrated. But if you see him stop for a minute to help another neighbor, his actions, in confirming your impressions, stand out in your mind.

Primacy Effect: The tendency for our judgments of others to be dominated by our first impression.

Social psychologists refer to the tendency of our judgments of others to be dominated by our first impression as the **primacy effect.** Simply put, the first information we receive about a person seems to carry more weight than subsequent information. Once we make up our minds about a person, it's hard to change. First impressions establish the general framework that we use to organize subsequent information about a person.

Because of the power of first impressions, people often make substantial errors in their evaluation of others. One way job interviewers overcome such errors is through training and instruction in combining all known information about a person before making a judgment (Leach, 1974). But, if we delay judgment and new information becomes available, our perception may be influenced by a **recency effect**—the tendency of our judgments of others to be dominated by our last, or most recent, impression. The lesson is that, in coming to know a person, we usually do not give equal weight to all the information we observe. Thus, an important aspect of social perception is its selectivity—we select and choose what is important and what is not.

Recency Effect: The tendency of our judgments of others to be dominated by our last, or most recent, impression.

Physical Appearance. One thing that is very important in first impressions is physical appearance. When we first observe a person we notice the person's clothes, facial features, hairstyle, grooming, approximate age, weight, race, sex, and physical attractiveness. Though most people may not be aware of it, their overall impressions of other persons depends heavily on their physical attractiveness. People who were asked to rate pictures of attractive men and women rated attractive persons of both sexes as more successful, more charming, more sociable, better poised, more independent, and more sexually warm than less attractive persons (Dion et al., 1972; Brigham, 1980). There is also a tendency to view less attractive people as deviant (for example, mentally ill), which perhaps explains why less attractive people are more likely to be convicted of a crime and to receive a harsher sentence than more attractive people (Jones et al., 1978; Unger et al., 1982). (See page 487.)

Of course, physical attractiveness doesn't influence all people in the same way (Andersen & Bem, 1981). But people do have a tendency to form judgments of others' morals, intelligence, and a number of other characteristics based solely on their physical appearance.

Nonverbal Communication. Another way we come to know and understand others is by observing their facial expressions, eye contact, gestures, tone of voice, and other nonverbal cues. Facial expressions provide a rich source of information. Another's smile signals friendliness or a willingness to have further social contact. A wrinkled nose and forehead and pursed lips, especially if accompanied by a clenched fist, signals anger. (For more on the face and emotion, see Chapter 9.)

A good example of the role of nonverbal communication in social perception is eye contact. Your reaction to a new acquaintance is influenced by both the level and the pattern of eye contact. If the person frequently gazes (looks directly at your face), you might take it as a sign of interest in establishing a new relationship. Indeed, when unacquainted college students were observed in a laboratory setting, it was found that they were most likely to begin a conversation if they had looked at each other at their initial encounter. And they were even more likely to converse after giving each other a second look following some distraction, like another student walking into the room (Cary, 1978). In another study, a researcher arranged to have assistants take job interviews. The assistants were instructed to make either high or low levels of eye contact with the interviewer. Those who made high levels of eye contact got the best ratings (Imada & Hakel, 1977). But one must not overdo it, because staring (continuous gazing) elicits a negative reaction. Whereas a brief gaze is a friendly sign, staring is often seen as a threat or sign of anger (Ellsworth & Carlsmith, 1973).

Another important form of nonverbal communication is touching. People touch each other all the time. If we consider the touch appropriate—a friendly handshake or a reassuring pat on the arm, for example—then we may respond positively. Under many circumstances, however, the touch is unwelcomed or unwanted, and we react negatively.

By recognizing the importance of nonverbal cues and consciously attending to them, a person can become better at reading such cues and in making better use of a major clue we use to know and understand others (Archer, 1980). But, in interpreting a person's nonverbal behavior, we most likely are getting information about their current mood or emotion—the temporary cause of their behavior. To know and understand them, we would be interested in their enduring dispositions and motives—the more lasting causes of their behavior. We infer whether their behavior is due to temporary or to more lasting causes through a process known as attribution.

Physical appearance plays a major role in first impressions.

The Process of Attribution

When we try to figure out the causes of other people's actions, we are engaging in what social psychologists call **causal attribution**—the process through which we infer causes and explanations of events or behavior. In studying causal attributions, social psychologists try to understand how we form our ideas of others' behavior. According to one theory, people try to understand the behavior of others as a scientist might: by observing an event, comparing the observation to previous experiences of similar occur-

Causal Attribution: The process through which we infer causes and explanations of events or behavior.

rences, and drawing conclusions (Heider, 1944, 1958). By analyzing other people's behavior as a scientist might, a person can draw inferences about the dispositional characteristics of others such as motives, traits, and intentions (Jones & Davis, 1965). Sometimes, however, the actions we observe do not reflect some dispositional tendency.

According to many social psychologists, in making causal attributions, people distinguish between dispositional causes and situational causes (Kelley, 1967, 1973). In making a **dispositional attribution,** we explain the cause of an observed behavior in terms of enduring dispositions. We say a person acted as such because of some personal characteristic, such as a motive or personality trait. In making a **situational attribution,** by contrast, we explain the cause of a person's behavior in terms of temporary, external causes. We say a person acted as such because of the situation. Behavior attributable to situational causes tells us little about a person.

According to Kelley (1972), there are three major factors that determine whether we will make a situational or a dispositional attribution: *consistency* (the extent that a person's behavior is the same under similar circumstances); *distinctiveness* (the extent to which a person's behavior occurs under a variety of circumstances); and *consensus* (the extent to which most people would engage in the behavior under similar circumstances). Kelley believes that dispositional attributions are made under conditions of low consensus, high consistency, and low distinctiveness; situational attributions are made when all three factors are high. (See Figure 13.1.)

When we attribute a person's behavior to dispositional causes, we can draw conclusions about what the person is like. If we attribute a waiter's friendly and outgoing behaviors to dispositional causes, then we will conclude that he is an outgoing, friendly person. Unfortunately, research on attributions shows that people often make serious errors in their attributions. As a general rule, people tend to attribute the behavior of others to dispositional causes, even in cases where there are very good reasons for making a situational attribution (Ross et al., 1977). Even though we know the waiter may be acting friendly and outgoing as a part of his job (and to get a bigger tip), we still have a stronger tendency to attribute his behavior to dispositional rather than to situational causes.

The tendency to overestimate the role of dispositional factors and underestimate the role of situational factors in making attributions is called the **fundamental attribution error** (Ross, 1977; Nisbett & Ross, 1980). Such attri-

Dispositional Attribution: Explaining the cause of an observed behavior in terms of enduring dispositions.

Situational Attribution: Explaining the cause of an observed behavior in terms of temporary, external causes.

Fundamental Attribution Error: The tendency to overestimate the role of dispositional factors and underestimate the role of situational factors in making attributions.

Figure 13.1 Schematic Summary of the Major Factors that Determine Our Attributions.

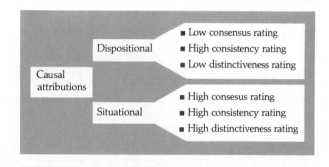

bution errors interfere with social perception: it's hard to get to know and understand Jennifer when your attributions of her behavior have led you to conclude that she is aloof and shy when, in fact, she's really quite sociable and caring. It was just the situation she was in when you observed her that caused you to think she was cold. What is more, your incorrect attribution may create a **self-fulfilling prophecy,** in which you act in a way to cause the very outcome you expect. Believing that Jennifer is shy and aloof, you avoid her. She responds to your avoidance as one might to a rejection, and so is, in fact, unfriendly and aloof toward you.

The study of how we acquire social knowledge reveals that the way we make judgments and form impressions of others is not always rational. Our judgments are usually based on very little information. What is more, our judgments are subject to many sources of bias. By becoming aware of biases such as the fundamental attribution error, we can take steps to correct for them. But a better understanding of how we acquire social knowledge can do more than help us view others more accurately; it can also give us some insights into how we come to know ourselves.

Self-Perception

Self-perception refers to the process through which we come to know ourselves—our own feelings, traits, motives, and the causes of our own behavior. Social knowledge is directly relevant to self-perception, because we come to know ourselves, at least in part, in relation to others. According to **social comparison theory,** when objective or physical standards are unavailable, people will use others as a standard by which to measure themselves (Festinger, 1954). Social psychologists have learned that people tend to compare themselves to others who are similar to themselves and, if possible, to select one who is just a notch or two above them in terms of ability (Wheeler et al., 1982).

Comparing yourself to someone who is only just slightly better gives you a good chance to observe personal progress. People tend to arrange things so as to achieve a reasonably good perception of themselves. The tendency is so strong that people often adopt strategies to protect themselves from failure and maintain their self-esteem by setting up excuses in advance. Social psychologists refer to these advance alibis as **self-handicapping strategies.** To demonstrate such strategies, Berglas and Jones (1978) asked one group of students to solve a set of problems for which there was no solution. Another group worked on solvable problems. Later, subjects in both groups were given the choice of continuing their work on the problems under one of two conditions: a drug that they were told would make them more alert and enhance performance or a drug that they were told would make them tired and lazy, impairing performance. The drug a subject selected depended on the type of problem he or she was asked to solve. Subjects who worked on solvable problems tended to select the enhancing drug. Subjects in the unsolvable group, by contrast, handicapped themselves by choosing the impairing drug.

In addition to comparing ourselves to others, we sometimes come to know ourselves in much the same way that we come to know others. According to Bem's (1967, 1972) **self-perception theory,** we come to know our

Self-Fulfilling Prophecy: A phenomenon in which an individual acts in a way that causes an expected outcome.

Self-Perception: The process through which we come to know ourselves— our own feelings, traits, motives, and the causes of our own behavior.

Social Comparison Theory: The theory that, when objective or physical standards are unavailable, people will use others as a standard by which to measure themselves.

Self-Handicapping Strategies: Strategies in which people protect themselves from failure and maintain their self-esteem by setting up excuses in advance.

Self-Perception Theory: Bem's theory that we come to know our attitudes and other personal characteristics by observing our own behavior and inferring causes, just as someone observing us might.

According to the self-perception theory, we come to know ourselves by observing our own behavior.

attitudes and other personal characteristics by observing our own behavior and inferring causes from the situations under which we behave in particular ways, just as someone observing us might. If you frequently help other people, you might soon observe your helpful behaviors and conclude by your own observations that you are a helpful person. The things you do, as opposed to the things you do not, provide the basis for what you observe and become aware of about yourself (Fazio, Sherman, & Herr, 1982).

In observing our own behavior and inferring causes, we seem to be subject to the same type of bias that occurs when we attribute other people's behavior to causes. Recall the fundamental attribution error in which we overestimate the role of dispositional factors and underestimate the role of situational factors in another person's behavior. We have a similar bias when observing our own behavior, only in reverse. We tend to attribute our own behavior to situational factors rather than to traits and other dispositional tendencies (Eisen, 1979; Taylor & Fiske, 1978). This tendency to attribute others' behavior to dispositional causes and our own to situational causes is referred to as the **actor-observer bias** (Jones & Nisbett, 1971). When you trip or fall, it isn't because you are clumsy; it is because of the toy some careless child left in the hall. Let Joan fall over the same toy and you conclude that she is clumsy.

We also tend to attribute positive outcomes to our own ability and effort and negative outcomes to external causes, a phenomenon known as the **self-serving bias** (Zuckerman, 1979). If you get an A, it's because of your talents and hard work; if you get a D, it's because you didn't have enough time to study, the room was noisy, the book was bad, and the teacher disorganized.

Attributional biases illustrate that the way we come to know ourselves and others depends to a large extent on how we think. In the next section

Actor-Observer Bias: The tendency to attribute others' behavior to dispositional causes and our own to situational causes.

Self-Serving Bias: The tendency to attribute positive outcomes to our own ability and effort and negative outcomes to situational causes.

■ Learning Check ■

Read the right side, then cover and try to recite. Repeat.

Three Types of Attributional Bias:	Definition
1. Fundamental Attribution Error	Overestimating dispositional factors and underestimating situational factors in others' behavior.
2. Actor-Observer Bias	Tendency to attribute others' behaviors to dispositional causes and our own to situational causes.
3. Self-Serving Bias	Tendency to attribute positive outcomes to our own ability and negative outcomes to external causes.

---

on social cognition we will look more closely at some of the ways we think about ourselves and others.

Social Cognition

Our perception of the social environment depends heavily on our interpretation of it. **Social cognition** refers to all cognitions and cognitive processes involved in social behavior. In studying social cognition, social psychologists seek to understand how we organize, interpret, and remember information about the social environment. Social cognition concerns more than attempts to understand the causes of behavior through social perception and self-perception. It concerns how we think of other people (and ourselves) generally.

The study of social cognition is based on the notion that the individual plays an active role in making sense of information provided by others (Fiske & Taylor, 1983). The individual is seen as an active problem solver, striving to understand, process, and assimilate feedback from the social environment. When you observe someone's actions, the information does not simply imprint on your brain. You attend to certain things more carefully than others, analyze the information, compare it to memories of similar experiences, and make sense of it.

In the process of making sense of what they observe, people begin to organize information into sets of interconnected frameworks called schemata. You are already familiar with the idea of schemata; we have used the concept as a learning device to present related clusters of information. A **social schema** (pl. schemata) is a cognitive framework about specific individuals or groups of individuals acquired through experience. As you come to know a person, you begin to form what might be described as a rough mental sketch of what the person is like. This rough sketch is analogous to a social schema. In later encounters with the person, you add information to fill in the details of your schema about him or her. Thus, social schemata serve as the structure for additional information about the person.

Social schemata for groups of individuals include a person's view of middle-class persons, the poor, the handicapped, the rich, the elderly, scientists, and so on. But, when we have a cognitive framework that represents a specific example of a person from a particular group, it is called a **prototype**. A prototype represents a specific, concrete example of a person from a particular group. For example, your prototype of scientists might re-

Social Cognition: All cognitions and cognitive processes that play a role in social behavior.

Social Schema (pl. schemata): A cognitive framework about specific individuals or groups of individuals acquired by experience.

Prototype: A cognitive structure that represents a specific example of a person from a particular group.

semble a grey-haired man or woman wearing a white laboratory coat and holding a test tube; your prototype of used car salesmen, a slick-looking, fast-talking, dark-haired man dressed in a cheap suit.

Self-Schemata: Schemata that pertain to the way we view ourselves; generalizations and expectations that we have about our own dispositions and behavior.

Another type of schemata are those that pertain to the way we view ourselves, or **self-schemata.** Self-schemata are generalizations and expectations that we have about our own dispositions and behavior. If your self-schemata include the generalization that you are good at leading others, you would tend to see yourself as a likely candidate for a leadership position. If others criticize your leadership role, you might ignore their feedback or view them in a negative light (for example, they are untrustworthy, don't understand how hard it is to lead, don't appreciate your value as a leader, etc.).

Script: A social schema that pertains to social situations; a cognitive framework for the normal characteristics and course of events of a social situation.

Another type of social schema pertains to social situations. A **script** is a cognitive framework for the normal characteristics and course of events of a social situation. Through experience, we come to acquire general ideas and expectations toward a variety of social situations—family gatherings, shopping at department stores, going to the hairdressers, and so on. Thus, when you go shopping, you expect the store clerk to help you find what you are looking for. You don't expect other shoppers to ask you for help. If one does, you are likely to say something like, "But I don't work here."

Cognition plays a major role in social behavior. It influences the way we gather social information and our interpretation of it. Our view of others and ourselves depends heavily on it. In the next section we will continue to explore the relationship between social behavior and cognition as we examine the nature of attitudes.

ATTITUDES

Attitude: A relatively enduring cluster of feelings, beliefs, and action tendencies toward specific persons, groups, ideas, or objects.

When stopped and asked by a reporter what she thought of the chances of an incumbent in an upcoming election, an elderly woman became tense and raised her voice. "I've been in this state for a long time," she said, "and never have I seen a more dishonest and self-serving politician. I don't like him and I, for one, am voting against him." In this woman's statement, we can see each of the three major components of an **attitude,** which can be defined as a relatively enduring cluster of feelings, beliefs, and action ten-

■ Learning Check ■

Read the right side, then cover and try to recite. Repeat.

For each of the following cognitive frameworks, try to indicate whether it pertains to (1) another person or group of persons; (2) a specific example of a person from a particular group; (3) to oneself; and (4) to events. (Answers are on the right.)

Prototype	Specific example of person from a particular group
Self-Schemata	Oneself
Social Schemata	Person or group of persons
Script	Events

In understanding ourselves, we must also understand the people we encounter throughout our lives. We do not exist in isolation, but instead interact with and respond to those around us. Our family, friends, co-workers, and even strangers affect our behavior, and our study of psychology is not complete without looking at our actions within this social context.

Just as we come to know ourselves by observing our own behavior, we develop perceptions of others by judging their likes and dislikes, and their attitudes towards us. We choose friends who share our interests, and respond warmly when they express their own caring and admiration.

Our parents also have a strong influence on our attitudes. From a very young age, we are taught to believe as they do, and even to imitate their actions.

Often, we respond closely to pressure from our peers, and follow their lead, no matter how strange the behavior seems at the time.

Group influence can be quite intense, and at times, we feel as if there is no retreat. The pressure to conform can be so great that workers may agree to strike, though they do not feel strongly about the cause. Even passive sports fans, caught in a violent mob, can be swept up by a wave of aggression.

Sometimes, it only takes one persuasive leader to change how we feel; at other times, a whole society can impose its beliefs on us.

Whether we are responding to one close friend or a crowd of strangers, our attitudes and actions are influenced by those around us. We must remember, as we come to understand ourselves, that our social behavior plays an important part in our lives.

dencies toward specific persons, groups, ideas, or things (Eagly & Himmelfarb, 1978; Rajecki, 1982). In her statement, the woman expressed her feelings ("I don't like him"), her belief ("he's dishonest and self-serving"), and her action tendencies ("I'm voting against him").

The study of attitudes and attitude change is a central topic in social psychology. In our discussion of attitude, we will begin by considering how we form our attitudes and how social psychologists measure them. Next, we will examine the question of how attitudes are changed and the relationship between attitudes and behavior. Finally, we will consider prejudice—a special type of attitude with social implications.

How Attitudes Are Formed and Measured

Social learning experiences play a major role in the attitudes a person acquires. Through observational learning, we observe, as children, the reactions of the members of our families and other adults and learn from their experience. We imitate others and follow their example as models. We also acquire attitudes as a result of direct conditioning experiences. A child salutes during the raising of the flag at a parade, and the parents reinforce a positive attitude toward flag and country with praise, approval, or other rewards, as in operant conditioning (see Chapter 6). Later, the child may be punished for playing with another child of a certain religious or ethnic orientation. The child also learns by association, as in classical conditioning (see Chapter 6). For example, if the parents frequently associate Cubans with words like cruel, bad, mean, dirty, etc., then the child may soon acquire a rather negative attitude toward Cubans. Indeed, children's attitudes toward political, economic, and religious affairs are quite similar to their parents' (Stone, 1974; Jennings & Niemi, 1968).

Parents do not, however, have a monopoly on their children's attitudes. In addition to providing information, peers have the power to reward and punish by giving acceptance and approval or withholding it. A child who fails to adopt "popular" attitudes—those that are in fashion and widely held—is ignored or excluded. Junior high school students are especially susceptible to such pressures to adopt the attitudes of their peers (Costanzo, 1970).

In sum, attitudes are learned behavior. Through social learning experiences and conditioning, we acquire clusters of feelings, beliefs, and action tendencies toward people, groups, ideas, and so on.

Because an attitude can encompass so many different aspects of behavior, social psychologists have had to be creative in finding ways of measuring them. One such approach is called the Likert Scale. In the **Likert Scale,** individuals are asked to indicate their degree of agreement or disagreement with a variety of statements that pertain to their views about a particular person, group, idea, or thing (Likert, 1932). (See Figure 13.2.) Another approach is the **semantic differential.** In this procedure, the individual is asked to indicate his or her attitude by rating his or her reaction to each of a series of paired opposites, as in Figure 13.2 (Osgood et al., 1957).

The Likert Scale and semantic differential can be used to measure people's attitudes toward just about anything. They also can be used to measure attitude change.

Likert Scale: A technique used to measure attitudes, in which individuals are asked to indicate their degree of agreement or disagreement with a variety of statements that pertain to their views about a particular person, group, idea, object, or event.

Semantic Differential: A method of measuring attitudes in which the individual is asked to indicate his or her attitude toward a person, group, idea, object, or event by rating it on a seven-point scale for each of a series of paired opposites.

Figure 13.2 Measuring Attitudes: The Likert Scale and Semantic Differential.

Likert Scale

The individual is given a series of questions and asked to indicate level of agreement or disagreement as in the following:

1. I prefer large cars over small ones even though they cost more to purchase and maintain.
   (Circle One)

1	2	3	4	5
Strongly Disagree	Disagree	Undecided	Agree	Strongly Agree

Semantic Differential

Subjects asked to rate a person, group, idea or thing in terms of a series of paired opposites. For example, to sample a person's attitudes toward a new perfume or cologne, a company might ask people to rate it in terms of the following:

Sweet .   .   .   .   .   . Bitter

Light .   .   .   .   .   . Heavy

Warm .   .   .   .   .   . Cold

Fashionable .   .   .   .   .   . Silly

Attitude Change Through Persuasive Communication

Social psychologists are not only interested in measuring a person's attitude, they also want to understand the conditions that lead to attitude change. Among the conditions that have been studied in detail are those relating to **persuasive communication**—written, spoken, televised, or filmed messages intended to persuade or promote attitude change.

The first intensive, large-scale investigation of persuasive communication began during the Second World War, when the military invited psychologist Carl Hovland to help solve training and morale problems. Hovland and colleagues identified a number of factors critical to effective persuasion. These included the source of the communication, the type of message, and characteristics of the audience. In other words, who says what to whom (Hovland et al., 1949, 1953).

The Source of the Communication. As you might suspect, the characteristics of the communicator can have a substantial impact on his or her persuasiveness. People respond best to communicators who they believe to be sincere, trustworthy, competent, and knowledgeable (Eagly & Himmelfarb, 1978; Wood & Eagly, 1981). Audiences also respond to communicators who are attractive, similar to themselves, or of high status (Eagly et al., 1978; Zimbardo et al., 1977). Communicators who are not viewed as sincere, trustworthy, or competent, or who do not seem to know what they are talking

Persuasive Communication: Written, spoken, televised, or filmed messages intended to persuade or promote attitude change.

about, or who are personally unappealing, lack credibility and hence are unconvincing.

One advantage of attractive or high status communicators is that they arouse more interest and attention, which, in turn, increases the chances that people in the audience will think more carefully about their message. Or, the more credible or famous a communicator, the more likely the audience will listen to and think about the message and associate it with the communicator's positive attributes. Thus, the power of effective communicators stems in part from their ability to affect cognitions (Jaccard, 1981).

The Type of Message. The kind of argument a communicator makes can affect the way an audience responds. Emotional appeals, for example, attempt to alter attitudes by arousing the audience's emotions. In some cases the emotions are positive, such as a heart-warming or inspiring story. In other cases, the intent of the message is to arouse fear, shame, or guilt. In general, messages that arouse emotion are more effective in inducing attitude change than the nonemotional, logical presentations of rational arguments (Higbee, 1969; Leventhal, 1970). Appealing to one's fear of a premature death and desire for family security is usually more effective in persuading people they need more life insurance than presenting a table of statistical probabilities, for instance.

Politicians are often persuasive communicators due to their attractiveness, high status, and ability to use emotional appeal.

If appealing to people's fears enhances the persuasiveness of a message, can we assume that the most effective messages are those that induce the most fear? Comparisons of high and low fear messages have shown that determining the ideal amount of fear in a message can be quite tricky. In a classic study, Janis and Feshbach (1953) found that a low fear message that warned of possible tooth decay and cavities produced more positive attitudes toward proper dental care than a high fear message that included graphic pictures of advanced gum disease. Based on these findings it was concluded and widely believed that the most effective messages are those that arouse low or moderate levels of fear. A study of attitudes about the dangers of smoking, however (Leventhal et al., 1967), found that a high fear film depicting blackened, diseased lungs was more effective than a low fear film that was far less gruesome. Subsequently, several other investigators reported a similar superiority for high fear messages, contradicting the original classic study.

In an attempt to resolve the inconsistencies, social psychologists learned that high fear messages fail when the audience finds the message so disturbing that to cope with it they must either reject it or convince themselves it couldn't happen to them. If, however, the audience can be convinced that there is a good chance the negative outcome can happen to them, and the message includes specific recommendations for preventing the negative outcome, the high fear message can be extremely persuasive (Eagly, 1974; Rogers, 1975). The next time you are confronted by an emotional appeal, you might ask yourself if it makes use of findings from social psychology. If it is a high fear appeal, then it should provide specific recommendations or steps one can take to prevent or reduce the threat.

Information-processing explanations of emotional appeals hold that the effect of a message depends on how it is processed (Wood & Eagly, 1981). Again, the key to enhancing the effectiveness of a message is to present it so as to maximize the chances the individual will think about it (Jaccard, 1981). People are likely to think more about messages that are personally relevant, thus the power of the impression that the negative outcome *is something that can actually happen to the person.* Similarly, fear may induce a person to think more carefully about the pros and cons of a message.

The Audience. Although the extent to which one processes a message plays a key role in its effectiveness, more isn't always better. If the audience already knows and favors a certain attitude, then encouraging them to think about it by presenting counterarguments just might lead them to change their minds. Thus, when an audience is already favorably disposed, there is no sense in arousing them to think about the other side. If, however, the audience is undecided, knows there are two sides to the argument, or is certain to hear the other side and is relatively intelligent, presenting only your side may reduce your credibility or make them wonder about the counterarguments. In a debate, for example, it usually is best to warn the audience by presenting your opponent's arguments in relatively weak form and then refuting them. In this way, the audience has time to think about the problems with your opponent's position and become more resistant to it. For example, in arguing against a tuition increase, you might say something like this: "Some say that more tuition will mean better services for all; but what about the students who can't afford to register—how will they get better service?" In sum, sometimes the most effective message is one that increases processing; other times, it is one that limits it or directs it in a certain way. (Figure 13.3 summarizes some of the major aspects of persuasive communication.)

Attitudes and Behavior

Social psychologists have learned that attitudes predict actions only under certain conditions. First, the attitude must be strong; in general, the stronger the attitude, the better it will predict a person's actions (Fazio et al., 1982; Snyder & Kendzierski, 1982). Second, the more specific the attitude,

Figure 13.3 Schematic Summary of the Factors Related to Persuasive Communication.

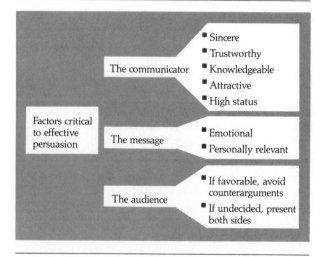

the better it predicts behavior (Borgida & Campbell, 1982). For example, you may have a strong negative attitude toward large corporations. Yet if you are employed by one, you might work as hard as you can for it because of your more specific attitudes toward excellence. Finally, attitudes are most likely to predict action when the outcome of an event affects you personally (Sivacek & Crano, 1982). For example, you may be against overdevelopment in the cities. But you don't bother to fight plans for new development unless the city informs you of a plan to build a large apartment complex in your neighborhood. Thus, a person's attitudes and actions don't necessarily correspond. What is more, the relationship between attitudes and actions is not always a one-way street.

Changing Attitudes Through Behavior Change and Cognitive Inconsistencies

In a classic experiment, college students were given various rewards for engaging in **attitude-discrepant actions** (actions inconsistent with one's attitudes). The students were paid to convince others to participate in boring, useless tasks, like circling all the vowels in an old newspaper. Students who were paid only a dollar an hour to convince others to perform the task showed a considerable change in attitude after the experiment. Though they had begun with a negative attitude toward the task, they came to see it as interesting and worthwhile. In contrast, students who were paid twenty dollars an hour to convince others to perform the task showed little change in attitude.

In interpreting their findings, Festinger and Carlsmith (1959) argued that engaging in attitude-discrepant actions had created a state of discomfort, which they called dissonance, in the students. Such dissonance, they argued, results from holding two inconsistent beliefs or ideas at the same time. This dissonance acts as a drive, urging a person to reduce the cognitive inconsistency. Those students who were paid twenty dollars for the task reduced the inconsistency by reasoning that inducing others to perform the futile ordeal was justified by their reward. But the students who were paid only one dollar had trouble justifying their attitude-discrepant behavior. Thus, they could not easily resolve that the task was boring but that they had told others it was fun. To reduce their dissonance, these students changed their attitude toward the task.

Festinger and Carlsmith (1959) hypothesized that dissonance caused by attitude-discrepant actions can be reduced in one of three ways. First, one may alter one's action to fit the original attitude. For example, the students who were paid only $1.00 might have dropped out of the experiment or told others what they really thought of the task. Second, one may change the attitude to fit the actions, just as those that were paid $1.00 adopted a more favorable attitude toward the task. Finally, dissonance can be reduced by reevaluating the importance of the attitude or actions, just as the students who were paid $20.00 convinced themselves that their actions were of little importance relative to the reward.

Subsequent work revealed that Festinger and Carlsmith were only partially correct, however. Attitude-discrepant actions cause attitude change only under certain conditions. First, the individual has to believe that there

Attitude-Discrepant Actions: Actions inconsistent with one's attitudes.

Figure 13.4 Schematic Summary of Cognitive Dissonance Theory.

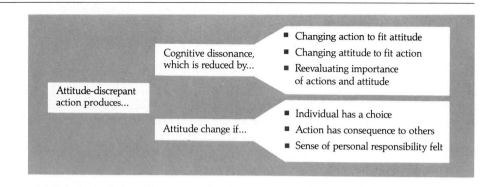

is a choice whether or not to perform the act. Individuals who are forced to engage in attitude-discrepant actions at gunpoint, for example, show little attitude change. Moreover, the actions must be of some consequence to others—someone else has to be affected. Finally, one must feel a sense of personal responsibility for these consequences (Cooper, 1980; Oskamp, 1977). (See Figure 13.4 for a summary.)

A special case of cognitive inconsistency occurs when somebody we like has an attitude in strong disagreement with one of our own. For example, you may be for capital punishment and find that one of your best friends is totally against the death penalty. According to balance theory, people are comfortable when the people they like share their views on issues that both consider important. When they don't, it creates a state of imbalance—a discomfort similar to cognitive dissonance (Heider, 1958; Newcomb, 1981). To restore the balance, the relationship or the attitude must undergo some change. Either you will like your friend less, or she you, or one of you will change your attitude when you disagree on an important issue, according to balance theory.

Prejudice and Related Concepts

A special type of attitude, an unjustifiable negative attitude toward members of some distinct social group, has a special name, prejudice. More specifically, **prejudice** refers to an intolerant, unfair, or unfavorable attitude toward a group of people (Harding et al., 1969). Prejudice involves a prejudgment. A person with a prejudice has negative feelings toward others only because they happen to be members of a particular group. For example, people with a prejudice against Jews would tend to respond to each individual Jew on the basis of his or her negative feelings and preconceived

Prejudice: An intolerant, unfair, or unfavorable attitude toward the members of a specific group.

■ Learning Check ■

Read the right side, then cover and try to recite. Repeat.

When attitudes predict behavior:

1. The attitude is strong.
2. The attitude is specific.
3. The outcome of an event affects you personally.

notion about Jews rather than on the basis of the individual's behavior and deeds.

When the action tendencies of a prejudiced attitude are actually expressed in overt behavior, they too have a special name, discrimination. **Discrimination** refers to unjustified negative actions against the members of a specific group. Discrimination sometimes involves unfair hiring practices. For example, when the Irish first began immigrating to the United States in large numbers to avoid the scourge of Ireland's potato famine, many business owners hung a sign on their doors with the letters INNA, which meant, "Irish need not apply."

The specific beliefs that accompany a prejudice also have a special name, stereotype. A **stereotype** is a set of beliefs and expectations about the members of a specific group. For example, a person who stereotypes Italians as hot-tempered attributes this characteristic to each individual Italian and automatically expects an Italian to act in accordance with the stereotype regardless of his or her actual temperament.

In sum, there is a close correspondence between the feeling, action, and belief components of attitudes and prejudice, discrimination, and stereotypes, respectively. Because prejudice is a negative attitude, it reflects a negative feeling. When you add discrimination and a set of negative beliefs, you get such complex problems as racism and sexism—negative attitudes, beliefs, and actions toward an individual because of race or sex.

Sources of Prejudice. Social psychologists are concerned with how people acquire their prejudices, discriminatory practices, and stereotypes. Many different factors have been implicated. Social learning experiences and direct conditioning may be involved in the formation of a prejudiced attitude. People acquire their prejudices by observing others, by rewards and punishments, and by association (see page 463 on attitude formation).

A second factor that has been implicated in prejudice is competition between groups (Esman, 1970). New groups can threaten the security and economic well-being of an established group, just as each new wave of immigrants to the United States were viewed as a threat to job security by those that had come before and were already established. To protect itself from the intruding new group, the established one develops negative feelings and discriminatory practices.

A third possible source of prejudice is a tendency of people to divide the social world into "those that are with us" and "those that are not with us, or against us." Those that are with us are considered the in-group; those that are not, the out-group (Tajfel & Turner, 1979). Before long, people in the in-group develop negative attitudes toward those in the out-group (Wilder, 1981).

Some social psychologists link prejudice to a particular cluster of dispositional traits and tendencies (Adorno et al., 1950). Many prejudiced people, regardless of the target of their prejudice—Jews, blacks, women, Irish, Italians, Catholics, or whichever—seem to have one thing in common. They possess what Adorno and colleagues (1950) call the **authoritarian personality.** According to these researchers, authoritarian personalities are rigid, hostile, and overconventional. They feel justified in hurting anyone who doesn't fit into their preconceived notions of proper conduct. They are over-

Discrimination: Unjustified negative actions against the members of a specific group.

Stereotype: A set of beliefs and expectations about members of a specific group.

Authoritarian Personality: A rigid, hostile, overconventional individual who is overconcerned with issues of power and authority and prone toward prejudice.

concerned with issues of power and authority. They believe firmly that one should follow the orders of one's superior.

Reducing Prejudice. In addition to understanding the causes of prejudice, social psychologists are concerned with techniques that can be used to reduce it. One promising approach involves **intergroup contact** (Simpson & Yinger, 1972; Stephan, 1978). People with a prejudice toward one another are brought together in small groups. An unbiased third party helps them to communicate with and understand each other better. A number of studies have found that, under certain conditions (for example, the two groups engage in informal contact and meet under cooperative conditions), such direct contact between members of different racial or ethnic groups is often followed by a substantial reduction in prejudice (Aronson et al., 1978).

> **Intergroup Contact:** A technique of reducing prejudice by bringing together people with a prejudice toward each other.

SOCIAL INFLUENCE

The ways in which we are influenced by others are many. In this section we examine four specific types of such social influence: obedience, compliance, comformity, and group pressures.

Obedience

Obedience is a form of social influence in which an individual is commanded to act in accordance with an order from an authority. If a traffic officer signals a driver to proceed through a red light, the driver usually obeys. But what are the limits of obedience? Is there a point at which an individual won't obey the commands of authority? Let's consider this question by putting you in the position of the subjects who participated in a classic social psychological experiment on obedience.

> **Obedience:** A form of social influence in which an individual is commanded to act in accordance with an order from an authority.

*This photo shows the shock machine used by Milgram (left),
and the actor (learner) being strapped in (right) before the experiment.*

Imagine you've decided to respond to an ad in the newspaper asking for volunteers for a psychological experiment. You make your way to the science building of a university, where you meet a friendly, middle-aged man who is also responding to the ad. The experimenter explains that he is conducting a learning experiment to test his theory that people learn faster when punished. Your heart skips a beat when you see his shock machine with dials numbered 15, 30, 45, and so on up to 450 volts. You are especially alarmed by the warning *Danger: Severe Shock* under the dials marked 375, 390, 405, and 420, and by the XXX under the dials marked 435 and 450. Luckily, you are selected as the teacher and the middle-aged man is strapped to a chair and hooked up to the shock machine.

Your job is to read a list of word pairs to the learner (apple–red, baby–cries, etc.). After reading the whole list, you then read the first word of each pair and he is to tell you the second. Each time he is wrong you are to give him a shock, increasing the strength of the shock with each new wrong answer.

You read the list and then test the learner. After a few correct responses he makes an error, and the experimenter instructs you to give him a 15-volt shock. As you proceed, the learner continues to make errors; soon you are up around the 150-volt level. The poor man finally begins to moan and begs to be let free. But the experimenter assures you that he will take responsibility for the man's safety and insists that you continue. "The man is not being permanently injured," he responds. "It is absolutely essential that you continue."

Stanley Milgram (1963) placed people in this very predicament. The machine he used was a fake—it didn't really shock the learner—and the learner only pretended to be hurt. Before conducting the experiment, Milgram had asked psychiatrists and other professionals how far people might go in such a situation. Few believed that free American citizens would obey the experimenter and shock the learner at the 450-volt level. Yet in the first trial, 65

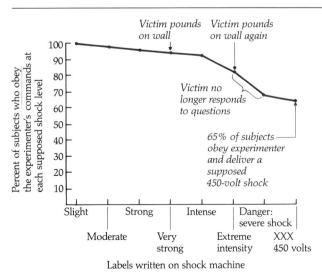

Figure 13.5 Despite predictions to the contrary, 65 percent of Milgram's subjects followed the commands of authority and continued delivering shocks through the 450-volt level. (After Milgram, 1963).

percent of the forty volunteers obeyed and delivered shocks through the highest level (see Figure 13.5).

Milgram tried altering the conditions of the experiment to see if the results would stand up. He moved the laboratory to a run-down old building; he used students as volunteers. Results were about the same. Some 62.5 percent of the subjects followed the experimenter's commands to the end, even when the learner feigned extreme pain and begged to be released (Milgram, 1965a).

Milgram's subjects were far more obedient than anyone would have believed or predicted. When the learner was placed in the same room as the teacher, 40 percent of the subjects still obeyed to the end. Some 30 percent obeyed to the end even when the learner partially freed himself and the subject had to force the learner's hand down on the shock plate; and 22 percent obeyed to the end when the experimenter was not actually present but gave the orders over the telephone (Milgram, 1970, 1974).

Milgram's obedience studies immediately raised concerns about the ethics of his experimental procedures (Baumrind, 1964). Some questioned his use of **deception**—deceiving subjects by deliberately withholding information about the true nature of the experiment. In his defense, Milgram argued that the extreme tension subjects experienced during the experiment, as revealed by their quivering voices, shaky hands, and heavy breathing, could not have been anticipated. The professionals Milgram had questioned before the experiment had greatly underestimated the level of obedience Milgram was to find as well as the stress such a situation could invoke. Also in his defense, Milgram used a **debriefing** procedure to undo any damage. After the experiment, he explained the real purpose, reassured subjects, and provided a friendly reconciliation between the subject and unharmed victim. When the experiment was complete, subjects were given a written report of the results and the opportunity to respond to a questionnaire pertaining to their experiences as subjects. A large majority (84 percent) indicated they were glad they participated and that experiments of this type should continue (Milgram, 1964, 1974).

Today, the use of deception in psychological experiments remains a matter of controversy (Baumrind, 1985). According to the Ethical Code of the American Psychological Association (1982), subjects cannot be exposed to deception unless: (1) it can be justified by the potential scientific benefits; (2) precautions are taken to reduce possible harm to subjects; (3) there is not another way of answering the question posed by the experiment; (4) subjects are warned in advance of possible dangers; (5) and subjects provide informed consent in which they sign an agreement that specifies the potential risks of the experiment.

Is it possible to protect oneself from the coercive power of authority? Milgram (1965b) learned that, if just one disobedient person were added to his experimental situation, there was a significant decrease in obedience. If one person has the courage to resist, others may follow. But in the absence of defiant models, resistance to authority stems from taking responsibility for one's actions. In post-experimental interviews, the most common rationale Milgram's subjects provided for their obedience was that the experimenter "took" responsibility. Awareness of one's susceptibility to authority can also help one be more resistant to unreasonable or inappropriate commands. Obedience can, but need not, be blind. In Box 13.1 we observe the

Deception: Deceiving subjects by withholding information about the true nature of the experiment.

Debriefing: Explaining the true nature of an experiment in which deception was used.

Box 13.1 PSYCHOLOGY IN ACTION: Understanding Power

Suppose that, as floor supervisor in the jewelry department of a department store, you have received several complaints that one of your clerks, John M., is rude and discourteous. You subsequently keep an eye on him. You notice that he always seems to wear a frown and rarely uses words like "please" or "thank you." How might you, as a person and as John's supervisor, use social influence to change John's behavior? Let's look at five different types of power you might use: legitimate power, expert power, referent power, coercive power, and reward power.

Legitimate power refers to the influence an individual holds over another because of his or her role or position. An instructor has legitimate power over students. A general has legitimate power over a captain. A manager has legitimate power over a subordinate. Legitimate power stems from the position one holds rather than from the characteristics of the individual who holds the position. As John's supervisor, you have legitimate power over him. In using legitimate power, you could simply tell John that, as his supervisor, you are ordering him to make an effort to be more courteous with the customers. Legitimate power can be quite influential, as we just learned in examining Milgram's studies of obedience to authority. But you could use other types of power as well.

Expert power refers to the influence an individual holds over others by virtue of knowledge or expertise in a given area. An instructor exerts influence over students not only because of position but also because of knowledge and training in a particular field of study. In using expert power to influence John, you could argue that, through your experience and training, you know that it is best to be courteous to customers. But if John has been working for the company

longer than you he might reject your argument. So you might want to use referent power instead.

Referent power refers to the influence an individual holds over another because of a close interpersonal relationship. Friends have referent power over each other. If you had made the effort to develop a working relationship with John, you might have used referent power. You could say something like, "Look, John. I know it doesn't seem important to you, but *do me a favor; do it for me*; be courteous." But, if you have no interest in a relationship with John, you could resort to coercive power.

Coercive power refers to influence that stems from the ability to withhold rewards or punish others. As John's supervisor you could use coercive power by threatening to terminate or demote him. You could also make his job less satisfying by restricting his duties to dusting display cases. In using coercive power, you would be applying a technique of learning. Punishing John for being discourteous is one way of suppressing such behavior.

A more positive approach would be to use reward power—influence derived from one's ability to dispense rewards. You might try, for example, to shape John's behavior by observing him carefully and praising him for being courteous. You also might try to use your reward power to motivate John by telling him that more courteous behavior on his part might lead to a pay increase. You could use observational learning and modeling by assigning him to work in the presence of a courteous worker. John could then observe the desired behaviors and might be encouraged to model them if he sees you reward the courteous worker with a bonus.

---

power of authority from a somewhat different perspective by examining various forms of power and how they might be used in real-life situations.

■ **Learning Clue** ■

Keep in mind that the various techniques of compliance involve multiple requests. The first request sets up a second or additional request.

Compliance

Compliance differs from obedience in that what is asked of an individual comes in the form of a request, rather than an order or command. Because a request does not usually carry the same weight as an order, people

Compliance: A form of social influence in which an individual is requested, rather than commanded, to perform some act.

Foot-in-the-Door Technique: Getting a person to agree to a small request to increase the chances he or she will later comply with a larger one.

have found some clever, and sometimes devious, techniques to induce others to comply with their requests. Three such techniques are called the "foot-in-the-door," the "door-in-the-face," and the "low ball procedure."

The idea of the **foot-in-the-door technique** is that, when you get a person to agree to a small request, he or she is much more likely to comply subsequently to a larger one. For example, homeowners who agreed to place a small "Keep America Beautiful" sign in their front windows were much more likely to agree to a later request to place a large sign in their front yard than were others from the same neighborhood who were only subjected to the larger request (Freedman & Fraser, 1966). And people who agreed to a request for a 5-minute telephone interview were more likely to agree to a 25-minute interview than people who did not receive the smaller request (Zuckerman et al., 1979).

Door-in-the-Face Technique: Enhancing compliance by asking a very substantial request which, if refused, can be followed by a smaller request.

In the **door-in-the-face technique,** by contrast, one begins with a very substantial request. Then, if refused, a much smaller request is made. A number of studies have shown that people who refuse a large request often are more likely to comply with a smaller request. To be effective, however, the first request must be relatively large and related to the second (DeJong, 1979).

Low Ball Procedure: Altering the nature of a request to which someone has already complied, such as adding on charges after a sale has been made.

In the **low ball procedure,** one alters the nature of a request to which someone has already complied. It is sometimes used in direct sales to snarl an unsuspecting buyer. A product is offered at an unbelievably low price. After the customer agrees to buy it, he learns that the price doesn't include certain accessories, without which the product is of no value. After you agree to buy a vacuum cleaner for $45.00, a third of the usual cost, the salesperson says, "These five attachments go with the cleaner." "Good," you say, "wrap it up." The salesperson hands you a bill for $135.00 and, before you have a chance to protest, casually informs you that the accessories are not included in the price.

Conformity

Conformity: A form of social influence in which an individual acts in accord with accepted standards and beliefs. The pressure to yield to the wishes of others is indirect—in the form of group expectations and group pressure.

In compliance, the pressure on the individual is direct. In **conformity,** by contrast, an individual acts in accord with accepted standards and beliefs. The pressures to yield to the wishes of others thus come indirectly in the form of group expectations and group pressure.

To get an idea of the power of the group on an individual, put yourself in the place of subjects who participated in a classic series of experiments on conformity (Asch, 1951). You have volunteered to participate in what you have been told is an experiment on human visual perception. You are seated at a round table along with six others. You and the others are to match the line on one flashcard with one of three other lines on another card. By the apparent luck of the draw, you are seated so that you are next to the last to respond.

The experimenter holds up the first flashcard. The first five subjects all say line C provides the best match. Indeed, line C is obviously the correct choice, so you too choose line C. The same procedure is repeated several times. The task seems so easy that you begin to get bored. Then the experimenter presents another trial. Line A is obviously the best match this time, but the first person to respond chooses B. You take a second hard look at the cards when the next three subjects also choose B. Then, without hesitation, the person just before you says B. Now it's up to you. Do you conform and say "B" like everyone else, or do you step out of the group and choose A? Asch found that subjects went along with the group's obviously incorrect judgments on 32 percent of the trials.

In the actual experiment, the other subjects were confederates who responded according to prearranged instructions. Earlier results had shown that, when subjects were tested individually, they selected the incorrect line less than 5 percent of the time. In the context of the group and Asch's experimental procedure, however, subjects either questioned their own judgments or simply went along with the group. Roughly three out of four subjects agreed with a false judgment at least once (Asch, 1951, 1955).

Asch's experiment, the results of which have since been confirmed (Allen & Wilder, 1980; Nicholson et al., 1985), has a number of everyday applications. Jury murder trials, for instance, sometimes boil down to situations in which eleven jurors are convinced that the accused is guilty and one disagrees. To reach a unanimous verdict, the eleven pressure the dissenter to comply with their decision. The dissenter may start to doubt his or her original judgment, yield to the group, and vote to condemn someone who he or she believes is innocent. With two dissenters, however, the power of the majority is not as strong. (For more on psychology and law see the last section of this chapter.)

Just as the presence of disobedient models can reduce the tendency of others to obey, so can nonconformists reduce the pressure to conform. Asch (1956) found that, if even one confederate disagreed with the rest, subjects would conform with the group's incorrect judgments much less often—only about 5 percent of the time. And actual studies indicate that a small dissenting minority of jurors do not always submit to the will of the majority (Davis et al., 1981). In the next section we will look more closely at the nature of groups and group influences.

Groups and Group Influences

A **group** can be thought of as two or more people who interact so that each person influences and is influenced by the other (Shaw, 1981). The processes that operate in a group to influence its members are called **group dynamics.** Group dynamics include written and unwritten standards of behavior, or **group norms.** A code for how the members of a group should dress, written or unwritten, is a group norm. Such norms guide and regulate group behavior, and the pressure to act in accordance with them can be quite intense.

Social psychologists have learned that groups often cause a person to act quite differently from how he or she would act alone, as an individual. For one thing, group decisions tend to be either more risky or more conservative than those of any individual member working alone (Fraser, 1971). For another, in a group there is a tendency to relax and let others do the work (Latané et al., 1979). Consequently each individual member contributes less than they would if acting alone when solving a problem or completing a task, a phenomenon known as **social loafing.** As group size increases, each individual's level of **perceived dispensability** also increases. Feeling that he

Group: Two or more people who interact so that each person influences and is influenced by the other.

Group Dynamics: The processes that operate in a group to influence its members.

Group Norms: The written and unwritten standards of behavior of a group.

Social Loafing: The tendency of each individual member of a group to contribute less than they would if acting alone.

Perceived Dispensability: The feeling that one is less needed in a group, which leads to a reduced effort.

Cooperation: Two or more persons working together to reach a common goal. (See Box 13.2.)

or she is less needed, the person makes less effort. To minimize social loafing, social psychologists recommend making each individual believe that his or her individual effort is critically important or informing them that individual performance will be recorded (Kerr & Bruun, 1983).

Box 13.2 PSYCHOLOGY IN ACTION: Groups and Real-World Problems: The Robber's Cave Study

It was a beautiful summer afternoon when a group of eleven- and twelve-year-old boys arrived at the Robber's Cave Summer Camp. The boys were anticipating about six weeks of swimming, hiking, camping-out, and other typical summer camp activities. Little did they know that behind the scenes researchers were observing their behavior and had prepared some interesting little twists that would add spice to their experience (Sherif, 1966; Sherif et al., 1961).

The boys were assigned to a cabin located at the upper end of the camp. A second group of boys, who arrived a few hours later, were assigned to a cabin at the lower end of the camp. The two groups of boys were unaware of each other's presence. They were also unaware that the camp counselors and other camp staff were all part of a research team.

The researchers planned activities for each group that required mutual assistance, or **cooperation**—two or more persons working together to reach a common goal. Each group worked as a team to clear the beach, prepare a campsite, and build a campfire. Boys who had a flair for getting things done and assigning tasks soon emerged as leaders. The boys in each group developed a sense of mutual liking, or **cohesiveness**—the attraction and feeling of mutual concern that group members have for each other; the force that holds a group together. One group named itself the "Eagles"; the other called themselves "Rattlers."

Within each group, the boys' behavior toward each other was clearly positive. They helped each other, often for no apparent personal gain (e.g., one of the boys lost his pocketknife and three others spent several hours helping him find it). And they cooperated. But the boys' prosocial behavior was soon to change.

The Eagles and Rattlers had co-existed independently, each group unaware of the other. This state of peace soon ended, however, when the researchers brought the two groups together and forced them into **competition**—in which two individuals or groups strive for a goal that only one person or group can win. Relay races were held with desirable prizes only for the winning team. It was like a real-life situation in which two countries fight over the same territory, two people for the same lover, or two companies for the

same customers. One can only win at the other's expense. The groups soon found themselves in conflict. Members of each group would pick fights and called each other derogatory names. They planned raids on each other's campsites.

In the real world, such as in labor-management disputes or disagreements among nations, conflict is often settled through **negotiation**—the process of a mutual trading of offers and counter-offers until a consensus is reached. However, the Eagles and the Rattlers refused to negotiate. When the Eagles proposed that the leaders of each group meet and discuss their differences, the boys declined on the grounds that such would be a show of weakness.

Just before things really got out of hand, the researchers introduced a **superordinate goal**—an important goal that can only be achieved through cooperation. The truck that brought food for both groups "fell" into a ditch. It required the combined effort of both groups to pull it out with ropes. The researchers also arranged a break in the waterline. The two groups again had to combine their efforts to find the leak and restore their water. Through a series of superordinate goals, in which the two groups had to combine their efforts to achieve a common objective, the members of the two groups began talking to each other. Soon they actually began to like each other. The conflict was resolved.

As in the Robber Cave's Study, these boys are "pulling together" as a group to defeat a rival team.

More dangerous than social loafing is a problem that sometimes occurs in groups whose members place a high priority on uniformity and consensus. Such groups seem to take on a life of their own, independent of the control of any one, or even most, members. A case in point is the phenomenon of **groupthink,** the tendency of small, closely knit groups to quiet all dissent and to take a course of action without giving full consideration to the consequences or alternatives (Janis, 1972). Have you ever been in a situation where you did something because you thought that's what another person wanted to do? Then later you learn that the other person really didn't want to do it but did so, thinking that's what you wanted. Groupthink is something like that: nobody speaks up.

Groups can guard against the groupthink phenomenon by making a purposeful effort to encourage dissent and to examine both sides of an argument before making a decision. Individual members can play "devil's advocate," and those who disagree can be rewarded rather than criticized.

Another dangerous group dynamic is a loss of individual awareness and apprehension, or **deindividuation.** Being in a group can draw one's attention away from oneself and weaken restraints against impulsive or unacceptable behavior (Prentice-Dunn & Rogers, 1983). A person can get caught up in the ongoing situation and will of the group. There is a lowered ability to regulate one's own behavior and an increased tendency to follow the actions of others. Deindividuation helps us to better understand how law-abiding citizens can turn into a riotous mob that burns down neighborhoods or participates in a lynching.

Studying groups is not easy. Indeed, social psychologists have devised a number of ingenious ways to study them. One example, which illustrates a number of important aspects of group functioning, is a classic investigation known as the Robber's Cave Study, which we discuss in Box 13.2. In the Robber's Cave Study we see three major types of social interaction: the liking or attraction that developed between some of the boys, their helping of each other, and their aggression against one another. In the next section we will examine these three types of social relations in greater detail.

SOCIAL RELATIONS

What are the factors that cause people to like or dislike each other and treat each other as they do? In this section we will try to answer this question. We will discuss three major types of social relations: interpersonal attraction, aggression, and helping.

Interpersonal Attraction

Interpersonal attraction refers to an attitude of liking or disliking between two people. In an effort to understand why people like or dislike each other, social psychologists have proposed a number of theories. They have also identified a number of specific factors that exert a powerful influence on interpersonal attraction.

Cohesiveness: The attraction and feeling of mutual concern among group members.

Competition: Two individuals or groups striving for a goal that only one person or group can win.

Negotiation: The process of a mutual trading of offers and counter-offers until a consensus is reached.

Superordinate Goal: An important goal that only can be achieved through cooperation.

Groupthink: The tendency of a small, closely knit group to quiet all dissent and to take a course of action without giving full consideration to the consequences or alternatives.

Deindividuation: A loss of individual awareness and apprehension that occurs when a person is in a group.

Interpersonal Attraction: An attitude of liking or disliking between two people.

Theories of Interpersonal Attraction. Two major theories of interpersonal attraction are reward theory and equity theory. According to the reward theory, interpersonal attraction depends on learning (Byrne & Clore, 1970). Simply stated, we like people whose behavior we associate with rewards and positive feelings; we dislike people whose behavior we associate with negative feelings. The reward theory is based on the idea that people can become conditioned to like or dislike others. When we are with another person and we experience positive feelings, we associate the two and eventually become conditioned to respond to the person with positive feelings.

Equity theory carries the role of reward in attractions a step further and emphasizes trade-offs and balance. According to this theory, interpersonal attraction depends on both parties getting roughly the same degree of benefit (Hatfield & Traupmann, 1981). To the extent that there is equity in what each person gets and gives in a relationship, there is balance and the relationship should be enhanced. For example, Traupmann and colleagues (1981) found that the more husbands and wives saw their relationship as roughly equal in terms of give and take, the more they reported feeling satisfied and happy. Those that thought they were getting more than their share out of the relationship were less happy and satisfied; and those that were getting less than their share were even less satisfied and happy.

Factors in Interpersonal Attraction. Social psychologists have identified a number of processes that play a major role in interpersonal attraction. Among the most important of these are physical proximity (propinquity), personal characteristics, reciprocity, and intentions (see Figure 13.6).

It should come as no surprise that the people we come to like are those with whom we come into contact. **Propinquity,** or physical proximity, is one of the most powerful predictors of whether a friendship will develop. We are most apt to become attracted to those who cross our paths—in parking lots, at entrances, in supermarkets, at work, and so on (Newcomb, 1961; Monge & Kirste, 1980). In fact, anything that increases the likelihood that two people will meet increases the chances that they will get to know and like each other (Festinger et al., 1950). Thus, the closer a person lives to your

Propinquity: Physical proximity. An important factor in interpersonal attraction.

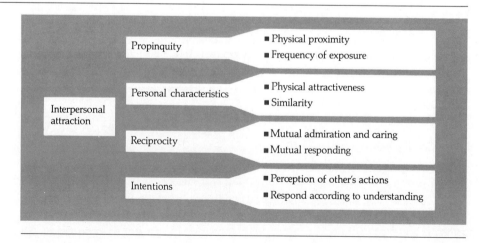

Figure 13.6 Schematic Summary of the Factors Involved in Interpersonal Attraction.

home, the more likely he or she will become your best friend (Ebbesen et al., 1976). And the person you are most likely to become romantically involved with and marry is someone you will meet in your neighborhood, at work, or in school (Burr, 1973). A number of studies have revealed, in fact, that the more we are exposed to just about anything—a meaningless word, a billboard, a song, another person—the more we like it (Zajonc, 1968). The main exception appears to occur when our initial impression is extremely negative. In such cases, repeated exposure can lead to decreased attraction (Swap, 1977).

Of course, mere exposure is not the only thing that matters. The person's personal characteristics—physical attractiveness, opinions and attitudes, needs and desires—count, too. In one study, students were led to believe that they were being matched by a computer for a school dance. Actually, they were assigned partners at random. About halfway through the dance they were asked to rate each other. The only factor that related to the students' attraction to each other and desire for future contact was physical appearance (Walster et al., 1966).

But people do not always choose the most beautiful or handsome person they can find for their partner. Instead, we tend to choose for a partner someone who is similar to ourselves. A number of studies have revealed that couples ranging from those on a first date to husbands and wives of all ages are roughly similar in physical attractiveness as rated by independent judges (Murstein, 1972). This tendency for people to choose a partner who is similar in attractiveness is known as the **matching phenomenon** (Berscheid et al., 1971). Even same-sex friends for both sexes have been found to be similar in attractiveness (Cash & Derlega, 1978). People are also attracted to others who are similar to them in interests, attitudes, abilities, and opinions (Newcomb, 1961; Hill & Stull, 1981).

Another major factor in interpersonal attraction is **reciprocity**—a mutual admiration and caring. Simply stated, we respond to others the way they respond to us. People like (or dislike) others to the extent that others like (or dislike) them (Byrne, 1971). People will tend to like you if you speak approvingly about them, do them a favor, or treat them kindly (Sigall & Aronson, 1969). Conversely, they are likely to reject you if you reject them (Byrne & Rhamey, 1965).

You may be thinking that there have been times when you liked or were kind to someone who rejected you. One reason people won't always respond in kind is that they don't always understand others' intentions. If others interpret your kind words as insincere flattery, they are likely to react negatively. This is because, although they often respond favorably to genuine praise, people do not like to be manipulated (Brehm & Cole, 1966; Colman, 1980).

Matching Phenomenon: The tendency for people to choose a partner who is similar to themselves in attractiveness.

Reciprocity: A mutual admiration and caring; the tendency to respond to others the way they respond to us.

Aggression

Many of the factors that play a role in interpersonal attraction—proximity, reciprocity, and intentions—also are involved in aggression. For example, many assaults and murders involve people who live in close proximity. And people tend to respond to aggression with aggression. Direct verbal or physical provocation—anything from calling names through direct physical attack—is a good way to elicit aggression in another (White & Gruber, 1982). Aggression can also stem from the way we perceive another's intentions (Goldstein et al., 1975). For example, if someone cuts in front of you on the highway, you're less likely to want to strangle the person if you think he or she is ill and on route to a hospital.

Aggression: Behavior directed toward the goal of harming or injuring another living being.

Aggression can be defined as behavior directed toward the goal of harming or injuring another living being (Baron, 1977). A number of theories have been advanced to explain aggression. One holds that aggression is due to inborn, genetically transmitted characteristics. According to this instinct theory, aggression within the members of a species is instinctual, the product of evolution and survival of the fittest (Lorenz, 1966).

Another view of aggression is that it is a drive (Dollard et al., 1939). According to the frustration-aggression hypothesis, for example, the thwarting of one's goals increases the strength of an aggressive drive that may then lead to aggression. The frustration-aggression hypothesis is subject to at least two limitations, however. First, people don't always respond to frustration with aggression. Sometimes people respond to thwarting with resignation or despair (Bandura, 1973). Second, there are many cases in which aggression occurs in the absence of frustration. For example, killings by hired assassins, professional soldiers, and even that of public executioners meet the definition of aggression but do not stem from frustration. (For more on instinct and drive theories of behavior, see Chapter 9, on motivation and emotion.)

A more prevalent theory of aggression is based on social learning theory, which emphasizes learning in the social context (see Chapter 6). Social learning interpretations hold that aggression is multiply determined, the product of observational learning, modeling, rewards and punishments, past experiences, and the immediate social environment (Bandura, 1973). Social learning theory also acknowledges the role of cognitions, such as our expectations and interpretations, in aggression.

Aggressive Model: Another person behaving in an aggressive manner.

According to social learning theory, when we are exposed to an **aggressive model**—another person behaving in an aggressive manner—we too can learn to be aggressive. Aggressive models provide examples of aggressive behavior for us to imitate. They may also show us that it pays to be aggressive. When we observe another person's aggression succeed in obtaining a reward or accomplishing a goal (for instance, gaining prestige, status, friendship, or self-respect by beating up a bad guy or bully), we obtain what is called vicarious gratification. We experience a reward indirectly. When we observe aggressive models whom we respect and admire—fighting on the football field and baseball diamond, for instance—we may imitate their behavior because we want to be like them (Bandura, 1973).

A controversial implication of the social learning view relates to the relationship between television and aggression. If exposure to aggressive models causes aggression, then viewing violence on television may be linked to the killings, beatings, shootings, muggings, and destruction that occur in the real world. In particular, is there a relationship between the viewing of TV violence and the amount of aggression exhibited by children?

To answer this question, Eron (1982) and Huesmann (1983) studied large groups of children over several years. The researchers conducted careful interviews of some 748 first- and third-grade children to determine how much

TV violence they observed. They also took note of other factors, such as the extent to which the children were punished or rejected by their parents and the attitudes of their parents toward aggression. In addition, they asked the classmates of these students to rate them in terms of how much aggression they observed in their actual behavior (fighting, hitting, verbal threats, and so on). The researchers found that, for both boys and girls, the more televised aggression they watched, the higher their level of aggression toward others. In fact, this relationship became even stronger year after year. But other factors—parental attitudes and treatment of the children—also contributed to the level of aggression exhibited by the children (Eron, 1982).

The evidence supporting the notion that watching violence on television promotes aggression is strong but not conclusive. Aggression, according to the social learning view, is multiply determined; evidence collected to date points to exposure to televised violence as among the determinants (Liebert et al., 1982).

The consequences of aggression are serious, no matter what its cause. And psychological research has a number of implications for how we might reduce it—avoid being a victim of it or suffering from the consequences of one's own aggressive acts. Studies have indicated, for example, that the mere presence of a gun or other weapon can stimulate aggressive behavior in a person prone to aggression (Berkowitz, 1981). This fact provides a good argument against having a dangerous weapon in the home. According to police reports, few people with handguns are ever able to use them for self-protection. Instead, a criminal uses the gun against the owner—or, more likely, the owner uses it against a friend or relative in the heat of an argument. Thus, one way to reduce the chances that you will be involved in an aggressive incident is to remove yourself from the instruments of aggression (Berkowitz, 1981).

Assertiveness training (see Chapter 15, Treatment of Abnormal Behavior) can also help to prevent aggression by giving people more constructive ways of expressing negative feelings. You might, for example, imagine yourself in a situation that might lead you to aggress against another. Then think of alternative ways of handling the same situation. Periodic mental rehearsal of such techniques can help you to remain calm in trying situations. (See Chapter 11 on coping, life-style, and stress for more on how to use mental rehearsal.)

One way to handle a person on the brink of aggression is by trying to communicate empathy or understanding—to acknowledge his or her anger. Have you ever expressed your anger, only to be ignored or told not to be angry? Telling someone not to be angry is a good way to make the person even more angry. Likewise, ignoring a person's anger may frustrate the person. Instead, an understanding response like "You seem really angry" can, in some situations, communicate a sense of empathy and defuse the person's anger.

Another way to defuse a person's anger is to elicit an incompatible response like humor (Zillman, 1971, 1979). In one study, exposure to humorous material reduced aggression in angry subjects (Mueller & Donnerstein, 1977). Mild sexual arousal (see Chapter 10 on sexuality) is also incompatible with aggression. And some studies have suggested that exposure to mild erotica can reduce future aggressive behavior (Baron, 1983; Frodi, 1977).

Finally, don't forget the tendency of expectations to become self-fulfilling prophecies. If you expect a person to be aggressive, you may inadvertently act in a way that encourages such behavior. Conversely, if you expect someone to behave in a reasonable manner and behave accordingly, your expectation may be fulfilled.

Altruism

Altruism: Concern and help for others that have no apparent benefit for the person who carries them out.

Whereas aggression shows the darker side of social behavior, altruism reveals the positive. **Altruism** refers to concern and help for others that have no apparent benefit for the person who carries them out (Staub, 1978). Altruism is thus a positive act which is performed regardless of whether or not there is a reward. When you help another person without any expectation of a reward, you are displaying altruistic behavior (Brown, 1975). Examples of such behavior include helping a stranded motorist fix a flat tire, providing assistance to the victim of an emergency or natural disaster, and helping a lost child find his or her mother, asking for nothing in return.

But sometimes people often fail to help others, even when they are in dire need. Early one morning in Queens, New York, a young woman was stabbed to death while some thirty-eight neighbors did nothing to help. The woman pleaded and screamed, but no one came to her aid, or so much as called the police. Following this incident, social psychologists began a series of investigations to understand why these bystanders failed to help the woman.

Bystander Effect: The phenomenon in which people are less likely to help someone in distress when others are present.

The researchers found that the number of people who heard the woman's cries may have worked against her. People are less likely to help someone in distress when others are present (Latané & Nida, 1981), a phenomenon known as the **bystander effect.** In one demonstration of the bystander effect, subjects were asked to fill out a questionnaire, presumably as part of an experiment. After several minutes, a pungent smoke was blown through a vent in the testing room. In one condition, subjects were alone. In another condition, two other persons, confederates of the experimenter, were present. The confederates were instructed to shrug their shoulders in response to the smoke and continue writing. When subjects were alone, 75

The chances of these down and out individuals receiving help from passers-by are especially slim due to the presence of others and their unkempt appearance.

percent acted to investigate the smoke. Only 10 percent acted, however, when they were with the two confederates (Latané & Darley, 1968).

In a group, each person seems to wait for someone else to do something. There is a **diffusion of responsibility**—a feeling that responsibility is shared by the group. Consequently, each person feels less responsible than they would as individuals. People also seem to want to make sure that someone who appears to be in distress does actually need help (Shotland & Huston, 1979). It's embarrassing to run to the aid of a person who yells in pain, only to learn that the person was just joking or overreacting. But there is a practical lesson here. If you need help, make sure you make your needs as clear as possible.

Some experts have hypothesized that helping behavior is due to a specific emotional reaction—empathy (Archer et al., 1981). Empathy can be defined as the vicarious experiencing of another's emotions (Hoffman, 1981). People who are high on measures of empathy are the most likely to help a person in need (Coke et al., 1978). Presumably, his or her tendency to see the world from another's perspective motivates the empathic individual to help.

Interpersonal attraction also plays a role in altruistic behavior. For instance, individuals were more likely to return an application for graduate school that had been left in a telephone booth by researchers if an attractive person's photo was attached to the application than if the photo of an unattractive person was attached (Benson et al., 1976). There is also a relationship between similarity and helping behavior (Krebs, 1975). Finally, people are likely to help others if they believe there is a good chance for reciprocity; that is, that the favor will be returned. Of course, if there is a motive for helping, we can't really call it altruism.

In studying topics such as altruism and aggression, we can see the relevance of social psychology to everyday behavior. Indeed, in their effort to understand social behavior, social psychologists have become increasingly interested in studying people in the context of real-world settings, and a relatively new subfield called Applied Social Psychology has emerged.

APPLICATIONS OF SOCIAL PSYCHOLOGY

When social psychologists talk about **applied social psychology,** they are referring to attempts to understand human social behavior in real-world settings (Fisher, 1982). A major goal of the research in applied social psychology is the solution of social problems. In this section we will briefly discuss two major applications of social psychological research to real-world settings: the physical environment and the legal system.

Environmental Psychology

Environmental psychology refers to the study of the interrelationship between individual behavior and the environment (Fisher et al., 1984). So-

Diffusion of Responsibility: A feeling that responsibility is shared by all members of a group; consequently each person feels less responsible than they would as individuals.

Applied Social Psychology: Attempts to understand human social behavior in real-world settings; a major goal of research in applied social psychology is the solution of social problems.

Environmental Psychology: That branch of psychology concerned with the interrelationship between individual behavior and the environment.

cial psychologists who study this field are interested in understanding how environments affect people and how people affect environments.

How Environment Affects Social Behavior. Temperature, sound, air quality, and other aspects of the physical environment affect our behavior in many ways. Soft music can have a soothing effect or make us more open to persuasive communications. When it gets too hot or humid, we tend to become irritable. Heat also affects aggression. As the temperature rises, tempers begin to flare and aggression becomes more likely. But when it gets extremely hot, all a person wants to do is seek comfort and be alone. Thus, the relationship between heat and aggression is what psychologists call *curvilinear*—as the temperature increases, so does aggression, but only up to a point, after which temperature increases actually lead to reduced aggression (Baron & Bell, 1976; Bell & Baron, 1976) (see Figure 13.7).

Noise: Unwanted sounds.

Noise, or unwanted sounds, also affects us in many ways. Blasting stereos, jet planes overhead, street repair and construction sounds are irritating. They can impair our performance. When children attend schools close to airports, or are subjected to other types of noise, they perform their work less well (for example, do poorer on arithmetic problems) and give up more quickly on problem-solving tasks than children who attend schools in quiet neighborhoods or who aren't subjected to noise (Loeb et al., 1982). When noise is loud, unpredictable, and uncontrollable, it becomes detrimental to performance, stressful, and detrimental to one's health (Glass & Singer, 1972). (For more on stressors, stress, and health, see Chapter 11.)

Noise also reduces helping behavior and increases aggression. In a study on noise and altruism, for example, students who had been exposed to uncontrollable noise were less likely to help a confederate of the experimenter (who posed as a stranger asking for help in solving a math problem) than students who had not been exposed to the noise (Sherrod & Downs, 1974). In another study, the researchers pretended to have an accident (dropping packages) near a construction site. They received less help from

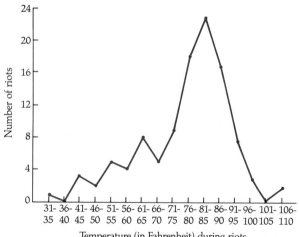

Figure 13.7 This graph shows the relationship between heat and riots. Contrary to popular belief, riots do not necessarily increase as the temperature rises; at very high temperatures, the number of riots occurring is less than at moderately high temperatures. (After Baron & Bell, 1976).

others under noisy conditions than when it was more quiet (Page, 1977). Studies of aggression and noise, on the other hand, have shown that people are more likely to respond with aggression when subjected to loud noise (Geen, 1978).

Human Spatial Behavior. Another area of concern in environmental psychology is the study of human spatial behavior, or **proxemics.** People use physical space to regulate social interactions in a number of ways. These include personal space, territoriality, and privacy (Fisher et al., 1984; Stokols, 1978a). We will continue our discussion of environmental psychology by considering briefly each of these three aspects of human spatial behavior.

A person's **personal space** can be defined as an invisible boundary or zone surrounding one's body that is thought of as a part of oneself. We normally don't like it when others invade our personal space. Moving physically close to another is usually a way of communicating intimacy. We consider it rude or threatening if a stranger moves into our intimate zone of personal space—the distance from about 0 to 1.5 feet that we reserve for such intimate behaviors as comforting a close friend and making love (Hall, 1966). An appropriate distance for friends and acquaintances is more like 1.5 to 4 feet; and for impersonal business contacts, more like 4 to 12 feet (Hall, 1966). Psychological studies suggest that one's response to an invasion of personal space depends heavily on attributions. When we interpret a person's attempts to come physically closer as a friendly, complimentary, or helpful gesture, our response tends to be positive; when we interpret it as rude, aggressive, or inappropriate, we react negatively (Konečni et al., 1975; Baron, 1978).

Another aspect of human spatial behavior is **territoriality**—the ownership, use, and defense of areas by persons or groups (Altman, 1975). When you say, "This is my room" or "This is my desk," you are displaying territoriality. Social psychologists study territoriality by such techniques as placing sweaters and books to mark off part of a library desk to see how and when people will invade the territory. They also use the concept of territoriality to explain such phenomena as the home field advantage in sports like football, baseball, and basketball. The fact is, sports teams tend to play better when on their own territory, and people tend to be more effective in performing a

Proxemics: The study of human spatial behavior.

Personal Space: An invisible boundary or zone around a person's body that is thought of as part of oneself.

Territoriality: The ownership and defense of areas by persons or groups.

A person's personal space is the invisible boundary or zone surrounding one's body that is thought of as part of oneself. In a business relationship, a comfortable distance is about 4–12 feet.

task or competing with others when on their own turf (room, home, dorm, etc.) (Edney, 1975; Martindale, 1971).

According to Altman (1975), the main function of territoriality in human behavior is to obtain privacy. **Privacy** refers to intentionally retreating from social contact in order to be alone or with a specific person or group of people. Having an area that we can call our own gives us a place to retreat from social contact. Without such a place, we would have less control over our social contact.

Our discussion of spatial behavior has been no more than a short glimpse at the many areas of concern in environmental psychology and the practical application of social psychological research to social problems and issues. In our concluding section, we will take a glimpse at still another area of application in social psychology.

The Legal System

In this chapter we have considered everything from how people come to know and understand others through how they use persuasion to change others' attitudes and various forms of social influence to control others' actions. Just about all of the topics we've discussed have a special relevance to our laws, judicial system, and system of justice. Consider what happens during a police interrogation.

The interrogator points a threatening finger at the accused and demands a confession. The accused doesn't obey, so the interrogator says, "We know you did it. An eyewitness identified you." Or, the interrogator may try the friendly approach. He sympathizes with the accused, tries to increase interpersonal attraction through flattery, or communicates friendship with a touch on the arm or a small favor—a cup of coffee or a cigarette. Perhaps you can think of other tactics that might be used, based on your knowledge of social behavior.

According to Tapp (1976), there are three key areas in which psychology interfaces with the law: legal socialization, the judicial processes, and the criminal justice system. Legal socialization refers to how we acquire attitudes about the law and our standards of right and wrong. The judicial processes include such topics as police interrogation methods, jury selection, eyewitness testimony, and jury decision making. Psychology's interface with the criminal justice system includes understanding the prison system

Privacy: Intentionally retreating from social contact in order to be alone or with a specific person or persons.

■ **Learning Check** ■

For each of the following three aspects of human spatial behavior, read the definition, then cover the right side and try to recite it. Repeat.

Personal Space	An invisible boundary or zone surrounding one's body that is thought of as part of oneself
Territoriality	The ownership, use, and defense of areas by persons or groups
Privacy	Intentionally retreating from social contact in order to be alone or with a specific group of people

and its methods. We won't be able to discuss all of these areas, or even a large chunk of them. We will be able to see, however, why the legal system is a major concern of applied social psychology.

In studying the judicial process, for example, social psychologists have examined attorneys, defendants, and witnesses. The attorney's opening arguments set the tone of a trial. When attorneys provide relatively long opening statements, assure the jurors of their client's innocence, and confidently promise to provide evidence of his or her innocence, jurors are more likely to find the accused not guilty, even if the promised evidence is never produced (Pyszczynski & Wrightsman, 1981). The effect of opening statements may be attributable to the power of first impressions, or the primacy effect. (But don't tell your lawyer to make promises that can't be kept, for it may boomerang if the prosecutor points it out to the jury in the closing arguments.)

Interpersonal attraction also operates in the courtroom. Juries tend to be easier on defendants who are physically attractive and similar to themselves (Stewart, 1980; Shepherd & Sloan, 1979). They are more persuaded by witnesses whom they perceive as credible—those who are confident and sincere, for example. Unfortunately, a jury's willingness to believe a sincere eyewitness can send an innocent person to jail; numerous studies have, in fact, attested to the unreliability of eyewitness testimony. In one, a mock crime was televised on a news program. Viewers were subsequently shown photographs of six suspects, including the real mugger. The result—only about 200 of the 2,000 eyewitnesses correctly identified the mugger (Buckhout, 1980). (For more on eyewitness testimony, see Chapter 7 on memory.)

Social psychological research has also profoundly affected the process of jury selection. Both defense lawyers and prosecutors take social psychological findings (for example, those relating to interpersonal attraction) into account when selecting jurors. But that is not all. Recently, the Courts, in the case of *Lockhart* v. *McCree*, made a major decision on jury selection based on social psychological findings.

In most states that allow capital punishment, prospective jurors who are against capital punishment are routinely excluded from murder trials in which the death penalty is possible. The argument is that, since they are against the death penalty, such jurors would not vote guilty even if they believed the accused is guilty (Turkington, 1986). Over 1,300 people have been sentenced to death in courtrooms where such jurors were excluded.

Social psychologists studied the issues. They found a definite difference between individuals who favor the death penalty and those against it (Rokeach & Vidmar, 1973). They found that those in favor of the death penalty were more likely to have an authoritarian personality (see the section on prejudice, p. 469). Such personalities are more likely to base their verdicts on how much they like the defendant, and to be especially punitive against those they don't like, regardless of the facts (Mitchell & Byrne, 1982). Other studies revealed that, in general, a person for capital punishment is more likely to vote for conviction than one who is not (Jurow, 1971).

Along with a number of judges, lawyers, and other professionals, social psychologists began to question the fairness of excluding jurors against capital punishment in murder trials. They conducted studies involving mock videotaped trials and found that the verdict often depended on who was in the jury. When at least two of its members were against the death penalty, the entire jury was more likely to come to an innocent verdict (Cowan et al., 1985).

Based on these and related findings, the 8th U.S. Circuit Court of Appeals ruled that the exclusion of jurors in capital punishment cases deprived defendants of a right to a fair trial. An all pro-capital punishment jury, the Court argued, was biased toward conviction. Then, on May 5, 1986, the U.S. Supreme Court reversed the ruling. According to the Supreme Court, even though studies may show that people who support the death penalty are more apt to convict suspected criminals, it is necessary to keep off juries those citizens who say their attitudes toward the death penalty might affect their impartiality. Despite the Supreme Court's reversal, this case illustrates psychology's influence on the judicial system and, in a broader context, on just about every area of our lives.

LEARNING FRAMEWORK

I. People acquire knowledge about themselves and others through direct experiences, interpretations, and cognitive frameworks.
  A. Social perception—the process through which we come to know and understand others—is strongly influenced by first impressions, physical appearance, and nonverbal communication. (Review: *Primacy Effect; Recency Effect*)
  B. Social psychologists have found that, in making attributions of other people's behavior, people have a tendency to overestimate the role of personal dispositions and underestimate the role of external pressures. (Review: *Fundamental Attribution Error; Figure 13.1*)
  C. In coming to know ourselves in relation to others, we are also subject to making attributional errors. (Review: *Self-Perception Theory; Actor-Observer Bias; Self-Serving Bias*)
  D. Our social cognition includes a number of specific frameworks for organizing information about people, ourselves, and social events. (Review: *Social Schemata; Self-Schemata; Prototype; Script*)
II. Attitudes are feelings, beliefs, and action tendencies toward persons, groups, ideas, or things.
  A. Attitudes are formed through social learning experiences and direct conditioning. (Review: *Figure 13.2*)
  B. Three major factors in the effectiveness of persuasive communication are the characteristics of the communicator, the kind of argument that is used, and the characteristics of the audience. (Review: *Figure 13.3*)
  C. Attitudes affect actions and actions affect attitudes, but only under certain conditions. (Review: *Attitude-Discrepant Actions; Figure 13.4*)
  D. Prejudice, stereotypes, and discrimination parallel the feeling, belief, and action components of attitudes. (Review: *Authoritarian Personality; Intergroup Contact*)
III. Social influence comes in many forms.
  A. A person's willingness to obey the commands of authority may be far greater than he or she realizes. (Review: *Obedience; Milgram's Studies; Figure 13.5*)
  B. People use a number of techniques to pressure others to comply with

their requests. (Review: *Compliance; Foot-in-the-Door Technique; Door-in-the-Face Technique; Low Ball Procedure*)

C. People often deny their own perceptions or act contrary to their beliefs in the face of group pressures. (Review: *Asch Experiments*)

D. People often make errors of judgment in a group. (Review: *Group Norms; Groupthink; Deindividuation*)

IV. Social psychologists have identified a number of factors that influence how we feel about and treat each other.

A. Theoretically we come to like or dislike people because of the rewards and punishments we associate with them, but a number of very specific factors also play a major role in interpersonal attraction. (Review: *Figure 13.6; Matching Phenomenon*)

B. Aggression—behavior directed toward the goal of harming or injuring others—is complex and multi-determined. (Review: *Aggressive Model*)

C. Social psychologists try to understand when and why a person will (or will not) help a stranger for no apparent benefit. (Review: *Bystander Effect; Diffusion of Responsibility*)

V. Social psychology is of applied relevance to real-world settings.

A. Two important aspects of the physical environment that affect social behavior are noise and physical space. (Review: *Environmental Psychology; Proxemics*)

B. Social psychological findings have had a major impact on jury selection.

Psychological Disorders
and Their Treatment

Abnormal Behavior

Chapter Outline

As a teenager, Karen Carpenter had loved tacos and chili, and had even been a little overweight. When she was in her mid-twenties, however, the famous singer's weight dropped well below normal. "She lived on salads, maybe dry toast for breakfast," her brother recalled. Soon, exhausted by her demanding schedule of recording and performing, Karen landed in a hospital bed. It was two months before she recovered.

Still, despite pleas from family and friends, Karen would not eat normally. Six years passed before she was willing to listen, and by that time her poor eating habits were so ingrained she could not change them without the help of mental health professionals. Karen did eventually overcome her resistance to eating, and she regained most of her lost weight. But it was too late; years of undereating followed by sudden weight gain had put an unusual strain on her heart. At the age of thirty-two, Karen Carpenter died of heart failure.

Anorexia Nervosa: An abnormal pattern of behavior marked by a morbid fear of becoming fat and by self-starvation.

Karen's death was an apparent complication of **anorexia nervosa,** an abnormal behavior pattern marked by a morbid fear of becoming fat and by self-starvation. Cases of anorexia nervosa were documented as early as the seventeenth century, but not until the 1960s and 1970s has the disorder become fairly common. Curiously, the disorder seems to occur almost exclusively in females; only about 5 percent of the reported cases involve males. An estimated 1 percent of women between the ages of twelve and twenty-five—approximately 260,000 women—experience anorexic symptoms (U.S. News and World Report, August 1982). The disorder claims the lives of as many as one in five victims.

What causes a person to literally starve herself to death? According to some experts, the behavior stems from a stifling of the child's initiative by the parents, which leads to a blurred sense of individuality (Bruch, 1973; Selvini-Palazzoli, 1974). To obtain a feeling of control or mastery, such children may stubbornly refuse to eat (Guidano & Liotti, 1983). Other experts have pointed to early traumatic experiences or deep, unconscious feelings of

Singer Karen Carpenter, seen here with Herb Alpert and her brother Richard, was a victim of anorexia nervosa.

guilt as a major factor in the development of the disorder (Friedman, 1985). Yet not every woman who experiences early parental stifling or trauma develops anorexia nervosa. Some scientists have speculated that the disorder involves a physiological disturbance in the areas of the brain and the chemical transmitters that regulate eating. People may inherit a predisposition for the disorder, this reasoning goes (Gwirtsman et al., 1983). Support for a biological explanation of anorexia nervosa is at best incomplete, however.

Researchers have recently found an interesting parallel to anorexia nervosa in the behavior of men who compulsively jog one hundred miles per week or compulsively lift weights. Like women who starve themselves, these "obligatory" runners and weight lifters ignore pain, illness, and other serious physical symptoms in a relentless pursuit of perfection. In fact, many obligatory runners fear that if they stop running they will cease to exist. They become depressed if they cannot run for one day, and will sacrifice personal needs and social and vocational pursuits to maintain their self-imposed regime. Like anorexic women, these obligatory runners and weight lifters tend to come from upper-class families, to be perfectionistic, and to have extremely high self-expectations (Yates et al., 1983).

Karen Carpenter's self-starvation dieting and the compulsive running of obligatory runners raise a number of important issues. In particular, such behaviors lead us to ask the question of how or when is any given behavior abnormal. When is a particular behavior "too much"? Such behaviors also reveal how physiological conditions such as heart failure can be interlocked with a behavioral pattern, which leads to another question: At what point is a given problem a physiological problem or a behavioral one? In this chapter we attempt to answer these and other questions.

We begin with a discussion of what abnormal behavior is and how such behaviors are classified. Second, we will consider the problems of alcohol and substance abuse. Such problems help us to explore the issues of "when is too much" and when is the problem physical and when behavioral. Then we will examine four major classes of abnormal behavior and the various forms of abnormal behavior within each class. Two major goals of this chapter are to introduce you to the concepts and research in the field of abnormal psychology and to help you to comprehend psychological terms that you read in magazines and books and hear on television.

WHAT ABNORMAL BEHAVIOR IS

Statistical Criterion: A criterion for abnormal behavior that states that behavior is abnormal if it deviates from the average.

Running is a behavior that most people in our society would consider normal. So how does someone tell when a behavior is abnormal? That question is not easy to answer. Defining abnormal behavior is like trying to define intelligence; there are many definitions, but no consensus on which should prevail. A common approach is based on statistical frequency. According to the **statistical criterion,** a behavior is abnormal if it deviates from the average and therefore is rare. Behaviors that are found most frequently among a particular social group are considered normal; those that occur infrequently are considered abnormal. The problem with the statistical definition is that infrequent behaviors aren't always abnormal. Exceptional artistic or musical talent, though relatively rare, certainly isn't abnormal; nor is exceptional intellectual or creative ability.

Moral Criterion: A criterion for abnormal behavior that states that behavior is abnormal if it deviates from socially acceptable norms.

According to the **moral criterion,** behaviors that deviate from socially acceptable norms are abnormal. Every society has a set of written or unwritten social norms that specifies the appropriate behavior in a given situation. Under the moral criterion, behaviors that violate those norms would be considered abnormal. The problem with a moral definition is that social norms vary from time to time within a culture and across cultures—witness the different attitudes that have emerged toward human sexual behavior (see Chapter 10). Moreover, like deviations from the statistical average, not all deviations from the social norm can be considered abnormal. Otherwise, people who merely express disapproval of social norms would be branded abnormal. (In the Soviet Union, they are; those who speak out against government-imposed social order are labeled deviant and confined to a psychiatric prison for "rehabilitation".)

Maladaptive Criterion: A criterion for abnormal behavior that states that behaviors that enhance a person's well-being are adaptive and normal; behaviors that undermine it are maladaptive and abnormal.

A third standard for abnormal behavior is based on its maladaptiveness. According to the **maladaptive criterion,** behaviors that enhance a person's well-being are considered adaptive and normal; behaviors that undermine it are considered maladaptive and abnormal. Thus, going on a diet or exercising regularly in order to maintain good health would be considered normal; dieting or exercising to the point of impairing one's health, abnormal. The problem with this criterion is that some behaviors that are adaptive in the short run can be maladaptive over the long run. Some people drink relatively small amounts of alcohol to enhance their sociability; but, for those who eventually come to rely on alcohol in order to function, the short-term benefit can lead to long-term problems.

Personal Distress Criterion: A criterion for abnormal behavior that states that behaviors that cause a person psychological pain or distress are abnormal.

A fourth criterion of abnormal behavior is based on **personal distress.** Behaviors that cause a person psychological pain or distress would thus be considered abnormal. Pain or grief over the loss of a loved one is quite nor-

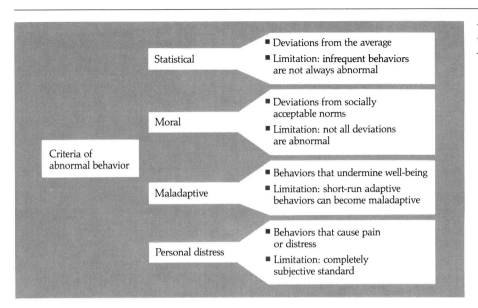

Figure 14.1 Schematic Summary of Criteria of Abnormal Behavior.

mal—even healthy—however, and most people experience bouts of despair or apprehension at one time or another. Like the other criteria, this one has its limitations; since everyone has different stress reactions (see Chapter 11), this criterion is very subjective. (Figure 14.1 summarizes the four criteria for abnormal behavior.)

Today, most psychologists would agree that a definitive description of abnormal behavior is not yet possible. Years—perhaps even decades or centuries—are needed in which to collect more data about psychological health before the boundaries of abnormal behavior can be sharply delineated. But for now a composite of the definitions just described will provide us with a plausible working definition: **Abnormal behavior** is a pattern of thought, feeling, or action that is deemed inappropriate or maladaptive in a given context, either by the individual who experiences it or by the majority of his or her peers. Such behavior often involves a violation of social norms, and it usually impairs a person's ability to function or causes personal distress.

Abnormal Behavior: A pattern of thought, feeling, or action that is deemed inappropriate or maladaptive in a given context, either by the individual who experiences it or by the majority of his or her peers. Such behavior often involves a violation of social norms, and it usually impairs a person's ability to function or causes personal distress.

■ Learning Check ■

Read the definitions, then cover the right side and try to recite them. Repeat.

Statistical Criterion	Behaviors that deviate from the average are abnormal.
Moral Criterion	Behaviors that deviate from socially acceptable norms are abnormal.
Maladaptive Criterion	Behaviors that undermine well-being are maladaptive and abnormal.
Personal Distress Criterion	Behaviors that cause a person psychological pain or distress are abnormal.

Abnormal Behavior as Due to Natural Causes

Throughout much of the history of Western civilization, disorders like Karen Carpenter's anorexia nervosa were attributed to supernatural causes, and the primary treatment for them was the ritual casting out of demons. By the fifteenth century, the demonic theory of abnormal behavior had reached such extreme proportions, the mentally ill were thought to be working with the devil or suffering God's punishment for their sins. No retaliation against the devil was considered too severe; sufferers were mercilessly flogged, placed in steaming ovens, plunged into icy lakes, or burned at the stake as witches. While later eras adopted a more reasonable view, it was not until the nineteenth century that a scientific position was developed. Gradually it became accepted that abnormal behavior is a result of natural causes (see Figure 14.2).

Once a scientific view had been established, the way was open, not just for humane treatment, but for the systematic study of disordered behavior. Toward the end of the last century the German psychiatrist Emil Kraepelin (1856–1926) noted that there were distinct types of abnormal behavior, or **syndromes,** which are groups of symptoms that define a particular pattern of abnormal behavior. He proposed that the first step in the study of abnormal behavior should be to identify the major syndromes and the specific

Syndrome: A group of symptoms that define a particular pattern of abnormal behavior.

Figure 14.2 Early Approaches to Abnormal Behavior. In Medieval times, the mentally ill were brutally treated. However, by the end of the 18th century, more humane solutions were recognized, as is illustrated by this painting of the Frenchman Pinel releasing the insane from their manacles in 1795.

Reproduced by permission of Goupil et Cie, Paris.

PINEL AT LA SALPÊTRIÈRE, IN 1795, RELEASING THE INSANE FROM THEIR MANACLES.
From the painting by Tony Robert-Fleury at the Salon of 1876.

symptoms that define a distinct type of abnormal behavior. The work that he began continues to this day.

The Classification of Abnormal Behavior

Kraepelin's main contribution was distinguishing one kind of abnormal behavioral pattern from another. Research since his time has become more refined in its focus on isolating specific abnormal patterns. To date, no one has come up with a system of classification for abnormal behavior that everyone can agree on. The most widely used system is the American Psychiatric Association's (1980, 1985) *Diagnostic and Statistical Manual of Mental Disorders* (DSM).

The DSM tries to answer the question of when a behavior is abnormal by specifying a list of behavioral criteria upon which to base a diagnosis. Table 14.1 provides a list of the major categories of disorders in the DSM.

Table 14.1 Categories of Mental Disorders from the DSM

Category	Examples
1. Disorders Usually First Evident in Infancy, Childhood, or Adolescence	Mental retardation; anorexia nervosa
2. Organic Mental Disorders	Dementia; Alzheimer's Disease
3. Psychoactive Substance Use Disorders	Alcohol dependence; cocaine dependence
4. Sleep Disorders	Sleep-walking; insomnia
5. Schizophrenic Disorders	Paranoid schizophrenia; catatonic schizophrenia
6. Delusional Disorders	Delusions of jealousy or persecution
7. Mood Disorders	Depression; excessive elation
8. Anxiety Disorders	Phobia
9. Somatoform Disorders	Psychogenic pain (pain with no physical cause)
10. Dissociative Disorders	Multiple personality; psychogenic amnesia
11. Psychosexual Disorders	Child molester (pedophilia)
12. Fictitious Disorders	Voluntarily faking a mental disorder
13. Disorders of Impulse Control	Fire-setting
14. Adjustment Disorders	Severe anxiety and depression occurring three months following a trauma (for example, being raped)
15. Psychological Factors Affecting Physical Condition	Psychosomatic disorders such as ulcers or skin rash
16. Personality Disorders	Dependent personality; hysterical personality

Source: Adapted from the American Psychiatric Association Diagnostic and Statistical Manual of Mental Disorders, Third Edition. Washington, DC, American Psychiatric Association, 1980, and the DRAFT of the DSM-III-R in Development, (subject to change), by the Work Group to Revise DSM-III, 1985.

The DSM has been criticized on the grounds that it stigmatizes people with unnecessarily negative labels (Abeles, 1981; Smith, 1981). Other critics argue that only the individual is singled out, while disturbed families and subcultures are ignored (Weary & Mirels, 1982). What is more, in a woman's view of the DSM, one psychologist has charged that the manual suffers from sex-biased assumptions about what constitutes healthy behavior (Kaplan, 1983). Despite its limitations, weaknesses, and possible biases, the DSM is in fact widely used and will probably continue to be for some time. In response to critics, its authors are continually updating and refining it. (The versions cited here are from the *DSM-III* (APA, 1980) and the *DSM-III-R* (APA, 1985)). And it does provide a framework for distinguishing among the various types of abnormal behavior.

Consistent with the work begun by Kraepelin, the DSM attempts to divide abnormal behavior into distinct categories. In all, some sixteen distinct categories of mental disorders have been designated. Some of these we have already discussed. Sexual dysfunctions, for example, are classified among the psychosexual disorders. (See Chapter 10.)

Each category in the DSM is further divided into a number of subcategories. For example, the psychoactive substance use disorders are subdivided into those associated with alcohol, those associated with cocaine, those associated with barbiturates, and so on. Let's begin by taking a closer look at these substance use disorders as well as some of the behaviors that define them.

■ Learning Clue ■

Each disorder is associated with a group of symptoms that distinguishes it from the others. In studying them, ask yourself how they are alike, how they differ, and what is *distinctive* about each.

ALCOHOLISM AND OTHER PSYCHOACTIVE SUBSTANCE USE DISORDERS

Psychoactive substances refer to drugs and other chemicals (for example, paint thinner, airplane glue, gasoline fumes) that alter a person's behavior—action, feelings, and cognitions. Such substances include alcohol, sedative drugs, heroin, amphetamine, cocaine, LSD, and marijuana. The use of such substances is common, widespread, and, under certain conditions, normal. Some are used for medical reasons; others are widely used at social gatherings. But the use of psychoactive substances can also cause serious physical, mental, and social problems for the user, for the user's family, and for society.

Substance use disorders provide a good starting point for our discussion of abnormal behavior. They illustrate two key issues: the interlocking of a physiological condition and a behavioral pattern, and the problem of telling when "too much" begins. In this section we will see how the DSM attempts to delineate such abnormal patterns of substance use and consider how such patterns develop. Our discussion will focus on the most widespread of the substance use disorders, alcohol dependence. (See Chapter 5 for a discussion of the psychological and physiological effects of psychoactive drugs.)

Substance Dependence

Each psychoactive substance is associated with a particular pattern of physiological and psychological effect, depending on the dose that is taken. For a person weighing about 150 pounds, two to three drinks (with one drink roughly equivalent to an ounce of spirits, one beer, or one glass of wine) produces a feeling of relaxation and sense of well-being. As more alcohol is ingested, the individual becomes further intoxicated. Inhibitions are lowered; speech may become slurred.

With repeated use of a substance, the individual may develop a tolerance for it, which means greater quantities must be taken in order to obtain the desired effects. Instead of two to three drinks, five may be required to produce a feeling of relaxation and sense of well-being. If the individual stops using the substance, he or she may experience withdrawal symptoms such as nausea, weakness, anxiety, depression, and irritability. (For more on tolerance and withdrawal, see Chapter 5.)

Tolerance and withdrawal symptoms are two of the more dramatic symptoms of substance dependence. A complete list of the defining criteria for such a dependence is presented in Table 14.2. According to the DSM, an individual who has any three of the nine symptoms listed in Table 14.2 is suffering from a psychoactive substance dependence.

The criteria listed in Table 14.2 can apply to the use of any substance. For example, a person who is preoccupied with seeking or using cocaine, who takes larger quantities of cocaine or uses the drug over a longer period than originally intended, and who continues to use cocaine even though, in

Table 14.2 Criteria for a Psychoactive Substance Dependence Disorder (According to the DSM, any three criteria define a psychoactive substance dependence disorder.)

1. Preoccupation with seeking or taking the substance
2. Often takes larger quantities or uses the substance over a longer period than intended
3. Tolerance
4. Withdrawal symptoms
5. Takes substance to relieve or prevent withdrawal symptoms
6. Persistent desire or repeated efforts to cut down
7. Frequent inability to fulfill social or occupational obligations due to substance
8. Has given up some important social, occupational, or recreational activity to seek or use substance
9. Continued taking of substance despite significant social, occupational, legal, or physical problems due to its use

Source: Adapted from the American Psychiatric Association Diagnostic and Statistical Manual of Mental Disorders, Third Edition. Washington, DC, American Psychiatric Association, 1980, and the DRAFT of the DSM-III-R in Development, (subject to change), by the Work Group to Revise DSM-III, 1985.

so doing, jeopardizes his or her job or family relationships suffers from cocaine dependence.

Consequences and Causes of Substance Dependence: The Example of Alcoholism

Substance dependence disorders are serious problems. They cause personal suffering to millions of victims; the toll they exact is staggering. Some 10 million Americans suffer from dependence on alcohol alone. Such individuals are at risk for a host of medical problems (for example, cirrhosis of the liver) and fatal accidents. According to various estimates, about half of all auto fatalities, 80 percent of all home violence, thirty percent of all suicides, 60 percent of all child abuse, and 65 percent of all drownings involve someone who is dependent on alcohol (Newsweek, 1983).

Though substance use disorders are relatively easy to diagnose and their consequences well-known, their cause remains a matter of controversy. The fact is, there is no one personality, life-style, or environmental condition associated with dependence on alcohol or other substances. Just about anyone—rich–poor, labor–manager, male–female—can be a victim (Shore, 1985). Some point to genetic influence; others to family factors such as parental drug use (Gabrielli & Plomin, 1985; Jurich et al., 1985). While genetic and family factors may contribute to some cases of alcohol and other types of substance dependence, there are many cases that cannot be attributed to either of these factors. And a careful study of the literature reveals that people do not take alcohol simply to reduce stress. In fact, alcohol abuse can be a major cause of stress in a victim's life (Powers & Kutash, 1985).

According to some experts, the development of alcoholism occurs in stages (Jellinek, 1952). The first stage is characterized by periodic drinking for one of a variety of reasons (relieve stress, peer pressure, etc.). In the sec-

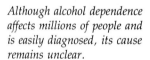

Although alcohol dependence affects millions of people and is easily diagnosed, its cause remains unclear.

ond stage, heavy drinking often produces blackouts (see Chapter 5), in which the drinker forgets what he or she did while intoxicated. In the third stage the drinker loses control; one drink and he is unable to stop until either the liquor or his consciousness gives out. In the final stage the drinker's behavior becomes chronic. He or she is intoxicated almost constantly, to the point where family, job, and even personal hygiene are subordinated to the habit.

Others have argued, however, that alcoholism is not a single disease. According to this multidimensional view, alcohol dependence is a problem that may stem from several different causes or combinations of causes and that may be manifested by any one of several different patterns (Wanberg & Horn, 1983). For some people, the critical point may be signified by several driving offenses because of alcohol. For others, the pattern may involve drinking on the job or marital problems because of their drinking. Thus, alcohol dependency can manifest itself in many different ways.

The study of alcohol and other types of substance dependence in many ways exemplifies the entire field of abnormal behavior. Millions of people are affected, but the cause and even the exact nature of the affliction remains unclear. In the sections ahead we will examine several other major disorders, such as those relating to anxiety.

ANXIETY, SOMATOFORM, AND DISSOCIATIVE DISORDERS

Anxiety, somatoform, and dissociative disorders are each considered separate categories in the DSM. At one time they were grouped together under the heading **neurosis,** a psychoanalytic term for disturbances associated with **anxiety**—a feeling of apprehension, tension, or uneasiness. That term, neurosis, is no longer used in the DSM because of its connection with Freudian theory, which, as we have seen (see Chapter 12), has become particularly controversial in recent years.

Though the behavioral patterns of these three categories of disorders are actually quite different, they do share some significant similarities. These patterns typically are associated with intense and subjectively distressing symptoms. All are seriously disruptive to the lives of those affected. None involves a loss of contact with reality, however; though the symptoms are distressing, the person can still distinguish what is real from what is not. There are no hallucinations associated with these disorders; no blatant violation of social norms.

Neurosis: A psychoanalytic term for disturbances associated with anxiety.

Anxiety: A feeling of apprehension, tension, or uneasiness.

■ Learning Check ■

Distinctive features of substance dependence:

1. The repeated use of a psychoactive substance

2. A variety of physical, mental, social, and/or occupational problems associated with use or cessation of the substance

Anxiety Disorders

Patterns in which anxiety is the predominant symptom are referred to as anxiety disorders. The experience of anxiety is normal in a variety of situations—before an exam, a public speech, or a job interview, for instance. Anxiety is also a normal reaction to threat—a danger signal that alerts us to emergencies. But the intense fear and panic associated with anxiety disorders is way out of proportion to the situation. The victim suffers heart palpitations, breathlessness, dizziness, apprehension—sometimes even a vague feeling of impending catastrophe—in response to everyday situations.

There are two major subclasses of anxiety disorders: phobic disorders and anxiety states. Each subclass, in turn, is associated with one or more specific disorders (see Figure 14.3).

Phobic Disorders: A subcategory of anxiety disorders in which the victim's anxiety is attached to a particular object or situation, toward which the person manifests unrealistic or illogical fear.

Phobic Disorders. In the **phobic disorders** the victim's anxiety is attached to a particular object or situation, toward which the person manifests unrealistic and illogical fear. Phobic anxiety disorders are defined by three criteria. First, the anxiety must be way out of proportion to reality. Fear of a potentially dangerous snake or spider is appropriate and normal, as is fear of driving through an unfamiliar city in the middle of the Friday afternoon rush hour. But extreme fear of familiar small worms or of entering a parked automobile is unrealistic and illogical. Second, the victim must recognize or be persuaded that the anxiety is irrational. Otherwise the person would have to be considered "out of contact" with reality, unable to distinguish real fears from those that are illogical or imagined. Third, the anxiety must incite a compelling desire to flee from or otherwise avoid the feared stimulus.

Although, in theory, a person can develop a phobic fear of just about anything, in practice phobic responses tend to fall into what are called "stimulus classes," or groups, such as an irrational fear of heights (acrophobia) or of closed places (claustrophobia). Very rarely would a person develop, say, a table phobia. One may be phobic for a particular item within a stimulus class, such as a claustrophobic who experiences panic only in elevators; or the fear may spread (generalize) to related items within a stimulus class. Thus, many claustrophobics will avoid the back seat of Volkswagens, small bathrooms without windows, sleeping bags, or even wearing a turtleneck sweater.

Figure 14.3 Schematic Overview of Anxiety Disorders.

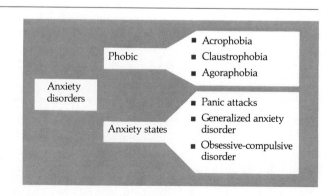

One particularly debilitating phobia is **agoraphobia,** the fear of too much unprotected space, sometimes known as "the fear of fears." Some agoraphobics experience anguish only when boundaries are not visible, such as in the middle of a vast desert or on the ocean. For others, the fear has generalized to such an extent that even a solitary walk to the corner mailbox is terrifying; there is too much danger outside the safe confines of home.

Most people have a minor fear of traveling, walking, or being left alone, particularly in unfamiliar places. But such fears dominate the agoraphobic's life. To avoid being alone or left without help, the victim restructures her entire existence. Consider the case of B.C.:

> B.C., aged 34, had been severely agoraphobic for 9 years, the last 2 of which she had been entirely unable to leave her home unless accompanied by her husband or by a guide dog. Although of normal sight, B.C. had undertaken to help train a guide dog for the blind; during the course of its stay with them, the dog had become indispensable to her. (Hafner, 1982, p. 100)

This woman was referred to treatment soon after the guide dog had been trained and returned to its owners.

Because the symptoms are so severe, agoraphobics make up an estimated 50 to 80 percent of those who seek treatment for phobia (Chambless & Goldstein, 1980).

Anxiety States. Anxiety states are characterized by chronic anxiety and apprehension. The victim's anxiety cannot be so neatly tied to a specific object or boundary, as in the phobic disorders. Instead, the anxiety typically is more general and pervasive, and it can strike at any time or place. There are three major specific anxiety state disorders: panic attacks, generalized anxiety disorder, and obsessive-compulsive disorder (see Figure 14.3).

Panic attacks are sudden episodes of terror accompanied by physical reactions like palpitations, choking or smothering sensations, dizziness, vertigo, faintness, trembling, and nausea. The attacks last from a few minutes to half an hour, and are so unsettling that the victim often develops a sec-

Agoraphobia: The fear of too much unprotected space, sometimes known as "the fear of fears.".

Anxiety States: A subcategory of anxiety disorders characterized by chronic anxiety and apprehension (including panic attacks and generalized anxiety disorders).

Panic Attacks: Sudden episodes of terror accompanied by physical reactions like palpitations, choking or smothering sensations, dizziness, vertigo, faintness, trembling, and nausea.

Looking down from the top of this spiral staircase would be horrifying to someone with acrophobia—an irrational fear of heights.

ondary fear that the attack will recur—a dread called *anticipatory anxiety.* Even a single attack may incapacitate a person for months. Panic attacks are frequently associated with agoraphobia, which is why agoraphobia is sometimes called the fear of fears. Consider the following case:

> I was on a bus going into the city to work when all of a sudden I couldn't feel my arms and legs, as if my arms and legs didn't exist. I thought I was going to pass out. I was terrified. I wanted to get to the office so as not to faint in public. (Hafner, 1982, p. 104)

When this woman got to her office, she became convinced that she was dying of a brain hemorrhage and was taken to a doctor. The episode lasted about an hour. Subsequently she avoided city buses, due to anticipatory anxiety that she might experience another similar attack. Thus, following her panic attack, she developed agoraphobia.

Generalized Anxiety Disorder: An anxiety state disorder that involves persistent, uncontrollable anxiety that is unconnected to any particular stimulus.

A second anxiety state disorder, **generalized anxiety disorder,** involves persistent, uncontrollable anxiety that is unconnected to any particular stimulus. The victim feels a powerful but vague sense of apprehension and uneasiness, for no apparent reason. In contrast to panic attacks, generalized anxiety disorder involves a pervasive feeling of anxiety that the victim experiences more or less continuously for at least six months. The anxiety may vary in intensity, but the pervasive feeling of fear or worry is almost always present.

Obsessive-Compulsive Disorder: An anxiety state disorder involving a compelling urge to engage in unnecessary or repetitive actions (compulsions) or nagging, unpleasant thoughts (obsessions).

Another anxiety state disorder, **obsessive-compulsive disorder,** involves a compelling urge to engage in unnecessary and repetitive actions (called compulsions) or nagging, unpleasant thoughts (obsessions). Resisting the impulse to do so causes the victim anxiety. Obsessive-compulsive disorders are somewhat like the flip side of a phobia. While a phobia is a ritual of avoidance, of not doing in order to avoid anxiety, an obsessive or compulsive behavior is a ritual of thinking or doing to control anxiety (Salzman, 1982). Obsessions and compulsions are usually automatic, and they often run counter to the person's real goals or feelings. Though the victim doesn't wish to perform the behavior or entertain the thought, he or she is unable to prevent it. For example, the mother of a newborn baby cannot rid herself of the thought that she will drop the child and injure it. In the end, such actions or thoughts often generate more anxiety than they were supposed to control.

■ Learning Check ■

Read the distinctive features for each of the following disorders, then cover the right side and try to recite it. Repeat.

Agoraphobia	Fear of too much unprotected space (the fear of fears)
Panic Attacks	Sudden episodes of terror accompanied by physical reactions
Generalized Anxiety Disorder	Persistent, uncontrollable anxiety
Obsessive-Compulsive Disorder	Compelling thoughts (obsessions) or actions (compulsions)

Somatoform Disorders

Somatoform means "bodylike." The category, **somatoform disorders,** is characterized by physical symptoms—paralysis, blindness—for which there is no apparent physical cause or damage, but for which there is evidence of a psychological cause. These physical symptoms tend to appear to worsen during times of stress.

People with somatoform disorders tend to elicit attention or assistance by exaggerating the severity of their symptoms. This **secondary gain,** or indirect benefit of reassurance and support, either helps to maintain the symptoms or encourages their recurrence when the person feels neglected.

One of the most elusive and perplexing of the somatoform disorders is the **psychogenic pain disorder,** in which no detectable physical damage can be found to account for a person's complaints of pain. Some psychologists question whether such pain is actually **psychogenic** (meaning caused by psychological factors); they suspect that medical technology is simply not sensitive enough to detect some sources of pain. And it is true that, while technicians can easily detect physical damage to the bones and spinal column, they find it difficult to assess damage to the soft muscle tissue of the back and thighs. Psychogenic pain does not follow the patterns normally associated with physical damage, however. A patient may report that the pain "floats around"—appearing sometimes in the left shoulder, sometimes in the right thigh, and at other times between the shoulder blades. Such complaints do not seem to indicate a physical source for the pain. Moreover, like psychogenic blindness or paralysis, psychogenic pain yields important secondary gains for the patient—freedom from difficult tasks, sympathy, an excuse for avoiding uncomfortable situations.

Somatoform disorders should not be confused with **psychosomatic disorders** such as ulcers, hives, and hypertension (see Chapter 11). Psychosomatic disorders are stress-related physical problems with a physiological basis caused by psychological factors. Somatoform disorders, by contrast, are physical symptoms for which there is no apparent physical cause but evidence for psychological conflicts.

Dissociative Disorders

Dissociative disorders involve a sudden but usually temporary change in normal cognitive activity or motor behavior, such as selective memory loss or sudden, unexpected travel away from home with the assumption of a new identity and an inability to recall one's previous identity. These disorders, which include psychogenic amnesia, fugue states, and multiple personality, are among the most highly publicized and sensationalized of the psychological disorders. (See Figure 14.4.)

In **psychogenic amnesia,** past memories are forgotten for no apparent physical reason (such as head injury). Suddenly the victim is unable to recall important, well-learned information. Most people experience forgetfulness once in a while—a name on the tip of the tongue or a forgotten appointment. But the psychogenic amnesiac's forgetting is far more extensive.

An enlisted man in the air corps had some previous experience as a private pilot. After a disagreement with his wife, he decided to punish her by

Somatoform Disorders: A category of disorders characterized by physical symptoms (for example, paralysis or blindness) for which there is no apparent physical cause or damage, but for which there is evidence of a psychological cause.

Secondary Gain: An indirect benefit of reassurance, support, attention, or assistance, which helps to maintain symptoms of disordered behavior or encourages their recurrence.

Psychogenic Pain Disorder: A somatoform disorder in which there is no detectable physical damage to account for a person's complaints of pain.

Psychogenic: Caused by psychological factors.

Psychosomatic Disorders: Stress-related disorders such as ulcers, hives, and hypertension, which involve physical problems with a physiological basis caused by psychological factors.

Dissociative Disorders: Disorders that involve a sudden but usually temporary change in normal cognitive activity or motor behavior (including psychogenic amnesia, fugue states, and multiple personality).

Psychogenic Amnesia: A dissociative disorder in which past memories are forgotten for no apparent physical reason (such as head injury).

Figure 14.4 Schematic Overview of Dissociative Disorders.

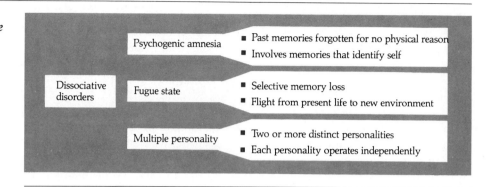

committing suicide. Choosing the most dramatic method he could think of he took off in a large, unattended aircraft and made several passes at the local river, each time pulling up before he plunged in. Very soon, all other aircraft were diverted to other cities, and the local control tower was concentrating on trying to persuade him to change his mind. He finally agreed, but then he discovered that although he knew how to take off, he did not know how to land the unfamiliar plane. After some tense interchanges with the control tower, however, he managed to get the plane down. When the welcoming party of military police arrived at the plane, he found himself unable to remember his name or anything about his identity, his present situation, or the events leading up to it. (Aldrich, 1966, p. 238)

This case illustrates a common problem in diagnosing psychogenic amnesia: the therapist cannot tell for sure whether the memory loss is real or feigned. The symptoms occur so suddenly, and their secondary gains are often so convenient, that most people have difficulty believing they are real. Extensive case reports such as the one above have convinced most experts that sudden selective memory loss can be induced by psychological factors, however. Typically, the memory loss in psychogenic amnesia involves only those memories that would identify the self, such as one's name, occupation, residence, and recognition of friends and relatives. However, there is no known sure-fire way of distinguishing real from feigned psychogenic amnesia (Schacter, 1986).

Fugue State: A dissociative disorder involving selective memory loss as well as flight from one's present life situation to a new environment.

A **fugue state** is a dissociative disorder involving selective memory loss as well as flight from one's present life situation to a new environment. People with this condition wander away, forget their old identity, and assume a new one—like the man who went out to buy a loaf of bread and didn't come back for twenty years. Such people are sometimes discovered living in different states under an entirely new name with an entirely different occupation. Some eventually recall their old identity as suddenly as they lost it; others may never regain their former selves.

Multiple Personality: A dissociative disorder in which a person has two or more distinct personalities, each of which operates independently and often without the awareness of the others.

The rarest and most dramatic of the dissociative disorders is **multiple personality,** a condition in which a person has two or more distinct personalities, each of which operates independently and often without the awareness of the others. The individual personalities are usually quite different, often opposites. Different ones dominate at different times, bringing their own memories, behavior patterns, and social friendships with them. The

In the movie "The Three Faces of Eve," Joanne Woodward played the dramatic role of a woman with a multiple personality.

transition from one personality to another usually occurs suddenly and is often associated with psychosocial stress.

The existence of multiple personalities has been amply documented by case studies (Bowman et al., 1985). In the classic report of the three faces of Eve, a woman possessed three distinct personalities, one of which was aggressive and strongly disliked her more gentle, conventional personality as well as her submissive personality. Eve first went to her therapist complaining of severe headaches accompanied by blackouts. For several months the therapist knew her only as a retiring, gentle, and conventional person. But one day Eve's personality changed abruptly:

> As if seized by sudden pain, she put both hands to her head. After a tense moment of silence, both hands dropped. There was a quick, reckless smile, and, in a bright voice that sparkled, she said, 'Hi, there, Doc!' The demure and constrained posture of Eve White had melted into buoy and

■ Learning Check ■

Read the questions and answers, then try answering the questions with the answers covered.

1. *Question*: What are the clues that indicate pain is psychogenic (caused by psychological factors)?

1. *Answer*: Psychogenic pain does not follow patterns normally associated with physical damage and typically provides secondary gains (support, reassurance, attention, etc.).

2. *Question*: Identify a major similarity and a major difference between somatoform disorders and psychosomatic disorders.

2. *Answer*: Both are caused by psychological factors. However, in somatoform disorders there is no physical damage; in psychosomatic disorders, there is.

repose . . .This new and apparently carefree girl spoke casually of Eve White and her problems, always using she or her in every reference, always respecting the strict bounds of a separate identity . . .When asked her name, she immediately replied, 'Oh, I'm Eve Black,' (Thigpen & Cleckley, 1954, p. 137)

Causes of Anxiety, Somatoform, and Dissociative Disorders

As with the substance use disorders, the causes of anxiety, somatoform, and dissociative disorders remain a matter of theory and debate. Some point to biological factors, others to psychological or environmental factors, and still others to an interaction between genetic dispositions and environment.

Biological Theories. Biological theories emphasize the role of genetic predispositions and inherited characteristics. For example, inherited factors play a major role in the reactivity of the autonomic nervous system, in the balance of neurotransmitter substances that play a role in anxiety, and in brain sensitivity to the chemical messengers that signal anxiety. Certain individuals are thus genetically predisposed to experience stronger, more frequent, or more intense anxiety responses than others. In some cases, the response to anxiety may be so extreme (compared to the norm) as to be considered disordered, as in a generalized anxiety state. In other cases, the anxiety response may run haywire, as in panic attacks.

Support for the biological theory has come from a recent discovery of an association between panic attacks and mitral valve prolapse, a genetic heart disorder in which blood can sometimes seep back into the pumping heart. Some 50 percent of patients with severe, frequent panic attacks have this heart condition (Hartman et al., 1982). Thus, at least for some persons, intense, unpredictable bouts of anxiety are related to an inherited heart defect. However, the actual mechanism that links mitral valve prolapse and panic attacks remains unclear. Moreover, the existence of a relationship between the heart defect and panic attacks for half the affected persons leaves an unanswered question: what is the cause of panic attacks in the 50 percent who do not have the heart defect?

Psychological Theories. Psychological theories of the causes of anxiety, somatoform, and dissociative disorders can be broadly divided into those based on the concepts of Freudian theory and those based on learning theory. According to Freudian theory, the anxiety, somatoform, and dissociative disorders are due to an inappropriate or maladaptive response to anxiety. According to learning theory, the behaviors that characterize these disorders are learned.

Panic attacks and generalized anxiety disorders, according to Freudian theory, are due to the surfacing of previously repressed anxiety; that is, anxiety hidden from awareness in the unconscious (see Chapter 12). In phobic disorders, the anxiety becomes attached to a specific object or situation while its real source remains buried in the unconscious. In obsessive-compulsive disorders, the nagging thoughts or repetitive actions are psychological defenses whose purpose is to "bind" the anxiety, preventing it from reaching conscious awareness. And while the thoughts or actions them-

Table 14.3   Causes of Anxiety, Somatoform, and Dissociative Disorders According to Freudian Theory

Disorder	Theoretical Cause
Panic Attacks	Surfacing of repressed anxiety
Phobic Disorders	Unconscious anxiety becomes attached to a specific object or situation
Obsessive-Compulsive Disorders	Nagging thoughts and repetitive actions are defenses against unconscious anxiety
Somatoform Disorders	Physical symptoms are a defense against anxiety
Dissociative Disorders	Sealing one part of the mind from other parts provides a defense against anxiety

selves may generate anxiety, the original source of anxiety remains buried in the unconscious. In the somatoform disorders, the physical symptom is actually a defensive maneuver against anxiety. Blindness prevents the individual from seeing a painful reality, for instance. The dissociative disorders, by contrast, are viewed as a sealing off of one part of the mind from other parts, again as a defense against anxiety. In psychogenic amnesia, for example, painful memories are sealed off from consciousness and thus are no longer disturbing (see Table 14.3).

Learning theory explanations argue that all of the so-called abnormal patterns of behaviors are acquired through the same principles of conditioning and reinforcement as any other behavior. Where they differ from other behavior is in their intensity, frequency, or adaptiveness. A phobia, for instance, can be viewed as a learned avoidance. A child who was once punished by being locked in a closet, for example, avoids them. His behavior is maintained because, in avoiding the closet, he is reinforced by a reduction in the anxiety he experiences whenever he is near the closet. Later his fear of closets can generalize to fear of any enclosed area. Social learning explanations emphasize the role of modeling in the acquisition of an abnormal behavioral pattern. A child who observes a parent become pale, tense, faint, and apprehensive as he enters an elevator acquires a similar response through observation. (For more on learning theory explanations, see Chapter 11 on the behaviorist and social learning theories of obesity.)

As with the biological theories, support for psychological explanations of abnormal behavior is mixed and incomplete. In subsequent sections we will examine both types of explanations in greater depth and consider how they might apply to other categories of disorders, such as those involving depression.

MOOD DISORDERS

Mood disorders (also known as affective disorders) involve a pervasive and sustained emotion that produces the prolonged low of a depression, the extended high of elation, or alternating cycles of depression and elation.

Mood Disorders: (Also known as affective disorders). Disorders that involve a pervasive and sustained emotion that produces the prolonged low of a depression, the extended high of elation, or alternating cycles of depression and elation.

Figure 14.5 Schematic Overview of Mood Disorders.

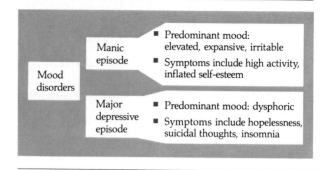

Like anxiety, emotional ups and downs are normal and appropriate when they signal certain experiences. After a personal victory, a feeling of elation, euphoria, and well-being is natural; after a defeat or loss, sadness, disappointment, and even despondency are common. But just as anxiety can grow far out of proportion to the circumstances, so can depression and elation reach abnormal proportions.

Mood disorders as a group are among the most prevalent of abnormal behaviors. The National Institute of Mental Health estimates that, during their lifetimes, approximately one in four people in the United States will suffer some form of depression severe enough to warrant treatment. Every year approximately 3–4 percent of the population are affected, amounting to 4,035 women per 100,000 and 1,698 men per 100,000 (Stoudemire et al., 1985). Depression is also the most prevalent psychological disorder in the elderly, affecting one in ten (Munoz et al., 1985). Because of the prevalence and debilitating effects of these disorders, they have been the focus of considerable research.

Our discussion of mood disorders begins with a description of the behaviors that define abnormal elation (manic episode) and abnormal depression (major depressive episode) (see Figure 14.5). Then we will consider some specific mood disorders. Finally, we will examine how these disorders are caused.

Manic and Major Depressive Episodes

A **manic episode** is a mood disturbance characterized by one or more distinct periods in which the predominant mood is either elevated, expansive, or irritable in conjunction with a number of associated symptoms (see Figure 14.5). Such symptoms include an extremely high level of activity and inflated self-esteem. One may see **flight of ideas,** a nearly continuous flow of accelerated speech with abrupt changes in topics. Victims of a manic episode also experience a decreased need for sleep, in severe cases going for days with only two or three hours of sleep per day, if any. Increases in appetite and sexual activity, without regard for the consequences, are common as well. Characteristically, the victim will engage in actions that have very damaging consequences, such as going on a buying spree, foolish business investments, or reckless driving. In one case, the owner of a prosperous restaurant almost went bankrupt during a manic episode in which she

Manic Episode: A mood disturbance characterized by one or more distinct periods in which the predominant mood is either elevated, expansive, or irritable in conjunction with a number of associated symptoms (e.g., high activity and inflated self-esteem).

Flight of Ideas: A nearly continuous flow of accelerated speech with abrupt changes in topics.

served drinks and expensive wines to all customers "on the house." Speech typically becomes loud, rapid, and difficult to interrupt. The victim may become hostile, stubborn, or even impossible to deal with, as the following case study illustrates.

Depression can be an overwhelming experience, characterized by feelings of worthlessness and despondency.

> Alan C. was a 43-year-old, unmarried computer programmer who had led a relatively quiet life until two weeks before. After a short absence for illness, Alan returned to work unusually happy and energetic, greeting everyone at work. A few days later, during the lunch hour, Alan bought a huge cake and insisted that his fellow workers eat some of it. At first, everyone was amused and surprised by his antics. But two colleagues working with him on a special project became increasingly irritated, because Alan failed to devote any time to the project.
>
> On the day the manager decided to inform Alan of his colleagues' concern, Alan exhibited delirious manic behaviors. When he came to work, he immediately jumped on top of a desk and yelled, 'Listen, listen! We are not working on the most important aspects of our data! I know since I've debugged my mind. Erase, reprogram, you know what I mean. We've got to examine the total picture based on the input!' Alan then proceeded to spout profanities and address obscene remarks to several of the secretaries. Onlookers thought that he must have taken drugs. Attempts to calm him down brought angry and vicious denunciations. The manager who had been summoned also failed to calm Alan. Finally, he threatened to fire Alan. At this point, Alan called the manager an incompetent fool and stated that he could not be fired. His speech was so rapid and disjointed that it was difficult to understand him. Alan then picked up a chair and said he was going to smash the computers. Several coworkers grabbed him and held him to the floor. Alan was yelling so loud that his voice was quite hoarse, but he continued to shout and struggle. Two police officers were called and had to handcuff him to restrain his movements.
>
> Within hours, he was taken to a psychiatric hospital for observation. (Sue, Sue, & Sue, 1981, p. 246)

A **major depressive episode** is mood disturbance characterized by a prominent and relatively persistent **dysphoric mood**—sad, discouraged, down in the dumps, or loss of interest and pleasure for all or most usual activities, in conjunction with a number of associated symptoms (see Figure 14.5). Such symptoms include decreased energy, feelings of worthlessness, and thoughts of death or suicide. The victim feels hopeless and despondent and may be unable to concentrate. Though the person is constantly fatigued, even without any physical exertion, he complains of sleep disturbances, typically early morning awakenings or severe **insomnia**—difficulty falling asleep or staying asleep. Loss of appetite and substantial weight loss are also common. The person is at increased risk of suicide (see Box 14.1). In general, the person seems to slow down—body movements become sluggish, speech drags, and pauses increase in duration and frequency.

Major Depressive Episode: A mood disturbance characterized by prominent and relatively persistent dysphoric mood (sad, discouraged, down in the dumps), or loss of interest and pleasure for all or most usual activities, in conjunction with a number of associated symptoms (e.g., decreased energy and feelings of worthlessness).

Dysphoric Mood: A mood that is characterized by being sad, discouraged, or down in the dumps.

Insomnia: Difficulty falling asleep or staying asleep.

> Mr. T. S., aged forty, married and father of three children, was hospitalized following a rather sudden onset of severe depressive symptoms that had persisted for the previous two months. In the hospital, if left to his own devices, he would spend most of his time sitting on a chair by the side of his bed, moaning and wringing his hands. His facial expression was one of the deepest dejection, and his eyes were reddened from weeping. At times he would get up and pace the floor heavily. All of his pos-

Box 14.1 PSYCHOLOGY IN ACTION: Suicide Prevention

This year more than 200,000 Americans will attempt suicide, according to the National Center for Health Statistics. Nearly 30,000 of them will succeed. Calculated another way, a suicidal death occurs on the average of once every twenty minutes. Just over half the victims, some 16,000 of them, suffer from a depressive disorder (Stoudemire et al., 1985). For the others, it is usually not possible to pinpoint any specific factor in their decision to end their lives. Some experts believe that suicidal people do not particularly want to die; they have just stopped caring about whether or not they are alive (Schneidman et al., 1970). No matter what their reason, these suicide victims are from all walks of life.

Although it is very difficult to predict who will commit suicide, there do appear to be a few general behavior patterns characteristic of suicidal individuals. Three-quarters of them discuss their intentions beforehand—as if calling for help from others. If someone you know confides in you of a plan or of frequent thoughts of suicide, there are some things that you can do that are better than ignoring the warning.

First, try to show composure. In so doing you communicate a sense that someone is in control of the situation. Second, take the threat seriously and listen to the person. Try to understand why the individual has been driven to such drastic action. Accept each complaint or feeling—do not minimize the importance of the person's difficulties. Something that may seem insignificant to you may be a life and death matter to someone else. Do not tell the person that he or she shouldn't feel so bad. He or she is probably trying to illustrate just how bad things really are (Saccuzzo & Kaplan, 1984, p. 79).

Above all, you should not try to take matters into

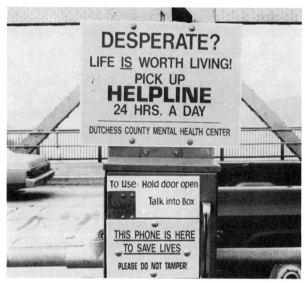

An important aspect of suicide prevention is letting the individual know that help is available.

your own hands. Your primary goal should be to help get the person to a trained professional. Perhaps you can persuade the person to go with you to the college counseling center. Another possibility is to call information and get the number of a crisis hotline center. Do not abandon the potential victim until you've obtained outside help. Many victims often experience temporary relief after talking about the suicide and mistakenly say the crisis is over (Frederick, 1981). Although you can make a difference in preventing a suicide, you cannot do it alone.

---

tural muscles seemed to sag, giving him the appearance of a much older man. Mr. T. S. was anorexic and, if left to himself, would not eat. He was severely constipated. He tended to ignore his personal appearance and hygiene completely. He was insomniac although appearing to be very fatigued. As a rule, Mr. T. S. would not speak unless spoken to, but occasionally he would address another patient or member of the ward staff. At such times he would usually berate himself in the harshest terms, saying that he did not deserve to live. (Adapted from Hofling, 1968, pp. 360–361)

It is important to distinguish between a major depressive episode and normal grief. Although both involve intense pain and despair, the depressive episode is not appropriate to the situation. Self-blame may be totally out of proportion to the circumstances, as in the woman who refused to forgive herself for the serious accident her husband experienced while driving under the influence of alcohol. Though she was not in the car, she blamed herself for not doing something about her husband's drinking. Moreover, people who experience normal grief typically bounce back quickly from their lows, as in the following example:

> A man of 52, successful in business, lost his wife. He responded with a severe grief reaction, with which he was unable to cope. He did not want to see visitors, was ashamed of breaking down, and asked to be permitted to stay in the hospital on the psychiatric service, when his physical condition would have permitted his discharge, because he wanted further assistance. Any mention of his wife produced a severe wave of depressive reaction, but with psychiatric assistance [he was willing to talk about his feelings], and after three days . . . he seemed well enough to go home.
>
> As soon as he returned home he took an active part in his business, assuming a post in which he had a great many telephone calls. He also took over the role of amateur psychiatrist to another bereaved person, spending time with him and comforting him for his loss. (Lindemann, 1982, p. 59)

Specific Mood Disorders

Specific mood disorders are based on two main distinctions. The first is based on the severity and range of symptoms. The second distinction concerns whether the individual has, or has ever had, manic symptoms, or has only depressive symptoms with no history of manic symptoms.

A **bipolar disorder** (formerly known as manic-depressive illness) is very severe and involves manic symptoms or a history of them. The individual may have any of the following: the full range of symptoms of a manic episode with no history of depressive symptoms; a mixture or alternating sequence of manic and depressive symptoms; or the full range of symptoms of a major depressive episode and a history of at least one manic episode. In **major depression,** by contrast, the individual shows the full range of symptoms of a major depressive episode with no history of a manic episode. The two less severe mood disorders are the **cyclothymic disorder,** in which the individual may show only manic symptoms, a mixture or alternating sequence of manic and depressive symptoms, or depressive symptoms with a history of manic symptoms; and **dysthymic disorder,** in which the individual shows only depressive symptoms and no history of manic symptoms.

Causes of Mood Disorders

Attempts to explain the causes of mood disorders fall into one of two broad categories: biological and psychological theories. Biological explanations blame genetic dispositions and physiological disturbances; psychological explanations emphasize early childhood experiences, environmental stress, learning, and faulty cognition.

Biological Theories. Numerous studies have supported the role of heredity, especially in bipolar disorder and major depression (Reich et al., 1985). For example, studies of twins have shown that, if one of a pair of **monozygotic twins** (twins who develop from the same egg and thus share the same genes) develops bipolar disorder, the other twin is likely to do so as well (Egeland, 1985). The degree of risk that both will manifest the disor-

Bipolar Disorder: A mood disorder in which the individual may have any of the following: the full range of symptoms of a manic episode with no history of depressive symptoms; a mixture or alternating sequence of manic and depressive symptoms; or the full range of symptoms of a major depressive episode and a history of at least one manic episode.

Major Depression: A mood disorder in which the individual shows the full range of symptoms of a major depressive episode with no history of a manic episode.

Cyclothymic Disorder: A mood disorder (less severe than bipolar disorder) in which the individual may show only manic symptoms, a mixture or alternating sequence of manic and depressive symptoms, or depressive symptoms with a history of manic symptoms.

Dysthymic Disorder: A mood disorder (less severe than major depression) in which the individual shows only depressive symptoms and no history of manic symptoms.

Monozygotic Twins: Twins who develop from the same egg and thus share the same genes.

Dizygotic Twins: Twins who develop from different eggs and are no more genetically alike than siblings.

der is much greater than it is for **dizygotic twins,** who develop from different eggs and are no more alike genetically than siblings (Wierzbicki, 1985). If one of a pair of monozygotic twins develops a bipolar disorder, chances are about seven in ten (70 percent) that the other will (Perris, 1982). The chance of two dizygotic twins developing a bipolar disorder is only about 15 percent (Allen, 1976). The risks are similar for major depression (Winokur et al., 1971). When all disorders involving depression are considered together, however, the rates go down—to about 40 percent for monozygotic twins and 10 percent for dizygotic twins (Baker et al., 1972; Gershon et al., 1971). Thus, the case for heredity is strongest for the most severe disorders and weaker for the less severe disorders.

Supporters of the biological theory speculate that people may inherit a physiological tendency toward disturbances in their biochemical processes. Indeed, there is considerable evidence of biochemical abnormalities in all the mood disorders. The major culprits appear to be neurotransmitters, the chemical substances that transmit messages from one part of the brain to another. Two that have been implicated in mood disorders are norepinephrine and serotonin.

Norepinephrine and serotonin are concentrated in two areas of the brain that play an important role in regulating emotional behavior, the hypothalamus and the limbic system (see Chapters 3 and 9). In the 1950s, doctors observed that drugs that reduced the brain level of norepinephrine and serotonin (like reserpine, a drug used in treating high blood pressure) often caused patients to become severely depressed. Drugs that increased brain levels of those neurotransmitters, such as iproniazid, which was once used to treat tuberculosis, frequently made patients elated or euphoric. Scientists set to work to test the hypothesis that depression stemmed from a deficiency of norepinephrine, serotonin, or both, and mania from an excess of those substances. They found that drugs that increase the brain levels of these two neurotransmitters help to alleviate depression (Mindham, 1982; Nies & Robinson, 1982). (We will discuss these drugs in greater detail in the next chapter on the treatment of abnormal behavior.)

Recently support for the role of biochemical factors has come from tests of the level of dexamethasone in depressive subjects (Kronfol & House, 1985). Dexamethasone is a drug that normally suppresses the production of the hormone cortisol, which plays a role in stress (see Chapter 11). For reasons not clearly understood, dexamethasone does not suppress cortisol during a depressive episode (Jaffe et al., 1983). When the depression clears up, however, the drug resumes its suppressant function (Evans & Nemeroff, 1983).

Evidence for the biological origin of affective disorders, though it is persuasive, is incomplete. Twin studies are far from conclusive, partly because identical twins are treated differently from fraternal twins. Because identical twins look alike, they tend to be treated alike—more so than fraternal twins, who may not even be of the same sex. Thus, the greater risk of both identical twins succumbing to a mood disorder may be due to environment. Moreover, genetic studies do not explain how a person acquires an excess, deficiency, or imbalance of neurotransmitters. Disturbances in neurotransmitter levels may be the effect rather than the cause of a mood disorder. For example, the loss of sleep or appetite associated with depression or the overactivity associated with a manic episode may trigger biochemical changes. In one study, normal people who merely acted as if they were experiencing a manic episode sustained changes in their neurotransmitter levels that resembled those of individuals actually experiencing a manic episode (Post et al., 1973).

Psychological Theories. Several theories of the cause of mood disorders concentrate on psychological factors. Psychoanalytic theory interprets depression as a reaction to a loss—loss of a loved one, of status or job, or of support from others. According to theory, the loss provokes anger, which the person turns inward out of inability or unwillingness to express it. Thus, depression is viewed as anger directed at the self (Abraham, 1960). Have you ever felt angry without being able to express it, for example, and soon after found yourself feeling frustrated and depressed? Such experiences are common. Mania, on the other hand, is interpreted as a defense against depression—a reaction formation in which the person takes a position opposite to his or her real feelings and expresses anger outwardly. (For more on defense mechanisms and psychoanalytic theory, see Chapter 12.)

A learning theorist, on the other hand, would attribute depression to a lack of or loss of reinforcement (Ferster, 1966; Zueck & Katkovsky, 1985). For instance, college students who set extremely high goals for themselves and then miss them sometimes become depressed. When they obtain "only" a B− average while working part-time and maintaining family relationships, they brand themselves a failure, punishing themselves instead of rewarding

Figure 14.6 Items from the Beck Depression Inventory. [Three items (Sadness, Self-Dislike, and Crying Spells) from Beck Depression Inventory. From Beck, A. T. DEPRESSION: Causes and Treatments. Philadelphia, Univ. of Pennsylvania Press, 1967. Reprinted by permission of the Univ. of Pennsylvania Press.]

Sadness

0 I do not feel sad.
1 I feel sad.
2 I am sad all the time and I can't snap out of it.
3 I am so unhappy that I can't stand it.

Self-Dislike

0 I don't feel disappointed in myself.
1 I am disappointed in myself.
2 I am disgusted with myself.
3 I hate myself.

Crying Spells

0 I don't cry any more than usual.
1 I cry more now than I used to.
2 I cry all the time now.
3 I used to be able to cry, but now I can't even cry even though I want to.

themselves for their hard work. Once depressed, they become less active, reducing their chances of succeeding still further. A vicious cycle develops, in which the lack of reinforcement leads to depression and inactivity, and the inactivity to further reduction of reinforcement (Lewinsohn et al., 1980).

Perhaps the most influential of the psychological theories of depression is based on cognitive theory, which focuses on what people think, believe, and expect rather than on what they do (Ingram & Hollon, 1986). According to this theory, disturbed cognitions—negative expectations, faulty beliefs, and the like—are the main cause of depression (Beck, 1967; Beck & Young, 1985).

To test the cognitive theory, psychologists use questionnaires such as the **Beck Depression Inventory,** a measure of a person's current thoughts and feelings that evaluates a person's level of depression. Subjects are asked to choose the statements that best describe them. For each answer they receive a certain number of points; the more negative the answer, the higher its point value. (See Figure 14.6.)

In support of cognitive theory, numerous studies have shown that people who score high on the Beck Inventory are, in fact, depressed (Hatzenbuehler et al., 1983). The higher the score, the more severe the depression (Cavanaugh & Wettstein, 1983). Such evidence is useful in helping us to understand mood disorders; but, like biological theories, psychological approaches such as cognitive theory do not explain these disorders completely.

Beck Depression Inventory: A measure of a person's current thoughts and feelings that evaluates a person's level of depression.

■ Learning Clue ■

The symptoms of schizophrenia can be divided into four major categories. These are: (1) cognitive disturbances; (2) emotional disturbances; (3) social disturbances; and (4) perceptual disturbances.

SCHIZOPHRENIA

Schizophrenia: A family of disorders characterized by cognitive, emotional, social, and perceptual disturbances.

Of all the abnormal behavior patterns, **schizophrenia,** a family of disorders characterized by cognitive, emotional, social, and perceptual disturbances, is the most puzzling. Because schizophrenia involves a loss of contact with reality—a seriously distorted view of the environment—it is far more crippling than most other abnormal behaviors. Victims cannot communicate well or maintain normal social relationships and may withdraw completely from others. Schizophrenia is so severe that even though only 1 percent of the population succumbs to it, it accounts for about 20 percent of all admissions to mental health facilities (NIMH, 1977).

Schizophrenia may strike any time between adolescence and middle adulthood, though it occurs most often in the early adult years. It can take so many different forms, however, that it is almost an error to refer to it as a single disorder. The onset may be rapid or gradual. The victim may seem relatively normal prior to the appearance of the first symptoms, or may always have seemed a bit strange. Symptoms may last indefinitely or disap-

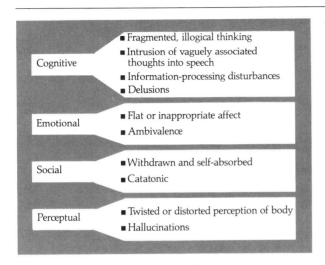

Figure 14.7 Schematic Overview of Four Main Categories of Schizophrenic Symptoms.

pear and then recur suddenly. Over the years the symptoms tend to vary in severity (Szymanski et al., 1983). In this section we will examine schizophrenia in terms of its four main categories of symptoms (see Figure 14.7).

Cognitive Disturbances

The schizophrenic's thinking is fragmented and illogical; to the point where communication is difficult if not impossible. Consider this comment, made by a schizophrenic to his doctor:

> Doctor, I have pains in my chest and hope and wonder if my box is broken and heart is beaten for my soul and salvation and heaven, Amen. (Chapman & Chapman, 1973).

How are such utterances to be explained? According to some researchers, schizophrenics have difficulty filtering out thoughts that are vaguely associated with, but not relevant to, their messages. When a

These Louis Wain drawings seem to illustrate the disordered thought patterns of a man who developed elements of a schizophrenic personality in the latter part of his life. However, though the cat drawings are distorted and confusing, there is no known relationship between their creation and the artist's eventual mental decline.

schizophrenic attempts to express an idea, these associated ideas intrude into his speech (Chapman & Chapman, 1973). Look again at the example printed above. What the patient really wanted to say was this:

> I have pains in my chest and wonder if there is something wrong with my heart.

But the patient also hoped nothing was wrong with him, and in his speech, the word *hope* got mixed in with worry. Similarly, the word *box* is associated with chest; *broken* and *beaten* with wrong; *soul* with heart; and *salvation* and *heaven*, in turn, with *soul*. Put it all together and you get a highly confusing statement (Chapman & Chapman, 1973).

To get a better understanding of the schizophrenic's problem with associated ideas, try answering the following questions from the Rattan-Chapman test (1973):

1. SHOOT means the same as:
   a. Rifle
   b. Rug
   c. Sprout
   d. None of the above
2. SHIP means the same as:
   a. Ocean
   b. Transport
   c. Book
   d. None of the above

In the first item, the correct answer is sprout. Rifle is associated with shooting, but doesn't mean the same thing. Likewise, ship is associated with ocean but doesn't mean the same. Numerous experiments with items like these have shown that schizophrenics choose the tricky associated words much more often than control subjects (Chapman & Chapman, 1973).

Many researchers have attributed the breakdown of the schizophrenic's thought process to a disturbance in normal information processing (Saccuzzo, 1986; Saccuzzo & Braff, 1986). According to one such view, for example, schizophrenics are unable to filter out irrelevant information and attend only to relevant thoughts. As a result, inappropriate ideas become mixed with appropriate ones. And, indeed, schizophrenics often complain of such difficulties, as in the following tape-recorded comments from schizophrenic patients:

> It's as if I am too wide awake, very, very alert. I can't relax at all. Everything seems to go through me. I just can't shut things out. I listen to sounds all the time. I let all the sounds come in that there are. I should really get an earphone and a wireless and control these sounds coming in so that at least I know they are separate from me. (McGhie & Chapman, 1961, p. 105)

Delusion: A strong but incorrect belief maintained in the face of contrary evidence.

Delusions of Persecution: A delusion in which the central theme is a false belief that one is being attacked, cheated, or persecuted.

One of the most dramatic and characteristic cognitive disturbances in schizophrenia is the **delusion,** a strong but incorrect belief maintained in the face of contradictory evidence. Common delusions include the belief that foreign thoughts, feelings, or actions are being imposed on one by some external force, or that one's thoughts are being removed from one's mind and broadcast to others. In **delusions of persecution,** for example, the central theme is a false belief that one is being attacked, cheated, or persecuted.

Delusions also occur in a major DSM category called paranoia. In paranoia, delusions occur without other evidence of cognitive impairment, such as disordered language. When delusions are found in schizophrenic disorders, the term paranoid schizophrenic is used.

Emotional Disturbances

Though schizophrenics may sometimes have outbursts of anger, their **affect**—immediately expressed and observed emotion—is either inappropriate or flat. The victim may giggle or laugh when talking about how her sister was seriously injured and had to have her arm amputated. She may weep uncontrollably when telling of a little kitten that was unable to catch a sparrow. Or she may show no emotion, talking in a controlled monotone that is devoid of emotional coloring.

Another characteristic emotional disturbance is **ambivalence**—strong but contradictory feelings toward the same person, place, activity, or idea. Thus, a schizophrenic may simultaneously express strong feelings of love and hate for his family. Or he may desperately want treatment but avoid it at all costs. Always the feelings are strong and drive the victim in two different directions at the same time.

Affect: Immediately expressed and observed emotion (as opposed to mood, which refers to a pervasive and sustained emotion).

Ambivalence: Strong but contradictory feelings toward the same person, place, activity, or idea.

Social Disturbances

Socially, schizophrenics withdraw from others. Either they are painfully shy and awkward around others, and therefore avoid them, or they have no interest in other people. Some become completely self-absorbed, and in extreme cases a schizophrenic may become withdrawn to the point of a **catatonic stupor**—a reduction in spontaneous movements, sometimes to the point of becoming motionless. (Such schizophrenics are referred to as catatonic schizophrenics.)

Catatonic Stupor: A reduction in spontaneous movements and activity; sometimes to the point of becoming motionless.

A 33-year-old man was admitted to the hospital after his wife became alarmed over his complete inactivity. He had been unemployed for two months and had become progressively more uncommunicative, responding to her only minimally. A few days previously he stopped talking altogether and sat in his chair all day long with his eyes closed. His wife thought that he might be sick, but a physical examination failed to reveal any disease or physical difficulties. While he was in the hospital, he did open his eyes and talk for brief periods of time, although it was difficult to understand what he was trying to say. (Sue, Sue, & Sue, 1981, p. 293)

Perceptual Disturbances

Schizophrenia is often accompanied by a variety of perceptual disturbances. Colors may appear brighter and noises sound louder. The patient may not recognize himself in a mirror, or may perceive his body to be twisted or distorted.

In the most dramatic of these disturbances, **hallucinations,** the schizophrenic experiences false perceptions, seeing or hearing things that aren't there. A hallucination may involve any sense. The patient may discern huge, ugly faces or unfamiliar figures pointing at her. She may smell peculiar odors or taste poison in her food. The most common hallucination

Hallucinations: False perceptions; seeing or hearing things that aren't there.

In a catatonic stupor, a schizophrenic may become totally motionless, yet still be aware of his or her surroundings.

is auditory. Typically the schizophrenic hears someone scolding her for some misdeed, or commanding her to do something evil. These hallucinations are not experienced as voices in the head, however, but as sounds emanating from an external source, such as God or the devil.

Causes of Schizophrenia

Schizophrenia is perhaps the most thoroughly investigated of all abnormal behavior patterns. Every year hundreds of papers are published on the subject; until fairly recently, in fact, more time, money, and energy had been spent on schizophrenia than on all the other disorders combined (Grinker, 1969). Not only in psychology but in chemistry, biology, medicine, and anthropology, scientists are working to unravel the mysteries of this complex disorder. Again the theories fall into two broad categories, biological and psychological. We will discuss each of these as well as a promising theory that points to the interaction of biological and psychological factors.

Biological Theories. Schizophrenia seems to have a genetic predisposition. Studies done all over the world have documented an increased incidence of the disorder among close relatives of schizophrenics (Rodnick et al., 1984). If one person in a family has schizophrenia, close relatives are ten to fifteen times more likely than others to develop it. The more genes one holds in common with a person who has schizophrenia, the greater the risk (Kessler, 1980). A person whose identical twin is schizophrenic or whose parents are both schizophrenic bears a 50–50 risk for the disorder—a liability three to six times greater than that of fraternal twins and 50 times greater than that of the general population (Gottesman & Shields, 1976; Rosenthal, 1977). A child born to schizophrenic parents is at high risk even if adopted and raised by normal parents (Heston, 1966, 1970; Wender et al., 1968, 1974).

As with mood disorders, supporters of the biological theories believe that the schizophrenic inherits some disturbances in the balance, concentration, or capacity to make use of certain neurotransmitters (Snyder, 1980). The neurotransmitter most strongly implicated is dopamine, which, like norepinephrine and serotonin, is heavily concentrated in the limbic system. Theory holds that the schizophrenic's brain either suffers from an excess of dopamine or is exceptionally sensitive to it (Snyder, 1980).

The evidence for biological theories of schizophrenia is strong but not conclusive, however. Family studies are flawed in that relatives share not only the same genes but the same environment (Lidz & Blatt, 1983). That is especially true of identical twins, who, as we've learned, tend to be treated alike because of their close resemblance. Moreover, twins who are reared apart usually are not separated for at least six weeks, sometimes for as long as nine months after birth. And even if they were separated at birth, they still shared for nine months the environment of their mother's womb. Thus, they share the same environment during a formative early period. But even if the results of all such studies were taken as accurate, heredity could not be considered the only cause of schizophrenia. Otherwise, why would the identical twin of a schizophrenic run only a 50-percent rather than a 100-percent risk of developing the disorder? Clearly inherited factors alone are insufficient to account for schizophrenia's cause.

Psychological Theories. Psychological theories have emphasized the role of learning, family background, and stress in the cause of schizophrenia. In support of the role of learning, the symptoms of schizophrenia vary from culture to culture and from generation to generation, though the disorder occurs worldwide. (Pfohl & Winokur, 1983). The delusion that one's mind is being controlled by the Nazis, once common during the Second World War, has been replaced by the delusion of control by the communists, for example. And delusions of invaders from Mars have been replaced by delusions that computers are trying to take control of one's mind or the world.

Family background and stressful life events may also contribute to the development and maintenance of the disorder. The idea that schizophrenia might be caused by abnormal family interactions dates back to the 1950s, when researchers proposed that schizophrenia might be caused by double messages from the parents (Bateson et al., 1956). For example, a mother might ask her child to hug her and then react rigidly, or punish the child shortly thereafter. A child in such a double bind would eventually become confused, unable to decipher the messages of others or communicate effectively with them. Though the double bind theory remains controversial, severe communication problems in the family do seem to contribute to the development of some cases of schizophrenia (Liem, 1980).

Studies also show that many hospitalized schizophrenics have experienced more than their share of stressful life events—unemployment, financial difficulties, family problems, and unexpected setbacks (Spring & Coons, 1982). Stress can contribute to many disorders, however; and schizophrenics are no more stressed than patients with other problems (Rabkin, 1980). The question is, why does stress contribute to the development of schizophrenia in some people, but not in others?

The Diathesis–Stress Theory. According to the diathesis–stress theory, schizophrenia results from the interaction of genetic predisposition or, diathesis, and stress (Meehl, 1962; Spring & Zubin, 1978). Presumably, in order to become schizophrenic, one must inherit at least some tendency for the disorder. This tendency may be either strong or weak, depending on one's biological makeup. Stress in the form of impaired communication or catastrophic events can then kick off a schizophrenic episode in these people. The stronger one's inherited disposition for the disorder, the less stress is needed to induce the symptoms. People who inherit no tendency toward the disorder will never develop it, even under the severest stress.

The diathesis–stress theory is currently one of the most influential views of schizophrenia. It explains how only one of a pair of identical twins might become schizophrenic, and it is consistent with a broad range of findings. The theory is far from proven, however. Its major value is that it provides a useful model of the interaction of biological and psychological factors in the development of abnormal behavior.

Personality Disorders: Deeply ingrained, inflexible patterns of actions and thoughts that halt the normal adjustment process, creating a maladjusted style of behavior that becomes a central, enduring aspect of the personality.

PERSONALITY DISORDERS

Personality disorders are deeply ingrained, inflexible patterns of behavior and thinking that halt the normal adjustment process, creating a malad-

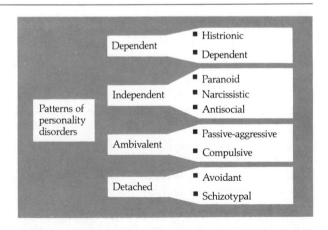

Figure 14.8 Schematic Overview of Patterns of Personality Disorders.

justed style of behavior that becomes a central, enduring aspect of the personality. Such disorders generally involve more subtle symptoms than any of the disorders discussed thus far, and there usually is less internal anguish. There is no loss of contact with reality, as in schizophrenia. Yet there is a twist, a characteristic distinctive feature, which permeates the interpersonal relationships of these individuals.

The classification of personality disorders used in the DSM is based heavily on the work of the psychologist Theodore Millon, who developed a model of personality that is based on how people handle dependency (Millon, 1969, 1981). Specifically, Millon described personalities in terms of their primary source of reinforcement, themselves or others. He identified four extreme patterns: dependent, independent, ambivalent, and detached (see Figure 14.8). The specific DSM personality disorders described below are based on these four patterns.

Dependent Patterns: Histrionic and Dependent Personalities

For people with personalities of the dependent pattern, the primary source of reinforcement is other people. These personality types have somehow learned that approval—feelings of security, confidence, acceptance, and the like—is best provided by others. Such people possess a powerful need for external support and attention, but are unable to rely on themselves for the approval and reassurance they desperately desire. They simply cannot look at their own accomplishments and say, "I'm proud of myself, no matter what other people think." Instead, they let others define their worth.

Personalities of the dependent pattern fall into one of two categories, depending on whether they actively manipulate others to secure approval or just passively wait for it. The first type, the manipulative **histrionic personality,** is typically sociable, talkative, and affectionate. These people are forever on the alert for an opportunity to demonstrate their charm or talent, so that others might reward them with compliments or encouragement. Histrionic personalities tend to be intense and exhibitionistic, prone to overdramatization of their feelings and experience. Because they love being the center of attention, to most observers they appear independent and confident. But they behave as they do because that is the only way they know to elicit attention from others. They will quickly change their strategy, if that is what is needed to win praise or avoid criticism.

> They are fickle, emotionally labile, irresponsible, shallow, love-intoxicated, giddy and shortsighted . . . Seductive, manipulative, explosive and sexually provocative, they think emotionally and illogically. Easy prey to flattery and compliments . . . they are possessive, grasping, demanding, romantic . . . When frustrated or disappointed, they become reproachful, tearful, abusive and vindictive . . . Rejective sensitivity is perhaps their outstanding common clinical feature. (Klein, 1972, p. 237)

In contrast to the histrionic personality, the passive **dependent personality** attempts to secure attention and support by subordinating his or her own needs to the needs of others. Lacking self-confidence and ambition, these people sit back and wait for others to assume responsibility for their

Histrionic Personality: A personality disorder in which the individual actively manipulates others to secure approval.

Dependent Personality: A personality disorder in which the individual attempts to secure attention and support by subordinating his or her own needs to the needs of others.

lives. They rarely display initiative, but instead passively comply with the leadership of others to secure approval and support. If left alone, with no other source of approval but themselves, they experience intense discomfort. They are prone to anxiety disorders and depression (Millon, 1969, 1981).

Independent Patterns: Paranoid, Narcissistic, and Antisocial Personalities

For personalities of the independent pattern, the primary source of reinforcement is within the self. In contrast to personalities of the dependent pattern, these people have somehow learned not to rely on others. Like dependent-pattern personalities, they fall into two main categories, depending on whether they are active or passive in asserting themselves. A third category, the antisocial personality, shows some of the characteristics of each of these two main categories.

Paranoid Personality: A personality disorder marked by suspicion and mistrust of others.

The active **paranoid personality** harbors a marked suspicion and distrust of others. To counter the opposition these people expect from others, they develop a repertoire of assertive, aggressive behaviors. Their aim is to dominate and conquer; their motto, "Do unto others before they do unto me." Needless to say, these are people who do not take criticism well; they are easily slighted. Ever alert to signs of rejection or disapproval, they soon find it, thus reinforcing their suspicions.

Paranoid personalities are excessively concerned with loyalty on the part of those who are close to them. They are constantly on guard against deceit, ever ready to find hidden motives. Generally these people are argumentative, excitable, and tense. Though they are hypercritical of others, they avoid any personal blame, even when warranted, and they refuse to admit to weakness. Instead, they strive to prove their power by shows of force and strength. Although others initially may see these personalities as ambitious, capable, and energetic, their defensiveness, suspicion, and jealousy ultimately prevent them from realizing their potential (Millon, 1981).

Narcissistic Personality: A personality disorder marked by an inflated sense of self-importance.

The passive **narcissistic personality,** on the other hand, marked by an inflated sense of self-importance, is blissfully secure. Like Narcissus, the

Theodore Bundy is considered to be an individual with an antisocial personality. Throughout his arrest and trial, he maintained an inappropriate, jovial attitude, though he was convicted of having committed several brutal murders.

youth who according to Greek legend fell in love with his own reflection, these people love themselves. Confident that others will just naturally recognize their specialness, they make no effort to prove themselves. "I'm great and I know it, and so does everybody else" is their motto. Narcissistic personalities can be recognized by their pretentious air of snobbishness. Not surprisingly, these people's interpersonal relations are shallow.

The **antisocial personality** is an independent pattern that can involve both the hostility and aggression characteristic of the paranoid personality and the shallowness of interpersonal relationships characteristic of the narcissistic personality. Major characteristics of the antisocial personality include irresponsibility, impulsiveness, and callous exploitation of others. Such individuals commonly engage in delinquent or criminal acts; they typically are unable to sustain consistent work behavior; they fail to plan ahead; and they deceive or use others without remorse.

Antisocial Personality: A personality disorder involving irresponsibility, impulsiveness, and callous exploitation of others.

Ambivalent Patterns: Passive-Aggressive and Compulsive Personalities

Personalities of the ambivalent pattern are ruled by a conflict over dependency. They vacillate between an "elbows-out" independence and a clinging dependence. These personality patterns fall into one of two categories, depending on how the conflict is expressed.

The **passive-aggressive personality** vacillates between relying on others and relying on self. These people's behavior can change dramatically at a moment's notice. First they are agreeable and compliant, next stubborn and negativistic. The change in attitude is often accompanied by a change in emotional tone. At one moment the person is charming, pleasant, and sociable, like the histrionic personality; at the next, moody, complaining, suspicious, and angry, like the paranoid personality. Because the passive-aggressive never sticks with one attitude for long, though, angry outbursts are often followed by deep remorse. Overall, these people tend to be restless and discontented, always finding fault and complaining, never satisfied.

Passive-Aggressive Personality: A personality disorder in which the individual vacillates between relying on others and relying on self.

Because of their ambivalence—their simultaneous needs to submit to and to dominate others—passive-aggressive personalities typically discharge their hostility in indirect ways. They are masters of procrastination, especially when others are depending on them; just for spite they will frustrate the well-laid plans of family and friends. These are the workers who are intentionally inefficient, the group members who make everyone late by not being ready on time. Their behavior alienates others and prevents them from functioning effectively in social or occupational situations.

> Mrs. G., a 47-year-old laboratory technician, was fired from her job because her boss felt she was 'sabotaging' the research project, as she would 'forget' to enter data, miss the time for obtaining samples, or fail to notify the lab chief when there was a technical problem that required intervention. She was seen in the Psychiatry Outpatient Department because she complained of feeling unproductive and uncertain about her future. She reluctantly revealed that she had been angry and jealous because her boss, a younger woman, was successful and well recognized, while the patient had not been able to attain the recognition she felt she deserved. (Guggenheim & Nadelson, 1982, p. 139)

Compulsive Personality: A personality disorder characterized by rigid outward conformity and ambivalence.

The **compulsive personality's** ambivalence is reflected not in passive resistance or in extreme swings in behavior, but in rigid outward conformity. Caught in a conflict between fear of social disapproval and the need for self-expression, these people overcontrol themselves, suppressing all outward signs of independence. Though their behavior is dependent, their need to be assertive, original, and free of restrictions imposed by others cannot be fully squashed. The approval they obtain by conforming is bought at the cost of great inner resentment and hostility (Millon, 1981).

Because compulsive personalities must constantly inhibit their desires and deny their feelings through self-discipline and self-restraint, they suffer from an inability to express warmth and tenderness. They become perfectionistic, preoccupied with rules, order, efficiency, and detail, and may insist that others adhere to their punishing standards as well. Commonly these people devote themselves to work and productivity to the exclusion of pleasure.

Detached Patterns: Avoidant and Schizotypal Personalities

Personalities of the detached pattern rely neither on self nor on others. Abandoning or denying their need for both dependence and independence, they avoid all close or competitive relationships and withdraw into an isolated world of their own. Detached personalities may be divided into two categories, the simple avoidant personality and the more severe schizotypal personality.

Avoidant Personality: A personality disorder in which the individual is extraordinarily sensitive to rejection.

Avoidant personalities are highly sensitive to rejection; the slightest rebuff can cause them unbearable humiliation. Consequently, these people avoid all but the safest relationships. They may withdraw from contact with anyone except for a totally accepting and uncritical mother, for example. Underneath it all, though, avoidant personalities really want to join the group; they are simply too shy and fearful of doing so. Their social awkwardness and intense anxiety are apparent to all around them, who may see them as social misfits. As children, these people are usually teased mercilessly by their peers. Greatly distressed by their inability to socialize and to relate comfortably to others, they tend to develop a poor self-image, attributing their difficulties to personal inadequacy. Unlike schizophrenics, who often share in their social sensitivity and awkwardness, avoidant personalities do not lose contact with reality; nor is there evidence that such personalities are especially prone to develop a schizophrenic disorder (Shapiro, 1978).

Schizotypal Personality: A personality disorder in which the individual manifests odd thoughts, perceptions, and communications similar to, but not as severe as, the symptoms of schizophrenia.

The **schizotypal personality** manifests a variety of odd thoughts, perceptions, and communications similar to, but not as severe as, the symptoms of schizophrenia. These people have difficulty forming and maintaining interpersonal relationships, controlling anxiety, communicating with others, and thinking clearly. They are prone to eccentric convictions.

In contrast to the avoidant personality, the schizotypal personality is often viewed as a latent or borderline form of schizophrenia (Saccuzzo & Schubert, 1981; Nakano & Saccuzzo, 1985). If one of a pair of identical twins is schizophrenic, frequently the other is a schizotypal personality (Heston, 1970). Schizotypal personalities generally do not lapse into full-blown schizophrenia, however. Seldom do they reach the point where hospitalization is necessary. They may, however, experience brief periods of bizarre behavior or distortions of reality, which can sometimes reach delusional proportions (Eckblad & Chapman, 1983).

We have discussed the problems of abnormal behavior throughout this book, and in this chapter we focused exclusively on the nature, classification, and possible causes of such behavior. In the next chapter we will consider how such behaviors are treated. As we shall see, treatment generally follows from the theory of what causes a specific disorder. For example, those who follow a Freudian theory of depression try to help a person ventilate or express bottled up self-anger. Those who follow a cognitive theory, by contrast, concentrate on changing cognitions.

LEARNING FRAMEWORK

I. Abnormal behavior often violates social norms, impairs functioning, and causes personal distress. (Review: *Figure 14.1*)
   A. Abnormal behavior is due to natural causes, not supernatural ones.
   B. Abnormal behavior is classified in a manual called the *Diagnostic and Statistical Manual of Mental Disorders* (DSM).
II. Alcohol and substance use disorders illustrate the interlocking of a physiological condition and a behavioral pattern.
   A. Repeated use of a substance often leads to withdrawal symptoms—nausea, weakness, anxiety, and so on—which occur if the individual abruptly stops using the substance.
   B. The cause of substance use disorders is a matter of theory, but the medical and personal consequences are well documented.
III. Anxiety, somatoform, and dissociative disorders share some significant similarities, but the behavioral patterns associated with each are quite different.
   A. In anxiety disorders, inappropriate anxiety is the predominant symptom. (Review: *Figure 14.3; Agoraphobia; Panic Attacks; Obsessive-Compulsive Disorder*)
   B. In somatoform disorders there are physical symptoms with no apparent physical cause. (Review: *Secondary Gain; Psychogenic; Psychosomatic Disorders*)
   C. In dissociative disorders, there is a change in normal mental activity. (Review: *Figure 14.4; Psychogenic Amnesia; Fugue State; Multiple Personality*)
   D. Both biological and psychological theories have been proposed to account for the cause of anxiety, somatoform, and dissociative disorders, but no single theory prevails at this time. (Review: *Table 14.3*)
IV. Mood disorders involve elation or depression that is inappropriate (out of proportion to the situation).
   A. A manic episode involves inappropriate elation or irritability plus a number of associated symptoms. A major depressive episode involves inappropriate depression, loss of interest and pleasure, and a number of associated symptoms. (Review: *Figure 14.5; Flight of Ideas; Dysphoric Mood*)
   B. Mood disorders are distinguished in terms of severity, range of symptoms, and the presence or absence of manic symptoms.
   C. Twin and drug studies have supported a biological contribution to the

cause of mood disorders. Questionnaire studies have supported the role of cognition. (Review: *Beck Depression Inventory*)

V. The major symptoms of schizophrenia can be divided into four categories. (Review: *Figure 14.7*)

A. Cognitive: the schizophrenic's thinking may be fragmented and illogical. (Review: *Delusion*)

B. Emotional: the schizophrenic's emotional expressions may be inappropriate or devoid of feeling. (Review: *Affect; Ambivalence*)

C. Social: the schizophrenic is uncomfortable around people and so withdraws from them. (Review: *Catatonic Stupor*)

D. Perceptual: the schizophrenic may distort the world or have sensory experiences without external stimulation. (Review: *Hallucinations*)

E. One prevalent theory holds that people may inherit a weak, strong, or no predisposition to develop the disorder. The greater the disposition, the less environmental stress needed to trigger the disorder. (Review: *Diathesis–Stress Theory*)

VI. Personality disorders fall into four categories, each of which has at least two related personality disorders, one active, one passive. (Review: *Figure 14.8*)

A. Dependent patterns rely on others for approval, feelings of security, support, and attention. (Review: *Histrionic Personality; Dependent Personality*)

B. Independent patterns rely only on themselves; they lack give and take skills. (Review: *Paranoid Personality; Narcissistic Personality; Antisocial Personality*)

C. Ambivalent patterns cannot find a balance between relying on themselves and relying on others. (Review: *Passive-Aggressive Personality; Compulsive Personality*)

D. Detached patterns cannot rely on themselves; nor can they rely on others. (Review: *Avoidant Personality; Schizotypal Personality*)

15

Treatment of Abnormal Behavior

Chapter Outline

Psychotherapy: Techniques developed by observation, experience, and experimental research to help people solve their problems, change their behavior, or cope more effectively.

Psychiatrists: Physicians who specialize in the diagnosis and treatment of abnormal behavior. As medical doctors (M.D.'s), psychiatrists are licensed to prescribe drugs and use other forms of medical interventions in treating abnormal behavior.

J ulia L., an intelligent and attractive twenty-three-year-old woman, could remember feeling insecure as far back as she could recall. As a child she had been afraid to stand up to her strict father and overprotective mother. Instead, she had been a "good girl," always doing what she was told. Julia did well in school and wanted to go to college, but her parents thought that what was good enough for them was good enough for her. They always insisted that her major objective be to find a husband. Her father also thought she should work and contribute to the upkeep of her family's home.

Though her parents didn't really force her, Julia decided not to enter college after graduating from high school. Instead, she began working under the direction of her mother in the dry cleaning business her father owned and operated. On the one hand, she was miserable having to deal with her parents at home and at work. She thought often of moving as far away as she could. On the other hand, the thought of leaving gave her a vague feeling of uneasiness.

As the months passed, Julia began to feel more and more frustrated and trapped. And to make matters worse, her parents had become increasingly critical of her. It seemed like nothing she did was right as far as they were concerned. Her father said that she had become careless. Her mother said that she was just like a baby. All Julia knew was that something was terribly wrong. For a long time she had wanted to talk to somebody about her problems. A friend confided that she had once benefited greatly by talking to a professional therapist. That was the final nudge Julia needed to seek treatment.

In seeking help for her problem, Julia would have to make a number of important decisions, as there are many different approaches to **psychotherapy**—techniques developed by observation, experience, and experimental research to help people solve their problems, change their behavior, or cope more effectively. In this chapter we will look at four main approaches used in psychotherapy: psychoanalytic, behavioral, cognitive, and humanistic. Each is based on a different set of assumptions. Each has its own set of techniques to bring about change. And, from the point of view of the person seeking help, each has its own unique features. After examining the basic assumptions, techniques, and unique features of each of the four models of psychotherapy, we will consider medical approaches, which use drugs and

Clinical Psychologists:
Psychologists trained in the specialty concerned with the study, diagnosis, and treatment of abnormal behavior.

Box 15.1 PSYCHOLOGY IN ACTION: Being a Good Consumer: I. Selecting a Therapist

Suppose you believed that you or someone in your family might require the services of a psychotherapist. Here are some things you might consider.

First, there are many types of professionals involved in the process of helping others to change their behaviors, to cope, and to live more effectively. **Psychiatrists,** as we have learned, are medically trained specialists. Because they hold an M.D. degree, psychiatrists can prescribe medication, admit people to hospitals, and use any of the other medically oriented forms of treatment discussed later in the chapter. A **clinical psychologist** is a psychologist who also specializes in treatment. Clinical psychologists receive general training in the science of behavior as well as specific training in psychotherapy, psychological testing, and other clinical interventions. Most hold a Ph.D. (Doctor of Philosophy) degree and must complete at least one year of internship and an additional year of post-doctoral training under the direction of an experienced practitioner before they are licensed to practice. Many of the techniques of therapy we will discuss were developed by clinical psychologists or based on psychological research. A third type of health professional is the social worker. Social workers are trained in the field of social work, which emphasizes the individual in relation to the social system. Social workers hold the M.S.W. (Master of Social Work) degree and usually must have a year or two of additional supervised experience before they are licensed to practice.

In searching for a psychotherapist, you can begin by asking around. Although a therapist who has helped a friend or family member might not be suitable for you, a strong recommendation from a satisfied client is a good beginning. In addition, you can call the psychology or counseling department of your college, ask your professors, or visit your family physician. Many universities and colleges have free or low-cost counseling centers for their students. County mental health centers also offer services, based on ability to pay.

When you first contact a prospective therapist, there are a number of issues to discuss before you

Before committing yourself to therapy, it is important to talk openly with the therapist in order to establish a trusting relationship.

commit yourself to treatment. Ask the therapist to describe his or her qualifications and experience. What medical school or university did the therapist graduate from? How much training did the therapist receive after completing his or her degree? Because of the importance of establishing an open and trusting relationship, qualified therapists should be happy to discuss your questions. Be cautious of one who won't.

Ask your therapist about fees. The fees should be reasonable and within your means. If not, ask the therapist about other options, such as community mental health clinics. If you have insurance, it probably has limitations. You'll need to check into these and determine whether your prospective therapist qualifies for reimbursement by your insurance company.

Of particular importance is the therapist's orientation. In the pages ahead we will discuss the major approaches to therapy. By examining these from the standpoint of the person receiving help, you can evaluate how well the approach might be suited to you. As you will see, no one approach is best for everyone. A person in therapy should feel free to discuss doubts about the treatment with the therapist and to get a second opinion or request a referral to another therapist.

other medically based techniques in treatment. Finally, we will consider other aspects of treatment, such as those that combine more than one model, those that combine psychotherapy and medical procedures, and those that use the various treatment techniques to treat families and groups.

Because the approaches to treatment are so varied, selecting a therapist is not an easy process (see Box 15.1). Julia finally decided on one who was psychoanalytically oriented. He was the same therapist who had helped her friend.

Psychoanalytic Approaches: Approaches to treatment that are aimed at relieving a patient of an underlying emotional disorder, which is presumed to be the cause of a patient's symptoms. These approaches are based on the Freudian technique of psychoanalysis, a process of bringing into awareness unconscious conflicts presumed to be at the root of problem behaviors.

Psychodynamics: Psychic (mental) forces and processes that develop through childhood experiences and which influence adult thinking and behavior.

Insight: An understanding of the roots of one's psychological problems.

Free Association: A psychoanalytic technique in which patients are encouraged to talk freely about themselves without censoring or evaluating their monologue.

In traditional psychoanalysis, the patient lies on a couch while the analyst sits behind, remaining anonymous and encouraging the patient to engage in "free association."

PSYCHOANALYTIC APPROACHES

Psychoanalytic approaches are aimed at relieving an underlying emotional disorder, which is presumed to be the cause of a patient's symptoms. Psychoanalytic approaches are based on the Freudian technique of psychoanalysis, a process of bringing into awareness unconscious conflicts presumed to be at the root of problem behaviors. These approaches focus on a patient's **psychodynamics**—psychic (mental) forces and processes that develop through childhood experiences and which influence adult thinking and behavior. (Whether a person seeking help is called a patient or a client depends on the therapist's orientation. For psychoanalytically oriented therapists, the preferred term is patient.) Psychoanalytically oriented therapists, also known sometimes as psychodynamic, attempt to help patients achieve **insight**—an understanding of the roots of their psychological problems—by exploring the past in depth and uncovering deeply buried unconscious conflicts and childhood anxieties. These therapists assume that abnormal actions and cognitions are the result of an underlying emotional disturbance that stems from such conflicts and anxieties. (For more background on psychoanalytic approaches, see Chapter 12.)

Techniques and Goals of Treatment

Patients are encouraged to engage in a process known as **free association,** in which they are encouraged to talk about themselves freely, giving a running account of their every thought and feeling no matter how in-

significant. To accomplish this, patients are cautioned not to censor or evaluate their monologue. Free association is like free flowing thought, spoken out loud.

The therapist then analyzes these thoughts for clues to unconscious conflicts that may lie behind the patient's problem behavior. Through **dream analysis**—a process in which the patient is asked to recall and describe his or her dreams—the therapist searches for additional clues in the symbolic events of the patient's dreams.

As therapy progresses, the therapist prepares the patient to understand how early childhood experiences and unconscious conflicts affect present behavior. In a process known as **laying the groundwork,** the therapist highlights patient statements that he or she believes the patient must be aware of in order to gain insight. Similarities and contradictions are noted. Gradually the patient is prepared for an **interpretation**—an explanation of the problem or of the patient's motives for behaving in a certain way. Throughout the entire process, however, the therapist remains anonymous and neutral, revealing as little personal information as possible.

Such anonymity is central to treatment, as it is necessary to the development of a phenomenon known as **transference**—a process in which the patient transfers the feelings and attitudes formed in an earlier relationship to the therapist. Although the therapist remains neutral, the patient begins to have uncalled-for emotions, ideas, and fantasies about the therapist. For instance, the patient may for no apparent cause become angry at the therapist. Such feelings, according to psychoanalytic theory, represent childhood conflicts long buried in the unconscious, surfacing as a result of therapy. In transferring these feelings to the therapist, the patient is able to vent them in a safe context, without risk of retaliation from the person to whom they are actually directed. And, because the therapist has remained neutral, the patient's strong feelings become material that the therapist can interpret in helping the patient achieve insight. (Figure 15.1 provides a summary of the psychoanalytic approach.)

Free association, dream analysis, and the interpretation of transferred conflicts are all based on the Freudian principle of repression. Theoretically,

Dream Analysis: A psychoanalytic technique in which the patient is asked to recall and describe his or her dreams.

Laying the Groundwork: A psychoanalytic technique in which the therapist highlights patient statements that he or she believes the patient should be aware of in order to gain insight.

Interpretation: An explanation of the patient's problems or of the patient's motives for behaving in a certain way.

Transference: A process in which the patient transfers the feelings and attitudes formed in an earlier relationship to the therapist.

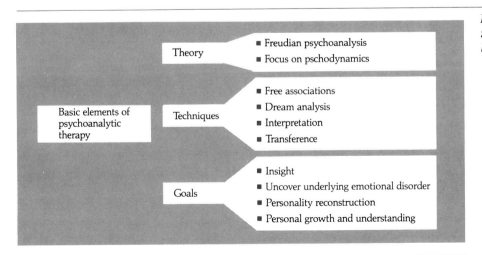

Figure 15.1 Schematic Summary of Psychoanalytic Therapy.

overt manifestations of a conflict are only symptoms, a surface expression of some deeper emotional problem. Treating the symptom and not its cause would be like treating a strep throat or other bacterial infection with throat lozenges. The lozenges may relieve the throat pain temporarily, but they have no effect on the cause of the pain, a respiratory infection. Consequently, a new symptom, like a fever, may develop—a phenomenon called **symptom substitution,** or the replacement of one symptom with another. Thus, in psychoanalytically oriented treatment, the primary target of change is the underlying emotional disorder, which is presumed to be the cause of the patient's symptoms.

> **Symptom Substitution:** The replacement of one symptom with another.

Psychoanalytically oriented therapy is practiced today in many variations. In traditional psychoanalysis, the patient is seen individually for an hour a day, four or five times a week. The goal is reconstruction of the personality, from a conflict-ridden one ruled by unconscious anxieties to a mature one with deep insight into how early experiences and unconscious conflicts affect adult behavior and with the ability to choose behavior based on present circumstances rather than past experiences (Wolberg, 1967). In the less-intense versions of psychoanalytically oriented psychotherapy practiced by most therapists today, however, the patient may be seen only once a week; the goal is personal growth and self-understanding (Chessick, 1985). Because of the richness and complexity of the psychoanalytic approach, it is not possible to capture the essence of what a patient experiences in our brief presentation. But, by looking at how the psychoanalytic approach was used in Julia's case, perhaps it is possible to get a better feel for it than might be achieved by a mere description of its basic technique.

A Psychodynamic Analysis of Julia's Problem

The therapist Julia was referred to attended a well-known midwestern university. After obtaining his Ph.D. degree in psychology with a specialty in clinical psychology, he trained for two additional years at a psychoanalytically oriented medical center under experienced practitioners.

The therapist began by taking a careful case history. Julia lay on a couch; the therapist sat behind her and listened thoughtfully, noting her hesitations, change in tone, and other nonverbal signs of emotion. Talking about her symptoms upset Julia, so she cried on and off; but she managed to explain her problem without prompting from the therapist.

After about forty minutes, the therapist explained his fees and orientation. He asked Julia to come back for an additional session so that he could better evaluate her problem. After the second session the therapist accepted her as a patient. He had had relatively good success in dealing with people like Julia. Indeed, research has revealed that psychoanalytically oriented therapy works best with adults who are anxious, young, intelligent, and verbal (Luborsky & Spence, 1978; Kernberg et al., 1972). So Julia was an excellent candidate for treatment. The therapist arranged to see her twice a week, from 2 to 2:45 p.m. on Monday and Thursday.

The therapist diagnosed Julia's problem in terms of her overreliance on her parents and inability to assert herself. In short, she suffered from overdependency. According to Freudian theory, such overdependency stems from the individual's failure as a child to learn to function independently of a powerful, protective adult. At first, every child suffers separation anxiety when left for even brief periods by the parents. Most learn to control and finally overcome it. But some, like Julia, never fully overcome the feelings of exposure or vulnerability provoked by separation from parental or other powerful figures.

The fact that Julia recalled feeling insecure for as long as she could remember convinced the therapist that the origins of her conflict were to be found in her early experiences. Julia had been strictly toilet trained; her mother once proudly informed her that she had been trained before she was two. The therapist suspected that a repressed urge for independence lay beneath her submissiveness. In order to receive her mother's love and attention and to maintain her support, Julia had had to deny her impulse for pleasure and learn to control her bowels before she was emotionally ready. At a formative age, she had learned to give up her own desires and conform to the expectations of others.

Julia's father, a rigid man who imposed his will on her and everyone else in the family, also seemed to be part of the problem. He had never given Julia the opportunity to be independent. Instead, as she grew from childhood to womanhood he contributed to her tendency to deny herself through his demands and arbitrary rules. As a result, she failed to learn to rely on her own judgment. By the time she graduated from high school she had become excessively dependent on both her parents for direction and support. Moreover, Julia was unable to express resentment and anger for fear of driving away those on whom she depended for protection. So strong was her fear of separation, in other words, that she could not risk losing control of her emotions, even when she had a right to be angry. Her therapist suspected that her carelessness and mistakes at work were symbolic of the anger she felt but could not express.

Treatment of Julia's Case with Psychoanalytically Oriented Techniques

Julia's therapist laid the groundwork for her recovery by underscoring those of her comments that were especially relevant to her conflicts. For instance, in the third session, while Julia was free associating about what she would give her mother for a birthday present, she said, "She needs a sharp knife to cut herself—no, I mean bread; she likes crusty French bread, but none of her knives are sharp enough." The therapist noticed that Julia had become upset and gone out of her way to clarify her remark, and he suspected that she was threatened by the hint of hostile feelings toward her mother. "The thought that you might want to see your mother injured disturbs you," he commented. Julia disagreed, however; and the therapist did not pursue the matter. In psychoanalytically oriented therapy, the patient must be slowly and carefully prepared for an interpretation of the underlying problem.

> In her twelfth session, Julia recalled the following dream: I was running and running but not getting anywhere. Why I was running, I don't know; all I knew was that I wanted to get away but couldn't. Suddenly I realized I was bound to a sinister old witch. She was laughing at me as I struggled

to break away. The next thing I knew I had a knife in my hand. At first I thought I could cut myself free. Then it occurred to me to stab the witch. She was laughing and mocking me. Then I woke up. "How did you feel?" queried the therapist.

"I don't know," replied Julia. "Angry, I guess. I really wanted to stab her."

"And who might that witch be?" the therapist inquired.

"I don't know," Julia retorted angrily. "Who do you think it might be?"

"Perhaps talking about this makes you feel angry at me?" the therapist responded.

"No," Julia answered, and changed the subject.

The therapist suspected that Julia's anger toward him was a transference of the anger that she would have liked to express toward her mother. She wasn't yet ready to face her old resentments, however, so she denied them. In changing the subject, Julia manifested what psychoanalytically oriented therapists call **resistance:** an attempt to resist treatment by blocking the exploration of a sensitive topic, failing to provide information, or an unwillingness to cooperate with the therapist.

Over the months Julia's free associations produced numerous slips expressive of hostility toward her mother. Gradually Julia began to agree with her therapist that she might be angry at her mother, and that the witch in her dream might symbolize her mother. She also began to experience intense feelings of anger at the therapist. The therapist encouraged her to express this transferred anger to him so that she might work through and resolve it.

The experience was an emotional one for Julia. She screamed and yelled and told her therapist all the things she presumably wanted to tell her mother. The long overdue release of her deep resentment and anger made Julia feel as if a huge weight had been lifted from her. As the therapist gradually helped her to become aware of deeply buried anger and feelings of insecurity rooted to her childhood anxieties, Julia was able to deal with them from a mature, adult perspective. Because they had been so deeply buried, she had not been able to deal with the roots of her problem before.

Julia's insight was also evident in her behavior. Even she was surprised by how well she handled herself the day she told her parents that she was moving to her own apartment and had found another job. She had matured considerably in the course of her treatment and was ready to go off on her own. She still felt insecure from time to time, but she was very much improved.

There is considerable controversy among researchers as to what constitutes a cure in psychotherapy (Bergin & Lambert, 1978). Often a patient, as judged by the therapist or by the patient's own subjective experience, is somewhat improved or even very much improved as a result of treatment, but not completely free of symptoms. Many depressed patients who undergo treatment experience increased self-esteem, learn to deal with guilt, and have less intense or prolonged episodes of dysphoric (sad, down, depressed, etc.) affect. Yet they still get depressed from time to time. In Julia's case, it is difficult to say whether or not she had been cured, or even what would constitute a cure for her. But, as far as her therapist was concerned,

Resistance: An attempt to resist treatment by blocking the exploration of a sensitive topic, failing to provide information, or an unwillingness to cooperate with the therapist.

■ Learning Check ■

For each of the following techniques of psychoanalytically oriented therapy, read the definition, then cover the right side and try to recite. Repeat.

Free Association	Patient encouraged to talk freely without evaluating the monologue
Dream Analysis	Patient recalls and describes dreams; therapist looks for symbolic clues to patient's problem
Laying the Groundwork	Therapist highlights statements that patient must be aware of to achieve insight
Interpretation	Therapist explains patient's problems or motives for behaving in a certain way
Transference	Patient transfers feelings and attitudes to therapist; therapist interprets these feelings to help patient achieve insight

she was no longer in need of treatment. In their last few sessions, Julia and her therapist dealt with her feelings about terminating therapy.

BEHAVIOR THERAPY

Behavior therapy is an approach to treatment aimed at modifying the overt actions that define a person's problem; behavior therapists use the principles of learning to change problem behaviors. They assume that abnormal behaviors are learned, and learned according to the same principles as are normal behaviors. Individuals seeking help are called "clients" rather than patients because they are not considered ill. Using the same principles that established the problem behaviors in the first place, behavior therapists attempt to create new, more acceptable behaviors to replace the old.

The style of a behavior therapist differs noticeably from that of a psychoanalytic therapist. There is no couch; client and therapist sit face to face, separated by a desk. The therapist is much more direct in asking questions and seeking information. The more direct questioning reflects behavior therapists' more direct approach to treatment.

A behavior therapist does not assume that problem behaviors—compulsive gambling, excessive shyness, unrealistic fears, and the like—are symptoms of some underlying emotional problem, as the psychoanalytically oriented therapist does. Instead, the therapist assumes that the behaviors themselves are the problem and should be the direct target of treatment. According to these therapists, problem behaviors differ from normal behaviors mainly in their extreme or maladaptive nature. Everyone bathes and showers, but not ten to fifteen times a day as might a compulsive washer. And, whereas taking a shower is adaptive, compulsively taking a shower every two hours interferes with practically all other areas of a person's life.

Behavior Therapy: An approach to treatment aimed at modifying the overt actions that define a person's problem.

Figure 15.2 Schematic Summary of Behavior Therapy.

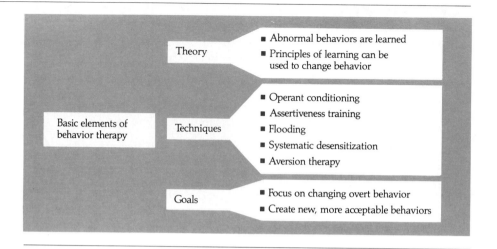

Thus, in behavior therapy, the primary target of change is overt behavior—the actions that are presumed to be maladaptive. If the client is afraid to drive alone, the therapist trains the client to do so. Once behavior has changed, the client is considered to be cured. In this section we will discuss five specific techniques of behavior therapy: operant conditioning, assertiveness training, flooding, systematic desensitization, and aversion therapy. (Figure 15.2 provides a summary of behavior therapy.)

Operant Conditioning Techniques

Operant conditioning techniques are based on the principles of learning and operant conditioning developed by E. L. Thorndike (1898) and B. F. Skinner (1938) and colleagues (see Chapter 6). The therapist uses reinforcement—the presentation or removal of rewards and punishments—to help clients acquire new behaviors or strengthen healthy ones. The therapist begins by identifying the behavior most in need of change. That behavior then becomes the target for treatment and is referred to as the **target behavior.**

After a target behavior is selected, the therapist attempts to establish a baseline, which means evaluating its strength—how frequently the behavior occurs within a given time frame—before making any attempt to alter it. This is done by direct observation or by asking the client to keep a record of the target behavior's occurrence. Then, during the next—or reinforcement—phase, the client is rewarded for performing the target behavior. If the reinforcement is effective, it should increase the strength of the behavior beyond the baseline (see Table 15.1).

The experience of an agoraphobic individual who was afraid to walk alone will illustrate how the procedure works. (Agoraphobia involves the fear of too much unprotected space—see Chapter 14.) To evaluate the strength of this target behavior, the therapist recorded how far the client was willing to walk alone on a one-mile course. During the baseline period the client walked an average of less than 400 yards. His walking increased markedly, however, when he was praised for going just a little farther each time (see Figure 15.3). Soon he was averaging about 10,000 yards per walk—

Operant Conditioning Techniques: A type of behavior therapy, based on the principles of learning and operant conditioning developed by B. F. Skinner and colleagues, in which the therapist uses reinforcement to help clients acquire new behaviors or strengthen healthy ones.

Target Behavior: In operant conditioning approaches to treatment, the behavior that the therapist identifies as in need of change and that becomes the target for treatment.

Table 15.1 Steps in Operant Conditioning Approaches

		Example
Step 1	Identify Target Behavior	Walking alone
Step 2	Establish Baseline	Record how far the client is able to walk alone before initiating treatment
Step 3	Reinforcement	Client praised for walking alone
Step 4 (optional)	Remove Reinforcement	Stop praising client
Step 5	Reinstate Reinforcement	Client praised for walking alone

a 25-fold increase over baseline levels. When reinforcement was withdrawn, however, the strength of the behavior dropped sharply; when it was reinstated, the strength of the behavior increased again (Agras et al., 1968).

Operant techniques have been applied to a wide range of problems. In a *token economy* program, for instance, operant techniques are used in institutions such as mental hospitals and homes for juvenile delinquents and in the schools. After a target behavior has been identified and a baseline taken, people are rewarded with tokens, which can be exchanged for more tangible rewards such as candy bars, magazines, passes, special privileges, shows, and the like.

In one classic study, a token economy program was applied to a group of mental patients who had been hospitalized for twenty years (Atthowe &

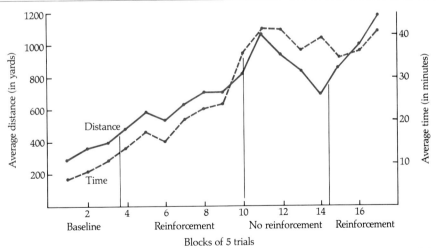

Figure 15.3 In this figure, the heavy line indicates the average distance, and the dotted line the average amount of time, an agoraphobic spent walking alone. As the figure shows, both measures indicate a strengthening of the target behavior over baseline levels during the reinforcement phase of treatment. When reinforcement is withdrawn, there is a decrease in strength, but not to previous baseline levels. When reinforcement is reinstated, however, the strength of the behavior increases to its previous high during the original reinforcement period (Adapted from Agras et al., 1968).

Krasner, 1968). Observation of these patients revealed they did nothing but sit or sleep in large overstuffed chairs on the hospital ward. They typically did not move except to get their meals. A few would not get up even for meals without prodding. Others wouldn't leave their chair to go to the bathroom.

As a first step in setting up a token program for the patients, the researchers selected behaviors related to good personal hygiene (shaving, bathing daily, using the toilet as needed, wearing clean clothes, and the like) and appropriate table manners (eating with a fork and spoon instead of by hand, chewing with the mouth closed, etc.). They took a baseline and found a very low frequency for all target behaviors. Then they implemented a token program. Patients were told what behaviors would be rewarded with tokens; they were also told what rewards the tokens could be exchanged for. The entire hospital staff then observed the patients and gave them tokens following each targeted behavior. At first, the program had little effect. Then the researchers used a little ingenuity. Sitting in the large comfortable chairs as most of the patients liked to do was changed from a "routine right" to a privilege. If they wanted to sit, the patients would have to earn the right by accumulating a sufficient number of tokens. Soon there was a dramatic rise in almost all target behaviors. To many, the results were truly amazing. Patients who seemed all but hopeless were acting more like responsible human beings than they had for some twenty years (Atthowe & Krasner, 1968).

The use of rewards to change behavior, as in a token economy, is called **contingency management.** The idea behind contingency management is to change a behavior by altering its consequences. Getting a reinforcer is made contingent on making the desired behavior change. Contingency management is the heart of the therapeutic use of operant conditioning. In addition, as we saw in Chapter 11, contingency management is sometimes used in conjunction with other major techniques of behavior therapy. Consider assertiveness training.

Contingency Management: The use of rewards to change behavior; attempting to change behavior by altering its consequences.

Assertiveness Training

People who are anxious and insecure in social situations tend to be underassertive. If someone steps in front of them in a waiting line, they are more likely to feel intimidated than to confidently say, "This is a line. The back of it is over there." In **assertiveness training,** such people learn to communicate their feelings and needs to others with more confidence; to be assertive without being aggressive. The therapist literally teaches clients how to respond effectively in troublesome situations. Helping the client to act more effectively in such situations is the target of treatment.

First the client describes the situation and the therapist suggests specific ways of handling it. Then the client and therapist act out the situation, a technique known as **role playing.** The therapist may demonstrate the appropriate behaviors, providing a model for the client to follow; or she may play the other role, allowing the client to practice the new response. In the case of a twenty-eight-year-old grocery store clerk named Jim, the procedure went this way:

Assertiveness Training: A technique of behavior therapy in which people learn to communicate their feelings and needs to others with more confidence; to be assertive without being aggressive.

Role Playing: A technique in which client and therapist act out a situation. In role play, a therapist may demonstrate the appropriate behavior or play the other role and allow the client to practice the new response.

Therapist: Suppose you and your wife go to a very expensive French restaurant. You order your steak rare, and the waiter replies, "Yes

sir, rare." But he brings you a steak that is well-done. What would
you do?

Jim: I don't know; probably just eat it.

Therapist: Can you tell me what your reason would be?

Jim: I don't like to cause any trouble; it would be too embarrassing to make a fuss.

Therapist: But how would you feel?

Jim: I'd be pretty damn mad at the waiter, and even madder at myself for not doing something.

Therapist: It sounds to me as if you feel you should take some kind of action.

Jim: That's right.

Therapist: I agree. There are many things you could do. For example, you could tell the waiter, "I ordered this rare and I think you wrote that down. Please take this back and bring me a steak cooked rare." Fear is what prevents people from speaking up in these situations—fear of embarrassment, of creating a scene, and so on. However, if you do attempt to speak up and express your true feelings whenever possible, each time you do you'll feel less afraid. Now let's practice. Pretend I'm the waiter and I've just brought your steak well-done.

The therapist works with the client until he is able to express his anger appropriately. She may offer suggestions on the right posture, tone of voice, eye contact, and choice of words. (Figure 15.4 shows examples of the statements clients learn to use.) Once the client has mastered one situation, the two repeat the procedure with a different situation. When the client has mastered a variety of assertive responses, and has learned to identify situations in which assertiveness is appropriate, he is encouraged to practice it in real life. In later sessions, the therapist and client discuss the client's performance in these real-life situations, and the therapist continues to give the client direct suggestions on how to handle himself more effectively.

As the individual becomes more effective, appropriate assertiveness in real life leads to rewarding consequences—a better-tasting steak, a good feeling for not being taken advantage of, or whatever. When this occurs, assertive behaviors are strengthened, as in contingency management. The naturally occurring positive consequences serve to maintain the client's newly acquired assertive behaviors even after the therapy has been completed.

Assertion training is just one of the many behavior therapy techniques that help people deal more effectively with difficult situations. Flooding is another.

1. Would you please call me back. I can't speak to you now.
2. Excuse me. You're obstructing my view.
3. Will you kindly stop talking during the play/movie/music.
4. This is a line. Please go to the back of it.
5. You have kept me waiting 20 minutes.

Figure 15.4 Assertive Statements. (Adapted from Wolpe, 1982).

Flooding

Flooding: A technique of behavior therapy in which clients are given long exposures to stimuli that are highly disturbing to them, with the aim of reducing their anxiety and avoidance response to these stimuli so that they can respond more effectively to them.

In Vivo Exposure: Real-life exposure to feared situations, as opposed to imagined exposure.

Avoidance Responses: The avoidance of a stimulus because of unpleasant experiences with it.

Flooding is a technique of behavior therapy in which clients are given long exposure to stimuli that are highly disturbing to them. The goal of the technique is to reduce anxiety and avoidance responses to these stimuli and so increase the likelihood of more effective responses. A person who avoids going into the garage at night because of a fear of rats might be asked to imagine that he has just gone into the garage when suddenly a large rat comes out of nowhere and crawls up his leg. When he tries to shake it off, it jumps onto his head; all efforts to remove the rat fail. Or an agoraphobic with a deathly fear of crowds might be taken into a large department store at the peak of the winter holiday season. The technique of real-life exposure to feared situations, as opposed to imagined exposure, is called **in vivo exposure.**

The rationale for flooding is based on the results of learning experiments with **avoidance responses**—that is, the avoidance of a stimulus because of unpleasant experiences with it (Solomon, 1964). If a cat is placed in a box with an electric grid at the bottom and is shocked three seconds after a bell rings, it will soon learn to jump out of the box at the sound of the bell, to avoid being shocked again. Once such avoidance responses are learned, they are extremely difficult to extinguish. Normally, extinction occurs when we withdraw reinforcement. The unrewarded response becomes gradually weakened until finally extinction occurs, which means the response is no more likely to occur than it did before it was rewarded.

But how can we extinguish an avoidance response? Even if the electric grid is removed, the cat will still jump out of the box at the sound of the bell. It won't wait around to see if the shock will follow. In the same way, humans who have had unpleasant experiences in crowded places don't wait around in a crowd for a repeat experience. If we want the subject, cat or human, to unlearn an avoidance response, we must expose it to the feared stimulus without negative consequences. We rig the box so the cat cannot escape, ring the bell, but do not shock the cat. Or we expose humans to the very stimuli they fear, under conditions in which negative consequences will not follow. By confronting a situation they would normally avoid, clients can learn that it will not necessarily produce dire consequences, and thus they unlearn their avoidance response.

Though flooding and related techniques have been successful in the treatment of many types of fears, the procedure does have some drawbacks. Besides causing the client distress and discomfort, it can actually cause some clients to get worse (Levis, 1980):

> Dr. K. was a physician with a severe phobia for insane people and insane behavior. He was in military service, and soon after he began to consult me was offered a transfer to a psychiatric hospital. I encouraged this, thinking that the phobia might be overcome by flooding. On my advice, he exposed himself continuously to the presence of schizophrenic patients, sometimes for hours at a stretch. Far from decreasing, his reactions to these patients grew progressively worse, and in addition, he developed a rising level of pervasive anxiety. By the end of the second day he was so extremely anxious that he had to be relocated. He had become much more sensitive than ever before to "insane stimuli." He was now a far more difficult problem than when I had first seen him . . . (Wolpe, 1982, p. 245)

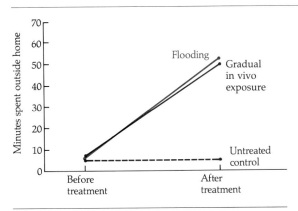

Figure 15.5 *Two groups of agoraphobic subjects indicated the number of minutes they spent outside the home without feeling tense before and after one of two kinds of treatment: flooding and gradual in vivo exposure. Both groups showed an increase·in average minutes compared to an untreated control group of agoraphobics, but neither treatment was superior to the other. (Adapted from Emmelkamp, 1974).*

Studies show that, for some cases, alternatives to flooding are just as effective but less risky (Marshall, 1985). In one, a group of agoraphobic subjects was treated with flooding and another group with gradual in vivo exposure. A third, the control group, received no treatment at all. Clients rated their own progress by recording how much time they could spend outside the house without feeling tense. Before treatment, the three groups rated their time outside about equally. After seven sessions in therapy, the two groups receiving treatment showed significant improvement over the untreated control group. Neither treatment proved more effective than the other, however (see Figure 15.5) (Emmelkamp, 1974).

Flooding illustrates how the behavior therapist uses principles of learning—extinction of an avoidance response in the case of flooding—to change behavior. The technique does have a place in clinical practice. Because it can prove to be distressing to certain individuals, however, a behavior therapist would be inclined to use an alternative approach, if an equally effective one is available. One such approach is systematic desensitization.

Systematic Desensitization

Systematic desensitization is a gradual step-by-step technique for training clients to react to a troubling stimulus with a new response, one that is incompatible with anxiety. In contrast to flooding, the client is gradually ex-

Systematic Desensitization: A gradual step-by-step technique for training clients to react to a troubling stimulus with a new response, one that is incompatible with anxiety.

Systematic Desensitization. *In systematic desensitization, the client is gradually exposed to real or imagined stimuli that elicit anxiety, and learns to replace his or her fear with relaxation. This group is first learning to identify the symptoms of their anxiety.*

posed to stimuli that elicit anxiety. More specifically, while the client is relaxed, the therapist gradually exposes him to a weak form of the feared stimulus. When the client can remain relaxed in the presence of this weak stimulus, the therapist introduces a stronger one, and so on until the client can relax in the presence of the full-strength stimulus. The idea is that relaxation competes with and inhibits anxiety. If a client can learn to face a feared stimulus with relaxation, anxiety will be blocked, or significantly reduced, and the client will be able to respond more effectively to the stimulus.

As in operant conditioning, the therapist must first identify the target behavior—such as poor test performance due to extreme anxiety while taking a test (test anxiety). Then the therapist identifies the stimuli that elicit anxiety and impair behavior. These stimuli are broken down into a **fear hierarchy,** a list of situations involving the feared stimulus, arranged according to the amount of anxiety they cause. For example, a hierarchy for fear of bugs might be arranged according to number (1 bug, 10 bugs, 50 bugs), size (small bugs, medium-sized bugs, large bugs), or distance (distant bugs, close bugs). The number of items on the hierarchy varies, depending on the nature and complexity of the client's problem. Figure 15.6 shows a hierarchy for test anxiety, arranged according to time.

To simplify the construction of a fear hierarchy, behavior therapists help clients to quantify their fears. They ask the client to think of the worst anxiety he has ever experienced or can imagine experiencing, and to assign it a rating of 100. Absolute calm is assigned a rating of zero. The client then practices expressing the level of anxiety he is experiencing at any given time with a number on this scale—20, 50, 70, and so on. Each point on the scale is called a **SUD,** short for "subjective unit of disturbance." The sud scale is a subjective rating system in which clients express the strength of their anxiety to a given stimulus on a scale from zero (no anxiety) to 100 (highest possible level of anxiety). It provides a simple, straightforward way for clients to communicate the strength of their anxiety to a therapist (Wolpe, 1958, 1982).

Fear Hierarchy: A list of situations involving a feared stimulus, arranged according to the amount of anxiety they cause.

SUD: Subjective unit of disturbance, a subjective rating system in which clients express the strength of their anxiety to a given stimulus on a scale from zero (no anxiety) to 100 (highest possible level of anxiety).

Figure 15.6 Fear Hierarchy for Test Anxiety. (Reprinted with permission J. Wolpe, The Practice of Behavior Therapy, *1982, Pergamon Press.)*

1. Two weeks before an examination
2. A week before an examination
3. Four days before an examination
4. Three days before an examination
5. Two days before an examination
6. One day before an examination
7. The night before an examination
8. The examination paper lies face down before her
9. Awaiting the distribution of examination papers
10. Standing before the unopened door of the examination room
11. In the process of answering an examination paper
12. On the way to the university on the day of an examination

Hierarchy construction usually begins about the same time as training in deep-muscle relaxation. The client learns how to tense and then relax each of his major muscle groups, and practices it for ten to fifteen minutes, twice a day. After a few weeks of practice, most people can learn to induce a state of deep relaxation and calmness in themselves (Wolpe, 1958, 1982). (For a more detailed description of deep muscle relaxation, see Chapter 11.)

Finally, the client is exposed to items on the completed fear hierarchy in a relaxed state, either through imagery or in vivo. When imagery is used, the therapist asks the client to imagine the weakest item on the hierarchy for about five seconds. When the client can tolerate the idea without anxiety (zero suds), the therapist moves to the next item. In the case of a twenty-four-year-old art student who suffered from an extreme fear of examinations, the procedure went this way:

> *Therapist:* I am going to ask you to imagine a number of scenes. If at any time you feel disturbed or worried and want to draw my attention, feel free to do so. As soon as a scene is clear in your mind, raise your left index finger about an inch. First, I want you to imagine that you are standing at a familiar street corner on a pleasant morning, watching the traffic go by. You see cars, motorcycles, trucks, bicycles, people, and traffic lights; and you hear the sounds associated with all those things. (The client raises her finger and the therapist pauses for five seconds.) Now stop imagining that scene. By how much did it raise your anxiety level?
>
> *Miss C.:* Not at all.
>
> *Therapist:* Now give your attention once again to relaxing. (The therapist gives the client instructions to relax for about twenty to thirty seconds.) Now imagine that you are home studying on the evening of April 20th, exactly one month before your first final exam. (After about fifteen seconds Miss C. raises her finger. The therapist pauses

---

▪ Learning Check ▪

For each question: read, cover, try to recite, repeat.

Q: How are flooding and systematic desensitization alike?

A: Both expose client to anxiety-provoking stimuli. Use either imagined or in vivo exposures. Attempt to help client respond more effectivity to an anxiety-provoking stimulus.

Q: How are flooding and systematic desensitization different?

A: Exposure is prolonged and intense in flooding; gradual and mild in desensitization. In desensitization the disturbing stimulus is broken down into a hierarchy; in flooding no hierarchy is used. In desensitization exposure takes place while client is relaxed and calm; in flooding the client is not relaxed and may experience distress.

for another five seconds.) Stop that scene. By how much did it raise your anxiety?

Miss C.: About 10 units.

Therapist: Now give your attention once again to relaxing. (pause) Now imagine the same scene again—a month before your examination.

On the third presentation of this scene, Miss C. reported no anxiety. The therapist then exposed her to the next item on the hierarchy (adapted from Wolpe, 1982, pp. 158–159).

With this procedure, each new item on the hierarchy is no more disturbing than the last. Once a person has conquered one item, the next simply isn't as terrifying. When Miss C. began treatment, imagining herself four weeks before an exam generated about 10 suds worth of anxiety in her. When she reached the point where that scene generated zero suds, she could progress to a scene two weeks before the exam without going above 10 suds. (She had rated it 20 suds before.) Thus working through the items on a hierarchy is like climbing a ladder. The client conquers an anxiety in a manageable way, one step at a time, and learns a new response (relaxation) to stimuli that once elicited anxiety.

Sometimes behavior therapy techniques are used not to reduce a fear but to create one. Consider aversion therapy.

Aversion Therapy

Aversion Relief: A technique of cognitive behavior therapy in which the therapist uses learning techniques to condition a client to respond to certain words or thoughts with a feeling of relief by pairing a word with the termination of an unpleasant stimulus.

Aversion therapy is a type of behavior therapy in which an unpleasant (aversive) stimulus is paired with the cues associated with an undesired response. For example, a child molester may be shocked while being shown pictures of children playing. The idea is not to punish the molester, but to change the effect of the cue on his behavior. Presumably, the sight of children playing acts as a cue for the molester to begin making sexual advances toward children. By pairing shock with this same cue, the molester will respond to it in a different way. Specifically, the sight of children will become associated with the fear and pain of shock.

In aversion therapy, an attempt is made to associate the stimuli that lead to an undesired response with an aversive stimulus. The therapy has been used with mixed success in an effort to treat alcohol and drug addiction, inappropriate sexual behaviors, and overeating and smoking (Rachman & Teasdale, 1968). But even if it were 100 percent effective, the procedure raises some important ethical issues.

The use of an aversive procedure involves the infliction of pain. Of all the techniques we've discussed, none have a greater possibility of causing harm to a person than aversion techniques. When is it ethical and moral to inflict such pain on a person to control his or her behavior? Psychologists do not have the answer.

All approaches to therapy involve values, ethics, and sensitive personal issues (London, 1964). In using their behavior change techniques, behavior therapists are making a judgment that a person would be better off by learning some new response or unlearning an old one. But what if the judgment involved changing or even controlling a person's thoughts? Such judgments are, in fact, a major feature of the cognitive approaches.

In the psychoanalytic approaches, the primary target of change is an underlying emotional response. In behavior therapy, the presenting behavior is considered to be the problem. Cognitive approaches attempt to modify cognitions.

COGNITIVE APPROACHES

Treatments that attempt to change or modify a client's cognitions—thoughts, beliefs, expectations, and the like—are called **cognitive approaches.** Such approaches fall into one of two major categories, depending on whether cognitions are viewed as behavior to be modified (cognitive behavior therapy) or as the underlying cause of disordered actions and emotions (classical cognitive therapy). (See Figure 15.7.)

In **cognitive behavior therapy,** cognitions are viewed as behavior and the therapist uses learning principles to modify a client's cognitions. Cognitive behavior therapy is based on the same philosophy as behavior therapy in that the presenting behavior, rather than some underlying emotional problem, is considered the direct target of treatment. Cognitive behavior therapy extends the definition of behavior to include cognitions as well as overt actions. In using cognitive behavior therapy, the therapist assumes that, like overt actions, cognitions are learned responses that are subject to modification by reinforcement, conditioning, and other learning-based procedures. The idea behind cognitive behavior therapy is the same as it is in behavior therapy—that problem behavior, not hypothetical underlying emotional problems, should be the focus of treatment.

Classical cognitive therapy, by contrast, refers to those approaches in which cognitions are considered the primary target of treatment because they are presumed to be the cause of abnormal actions or emotions. Classical cognitive therapy attempts to modify a client's premises, assumptions, attitudes, and other cognitions, because these are believed to be the primary source from which disturbed actions and emotions stem. This is in direct

Cognitive Approaches: Approaches to treatment that attempt to modify a client's cognitions—thoughts, beliefs, expectations, and the like.

Cognitive Behavior Therapy: A cognitive approach to treatment in which cognition is viewed as behavior and the therapist uses learning principles to modify a client's cognitions (aversion relief, covert sensitization, thought stopping, and self-instructional training).

Classical Cognitive Therapy: Approaches to treatment in which cognitions are considered the primary target of treatment because they are presumed to be the cause of abnormal actions or emotions.

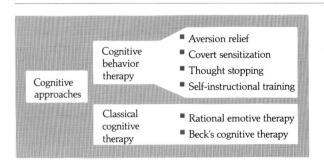

Figure 15.7 Schematic Overview of Cognitive Approaches to Therapy.

contrast to the psychoanalytic view that holds an emotional problem to be the underlying cause of disturbed actions or cognitions; and in contrast to behavior therapy and cognitive behavior therapy, which view the behavior itself as the problem.

In this section, we will examine both categories of the cognitive approaches, beginning with cognitive behavior therapy. Then we will consider the classical cognitive therapies, which also modify cognitions but which developed independently of learning theory and hold a different philosophy concerning the fundamental target of treatment.

Cognitive Behavior Therapy

Four techniques of cognitive behavior therapy are: aversion relief, covert sensitization, thought stopping, and self-instructional training (see Figure 15.7). Each treats cognitions as a behavior that can be modified through the application of learning principles.

Aversion Therapy: A type of cognitive behavior therapy in which an unpleasant stimulus is paired with the cues associated with an undesired response.

In **aversion relief,** the therapist uses learning techniques to condition a client to respond to certain words or thoughts with a feeling of relief by pairing a positive word with the termination of an unpleasant stimulus. The word *calm* might be paired with relief from a mild but unpleasant electric shock to the forearm, for example. First the therapist places an electrode on the client's arm and switches on the current. To stop the shock, all the client has to do is say "calm"; the therapist immediately switches off the current. The idea is that the word *calm* becomes associated with the relief that follows when the shock is terminated. After several trials, saying the word *calm* thus becomes a conditioned stimulus for the feeling of relief. Eventually, just thinking "calm" can be enough to elicit the conditioned feeling of relief (Wolpe, 1958, 1982). Unlike aversion therapy, the shock that is used in aversion relief is relatively mild and painless. Nevertheless, the use of shock does pose some risks (for example, faulty equipment, hurting a person with a low sensitivity to pain, etc.). Another cognitive procedure, covert sensitization, eliminates the shock completely through the use of aversive imagery.

Covert Sensitization: A technique of cognitive behavior therapy in which the client is taught to associate the stimuli that elicit problem behaviors with aversive thoughts and images.

In **covert sensitization** the client is taught to associate the stimuli that elicit problem behavior with aversive thoughts and images. The thought of drinking alcohol might be paired with an image of the consequences of uncontrolled drinking—seeing oneself doing something terribly embarrassing, being arrested for drunk driving, or the like. The idea is that a new response will become associated to the stimuli that elicit drinking. Instead of responding to the thought of liquor by drinking, the person will respond to it as he might to the image—with disgust. Covert sensitization is just like aversion therapy, except that no shock is used and the individual, through thoughts and images, controls the aversive stimulus. Sometimes, however, the problem is not one of creating aversive thoughts, it is stopping unwanted ones.

Thought Stopping: A technique of cognitive behavior therapy in which the therapist teaches the client to disrupt or eliminate maladaptive thoughts.

In **thought stopping,** the therapist teaches the client to disrupt or eliminate maladaptive thoughts. The typical procedure involves having the client shout "Stop!" whenever the disturbing thoughts appear. Next, the client learns to terminate the undesirable thoughts by mentally thinking, "Stop." The goal is to use the technique every time the undesired cognitions recur, as soon as they reach awareness. For example, a person with obsessional

> 1. I can remain calm and cool no matter what he says.
>
> 2. I don't have to let this upset me because I know I can control my anger.
>
> 3. I handled difficult problems before, so I know I can handle this one.
>
> 4. Instead of dwelling on the negative, I can concentrate on ways of dealing with this mess.
>
> 5. Getting into a shouting match won't accomplish anything, so I'm going to stay in control of myself.

Figure 15.8   Examples of Positive Self-statements.

thoughts—persistent, irrational, or disturbing thoughts that the person cannot control—might use thought stopping to get some relief. Then self-instructional training might be used.

Self-instructional training is a technique aimed at modifying a client's **internal dialogue**—the mental conversation that people carry on more or less habitually throughout their waking hours (Meichenbaum, 1977). The procedure goes a step beyond thought stopping in that it seeks to replace maladaptive thoughts with new, more adaptives ones. The therapist begins by helping the client to become aware of his internal dialogue and its influence on his actions and feelings. She teaches the client that such dialogue, and in particular **self-statements**—the things a person mentally tells himself about himself—has a profound effect on behavior (see Figure 15.8).

The therapist then concentrates on identifying negative, detrimental, or self-defeating parts of the internal dialogue. Once they are identified, the client can unlearn them and rehearse new, more effective statements. The therapist may also suggest self-statements that increase the client's productivity or that facilitate coping. (Figure 15.8 lists positive self-statements that are helpful in dealing with a variety of stressful situations.) That done, the client learns to reinforce the new statements, such as with approving thoughts like, "Good, I'm getting better."

Self-instructional training, like other techniques of cognitive therapy, relies on principles of learning and conditioning (for example, rewards) to modify thoughts. Classical cognitive therapy takes a somewhat different approach.

Classical Cognitive Therapy

In this section we will discuss two major techniques of classical cognitive therapy: rational emotive therapy and Beck's cognitive therapy. Both assume that cognitions are the fundamental cause of maladaptive actions and disturbed emotions; both attempt to modify a client's basic premises, assumptions, attitudes, or other cognitions that are presumed to be at the root of the problem. Clients don't simply learn new self-statements, for instance; they come to evaluate their experiences differently.

In **rational emotive therapy,** an approach to therapy developed by clinical psychologist Albert Ellis (1962), it is assumed that problem behaviors stem from one or more irrational beliefs. Rational emotive therapy can be summarized in terms of an A (Activating Event), B (Belief System), C (Consequences), D (Disputing) format (Ellis, 1984). According to this format, the

Self-Instructional Training: A technique aimed at modifying a client's internal dialogue—the mental conversation that people carry on more or less habitually throughout their waking hours.

Internal Dialogue: The mental conversation that people carry on more or less habitually.

Self-Statements: The things a person mentally tells himself about himself.

Rational Emotive Therapy: A classical cognitive therapy approach developed by Albert Ellis that assumes that problem behaviors stem from one or more irrational beliefs.

emotional consequences (C) of an activating event (A) depend on a person's belief system (B). A person who believes that it is terrible whenever things aren't the way he or she wants them overreacts to each minor setback as if it were a major catastrophe. The person's emotional response to the setback is determined by the person's irrational belief. In rational emotive therapy, the therapist disputes (D) the belief by challenging it rationally. When the belief changes, the individual will react differently to setbacks. Here are some examples of the kind of irrational beliefs identified by Ellis (1962):

- The notion that a person must be loved or approved of by virtually everyone in his community.
- The idea that, to consider oneself worthwhile, a person must be thoroughly competent, adequate, and achieving in all possible respects.
- The idea that, when life doesn't go the way one would like, catastrophe has struck.
- The idea that certain difficulties and responsibilities are easier to avoid than to face.

A major premise of rational emotive therapy is that emotions are the product of thinking. We feel bad about something because we think it is bad. Rational emotive therapists attempt to change a person's distressing emotional responses by changing the thinking upon which they are based. They deliberately direct the client's behavior, teaching him to think rationally about his experiences. Therapy begins with a direct assault on the client's belief system. The therapist pulls no punches in trying to expose an irrational belief, as in the following case:

> *Therapist:* Johnny, it sounds to me as if you believe everyone controls you. No matter what happens to you, it's someone else's fault. They make you angry, they make you sad, they make you unhappy. Well, I have a great idea! Why don't we create a Johnny doll? We could probably get Mattel to market it. You know, we have this little doll with a set of remote controls, and every time we press a button we can make it happy, sad, depressed. We can make it dance or sing. We control the doll through remote control. Or maybe we can make a puppet and call it a Johnny puppet. Other people pull the strings and Johnny does what they want. What do you think?
>
> *Johnny:* (laughs) That's funny. But that's not how it is. I don't sound that way!
>
> *Therapist:* Oh, yes, you do. You sound as if you believe you're a puppet and other people control you. (Walen et al., 1980, p. 17)

Not all practitioners of rational emotive therapy are as confrontive as in this example, but all of them offer direct guidance and ask direct questions in their effort to point out the irrational beliefs at the root of ineffective behaviors or negative emotions. Because of the focus on cognition, the therapist often takes the role of teacher and uses absurdity and humor to confront the irrationality of the client's thinking (Ellis, 1984).

In another form of classical cognitive therapy called **Beck's cognitive therapy,** the therapist focuses on changing the client's negative views about self, the world, and others. In this approach, which was developed by Aaron Beck (1976), the therapist challenges beliefs such as, "I'm good for

Beck's Cognitive Therapy: A classical cognitive therapy, developed by Aaron Beck, that focuses on changing the client's negative views about self, the world, and others.

nothing," "I was meant to suffer," "The world is a cruel and hostile place," and "Nobody cares." Beck believes that such beliefs either cause or contribute to feelings of depression. And indeed, studies have indicated that Beck's and other cognitive therapy approaches are particularly effective in treating depression (Beck & Young, 1985; Teasdale, 1985).

Beck's cognitive approach also helps clients to become aware of distorted or inappropriate habits of thought or reasoning. Many people tend to magnify or exaggerate the meaning of an event, a cognitive distortion called *magnification*. When relatively minor setbacks and difficulties are blown up out of proportion to their real significance, they can block personal development. Constructive criticism becomes a major insult, and failure to receive a promotion means one's career is ruined.

Another common distortion is *overgeneralization*, which involves the creation of a general rule from a single incident. A single failure is interpreted as a sign of personal incompetence. One professor is unfair; therefore all professors are unfair. One man can't be trusted; therefore all men can't be trusted.

In yet another common distortion, *arbitrary inference*, a person draws a conclusion that is unwarranted by the facts. Typically, an isolated or insignificant event is taken as proof for the incorrect conclusion. Someone turns down your invitation to dinner; therefore he doesn't like you. In Beck's approach, the client is taught to recognize such inappropriate or distorted habits of thought, to challenge and correct them.

Client: I can't do anything right.
Therapist: What makes you say that?
Client: It was my parents' fiftieth anniversary, and I totally forgot.
Therapist: From this you conclude you can't do anything right?
Client: It was one of the most important days of their lives. I shouldn't have forgotten.
Therapist: But how can you conclude you can't do *anything* right just because of a single mistake?
Client: It's just that I'm ticked off at myself.
Therapist: Right—you are upset with yourself. But can you really say nothing you do is right? Did you remember your parents' anniversary last year? How many things have you done to show your love for your parents?
Client: A lot, I guess.
Therapist: Do you see how you've taken a single incident and from it drawn general conclusions that really aren't true?
Client: Yes.
Therapist: Next week I want you to keep track of all of your thoughts and conclusions, especially those in which you seem to take a single incident and exaggerate its significance, or draw general conclusions about yourself and others. I want you to write them down and think about them.

Though the various cognitive therapies differ in theory, in practice a therapist often combines the ideas from Beck's and Ellis's approaches together with techniques of cognitive behavior therapy (Lazarus, 1981; Wilson, 1984). Later on in the chapter we will discuss in greater detail the modern

■ **Learning Check** ■

Read, try to recite, repeat.

Q: Cognitive behavior therapy and classical cognitive therapy both attempt to change or modify a client's cognitions. In what important ways do these two main categories of cognitive approaches to treatment differ?

A: Cognitive behavior therapy follows the philosophy of behavior therapy, which states that behavior is the problem; classical cognitive therapy takes the philosophy that disordered actions and emotions stem from cognitions.

Cognitive behavior therapy, like behavior therapy, views behavior as its primary target of treatment; classical cognitive therapy views cognitions as the primary target of treatment.

---

tendency for therapists to use a combination of techniques. For now, let us turn to the humanistic therapies and examine some of the techniques used in this major approach.

HUMANISTIC THERAPIES

Humanistic Therapies: Approaches to treatment in which the primary target of treatment is the self—those conscious aspects of an individual's world that the individual associates with "I" or "me."

Self: Those conscious aspects of an individual's world that the individual associates with "I" or "me," including a person's sense of personal identity, self-awareness, self-definition, and personal beliefs.

Gestalt Therapy: A humanistic therapy developed by Fritz Perls, which emphasizes the wholeness of the person and the integration of thoughts, feelings, and actions into a unified whole.

In the **humanistic therapies,** the primary target of treatment is the **self**—those conscious aspects of an individual's world that the individual associates with "I" or "me," including personal identity, self-awareness, self-definition, and personal beliefs (see Figure 15.9). Humanistic therapists assume that a client's emotions, actions, and cognitions are directed by the self. In helping a client to become aware of his or her self, and to experience events realistically instead of denying or distorting them, humanistic therapists help a client gain better control of distressing actions, emotions, and cognitions. In so doing, they seek to enhance a client's personal growth, self-awareness, and sense of personal responsibility. In this section we will briefly discuss Gestalt therapy. Then we will look at a second humanistic therapy, the person-centered approach, as a more detailed illustration of the humanistic therapies.

Gestalt Therapy

Gestalt therapy, developed by Fritz Perls (1894–1970), emphasizes the wholeness of the person and the integration of thoughts, feelings, and actions into a unified whole, the self. The therapist strives to keep the client attuned to the "now"—the immediate moment. The emphasis is on what is, as opposed to what was, what might be, or what ought to be. The client who is dominated by past mistakes, defeats, or failures—events that have already happened and can't be changed—misses the present, just as does the person who constantly worries about future events which may never come to pass.

To keep the client in the present, the Gestalt therapist strives to keep the dialogue in the present tense. Instead of examining what has happened or what might happen, she encourages the client to explore his present feelings. "How do you feel now?" the therapist might ask. If the client frowns, the therapist might ask, "What does that mean?" To focus the experience, the therapist might have the client exaggerate his frown, attuning him to his bodily feelings and their significance. Always the therapist focuses on the here and now, as in the following example from Simkin and Yontef (1984):

> *Client:* I don't know what to work on.
> *Therapist:* What are you aware of right now?
> *Client:* I am glad to see you, but I'm tense about a meeting tonight with my boss.
> *Therapist:* What do you need right now? (p. 290)

In keeping the client in the here and now, the Gestalt therapist uses a number of specific techniques such as encouraging the person to use "I" instead of words like "You," or "It," when talking about himself. Instead of saying, "It makes you feel embarrassed talking about feelings" the person would be instructed to say, "I feel embarrassed talking about my feelings." Another Gestalt therapy technique is to instruct the person to convert questions to statements. Instead of, "Do you really think that's a good idea?" The client might learn to say, "I don't believe you think that's a good idea." In still another technique, called the empty chair, the person acts the way he or she would like to toward another person, who is pictured sitting in an empty chair. The empty chair technique can also be used to work out a personal conflict or indecision. The person sits in one chair, taking one side of the issue, and changes chairs to take the other.

The Gestalt techniques are just one approach to enhancing self-awareness. In the person-centered approach, the therapist concentrates on providing the conditions that are believed to foster personal growth and personal awareness.

Person-Centered Therapy

One of the best known and most widely used humanistic therapy is the **person-centered** (formerly known as client-centered) approach developed by Carl Rogers (1942, 1951). This type of treatment attempts to help people get "in tune" with their real self—to see the world and themselves and to act from their own perspective, rather than according to a distorted or unrealistic view. It is based on the humanistic assumption of an inborn urge toward growth and fulfillment—what Maslow called the tendency toward self-actualization (see Chapter 12). Rogers believes that, when people get out of touch with their selves, which happens when they persistently act the way others think they should rather than according to the way they feel, their actualizing tendency becomes blocked. Having lost contact with this natural guidance system, which directs them toward growth and fulfillment, they have difficulty deciding what is right for them and what is not. Person-centered therapy is designed to put the person back in touch with his or her self, so that the person can again learn to act according to the natural guidance system of the actualizing tendency and resume the road toward growth and self-fulfillment.

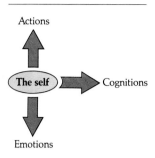

Figure 15.9 Humanistic therapies focus on the self— the person's sense of personal identity and awareness. They assume that one's cognitions, actions, and emotions are integrated and directed by the self.

Person-Centered Therapy: A humanistic therapy (formerly known as client-centered therapy) developed by Carl Rogers that attempts to help people get "in tune" with their real self—to see the world and themselves and to act from their own perspective, rather than according to a distorted or unrealistic view.

To remove blocks to the actualizing tendency, Rogers recommended that therapists provide a special kind of interpersonal relationship with their clients. Of particular importance, he felt, were three qualities that he called conditions for growth.

The three conditions Rogers urged therapists to provide are genuineness, acceptance (often called unconditional positive regard), and empathy. By genuineness, Rogers meant personal honesty on the therapist's part. Instead of assuming the role of the all-knowing, uncommunicative authority figure, as in psychoanalytic therapy, the therapist behaves naturally, as she normally would. Rogers learned of the importance of genuineness from his own clinical experience; he felt that as a therapist he achieved far better results by being himself than by attempting to assume the role of an authority (Rogers, 1951, 1980).

By acceptance (unconditional positive regard), Rogers meant that the therapist should accept, approve of, and support the client wholeheartedly, without reservation. Most personal relationships are judgmental; people evaluate each other's actions as good or bad. But an accepting therapist refrains from judging the client's confidences. Relieved of the fear of being judged, the client is free to explore present feelings, past experiences, and future courses of action. The therapist's unqualified acceptance also encourages self-acceptance on the client's part.

The importance of acceptance in a therapeutic relationship cannot be overestimated. To give an example, suppose a client and therapist have met several times and are just getting to know each other better. One day, frustrated by his past experiences in therapy, he confides to the therapist, "You know, I really think these sessions are getting me nowhere." If the therapist responds judgmentally, contradicting or scolding him, will he feel free to tell the therapist his attitudes about sex or morality? Probably not. Having been evaluated, he is no longer completely willing to confide in the therapist, for fear of disapproval. He will tend to hold back, limiting what he reveals about himself and restricting the depth of his relationship with the therapist. For this reason most therapists, whether or not they follow Rogers's approach, avoid judging the client's behavior, during the early phase of treatment.

In person-centered therapy, it is important for the therapist to communicate an acceptance and understanding of the client's thoughts and feelings.

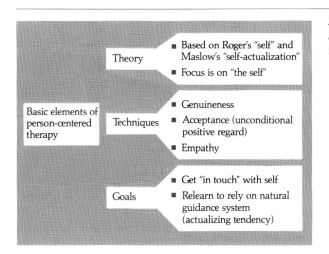

Figure 15.10   Schematic Summary of Person-Centered Therapy.

By empathy, or understanding, Rogers meant that the therapist should sense accurately the feelings the client is experiencing and communicate his understanding to the client. It isn't enough for the therapist to say, "I understand." He must communicate his understanding in words, tone of voice, and other nonverbal signs.

According to Rogers, the three conditions for growth—genuineness, acceptance, and empathy—are essential to any kind of relationship that fosters personal development: therapist–client, parent–child, leader–group. Without them, the client will not grow. With them, change and growth, he believes, are virtually guaranteed (Rogers, 1980). For when people are accepted and prized, they tend to develop a more caring attitude toward themselves. When they are listened to with empathy, they begin to hear their own inner voice more accurately. They get back in tune with their tendency toward self-actualization (Rogers, 1951). (See Figure 15.10.) Indeed, a wide body of literature supports the importance of the three conditions for growth and positive outcome in psychotherapy (Truax & Mitchell, 1971).

Levels of Empathy in Person-Centered Therapy

Rather than using specific techniques, the person-centered therapist concentrates on forming a relationship in which the therapist provides the three conditions for growth. There is no way that this process of relationship formation can be condensed. We can, however, look at some examples of what a person-centered therapist might or might not say, based on a rating system that is used to evaluate empathy (Truax & Carkhuff, 1967).

Empathy is evaluated in terms of one of five levels, depending on how well the therapist communicated understanding to the client. Responses at level 1 show no empathy at all. They do not attend to what the client communicates. Such responses are avoided in person-centered therapy:

Client: I feel terrible about what happened.
Level 1 Response: There's nothing to worry about. Tomorrow is the first day in the rest of your life.

Comment: The level 1 response has little to do with what the client is trying to communicate.

Level 2 responses are also inadequate from the standpoint of a person-centered therapist. Such responses communicate some awareness of the obvious, surface feeling, but do not capture the client's full meaning:

Client: I feel terrible about what has happened.
Level 2 Response: It's not as terrible as you say. I think there is something you can do to make things right.
Comment: The level 2 response subtracts from the client's expressions. It does not look at things from the standpoint of the client.

Responses at level 3 are essentially interchangeable with the client's expressions. For the person-centered therapist, level 3 constitutes the minimum level of empathy to foster growth. This level is used most during the early phase of treatment, when the therapist and client are getting to know each other.

Client: I feel terrible about what has happened.
Level 3 Response: You feel really bad about how this whole thing turned out.
Comment: Level 3 responses neither add nor subtract from the client's expression. They reflect the surface feelings, but not the deeper ones expressed by the client.

Level 4 responses add noticeably to a client's expressions. A person-centered therapist uses level 4 responses to express a feeling at a deeper level than the client was able to do. Such responses foster self-awareness and help the client to explore his or her feelings at still deeper levels (Truax & Carkhuff, 1967):

Client: I feel really bad about what has happened.
Level 4 Response: The outcome has been more than disturbing. Underneath you feel a deep sense of guilt and shame.
Comment: Level 4 responses go beyond the surface to capture some of the underlying feelings of a client's expressions.

Level 5 responses are the deepest level of empathy. In making a level 5 response, the person-centered therapist adds to the feeling and meaning of a client's expression and captures the full significance. In making level 5 responses, the person-centered therapist communicates that he or she is fully in tune with the client's experience:

Client: I feel really bad about what has happened.
Level 5 Response: Looking back on how you hurt her feelings, you feel deeply saddened. And behind your feelings of guilt there is a realization of how much she really means to you.
Comment: Level 5 responses reflect the deepest meaning of a client's expressions.

All approaches to psychotherapy involve some type of psychological intervention. In the person-centered approach, such intervention involves the formation of a special type of relationship. But there are approaches to treatment that do not rely exclusively on psychological techniques and principles of behavior change. No discussion of treatment would be complete without mention of these medical approaches.

MEDICAL TREATMENTS

Medical treatments rely on the tools of the medical profession: drugs, hospitalization, and a number of techniques that can only be used in a hospital, such as surgery. Of these, drugs are by far the most widely used.

Drug Therapy

Three major classes of drugs used in the treatment of abnormal behavior are called antipsychotics, antidepressants, and antianxiety drugs. Each is intended to compensate for a physiological imbalance in the patient's body, which is assumed to be the cause of the abnormal behavior.

Antipsychotic drugs, sometimes called major tranquilizers, are used to treat conditions in which a person has lost contact with reality. The term *psychotic* refers to an impairment in reality testing—an inability to distinguish what is real from what is not; antipsychotics counteract impaired reality testing. The primary use of antipsychotics is in the treatment of schizophrenia. They are generally effective in reducing the cognitive disorganization and distortions associated with this severely impairing disorder. Antipsychotics are also sometimes used in very low doses in the treatment of other conditions such as severe involuntary tics and alcoholism. In the treatment of schizophrenia, they appear to work by blocking the activity of dopamine, a neurotransmitter implicated in the cause of schizophrenia (Snyder, 1977). Among the most widely used antipsychotics are Thorazine, Mellaril, Stelazine, and Haldol.

When antipsychotics were discovered in the 1950s, they were a major breakthrough in the treatment of schizophrenia. Up to that time, most people suffering from delusions, hallucinations, and other symptoms of loss of contact with reality were doomed to a lifetime of hospital confinement. With the discovery of these new drugs, however, patients who had once been restrained or locked behind closed doors improved dramatically, sometimes to the point where they could return to the community or even hold a job. Today, many schizophrenic patients can be treated as outpatients, with only relatively brief (two to four months) periods of hospitalization when their symptoms flare up or become active (Caton et al., 1985).

Antipsychotics are not without drawbacks. They can produce a number of unpleasant side effects, including loss of memory, trembling, stiffening of the muscles, and drooling. Some of these side effects can be permanent, even for patients who no longer need the drug to prevent a recurrence of their symptoms. For the majority of these patients, however, the side effects are far less objectionable than the symptoms the drugs prevent.

Antidepressants are used to treat depressions. Among the more widely used are Imipramine, Tofranil, Elavil, and a class of drugs known as

Medical Treatments: Approaches to the treatment of abnormal behavior that rely on the tools of the medical profession, such as drugs, hospitalization, and surgery.

Antipsychotic Drugs: Drugs used to treat conditions in which a person has lost contact with reality (Thorazine, Mellaril, Stelzine, Haldol).

Antidepressant Drugs: Drugs used to treat depressions (Imipramine, Tofranil, Elavil, monoamine oxidase (MAO) inhibitors).

Table 15.2 Summary of Three Major Classes of Drugs Used in Treatment

General Class	Examples	Used Primarily For
Antipsychotics	Thorazine Mellaril Stelazine Haldol	Schizophrenic symptoms (loss of reality contact; hallucinations; delusions)
Antidepressants	Imipramine Elavil Monoamine Oxidase (MAO) Inhibitors	Depression and depressive symptoms
Antianxiety	Librium Valium Serax	Anxiety and anxiety-related disorders

monoamine oxidase (MAO) inhibitors. These drugs increase the brain levels of the neurotransmitter norepinephrine by preventing its breakdown by enzymes or by preventing its reabsorption into the body (Berger, 1978).

Antidepressants are most effective in treating major depressive disorders, in which symptoms are severe and relatively sudden in onset. In these cases, antidepressant drugs often can produce dramatic improvements in two weeks or less. For chronic depressive disorders, antidepressants are less effective (Mindham, 1982; Nies & Robinson, 1982).

In general, patients who are treated with antidepressants do not have to take the drug for life. Usually they begin by taking gradually increasing doses, until a therapeutic level has been reached and their symptoms have improved. Then they maintain that dosage for an average of several months (specific uses vary widely) before gradually reducing it.

Like antipsychotics, antidepressants can produce several side effects. They make some patients feel overstimulated, as if they are "jumping out of their skin." Trembling, blurred vision, and weight gain are also common. Patients run an increased risk of stroke as well, especially if they mix these drugs with others, including many over-the-counter medicines (Mindham, 1982; Nies & Robinson, 1982). As with antipsychotics, however, the benefits of these drugs far outweigh their negative side effects, which often disappear in a few weeks.

Antianxiety Drugs: Drugs used to treat disorders in which anxiety is the major symptom (Librium, Valium, Serax).

Antianxiety drugs, sometimes called minor tranquilizers, are used to treat disorders in which anxiety is the major symptom. Among the most widely used are Librium, Valium, and Serax. If taken in moderate doses, these drugs have only a mild sedating effect, yet they are highly effective in reducing anxiety. A major problem with antianxiety drugs is that they have a high potential for leading to physical and psychological dependence if used unwisely or to excess (Levenson, 1981). Table 15.2 summarizes the three major classes of drugs and their effects.

Hospital Treatment

Hospitalization is a treatment usually reserved for patients who have lost contact with reality, or who represent a danger to themselves or others.

It is sometimes the only way, short of jail, of preventing a person from doing serious injury or engaging in highly irresponsible behaviors, such as squandering years of hard-earned savings in a day. For a few people, the hospital is a refuge, a place to escape the demands and stresses of daily life. To them, the benefits more than compensate for the confinement and temporary loss of freedom.

Perhaps the most frequently heard complaints about hospital treatment are that far too many patients don't really need to be there, and that the treatment they receive is minimal. These criticisms were dramatized in a controversial study conceived by the psychologist David Rosenhan (1973). Rosenhan and seven others went to a variety of hospitals in five different states complaining of hearing voices that said, "empty," "hollow," and "thud." Nearly every hospital the group went to admitted them and kept them from seven to fifty-two days, despite the fact that, once they were admitted, they acted perfectly normal.

Unfortunately, only the patients seemed to realize that there was nothing wrong with Rosenhan and his colleagues. Apparently, once a person is admitted to a hospital as a patient, just about anything he or she does can seem abnormal to the staff. Rosenhan openly took notes on his experiences; the staff duly recorded his "writing behavior" as a symptom. The researchers received little if any psychotherapy. Instead, the staff "treated" them with over two thousand pills (which they did not take) and discharged them with the diagnosis, "Schizophrenia, in remission" (Rosenhan, 1973).

Rosenhan's study generated considerable criticism. His ethics, scholarship, methods, and conclusions were all questioned. One of the arguments made against his approach was that, if a person fakes a symptom, he or she will nevertheless be diagnosed accordingly, and legitimately so (Kety, 1974). For example, if you go to your physician complaining of severe stomach cramps, which you state are caused by some cleaning fluid you swallowed, the physician will assume you are telling the truth and treat you for poisoning. He or she will not wait to see whether you get worse before responding.

Since the 1960s, with the passage of the Community Mental Health Center Act, which provided funds for the establishment of treatment centers in local communities, there has been less need for hospitalization. Community mental health centers provide affordable treatment services in towns and cities across the United States. The philosophy behind these centers is that, by providing rapid treatment in the community, much hospitalization, especially long-term hospital care in state institutions, can be avoided (Iscoe, 1982). Indeed, as Figure 15.11 shows, with the growth of community mental health centers has come a dramatic decrease in the percentage of people in mental hospitals.

For some individuals, hospitalization cannot be avoided and, in fact, is desirable. Hospitalization can remove a person from a stressful environment. It also provides respite for weary family members who must deal with a severely disturbed relative on a daily basis. However, just as hospital treatment can sometimes be controversial, so too can some of the procedures that are used only in hospitals, like electroconvulsive therapy.

One of the most controversial of all hospital treatments is **electroconvulsive (shock) therapy (ECT)**—the use of electricity to produce convulsions and unconsciousness in the treatment of abnormal behavior. This treatment,

Halfway houses provide an "in-between" living situation. The patient is no longer in need of hospitalization, but is not quite ready to return home.

Electroconvulsive Therapy (ECT): The use of electricity to produce convulsions and unconsciousness in the treatment of abnormal behavior.

Figure 15.11 *The percentage of patients in mental health hospitals decreased dramatically between 1955 and 1975. Data from National Institutes of Mental Health. (Adapted from Saccuzzo & Kaplan, 1984).*

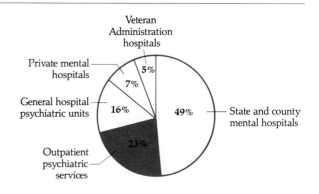

1955 Total (1.7 million)

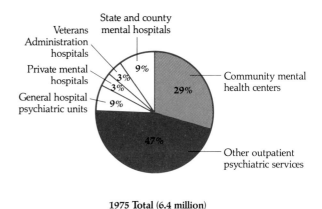

1975 Total (6.4 million)

☐ Inpatient   ■ Outpatient   ▨ Inpatient and Outpatient

which was developed before the discovery of antipsychotic drugs, was based on the observation that epileptics rarely develop the symptoms of schizophrenia. Researchers reasoned that convulsions might somehow "protect" a person from schizophrenia, and that inducing convulsions by running an electric shock through a schizophrenic's body might somehow cure the disorder.

Because of the effectiveness of antipsychotic drugs, electroconvulsive therapy is generally used only as a last resort in the treatment of schizophrenia. It is more commonly used in treating cases of severe depression (Kiloh, 1982). The treatment is not as traumatizing as it was when it was first developed, for patients are given sedatives to calm them and muscle relaxants to prevent injury. Then a brief current of 70 to 130 volts is passed through the patient's body. Patients are usually given six to twelve treatments over as many days. The procedure apparently causes brain damage that results in short-term (sometimes long-term) memory loss (Squire, 1977), but does relieve severe depression at least temporarily (Coryell, 1978). Critics argue that it is overused and dangerous because of the brain damage it can cause (Breggin, 1979). Supporters argue that the treatment can be lifesaving, as, for example, in eliminating depression-related suicide (Kramer, 1985).

Another hospital treatment, rarely used today, is **psychosurgery,** the surgical destruction of selected parts of the brain. In an operation called a frontal lobotomy, for example, the frontal lobes are severed from the thalamus. A frontal lobotomy eliminates most of the symptoms of schizophrenia, but produces irreversible personality changes as well. With the discovery of antipsychotic drugs in the 1950s, the procedure became all but obsolete except when all else has failed (Kelly, 1982).

Medical treatments, particularly the use of drugs, are often used in combination with one or more approaches to psychotherapy. In our final section, we will look more closely at such combination approaches as we look beyond the basic models of treatment.

Psychosurgery: The surgical destruction of selected parts of the brain in the treatment of abnormal behavior.

BEYOND THE BASIC MODELS OF TREATMENT

Each of the basic approaches to psychotherapy can be used alone or in combination with other approaches and medical treatment. We have discussed treatment primarily from the standpoint of individual therapy, in which there is a one-to-one relationship between the therapist and person being treated. In addition, however, people are sometimes treated in the context of a group or family.

Eclectic Treatments

Eclectic treatments are those that draw on more than one approach. A therapist using an eclectic treatment uses any one of a number of techniques in helping people solve their problems or cope more effectively. An example of eclectic treatment is the multimodal therapy developed by Arnold Lazarus (1971, 1976). The premise of multimodal therapy is that patients or clients are usually troubled with a multitude of specific problems, each of which requires a specific treatment (Lazarus, 1984). In using multimodal therapy, a therapist may use a behavior therapy technique such as systematic desensitization to remove a specific fear in conjunction with a cognitive technique such as self-instructional training to modify self-defeating statements. In using multimodal therapy to treat alcoholism, Lazarus (1965) lists the following components of treatment:

Eclectic Treatments: Treatments that draw on more than one approach (for example, psychoanalytic and behavior therapy; or psychoanalytic therapy in conjunction with drug therapy).

1. Medical care
2. Aversion therapy to control drinking behavior
3. Systematic desensitization to deal with specific anxieties
4. Assertiveness training
5. The development of a cooperative relationship with the patient's spouse

In multimodal treatment, the therapist tries to identify all aspects of a person's life in need of change and to use the best technique possible for each area in need of change.

Another example of an eclectic approach is a treatment program developed by the New York State Psychiatric Institute to treat victims of panic attack—sudden, unexpected periods of extreme apprehension accompanied by such symptoms as heart palpitations, choking or smothering sensations, trembling, dizziness, faintness, and fear of dying or of losing control. Such attacks are associated with agoraphobia, sometimes known as the fear of fear because its victims live in fear of having a panic attack. This fear prevents them from venturing out in the world.

The eclectic treatment of the New York Institute includes medication to prevent panic attacks. Specifically, low doses of antidepressant drugs such as Imipramine are used, as they have been found to effectively eliminate panic attacks in most patients (Gorman et al., 1981). The drug alone cannot really cure patients, however, because of the numerous secondary fears and anticipatory anxiety that generally develop from panic attacks. A full plan for recovery may include antianxiety drugs and a variety of therapy techniques, such as in vivo desensitization and assertion training. Many patients also need help in restructuring or redefining their view of themselves and their symptoms. Cognitive techniques are helpful in getting them out of the habit of interpreting their symptoms as a sign of weakness, and into the habit of making positive self-statements. The effects of years of fear, intense panic, and even the feeling of losing one's mind have to be overcome. The eclectic program of the New York State Institute provides for the specific needs of each patient, using whatever combination of approaches that appears best suited to the patient's problems. In some cases, group or family approaches are used in conjunction with other techniques.

Group and Family Approaches

In group approaches, people receive treatment as a group. In using group approaches, a therapist may concentrate on one person at a time, while the others in the group observe and benefit by the experience of the other patients. Most group approaches, however, focus on the individual as a member of the group. As such, the person comes under the influence of the processes that affect any small group. For example, the members may form a sense of group identity. The forces of the group, such as a group standard of assuming personal responsibility, operate to help the person change.

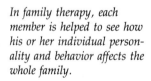

In family therapy, each member is helped to see how his or her individual personality and behavior affects the whole family.

Sometimes all of the group members share a common problem. In such **self-help groups,** people with a particular problem meet together to share experiences to support each other. The self-help group may or may not involve a professional therapist. TERRAP (a contraction of the phrase, "Territorial Apprehensiveness") is a self-help group for people suffering from anxiety, panic, and phobias. It has centers located in major cities throughout the United States, where people with such problems meet in groups directed by a professional therapist. Alcoholics Anonymous (AA), by contrast, is a self-help group for alcoholics run entirely by its members without professional therapists. The effectiveness of self-help groups and the support they provide is attested to in the high rate of success of AA, even when compared to professional treatment programs (Leach & Norris, 1977; McCrady, 1985).

Another special type of group treatment is family therapy—in which treatment is aimed at improving the functioning of the family as a unit and

Self-Help Groups: Treatment groups in which individuals who share a particular problem meet together to share experiences and support each other.

Box 15.2 PSYCHOLOGY IN ACTION: Being a Good Consumer: II. The Effects of Psychotherapy

Our study of the various approaches to psychotherapy raises some important questions from the standpoint of the consumer. In particular, the consumer wants to know what evidence exists in support of psychotherapy's effectiveness and whether any one approach has proven more effective than any other.

The issue of the effectiveness of psychotherapy first became prominent in 1952, when British psychologist Hans Eysenck challenged psychotherapists to show that their treatment was, in fact, better than no treatment at all. Eysenck's challenge, which he has periodically reissued, stimulated a plethora of studies that have compared psychotherapeutic outcome for individuals receiving treatment versus those receiving none.

Numerous studies and literature reviews have supported that, on the whole, psychotherapy is, in fact, superior to no treatment at all. A book (Meltzoff & Kornreich, 1970), which reviewed over 100 studies, found support for therapy in the majority (about 80 percent) of them. Another review (Bergin & Lambert, 1978) found that, while most people (more than 90 percent) show at least some improvement, a small but significant number actually get worse. This review revealed that, when people undergoing treatment are bunched together in a group and compared to an untreated control group, the gains shown by those who do improve are sometimes cancelled out and thus obscured by the worsening of symptoms found by others. Such findings reveal that psychotherapy is a very powerful tool indeed, but that it can be for better or for worse. Therapists who seem to have a far larger than normal share of clients whose condition worsens are called "psychonoxious" therapists.

The general effectiveness of psychotherapy is also supported by a large-scale analysis of 375 studies. Smith and Glass (1977), using a technique called meta-analysis, a statistical method for combining the results of many different studies, found that the average client who had received psychotherapy is better off than 75 percent of the individuals who had not received psychotherapy. Though such large-scale studies have been criticized on the grounds that they blindly combine well-done studies with those that may be seriously flawed (Eysenck, 1978; Wilson & Rachman, 1983), the preponderance of weight appears to remain in support of psychotherapy (Landman & Davies, 1982; VandenBos, 1986) in adults as well as children (Casey & Berman, 1985).

The issue of which type of treatment, if any, is most effective is far less clear. While some studies have supported one kind of treatment over another (Wolpe, 1981), others have not (Garfield, 1981; also see Stiles et al., 1986). The problem in comparing the therapies is that they have different goals. It is difficult to compare the effectiveness of an assertion training program for a person whose only problem is a lack of assertiveness to psychoanalytic therapy for someone with a wide range of interacting problems. And, as we have seen, different therapies are better than others, depending on the nature of the problem.

At this time, there is not enough evidence to say that one type of therapy is better than another for any given unique individual. The decision of which type of therapy might be best for you, or for someone you know, is in part personal (which approach do you favor the most?) and in part a matter to discuss with the therapist you might be considering.

improving the family members' relationships with each other (Fox, 1976). Family therapy differs from other group approaches in that the group members have a history together and are involved in an ongoing day-to-day relationship (Margolin, 1982).

There are numerous approaches to family therapy. Bowen's (1971) family systems approach attempts to help a family member learn both to be an individual and a member of a complex family system. Family relationships are seen in terms of interlocking triangles—father, mother, and child or wife, husband, and mother-in-law, for example. The family is analyzed in terms of such triangles. Family members are helped to see how the behavior of one member of such a triangle affects the others.

In the strategic intervention approach pioneered by Don Jackson and Jay Haley, the critical issue of therapy involves control. The family member identified as patient uses his or her problem to control the other members of the family. The therapist attempts to develop a strategy for changing the balance of power within the family, hence the term *strategic intervention* (Haley, 1980).

There are many approaches to treatment. Each has its advantages and disadvantages; its strengths and limitations. No single approach is best for all problems. And no therapist is an expert in all techniques. Nevertheless, regardless of the approach, millions of people can and do find help for their problems. (In Box 15.2 we look more closely at the issue of the effectiveness of psychotherapy.)

LEARNING FRAMEWORK

I. Psychoanalytic approaches to treatment attempt to help a person understand the roots of his or her problem and to deal with it from a mature, adult perspective. (Review: *Figure 15.1; Psychodynamics; Insight; Transference; Resistance*)

II. Behavior therapy is based on the assumption that abnormal behaviors are learned and therefore can be unlearned. (Review: *Figure 15.2*)

A. In operant conditioning approaches, the therapist identifies a specific behavior in need of change and uses reinforcement to modify its frequency or strength. (Review: *Table 15.1; Figure 15.3; Target Behavior; Token Economy*)

B. In assertiveness training, the therapist uses learning techniques to help people to express their feelings, especially those of anger, in an appropriate way. (Review: *Figure 15.4; Role Playing*)

C. In flooding, clients are exposed to real or imagined stimuli that are highly disturbing to them. (Review: *Avoidance Responses*)

D. In systematic desensitization, clients are gradually exposed to a relatively mild form of a disturbing stimulus while in a state of relaxation. (Review: *Figure 15.6; Fear Hierarchy; SUD*)

E. In aversion therapy, an aversive stimulus is paired with the cues that lead to an undesired behavior. The infliction of pain in aversive therapy raises some ethical issues, however.

III. The two cognitive approaches attempt to change patterns of thinking or other cognitions that interfere with a client's well-being. (See *Figure 15.7*)

    A. Cognitive behavior therapy uses learning to modify cognitions and follows the behaviorist philosophy that the target of treatment is behavior. (Review: *Figure 15.8; Aversion Relief; Covert Sensitization; Thought Stopping; Self-Instructional Training*)

    B. Classical cognitive therapy views cognition as the ultimate target of treatment with the assumption that disturbed actions and emotions stem from cognition. (Review: *Rational Emotive Therapy; Beck's Cognitive Therapy*)

IV. In the humanistic therapies, the self is the primary target of treatment. Humanistic therapies assume that actions, emotions, and cognitions are orchestrated by the self. (Review: *Figure 15.9; Self*)

    A. Gestalt therapy is a humanistic therapy that focuses on the client's immediate experience and emphasizes that thoughts, feelings, and actions are an integrated whole.

    B. Person-centered therapy is a humanistic therapy that emphasizes natural growth, the conditions for which the therapist provides. (Review: *Figure 15.10; Genuineness; Acceptance; Empathy*)

V. Medical treatments include drugs and hospitalization.

    A. Drugs are used to combat impairments in reality testing, depression, and anxiety. (Review: *Table 15.2; Antipsychotic Drugs; Antidepressant Drugs; Antianxiety Drugs*)

    B. Hospitalization is often the only safe treatment for a severely disturbed person, one who has lost contact with reality or who is a danger to self or others. (Review: *Rosenhan Study; Figure 15.11; Electroconvulsive Therapy (ECT); Psychosurgery*)

VI. Two important aspects of treatment involve combination and group approaches.

    A. Eclectic approaches combine two or more techniques. (Review: *Eclectic Treatments; Multimodal Therapy*)

    B. There are a variety of group approaches to treatment. (Review: *Self-Help Groups; Family Therapy*)

Statistical Appendix

It's the week following your first exam in psychology, and your instructor is passing out the graded answer sheets. You feel butterflies in your stomach as she calls out your name. When she hands you your test, you find that you got an 83. Is that good or bad? You don't know, because you don't know what the score is based on.

In order to evaluate your score, what would you need to know? One thing you would want to determine is whether your instructor based your grade on a straight percentage system or on a curve. With straight percentages, the numerical equivalents of the letter grades are specified in advance: 90 to 100 equals an A, 80 to 89 a B, and so on. With a curve, numerical scores are translated into letter grades according to their position in relation to other scores. Students with the highest scores, say, those that score in the top 5 percent of the class, receive As; the next 15 percent of the students receive Bs, and so on.

If you were graded on a curve, the value of your 83 would depend on its relation to the scores obtained by all other students in the class. If fifty students took the test and only one obtained a score higher than yours, you would have reason to be proud of your performance. If forty-eight students obtained scores higher than yours, however, you would have little reason to rejoice.

When you compare your score to the scores obtained by others on the same test, you are using **statistics**—methods of describing, analyzing, and interpreting numerical data. You are analyzing the class's score to determine the relative meaning of your own. In more complicated ways, psychologists use statistics to make sense of the raw data they obtain in their surveys and experiments.

Psychologists use statistics to describe their data and to make inferences about the meaning of their data for individuals or groups other than the ones who participated in their investigation. The methods used in describing numerical data are called **descriptive statistics.** Those used in making in-

Statistics: Methods for describing, analyzing, and interpreting numerical data.

Descriptive Statistics: Methods used in providing a concise description of numerical data.

ferences are called **inferential statistics.** In using inferential statistics, a psychologist may observe a small group of people, known as a *sample,* in order to draw conclusions about the characteristics of a larger group of individuals, known as a *population.* For example, pollsters question a small sample of voters in order to make statements about the entire population of voters. Based on the response of the sample, they might conclude that 48 percent of the voters prefer candidate X, give or take five percentage points. In a similar way, psychologists may study the relationship between life-style and health for 5,000 men and women in order to draw inferences about the relationship between life-style and health for the general population.

In our discussion, we will examine basic concepts of descriptive and inferential statistics. We will also look more closely at the nature of correlation, which, you may recall, enables a psychologist to determine the extent to which two variables are related.

Inferential Statistics: Methods used in making inferences from observations of a small group of individuals, known as a sample, to a larger group of individuals, known as a population.

DESCRIPTIVE STATISTICS

Think for a moment about the mountains of data researchers must deal with in evaluating the results of a survey or an experiment. Experiments using equipment that measures heart rate or blood pressure or that records the bar presses made in a Skinner box typically produce roll upon roll of scores. To get a clear picture out of this voluminous detail, scientists must somehow summarize it. Statistics provide both the tools, or formulas, for doing so and the language for expressing the results. They enable researchers to describe their findings in a few precise sentences rather than in several volumes of unsorted data.

Typically, a statistical description of a body of data will include an estimate of the most common score or read-out, as well as the degree to which other scores varied from it. It will also provide a measure of how often a particular score or read-out occurred. Take the results of your exam. Using descriptive statistics, your professor can determine what the most common score was; how much the other scores varied from it; and how many other students got the same score you did. To do so, she might begin by making what is called a frequency distribution.

Frequency Distributions and Percentiles

Measures of the frequency of each score obtained by a group of people—how many people scored 83 on an exam, how many 84, and so on—are called **frequency distributions.** A typical frequency distribution lists all the

Frequency Distribution: A measure of the frequency of each score obtained by a sample of people.

■ Learning Check ■

Read the definition, then cover the right side and try to recite. Repeat.

Descriptive Statistics Methods used in describing numerical data
Inferential Statistics Methods used in making inferences

scores along with the number of times they occurred. The frequency distribution for the exam scores in your class might look like this:

Score	Number of People Who Obtained Score
96	1
94	2
91	3
88	2
86	4
83	2
81	3
79	3
78	4
77	2
76	6
74	3
70	4
69	2
66	3
60	4
58	1
53	1

Such data can also be graphically represented in the form of a frequency
polygon (see Figure A.1). To plot a frequency polygon, list all of the possible
scores (beginning with the lowest) on the horizontal axis as shown in Figure
A.1. On the vertical axis, make a list from 1 to the largest frequency that occurred. In our example, 6 people obtained a score of 76. More people obtained a score of 76 than any other score. Therefore, on the vertical axis we
list from 1 through 6 and can now use the vertical axis to record how many
times each of the values on the horizontal axis occurred.

The next step in plotting the frequency polygon is to indicate how many
people (the frequency) obtained each score. One person obtained a score of
53, so we plot a point above the 53 and in the same column as the one as
shown in Figure A.1. One person also obtained a score of 58, so we plot another point just above the 58 and in the same column as the one. Since four
people obtained a score of 60, the point we plot above the 60 goes in the
same column as the four. We continue until we've indicated how many people obtained each possible score by putting a point above each score and in
the column of the frequency that corresponds to the number of people who
obtained that particular score. Finally, we can connect the points.

Interpreting a Frequency Polygon. As you can see from our frequency
polygon in Figure A.1, two people scored 83. Since your score was 83, you
know that one other person got the same score. Can you tell anything else
from the frequency distribution? You can easily determine the highest and
lowest scores and general shape of the distribution of scores. Another thing
you should be able to see by doing some quick arithmetic is that twelve people did better than you and thirty-six did worse. You could then use this information to determine your **percentile rank**—the percentage of scores that

Percentile Rank: The percentage of scores that fall
below a particular score.

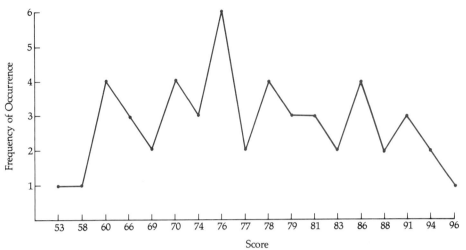

Figure A.1 A Frequency Polygon. A frequency polygon provides a graphic representation of the frequency of occurrence of a set of scores. Examination of this frequency polygon reveals that the score of 76 occurred six times. A score of 53 (the lowest score) and a score of 96 (the highest score) each occurred only once.

fall below a particular score. You can calculate a percentile rank in four simple steps.

1. Determine how many people obtained a score below the score of interest (in your case, 36)
2. Determine how many people took the test (in your case, 50)
3. Divide the number of people who scored below (Step 1) by the number of people in the group (Step 2). (in your case, 36 ÷ 50 = .72)
4. Multiply the result of this division (Step 3) by 100. (in your case, 100 × .72 = 72)

A percentile rank tells you the percentage of people who obtained a score below any given score. In your case, being in the 72nd percentile means that 72 percent of the individuals in the class obtained a score below yours.

Major Tendencies in a Frequency Distribution. To emphasize the major tendencies in a frequency distribution, data can be summarized and presented in terms of ranges of scores. A frequency distribution of your class's exam scores by ten-point ranges would look like this:

Range of Scores	Number of People Who Scored in This Range
90–100	6
80–89	11
70–79	22
60–69	9
50–59	2

These scores can also be represented graphically as a histogram (see Figure A.2).

The method of plotting a histogram is analogous to plotting a frequency polygon. We use the horizontal axis to indicate the range of scores from the

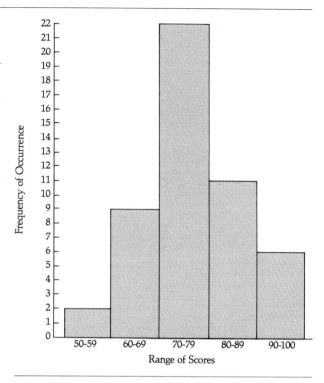

*Figure A.2   A His-
togram.   A histogram is
like a frequency polygon except that the frequency of occurrence is indicated by bars
rather than by points. In
this histogram, the scores
listed on the horizontal axis
are grouped according to
ranges, which provides a
more condensed summary of
the data represented in Figure A.1.*

lowest to the highest value. We use the vertical axis to record frequency—
how many times each of the values on the horizontal axis occurred. Instead
of plotting the points, in a histogram we draw a bar above each score or
range of scores. The height of the bar corresponds to the frequency that a
given range of scores occurred.

When frequency data are summarized, you lose some information.
However, the major tendencies are easier to spot. For example, you can see
at a glance that only six people scored between 90 and 100, while eleven
scored between 80 and 89 (your range).

Shapes of Frequency Distributions. Graphs of frequency data can take
many shapes. Figure A.3 shows four: symmetrical, bimodal, positively
skewed, and negatively skewed.

As you can see, in a symmetrical distribution, one side is the mirror image of the other. A symmetrical distribution tells us that just as many people
scored above the average as below the average. A special type of symmetrical distribution is called a *normal distribution*. In a normal distribution, the
curve is perfectly symmetrical and bell-shaped (see Figure A.4). As you will
see later (page 580–582), this curve, known as the normal curve, is useful in
understanding the relationship between any given score and the average
score.

In contrast to symmetrical distributions, bimodal distributions tell us
that there are two high points in the distribution. You might see such a distribution when most people either obtain a very high score or a very low
score, but not one in the middle.

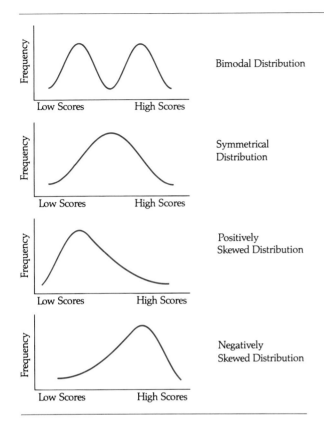

Figure A.3 Types of Frequency Distributions.
This figure illustrates four types of frequency distributions. A bimodal distribution has two high points. In a symmetrical distribution, most scores tend to be in the middle of the distribution. In a positively skewed distribution, the peak of the distribution clusters around low scores. In a negatively skewed distribution, the peak is around high scores.

In a skewed distribution, most people obtain scores at one end of the distribution or the other. For example, on a very difficult test many people obtain a low score and relatively few obtain a high score. Such distributions are said to be positively skewed. In a negatively skewed distribution, the reverse occurs: there are many high scores and relatively few low ones.

Measures of Central Tendency

One way of describing distributions is in terms of measures of central tendency—numbers that represent the typical score. One such measure is the **mode,** which refers to the most common, or frequently occurring, score.

Mode: The most common, or frequently occurring, score in a distribution.

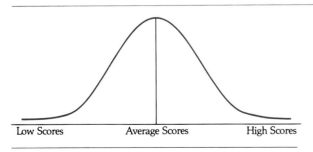

Figure A.4 A Normal Distribution. *In a normal or bell-shaped distribution, the curve is perfectly symmetrical, with most scores clustering around the average and just as many scores above the average (mean) as below it.*

Box A.1 The Formula for the Mean

The formula for obtaining the mean can be represented as follows: $\overline{X} = \dfrac{\Sigma X}{N}$

In this formula, $\overline{X}$ refers to the mean; the Greek letter sigma (Σ) means summation; X refers to each individual score; and N refers to the number of scores. The formula says the mean equals the sum of each individual score divided by the number of scores.

Median: The middle score in a distribution; the score where half the people score above, half below.

Mean: The arithmetic average, determined by taking the total of all the scores and dividing by the number of scores.

In our hypothetical frequency distribution of exam scores, 76 was the score that occurred most often: six people got that score.

A second measure of central tendency is the midpoint of a distribution, which is called the **median.** The median is the quantity that would fall in the middle were the individual scores arranged in a column from highest to lowest. In our hypothetical distribution, twenty four-people scored above 77 and twenty-four people below; the median is therefore 77.

A third measure of central tendency is the arithmetic average, or **mean.** To obtain the mean, add up all your scores and divide by the number of scores that you added. In the case of your exam, the total is 3,834 (remember, you have to add in each score as many times as it occurs; 86 occurs four times, for instance). To obtain the mean you would divide 3,834 by 50, the number of scores that you added to get your total. Thus, the mean is 76.68.

Why three measures of central tendency instead of just one? Depending on the nature of the distribution, the most commonly used measure, the mean, may not indicate the true center. For instance, in a skewed distribution (see page 577) the median may provide a better measure of central tendency than the mean. More scores typically will cluster around the median than the mean in a skewed distribution. Thus, while the mean may provide a good measure of central tendency for the symmetrical distribution, the median often provides a somewhat better measure for a central tendency for the skewed distribution as more scores will tend to cluster around the median than the mean in a skewed distribution.

Let's consider a relatively simple example to illustrate how a mean is calculated. Suppose five people took a 10-point quiz and obtained the following scores:

Person 1	2
Person 2	3
Person 3	4
Person 4	5
Person 5	6

■ Learning Check ■

Read the right side, then cover and try to recite. Repeat.

Three measures of central tendency

1. Mode—the most frequently occurring score
2. Median—the middle score
3. Mean—the arithmetic average

To calculate the mean, we begin by adding up all the scores: 2 + 3 + 4 + 5 + 6 = 20. Next we divide by 5, the total number of scores. The mean is equal to 20 divided by 5, or 4. Thus, the average score for the quiz is 4.

Measures of central tendency are useful in summarizing a distribution because they describe a tendency common to a large number of scores. But a set of scores can also be viewed in terms of how different individual scores are from each other—that is, how much they vary.

Measures of Variability: The Range

Variability is a measure of the degree of difference, or variation, among scores. A simple measure of variability is the **range,** or the difference between the highest and the lowest scores in a distribution. The wider the range, the greater the variability. Suppose five people have taken a 10-point quiz, and their scores are as follows:

Person 1	6
Person 2	7
Person 3	8
Person 4	9
Person 5	10

Variability: Differences or variations within a set of scores.

Range: The difference between the highest and the lowest score in a distribution.

The scores go from 6 to 10, so the range is 4 (10 − 6 = 4). If the scores had ranged from 3 to 10 (a range of 7), the variability would have been greater. On the other hand, if everyone had obtained the same score—say, 8—the range would be zero, and there would be no variability in the distribution.

What was the range in the distribution of exam scores for your class? The highest score was 96; the lowest, 53. Therefore the range was 43 (96 minus 53).

Measures of Variability: The Standard Deviation

A more precise indicator of variability is called the standard deviation. The standard deviation indicates how much scores vary about the mean. Whereas the range only involves the highest and lowest scores, the standard deviation involves all scores. But the meaning of the standard deviation is not intuitively obvious. Let's begin our discussion of the standard deviation by considering the formula for determining it.

The Formula for Standard Deviation. The formula for the standard deviation can be represented as follows:

$$SD = \sqrt{\frac{\Sigma(X - \overline{X})^2}{N}}$$

In this formula, *SD* refers to the standard deviation; *X* refers to each individual score; $\overline{X}$ refers to the mean; the Greek letter sigma (Σ) means summation; *N* refers to the number of scores; and the mathematical symbol $\sqrt{}$ stands for square root.

Steps for Calculating the Standard Deviation. The formula for the standard deviation can be broken down into five steps as follows:

1. Subtract the mean from each score. ($X - \overline{X}$, where X = the score and $\overline{X}$ the mean)
2. Square the results (that is, multiply each result by itself). ($X - \overline{X}$)^2
3. Add all the results ($\Sigma(X - \overline{X})^2$)
4. Divide by the number of scores. (N)
5. Find the square root of the results.

As an example, consider the 10-point quiz we discussed in reference to the range (page 579). The mean for the five scores in this example is 8 ($6 + 7 + 8 + 9 + 10$, divided by 5). Following our five steps to calculate the standard deviation, we would proceed as follows:

Step 1. Subtract the mean from each score.

Score	Mean	Result
6	8	$6 - 8 = -2$
7	8	$7 - 8 = -1$
8	8	$8 - 8 = 0$
9	8	$9 - 8 = 1$
10	8	$10 - 8 = 2$

Step 2. Square the results.

$$-2 \times -2 = +4*$$
$$-1 \times -1 = +1$$
$$0 \times 0 = 0$$
$$1 \times 1 = 1$$
$$2 \times 2 = 4$$

*(Remember, a minus times a minus is a plus)

Step 3. Add all the results.

$$4 + 1 + 0 + 1 + 4 = 10$$

Step 4. Divide by the number of scores.

$$10 \text{ divided by } 5 = 2$$

Step 5. Find the square root of the results.

$$\sqrt{2} = 1.414$$

Standard Deviation: A mathematical expression of the degree of variability around the mean in a set of scores; the square root of the average squared deviation around the mean given by

$$\sqrt{\frac{\Sigma(X - \overline{X})^2}{N}}$$

The Meaning of Standard Deviation. The **standard deviation** can be more precisely defined as a mathematical expression of the degree of variability around the mean in a set of scores. The larger the standard deviation, the more the scores vary from the mean; the smaller the standard deviation, the less they vary. This relationship can be shown graphically (see Figure A.5). The smaller the standard deviation, the more closely packed the scores are at the center of the distribution, and the steeper the curve that results.

The standard deviation is particularly useful in analyzing scores that form a normal distribution (that which produce a normal, or bell-shaped,

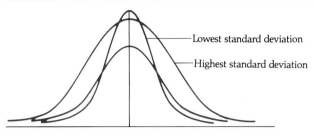

Figure A.5 Superimposed Symmetrical Curves with Different Standard Deviations. This figure illustrates three symmetrical curves. Each has a different standard deviation depending on the form of the distribution. The curve in which scores are spread out widely across the distribution has the highest standard deviation; the "skinny" curve in the center (in which most scores are in the center of the distribution) has the lowest standard deviation.

Lowest standard deviation

Highest standard deviation

curve as in Figure A.4). The data of a normal curve are distributed according to a mathematical relationship, expressed in terms of the standard deviation. That relationship is:

1. 68.26 percent of all scores fall between plus and minus one standard deviation of the mean.
2. 95.44 percent of all scores fall between plus and minus two standard deviations from the mean.
3. 99.72 percent of all scores fall between plus and minus three standard deviations from the mean.

For example, we know that IQs are a normally distributed characteristic. We also know that the mean IQ on the Wechsler Intelligence Scale is 100, and the standard deviation is 15. Thus 68.26 percent of all IQ scores on the Wechsler Intelligence Scale will fall between 115 (one standard deviation above the mean) and 85 (one standard deviation below the mean). (If the mean were 50 and the standard deviation 10, 68.26 percent of all the scores would fall between 60 and 40). We can know that 95.44 percent of all Wechsler IQ scores fall between 130 and 70, and that 99.72 percent of all the

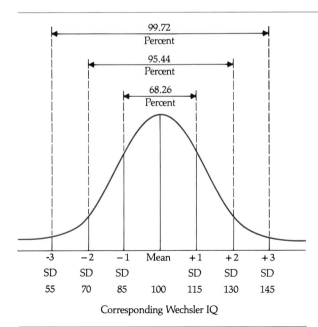

Figure A.6 Normal Distribution. This figure shows the normal distribution and the corresponding percent of the distribution that falls between ±1 SDs, ±2 SDs, and ±3 SDs. It also shows the corresponding Wechsler IQ.

scores fall between 145 and 55. IQs above 145 or below 55 are extremely rare, then. Only about .28 percent of all scores fall into those ranges. (See Figure A.6.)

INFERENTIAL STATISTICS

Just as descriptive statistics allow scientists to describe large bodies of data with just a few numbers, inferential statistics allow them to draw conclusions from that data. Using data obtained from experiments, they can determine whether or not observed differences in the scores obtained by two or more groups of subjects are due to chance.

Suppose, for example, that a psychologist is studying the effects of amount of sleep on memory recall. One group of subjects is allowed to sleep a full 8 hours within a 24-hour period. A second group is allowed to sleep only 4 hours within the same period. Subjects in both groups are then read lists of digits of varying lengths to determine the longest list each can recall on a single presentation. The psychologist then finds the average length of the list recalled by the subjects. For subjects who slept 8 hours the average was 7 digits. The average for the subjects who slept 4 hours was 6 digits. How can the psychologist tell that the observed differences between the two groups of subjects was not due to some chance occurrence such as an unusual number of lucky guesses in the group that got 8 hours of sleep? To make sure that their results are not due to chance, scientists have developed what are called tests of statistical significance. Such tests tell the psychologist the probability of obtaining the outcome assuming chance alone is working. If the outcome is rare, the psychologist rejects chance as an explanation.

Statistically Significant Result: A result whose odds of occurring by chance are less than 5 out of 100.

To determine what is rare, scientists have established a general rule. If the odds of getting a particular result by chance alone are less than 5 out of 100, the result is considered **statistically significant,** or due to something other than chance. In experimental literature, a significant result is indicated by the statement $p < .05$, a short way of saying "The probability (p) of obtaining the result by chance is less than ($<$) five out of 100." This statement tells the psychologist that the results of the study are dependable: if the experiment were repeated, similar results would most likely be found.

CORRELATION

You may recall from Chapter 1 that the correlational method involves the compiling of data on two or more variables through such devices as surveys or tests. The data are then analyzed statistically to reveal possible relationships among the variables. If a relationship is discovered, the extent of the relationship, called a correlation coefficient (designated by the symbol r), can then be expressed mathematically as a number between +1 and −1. The closer the number is to +1 or −1, the stronger the relationship. Thus, a correlation of −.87 would indicate a stronger relationship than .5.

For example, consider these scores on the Scholastic Aptitude Test (SAT) and the freshman grade point averages (GPA) of students who received them:

	Score on SAT	Freshman GPA
Student 1	1300	3.6
Student 2	1150	2.9
Student 3	1050	3.3
Student 4	950	2.4
Student 5	800	2.6

These scores are related because students with higher scores on the SAT also have the highest GPAs, and conversely, those with lower SAT scores have relatively low GPAs. Thus, SAT and GPA are correlated. However, the relationship is not perfect, because the student who obtained an SAT score of 1150 had a lower GPA than the one with a score of 1050, and the student with a score of 800 had a slightly higher GPA than the one with a score of 950.

In evaluating the degree of relationship between two variables, it is helpful to plot a graph. Figure A.7 illustrates such a graph. In Figure A.7, SAT scores are plotted along the Y-axis; Freshman GPA is plotted along the X-axis.

Each point on the scatter diagram reveals where a particular person scored on both the SAT (Y) and GPA (X). The line in Figure A.7 describes the relationship between all the points. More specifically, this line is an expression of the best linear (straight line) relationship between SAT and GPA for the five individuals. Using a mathematical formula, a psychologist can determine that the correlation between the two variables in the above example is .8 (expressed as $r = +.8$).

The correlation between GPA and SAT is positive. In a **positive correlation,** as scores for one variable increase, the scores for a second increase in

Positive Correlation: In a positive correlation, as scores for one variable increase, scores for a second increase in some proportion.

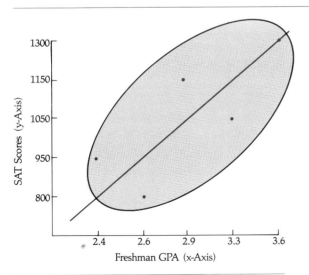

Figure A.7 A Scatter Plot.   *This figure shows a scatter plot of five peoples' scores on the Scholastic Aptitude Test and their Freshman Grade Point Average. The SAT score for each person is plotted on the Y-axis, while their GPA is plotted on the X-axis.*

some proportion. People who obtain high scores on one variable obtain high scores on a second, and vice versa. In other words, in a positive correlation people maintain a similar relative position on two variables. Students who do well on the midterm also do well on the final. The more outgoing the salesperson, the better he or she is at selling (see Figure A.8).

But correlation can also be negative. In a **negative correlation,** as scores on one variable increase, scores on the other decrease, and vice versa. This would occur if the people who did best on the midterm got relatively low scores on the final. If there were a negative correlation between an outgoing nature and sales ability, the more outgoing the salesperson, the less successful he or she would be. There is a negative correlation between smoking in pregnant women and the birth weight of their infants. The more cigarettes they smoke, the lower the birth weight (see Figure A.8).

Negative Correlation: In a negative correlation, as scores on one variable increase, scores on a second decrease in some proportion.

Negative correlation should not be confused with the lack of a relationship. A negative correlation indicates a predictable relationship between two variables—namely, that as one increases, the other decreases. If there is *no* correlation between variables, there is no predictable relationship between them, positive or negative (see Figure A.8). There may be no correlation between the number of hours that you daydream each day and the grades you get in school. You may be able to daydream for hours on end without adversely affecting your grades. On the other hand, there may well be a negative correlation (that is, the more you daydream, the worse your grades).

The correlation, or relationship, between variables may be of any degree. A high correlation coefficient indicates a strong relationship between variables; a low coefficient, a weak relationship. Most surveys and tests yield correlation coefficients that are far from perfect. A typical strong correlation, that between the Stanford-Binet intelligence test and reading ability in children, is approximately .6 in most relevant studies (Sattler, 1982).

In closing, it is important to remember a point that has been made throughout this book; namely, that a correlation between two variables doesn't mean that one caused the other. A person's IQ alone does not determine his or her score on an exam; other factors, such as study time, also contribute. What correlation does indicate is that the factors are in some way related. People with high IQs might simply be good test takers, for instance. Or they might actually be better learners. You can't tell by looking at the correlation.

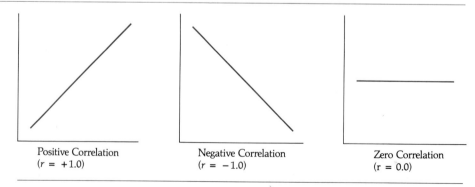

Figure A.8 Scatter Plots for Positive, Negative, and Zero Correlations.
This figure shows the scatter plots for a perfect positive correlation (r = +1.0), a perfect negative correlation (r = −1.0), and a zero correlation (r = 0.0).

Positive Correlation
(r = +1.0)

Negative Correlation
(r = −1.0)

Zero Correlation
(r = 0.0)

LEARNING FRAMEWORK

I. Descriptive statistics provide the tools for summarizing and expressing numerical data.

  A. Frequency distributions summarize how many times each possible score occurred. (Review: *Frequency Distribution; Percentile Rank; Figure A.1; Figure A.2; Figure A.3*)

  B. Measures of central tendency summarize data in terms of the center of a distribution of scores. (Review: *Mode; Median; Mean*)

  C. Measures of variability summarize the extent to which the scores of a distribution vary from each other. (Review: *Range; Standard Deviation; Figure A.4; Figure A.5*)

II. To draw dependable inferences, it is necessary to determine within a reasonable doubt that the findings are not simply due to chance. (Review: *Statistically Significant Result*)

III. Correlations express the extent of relationship between two variables. They do not reveal cause-effect relationships, however. (Review: *Positive Correlation; Negative Correlation; Figure A.7; Figure A.8*)

Glossary

Abnormal Behavior: A pattern of thought, feeling, or action that is deemed inappropriate or maladaptive in a given context, either by the individual who experiences it or by the majority of his or her peers. Such behavior often involves a violation of social norms, and it usually impairs a person's ability to function or causes personal distress.

Absolute Threshold: The minimum amount of stimulus energy necessary to activate a sensory system.

Accommodation: In Piaget's theory, the development of a new schema (organized pattern of thought or behavior) or modification of an existing one.

Accommodation: In vision, changes in the curvature of the lens of the eye to focus light from objects onto the retina at the back of the eye.

Acoustic Code: Coding in terms of sounds; mentally repeating words or sounds or transforming visual information into words, as when the sight of a book is coded mentally in terms of the word "book."

Acquired Immune Deficiency Syndrome (AIDS): A sexually transmitted viral disease that drastically lowers the body's resistance to ward off infections.

Acquisition: In operant conditioning, an increase in the frequency of an emitted response or the appearance of a new (i.e. previously unobserved) response.

Actor-Observer Bias: The tendency to attribute others' behavior to dispositional causes and our own to situational causes.

Actualizing Tendency: According to Rogers, an inborn tendency of the individual toward growth and the development of his or her capacities.

Additive Color Mixing: The mixing of lights of two or more different wavelengths (colors) to form a new color.

Adolescence: The period of development that begins about the time the individual becomes biologically mature and ends by young adulthood (usually twelve–eighteen years).

Affect: Immediately expressed and observed emotion (as opposed to mood, which refers to a pervasive and sustained emotion).

Aggression: Behavior directed toward the goal of harming or injuring another living being.

Aggressive Model: Another person behaving in an aggressive manner.

Agoraphobia: The fear of too much unprotected space, sometimes known as the "fear of fears."

Alcohol: A depressant drug found in alcoholic beverages such as beer and wine or in more concentrated forms in whiskey, rum, vodka, gin, scotch, and brandy.

Alpha Waves: Brain waves that appear in the EEG of a relaxed subject with eyes closed. (These waves are larger and slower than beta waves.)

Altered States of Consciousness: States of consciousness other than those that occur during normal waking (for example, drug-induced states, hypnosis, and meditation).

Altruism: Concern and help for others that have no apparent benefit for the person who carries them out.

Ambivalence: Strong but contradictory feelings toward the same person, place, activity, or idea.

Amnesia: Loss of memory due to brain injury, surgery, or trauma.

Amniocentesis: Withdrawing and analyzing amniotic fluid from a pregnant woman to determine if the fetus has a genetic defect.

Amplitude: A physical property of a sound wave determined by the height of the wave from crest to base or from trough to base, which is perceived as loudness.

Analogy: A heuristic in which one attempts to solve a problem using the ideas behind a previous solution to a similar problem.

Anal Stage: The second of Freud's stages of psychosexual development (ages two to three), which is dominated by a need to obtain gratification through bowel movements and in which the energies of the libido are redirected to the anal zone of the body.

Anatomical Sex: A biological aspect of sex determined by the presence of male or female genitals.

Anima: In Jungian theory, the feminine archetype, which both males and females possess.

Animistic Thinking: Attributing life and consciousness to inanimate objects or natural phenomena.

Animus: In Jungian theory, the masculine archetype, which both males and females possess.

Anorexia Nervosa: An abnormal pattern of behavior marked by a morbid fear of becoming fat and by self-starvation.

Anterograde Amnesia: An inability to learn or remember new information following brain injury or surgery.

Antianxiety Drugs: Drugs used to treat disorders in which anxiety is the major symptom (Librium, Valium, Serax).

Antidepressant Drugs: Drugs used to treat depressions (Imipramine, Tofranil, Elavil, monoamine oxidase (MAO) inhibitors).

Antipsychotic Drugs: Drugs used to treat conditions in which a person has lost contact with reality (Thorazine, Mellaril, Stelzine, Haldol).

Antisocial Personality: A personality disorder involving irresponsibility, impulsiveness, and callous exploitation of others.

Anxiety: A feeling of apprehension, tension, or uneasiness.

Anxiety States: A subcategory of anxiety disorders characterized by chronic anxiety and apprehension (including panic attacks and generalized anxiety disorders).

Aphagia: Cessation of eating; refusal to eat.

Applied Social Psychology: Attempts to understand human social behavior in real-world settings; a major goal of research in applied social psychology is the solution of social problems.

Approach-Approach Conflict: Having to choose between two equally desirable but mutually exclusive alternatives.

Approach-Avoidance Conflict: Having to choose whether to pursue a goal that has both positive and negative qualities.

Archetypes: According to Jung, universal thought forms and emotions which predispose the individual to perceive the world in particular ways.

Arousal: A general state of the organism involving excitation, or a feeling of being stimulated.

Assertiveness Training: A technique of behavior therapy in which people learn to communicate their feelings and needs to others with more confidence; to be assertive without being aggressive.

Assimilation: Incorporating new experiences into existing organized patterns of behavior or thought (schemata).

Attachment: An enduring affectional bond between two people that produces a desire for close contact.

Attitude: A relatively enduring cluster of feelings, beliefs, and action tendencies toward specific persons, groups, ideas, or objects.

Attitude-Discrepant Actions: Actions inconsistent with one's attitudes.

Authoritarian Personality: A rigid, hostile, overconventional individual who is overconcerned with issues of power and authority and prone toward prejudice.

Autonomic Arousal: A heightened state of the autonomic nervous system, usually characterized by such physiological changes as a rise in heart rate, blood pressure, and skin temperature and an increased blood circulation.

Autonomic System: The division of the peripheral nervous system whose nerves lead from the CNS to the heart, smooth (generally involuntary) muscles of the internal organs, and glands. The autonomic system consists of two divisions, the sympathetic and the parasympathetic.

Autopsy: The dissection and examination of a dead body and its various parts.

Aversion Relief: A technique of cognitive behavior therapy in which the therapist uses learning techniques to condition a client to respond to certain words or thoughts with a feeling of relief by pairing a word with the termination of an unpleasant stimulus.

Aversion Therapy: A type of behavior therapy in which an unpleasant stimulus is paired with the cues associated with an undesired response.

Aversive Stimulus: A stimulus that is harmful, painful, noxious, or very unpleasant. Electric shock, extremes of hot and cold, bee stings, and snake bites are examples of aversive stimuli.

Avoidance: Behavior in which an organism terminates (avoids) an aversive stimulus by making an appropriate response before experiencing it.

Avoidance-Avoidance Conflict: Having to choose one of two equally undesirable options.

Avoidance Responses: The avoidance of a stimulus because of unpleasant experiences with it.

Avoidant Personality: A personality disorder in which the individual is extraordinarily sensitive to rejection.

Axon: The transmitting component of a neuron.

Axonal Transmission: Refers to the coordination of the neural impulse within a neuron. Axonal transmission begins with stimulation of receptor sites on the dendrites and cell body of a neuron.

Axon Terminals: Tiny knobs at the end of the axon that bear small structures called synaptic vesicles (the storage bins for the cell's chemical neurotransmitter substance).

Barbiturates: Depressant drugs chemically related to alcohol that are used to induce sleep.

Basal Metabolism: A measure of the amount of energy expended while at rest.

Basic Anxiety: A deep sense of anxiety in a child caused by a failure of the parents to provide a safe and secure environment.

Basilar Membrane: A layer of tissue in the inner ear that vibrates in response to sound.

Basket Cells: Receptor cells located at the bottom of each hair cell on the skin. Stimulation of these cells produces pressure sensations and indicates that something has come into contact with the skin.

Beck Depression Inventory: A measure of a person's current thoughts and feelings that evaluates a person's level of depression.

Beck's Cognitive Therapy: A classical cognitive therapy, developed by Aaron Beck, that focuses on changing the client's negative views about self, the world, and others.

Behavior: Any activity of an organism, whether shown outwardly or experienced inwardly—actions, feelings, and mental processes.

Behavioral Medicine: A field of psychology that focuses on the application of behavioral knowledge to problems of physical health (eg. coping with stress).

Behaviorism: A perspective in psychology based on J.B. Watson's position that the proper objects of study in psychology should be observable or overt behavior.

Behavior Potential: The probability that a person will display a certain behavior in any given situation.

Behavior Therapy: An approach to treatment aimed at modifying the overt actions that define a person's problem.

Beta Waves: Small fast brain waves that dominate the EEG of an alert, awake subject.

Bilaterally Symmetrical: The same on both sides; as the right half of the body is almost a mirror image of the left, the right half of the brain is almost a mirror image of the left half.

Binet-Simon Scale: The original version of the first modern measure of human intelligence. (In the United States, this scale has been revised into a test called the Stanford-Binet.)

Binocular Cues: Cues to depth perception that come from the use of both eyes.

Biofeedback: A technique for allowing people to gain control over bodily functions that are normally involuntary by providing them physiological feedback; a consciousness-altering technique in which feedback from instruments that monitor biological processes including brain wave activity is used to help a person learn to modify these processes; the use of conditioning techniques to help people learn to control responses traditionally regarded as involuntary.

Bipolar Disorder: A mood disorder in which the individual may have any of the following: the full range of symptoms of a manic episode with no history of depressive symptoms; a mixture or alternating sequence of manic and depressive symptoms; or the full range of symptoms of a major depressive episode and a history of at least one manic episode.

Bisexual: An individual who is sexually attracted to and has sexual contact with both male and female partners.

Bit: A single piece of isolated information; a unit of information.

Blackout: An episode that occurs after large amounts of alcohol have been consumed, in which the individual is unable to recall any of his or her actions during the episode.

Blocking Experiments: Experiments in which the signal value of a CS is blocked or masked due to an already established CS–US relationship.

Brain Stem: The inner core of the brain that begins where the spinal cord leaves off and continues like a stalk to the highest level of the brain, the cerebrum. The brain stem contains the structures responsible for most life-sustaining behaviors such as breathing and heartbeat.

Brightness Constancy: The phenomenon in which objects appear to maintain their appropriate color and brightness, despite physical changes in illumination.

Bystander Effect: The phenomenon in which people are less likely to help someone in distress when others are present.

Cardinal Traits: Pervasive traits that influence nearly every aspect of a person's life.

Case Study: A method of psychology that intensively explores the behavior of a single individual or specific group of individuals in great depth.

Castration Anxiety: A boy's fear that his father will retaliate against him for his sexual desire for his mother by cutting off his genitals.

Catatonic Stupor: A reduction in spontaneous movements and activity; sometimes to the point of becoming motionless.

Causal Attribution: The process through which we infer causes and explanations of events or behavior.

Cell Body: The information analysis component of a neuron, which contains the nucleus and carries out the life-sustaining functions of the cell.

Central Nervous System (CNS): The brain and the spinal cord. All the neurons that lie within the body structures of the skull and backbone.

Central Traits: Traits that influence major aspects of a person's life; less pervasive than cardinal traits.

Cerebellum: A brain structure attached to the brain stem that cooperates with other brain structures to permit muscular coordination and timing.

Cerebral Cortex: The outer covering of the cerebrum composed of deep infoldings called convolutions. Most complex human functions are carried out in the cerebral cortex.

Cerebral Dominance: An old concept that suggested that one hemisphere was superior to and dominated the other. Generally, the left hemisphere was believed to be the dominant one in right-handers.

Cerebrum: The highest level of the brain; the center for higher mental processes.

Chancre: A red, painless sore that appears on the genitals or in the vagina in the early stages of syphilis.

Chlamydia Trachomatis: A sexually transmitted disease that is transmitted through sexual contact of infected mucous membrane from either male or female.

Chromosomes: Particles containing genes, which are found in the nucleus of every cell in the body.

Chronological Age: An individual's actual age—the number of years and months since an individual was born.

Chunking: Translating two or more isolated bits of information into some larger unit through grouping, organizing, or coding them into something that can be treated as a whole.

Circadian Rhythms: Biological rhythms that occur over a 24-hour cycle.

Circumcision: Surgical removal of the foreskin of the penis.

Classical Cognitive Therapy: Approaches to treatment in which cognitions are considered the primary target of treatment because they are presumed to be the cause of abnormal actions or emotions.

Classical Conditioning: The process in which a neutral stimulus comes to elicit a conditioned response through repeated pairings with an unconditioned stimulus.

Clinical Psychologist: A psychologist who functions in mental health settings and is involved with the diagnosis, treatment, and understanding of problems of adjustment (abnormal behavior).

Clitoral Glans: The tip or head of the clitoris.

Clitoral Hood: A fold of skin that covers the clitoral shaft.

Clitoral Shaft: That part of the clitoris which is covered by the clitoral hood and ends in the clitoral glans.

Clitoris: A highly sensitive part of the female external genitals whose function is to focus and accumulate sexual pleasure.

Cochlea: A snail-shaped structure of the inner ear.

Cognitions: The mental aspects of behavior such as thoughts, images, evaluations, ideas, beliefs, expectations, and our awareness of these mental processes; thoughts, memories, symbols, mental representations, and all the processes and products involved in knowing.

Cognitive Appraisal: Interpreting an event in terms of its effect on well-being.

Cognitive Approaches: Approaches to treatment that attempt to modify a client's cognitions—thoughts, beliefs, expectations, and the like.

Cognitive Behavior Modification: An approach to psychotherapy and behavior change that attempts to modify or change an individual's internal dialogue (self-statements) and other cognitions.

Cognitive Behavior Therapy: A cognitive approach to treatment in which cognition is viewed as behavior and the therapist uses learning principles to modify a client's cognitions (aversion relief, covert sensitization, thought stopping, and self-instructional training).

Cognitive Psychology: The study of memory, consciousness, thought processes, and other cognitions.

Cognitive Restructuring: A cognitive approach to coping in which people learn to handle a stressful event by changing (restructuring) their interpretation of the event or by viewing it from a broader or different perspective.

Cohabitation: An unmarried adult couple living together.

Cohesiveness: The attraction and feeling of mutual concern among group members.

Coitus: Penile-vaginal intercourse.

Collective Unconscious: Inborn memories, instincts, and predispositions that the individual inherits.

Compartments Theory: A theory of memory, which holds that memory is made of a series of separate, distinguishable storage compartments.

Competition: Two individuals or groups striving for a goal that only one person or group can win.

Complementary Colors: Any two colors that are directly opposite to each other on the color wheel. If blended together as lightwaves they will cancel each other out, producing neutral gray or white.

Compliance: A form of social influence in which an individual is requested, rather than commanded, to perform some act.

Compulsive Personality: A personality disorder characterized by rigid outward conformity and ambivalence.

Concept: A symbol that represents a particular class of objects, words, or ideas that have something in common.

Conception: The fertilization of the female egg by the male sperm.

Concrete Operations: Piaget's 3rd stage of cognitive development (ages 7–11 or 12) in which the individual learns the principle of conservation.

Concrete Thinking: Thinking in terms of specifics rather than in terms of abstractions.

Conditioned Reinforcer: A stimulus that acquires reinforcing properties through conditioning. A stimulus that gains its power to reinforce because of its association with a stimulus already having that effect.

Conditioned Response (CR): The learned response to a conditioned stimulus, which has previously been paired with a US. The CR is similar, but not identical, to the UR.

Conditioned Stimulus (CS): A neutral stimulus that, when paired with an unconditioned stimulus, acquires the property to elicit a similar response.

Conditions of Worth: Rules for living that other people impose as a condition for their approval.

Cones: Receptor cells located in the eye that are sensitive to color.

Confederate: An assistant of the experimenter who pretends to be a subject in an experiment.

Conflict: A situation in which a choice must be made between two or more important goals.

Conformity: A form of social influence in which an individual acts in accord with accepted standards and beliefs. The pressure to yield to the wishes of others is indirect—in the form of group expectations and group pressure.

Confounding Variable: A variable that, if not controlled, might affect the results of an experiment. Variables other than the independent variable that might affect the dependent variable.

Connotative Meaning: The ideas or evaluations associated with a word.

Conscious: Those mental activities and phenomena of which an individual is aware at any given moment.

Consciousness: The process of knowing and of being aware.

Conservation: In Piaget's theory, the ability to recognize that certain properties (e.g., weight, volume) of an object or group of objects remain the same despite changes in the object's shape, length, or position.

Consolidation Theory: A theory that states experience sets up a trace, which requires a certain amount of time to become permanent. Forgetting is viewed as a failure in consolidation.

Consumer Psychologist: A psychologist who works in business and industry. Consumer psychologists are involved with activities such as product selection and packaging, marketing, advertising, and television programming.

Content Validity: The extent to which the content of a test is consistent with the definition or theory of what it is supposed to measure.

Contingency Management: Attempting to change behavior by altering its consequences; the use of rewards to change behavior; attempting to change behavior by altering its consequences.

Continuous Reinforcement: Reinforcement of every response.

Contraceptives: Devices for preventing pregnancy.

Contralateral: Refers to the fact that the left side of the brain receives input from and controls the right side of the body, and vice versa.

Control Group: The group in an experiment that is not exposed to the independent variable and provides a reference point against which the experimental group can be compared.

Conventional Morality: The stage in Kohlberg's theory of moral development (ages eight or nine to twenty) in which society's rules are followed because they are the rules.

Convergence: A binocular cue to depth perception caused when the eyes rotate inward to maintain focus.

Cooperation: Two or more persons working together to reach a common goal.

Coronal Ridge: A sensitive rim of tissue that separates the glans of the penis from the shaft.

Corpus Callosum: The major fibers that connect the right and left cerebral hemispheres and allow information to be passed back and forth between them.

Correlation: A statistical method that is used to determine the extent to which two variables or events are related.

Correlation Coefficient: A mathematical index between -1 and $+1$ that describes the direction and magnitude of the relationship between two variables.

Counseling Psychologist: A psychologist who works in mental health settings. Counseling psychologists administer occupational and interests tests and conduct vocational counseling to help people plan career goals.

Covert Rehearsal: Mentally practicing a desired behavior.

Covert Sensitization: A technique of cognitive behavior therapy in which the client is taught to associate the stimuli that elicit problem behaviors with aversive thoughts and images.

Creativity: The ability to be original, to combine known facts in new ways, or to find a new relationship between known facts.

Criterion Validity: A type of validity that tells what test scores mean by determining what criteria a test relates to or what kinds of behaviors it can predict.

Cross-Tolerance: An effect in which one drug can take the place of another. Taking one increases tolerance for the other, and taking one can usually satisfy the need for the other.

Cue-Dependent Theory: A theory of forgetting, which states that forgetting is due to a failure to retrieve the cues that were present at the time of encoding.

Curve of Forgetting: Ebbinghaus's curve, which plots the decline in savings as a function of the lapse of time since original learning.

Cyclothymic Disorder: A mood disorder (less severe than bipolar disorder) in which the individual may show only manic symptoms, a mixture or alternating sequence of manic and depressive symptoms, or depressive symptoms with a history of manic symptoms.

Dark Adaptation: Becoming accustomed to dark; increased sensitivity to light caused by a decrease in stimulation of the photoreceptors (receptors for light).

Data (singular—Datum): Evidence. The facts—usually numbers based on measurements that a psychologist uses to study behavior.

Death: The moment at which life ends.

Debriefing: Explaining the true nature of an experiment in which deception was used.

Decay Theory: A theory of forgetting that states that traces (hypothetical changes in the brain that result from experience) automatically fade away or "decay" with time.

Decentration: The ability of a child to consider more than one characteristic of an object at the same time.

Deception: Deceiving subjects by withholding information about the true nature of the experiment.

Decibels(dBs): The units of measure for the amplitude or energy of sound.

Deep Muscle Relaxation: A physical approach to coping with stress in which the individual systematically tenses then relaxes each of the major muscle groups.

Deep Processing: Encoding in terms of the meaning of an item.

Defense Mechanisms: Mechanisms used by the ego to control anxiety as it deals with the conflicting demands of the id, superego, and external world.

Deindividuation: A loss of individual awareness and apprehension that occurs when a person is in a group.

Delta Waves: Very large, slow brain waves usually associated with the deepest stages (3 and 4) of NREM sleep.

Delusion: A strong but incorrect belief maintained in the face of contrary evidence.

Delusions of Persecution: A delusion in which the central theme is a false belief that one is being attacked, cheated, or persecuted.

Dementia: A disease of old age involving losses of concentration, attention, and memory.

Dendrites: The receiving component of a neuron.

Denial: Defense mechanism in which the individual attempts to cope with threatening experiences by denying their existence.

Denotative Meaning: The dictionary definition of a word; what the word stands for.

Deoxyribonucleic Acid (DNA): The chemicals of which genes are made.

Dependent Personality: A personality disorder in which the individual attempts to secure attention and support by subordinating his or her own needs to the needs of others.

Dependent Variable: A variable that is presumed to be affected by the independent variable; the variable the scientist observes to see whether it changes, so called because it depends on what a subject does.

Depressants: Drugs that depress or reduce brain activity.

Depth Perception: The ability to see the world in three dimensions; the ability to perceive depth.

Desynchronized EEG: Brain waves that show no clear pattern.

Developmental Psychologist: A research psychologist who studies how people develop and change over the life span.

Developmental Psychology: The study of how individuals develop and change with age; the scientific study of how individuals and psychological processes develop over the life span, and the factors influencing their development.

Dichotic Listening: Listening to two different messages presented at the same time, one to each ear.

Dichromat: An individual who is partially color-blind, being insensitive to one of the two primary color pairs (red-green or blue-yellow).

Difference Threshold: The minimum amount of change in stimulus energy necessary for a person to determine that two stimuli are different, sometimes known as the **just noticeable difference (JND).**

Diffusion of Responsibility: A feeling that responsibility is shared by all members of a group; consequently each person feels less responsible than they would as individuals.

Discrimination: Unjustified negative actions against the members of a specific group.

Discriminative Stimuli: The conditions that signal the availability of reinforcement or set the occasion for responding.

Dispositional Attribution: Explaining the cause of an observed behavior in terms of enduring dispositions.

Dispositions: Tendencies to act, think, or feel in a certain manner.

Dissociative Disorders: Disorders that involve a sudden but usually temporary change in normal cognitive activity or motor behavior (including psychogenic amnesia, fugue states, and multiple personality).

Dizygotic (DZ) Twins: Twins who develop from different eggs and are no more genetically alike than siblings; fraternal twins, developed from two ova fertilized by two sperm. They may be of the same or opposite sex.

Dominant Gene: A gene whose effect on a trait is dominant over another (recessive) gene's and that will be manifest in the individual.

Door-in-the-Face Technique: Enhancing compliance by asking a very substantial request which, if refused, can be followed by a smaller request.

Double Approach-Avoidance Conflict: Having to choose between two alternatives, each of which possesses both positive and negative attributes.

Down's Syndrome: A form of mental retardation caused by a genetic abnormality, usually an extra chromosome no. 21.

Dream Analysis: A psychoanalytic technique in which the patient is asked to recall and describe his or her dreams.

Drive: An unpleasant state that results from need and that arouses and energizes the organism to satisfy the need.

Duct Glands: Glands that release their chemical substances into body cavities like the mouth or onto the surface of the body.

Dysphoric Mood: A mood that is characterized by being sad, discouraged, or down in the dumps.

Dysthymic Disorder: A mood disorder (less severe than major depression) in which the individual shows only depressive symptoms and no history of manic symptoms.

Eclectic Treatments: Treatments that draw on more than one approach (for example, psychoanalytic and behavior; or psychoanalytic therapy in conjunction with drug therapy).

Educational Psychologist: A psychologist who conducts research into techniques of teaching, student learning and motivation, and curriculum development.

Efferent Impulses: Neural impulses from the central nervous system going outward to the body (efferent means conducted outward from a center).

Ego: In Freudian theory, outgrowth of the id that is formed to provide direction for a person's impulses in accordance with reality.

Ego: According to Jung, the center of consciousness, a unifying force responsible for our feelings of identity and continuity as human beings.

Egocentric Thinking: Assuming others view the world as oneself, and an inability to take the view of another.

Eidetic Imagery: A visual image replica of an external stimulus that is no longer physically present; the ability to maintain a clear, vivid, and identical mental image of a stimulus after it has been experienced.

Ejaculation: The release of semen from the penis.

Ejaculatory Incompetence: A sexual dysfunction in which the male is unable to ejaculate in the vagina.

Elaborative Rehearsal: Elaborating upon an item by relating it to what one already knows.

Electra Complex: A young girl's (age three to five) sexual desire for her father and desire to eliminate her mother.

Electrical Brain Stimulation: A method of studying the brain in which a mild electric current is sent through a tiny wire called an electrode implanted inside the brain.

Electrocalogram EOG: The graphic recording of eye movement.

Electrochemical: Involving both electrical and chemical processes. Transmission of information in the nervous system is electrochemical.

Electroconvulsive Therapy (ECT): The use of electricity to produce convulsions and unconsciousness in the treatment of abnormal behavior.

Electrode: A tiny wire used in electrical brain stimulation and in obtaining electrical recordings of brain activity.

Electroencephalogram (EEG): A record of the electrical activity of the brain, recorded from the scalp; the actual graphic recordings of brain waves.

Electroencephalograph: A machine that records the brain's electrical activity through electrodes placed on the scalp; an instrument that enhances and records brain waves.

Electromagnetic Radiation: Energy waves of different lengths ranging from radio waves to very tiny gamma rays, a small portion of which are visible as light waves.

Electromyogram (EMG): The graphic recordings of changes in muscular tension.

Embryo: The earliest stages of growth, in humans beginning about four to seven days after conception and lasting to the end of the second month.

Emitted Response: A behavior that occurs spontaneously and originates from forces within the organism without obvious outside causes.

Emotional Conditioning: The process in which a previously neutral stimulus comes to elicit an emotional response by virtue of being paired with an unconditioned stimulus.

Encode (Encoding): Getting information into memory by transforming it into a code or internal representation; transforming input information into a form the memory system can use.

Encoding Specificity Principle: A principle that states that retrieval depends on the availability of the cues that were present at the time of encoding; something will be remembered only if the cues available during encoding are also available at the time of recall.

Endocrine Glands: Glands that release chemical substances called hormones into the bloodstream.

Engineering Psychologist: A psychologist who works in business and industry, often in collaboration with engineers to make machines and other mechanical products suited for the humans who use them.

Environmental Psychologist: Psychologists interested in the impact of the physical environment on the individual and behavior. These psychologists study such topics as the impact of pollution, noise, and crowding on health and behavior.

Environmental Psychology: That branch of psychology concerned with the interrelationship between individual behavior and the environment.

Epidemiology: The study of the health and disease of people in relation to their environment and way of living.

Epileptic Seizure: A sudden abnormal firing of brain cells that may result in uncontrollable convulsions of the body.

Epinephrine (Adrenalin): A hormone released by the adrenal medulla that mobilizes the body for action, especially in fear situations.

Episodic Memory: Memory for information pertaining to specific episodes or events—the time, place, or date of an experience (as opposed to semantic information). Episodic memory deals with one's personal experiences.

Equipotentiality: A principle of how the brain works, proposed by Karl Lashley, which states that different regions of the cerebral cortex are equal in their potential to assume any given function.

Erectile Dysfunction: An inability to obtain and/or maintain an erection firm enough for coitus; impotence.

Erection: An increase in the size of and hardening of the penis.

Erogenous Zones: In Freudian theory, areas of the body that are responsive to sexual stimulation.

Erogenous Zones: Areas of the body capable of producing pleasure when stimulated.

Erotica: Inanimate stimuli (literature, photos, art, etc.) that are sexually arousing.

Escape: Behavior in which the organism terminates (escapes from) an aversive stimulus by making an appropriate response after experiencing it.

Estrogen: A hormone present in both females and males; but usually considered a female hormone because it controls the development of female secondary sex characteristics and plays an important role in governing the menstrual cycle. In men, its function is unclear.

Ethology: That part of biological science concerned with the behavior of animals.

Eustress: Positive stress; converting a negative event into a positive one by adopting the right attitude.

Excitatory Stimulation: Stimulation that reduces permeability of a neuron's membrane, thus increasing its potential to fire.

Excitement: According to Masters and Johnson, the first of four stages of the human sexual response cycle, characterized by the vasocongestion (flow of blood to the pelvic region) that follows sexual arousal.

Exhaustion: The third and final stage of the general adaptation syndrome in which the body is no longer able to cope with prolonged stress.

Expectancy: An anticipated outcome; an individual's estimate of the probability that a behavior will lead to a desired result.

Expectation: A person's estimate of what is likely to happen in a given circumstance.

Experimental Group: The group in an experiment that is exposed to the independent variable. For example, if the effect of a drug is being studied, only the experimental group would receive the drug. A second, control group, would not be given the drug.

Experimental Psychologist: A research psychologist who studies how people learn, remember, solve problems, and perceive the world. These psychologists also study motivation and emotion, and they are concerned with developing new methods and approaches to psychological research.

External Locus of Control: The belief that the outcomes one obtains—rewards and punishments—come from powerful others or are the result of luck or circumstance.

External Theory: A theory of obesity proposed by Schachter, which states that obese people are more responsive to external cues for eating and less responsive to internal cues than people of normal weight.

Extinction: In classical conditioning, the reduction and gradual elimination of the conditioned response through unpaired presentations of the conditioned stimulus.

Extinction: In operant conditioning, the procedure in which reinforcement is withheld for a previously reinforced response, which results in a decrease in the rate of the response.

Extrinsic Motivation: Motivation inspired by the desire for some external reward or avoidance of punishment.

Extroversion: According to Jung, the outgoing, carefree, bold side of one's personality.

Extroversion: According to Eysenck, one end of a

basic introversion—extroversion dimension of personality. People who score high on the extroversion end tend to be sociable and outgoing, with many friends.

Facial Feedback Hypothesis: The theory that sensory feedback from the face generates the subjective experience of emotion.

Factor Analysis: A mathematical procedure for sorting trait items or test responses into clusters or related groups.

Fear Hierarchy: A list of situations involving a feared stimulus, arranged according to the amount of anxiety they cause.

Feature Detectors: Receptor cells in the eye that respond directly to certain visual patterns (such as a curve) as a unit.

Fetishism: A condition in which an individual's preferred source of sexual arousal and gratification is from masturbation with, or in the presence of an inanimate object.

Fetus: Prenatal organism from end of second month after conception until birth.

Figure-Ground Relationship: The relationship between a pattern or figure and the surrounding background.

Figure-Ground Reversal: A reversal in the relationship between a pattern (figure) and surrounding background (ground). The figure becomes ground and the ground becomes figure, resulting in a scene or picture that can be seen in two distinct ways.

Fixation: The attachment of the energies of the libido to a specific stage of psychosexual development.

Fixed Interval (FI): A schedule of intermittent reinforcement in which the first response occurring after a fixed time interval, measured from the preceding response, is reinforced.

Fixed Ratio (FR): A schedule of intermittent reinforcement in which a response is reinforced after a fixed number of responses. (Ratio refers to the ratio of responses per reinforcement.)

Fixed Schedule: A consistent schedule of reinforcement in which each reinforcement is based on the same numbers of responses or the same interval of time.

Flashback Attacks: The recurrence of the experiences that one had while under the influence of LSD long after the drug is no longer present in the body.

Flexibility: An aspect of creativity involving the ability to shift directions or change one's approach.

Flight of Ideas: A symptom in which the individual's ideas race so quickly that the logical relationship among thoughts break down and ideas are not evaluated against reality.

Flight of Ideas: A nearly continuous flow of accelerated speech with abrupt changes in topics.

Flooding: A technique of behavior therapy in which clients are given long exposures to stimuli that are highly disturbing to them, with the aim of reducing their anxiety and avoidance response to these stimuli so that they can respond more effectively to them.

Fluency: An aspect of creativity based on the total number of solutions one can generate for a given problem.

Foot-in-the-Door Technique: Getting a person to agree to a small request to increase the chances he or she will later comply with a larger one.

Forensic Psychologist: Psychologists who work in the criminal justice system. These psychologists study all aspects of crime from working with police to catch criminals to rehabilitation and prevention of crimes.

Foreskin: The skin that covers the glans of the penis.

Forgetting: The inability to make use of or retrieve information previously experienced.

Formal Operations: Piaget's fourth and final stage of cognitive development, which begins by age eleven or twelve and in which the individual develops the ability to deal with abstractions, form hypotheses, solve problems systematically, and consider hypothetical possibilities.

Fovea: The most sensitive part of the retina, which contains only cones; the point of greatest visual acuity, where fine details can be seen.

Free Association: A technique used in Freud's psychoanalytic approach to treatment to uncover unconscious content. In free association, a person is asked to express his or her feelings, experiences, and thoughts without evaluation or censorship; a psychoanalytic technique in which patients are encouraged to talk freely about themselves without censoring or evaluating their monologue.

Free Fatty Acids: The products of the breakdown of fat substances that build up in the blood when one has not eaten recently and that quickly diminish shortly after eating has begun.

Free Nerve Endings: Receptors that terminate in the outer layer of the skin, which are believed to produce painful sensation if stimulated.

Free Recall: Recalling, without the aid of notes or external cues, in any order of one's choosing.

Frenulum: A highly sensitive triangular fold of skin on the underside of the penis that connects glans and foreskin.

Frequency: The number of cycles per second of a sound wave, which is perceived as pitch.

Frequency Theory: A theory of hearing which states that hearing receptors on the organ of Corti on the basilar membrane fire at the same rate or frequency of the sound wave that stimulates them.

Frontal Lobes: The largest region of the cortex (in humans), lying at the front of the brain, which includes the motor strip involved in voluntary movements and may be the site of most higher mental processes.

Fugue State: A dissociative disorder involving selective memory loss as well as flight from one's present life situation to a new environment.

Functionalism: The term used to describe James's approach to psychology, which attempted to discover the functions or practical uses of the mind.

Fundamental Attribution Error: The tendency to overestimate the role of dispositional factors and underestimate the role of situational factors in making attributions.

"g": The symbol used by Spearman to denote general intelligence.

Galvanic Skin Response (GSR): A drop in the electrical resistance of the skin associated with sweating; a lowering of the resistance of the skin to the passage of electric current; an indicator of autonomic arousal.

Gender: Maleness or femaleness in a psychological or social sense.

Gender Identity: One's personal sense of being male or female.

Gender Role: All behavior socially expected of males or females in a given culture.

Gene: The basic unit of heredity composed of a biochemical substance called deoxyribonucleic acid (DNA).

General Adaptation Syndrome: A three-stage sequence in response to prolonged stress, identified by Selye: the alarm stage, the resistance stage, and exhaustion.

Generalized Anxiety Disorder: An anxiety state disorder that involves persistent, uncontrollable anxiety that is unconnected to any particular stimulus.

Generalized Expectations: Expectations that apply to a variety of situations.

Genetic Sex: A biological aspect of sex that is determined at conception by the presence of an XY chromosome pair (male), or an XX chromosome pair (female).

Genitals: Sex organs in the pelvic region; in males, the penis, testes, and scrotum; in females, the vulva and vagina.

Genital Stage: The fifth and last of Freud's stages of psychosexual development (ages 12 to adulthood), which is characterized by an awakening of sexual interests and mature sexuality; the stage of psychosexual development, beginning at puberty, which is characterized by mature sexuality—a desire for sexual intercourse, reproduction, and interest in other people.

Gestalt Psychology: The school of thought that emphasized the importance of studying the whole—that the properties of the parts depend on their relation to the whole.

Gestalt Therapy: A humanistic therapy developed by Fritz Perls, which emphasizes the wholeness of the person and the integration of thoughts, feelings, and actions into a unified whole.

Gland: An organ capable of manufacturing and releasing chemical substances.

Glans: The tip or head of the penis (glands of penis) or clitoris (clitoral glans).

Global Theory: A theory of brain functioning that emphasizes the workings of the brain as a whole and the interplay among the various structures of the brain.

Glucose: A sugar; the main source of energy for the brain.

Goal: A product that will reduce drive; water is the product that will reduce the drive of a thirsty person.

Gonorrhea: A sexually transmitted disease that is caused by a bacterium that is spread through genital, oral-genital, or anal-genital contact.

Grammar: The rules of a language for combining words into sentences.

Grasp Reflex: Inborn reflex found in the neonate characterized by tightening of the fingers around an object placed in the palm.

Group: Two or more people who interact so that each person influences and is influenced by the other.

Group Dynamics: The processes that operate in a group to influence its members.

Group Norms: The written and unwritten standards of behavior of a group.

Group Test: A test that can be administered to many people at the same time: a single examiner for many (a group of) subjects.

Groupthink: The tendency of a small, closely knit group to quiet all dissent and to take a course of action without giving full consideration to the consequences or alternatives.

Habituation: A gradual diminishing or disappearance of a response from the brain to continuous stimulation at a constant level.

Hallucinations: False perceptions; seeing or hearing things that aren't there.

Hallucinogens: Drugs that disrupt normal brain activity.

Heredity: Inborn or inherited—the transmission of a characteristic from parent to offspring.

Heritability: The extent to which differences between one group and another are due to genetic factors; the percentage of variability in a trait associated with differences in genetic composition of the individuals in the group.

Herpes: A sexually transmitted disease characterized by painful blisters on the genitals.

Hertz (Hz): The unit of measure of the frequency of a sound wave which specifies or indicates the cycles per second of a sound wave. One hertz equals one cycle per second.

Heuristics: Strategies for solving a problem that provide general guidelines but do not necessarily guarantee success.

Higher-Order Conditioning: The process in which

a conditioned stimulus is paired with a neutral stimulus in the formation of a new conditioned response.

Hippocampus: A structure of the limbic system believed to play a role in learning and memory.

Histrionic Personality: A personality disorder in which the individual actively manipulates others to secure approval.

Homeostasis: Processes that maintain internal stability by a system of checks and balances that correct for any deviation from an optimal or set level; the body's tendency to maintain a relatively constant internal state and to maintain its physiological balances.

Homologous Organs: The corresponding parts of the female and male sexual anatomy.

Homosexual: A preference for sexual partners of the same sex.

Hormones: Chemical messenger substances produced by the endocrine glands or brain which are released into the brain or bloodstream and can have a powerful effect on bodily functions and behavior.

Hue: The colors of the visible spectrum ranging from blue to red, measured in terms of the length of a lightwave.

Humanistic Psychology: A perspective in psychology that emphasizes the individual, personal awareness, and human qualities—characteristics that distinguish people from animals.

Humanistic Therapies: Approaches to treatment in which the primary target of treatment is the self—those conscious aspects of an individual's world that the individual associates with "I" or "me."

Hymen: A thin tissue that partially covers the opening of the vagina.

Hyperphagia: Continuous overeating; eating to excess.

Hypertension: Chronically high blood pressure; medically defined as a blood pressure above some given level, such as 160/95.

Hypothalamus: A peanut-sized structure below the thalamus that plays a critical role in emotional and motivational behavior and regulates the endocrine system.

Hypothesis: The expected relationship between two or more variables. An assumption about why something occurs or how things are related, which represents the end of a careful process of observation and thinking about behavior.

Icon: A hypothetical image or replica of an external stimulus, which was believed to be briefly retained in sensory memory while awaiting additional processing.

Id: All inherited biological needs and instincts; the ultimate source of all the mental energy that drives the individual.

Ideal Self: The self-concept we would like to have

or believe we should have; the way we think we should be.

Identity: Recognition of continuity and sameness in one's personality across situations and experiences; having a degree of self-understanding and self-acceptance.

Illusion: Discrepancy between what a person perceives and the physical world; perception that does not represent a stimulus as it exists in reality.

Immediacy of Reinforcement: The speed with which reinforcement follows a response.

Incentive Value: The attractiveness or desirability of a goal. The greater the incentive value of a goal, the greater the motivation to get it.

Incidental Learning: Learning without the intention to learn.

Independent Variable: The variable that a scientist manipulates or varies in an experiment, so called because it is changed independently of what a subject does.

Individual Test: A test that can only be administered to one person at a time: a single examiner for a single (individual) subject.

Individuation: According to Jung, a gradual, lifelong unfolding of one's unique characteristics and potentials.

Industrial Psychologist: A psychologist who works in business and industry. Duties include development of tools for employee selection, training, and evaluation.

Inhibition: The process in which an organism learns to withhold a response to a conditioned stimulus when it is not followed by an unconditioned stimulus. In inhibition, the CS becomes a signal that the US will not follow.

Inhibitory Stimulation: Stimulation that increases the permeability of a neuron membrane thus decreasing its potential to fire.

Insight: An understanding of the roots of one's psychological problems.

Insomnia: Difficulty falling asleep or staying asleep.

Instincts: Inborn inclinations to behave in a particular way under appropriate circumstances. Instinct requires no learning; it is transmitted genetically from parent to offspring.

Instrumental Conditioning: The term used by Thorndike to describe learning due to consequences. Responses that are instrumental in a given situation, that serve some purpose, become strengthened and are more likely to recur in that situation than responses that serve no purpose.

Intelligence Quotient (IQ): The ratio of mental age to chronological age. IQ = mental age divided by chronological age times 100 (IQ = MA/CA × 100).

Interactional Synchrony: The synchronization of a newborn's movements with the words and voice tone of others.

Interference Theory: A theory of forgetting that states that a trace (hypothetical changes in the brain that result from experience) will persist unless or until something occurs that interferes with it.

Intergroup Contact: A technique of reducing prejudice by bringing together people with a prejudice toward each other.

Intermittent Reinforcement: Noncontinuous reinforcement in which some, but not all, occurrences of a response are followed by a reinforcer.

Internal Consistency Reliability: The extent to which the items of a test correlate with each other.

Internal Dialogue: The mental conversation that people carry on more or less habitually.

Internalization: A process in which the child adopts as his or her own the rules, restrictions, and moral standards that were originally imposed by the parents.

Internal Locus of Control: The belief that the outcomes one obtains—rewards and punishments—are the result of one's own effort.

Interneurons: Neurons that carry messages from one neuron to another. Interneurons integerate the activities of incoming sensory input and coordinate outgoing messages.

Interpersonal Attraction: An attitude of liking or disliking between two people.

Interposition: A monocular cue for depth in which two objects are drawn such that one partially blocks out the other.

Interpretation: An explanation of the patient's problems or of the patient's motives for behaving in a certain way.

Interval Schedules: Intermittent schedules of reinforcement based on the time.

Intrinsic Motivation: Motivation to perform a task or activity when no apparent reward is received except that directly involved with the task itself; doing something because you like to.

Introspection: Looking inward. A method for analyzing consciousness by having observers report their experiences in response to a specific type of stimulation.

Introversion: According to Jung, the reserved, serious, introspective, shy side of one's personality.

Introversion: According to Eysenck, one end of a basic introversion–extroversion dimension of personality. People who score high on the introversion end of the dimension tend to be quiet, reserved, and contemplating.

In Vivo Exposure: Real-life exposure to feared situations, as opposed to imagined exposure.

Ion: An atom or molecule having a net positive charge or a net negative charge.

Just Noticeable Difference (JND): See **Difference Threshold.**

Kinesthesis: The sense of active movement; the sense of your limbs' position and movements through receptors located in the muscles, joints, and tendons.

Labia Majora: The outer lips of the vulva.

Labia Minora: The inner lips of the vulva.

Latency Period: The fourth of Freud's stages (ages six to twelve), which is a period of crystallization of the personality.

Latent Content: In Freudian theory, the symbolic meaning of a dream.

Lateral Hypothalamus (LH): An area of the hypothalamus from which signals to start eating are believed to originate; the hunger or "start" center for eating.

Lateralization: Refers to greater representation of some functions in one cerebral hemisphere than in the other.

Law of Closure: The Gestalt Law of Organization, that states that there is a tendency to fill in or close missing gaps in a figure and see it as complete.

Law of Effect: Thorndike's first law of learning, which states that stimulus–response connections are strengthened when accompanied or followed by satisfaction and weakened if accompanied by discomfort.

Law of Exercise: Thorndike's second law of learning, which states that, other things being equal, stimulus-response connections are strengthened by repetition.

Law of Proximity: The Gestalt Law of Organization that states that items that are near (close) to each other tend to be grouped together.

Law of Similarity: The Gestalt Law of Organization that states that items that are similar tend to be seen in groups.

Laying the Groundwork: A psychoanalytic technique in which the therapist highlights patient statements that he or she believes the patient should be aware of in order to gain insight.

Learned Helplessness: Learning that trying is of no use when exposed to inescapable pain.

Learning: Any relatively permanent change in behavior (or behavior potential) that stems from experience.

Left Hemisphere: The left half of the cerebrum or cerebral cortex, which is a near mirror image of the right half.

Lesion: An injury or loss. The brain can be studied by observing the behavioral effects of accidental injury (lesions) in specific parts of the brain or by systematically destroying certain parts of an animal's brain and observing the effects on behavior.

Libido: The sexual and life-preserving instincts of the id.

Likert Scale: A technique used to measure attitudes, in which individuals are asked to indicate their degree of agreement or disagreement with a variety of statements that pertain to their views about a particular person, group, idea, object, or event.

Limbic System: A group of brain structures that form a collar around the brain stem and that play an important role in emotional and motivational behavior like rage and sex.

Linear Perspective: A cue to depth perception based on the fact that two parallel lines will appear to come together as they recede in the distance.

Linguistic Relativity Hypothesis: The theory that language shapes the way people think—that people who speak different languages think differently because of differences in their language.

Liporeceptors: Specialized cells in the hypothalamus that respond to the level of fats (fatty acids) stored in the body.

Localization Theory: A theory of brain functioning that views the cortex as an array of discrete regions, each governing a different and specific behavioral output. That is, control of each kind of behavior is governed by a different but specific region of the brain.

Locus of Control: An expectation concerning the likelihood that one's behavior will lead to a desired outcome.

Long-Term Memory: Memory for long retention intervals; a hypothetical storage compartment in which permanent memories are held.

Low Ball Procedure: Altering the nature of a request to which someone has already complied, such as adding on charges after a sale has been made.

Maintenance Rehearsal: Repeating an item out loud or mentally to keep it in an activated state.

Major Depression: A mood disorder in which the individual shows the full range of symptoms of a major depressive episode with no history of a manic episode.

Major Depressive Episode: A mood disturbance characterized by prominent and relatively persistent dysphoric mood (sad, discouraged, down in the dumps), or loss of interest and pleasure for all or most usual activities, in conjunction with a number of associated symptoms (e.g., decreased energy and feelings of worthlessness).

Maladaptive Criterion: A criterion for abnormal behavior that states that behaviors that enhance a person's well-being are adaptive and normal; behaviors that undermine it are maladaptive and abnormal.

Manic Episode: A mood disturbance characterized by one or more distinct periods in which the predominant mood is either elevated, expansive, or irritable in conjunction with a number of associated symptoms (e.g., high activity and inflated self-esteem).

Manifest Content: In Freudian theory, the actual content of a dream; what the dreamer actually experiences or recalls.

Masochism: A preference for gaining sexual excitement through one's own suffering.

Mass Action: A principle of how the brain works, proposed by Karl Lashley, which states that the critical factor in learning ability and other higher mental processes is the total amount of tissue involved, not its location.

Masturbation: Self-stimulation of the genitals to orgasm.

Matching Phenomenon: The tendency for people to choose a partner who is similar to themselves in attractiveness.

Medical Psychologist: A psychologist who functions in medical settings. Medical psychologists are concerned with the behaviors that play a role in the development or maintenance of problems of physical health and in helping people alter these behaviors.

Medical Treatments: Approaches to the treatment of abnormal behavior that rely on the tools of the medical profession, such as drugs, hospitalization, and surgery.

Meditation: Conscious-altering techniques in which the individual uses a repetitive set of exercises or rituals (such as mentally repeating a sound over and over again) to achieve an altered state of consciousness.

Medulla: The first structure of the brain stem, which governs reflexes such as swallowing and a number of life-sustaining activities like heartbeat.

Memory: The process of encoding, retaining, and retrieving information and experience; the capacity that permits organisms to benefit from past experience.

Memory Structure: The organization of memory—the system by which memories are coded and stored.

Mental Age: A child's age-equivalent performance on a test. A child who can perform at the level of the average five-year-old, for example, has a mental age of five.

Method of Loci: A mnemonic device in which information to be remembered is placed within a very familiar sequence of events or locations. Items to be remembered are visualized in the familiar locations.

Mnemonic Device: Technique for improving memory; rules for encoding that enhance retrieval.

Monochromat: An individual who is totally color-blind.

Monocular Cues: Cues to depth perception that require the use of only one eye.

Monozygotic (MZ) Twins: Identical twins, developed from one ovum and one sperm, and sharing the same genes.

Mons veneris: A sensitive triangular area over the pubic bone in females consisting of a cushion of fatty tissue and covered by skin and pubic hair.

Mood Disorders: (Also known as affective disorders). Disorders that involve a pervasive and sustained emotion that produces the prolonged low of a depression, the extended high of elation, or alternating cycles of depression and elation.

Moral Criterion: A criterion for abnormal behavior

that states that behavior is abnormal if it deviates from socially acceptable norms.

Morpheme: The basic unit of meaning in a language.

Motion Parallax: A monocular cue to depth based on the fact that, in motion, nearer objects appear to move by faster than objects in the distance.

Motivation: The forces that energize and direct behavior.

Motor Cortex: Neurons in the cortex that execute output and are responsible for every voluntary movement.

Motor Neurons: Neurons that carry information from the central nervous system outward to the body (the output cables).

Multiple Orgasms: A series of two or more orgasms without dropping below the plateau level of arousal.

Multiple Personality: A dissociative disorder in which a person has two or more distinct personalities, each of which operates independently and often without the awareness of the others.

Nanometer (Nm): A billionth of a meter.

Narcissistic Personality: A personality disorder marked by an inflated sense of self-importance.

Naturalistic Observation: A method of psychology in which behavior is studied by observing or watching events as they occur naturally.

Nature: That side of the nature–nurture issue that represents the influence of heredity.

Need: An excess or deficiency in some product related to survival, such as air, food, or water.

Negative Afterimage: A sensory image following the termination of stimulus input, where the new image is the opposite of the initial image. For colors, the afterimage is the complement of the original stimulus (e.g., red is the complement of green. After looking at green, a red afterimage can be experienced by looking at a white surface).

Negative Reinforcer: A stimulus that strengthens a behavior by its disappearance; an aversive stimulus that has positive consequences by its removal. The removal or disappearance of an aversive stimulus (negative reinforcer) as a consequence of behavior is known as negative reinforcement.

Negotiation: The process of a mutual trading of offers and counter-offers until a consensus is reached.

Neural Transmission: The sending and receiving of information by neurons.

Neurohormones: Hormones released into the brain that act only on neurons.

Neuron: A nervous system cell; the functional or basic unit of the nervous system.

Neurosis: A psychoanalytic term for disturbances associated with anxiety.

Neurosurgeon: A physician specializing in brain surgery.

Neurotransmitters: Chemical substances that a neuron releases in transmitting messages to other neurons.

Noise: Unwanted sounds.

Nonrapid Eye Movement Sleep (NREM): Periods of sleep during which rapid eye movements are not occurring. There are four stages of NREM that vary from light to very deep sleep.

Nonsense Syllable: A meaningless three-letter word consisting of a consonant, a vowel, and another consonant (e.g., *zeg, bok, xac*).

Nonverbal Test: Tests that do not involve language or reading ability.

Norepinephrine (Noradrenalin): A hormone released by the adrenal medulla that mobilizes the body for action, especially in anger situations.

Nurture: That side of the nature–nurture issue that represents the influence of environment.

Obedience: A form of social influence in which an individual is commanded to act in accordance with an order from an authority.

Obese: Weighing 20 percent above one's ideal body weight.

Objective Personality Test: A test of personality that provides a self-report statement (for example, "I like rock and roll music") and requires an individual to choose between two or more alternative responses such as "True" or "False."

Object Permanence: The ability to be aware of the existence of objects even when they are not within the range of immediate sensory experience.

Observational Learning: Learning by watching; the acquisition of complex behavior by watching others.

Obsessive-Compulsive Disorder: An anxiety state disorder involving a compelling urge to engage in unnecessary or repetitive actions (compulsions) or nagging, unpleasant thoughts (obsessions).

Occipital Lobes: A region of the cortex lying at the rear of the brain that receives visual information.

Oedipus Conflict: A young boy's (age three to five years) sexual desire for his mother and desire to eliminate his father.

Olfactory Membrane: A layer of tissue high in the nasal cavity which contains the receptors for smell.

Operant Conditioning: The term Skinner used, in place of instrumental conditioning, which refers to the process in which the frequency of occurrence of any given emitted behavior is influenced by the consequences of the behavior.

Operant Conditioning Techniques: A type of behavior therapy, based on the principles of learning and operant conditioning developed by B. F. Skinner and colleagues, in which the therapist uses reinforcement to help clients acquire new behaviors or strengthen healthy ones.

Operants: Emitted behaviors (those that occur spontaneously) that operate on the environment to produce consequences.

Opiates: Depressant drugs that reduce or eliminate pain such as codeine, morphine, and the illegal drug heroin.

Optic Nerve: The bundle of fibers that join together in each eye and relay neural impulses to the brain.

Oral-Genital Contact: Mouth to genital sexual stimulation.

Oral Stage: The first of Freud's stages of psychosexual development (first eighteen months of life), which is dominated by a need to obtain gratification of the mouth, tongue, and gums; the stage of psychosexual development that occurs during the first year of life, in which the energies of the libido focus on the mouth, tongue, and gums, and the child demands pleasure through sucking, swallowing, and biting.

Organizational Psychologist: A psychologist who works in business and industry. Duties include making recommendations concerning the organizational structure of a company.

Orgasm: The sudden, highly pleasurable discharge of accumulated sexual tension characterized by muscular contractions in the pelvis; according to Masters and Johnson, the third stage of the human sexual response cycle.

Orgasmic Dysfunction: An inability for a woman to have orgasm.

Originality: An aspect of creativity referring to how new (novel) or unusual a person's solutions to a problem are.

Ossicles: Three small, connected bones in the middle ear, known as the hammer (malleus), anvil (incus), and stirrup (stapes), that act like levers to make sounds louder.

Oval Window: A structure in the inner ear that holds back the fluid that lies inside.

Ovaries: The pair of female sex glands that produce hormones such as estrogen.

Overtones: Multiples of the basic frequency of a sound wave, which result from vibrations in a musical instrument and are of a higher frequency than those played.

Panic Attacks: Sudden episodes of terror accompanied by physical reactions like palpitations, choking or smothering sensations, dizziness, vertigo, faintness, trembling, and nausea.

Paranoid Personality: A personality disorder marked by suspicion and mistrust of others.

Paraphilia: Sexual behaviors in which the individual's primary source of sexual gratification and arousal is a nonhuman or an inappropriate human partner.

Parasympathetic System: A division of the autonomic system that is concerned with recuperative life-sustaining functions. It is active during quiescence and often acts to counter the arousal-producing functions of the sympathetic division of the autonomic system.

Parietal Lobes: A region of the cortex that receives information from the body concerning touch sensations.

Partial Report Technique: A technique in which subjects are asked to report only a portion of a briefly presented stimulus, rather than the entire stimulus.

Passive-Aggressive Personality: A personality disorder in which the individual vacillates between relying on others and relying on self.

Pedophilia: A preference for sex with children to sex with adults (child molester).

Perceived Dispensability: The feeling that one is less needed in a group, which leads to a reduced effort.

Perceptual Organization: The automatic inclination to organize sensory elements into meaningful patterns.

Performance Tests: Tests that require the subject to perform in some activity (e.g., copy symbols, put blocks together, point to a missing object.)

Perineum: An area of hairless skin between the vagina and anus in females and between the scrotum and anus in males.

Peripheral Nervous System (PNS): All the neurons and neuron groupings that lie outside the central nervous system.

Persona: An archetype consisting of the role a person plays to meet the demands of others and express innermost feelings in an acceptable way.

Personal Distress Criterion: A criterion for abnormal behavior that states that behaviors that cause a person psychological pain or distress are abnormal.

Personality: Relatively stable and distinctive patterns of behavior that characterize an individual and his or her reactions to the environment.

Personality Disorders: Deeply ingrained, inflexible patterns of actions and thoughts that halt the normal adjustment process, creating a maladjusted style of behavior that becomes a central, enduring aspect of the personality.

Personality Psychologist: A research psychologist who studies how and why people differ in their dispositional tendencies and reactions to situations.

Personality Types: Basic dimensions that underlie traits.

Personal Space: An invisible boundary or zone around a person's body that is thought of as part of oneself.

Personal Unconscious: According to Jung, all personal experiences that are not in awareness, including those that can be brought into awareness by attending to them and those that are blocked from awareness.

Person-Centered Therapy: A humanistic therapy (formerly known as client-centered therapy) developed by Carl Rogers that attempts to help people get "in tune" with their real self—to see the world and themselves and to act from their own perspective, rather than according to a distorted or unrealistic view.

Persuasive Communication: Written, spoken, televised, or filmed messages intended to persuade or promote attitude change.

Phallic Stage: The third of Freud's stages of psychosexual development (ages three to five or six), in which the individual becomes acutely aware of sex differences.

Phobic Disorders: A subcategory of anxiety disorders in which the victim's anxiety is attached to a particular object or situation, toward which the person manifests unrealistic or illogical fear.

Phoneme: The smallest unit of sound that indicates a difference in meaning in a particular language (e.g., pit–bit); the simplest sound (smallest unit of speech) that serves to distinguish one utterance from another in a language; the basic unit of sound.

Photoreceptors: Receptor cells for vision; rods and cones, which are the receptor cells that respond to light.

Physical Dependence: An acquired physiological need for a drug.

Physiological Psychologist: A research psychologist who studies the relationship between biological processes and behavior.

Physiology: A branch of science concerned with how the body and its organs (e.g., the brain) function.

Pituitary Gland: An endocrine gland located at the base of the brain attached to the hypothalamus. Sometimes known as the master gland of the endocrine system, the pituitary gland releases hormones that influence other organs to release hormones.

Placenta: A membranous organ that lines the uterine wall and partially envelops the embryo.

Place Theory: A theory of hearing which states that pitch perception is determined by the place on the basilar membrane that is most strongly stimulated.

Plateau: According to Masters and Johnson, the second stage of the human sexual response cycle in which continued vasocongestion causes the tissues of the vagina and the testes to swell.

Pleasure Principle: The goal to obtain pleasure and avoid pain.

Pons: A structure of the brain stem above the medulla, which connects the outer layers of the cerebrum with the cerebellum.

Population: A group of organisms that can be categorized together because they hold certain characteristics in common.

Positive Regard: According to Rogers, the need to be valued, accepted, and cared for.

Positive Reinforcer: A stimulus that strengthens a behavior by its appearance. Its presentation or appearance as a consequence of behavior is called positive reinforcement.

Postconventional Morality: According to Kohlberg, a level of moral development in which the individual begins to challenge the validity of rules and develops a personal value system.

Posthypnotic Amnesia: Specific memory loss caused by a suggestion given to a person while under hypnosis to forget the specific information.

Preconscious: Those mental activities and phenomena of which an individual is not immediately aware but which can be brought into awareness by attending to them.

Preconventional Morality: According to Kohlberg, the first stage of moral development (typical of children up to about age nine), in which rewards and punishments are primary determinants of morality.

Prefix: A meaningful unit of language (morpheme) that can be put at the beginning of a word to modify its meaning (e.g., pre as in predetermine or predigest).

Prejudice: An intolerant, unfair, or unfavorable attitude toward the members of a specific group.

Premarital Sex: Coitus before marriage.

Premature Ejaculation: According to Masters and Johnson, the inability of a male to withhold ejaculation long enough to satisfy his partner in half or more of their sexual encounters.

Preoperational Stage: Piaget's second stage of cognitive development (ages two to six or seven), during which the individual has difficulty taking the vantage point of others (i.e., is egocentric).

Preparedness: An inherited predisposition to learn certain things. Prepared behaviors are behaviors that are learned rapidly due to an inherited predisposition.

Primacy Effect: In memory, the phenomenon in which items presented first in a list are more accurately recalled than those in the middle.

Primacy Effect: In social psychology, the tendency for our judgments of others to be dominated by our first impression.

Primary Appraisal: The initial evaluation of an event for its significance to personal well-being.

Primary Colors: A set of three colors, which, when mixed, can produce all other colors.

Primary Reinforcer: A stimulus that acts as a reinforcer without any previous experience; a stimulus that has the power to reinforce the first time it is used.

Principle of Simplicity: An explanation of the Gestalt Laws of Organization which states that humans group elements into their simplest form. Also referred to as the minimum principle (that we will perceive the simplest organization that will fit the stimulus).

Privacy: Intentionally retreating from social contact in order to be alone or with a specific person or persons.

Proactive Interference: The phenomenon in which previous learning can interfere with new learning.

Progesterone: A hormone present in both males and females but primarily known as a female sex hormone. It is present in high levels during pregnancy.

Projection: Defense mechanism in which the individual attributes his or her own unacceptable impulses to another person.

Projective Test: A test of personality that requires a person to respond to an ambiguous stimulus, thus projecting his or her feelings and needs.

Propinquity: Physical proximity. An important factor in interpersonal attraction.

Proprium: According to Allport, a sense of self; the unifying core of the personality.

Prototype: A cognitive structure that represents a specific example of a person from a particular group.

Proxemics: The study of human spatial behavior.

Psychiatrist: A medical doctor (M.D.) who specializes in the treatment of abnormal behavior and engages in psychotherapy; as medical doctors, psychiatrists are licensed to prescribe drugs and use other forms of medical interventions in treating abnormal behavior.

Psychoactive Drugs: Drugs that alter consciousness by producing subjective changes in mood, perceptions, or experience, by virtue of their effect on the chemistry of the brain.

Psychoanalysis: The technique of treatment for psychological disorders and the psychological theory developed by Sigmund Freud.

Psychoanalytic Approaches: Approaches to treatment that are aimed at relieving a patient of an underlying emotional disorder, which is presumed to be the cause of a patient's symptoms. These approaches are based on the Freudian technique of psychoanalysis, a process of bringing into awareness unconscious conflicts presumed to be at the root of problem behaviors.

Psychoanalytic Theory: The theory of personality developed by Sigmund Freud.

Psychodynamics: Psychic (mental) forces and processes that develop through childhood experiences and which influence adult thinking and behavior.

Psychogenic: Caused by psychological factors.

Psychogenic Amnesia: A dissociative disorder in which past memories are forgotten for no apparent physical reason (such as head injury).

Psychogenic Needs: According to Murray, needs acquired through experience; psychological or learned needs as opposed to physiological needs.

Psychogenic Pain Disorder: A somatoform disorder in which there is no detectable physical damage to account for a person's complaints of pain.

Psychological Dependence: A compelling need to take a drug even though the individual has no physical need to do so; a belief that normal functioning is not possible without regular use of a drug.

Psychologists: The scientists who study behavior.

Psychology: The science that studies behavior—the actions, mental processes, and experiences of humans and other organisms.

Psychosomatic Disorders: Physical diseases, such as ulcers and hypertension, that are traceable to psychological rather than physical factors; stress-related disorders such as ulcers, hives, and hypertension, which involve physical problems with a physiological basis caused by psychological factors.

Psychosurgery: The surgical destruction of selected parts of the brain in the treatment of abnormal behavior.

Psychotherapy: Techniques for helping people cope more effectively and deal with their problems; techniques developed by observation, experience, and experimental research to help people solve their problems, change their behavior, or cope more effectively.

Puberty: The period during which the individual becomes physically capable of reproduction; the stage of life during which the reproductive organs mature.

Punishment: The presentation of an aversive stimulus as a consequence of a response.

Q-Sort Technique: An experimental procedure in which individuals are asked to sort cards containing descriptive statements into piles ranging from those that are most characteristic to those that are least characteristic.

Radical Behaviorist: Psychologists who believe that psychology should restrict its inquiry to observable and directly measurable behavior.

Random Selection: A method for selecting subjects in which each individual has an equal chance of being chosen or assigned to a specific group.

Rape: Sex by force or the threat of force with an unwilling partner.

Rapid Eye Movements (REM): Rapid darting of the eyes under closed eyelids which occurs during sleep, usually associated with dreaming.

Rational Emotive Therapy: A classical cognitive therapy approach developed by Albert Ellis that assumes that problem behaviors stem from one or more irrational beliefs.

Rationalization: Defense mechanism in which the individual attempts to justify what otherwise would be unacceptable behavior.

Ratio Schedules: Intermittent schedules of reinforcement based on the number of responses emitted by an organism.

Reaction Formation: Defense mechanism in which the individual deals with unacceptable impulses by taking an extreme position against them.

Reality Principle: The goal of delaying gratification of instinctual urges until a suitable object and method are found.

Recency Effect: In memory, the phenomenon in which items presented at the end of the list are more easily recalled than those in the middle.

Recency Effect: In social psychology, the tendency of our judgments of others to be dominated by our last, or most recent, impression.

Receptor Cells: Specialized cells found in the eye,

ear, tongue, and other sensory organs designed to detect physical and chemical energy and convert it into a neural impulse.

Receptor Sites: Large molecules scattered across the surface of the dendrites and cell body of a neuron, which respond to chemical messages sent by other neurons.

Recessive Gene: A gene whose effect on a trait is only seen when there is no dominant gene.

Reciprocal Determinism: Bandura's term meaning that the individual and the environment affect each other in a mutual way.

Reciprocity: A mutual admiration and caring; the tendency to respond to others the way they respond to us.

Reflex: Automatic behavioral reactions to a stimulus that occurs without previous learning or experience; an inborn, automatic, involuntary, unlearned behavioral response to some event or condition.

Refractory Period: According to Masters and Johnson, a period of time following orgasm during which the male is physiologically incapable of having another orgasm.

Reinforcer: In operant conditioning, any stimulus that occurs as a consequence of an operant and increases its probability of recurrence.

Releasing Stimuli: Environmental cues that trigger instinctive behaviors. When an animal encounters a releasing stimulus, it instinctively engages in a genetically programmed behavioral pattern.

Reliability: The dependability or consistency of a test. The extent to which a test is free of errors due to measurement.

REM Rebound: An increase in the amount of time an individual spends in the REM stage of sleep, which follows REM deprivation.

Representative Sample: A sample that reflects all the major characteristics of the population from which it was drawn.

Repression: A defense mechanism in which anxiety-provoking thoughts, desires, or memories are made unconscious and thus inaccessible to conscious awareness.

Resistance: An attempt to resist treatment by blocking the exploration of a sensitive topic, failing to provide information, or an unwillingness to cooperate with the therapist.

Resistance Stage: The second of three stages of the general adaptation syndrome in which the body resists the effects of a prolonged stressor and temporarily adapts to it.

Resistance to Extinction: In classical conditioning, the strength of a conditioned response, measured in terms of the number of unpaired presentations needed to extinguish it. The stronger the response, the greater is its resistance to extinction.

Resistance to Extinction: In operant conditioning, the strength of a conditioned response measured in terms of the endurance of a response beyond the withdrawal of reinforcement.

Resolution: According to Masters and Johnson, the final stage of the human sexual response cycle during which the individual returns to a sexually unaroused state.

Response (R): The behavior of an organism, an observable and directly measurable behavior.

Response Bias: The tendency to respond to a test item in a particular way (e.g., agree or disagree) regardless of the content of the item.

Response Cost: The removal of a positive reinforcer following a behavior. In response cost, a form of punishment, we take something desirable away following a response in order to discourage that response (for example, we get charged a fine for parking illegally to discourage such behavior).

Resting Potential: The difference in charge between the inside and the outside of the cell membrane of a neuron in the resting state.

Resting State: The slight negative charge within a neuron compared to the outside when the cell is not firing. In its resting state, the cell membrane is said to be polarized.

Retention: Storage of information. Holding information in storage for later use.

Reticular Formation: A complex network of cells extending through the brain stem that participates with structures throughout the brain in carrying out their functions and that plays a role in waking and sleeping.

Retina: The light-receptive surface at the back of the inside surface of the eye.

Retinal (Binocular) Disparity: A binocular cue to depth perception in which viewing with two eyes produces two slightly different projected retinal images because of the distance between the eyes.

Retrieve (Retrieval): Recovering or extracting previously encoded information; to call back or recall; the act of bringing stored experiences into a conscious, activated state.

Retroactive Interference: The phenomenon in which new learning can interfere with previous learning.

Retrograde Amnesia: The inability to recall the events that preceded some injury or traumatic event.

Reverse Tolerance: An effect in which, after repeated regular use of a drug, less of the drug is needed to produce the same effects as when the drug was first taken.

Reversibility: The capacity to mentally reverse an operation and understand what a condition was like before it was changed.

Reward Mechanism: A central nervous system process whose excitation is rewarding.

Right Hemisphere: The right half of the cerebrum, which is a near mirror image of the left half.

Rods: Rod-shaped receptor cells located in the eye that are sensitive to light and dark.

Role Playing: A technique in which client and therapist act out a situation. In role play, a therapist may demonstrate the appropriate behavior or play the other role and allow the client to practice the new response.

Rooting Reflex: Neonate's reflexive turning of its head toward the side on which its cheek is touched.

Rote Rehearsal: Memorizing without regard to meaning or organization.

Sadism: The infliction of physical or psychological suffering on another person in order to obtain sexual excitement.

Sample: A subset or portion of a population.

Saturation: The intensity or pureness of a color.

Savings Method: A method for measuring forgetting by comparing the time (or number of repetitions) it originally took to learn to the amount of time (or number of repetitions) for relearning.

Scallop-Shaped Curve: A fan-like response curve that reflects an accelerated rate of performance as the end of an interval grows near in a fixed interval schedule of reinforcement.

Schedule of Reinforcement: The pattern and frequency of reinforcements that occur to strengthen a response.

Schemata (singular—Schema): Organized patterns of behavior or thought; a cognitive framework or mental representation of a sequence of related behaviors.

Schizophrenia: A family of disorders characterized by cognitive, emotional, social, and perceptual disturbances.

Schizotypal Personality: A personality disorder in which the individual manifests odd thoughts, perceptions, and communications similar to, but not as severe as, the symptoms of schizophrenia.

School Psychologist: A psychologist who works in the primary and secondary schools. Duties include counseling students and administering and interpreting psychological tests that measure abilities and interests.

Script: A social schemata that pertains to social situations; a cognitive framework for the normal characteristics and course of events of a social situation.

Scrotum: The sac of skin that contains the testes.

Secondary Appraisal: An evaluation of one's available options and resources for handling a stressful encounter that follows a primary appraisal.

Secondary Gain: An indirect benefit of reassurance, support, attention, or assistance, which helps to maintain symptoms of disordered behavior or encourages their recurrence.

Secondary Sex Characteristics: Physical characteristics that accompany the maturation of the sex organs, such as appearance of pubic hair, voice change, and breast development.

Secondary Traits: Traits that are highly specific and narrow; traits that apply to a restricted segment of an individual's life.

Self: In Jungian theory, an archetype that represents the person's inner potential and strivings.

Self: According to Rogers, those conscious aspects of an individual's world associated with "I" or "me" including a person's sense of personal identity, self-awareness, self-definition, and personal beliefs; an organized set of characteristics that the individual perceives as being peculiar to himself or herself, including a person's sense of personal identity, self-awareness, and self-definition.

Self-Actualization: According to Maslow, the inborn need for personal growth or for the fulfillment of one's potential. The highest of human needs, self-actualization moves the individual to attempt goals beyond mere survival.

Self-Concept: A person's self-definition. In Rogers's theory, an organized and relatively consistent set of assumptions that a person has about himself or herself.

Self-Control: The ability of a person to maintain or alter the course of his or her behavior independently of obvious external influences.

Self-Efficacy: The belief or expectation that one can successfully perform the behavior demanded by a situation; one's perceived ability to cope with situations in the environment.

Self-Fulfilling Prophecy: A phenomenon in which an individual creates or causes the conditions or outcomes that he or she expects, thus causing the expected outcome.

Self-Handicapping Strategies: Strategies in which people protect themselves from failure and maintain their self-esteem by setting up excuses in advance.

Self-Help Groups: Treatment groups in which individuals who share a particular problem meet together to share experiences and support each other.

Self-Instructional Training: A technique aimed at modifying a client's internal dialogue—the mental conversation that people carry on more or less habitually throughout their waking hours.

Self-Monitoring: Observing one's own behavior, including cognitions.

Self-Perception: The process through which we come to know ourselves—our own feelings, traits, motives, and the causes of our own behavior.

Self-Perception Theory: Bem's theory that we come to know our attitudes and other personal characteristics by observing our own behavior and inferring causes, just as someone observing us might.

Self-Reinforcement: Presenting rewards or punishments to oneself based on behavior.

Self-Schemata: Schemata that pertain to the way we view ourselves; generalizations and expectations that we have about our own dispositions and behavior.

Self-Serving Bias: The tendency to attribute positive outcomes to our own ability and effort and negative outcomes to situational causes.

Self-Statements: The things a person mentally tells himself about himself.

Semantic Code: Coding in terms of meaning.

Semantic Differential: A method of measuring attitudes in which the individual is asked to indicate his or her attitude toward a person, group, idea, object, or event by rating it on a seven-point scale for each of a series of paired opposites.

Semantic Memory: Memory in terms of language and words. The organization and structure of information stored in terms of language.

Semantics: The study of the meaning of language.

Semicircular Canals: Three fluid-filled tubes (canals) located in the inner ear that detect rotary motion.

Semipermeable: The condition of something that allows some things through but not others, as in a semipermeable cell membrane.

Senescence: Sensory and bodily declines with aging; growing old.

Sensate Focus: A technique used in the treatment of sexual dysfunctions. It involves touching and communication to enhance sexual pleasure and reduce sexual inhibitions and performance pressures.

Sensorimotor Stage: Piaget's first stage of cognitive development (0–2 years) in which organized patterns of behavior and thought (schemata) are acquired through sensory impressions and motor activities.

Sensory Adaptation: A reduction in the rate of firing of a receptor after continuous stimulation at a constant level.

Sensory Cortex: Neurons in the cortex that receive incoming information including the visual areas, the auditory areas, and the sensory strip that spans across the brain-like earphones.

Sensory Deprivation: Eliminating or greatly reducing input to the senses.

Sensory Memory: The initial representation of an external stimulus in the nervous system; the hypothetical storage compartment in which information is briefly retained in an unprocessed state while being transferred to short-term memory.

Sensory Neurons: Neurons that carry information from the body to the central nervous system (the input cables).

Separation Anxiety: The tendency of infants less than one year old to display discomfort and signs of anxiety when separated from their mothers.

Septum: A structure of the limbic system believed to play a role in pleasure.

Serial Learning: A technique of memory research in which items are presented in a specific order and must then be recalled in the same order.

Serial Position Effect: The phenomenon in which the percentage of errors is greater for items presented in the middle of a list than for those presented first or last.

Set Point Theory: The theory that the body will tend to stay within certain maximum and minimum weights, due to an internal mechanism that maintains a relatively constant weight over the years.

Sexual Aversion: An extreme or irrational fear and avoidance of sexual activity.

Sexual Dysfunction: Difficulties or inability at any stage of the normal sexual response cycle.

Sexually Transmitted Diseases: Diseases spread through sexual contact.

Shadow: In Jungian theory, an archetype that represents the inferior, evil, or dark side of a person.

Shallow Processing: Encoding in terms of sound or appearance rather than meaning.

Shape Constancy: The phenomenon in which objects of the same shape appear to be the same shape regardless of the angle or position from which they are viewed.

Shaping: The gradual reinforcement of responses that are similar to (approximate) the one you are interested in and the nonreinforcement of all other responses.

Short-Term Memory: Memory for short intervals, generally less than thirty seconds; a hypothetical compartment in which information is briefly held until it can be transferred to long-term memory.

Signal Detection Analysis: A method of eliminating nonsensory factors in evaluating an individual's ability to detect the presence of a stimulus (near the absolute threshold); both correct and incorrect judgments are taken into account.

Situational Disposition: Explaining the cause of an observed behavior in terms of temporary, external causes.

Size Constancy: The phenomenon in which objects of the same size appear to be the same size regardless of distance and in spite of differences in the size of the projected retinal image.

Skinner Box: A specially designed cubicle that gives an experimenter precise control over the environment in order to study operant behavior.

Sleep Spindle: A type of brain wave pattern that occurs during sleep, generally associated with the onset of stage 2 NREM sleep.

Slow Wave Sleep (SWS): The regular pattern of large slow delta waves that occurs during the deepest stage of sleep also known as stage 4 NREM.

Social Behavior: Behavior (overt actions, feelings, thoughts) of individuals in social situations.

Social Cognition: All cognitions and cognitive processes that play a role in social behavior.

Social Comparison Theory: The theory that, when objective or physical standards are unavailable, people will use others as a standard by which to measure themselves.

Social Interest: The impulse to relate to and be with others, and to adapt oneself to them.

Social Learning Theory: A viewpoint in psychology that focuses on learning in the social context through observation and emphasizes the importance of cognitions.

Social Loafing: The tendency of each individual member of a group to contribute less than they would if acting alone.

Social Perception: The process through which we come to know and understand others.

Social Psychologist: A psychologist who studies behavior in the social context. Social psychologists study such topics as the way people influence and affect each other in groups.

Social Psychology: The study of behavior within a social context.

Social Schema (pl. schemata): A cognitive framework about specific individuals or groups of individuals acquired by experience.

Somatic Arousal: The body's state of activation as measured by indicators such as heart rate, respiration, blood pressure, skin temperature, and oxygen consumption.

Somatic System: The division of the peripheral nervous system that includes all the input nerves that carry information from the skeletal (striated) muscles, joints, and skin to the central nervous system, plus all the output nerves leading to the skeletal or striated muscles, which control voluntary movement.

Somatoform Disorders: A category of disorders characterized by physical symptoms (for example, paralysis or blindness) for which there is no apparent physical cause or damage, but for which there is evidence of a psychological cause.

Source Traits: According to R. B. Cattell, the basic elements of personality.

Spinal Reflex: A reflex coordinated by the spinal cord in which neural impulses travel a circuit from sensory neurons to the spinal cord and back again to the motor neurons, without first going to the brain.

Split-brain Patients: Individuals who have had their corpus callosum severed, disconnecting the right and left hemispheres, in an effort to control severe epilepsy.

Spontaneous Recovery: In classical conditioning, the temporary reappearance of an extinguished conditioned response with rest.

Spontaneous Recovery: In operant conditioning, a temporarily higher rate of responding observed at the beginning of a subsequent experimental session following a session in which extinction has occurred.

Squeeze Technique: Method for preventing premature ejaculation in which the penis is firmly squeezed with the hand at the glans (or at the base of the shaft).

Stage: A distinct period of development within a sequence of levels.

Stages of Psychosexual Development: According to Freud, a fixed sequence of stages in which personality development proceeded.

Stanford-Binet Intelligence Scale: The United States version of the Binet-Simon Scale, first published by Lewis Terman of Stanford University in 1916.

State-Dependent Learning: The physiological state of the organism at the time of learning (for example, fatigued, on a drug, angry, etc.). Retrieval is impaired if the physiological state of an individual at the time of recall does not match that at the time of encoding.

Statistical Criterion: A criterion for abnormal behavior that states that behavior is abnormal if it deviates from the average.

Stereochemical Theory: The theory of smell that states that smell receptors are sensitive to molecules of similar shape and electrical charge.

Stereotype: A set of beliefs and expectations about members of a specific group.

Stimulants: Drugs that stimulate or increase brain activity.

Stimulus (stimuli)(S): Any type of physical or chemical energy (e.g., light, heat, pressure) to which an organism can respond. According to the behaviorists, the environmental condition that triggers or gives rise to a response.

Stimulus Control: The tendency for the probability or rate of responding to vary with the presence and absence of a signal (discriminative stimulus).

Stimulus Control Analysis: Identifying, through careful observation, the environmental stimuli that precede an undesired behavior.

Stimulus Discrimination: In classical conditioning, the process in which the organism comes to respond only to the original conditioned stimulus and not to similar stimuli. It is the opposite of stimulus generalization.

Stimulus Discrimination: In operant conditioning, a different rate of responding to two stimuli produced by a different rate of reinforcement for the two (for example, reinforce for pecking at a red key, don't reinforce for pecking at a green key).

Stimulus Generalization: In classical conditioning, the phenomenon in which stimuli similar to a conditioned stimulus elicit a similar response without prior learning, though to a lesser degree.

Stimulus Generalization: In operant conditioning, the phenomenon in which an organism that has been reinforced to emit a response to one stimulus emits the same response to similar stimuli; though to a lesser degree.

Stranger Anxiety: The tendency of infants less than one year old to show marked fear of strangers.

Stress: Exposure to a stressor.

Stressful Life Events: Situations that necessitate significant change in a person's life-style (marriage, divorce, graduation, changing jobs, etc.).

Stressor: Any demand placed on the individual.

Stress Response: The body's response to a stressor; the physiological changes induced by stress.

Striated Muscles: Muscles attached to the skeletal system that are involved in voluntary movement.

Stroboscopic Motion: The perception of movement from a series of rapidly presented still photos.

Structuralism: The name for Wundt's approach to psychology, whose aim was to analyze conscious experience in terms of its basic elements or structures.

Subgoals: A heuristic in which a problem is broken down into smaller, more manageable units.

Subjective Organization: Specific output order effects for unrelated information presented in a different input order for each presentation; recalling a list in an increasingly similar order, following each presentation of a randomly presented list.

Sublimation: Defense mechanism in which sexual and aggressive impulses are channeled into socially acceptable outlets.

SUD: Subjective unit of disturbance, a subjective rating system in which clients express the strength of their anxiety to a given stimulus on a scale from zero (no anxiety) to 100 (highest possible level of anxiety).

Suffix: A meaningful unit of language (morpheme) that can be put at the end of a word to modify its meaning (e.g., *ing* as in work*ing* or mov*ing*).

Superego: An outgrowth of the ego that represents the ideals and values of parents and society.

Superordinate Goal: An important goal that only can be achieved through cooperation.

Survey Method: A research method in which a representative sample of individuals are asked to respond to a set of questions, so that the opinions, attitudes, and the like of a population can be studied.

Sympathetic Arousal: A heightened state of sympathetic nervous system activity characterized by such physiological changes as rises in heart rate, increased blood pressure and blood circulation, and inhibition of digestion.

Sympathetic System: A division of the autonomic system that generally prepares the body for action. It is usually active during excitement, threat, or fear.

Symptom Substitution: The replacement of one symptom with another.

Synapse: The very tiny space between neurons; the area of functional contact between neurons.

Synaptic Transmission: Refers to the transmission of information between neurons (i.e., from one neuron to another).

Synaptic Vesicles: Tiny storage bins inside the axon terminals that contain a neuron's neurotransmitter.

Synchronized EEG: A brain wave pattern in which the majority of the waves are coordinated in frequency and peak—going up and down at about the same time.

Syndrome: A group of symptoms that define a particular pattern of abnormal behavior.

Syntax: The set of rules pertaining to the order of words in sentences and phrases.

Syphilis: A sexually transmitted disease that causes a chancre during the early stages and can lead to severe symptoms, such as blindness, and even death in later stages, if left untreated.

Systematic Desensitization: A gradual step-by-step technique for training clients to react to a troubling stimulus with a new response, one that is incompatible with anxiety.

Tachistoscope: An instrument used to present items for very brief durations (usually less than 200 milliseconds or two-tenths of a second).

Target Behavior: In operant conditioning approaches to treatment, the behavior that the therapist identifies as in need of change and that becomes the target for treatment.

Telegraphic Speech: Utterances from which all nonessential words are omitted.

Temporal Lobes: A region of the cortex that receives auditory information and transforms sounds into recognizable patterns.

Territoriality: The ownership and defense of areas by persons or groups.

Testes: The pair of male sex glands contained in the scrotum that produce hormones (such as testosterone) and sperm (the male's sex cells).

Testosterone: A hormone found in both sexes but generally referred to as the male sex hormone.

Test-Retest Reliability: The consistency of test results over time, based on two administrations of the same test to the same people.

Texture Gradient: A cue to depth perception based on the fact that, as objects recede into the distance, they appear to lose clarity and detail; a monocular cue for depth created by reducing clarity and detail.

Thalamus: A large complex brain structure that interconnects the brain stem and cerebral cortex and participates with other structures of the brain in carrying out such activities as relaying sensory information and participating in sleeping and waking behaviors.

Thought: All the mental operations or processes that go on in a person's head as the person attempts to solve problems, master the environment, or synthesize information.

Thought Stopping: A technique of cognitive behavior therapy in which the therapist teaches the client to disrupt or eliminate maladaptive thoughts.

Threshold: The point at which the amount of stimulation is sufficient to cause a neural impulse.

Thyroid Glands: A pair of endocrine glands located in the neck that release thyroxin, a hormone that influences the rate at which the body uses energy.

Timbre: The quality or richness of a sound; the quality that distinguishes one musical instrument from another.

Tolerance: An increase in the amount of a drug needed to obtain the same effect as when one first started using the drug.

Trace: The hypothetical physical changes in the brain that are the neurological correlates of learning and memory.

Traits: Relatively enduring dispositions (tendencies

to act, think, or feel in a certain manner in a given circumstance) that distinguish one individual from another.

Transduction: The translation of energy into neural impulses by sensory receptors; to change energy into a neural impulse.

Transference: A process in which the patient transfers the feelings and attitudes formed in an earlier relationship to the therapist.

Translocation: A genetic error in which all or part of one chromosome becomes attached to another during cell division.

Transsexualism: A strong desire to possess the genitals of the other sex which often leads the person to have a sex change operation.

Transvestism: A preference or desire to dress in the clothing of females (cross-dressing).

Trichromat: An individual with normal color vision.

Trichromatic Theory: A theory of color vision that states that the human eye has three types of color receptors, one for each of the additive color mixing primaries: red, green, and blue.

Trigram: A meaningless 3 consonant stimulus (e.g., DBL, DPS, LSH).

Tympanic Membrane: The eardrum.

Type A Behavior Pattern: A life-style characterized by competitiveness, achievement, striving, time urgency, and impatience.

Type B Behavior Pattern: A life-style characterized by the absence of Type A characteristics. People who exhibit the Type B pattern tend to be easygoing, relaxed, noncompetitive, and nonstriving.

Type E Behavior Pattern: A female life-style in which a woman spreads herself too thin and tries to be everything to everybody.

Ultradian Rhythms: Biological rhythms that occur in less than twenty-four hours, usually over 90-minute cycles.

Unconditioned Response (UR): The unlearned response to an unconditioned stimulus.

Unconditioned Stimulus (US): A stimulus that dependably produces (elicits) a response without the subject's prior experience.

Unconscious: According to Freud, mental processes that govern behavior without the individual's awareness; the wishes, thoughts, desires of which the person is unaware but which still affect behavior and cannot be brought into awareness except under special circumstances.

Vagina: An expandable muscular organ in the female that receives the penis during intercourse.

Vaginismus: A sexual dysfunction characterized by involuntary spastic contractions of the outer third of the vagina whenever penile insertion is attempted.

Valence: The value or importance of a goal or a particular outcome to an individual.

Validity: The meaning of a test. Extent to which a test measures what it claims to measure.

Validity Scales: Scales in the MMPI that evaluate the validity of a person's response to the test. The F scale, for example, can help determine if an individual exaggerated the extent of his or her problems.

Variable: Any measurable aspect of behavior that can take on two or more values. Any characteristic that can be observed dependably to differ in either quality (for example, good-bad) or quantity.

Variable Interval (VI): A schedule of intermittent reinforcement in which reinforcements are provided at irregular intervals.

Variable Ratio (VR): A schedule of intermittent reinforcement in which the number of responses necessary for each reinforcement varies after each reinforcement.

Variable Schedule: An inconsistent or irregular schedule of reinforcement in which each reinforcement is based on a different number of responses or on a different interval of time.

Vasocongestion: A rush of blood to the pelvic region that occurs during sexual arousal and results in penile erection in the male and vaginal lubrication in the female.

Ventromedial Hypothalamus (VMH): An area of the hypothalamus from which signals to stop eating are believed to originate; the satiety or "stop" center for eating.

Verbal Test: Tests that involve language, requiring reading ability or a verbal response.

Vestibular Sense: The sense of passive movement. Sensitivity to movements in the head and body as a whole; sensitivity to rotation, acceleration, deceleration, and the like.

Vestibule: The area of the vulva inside the labia minora and outside the vagina.

Vicarious Learning: Learning through observation alone, without direct experience.

Visual Cliff: A research apparatus designed to produce the optical illusion of a drop-off used to test depth perception in infants.

Volley Theory: A theory of hearing used to explain perception of high-frequency (high-pitched) sounds. According to the theory, groups of receptor cells fire in quick succession to achieve a faster-than-normal rate of firing.

Voyeurism: A preference for sexual excitement by spying on unwilling subjects as they undress or engage in sexual activity.

Vulva: The external sex organs of the female including the mons veneris, labia, clitoris, vestibule, and opening to the vagina.

Whole Report Technique: A technique in which subjects are asked to recall as much as they can from a briefly presented stimulus.

Withdrawal Symptoms: Physical illnesses (e.g., vomiting, the shakes) that occur when an individual stops taking a drug that he or she is physically dependent on.

Zoophilia: A preference for sex with animals instead of humans.

Zygote: A fertilized egg.

References

ABELES, N. (1981). Proceedings of the American Psychological Association, Incorporated, for the Year 1980. *American Psychologist, 36,* 552–586.

ABRAHAM, K. (1960). Notes on the psychoanalytic investigation and treatment of manic-depressive insanity and allied conditions (1911), in selected Papers on Psychoanalysis. (p. 137–156). New York: Basic Books.

ABRAHAM, S., COLLINS, G., & NORDSIECK, M. (1971). Relationship of childhood weight status to morbidity in adults. *HSMA Health Reports, 86,* 273.

ABRAHAM, S., & JOHNSON, C. L. (1979). *Overweight adults in the United States.* Vital and Health Statistics of the National Center for Health Statistics, No. 51.

ADAMS, F. M., & OSGOOD, C. E. (1973). A cross-cultural study of the affective meanings of color. *Journal of Cross-Cultural Psychology, 4,* 135–156.

ADKINS, E., & JEHU, D. (1985). Analysis of a treatment program for primary orgasmic dysfunction. *Behavior Therapy Research, 23,* 119–126.

ADLER, A. (1927). *Understanding human nature.* Hardcover English edition: New York: Greenberg, 1927. Paperback reprint: Greenwich, Conn.: Fawcett, 1957.

ADLER, A. (1933). *Social interest: A challenge to mankind.* Hardcover English edition: London: Faber & Faber, 1938. Paperback reprint: New York: Capricorn Books, 1964.

ADORNO, T. W., FRENKEL-BRUNSWIK, E., LEVINSON, D., & SANFORD, N. (1950). *The authoritarian personality.* New York: Harper.

AGRAS, S., & JACOB, R. (1979). Hypertension. In O. F. Pomerleau & J. P. Brady (Eds.), *Behavioral medicine: Theory and practice.* Baltimore: Williams and Wilkins.

AGRAS, W. S., LEITENBERG, H., & BARLOW, D. H. (1968). Social reinforcement in the modification of agoraphobia. *Archives of General Psychiatry, 19,* 423–427.

AHLSKOG, J., & HOEBEL, B. (1973). Overeating and obesity from damage to a noradrenergic system in the brain. *Science, 182,* 166–169.

AHLSKOG, J., RANDALL, P., & HOEBEL, B. (1975). Hypothalamic hyperphagia. Dissociation from hyperphagia following destruction of noradrenergic neurons. *Science, 190,* 399–401.

AINSWORTH, M.D.S. (1974). The development of infant-mother attachment. In B. M. Caldwell & H. N. Ricciuti (Eds.), *Review of child development research* (Vol. 3). Chicago: University of Chicago Press.

AINSWORTH, M.D.S. (1979). Infant-mother attachment. *American Psychologist, 34*, 932–937.

AINSWORTH, M.D.S., BLEHAR, M. C., WATERS, E., & WALL, S. (1978). *Patterns of attachment: A psychological study of the strange situation.* Hillsdale, N.J.: Erlbaum.

AINSWORTH, M.D.S., & WITTIG, B. A. (1972). Attachment and exploratory behavior of one-year-olds in a strange situation. In B. M. Foss (Ed.), *Determinants of infant behavior* (Vol. 4). New York: Wiley.

AKISKAL, H. S., & MCKINNEY, W. T. (1982). Overview of depression: Integration of ten conceptual models into a comprehensive clinical frame. In F. G. Guggenheim & C. Nadelson (Eds.), *Major psychiatric disorders.* New York: Elsevier Biomedical. (Originally published 1975, *Archives of General Psychiatry, 32*, 285–305).

ALDRICH, C. K. (1966). *An introduction to dynamic psychiatry.* New York: McGraw-Hill.

ALLEN, M. G. (1976). Twin studies of affective illness. *Archives of General Psychiatry, 35*, 1476–1478.

ALLEN, V. L., & WILDER, D. A. (1980). Impact of group consensus and social support on stimulus meaning: Mediation of conformity by cognitive restructuring. *Journal of Personality and Social Psychology, 39*, 1116–1124.

ALLPORT, G. W. (1937). *Personality: A psychological interpretation.* New York: Holt.

ALLPORT, G. W. (1961). *Pattern and growth in personality.* New York: Holt, Rinehart and Winston.

ALLPORT, G. W. (Ed.). (1965). *Letters from Jenny.* New York: Harcourt, Brace & World.

ALLPORT, G. W. (1967). Autobiography. In E. G. Boring and G. Lindzey (eds.), *A History of Psychology in Autobiography (Vol. 5).* New York: Appleton-Century-Crofts, 1–25.

ALLPORT G. W., & ODBERT, H. S. (1936). Trait-names: A psycholexical study. *Psychological Monographs, 47*, (211).

ALPERT, R. (1971). *Be here now.* San Cristobal, New Mexico: Lama Foundation.

ALTMAN, I. A. (1975). *The environment and social behavior.* Monterey, Calif.: Brooks/Cole.

AMERICAN CANCER SOCIETY. (1979). *Cancer Statistics.*

AMERICAN INSTITUTE FOR PREVENTATIVE MEDICINE. (1985).

AMERICAN PSYCHIATRIC ASSOCIATION. (1980). *DSM-III: Diagnostic and statistical manual of mental disorders. 3rd ed.* Washington, D.C.: APA.

AMERICAN PSYCHIATRIC ASSOCIATION. (1985). *DSM-III-R in development.* New York: APA.

AMERICAN PSYCHOLOGICAL ASSOCIATION, COMMITTEE FOR THE PROTECTION OF HUMAN PARTICIPANTS IN RESEARCH. (1982). *Ethical principles in the conduct of research with human participants* (2nd ed.). Washington, D.C.: Author.

AMODEO, J. (1981). Focusing applied to a case disorientation in meditation. *Journal of Transpersonal Psychology, 13*, 149–154.

AMOORE, J. E., JOHNSON, J. W., JR., & RUBIN, M. (1964). The stereochemical theory of odor. *Scientific American, 210*, 44–49.

ANAND, B. K., & BROBECK, J. R. (1951). Hypothalamic control of food intake in rats and cats. *Yale Journal of Biological Medicine, 24*, 123–140.

ANDERSEN, S. M., & BEM, S. L. (1981). Sex typing and androgyny in dyadic interaction: Individual differences in responsiveness to physical attractiveness. *Journal of Personality and Social Psychology, 41*, 74–86.

ANDERSON, E. G., & BONNYCASTLE, D. D. (1960). A study of the central depressant action of pentobarbital, phenobarbital, and diethyl-ether in relationship to increases in brain serotonin. *Journal of Pharmacological Experimental Therapy, 130*, 138–146.

ANGRIST, B., & GERSHON, S. (1970). The phenomenology of experimentally induced amphetamine psychosis: Preliminary observations. *Biological Psychiatry, 2*, 97–107.

ANOOSHIAN, L. J., & YOUNG, D. (1981). Developmental changes in cognitive maps of a familiar neighborhood. *Child Development, 52*, 341–348.

ARCHER, D. (1980). *How to expand your S.I.Q. (social intelligence quotient).* New York: M. Evans.

ARCHER, R. L., DIAZ-LOVING, R., GOLLWITZER, P. M., DAVIS, M. H., & FOUSHEE, H. C. (1981). The role of dispositional empathy and social evaluation in the empathic mediation of helping. *Journal of Personality and Social Psychology, 40*, 786–796.

ARLIN, P. K. (1975). Cognitive development in adulthood: A fifth stage? *Developmental Psychology, 11*, 602–606.

ARONSON, E., BLANEY, N., STEPHAN, C., SIKES, J., & SNAPP, M. (1978). *The jigsaw classroom.* Beverly Hills, Calif.: Sage.

ASCH, S. E. (1951). Effects of group pressure upon the modification and distortion of judgments. In H. Guetzkow (Ed.), *Groups, leadership, and men.* Pittsburgh: Carnegie Press.

ASCH, S. E. (1955). Opinions and social pressure. *Scientific American, 193*, 31–35.

ASCH, S. E. (1956). Studies of independence and conformity: A minority of one against a unanimous majority. *Psychological Monographs, 70*, (9, Whole No. 416).

ASCHOFF, J. (1981). Circadian rhythms: Interference with and dependence on work-rest schedules. In L. C. Johnson (Ed.), *Biological rhythms, sleep and shift work.* New York: SP Medical and Scientific Books.

ASERINKSY, E., & KLEITMAN, N. (1953). Regularly occurring periods of eye motility, and concomitant phenomena during sleep. *Science, 118*, 273–274.

ASERINSKY, E., LYNCH, J. A., MACK, M. E., TZANKOFF,

S. P., & HURN, E. (1985). Comparison of eye motion in wakefulness and REM sleep. *Psychophysiology, 22,* 1–10.

ATHANASIOU, R. (1980). Pornography: A review of research. In B. B. Wolman & J. Money (Eds.), *Handbook of human sexuality.* Englewood Cliffs, N.J.: Prentice-Hall.

ATHANASIOU, R., SHAVER, P., & TAVRIS, C. (1970). Sex. *Psychology Today,* July, 39–52.

ATKIN, C. (1982). Changing male and female roles. In M. Schwarz (Ed.), *TV and teens: Experts look at the issues.* Reading, Mass.: Addison-Wesley.

ATKINSON, J. W. (1964). *An introduction to motivation.* Princeton, N.J.: Van Nostrand.

ATKINSON, R. C., & SHIFFRIN, R. M. (1968). Human memory: A proposed system and its controlled processes. In K. W. Spence & J. T. Spence (Eds.), *The psychology of learning and motivation* (Vol. 2). New York: Academic Press.

ATTHOWE, J. M., JR., & KRASNER, L. A. (1968). A preliminary report on the application of contingent reinforcement procedures (token economy) on a "chronic" psychiatric ward. *Journal of Abnormal Psychology, 73,* 37–43.

ATTNEAVE, F. (1954). Some information aspects of visual perception. *Psychological Review, 61,* 183–193.

AX, A. F. (1953). The physiological differentiation between fear and anger in humans. *Psychosomatic Medicine, 15,* 433–442.

AXELROD, J., & REISINE, T. D. (1984). Stress hormones: Their interaction and regulation. *Science, 224,* 452–459.

AZRIN, N. H., & HOLTZ, W. (1966). Punishment. In W. K. Honig (Ed.), *Operant behavior.* New York: Appleton-Century-Crofts.

BAKER, M., DORZAB, J., & WINOKUR, G. (1972). Depressive disease: Evidence favoring polygenic inheritance based on an analysis of ancestral cases. *Archives of General Psychiatry, 27,* 320–327.

BAKER, R. W., MCNEIL, O. V., & SIRYK, B. (1985). Expectation and reality in freshman adjustment to college. *Journal of Counseling Psychology, 32,* 94–103.

BANCROFT, J. (1978). The relationship between hormones and sexual behavior in humans. In J. B. Hutchinson (Ed.), *Biological determinants of sexual behavior.* New York: Wiley.

BANDURA, A. (1969). *Principles of behavior modification.* New York: Holt, Rinehart, & Winston.

BANDURA, A. (1971). *Social learning theory.* New York: General Learning Press.

BANDURA, A. (1973). *Aggression: A social learning analysis.* Englewood Cliffs, N. J.: Prentice-Hall.

BANDURA, A. (1977a). Self-efficacy: Toward a unifying theory of behavioral change. *Psychological Review, 84,* 191–215.

BANDURA, A. (1977b). *Social learning theory.* Englewood Cliffs, N.J.: Prentice-Hall.

BANDURA, A. (1978). The self system in reciprocal determinism. *American Psychologist, 33,* 344–358.

BANDURA, A. (1982). Self-efficacy mechanism in human agency. *American Psychologist, 37,* 122–147.

BANDURA, A. (1986). *Social foundations of thought and action: A social cognitive theory.* Englewood Cliffs, N.J.: Prentice-Hall.

BANDURA, A., & ROSENTHAL, T. L. (1966). Vicarious classical conditioning as a function of arousal level. *Journal of Personality and Social Psychology, 3,* 54–62.

BARBER, T. X. (1979). Suggested ("Hypnotic") behavior: The trance paradigm versus an alternative paradigm. In E. Fromm & R. E. Shor (Eds.), *Hypnosis: Developments in research and new perspectives* (2nd ed.). New York: Aldine.

BARD, P. (1934). The neurohumoral basis of emotional reactions. In C. A. Murchison (Ed.), *Handbook of general experimental psychology.* Worcester, Mass.: Clark University Press.

BARLOW, J. S. (1985). Computer characterization of trace alternate and REM sleep patterns in the neonatal EEG by adaptive segmentation. *Electroencephalography and Clinical Neurophysiology, 60,* 163–173.

BARNETT, R. C., & BARUCH, G. K. (1985). Women's involvement in multiple roles and psychological distress. *Journal of Personality and Social Psychology, 49,* 135–145.

BARON, R. A. (1977). *Human aggression.* New York: Plenum Press.

BARON, R. A. (1978). Invasions of personal space and helping: Mediating effects of invader's apparent need. *Journal of Experimental Social Psychology, 14,* 304–312.

BARON, R. A. (1980). Olfaction and human social behavior: Effects of pleasant scents on physical aggression. *Basic Applied Social Psychology, 1,* 163–172.

BARON, R. A. (1983). *Human aggression.* New York: Plenum Press.

BARON, R. A., & BELL, P. A. (1976). Aggression and heat: The influence of ambient temperature, negative affect, and a cooling drink on physical aggression. *Journal of Personality and Social Psychology, 33,* 245–255.

BARTON, S., & HICKS, R. A. (1985). Type A–B behavior and incidence of infectious mononucleosis in college students. *Psychological Reports, 56,* 545–546.

BATESON, G., JACKSON, D., HAYLEY, J., & WEAKLAND, J. (1956). Toward a theory of schizophrenia. *Behavioral Science, 1,* 241–264.

BAUCOM, D. H., BESCH, P. K., CALLAHAN, S. (1985). Relation between testosterone concentration, sex role identity, and personality among females. *Journal of Personality and Social Psychology, 48,* 1218–1226.

BAUMEISTER, A., HAWKINS, W. F., & CROMWELL, R. L. (1964). Need state and activity level. *Psychological Bulletin, 61,* 438–453.

BAUMRIND, D. (1964). Some thoughts on the ethics of research after reading Milgram's "Behavioral study of obedience." *American Psychologist, 19,* 421–423.

BAUMRIND, D. (1975). The contribution of the family to the development of competence in children. *Schizophrenia Bulletin, 1,* 12–37.

BAUMRIND, D. (1985). Research using intentional deception: Ethical issues revisited. *American Psychologist, 40,* 165–174.

BAYLEY, N. (1965). Comparisons of mental and motor test scores for ages 1–15 months by sex, birth order, race, geographical location, and education of parents. *Child Development, 36,* 379–411.

BEACH, F. A. (1977a). Hormonal control of sex-related behavior. In F. A. Beach (Ed.), *Human sexuality in four perspectives.* Baltimore: Johns Hopkins University Press.

BEACH, F. A. (Ed.). (1977b). *Human sexuality in four perspectives.* Baltimore: Johns Hopkins University Press.

BECK, A. T. (1967). *Depression: Causes and Treatment.* Philadelphia: University of Pennsylvania Press.

BECK, A. T. (1976). *Cognitive therapy and emotional disorders.* New York: International Universities Press.

BECK, A. T., & YOUNG, J. E. (1985). Depression. In D. H. Barlow (Ed.), *Clinical handbook of psychological disorders.* New York: Guilford Press.

BÉKÉSY, G. VON. (1928). Theories des Hörens: Die Schwingungsform der Basilarmembran. *Physikalisch Zeitschrift, 29,* 739–810.

BÉKÉSY, G. VON. (1957). The ear. *Scientific American, 197,* 66–78.

BÉKÉSY, G. VON. (1960). *Experiments in learning.* New York: McGraw-Hill.

BELL, P. A., & BARON, R. A. (1976). Aggression and heat: The mediating role of negative affect. *Journal of Applied Social Psychology, 6,* 18–30.

BELL, R. Q., & HARPER, L. V. (Eds.). (1977). *Child effects on adults.* Hillsdale, N.J.: Erlbaum.

BELLACK, A. S. (1976). A comparison of self-reinforcement and self-monitoring in a weight reduction program. *Behavior Therapy, 7,* 68–75.

BEM, D. J. (1967). Self-perception: An alternative interpretation of cognitive dissonance phenomena. *Psychological Review, 74,* 183–200.

BEM, D. J. (1972). Self-perception theory. In L. Berkowitz (Ed.) *Advances in Experimental Social Psychology, (Vol. 6),* New York: Academic Press.

BENNETT, W., & GURIN, J. (1982). *The dieter's dilemma: Eating less and weighing more.* New York: Basic Books.

BENSON, H., & FRIEDMAN, R. (1985). A rebuttal to the conclusions of David S. Holmes's article: "Meditation and somatic arousal reduction." *American Psychologist, 40,* 725–728.

BENSON, H., KOTCH, J. B., CRASSWELLER, K. D., & GREENWOOK, M. M. (1977). Historical and clinical considerations of the relaxation response. *American Scientist, 65,* 441–443.

BENSON, P. L., KARABENICK, S. A., & LERNER, R. M. (1976). Pretty pleases: The effects of physical attractiveness, race, and sex on receiving help. *Journal of Experimental Social Psychology, 12,* 409–415.

BERENT, S. (1981). Lateralization of brain function. In S. B. Filskov & T. J. Boll (Eds.), *Handbook of clinical neuropsychology.* New York: Wiley.

BERGER, P. A. (1978). Medical treatment of mental illness. *Science, 200,* 974–981.

BERGIN, A., & LAMBERT, M. (1978). The evaluation of therapeutic outcomes. In S. Garfield & A. Bergin (Eds.), *Handbook of psychotherapy and behavior change.* New York: Wiley.

BERGLAS, S., & JONES, E. E. (1978). Drug choice as an externalization strategy in response to noncontingent success. *Journal of Personality and Social Psychology, 36,* 405–417.

BERKOWITZ, L. (1981). How guns control us. *Psychology Today, 15,* 11–12.

BERSCHEID, E., DION, K., WALSTER (HATFIELD), E., & WALSTER, G. W. (1971). Physical attractiveness and dating choice: A test of the matching hypothesis. *Journal of Experimental Social Psychology, 7,* 173–189.

BETTS, E. (1982). Relation of locus of control to aspiration level and to competitive anxiety. *Psychological Reports, 51,* 71–76.

BIRREN, J. E. (1974). Psychophysiology and speed of response. *American Psychologist, 29,* 808–815.

BIRREN, J. E. (1983). Aging in America. *American Psychologist, 38,* 298–299.

BIRREN, J. E., BUTLER, R. N., GREENHOUSE, S. W., SOKOLOFF, L., & YARROW, M. R. (Eds.). (1963). *Human aging: A biological and behavioral study.* Bethesda, Md.: U.S. Public Health Service.

BIRREN, J. E., & RENNER, V. J. (1977). Research on the psychology of aging: Principles and experimentation. In J. E. Birren & K. W. Schaie (Eds.), *Handbook of the psychology of aging.* New York: Van Nostrand Reinhold, 3–38.

BIRREN, J. E., & SCHAIE, K. W. (Eds.). (1977). *Handbook of the psychology of aging.* New York: Van Nostrand Reinhold.

BLAKESLEE, A. (1984). Brain's dream center located. *Science Digest, November,* 26.

BORGIDA, E., & CAMPBELL, B. (1982). Belief relevance and attitude-behavior consistency: The moderating role of personal experience. *Journal of Personality and Social Psychology, 42,* 239–247.

BORNSTEIN, M. H. (1975). Qualities of color vision in infancy. *Journal of Experimental Child Psychology, 19,* 401–419.

BORNSTEIN, M. H. (1979). Effects of habituation experience on posthabituation behavior in young infants. Discrimination and generalization among colors. *Developmental Psychology, 15,* 348–349.

BORNSTEIN, M. H., & MARKS, L. E. (January 1982). Color revisionism. *Psychology Today,* 64–66; 68–71.

BOTWINICK, J. (1973). *Aging and Behavior.* New York: Springer.

BOUCHARD, T. J., HESTON, L., ECKERT, E., KEYES, M., &

RESNICK, S. (1981). The Minnesota study of twins reared apart: Project description and sample results in the developmental domain. *Twin Research 3: Intelligence, Personality, and Development.* New York: Alan R. Liss.

BOUCHARD, T. J., JR., & MCGUE, M. (1981). Family studies of intelligence: A review. *Science, 212,* 1055–1059.

BOUSFIELD, W. A. (1953). The occurrence of clustering in the recall of randomly arranged associates. *Journal of General Psychology, 49,* 229–240.

BOWEN, M. (1971). The use of family therapy in clinical practice. In J. Haley (Ed.), *Changing families.* New York: Grune & Stratton.

BOWER, G. H. (1981). Mood and memory. *American Psychologist, 26,* 129–148.

BOWERMAN, M. F. (1976). Semantic factors in the acquisition of rules for word use and sentence construction. In D. M. Morehead & A. E. Morehead (Eds.), *Normal and deficient language.* Baltimore: University Park Press.

BOWKER, R. M. (1985). Variability in the characteristics of pontogeniculooccipital spikes during paradoxical sleep. *Experimental Neurology, 87,* 212–224.

BOWLBY, J. (1969). *Attachment and loss,* Vol. 1, *Attachment.* New York: Basic Books.

BOWMAN, E. S., BLIX, S., & COONS, P. M. (1985). Multiple personality in adolescence: Relationship to incestual experiences. *Journal of the American Academy of Child Psychiatry, 24,* 109–114.

BRADSHAW, J. L., & NETTLETON, N. C. (1981). The nature of hemispheric specialization in man. *Behavior and Brain Sciences, 4,* 51–91.

BRADY, J. V. (1979). Learning and Conditioning. In O. F. Pomerleau & J. P. Brady (Eds.), *Behavioral medicine: Theory and practice.* Baltimore: Williams and Wilkins.

BRAIKER, H. (1984). Are you a type E? Cited in C. S. Schneider, *Women & Stress, The San Diego Union,* March 18, 1984, 2–6.

BRAND, C. (1980). General intelligence and mental speed: Their relationship and development. In M. Friedman, J. P. Das, & V. O'Connor (Eds.), *Intelligence and learning.* New York: Plenum.

BRAY, G. A. (1976). *The obese patient.* Philadelphia: Saunders.

BRAZELTON, T. B. (1979). Effect of prenatal drugs on the behavior of the neonate. *American Journal of Psychiatry, 126,* 1261–1266.

BRECHER, E. (1975). Prevention of the sexually transmitted disease. *Journal of sex research, 11,* 318–328.

BREGGIN, P. R. (1979). *Electroshock: Its brain-disabling effects.* New York: Springer.

BREHM, J. W., & COLE, A. H. (1966). Effects of a favor which reduces freedom. *Journal of Personality and Social Psychology, 3,* 420–426.

BRELAND, K., & BRELAND, M. (1961). The misbehavior of organisms. *American Psychologist, 16,* 681–684.

BREWER, W. F. (1974). There is no convincing evidence for operant or classical conditioning in adult humans. In W. B. Weimer & D. S. Palermo (Eds.), *Cognition and the symbolic processes.* Hillsdale, N.J.: Lawrence Erlbaum Associates.

BRIDDEL, D., & WILSON, G. (1976). Effects of alcohol and expectancy set on male sexual arousal. *Journal of Abnormal Psychology, 85,* 225–234.

BRIGHAM, J. C. (1980). Limiting conditions on the "physical attractiveness stereotype": Attributions about divorce. *Journal of Research in Personality, 14,* 365–375.

BROADBENT, D. E. (1958). *Perception and communication.* New York: Pergamon.

BRODY, J. E. (February, 1977). How doctors can assure more perfect babies. *Woman's Day, 65,* 150; 152; 154.

BROWN, C. J. (1983). The job of F's: A student guide for getting lousy grades. *Teaching of Psychology, 10,* 176–177.

BROWN, J. (1958). Some tests of the decay theory of immediate memory. *Quarterly Journal of Experimental Psychology, 10,* 12–21.

BROWN, J. (1975). *The evolution of behavior.* New York: W. W. Norton.

BROWN, R. (1973). *A first language: The early stages.* Cambridge, Mass.: Harvard University Press.

BROWN, S. A. (1985). Expectancies versus background in the prediction of college drinking patterns. *Journal of Consulting and Clinical Psychology, 53,* 123–130.

BROWNELL, K. D. (1982). Obesity: Understanding and treating a serious, prevalent, and refractory disorder. *Journal of Consulting and Clinical Psychology, 50,* 820–840.

BROWNELL, K. D., & FOREYT, J. P. (1985). *Obesity.* In D. H. Barlow (Ed.), *Clinical handbook of psychological disorders.* New York: The Guilford Press.

BROWNELL, K. D., & STUNKARD, A. J. (1980). Physical activity in the development and control of obesity. In A. J. Stunkard (Ed.), *Obesity.* Philadelphia: Saunders.

BRUCE, D. (1985). The how and why of ecological memory. *Journal of Experimental Psychology: General, 114,* 78–90.

BRUCH, H. (1973). *Eating disorders: Obesity, anorexia nervosa and the person within.* New York: Basic Books.

BUCHSBAUM, M. T. (1984). The Genain quadruplets. *Psychology Today, 18,* 46–51.

BUCKHOUT, R. (1980). Nearly 2,000 witnesses can be wrong. *Bulletin of the Psychonomic Society, 16,* 307–310.

BULLOUGH, V., & BULLOUGH, B. (1977). *Sin, sickness, and sanity.* New York: New American Library.

BURGESS, A., & HOLMSTROM, L. (1979). Adaptive strategies and recovery from rape. *American Journal of Psychiatry, 136,* 1278–1282.

BURR, W. R. (1973). *Theory construction and the sociology of the family.* New York: Wiley.

BUSS, A. R., & POLEY, W. (1977). *Individual differences: Traits and factors.* New York: Gardner Press.

BUTCHER, J. (1986). Personal Communication.

BYRNE, D. (1971). *The attraction paradigm*. New York: Academic Press.

BYRNE, D. (1977). A pregnant pause in the sexual revolution. *Psychology Today*, July, 67–68.

BYRNE, D., & CLORE, G. L. (1970). A reinforcement model of evaluative responses. *Personality: An International Journal*, *1*, 103–128.

BYRNE, D., & LAMBERTH, J. (1971). The effect of erotic stimuli on sex arousal, evaluative responses, and subsequent behavior. *Technical Reports of the Commission on Obscenity and Pornography, 8*, Washington, D.C.; U.S. Government Printing Office.

BYRNE, D., & RHAMEY, R. (1965). Magnitude of positive and negative reinforcements as a determinant of attraction. *Journal of Personality and Social Psychology, 2*, 884–889.

CAIN, W. S. (1979). To know with the nose: Keys to odor identification. *Science, 203*, 467–470.

CALFEE, R. C. (1985). *Experimental methods in psychology*. New York: Holt, Rinehart and Winston.

CAMPOS, J. J., HAITT, S., RAMSAY, D., HENDERSON, D., & SVEJDA, M. (1978). The emergence of fear on the visual cliff. In M. Lewis & L. A. Rosenblum (Eds.), *The development of affect*. New York: Plenum.

CANNON, W. B. (1927). The James-Lange theory of emotion. *American Journal of Psychology, 39*, 106–124.

CANNON, W. B. (1929). *Bodily changes in pain, hunger, fear, and rage* (2nd ed.). New York: Appleton-Century-Crofts.

CARLSON, N. R. (1981). *Physiology of behavior* (2nd ed.). Boston: Allyn and Bacon.

CARLSON, R. A., & DULANY, D. E. (1985). Conscious attention and abstraction in concept learning. *Journal of Experimental Psychology: Learning, Memory, and Cognition, 11*, 45–58.

CARPENTER, E. (1985). Conditioning: It's the thought that counts. *Psychology Today, 19*, 8–10.

CARROLL, J. L., YOLK, K. D., & HYDE, J. S. (1985). Differences between males and females in motives for engaging in sexual intercourse. *Archives of Sexual Behavior, 14*, 131–139.

CARTWRIGHT, R. D. (1978). *A primer on sleep and dreaming*. Reading, Mass.: Addison-Wesley.

CARY, M. S. (1978). Does civil inattention exist in pedestrian passing? *Journal of Personality and Social Psychology, 36*, 1185–1193.

CASEY, R. J., & BERMAN, J. F. (1985). The outcome of psychotherapy with children. *Psychological Bulletin, 98*, 388–400.

CASH, T. F. & DERLEGA, V. J. (1978). The matching hypothesis: Physical attractiveness among same-sexed friends. *Personality and Social Psychology Bulletin, 4*, 240–243.

CASSETTY, J. (Ed.). (1983). *The parental child-support obligation*. Lexington, Mass.: Lexington Books.

CASTENELL, L. A. (1983). Achievement motivation: An investigation of adolescents' achievement patterns. *American Educational Research Journal, 20*, 503–510.

CATON, C. L. (1985). Rehospitalization in chronic schizophrenics. *Journal of Nervous & Mental Disease, 173*, 139–148.

CATTELL, R. B. (1957). *Personality and motivation, structure and measurement*. Yonkers-on-Hudson, N.Y.: World Book.

CATTELL, R. B. (1965). *The scientific analysis of personality*. London: Penguin.

CATTELL, R. B. (1973). Personality pinned down. *Psychology Today, 7*, 40–46.

CATTELL, R. B. (1976). *Comprehensive personality and learning theory*. New York: Springer.

CATTELL, R. B., & KLINE, P. (1976). *The scientific analysis of personality and motivation*. New York: Academic Press.

CAVANAUGH, S., & WETTSTEIN, R. M. (1983). The relationship between severity of depression, cognitive dysfunction, and age in medical inpatients. *American Journal of Psychiatry, 140*, 495–496.

CECH, C. G., & SHOBEN, E. J. (1985). Context effects in symbolic magnitude comparisons. *Journal of Experimental Psychology, 11*, 299–315.

CHAMBLESS, D. L., & GOLDSTEIN, A. J. (1980). Agoraphobia. In A. J. Goldstein & E. B. Foa (Eds.), *Handbook of behavioral interventions*. New York: Wiley.

CHAPMAN, L. J., & CHAPMAN, J. P. (1973). *Disordered thought in schizophrenia*. Englewood Cliffs, N.J.: Prentice-Hall.

CHESSICK, R. D. (1985). Psychoanalytic listening: II. *American Journal of Psychotherapy, 39*, 30–48.

CHEVALIER-SKOLNIKOFF, S. (1981). The Clever Hans phenomenon, cuing, and ape signing: A Piagetian analysis of methods for instructing animals. In T. A. Sebeok & R. Rosenthal (Eds.), *The Clever Hans phenomenon: Communication with horses, whales, apes, and people. Annals of the New York Academy of Sciences* (Vol. 364). New York.

CHRISTENSON, C. Y. (1971). *Kinsey: A biography*. Bloomington, Ind.: Indiana University Press.

CLARKE-STEWARD, K. A. (1978). Popular primers for parents. *American Psychologist, 33*, 359–369.

COHEN, H., ROSEN, R. C., & GOLDSTEIN, L. (1976). Electroencephalographic laterality changes during human sexual orgasm. *Archives of Sexual Behavior, 5*, 189–199.

COHEN, R. M., et al. (1980). Presynaptic noradrenergic regulation during depression and antidepressant drug treatment. *Psychiatric Research, 3*, 93–105.

COKE, J. S., BATSON, C. D., & MCDAVIS, K. (1978). Empathic mediation of helping: A two-stage model. *Journal of Personality and Social Psychology, 36*, 752–766.

COLMAN, A. (1980). Flattery won't get you everywhere. *Psychology Today, 14*, 80–82.

COMMITTEE ON MATERNAL NUTRITION, NATIONAL RESEARCH COUNCIL. (1970). *Maternal nutrition and the course of pregnancy*. Washington, D.C.: National Academy of Sciences.

CONDRY, J. C., & ROSS, D. F. (1985). Sex and aggression: The influence of gender label on the perception of aggression in children. *Child Development, 56*, 225–233.

CONRAD, R. (1964). Acoustic confusions in immediate memory. *British Journal of Psychology, 55*, 75–84.

COOPER, J. (1980). Reducing fears and increasing assertiveness: The role of dissonance reduction. *Journal of Experimental Social Psychology, 16*, 199–213.

CORDES, C. (1986). Intelligence: New definition lies beyond classroom and within mind. *APA Monitor, 17*, 7–9.

CORNSWEET, T. M. (1970). *Visual perception*. New York: Academic Press.

CORYELL, W. (1978). Intrapatient response to ECT and tricyclic antidepressants. *American Journal of Psychiatry, 135*, 1108–1110.

COSTANZO, P. R. (1970). Conformity development as a function of self-blame. *Journal of Personality and Social Psychology, 14*, 366–374.

COWAN, C., THOMPSON, W., & ELLSWORTH, P. C. (1985). The effects of death qualification on juror's predisposition to convict and on the quality of deliberation. *Law and Human Behavior, 2*, 112–118.

CRAIGHEAD, L. W., STUNKARD, A. J., & O'BRIEN, R. M. (1981). Behavior therapy and pharmacotherapy for obesity. *Archives of General Psychiatry, 38*, 763–768.

CRAIK, F.I.M. (1979). Human memory. *Annual Review of Psychology, 30*, 63–102.

CRAIK, F.I.M., & LOCKHART, R. S. (1972). Levels of processing: A framework for memory research. *Journal of Verbal Learning and Verbal Behavior, 11*, 671–784.

CRAIK, F.I.M., & TULVING, E. (1975). Depth of processing and the retention of words in episodic memory. *Journal of Experimental Psychology: General, 104*, 268–294.

CREWS, J., & ALDINGER, E. E. (1967). Effect of chronic exercise on myocardial function. *American Heart Journal, 74*, 536–541.

CROCKETT, D., CLARK, C., & KLONOFF, H. (1981). Introduction—An overview of neuropsychology. In S. B. Filskov & T. J. Boll (Eds.), *Handbook of clinical neuropsychology*. New York: Wiley.

CRONBACH, L. J. (1970). *Essentials of psychological testing* (3rd ed.). New York: Harper & Row.

CROOKS, R., & BAUR, K. (1983). *Our sexuality* (2nd ed.). Menlo Park, Calif.: Benjamin/Cummings.

CROWDER, R. G. (1976). *Principles of learning and memory*. Hillsdale, N.J.: Lawrence Erlbaum Associates.

CZEISLER, C., RICHARDSON, G. S., COLEMAN, R. M., ZIMMERMAN, J. C., MOORE-EDE, M. C., DEMENT, W. C., & WEITZMAN, E. D. (1981). Chronotherapy: Resetting the circadian clocks of patients with delayed sleep phase insomnia. *Sleep, 4*, 1–21.

CZEISLER, C., WEITZMAN, E. D., MOORE-EDE, M. C., ZIMMERMAN, J. C., & KNAUER, R. S. (1980). Human sleep: Its duration and organization depend on its circadian phase. *Science, 210*, 1264–1267.

DAHLKOETTER, J., CALLAHAN, E. J., & LINTON, J. (1979). Obesity and the unbalanced energy equation: Exercise versus eating habit change. *Journal of Consulting and Clinical Psychology, 47*, 898–905.

DANZIGER, K. (1985). The origins of the psychological experiment as a social institution. *American Psychologist, 40*, 133–140.

DARWIN, C. (1859). *Origin of species* (2nd ed.). London: Collier (revised edition, 1909).

DARWIN, C. (1859). *On the origin of species*. (Ed. by J. W. Barrow). New York: Penguin, 1969.

DARWIN, C. (1872). *The expression of the emotions in men and animals*. London: Murray.

DASHIELL, J. F. (1925). A quantitative demonstration of animal drive. *Journal of Comparative and Physiological Psychology, 5*, 205–208.

DAVIS, J. H., HOLT, R. W., SPITZER, C. E., & STASSER, G. (1981). The effects of consensus requirements and multiple decisions on mock juror verdict preferences. *Journal of Experimental Social Psychology, 17*, 1–15.

DAVIS, J. M. (1977). Central biogenic amines and theories of depression and mania. In W. E. Fann, I. Faracan, A. D. Pokorny, & R. L. Williams (Eds.), *Phenomenology and treatment of depression*. New York: Spectrum Publications.

DAVISON, G. C. (1973). Counter-control in behavior modification. In L. A. Hamerlynck, L. C. Handy, & E. J. Mash (Eds.), *Behavior change: Methodology, concepts, and practice*. Champaign, Ill.: Research Press.

DECI, E. L. (1972). Intrinsic motivation, extrinsic reinforcement, and inequity. *Journal of Personality and Social Psychology, 22*, 113–120.

DECI, E. L. (1980). *The psychology of self-determination*. Lexington, Mass.: Lexington Books.

DECI, E. L., & RYAN, R. M. (1980). The empirical exploration of intrinsic motivational processes. In L. Berkowitz (Ed.), *Advances in experimental social psychology* (Vol. 13). New York: Academic Press.

DEJONG, W. (1979). An examination of self-perception mediation of the foot-in-the-door effect. *Journal of Personality and Social Psychology, 37*, 2221–2239.

DEMPSTER, F. N. (1985). Proactive interference in sentence recall: Topic-similarity effects and individual differences. *Memory & Cognition, 13*, 81–89.

DENNIS, H. (Ed.). (1984). *Retirement preparation*. Lexington, Mass.: Lexington Books.

DETTERMAN, D. K. (1982). Does "g" exist? *Intelligence, 6*, 99–108.

DEVALOIS, R. L. (1965a). Analysis and coding of color vision in the primate visual system. *Cold Spring Harbor Symposia on Quantitative Biology, 30*, 567–579.

DEVALOIS, R. L. (1965b). Behavioral and electrophysiological studies of primate vision. In W. D. Neff (Ed.), *Contributions to sensory physiology* (Vol. 1). New York: Academic Press.

DEY, F. L. (1970). Auditory fatigue and predicted permanent hearing defects from rock and roll music. *New England Journal of Medicine, 282,* 467–470.

DIGMAN, J. M., & INOUYE, J. (1986). Further specification of the five robust factors of personality. *Journal of Personality and Social Psychology, 50,* 116–123.

DIGNAN, M., DENSON, D., ANSPAUGH, D., & C'MICH, D. (1985). Effects of sex education on sexual behaviors of college students. *Adolescence, 20,* 171–183.

DIMATTEO, M. R., & DINICOLA, B. D. (1982). Achieving patient compliance. The psychology of the medical practitioner role. New York: Pergamon.

DION, K. K., BERSCHEID, E., & WALSTER, E. (1972). What is beautiful is good. *Journal of Personality and Social Psychology, 24,* 285–290.

DIPBOYE, R. L., FROMKIN, H. L. & WILBACK, K. (1975). The importance of applicant sex, attractiveness, and scholastic standing in evaluation of job applicant resumes. *Journal of Applied Psychology, 60,* 39–43.

DOCTER, R. (1985). Transsexual surgery at 74: A case report. *Archives of Sexual Behavior, 14,* 271–277.

DOLLARD, J., DOBB, L. W., MILLER, N. E., MOWRER, O. H., & SEARS. R. R. (1939). *Frustration and aggression.* New Haven, Conn.: Yale University Press.

DOLLARD, J., & MILLER, N. E. (1950). *Personality and psychotherapy: An analysis in terms of learning, thinking, and culture.* New York: McGraw-Hill.

DONOVAN, W. L., & LEAVITT, L. A. (1985). Physiologic assessment of mother-infant attachment. *Journal of the American Academy of Child Psychiatry, 24,* 65–70.

DOUVAN, E., & ADELSON, J. (1966). *The adolescent experience.* New York: Wiley.

DULANY, D. E. (1968). Awareness, rules, and propositional control: A confrontation with S–R behavior theory. In T. R. Dixon & D. L. Horton (Eds.), *Verbal behavior and general behavior theory.* Englewood Cliffs, N.J.: Prentice-Hall.

DUNST, C. J., BROOKS, P. H., & DOXSEY, P. A. (1982). Characteristics of hiding places and the transition to stage IV performance in object performance tasks. *Developmental Psychology, 18,* 671–681.

EAGLY, A. H. (1974). Comprehensibility of persuasive arguments as a determinant of opinion change. *Journal of Personality and Social Psychology, 29,* 758–773.

EAGLY, A. H., & HIMMELFARB, S. (1978). Attitudes and opinions. In M. R. Rosenzweig & L. W. Porter (Eds.), *Annual review of psychology* (Vol. 29). Palo Alto, Calif.: Annual Reviews.

EAGLY, A. H., WOOD, W., & CHAIKEN, S. (1978). Causal inferences about communicators and their effect on opinion change. *Journal of Personality and Social Psychology, 36,* 424–435.

EARLE, J.B.B. (1981). Cerebral laterality and meditation: A review of the literature. *Journal of Transpersonal Psychology, 13,* 155–173.

EBBESEN, E., KJOS, G., & KONEČNI, V. (1976). Spatial ecology: Its effects on the choice of friends and enemies. *Journal of Experimental Social Psychology, 12,* 505–518.

EBBINGHAUS, H. (1885). *Ueber das gedächtnis: Untersuchen zur experimentellen psychologie* ("On memory") (H. A. Ruger & C. E. Bussenius, trans.). New York: Dover, 1964.

ECKBLAD, M., & CHAPMAN, L. J. (1983). Magical ideation as an indicator of schizotypy. *Journal of Consulting & Clinical Psychology, 51,* 215–225.

EDNEY, J. J. (1975). Territoriality and control: A field experiment. *Journal of Personality and Social Psychology, 31,* 1108–1115.

EGELAND, J. A. (1985). A family study of risk for bipolar disorders. Presented at the 1985 Annual Meeting of the American Psychiatric Association, Dallas.

EHRHARDT, A. A., & MEYER-BAHLBURG, H.F.L. (1981). Effects of prenatal sex hormones on gender-related behavior. *Science, 211,* 1312–1318.

EIBL-EIBESFELDT, I. (1972). *Love and Hate.* Holt, Rinehart and Winston.

EIBL-EIBESFELDT, I. (1975). *Ethology: The biology of behavior.* (2nd ed., trans. E. Klinghammer) New York: Holt, Rinehart and Winston.

EISEN, S. V. (1979). Actor-observer differences in information inferences and causal attribution. *Journal of Personality and Social Psychology, 37,* 261–272.

EISERT, D. C., & KAHLE, L. R. (1982). Self-evaluation and social comparison of physical and role change during adolescence: A longitudinal analysis. *Child Development, 53,* 98–104.

EKMAN, P., LEVENSON, R. W., & FRIESEN, W. V. (1983). Autonomic nervous system activity distinguishes among emotions. *Science, 221,* 1208–1210.

EKMAN, P., SORENSON, E. R., & FRIESEN, W. V. (1969). Pan-cultural elements in facial displays of emotion. *Science, 164,* 86–88.

ELLIOTT, G. R., & EISDORFER, C. (Eds.). (1982). *Stress and human health.* New York: Springer.

ELLIS, A. (1962). *Reason and emotion in psychotherapy.* New York: Lyle Stuart Press.

ELLIS, A. (1984). Rational-emotive therapy. In R. J. Corsini (Ed.), *Current psychotherapies* (3rd ed.). Itasca, Ill.: F. E. Peacock.

ELLIS, H. C., THOMAS, R. L., MCFARLAND, A. D., & LANE, J. W. (1985). Emotional mood states and retrieval in episodic memory. *Journal of Experimental Psychology, 11,* 363–370.

ELLSWORTH, P. C. & CARLSMITH, J. M. (1973). Eye contact and gaze aversion in an aggressive encounter. *Journal of Personality and Social Psychology, 28,* 280–292.

EMMELKAMP, P.M.G. (1974). Self-observation versus flooding in the treatment of agoraphobia. *Behaviour Research & Therapy, 12,* 229–237.

ENDICOTT, J. (1986). Diagnosis of schizophrenia. *Archives of General Psychiatry, 43,* 13–19.

EPSTEIN, A. W. (1985). The waking event-dream interval. *American Journal of Psychiatry, 142,* 123–128.

EPSTEIN, F., & ECKOFF, R. (1967). The epidemiology of high blood pressure—geographic distributions and etiological factors. In J. Stamler, R. Stamler, & T. Pullman (Eds.), *The epidemiology of hypertension.* New York: Grune and Stratton.

ERIKSON, E. H. (1950). In M. J. E. Senn (Ed.), *Symposium on the healthy personality.* New York: Josiah Macy, Jr., Foundation.

ERIKSON, E. H. (1963). *Childhood and society.* New York: Norton.

ERIKSON, E. H. (1972). Eight stages of man. In C. C. Lavatell & F. Stendler (Eds.), *Readings in child behavior and child development.* New York: Harcourt Brace Jovanovich.

ERIKSON, E. H. (1974). *Dimensions of a new identity.* New York: Norton.

ERLENMEYER-KIMLING, L., & JARVICK, L. F. (1963). Genetics and intelligence: A review. *Science, 142,* 1477–1479.

ERON, L. D. (1982). Parent-child interaction, television violence, and aggression of children. *American Psychologist, 37,* 197–221.

ESMAN, A. (1970). Toward an understanding of racism. *Psychiatry and Social Science Review, 4,* 7–9.

ETAUGH, C. (1980). Effects of nonmaternal care on children: Research evidence and popular view. *American Psychologist, 35,* 309–319.

EVANS, D. L., & NEMEROFF, C. B. (1983). The dexamethasone suppression test in mixed bipolar disorder. *American Journal of Psychiatry, 140,* 615–617.

EVANS, F. J. (1979). Hypnosis and sleep: Techniques for exploring cognitive activity during sleep. In E. Fromm & R. E. Shor (Eds.), *Hypnosis: Developments in research and new perspectives* (2nd ed.). New York: Aldine.

EVANS, R. I. (1979). Smoking in children and adolescents. Psychological determinants and prevention strategies. In *Smoking and health: A report of the surgeon general.* United States Department of Health and Human Services. Washington, D.C.: U.S. Government Printing Office.

EXNER, J. E., JR. (1974). *The Rorschach: A comprehensive system.* New York: Wiley.

EXNER, J. E., JR. (1981). But it's only an inkblot. *Journal of Personality Assessment, 44,* 562–577.

EYER, J. (1979). Hypertension as a disease of modern society. In C. A. Garfield, (Ed.), *Stress and survival.* St. Louis, Mosby.

EYSENCK, H. J. (1967). *The biological basis of personality.* Springfield, Ill.: Charles C Thomas.

EYSENCK, H. J. (1970). *The structure of human personality.* London: Methuen.

EYSENCK, H. J. (1975). *The inequality of man.* San Diego: Edits Publishers.

EYSENCK, H. J. (1978). An exercise in mega-silliness. *American Psychologist, 33,* 517.

EYSENCK, H. J. (Ed.). (1982). *A model for intelligence.* Berlin: Springer-Verlag.

EYSENCK, H. J., & EYSENCK, S.B.G. (1969). *Personality structure and measurement.* London: Routledge and Kegan Paul.

FANTZ, R. L. (1958). Pattern vision in young infants. *Psychological Record, 8,* 43–47.

FANTZ, R. L. (1965). Visual perception from birth as shown by pattern selectivity. *Annals of the New York Academy of Science, 118,* 793–814.

FARAH, M. J., GAZZANIGA, M. S., HOLTZMAN, J. D., & KOSSLYN, S. M. (1985). A left hemisphere basis for visual mental imagery? *Neuropsychologia, 23,* 115–118.

FAZIO, R. H., JEAW-MEI, C., MCDONEL, E. C., & SHERMAN, S. J. (1982). Attitude accessibility, attitude-behavior consistency, and the strength of the object-evaluation association. *Journal of Experimental Social Psychology, 18,* 339–357.

FAZIO, R. H., SHERMAN, S. J., & HERR, P. M. (1982). The feature-positive effect in the self-perception process: Does not doing matter as much as doing? *Journal of Personality and Social Psychology, 42,* 404–411.

FEDIO, P., & VAN BUREN, M. (1975). Memory and perceptual deficits during electrical stimulation in left and right thalamus and parietal subcortex. *Brain and Language, 1–2,* 78–100.

FEIN, G. G., SCHWARTZ, P. M., JACOBSON, S. W., & JACOBSON, J. L. (1983). Environmental toxins and behavioral development. *American Psychologist, 38,* 1188–1197.

FERGUSON, T. J., & RULE, B. G. (1982). Influence of inferential set, outcome intent, and outcome severity on children's moral judgments. *Developmental Psychology, 18,* 843–851.

FERGUSSON, D. M., HORWOOD, L. J., GRETTON, M. E., & SHANNON, F. T. (1985). Family life events, maternal depression, and maternal and teacher descriptions of child behavior. *Pediatrics, 75,* 30–35.

FERSTER, C. B. (1966). Animal behavior and mental illness. *Psychological Records, 16,* 345–356.

FERSTER, C. B., & SKINNER, B. F. (1957). *Schedules of reinforcement.* New York: Appleton-Century-Crofts.

FESHBACH, S. (1970). Aggression. In P. H. Mussen (Ed.), *Carmichael's manual of child psychology* (3rd ed., Vol. 2). New York: Wiley.

FESTINGER, L. (1954). A theory of social comparison processes. *Human Relations, 7,* 117–140.

FESTINGER, L., & CARLSMITH, J. M. (1959). Cognitive consequences of forced compliance. *Journal of Abnormal and Social Psychology, 58,* 203–210.

FESTINGER, L., SCHACHTER, S., & BACK, K. (1950). *Social pressures in informal groups: A study of human factors in housing.* New York: Harper.

FINCHER, J. (1981). *The brain: Mystery of matter and mind.* Washington, D.C.: U.S. News Books.

FISCHER, D. H. (1977). *Growing old in America.* New York: Oxford University Press.

FISHER, A. (1981). *The healthy heart.* Alexandria, Va.:

Time-Life Books.

FISHER, J. D., BELL, P. A., & LOOMIS, R. (1984). *Environmental psychology* (2nd ed.). New York: Holt, Rinehart & Winston.

FISHER, R. J. (1982). The professional practice of applied social psychology: Identity, training, and certification. In L. Bickman (Ed.), *Applied social psychology annual 3*. Beverly Hills, Calif.: Sage.

FISHER, S., & GREENBERG, R. P. (1977). *The scientific credibility of Freud's theories and therapy*. New York: Basic Books.

FISKE, S. T., & TAYLOR, S. E. (1983). *Social cognition*. Reading, Mass.: Addison-Wesley.

FLAVELL, J. H. (1977). *Cognitive development*. Englewood Cliffs, N.J.: Prentice-Hall.

FOLKINS, C. H., & SIME, W. E. (1981). Physical fitness training and mental health. *American Psychologist, 36*, 373–389.

FOLKMAN, S., & LAZARUS, R. S. (1985). If it changes it must be a process: Study of emotion and coping during three stages of a college examination. *Journal of Personality and Social Psychology, 48*, 150–170.

FOX, R. E. (1976). Family therapy. In I. B. Weiner (Ed.), *Clinical methods in psychology*. New York: Wiley.

FOUTS, R. S., KIMBALL, G. H., DAVIS, D. L., & MELLGREN, R. L. (1979). *Washoe and her children*. Paper presented at the Psychonomics Meeting, Phoenix, Ariz., Nov.

FRANKISH, C. (1985). Modality-specific grouping effects in short-term memory. *Journal of Memory and Language, 24*, 200–209.

FRASER, C. (1971). Group risk-taking and group polarization. *European Journal of Social Psychology, 1*, 493–510.

FREDERICK, C. J. (1981). Suicide prevention and crisis intervention in mental health emergencies. In C. E. Walker (Ed.), *Clinical practice in psychology*. New York: Pergamon Press.

FREDERICKS, L. E. (1980). The value of teaching hypnosis in the practice of anesthesiology. *International Journal of Clinical and Experimental Hypnosis, 28*, 6–15.

FREEDMAN, J. L., & FRASER, S. C. (1966). Compliance without pressure: The foot-in-the-door technique. *Journal of Personality and Social Psychology, 4*, 195–202.

FREIS, E. D. (1976). Salt, volume, and the prevention of hypertension. *Circulation, 53*, 509–594.

FREUD, S. (1915). Repression. In *standard edition*. Vol. 14. London: Hogarth Press. 1957.

FREUD, S. (1925). Character and anal erotism. In S. Freud, *Collected papers*. London: Institute for Psychoanalysis and Hogarth Press. Vol. 2.

FREUD, S. (1933). New introductory lectures on psycho-analysis. In *standard edition*. Vol. 22. London: Hogarth Press, 1964.

FREUD, S. (1940). An outline of psycho-analysis. In *standard edition*. Vol. 23. London: Hogarth Press, 1964. (First German edition, 1940).

FREUD, S. (1946). *The ego and the mechanism of defense*. New York: International Universities Press.

FRIEDMAN, H. S., HALL, J. A., & HARRIS, M. J. (1985). Type A behavior, nonverbal expressive style, and health. *Journal of Personality and Social Psychology, 48*, 1299–1315.

FRIEDMAN, M. (1985). Survivor guilt in the pathogenesis of anorexia nervosa. *Psychiatry, 48*, 25–39.

FRIEDMAN, M., & ROSENMAN, R. (1974). *Type A behavior and your heart*. New York: Knopf.

FRODI, A. (1977). Sexual arousal, situational restrictiveness, and aggressive behavior. *Journal of Research in Personality, 11*, 48–58.

GABRIELLI, W., & PLOMIN, R. (1985). Drinking behavior in the Colorado adoptee and twin sample. *Journal of Studies on Alcohol, 46*, 24–31.

GALANTER, E. (1962). Contemporary psychophysics. In R. Brown, E. Galanter, E. H. Hess, & C. Mandler (Eds.), *New directions in psychology* (Vol. 1). New York: Holt, Rinehart & Winston.

GARDNER, R. (1970). *The boys' and girls' book about divorce*. New York: Jason Aronson.

GARDNER, R. A., & GARDNER, B. T. (1975). Communication with a young chimpanzee: Washoe's vocabulary. In R. Chauvin (Ed.), *Edition du Centre National de la Recherche Scientifique*, Paris.

GARFIELD, S. L. (1981). Psychotherapy: A 40-year appraisal. *American Psychologist, 36*, 174–183.

GARRISON, W., EARLS, F., & KINDLON, D. (1984). Temperament characteristics and behavioral adjustment. *Journal of Clinical Child Psychology, 13*, 298–303.

GARROW, J. (1978). The regulation of energy expenditure. In G. A. Bray (Ed.), *Recent advances in obesity research* (vol. 2). London: Newman.

GATES, A. I. (1917). Recitation as a factor in memorizing. *Archives of Psychology, 6*, No. 40.

GAZZANIGA, M. S. (1970). *The bisected brain*. New York: Appleton-Century-Crofts.

GEEN, R. G. (1978). Effects of attack and uncontrollable noise on aggression. *Journal of Research in Personality, 12*, 15–39.

GEISELMAN, R. E., & BAGHERI, B. (1985). Repetition effects in directed forgetting: Evidence for retrieval inhibition. *Memory & Cognition, 13*, 57–62.

GELDARD, F. A. (1972). *The human senses* (2nd ed.). New York: Wiley.

GERSHON, E., DUNNER, D., & GOODWIN, F. (1971). Toward a biology of affective disorders: Genetic contributions. *Archives of General Psychiatry, 25*, 1–15.

GESCHWIND, N. (1982). Mathematical genius. *Science*. 141–144.

GIBSON, E. J., & WALK, R. D. (1960). The "visual cliff." *Scientific American, 202*, 67–71.

GIBSON, J. J. (1950). *The perception of the visual world*. Boston: Houghton Mifflin.

GIBSON, J. J. (1966). *The senses considered as perceptual systems*. Boston: Houghton Mifflin.

GILLIGAN, C. (1982). In a different voice: Psychological theory and woman's development. Cambridge, Mass.: Harvard University Press.

GLASS, D. C. (1977). *Behavior patterns, stress, and coronary disease.* Hillsdale, N.J.: Lawrence Erlbaum Associates.

GLASS, D. C., & SINGER, J. E. (1972). *Urban stress.* New York: Academic Press.

GLISKY, E. L., & RABINOWITZ, J. C. (1985). Enhancing the generation effect through repetition of operations. *Journal of Experimental Psychology: Learning, Memory, and Cognition, 11,* 193–205.

GLOVER, J. A. (1980). A creativity-training workshop: Short-term, long-term, and transfer effects. *The Journal of Genetic Psychology, 136,* 3–16.

GOLDSTEIN, J. H., DAVIS, R. W., & HERMAN, D. (1975). Escalation of aggression: Experimental studies. *Journal of Personality and Social Psychology, 31,* 162–170.

GOLDSTEIN, M. J. (1973). Exposure to erotic stimuli and sexual deviance. *Journal of Social Issues, 29,* 197–220.

GOODMAN, R. E., ANDERSON, D. C., BULLOCK, D. E. SHEFFIELD, B., LYNCH, S. S., & BUTT, W. R. (1985). Study of the effect of estradiol on gonadotrophin levels in untreated male-to-female transsexuals. *Archives of Sexual Behavior, 14,* 141–146.

GORDON & SNYDER (1986). *Personal issues in human sexuality.* Newton, Mass.: Allyn and Bacon.

GORMAN, J. M., FYER, A. F., GLICKLISH, J., KING, D. L., & KLEIN, D. F. (1981). Mitral valve prolapse and panic disorders: Effect of Imipramine. In D. F. Klein & J. Rabkin (Eds.), *Anxiety: New research and changing concepts.* New York: Raven Press.

GOTTESMAN, I. I., & SHIELDS, J. (1976). A critical review of recent adoption, twin, and family studies of schizophrenia: Behavioral genetics perspectives. *Schizophrenia Bulletin, 2,* 360–401.

GOULD, R. L. (1978). *Transformations.* New York: Simon & Schuster.

GRAF, P., SHIMAMURA, A. P., & SQUIRE, L. R. (1985). Priming across modalities and priming across category levels: Extending the domain of preserved function in amnesia. *Journal of Experimental Psychology: Learning, Memory, and Cognition, 11,* 386–396.

GREEN, D. M., & BIRDSALL, T. G. (1978). Detection and recognition. *Psychological Review, 85,* 192–206.

GREEN, D. M., & SWETS, J. A. (1966). *Signal detection theory and psychophysics.* New York: Wiley.

GREENE, J. W., WALKER, L. S., HICKSON, G., & THOMPSON, J. (1985). Stressful life events and somatic complaints in adolescents. *Pediatrics, 75,* 19–22.

GREENGLASS, E. (1985). A social-psychological view of marriage for women. *International Journal of Women's Studies, 8,* 24–31.

GREGORY, R. L. (1968). Visual illusion. *Scientific American, 219,* 66–76.

GREGORY, R. L., & WALLACE, J. G. (1963). Recovery from early blindness: A case study. *Experimental Psychology Society Monograph,* No. 2, whole.

GRIFFITHS, M., & PAYNE, P. R. (1976). Energy expendi-

ture in small children of obese and non-obese mothers. *Nature, 260,* 698–700.

GRIMES, A. M., GRADY, C. L., FOSTER, N. L., SUNDERLAND, T., & PATRONAS, N. J. (1985). Central auditory function in Alzheimer's disease. *Neurology, 35,* 352–358.

GRINKER, R. R. (1969). An essay on schizophrenia and science. *Archives of General Psychiatry, 20,* 1–24.

GRUBER, H. E. (1973). Courage and cognitive growth in children and scientists. In M. Schwebel & P. Raph (Eds.), *Piaget in the classroom.* New York: Basic Books.

GRUENEICH, R. (1982). The development of children's integration rules for making moral judgments. *Child Development, 53,* 887–894.

GUGGENHEIM, F. G., & NADELSON, C. (Eds.). (1982). *Major psychiatric disorders.* New York: Elsevier Biomedical.

GUIDANO, V. F., & LIOTTI, G. (1983). *Cognitive processes and emotional disorders: A structural approach to psychotherapy.* New York: Guilford Press.

GUILFORD, J. (1966). *Factors related to successful abstinence from smoking: Final report.* Los Angeles: American Institutes for Research.

GWINUP, G. (1975). The effect of exercise alone on the weight of obese women. *Archives of Internal Medicine, 135,* 676–680.

GWIRTSMAN, H. E., ROY-BYRNE, P., YAGER, J., & GERNER, R. H. (1983). Neuroendocrine abnormalities in bulimia (and anorexia nervosa). *American Journal of Psychiatry, 140,* 559–563.

GYNTHER, M. D., & GYNTHER, R. A. (1976). Personality inventories. In I. B. Weiner (Ed.), *Clinical methods in psychology.* New York: Wiley.

HABER, R. N. (1969). Eidetic images. *Scientific American, 220,* 36–55.

HABER, R. N. (1978). Visual perception. *Annual Review of Psychology, 29,* 31–59.

HACKMAN, J. R. (1977). Work design. In J. R. Hackman & J. L. Suttle (Eds.), *Improving life at work.* Santa Monica, Calif.: Goodyear.

HAFNER, R. J. (1982). The marital context of the agoraphobic syndrome. In D. L. Chambless & A. J. Goldstein (Eds.), *Agoraphobia: Multiple perspectives on theory and treatment.* New York: Wiley.

HALEY, J. (1980). *Leaving home.* New York: McGraw-Hill.

HALL, E. (1966). *The hidden dimension.* Garden City, N.Y.: Doubleday.

HALMI, K. A., FALK, J. R., & SCHWARTZ, E. (1981). Binge eating and vomiting: A survey of a college population. *Psychological Medicine, 11,* 697–706.

HAMER, B. (1982). All in the family. *Science Digest, 3,* (July/Aug.).

HANSEN, S. L., & DARLING, C. A. (1985). Attitudes of adolescents toward division of labor in the home. *Adolescence, 20,* 61–72.

HANSON, J. W. (1977). Unpublished paper.

HANSON, J. W., JONES, K. L., & SMITH, D. W. (1976). Fetal alcohol syndrome: Experience with 41 patients. *Journal of the American Medical Association, 235,* 1458–1460.

HARACKIEWICZ, J. M., SANSONE, C., & MANDERLINK, G. (1985). Competence, achievement orientation, and intrinsic motivation: A process analysis. *Journal of Personality and Social Psychology, 48,* 493–508.

HARDING, J., PROSHANSKY, H., KUTNER, B., & CHEIN, I. (1969). Prejudice and ethnic relations. In G. Lindzey & E. Aronson (Eds.), *Handbook of social psychology* (Vol. 5) (2nd ed.). Reading, Mass.: Addison-Wesley.

HARLOW, H. F. (1958). The nature of love. *American Psychologist, 13,* 673–685.

HARMON, L. R. (1963). The development of a criterion of scientific competence. In C. W. Taylor & F. Barron (Eds.), *Scientific creativity: Its recognition and development.* New York: Wiley.

HARRIS, M. B. (1983). Clothing: Communication, compliance, and choice. *Journal of Applied Social Psychology, 13,* 88–97.

HARTMAN, N., KRAMER, R., BROWN, W. T., & DEVEREUX, R. B. (1982). Panic disorder in patients with mitral valve prolapse. *American Journal of Psychiatry, 139,* 669–670.

HASS, E. J. & WHIPPLE, J. L. (1985). Effects of a concurrent memory task on hemispheric asymmetries in categorization. *Brain and Cognition, 4,* 13–26.

HATFIELD, E., & TRAUPMANN, J. (1981). Intimate relationships: A perspective from equity theory. In S. Duck & R. Gilmour (Eds.), *Personal relationships 1: Studying personal relationships.* New York: Academic Press.

HATFIELD, G., & EPSTEIN, W. (1985). The status of the minimum principle in the theoretical analysis of visual perception. *Psychological Bulletin, 97,* 155–186.

HATHAWAY, S. R., & MCKINLEY, J. C. (1943). *Manual for the Minnesota Multiphasic Personality Inventory.* New York: Psychological Corporation.

HATZENBUEHLER, L., PARPAL, M., & MATTHEWS, L. (1983). Classifying college students as depressed or nondepressed using the Beck Depression Inventory: An empirical analysis. *Journal of Consulting & Clinical Psychology, 51,* 360–366.

HAYDEN, B. C. (1981). Rorschach Cards IV and VII revisited. *Journal of Personality Assessment, 45,* 226–229.

HEARST, E. (1975). The classical-instrumental distinction: Reflexes, voluntary behavior, and categories of associative learning. In W. K. Estes (Ed.), *Handbook of learning and cognitive processes* (Vol. 2). Hillsdale, N.J.: Lawrence Erlbaum Associates.

HEARST, E. (1979). One hundred years: Themes and perspectives. In E. Hearst (Ed.). *The first century of experimental psychology.* Hillsdale, N.J.: Lawrence Erlbaum.

HEATH, R. G. (1972). Pleasure and brain activity in man. *Journal of Nervous and Mental Disease, 154,* 3–18.

HEBB, D. O. (1949). *The organization of behavior: A neuropsychological theory.* New York: Wiley.

HEBB, D. (1955). Drives and the CNS. *Psychological Review, 62,* 243–254.

HEBER, R., GARBER, H., HARRINGTON, S., HOFFMAN, C., & FARLENDER, C. (1972). Rehabilitation of families at risk for mental retardation. Progress report, December, Rehabilitation Research and Training Center and Mental Retardation, University of Wisconsin, Madison, Wisconsin.

HEIDER, F. (1944). Social perception and phenomenal causality. *Psychological Review, 51,* 358–374.

HEIDER, F. (1958). *The psychology of interpersonal relations.* New York: Wiley.

HELCOMB, H., & THOMAS, E. C. Nurturing productive thinking in able students. *The Journal of General Psychology,* 1981, *104,* 67–79.

HELMHOLTZ, H.L.F. VON (1896). *Handbuch der physiologischen optik* (2nd ed.). Hamburg: Voss.

HERBERT, J. R. (1977). Periodic suspension of respiration during the transcendental meditation technique. In D. Orme-Johnson & T. Farrow (Eds.), *Scientific research on the transcendental meditation program* (Vol. 1, pp. 134–135). Los Angeles: Maharishi European Research University Press.

HERON, W. (1957). The pathology of boredom. *Scientific American, 196,* 52–56.

HERRNSTEIN, R. J. (1982). IQ testing and the media. *Atlantic Monthly,* Aug., 68–74.

HESS, W. R. (1927). Stammgarglien-reizversuche. (Verh. Deutsch. physiol. Ges., Sept., Ber. ges. Physiol., 1928, *42,* 554. (Cited in Thompson, R. F., *Foundations of physiological psychology.* New York: Harper & Row.)

HESTON, L. L. (1966). Psychiatric disorders in foster home reared children of schizophrenic mothers. *British Journal of Psychiatry, 112,* 819–825.

HESTON, L. L. (1970). The genetics of schizophrenic and schizoid disease. *Science, 167,* 249–256.

HESTON, L., & SHIELDS, J. (1968). Homosexuality in twins. *Archives of General Psychiatry, 18,* 149–160.

HETHERINGTON, A. W., & RANSON, S. W. (1939). Experimental hypothalamohypophyseal obesity in the rat. *Proceedings of the Society for Experimental Biology and Medicine, 41,* 465–466.

HIGBEE, K. L. (1969). Fifteen years of fear arousal: Research on threat appeals: 1953–1968. *Psychological Bulletin, 72,* 426–444.

HIGGINS, S. T., & MORRIS, E. K. (1984). Generality of free-operant avoidance conditioning to human behavior. *Psychological Bulletin, 96,* 247–272.

HILGARD, E. R. (1979). Divided consciousness in hypnosis: The implications of the hidden observer. In E. Fromm & R. E. Shor (Eds.), *Hypnosis: Developments in research and new perspectives* (2nd ed.). New York: Aldine.

HILL, C. T., & STULL, D. E. (1981). Sex differences in effects of social and value similarity in same-sex friendship. *Journal of Personality and Social Psychology, 41,* 488–502.

HINES, D., GLISTA, J., & BYERS, B. (1985). Perceptual interference and hemispheric specialization. *Brain and Cognition, 4,* 76–89.

HITE, S. (1981). *The Hite report on male sexuality.* New York: Alfred A. Knopf.

HOBSON, J. A., & MCCARLEY, R. W. (1977). The brain as a dream state generator: An activation-synthesis hypothesis of the dream process. *American Journal of Psychiatry, 134,* 1335–1348.

HOCHBERG, J. E. (1978). *Perception* (2nd ed.). Englewood Cliffs, N.J.: Prentice-Hall.

HOCHBERG, J. E. (1979). Sensation and perception. In E. Hearst (Ed.), *The first century of experimental psychology.* Hillsdale, N.J.: Lawrence Erlbaum.

HOEBEL, B., & TEITELBAUM, P. (1962). Hypothalamic control of feeding and self-stimulation. *Science, 135,* 375–377.

HOFFMAN, L. W. (1979). Maternal employment: 1979. *American Psychologist, 34,* 859–865.

HOFFMAN, M. L. (1981). Is altruism part of human nature? *Journal of Personality and Social Psychology, 40,* 121–137.

HOFLING, C. K. (1968). *Textbook of psychiatry for medical practice* (2nd ed.). Philadelphia: Lippincott.

HOFMANN, A. (1980). *My problem child.* New York: McGraw-Hill.

HOGAN, R. M. & KINTSCH, W. (1971). Differential effects of study and test trials on long-term recognition and recall. *Journal of Verbal Learning and Verbal Behavior, 10,* 562–567.

HOLAHAN, C. J. & MOOS, R. H. (1985). Life stress and health: Personality, coping, and family support in stress resistance. *Journal of Personality and Social Psychology, 49,* 739–747.

HOLMES, D. S. (1974). Investigations of repression: Differential recall of material experimentally or naturally associated with ego threat. *Psychological Bulletin, 81,* 632–653.

HOLMES, D. S. (1984). Meditation and somatic arousal reduction: A review of the experimental evidence. *American Psychologist, 39,* 1–10.

HOLMES, D. S. (1985a). To meditate or to simply rest, that is the question: A response to the comments of Shapiro. *American Psychologist, 40,* 722–725.

HOLMES, D. S. (1985b). To meditate or rest? The answer is rest. *American Psychologist, 40,* 728–731.

HOLMES, K. (1982). *Natural history of herpes: Current trends in treatment.* Paper presented at the Herpes Symposium, Oregon Health Sciences University, Portland, April 2.

HOLMES, T. H., & RAHE, R. H. (1967). The social readjustment rating scale. *Journal of Psychosomatic Research, 2,* 213–218.

HOPEFUL-HARRIS, J. A. (1980). Rehabilitation of the cardiac patient: Improving compliance with an exercise program. *American Journal of Nursing, 3,* 449–451.

HOPSON, J. L. (1979). *Scent signals: The silent language of sex.* New York: Morrow.

HORN, J. L. (1979). Trends in the measurement of intelligence. In R. J. Sternberg & D. K. Detterman (Eds.), *Human Intelligence: Perspectives on its theory and measurement.* Norwood, N.J.: Ablex.

HORNE, J. A., & MOORE, V. J. (1985). Sleep EEG effects of exercise with and without additional body cooling. *Electroencephalograph and Clinical Neurophysiology, 60,* 33–38.

HORNEY, K. (1937). *The neurotic personality of our time.* New York: Norton.

HORNEY, K. (1942). *Self-analysis.* New York: Norton.

HORNEY, K. (1967). *Feminine psychology. New York:* Norton.

HOVLAND, C., JANIS, I., & KELLEY, H. H. (1953). *Communication and persuasion.* New Haven, Conn.: Yale University Press.

HOVLAND, C., LUMSDAINE, A. A., & SHEFFIELD, F. D. (1949). *Experiments on mass communication.* Princeton, N.J.: Princeton University Press.

HOWE, M.J.A. Biographical evidence and the development of outstanding individuals. *American Psychologist, 1982, 37,* 1071–1081.

HUBEL, D. H., & WIESEL, T. N. (1962). Receptive fields, binocular interaction, and functional architecture in the cat's visual center. *Journal of Physiology, 160,* 106–154.

HUBER, V. L. (1985). Comparison of monetary reinforcers and goal setting as learning incentives. *Psychological Reports, 56,* 223–235.

HUBERT, H. B., FABSITY, R. R., & FEINLEIB, M. (1980). Olfactory sensitivity in humans: Genetic versus environmental control. *Science, 208,* 607–608.

HUESMANN, L. R. (1983). Television violence and aggressive behavior. In D. Pearl & L. Bouthilet (Eds.), *Television and behavior: Ten years of scientific progress and implications for the 80's.* Washington, D.C.: U.S. Government Printing Office.

HUGHES, J., SMITH, T. W., KOSTERLITZ, H. W., FOTHERGILL, L. A., MORGAN, B. A., & MORRIS, H. R. (1975). Identification of two related pentapeptides from the brain with potent opiate agonist activity. *Nature, 258,* 577–579.

HULL, C. L. (1937). Mind, mechanism, and adaptive behavior. *Psychological Review, 44,* 1–32.

HULL, C. L. (1943). *Principles of behavior.* New York: D. Appleton-Century Co.

HUNT, H. T. (1985). Cognition and states of consciousness: The necessity for empirical study of ordinary and nonordinary consciousness for contemporary cognitive psychology. *Perceptual and Motor Skills, 60,* 239–282.

HUNT, M. (1974). *Sexual behavior in the 1970s.* Chicago: Playboy Press.

HUNT, W. A., & MATARAZZO, J. D. (1982). Smoking behavior. In R. J. Gatchell, A. Baum, and J. E. Singer (Eds.), *Behavioral medicine and psychology: Overlapping disciplines.* Hillsdale, N.J.: Lawrence Erlbaum.

HURD, P. D., JOHNSON, C. A., PECHACEK, T., BLAST, L. P., JACOBS, D. R., & LUEPKER, R. B. (1980). Prevention of cigarette smoking in seventh grade students. *Journal of Behavioral Medicine, 3,* 15–28.

HURVICH, L. M. (1978). Two decades of opponent

processes. In F. W. Billmeyer & G. Wyszecki (Eds.), *Color 77*. Bristol, England: Adam Hiler.

HURVICH, L. M., & JAMESON, D. (1974). Opponent processes as a model of neural organization. *American Psychologist, 29*, 88–102.

IMADA, A. S., & HAKEL, M. D. (1977). Influence of nonverbal communication and rater proximity on impressions and decisions in simulated employment interviews. *Journal of Applied Psychology, 62*, 295–300.

INGBER, D. (1982). The violent brain. *Science Digest*, April, 34–35.

INGRAM, R. E., & HOLLON, S. D. (1986). Cleaning up cognition in depression: An information processing perspective on cognitive therapy of depression. In R. E. Ingram (Ed.), *Information processing approaches to psychopathology and clinical psychology*. New York: Academic Press.

INSTITUTE OF MEDICINE. (1982). *Frontiers of research in biobehavioral sciences*. Washington, D.C.: National Academy of Sciences.

ISCOE, I. (1982). Toward a viable community health psychology: Caveats from experience of the community mental health movement. *American Psychologist, 37*, 961–965.

IZARD, C. E. (1971). *The face of emotion*. New York: Appleton-Century-Crofts.

IZARD, C. E. (1977). *Human emotions*. New York: Plenum Press.

IZARD, C. E., HEMBREE, E. A., DOUGHERTY, L. M., & SPIZZIRRI, C. C. (1983). Changes in facial expressions of 2- to 19-month-old infants, following acute pain. *Developmental Psychology, 19*, 418–426.

JACCARD, J. (1981). Toward theories of persuasion and belief change. *Journal of Personality and Social Psychology, 40*, 260–269.

JACKSON, D. K., & SCHNEIDER, H. G. (1985). Age, organization, and memory: Effects of presentation rate and rehearsal strategy. *Psychological Reports, 56*, 471–479.

JACKSON, M. K. (1985). The recognition of tachistoscopically presented words, varying in imagery, part of speech and word frequency, in the left and right visual fields. *British Journal of Psychology, 76*, 59–74.

JAFFE, K., BARNSHAW, H. D., & KENNEDY, M. E. (1983). The dexamethasone suppression test in depressed outpatients with and without melancholia. *American Journal of Psychiatry, 140*, 492–493.

JAMES, W. (1884). What is an emotion? *Mind, 9*, 188–205.

JAMES, W. (1890). *The principles of psychology* (2 Vols.). New York: Henry Holt.

JAMES, W.P.T., & TRAYHURN, P. (1981). Thermogenesis and obesity. *British Medical Bulletin, 37*, 43–48.

JANIS, I. L. (1972). *Victims of groupthink: A psychological study of foreign policy decisions and fiascoes*. Boston: Houghton Mifflin.

JANIS, I. L., & FESHBACH, S. (1953). Effects of fear-arousing communications. *Journal of Abnormal and Social Psychology, 48*, 78–92.

JEFFERY, R. W., SNELL, M. K., & FORSTER, J. L. (1985). Group composition in the treatment of obesity: Does increasing group homogeneity improve treatment results? *Behavior Research and Therapy, 23*, 371–373.

JELLINEK, E. M. (1952). Phases of alcohol addiction. *Quarterly Journal of Studies in Alcoholism, 13*, 673–678.

JENKINS, H. M. (1979). Animal learning and behavior theory. In E. Hearst (Ed.), *The first century of experimental psychology*. Hillsdale, N.J.: Lawrence Erlbaum Associates.

JENKINS, J. G., & DALLENBACH, K. (1924). Oblivescence during sleep and waking. *American Journal of Psychology, 35*, 605–612.

JENNINGS, M. K., & NIEMI, R. C. (1968). The transmission of political values from parent to child. *American Political Science Review, 62*, 169–184.

JENSEN, A. R. (1980). *Bias in mental testing*. New York: Free Press.

JENSEN, A. R. (In press for 1986.) The g beyond factor analysis. In J. C. Conoley, J. A. Glover, & R. R. Ronning (Eds.), *The influence of cognitive psychology on testing and measurement*. Hillsdale, N.J.: Lawrence Erlbaum Associates.

JOHNSON, L. C., SLYE, E., & DEMENT, W. C. (1965). EEG and autonomic activity during and after prolonged sleep deprivation. *Psychonomic Medicine, 27*, 415–423.

JONES, A. P., & FRIEDMAN, M. I. (1982). Obesity and adipocyte abnormalities in offspring of rats undernourished during pregnancy. *Science, 215*, 1515–1519.

JONES, E. E., & DAVIS, K. E. (1965). From acts to dispositions: The attribution process in person perception. In L. Berkowitz (Ed.), *Advances in experimental social psychology* (Vol. 2). New York: Academic Press.

JONES, E. E., & NISBETT, R. E. (1971). *The actor and the observer: Divergent perceptions of the causes of behavior*. Morristown, N.J.: General Learning Press.

JONES, R. T. (1971). Marijuana—induced 'high': Influence of expectation, setting, and previous drug experience. *Pharmacology Review, 23*, 359–369.

JONES, W. H., HANNSON, R. C., & PHILLIPS, A. L. (1978). Physical attractiveness and judgments of psychotherapy. *Journal of Social Psychology, 105*, 79–84.

JOUVET, M. (1967). Neurophysiology of the states of sleep. *Physiological Review, 47*, 117–177.

JOUVET, M., SASTRE, J., & SAKAI, K. (1981). Toward an etho-ethnology of dreaming. In I. Karacan (Ed.), *Psychophysiological aspects of sleep: Proceedings of the Third International Congress of Sleep Research*. Park Ridge, N.J.: Noyes Medical Publications.

JULESZ, B. (1964). Binocular depth perception without familiarity cues. *Science, 145*, 356–362.

JULIUS, S. (1977). Borderline hypertension: An overview. *Medical Clinical North American, 61*, 496–551.

JUNG, C. G. (1917). *Collected papers on analytical psychology*. New York: Moffat, Yard.

JUNG, C. G. (1943). The psychology of the unconscious. In *Collected works*. Vol. 7. Princeton: Princeton Univ. Press, 1953. (First German edition, 1943).

JUNG, C. G. (1961). *Memories, dreams, and reflections*. New York: Random House.

JUNG, C. G. (1963). *Memories, dreams, reflections*. London: Collins and Routledge & Kegan Paul.

JURICH, A. P., POLSON, C. J., JURICH, J. A., & BATES, R. A. (1985). Family factors in the lives of drug users and abusers. *Adolescence, 20,* 143–159.

JUROW, G. L. (1971). New data on the effect of a "death-qualified" jury on the guilt determination process. *Harvard Law Review, 84,* 567–611.

JUSTICE, A. (1985). Review of the effects of stress on cancer in laboratory animals: Importance of time of stress application and type of tumor. *Psychological Bulletin, 98,* 108–138.

KALLMAN, F. J. (1952). Comparative twin study on the genetic aspects of male homosexuality. *Journal of Nervous and Mental Disease, 115,* 283–298.

KAMIN, L. J. (1969). Predictability, surprise, attention and conditioning. In B. A. Campbell & R. M. Church (Eds.), *Punishment and aversive behavior*. New York: Appleton-Century-Crofts.

KAMIN, L. J. (1976). Heredity, intelligence, politics, and psychology: II. In N. J. Block & G. Dworkin (Eds.), *The IQ Controversy*. New York: Pantheon Books.

KAMIN, L. J. (1978). Transfusion syndrome and the heritability of IQ. *Annals of Human Genetics, 42,* 161–171.

KAMIN, L. J. (1982). Mental testing and immigration. *American Psychologist, 37,* 97–98.

KAMIYA, J. (1968). Conscious control of brain waves. *Psychology Today, 1,* 57–60.

KANDEL, D. B., DAVIES, M., & RAVEIS, V. H. (1985). The stressfulness of daily social roles for women: Marital, occupational and household roles. *Journal of Health and Social Behavior, 26,* 64–78.

KANIN, E. (1985). Date rapists: Differential sexual socialization and relative deprivation. *Archives of Sexual Behavior, 14,* 219–231.

KANNEL, W. B., CASTELLI, W. P., & MCNAMARA, P. M. (1968). Cigarette smoking and risk of coronary heart disease: Epidemiologic clues to pathogenesis. *National Cancer Institute Monograph, 28,* 9–20.

KANNEL, W., WOLF, P., VERTER, J., & MCNAMARA, P. (1970). Epidemiological assessment of the role of blood pressure in stroke: The Framingham study. *Journal of the American Medical Association, 214,* 301–306.

KAPLAN, M. A. (1983). A woman's view of DSM-III. *American Psychologist, 38,* 786–792.

KAPLAN, R., & SACCUZZO, D. P. (1982). *Psychological testing: Principles, applications, and issues*. Monterey, Calif.: Brooks/Cole.

KASAMATSU, A., & HIRAI, T. (1963). Science of Zazen. *Psychologia, 6,* 86–91.

KASAMATSU, A., & HIRAI, T. (1969). An electroencephalographic study of the Zen meditation (Zazen). *Psychologia, 12,* 205–225.

KATZ, J., & CRONIN, D. M. (1980). Sexuality and college life. *Change,* February–March.

KEESEY, R. E. (1980). A set-point analysis of the regulation of body weight. In A. J. Stunkard (Ed.), *Obesity*. Philadelphia: W. B. Saunders.

KELLEY, H. H. (1967). Attribution theory in social psychology. In D. Levine (Ed.), *Nebraska Symposium on Motivation*, (Vol. 15). Lincoln: University of Nebraska Press.

KELLEY, H. H. (1972). Attribution in social interaction. In E. E. Jones et al. (Eds.), *Attribution: Perceiving the causes of behavior*. Morristown, N.J.: General Learning Press.

KELLEY, H. H. (1973). The process of causal attribution. *American Psychologist, 28,* 107–128.

KELLOGG, W. N., & KELLOGG, L. A. (1933). *The age and the child*. New York: McGraw-Hill.

KELLY, D. (1982). Leucotomy. In E. S. Paykel (Ed.), *Handbook of affective disorders*. New York: Guilford Press.

KELLY, K. E., & HOUSTON, B. K. (1985). Type A behavior in employed women: Relation to work, marital, and leisure variables, social support, stress, tension, and health. *Journal of Personality and Social Psychology, 48,* 1067–1079.

KERNBERG, O. F., BURSTEIN, E., COYNE, L., APPLEBAUM, A., HOROWITZ, L., & VOTH, H. (1972). Psychotherapy and psychoanalysis: Final report of the Menninger Foundation's psychotherapy research project. *Bulletin of the Menninger Clinic, 36,* 1–275.

KERR, N., & BRUUN, S. E. (1983). Dispensability of member effect and group motivation losses: Free-rider effects. *Journal of Personality and Social Psychology, 44,* 78–94.

KESSLER, S. (1980). The genetics of schizophrenia: A review. *Schizophrenia Bulletin, 6,* 404–416.

KETY, S. S. (1974). "Commentary." *Journal of Nervous and Mental Disorders, 153,* 323.

KILMANN, R. H., & TAYLOR, V. A. (1974). Contingency approach to laboratory learning: Psychological types versus experiential norms. *Human Relations, 27,* 891–909.

KILOH, L. G. (1982). Electroconvulsive therapy. In E. S. Paykel (Ed.), *Handbook of affective disorders*. New York: Guilford Press.

KIMBLE, G. A. (1961). *Hilgard and Marquis' conditioning and learning* (2nd ed.). New York: Appleton-Century-Crofts.

KIMMEL, D. (1974). *Adulthood and aging*. New York: Wiley.

KINSEY, A., POMEROY, W., & MARTIN, C. (1948). *Sexual behavior in the human male*. Philadelphia: W. B. Saunders.

KINSEY, A., POMEROY, W., MARTIN, C., & GEBHARD, P. (1953). *Sexual behavior in the human female*. Philadelphia: W. B. Saunders.

KINTSCH, W. (1977). *Memory and cognition* (2nd ed.). New York: Wiley.

KINTSCH, W., & GREENO, J. G. (1985). Understanding and solving word arithmetic problems. *Psychological Review, 92,* 109–129.

KINTSCH, W., & MROSS, E. F. (1985). Context effects in word identification. *Journal of Memory and Language, 24,* 336–349.

KLEIN, D. F. (1972). *Psychiatric case studies: Treatment, drugs and outcome.* Baltimore: Williams and Wilkins.

KNITTLE, J. L., & HIRSCH, J. (1968). Effect of early nutrition on the development of rat epididymal fat pads: Cellularity and metabolism. *Journal of Clinical Investigation, 47,* 2091–2098.

KOHLBERG, L. (1963). The development of children's orientations toward a moral order: I. Sequence in the development of moral thought. *Vita Humana, 6,* 11–33.

KOHLBERG, L. (1969). Stage and sequence: The cognitive-developmental approach to socialization. In D. A. Goslin (Ed.), *Handbook of socialization theory and research.* Chicago: Rand-McNally.

KOHLBERG, L. (1976). Moral stages and moralization. In T. Lickona (Ed.), *Moral development and behavior.* New York: Holt, Rinehart & Winston.

KOHN, A. (1984). Teenagers under glass. *Psychology Today, 18,* 6.

KOLATA, G. (1984). Math genius may have hormonal base. *Science, 222,* 1312.

KOLB, B., & WHISHAW, I. Q. (1980). *Fundamentals of human neuropsychology.* San Francisco: W. H. Freeman.

KOLODNY, R. C. (1971). Plasma testosterone and semen analysis in male homosexuals. *New England Journal of Medicine, 285,* 1170–1174.

KOLODNY, R. C. (1980). *Adolescent sexuality.* Presented at the Michigan Personnel and Guidance Association Annual Convention. Detroit, November.

KOLTANOWSKI, G. (1986). *In the dark.* Corgopolis, Penn.: Chess Enterprises.

KONEČNI, V. J. (1975). Annoyance, type and duration of postannoyance activity, and aggression: The "cathartic" effect. *Journal of Experimental Psychology: General, 104,* 76–102.

KRAMER, B. A. (1985). Use of ECT in California, 1977–1983. *The American Journal of Psychiatry, 142,* 1190–1192.

KRAUSE, N., & GEYER-PESTELLO, H. F., (1985). Depressive symptoms among women employed outside the home. *American Journal of Community Psychology, 13,* 49–67.

KREBS, D. (1975). Empathy and altruism. *Journal of Personality and Social Psychology, 32,* 1134–1146.

KROGER, W. S. (1977). *Clinical and experimental hypnosis.* Philadelphia: J. B. Lippincott.

KRONFOL, Z., & HOUSE, J. D. (1985). Depression, DST and lymphocyte function. Presented at the 1985 Annual Meeting of the American Psychiatric Association, Dallas.

KÜBLER-ROSS, E. (1969). *On death and dying:* New York: Macmillan.

KURTINES, W., & GREIF, E. B. (1974). The development of moral thought: Review and evaluation of Kohlberg's approach. *Psychological Bulletin, 81,* 453–470.

KUTCHINSKY, B. (1970). Sex crimes and pornography in Copenhagen. A study of attitudes. *Technical Reports of the Commission on Obscenity and Pornography, 7,* Washington, D.C.: U.S. Government Printing Office.

LABOUVIE-VIEF, G. (1977). Adult cognitive development: In search of alternative interpretations. *Merrill-Palmer Quarterly, 23*(4), 227–263.

LANDMAN, J. T., & DAVIES, R. M. (1982). Psychotherapy outcome: Smith and Glass's conclusions stand up under scrutiny. *American Psychologist, 37,* 504–516.

LANGE, C. (1885). *Om Sindsbevaegelser.* Kjobenhavn.

LARRABEE, G. L., LEVIN, H. S., HUFF, F. J., KAY, M. C., & GUINTO, F. C. (1985). Visual agnosia contrasted with visual-verbal disconnection. *Neuropsychologia, 23,* 1–12.

LARSON, G. E., & SACCUZZO, D. P. (In press.) Gender, neuroticism, and speed-accuracy trade-offs. *Personality and Individual Differences.*

LASHLEY, K. S. (1929). *Brain mechanisms and intelligence.* Chicago: The University of Chicago Press.

LATANÉ, B., & DARLEY, J. M. (1968). Group inhibition of bystander intervention in emergencies. *Journal of Personality and Social Psychology, 10,* 215–221.

LATANÉ, B., & NIDA, S. A. (1981). Ten years of research on group size and helping. *Psychological Bulletin, 89,* 308–324.

LATANÉ, B., WILLIAMS, K., & HARKINS, S. (1979). Many hands make light the work: The causes and consequences of social loafing. *Journal of Personality and Social Psychology, 37,* 822–832.

LAZARUS, A. A. (1965). Toward the understanding and effective treatment of alcoholism. *South African Medical Journal, 39,* 736–741.

LAZARUS, A. A. (1971). *Behavior therapy and beyond.* New York: McGraw-Hill.

LAZARUS, A. A. (1976). *Multimodal behavior therapy.* New York: Springer.

LAZARUS, A. A. (1981). *The practice of multimodal therapy.* New York: McGraw-Hill.

LAZARUS, A. A. (1984). Multimodal therapy. In R. J. Corsini (Ed.), *Current psychotherapies* (3rd ed.). Itasca, Ill.: F. E. Peacock.

LAZARUS, R. S. (1982). Thoughts on the relations between emotion and cognition. *American Psychologist, 37,* 1019–1024.

LAZARUS, R. S. (1984). On the primacy of cognition. *American Psychologist, 39,* 124–129.

LAZARUS, R. S., AVERILL, J. R., & OPTON, E. M., JR. (1970). Toward a cognitive theory of emotions. In M. Arnold (Ed.), *Feelings and emotions.* New York: Academic Press.

LAZARUS, R. S., COHEN, J. B., FOLKMAN, S., KANNER, A., & SCHAEFER, C. (1980). Psychological stress and adaptation: Some unresolved issues. In H. Selye (Ed.), *Guide to stress research.* New York: Van Nostrand Reinhold.

LAZARUS, R. S., & MCCLEARY, R. A. (1951). Autonomic discrimination without awareness: A study of subception. *Psychological Review, 58,* 113–122.

LEACH, B., & NORRIS, J. L. (1977). Factors in the development of Alcoholics Anonymous (AA). In B. Kissin & H. Begleiter (Eds.), *The biology of alcoholism. Vol. 5. Treatment and rehabilitation of the chronic alcoholic.* New York: Plenum Press.

LEACH, C. (1974). The importance of instructions in assessing sequential effects in impression formation. *British Journal of Social and Clinical Psychology, 13,* 151–156.

LEDERMAN, S. J., KLATZKY, R. L., & BARBER, P. O. (1985). Spatial and movement-based heuristics for encoding pattern information through touch. *Journal of Experimental Psychology, 114,* 33–49.

LEFCOURT, H. M. (1976). *Locus of control: Current trends in theory and research.* Hillsdale, N.J.: Lawrence Erlbaum Associates.

LEIBOWITZ, H. W., & OWENS, A. (1986). We drive by night. *Psychology Today, 20,* 54–59.

LEIBOWITZ, H. W., & PICK, H. (1972). Cross-cultural and educational aspects of the Ponzo illusion. *Perception and Psychophysics, 12,* 403–432.

LEIDERMAN, H., & LEIDERMAN, G. (1974). Affective and cognitive consequences of polymatric infant care in the East African highlands. In A. Pick (Ed.), *Minnesota symposium on child development* (Vol. 8). Minneapolis: University of Minnesota Press.

LEVENSON, A. J. (1981). *Basic psychopharmacology.* New York: Springer.

LEVENTHAL, H. (1970). Findings and theory in the study of fear communications. In L. Berkowitz (Ed.), *Advances in experimental social psychology* (Vol. 5). New York: Academic Press.

LEVENTHAL, H., WATTS, J. C., & PAGANO, F. (1967). Effects of fear and instructions on how to cope with danger. *Journal of Personality and Social Psychology, 6,* 313–321.

LEVINE, L., COLL, C.T.G., & OH, W., (1985). Determinants of mother-infant interaction in adolescent mothers. *Pediatrics, 75,* 23–29.

LEVINSON, D. J. (1986). A conception of adult development. *American Psychologist, 41,* 3–13.

LEVINSON, D. J., DARROW, C. N., KLEIN, E. B., LEVINSON, M. H., & MCKEE, B. (1976). Periods in the adult development of men: Ages 18 to 45. *Counseling Psychologist, 6,* 21–25.

LEVINSON, D. J., DARROW, C. N., KLEIN, E. B., LEVINSON, M. H., & MCKEE, B. (1978). *The seasons of a man's life.* New York: Knopf.

LEVIS, D. J. (1980). Implementing the technique of implosive therapy. In A. Goldstein & E. B. Foa (Eds.), *Handbook of behavioral interventions.* New York: Wiley.

LEVY, J. (1985). Right brain, left brain: Fact and fiction. *Psychology Today, 19,* 38–45.

LEWINSOHN, P. M., MISCHEL, W., CHAPLIN, W., & BARTON, R. (1980). Social competence and depression: The role of illusory self-perceptions. *Journal of Abnormal Psychology, 89,* 203–212.

LEWIS, M. (1972). State as an infant-environment interaction: An analysis of mother-infant interaction as a function of sex. *Merrill-Palmer Quarterly, 18,* 95–121.

LIDZ, T., & BLATT, S. (1983). Critique of the Danish-American studies of the biological and adoptive relatives of adoptees who became schizophrenic. *American Journal of Psychiatry, 140,* 426–435.

LIEBELT, R. A., BORDELON, C. B., & LIEBELT, A. G. (1973). The adipose tissue system and food intake. In E. Stellar & J. M. Sprague (Eds.), *Progress in physiological psychology.* New York: Academic Press.

LIEBERT, R. M., SPRAFKIN, J. N., & DAVIDSON, E. S. (1982). *The early window: Effects of television on children and youth* (2nd ed.). New York: Pergamon.

LIEM, J. H. (1980) Family studies of schizophrenia: An update and commentary. *Schizophrenia Bulletin, 6,* 429–455.

LIKERT, R. (1932). A technique for the measurement of attitudes. *Archives of Psychology,* No. 140.

LIMBER, J. (1977). Language in child and chimp. *American Psychologist, 32,* 280–295.

LINDEMANN, E. (1982). Symptomatology and management of acute grief. In F. G. Guggenheim & C. Nadelson (Eds.), *Major psychiatric disorders.* New York: Elsevier Biomedical. (Originally published 1944, *American Journal of Psychiatry, 101,* 141–148.

LINDSAY, P. H., & NORMAN, D. A. (1977). *Human information processing* (2nd ed.). New York: Academic Press.

LINN, R. L. (1982). Admissions testing on trial. *American Psychologist, 37,* 279–291.

LIPSCOMB, D. M. (1969a). Ear damage from exposure to rock and roll music. *Archives of Otolaryngology, 90,* 545–555.

LIPSCOMB, D. M. (1969b). High intensity sounds in the recreational environment: Hazard to young ears. *Clinical Pediatrics, 8,* 63–68.

LIPSITT, L. P. (1977). The study of sensory and learning processes of the newborn. *Clinics of Perinatology, 4,* 163–186.

LIPSITT, L. P. (1979). Critical conditions in infancy: A psychological perspective. *American Psychologist, 34,* 973–980.

LIST, J. A., KEATING, D. P., & MERRIMAN, W. E. (1985). Differences in memory retrieval: A construct validity investigation. *Child Development, 56,* 138–151.

LIVSON, N., & PESKIN, H. (1980). Perspectives on adolescence from longitudinal research. In J. Adelson (Ed.), *Handbook of adolescent psychology.* New York: Wiley.

LOCKE, E. A. (1976). The nature and causes of job satisfaction. In M. D. Dunnette (Ed.), *Handbook of industrial and organizational psychology.* Chicago: Rand-McNally.

LOEB, M., HOLDING, D. H., & BAKER, M. A. (1982). Noise stress and circadian arousal in self-paced computation. *Motivation and Emotion, 6,* 43–48.

LOEHLIN, J. C., LINDZEY, G., & SPUHLER, J. N. (1975). *Race differences in intelligence.* San Francisco, W. H. Freeman.

LOFTUS, E. F., & PALMER, J. C. (1974) Reconstruction of automobile destruction: An example of the interaction between language and memory. *Journal of Verbal Learning and Verbal Behavior, 13,* 585–589.

LONDON, P. (1964). *The modes and morals of psychotherapy.* New York: Holt, Rinehart and Winston.

LORENZ, K. (1950). The comparative method in studying innate behavior patterns. *Symposia of the society for experimental biology, 4,* 221–268.

LORENZ, K. (1966). *On aggression.* New York: Harcourt Brace Jovanovich.

LUBORSKY, L., & SPENCE, D. P. (1978). Quantitative research on psychoanalytic therapy. In S. L. Garfield & A. E. Bergin (Eds.), *Handbook of psychotherapy and behavior change: An empirical analysis* (2nd ed.). New York: Wiley.

LUCE, G. G. (1965). *Research on sleep and dreams.* Bethesda, Md.: National Institute of Mental Health.

LUEGER, R. J., & HOOVER, L. (1984). Use of the MMPI to identify subtypes of delinquent adolescents. *Journal of Clinical Psychology, 40,* 1493–1495.

LURIA, A. R. (1968). *The mind of a mnemonist.* New York: Basic Books.

LYKKEN, D. T. (1982). Research with twins: The concept of emergencies. *The Society for Psychophysiological Research, 19,* 361–373.

MACCOBY, E. E., & JACKLIN, C. N. (1974). *Psychology of sex differences.* Stanford, Calif.: Stanford University Press.

MACKINTOSH, N. J. A new measure of intelligence? *Nature, 1981, 289,* (No. 5798), 529–530.

MACLUSKY, N. J., & NAFTOLIN, F. (1981). Sexual differentiation of the central nervous system. *Science, 211,* 1294–1295.

MACNICHOL, E. F. (1964). Three pigment color vision. *Scientific American, 211,* 48–56.

MADDUX, J. E., ROBERTS, M. C., SLEDDEN, E. A., & WRIGHT, L. (1986). Developmental issues in child health psychology. *American Psychologist, 41,* 25–34.

MAHARISHI YOGI, M. (1968). *Transcendental meditation: Serenity without drugs.* Bergenfield, N.J.: New American Library.

MAHONEY, M. J. (1974). *Cognition and behavior modification.* Cambridge, Mass.: Ballinger.

MAHONEY, M. J., & ARNKOFF, D. B. (1979). Self-management. In O. F. Pomerleau & J. P. Brady (Eds.), *Behavioral medicine: Theory and practice.* Baltimore: Williams and Wilkins.

MAIER, S. F., & LAUDENSLAGER, M. (1985). Stress and health: Exploring the links. *Psychology Today, 19,* 44–49.

MALMO, R. B. (1975). *On emotions, needs, and our archaic brain.* New York: Holt, Rinehart, & Winston.

MANNE, S., & SANDLER, I. N. (1984). Coping and adjustment to genital herpes. *Journal of Behavioral Medicine, 7,* 391–410.

MARCUS, M. D., WING, R. R., & LAMPARSKI, D. M. (1985). Binge eating and dietary restraint in obese patients. *Addictive Behaviors, 10,* 163–168.

MARGOLIN, G. (1982). Ethical and legal considerations in marital and family therapy. *American Psychologist, 37,* 788–801.

MARK, V., & ERVIN, F. (1970). *Violence and the brain.* New York: Harper & Row.

MARMOR, J. (Ed.). (1980). *Homosexual behavior.* New York: Basic Books.

MARSHALL, W. L. (1985). The effects of variable exposure in flooding therapy. *Behavior Therapy, 16,* 117–135.

MARTINDALE, D. A. (1971). Territorial dominance behavior in dyadic verbal interactions. *Proceedings, 79th Annual Convention, American Psychological Association, 6,* 305–306.

MASEK, B. J., FENTRESS, D. W., & SPIRITO, A. (1985). Behavioral treatment of symptoms of childhood illness. *Clinical Psychology Review, 4,* 561–570.

MASLOW, A. H. (1970). *Motivation and personality* (2nd ed.). New York: Harper & Row.

MASNICK, G., & BANE, M. J. (1980). *The nation's families, 1960–1990.* Cambridge, Mass.: Joint Center for Urban Studies of MIT and Harvard University.

MASSON, J. (1984). *The assault on truth: Freud's suppression of the seduction theory.* New York: Farrar, Straus, & Giroux.

MASTERS, W. H., & JOHNSON, V. E. (1966). *Human sexual response.* Boston: Little, Brown.

MASTERS, W. H., & JOHNSON, V. E. (1970). *Human sexual inadequacy.* Boston: Little, Brown.

MASTERS, W. H., JOHNSON, V. E., & KOLODNY, R. C. (1982). *Human sexuality.* Boston: Little, Brown.

MATARAZZO, J. D. (1972). *Wechsler's measurement and appraisal of intelligence* (5th ed.). Baltimore: Williams & Wilkins.

MATARAZZO, J. D. (1979). *Wechsler's measurement and appraisal of adult intelligence* (5th ed.). Baltimore: Williams & Wilkins.

MATTHEWS, K. A. (1982). Psychological perspectives on the Type A behavior pattern. *Psychological Bulletin, 91,* 293–323.

MATTHYSSE, S. (1974). Dopamine and the pharmacology of schizophrenia: The state of the evidence. *Journal of Psychiatric Research, 11,* 107.

MCARDLE, W. D., KATCH, F. I., & KATCH, V. L. (1981). Exercise physiology: Energy, nutrition, and weight control. Philadelphia: Lea & Febiger.

MCCARY, J. L. (1978). Human sexuality: Past, present and future. *Journal of Marriage and Family Counseling, 4,* 3–12.

MCCLELLAND, D. C. (1961). *The achieving society.* Princeton, N.J.: Van Nostrand.

MCCLELLAND, D. C. (1978). Managing motivation to

expand human freedom. *American Psychologist, 33,* 201–210.

MCCLELLAND, D. C., ATKINSON, J. W., CLARK, R. A., & LOWELL, E. L. (1953). *The achievement motive.* New York: Appleton-Century-Crofts.

MCCLINTOCK, M. K. (1971). Menstrual synchrony and suppression. *Nature, 229,* 244–245.

MCCRADY, B. S. (1985). Alcoholism. In D. H. Barlow (Ed.), *Clinical handbook of psychological disorders.* New York: Guilford Press.

MCDOUGALL, W. (1908). *Introduction to social psychology.* London: Methuen.

MCDOUGALL, W. (1933). *Energies of man.* London: Methuen.

MCGEER, P. L., & MCGEER, E. G. (1980). Chemistry and mood and emotion. *Annual Review of Psychology, 31,* 273–307.

MCGHIE, A., & CHAPMAN, J. (1961). Disorders of attention and perception in early schizophrenia. *British Journal of Medical Psychology, 34,* 103–116.

MCLAUGHLIN, J. A. (1981). Development of children's ability to judge relative numerosity. *Journal of Experimental Child Psychology, 31,* 102–114.

MEEHL, P. E. (1962). Schizotaxia, schizotypy, schizophrenia. *American Psychologist, 17,* 827–838.

MEICHENBAUM, D. (1977). *Cognitive-behavior modification: An integrative approach.* New York: Plenum Press.

MEICHENBAUM, D., & GENEST, M. (1980). Cognitive behavior modification: An integration of cognitive and behavioral methods. In F. H. Kanfer & A. P. Goldstein (Eds.), *Helping people change.* New York: Pergamon Press.

MELTON, G. B. (1983). Toward "personhood" for adolescents: Autonomy and privacy as values in public policy. *American Psychologist, 38,* 99–103.

MELTZOFF, J., & KORNREICH, M. (1970). *Research in psychotherapy.* New York: Atherton Press.

MELZACK, R. (1973). How acupuncture works. *Psychology Today, 7,* 28–38.

MELZACK, R., & WALL, P. D. (1965). Pain mechanisms: A new theory. *Science, 150,* 971–979.

MENAGHAN, E. G., & MERVES, E. S. (1984). Coping with occupational problems: The limits of individual efforts. *Journal of Health and Social Behavior, 25,* 406–423.

MERRELL-NATIONAL LABORATORIES. (1985). Norpramin. *American Journal of Psychiatry, 142,* A25.

MEYER-BAHLBURG, H. F. (1977). Sex hormones and male homosexuality in comparative perspective. *Archives of Sexual Behavior, 6,* 297–325.

MEYER-BAHLBURG, H. F. (1979). Sex hormones and female homosexuality: A critical examination. *Archives of Sexual Behavior, 8,* 101–120.

MILGRAM, S. (1963). Behavioral study of obedience. *Journal of Abnormal and Social Psychology, 67,* 371–378.

MILGRAM, S. (1964). Issues in the study of obedience: A reply to Baumrind. *American Psychologist, 19,* 848–852.

MILGRAM, S. (1965a). Liberating effects of group pressure. *Journal of Personality and Social Psychology, 1,* 127–134.

MILGRAM, S. (1965b). Some conditions of obedience and disobedience to authority. *Human Relations, 18,* 57–76.

MILGRAM, S. (1970). The experience of living in cities. *Science, 167,* 1461–1468.

MILGRAM, S. (1974). *Obedience to authority.* New York: Harper & Row.

MILLER, G. (1981). *Language and speech.* San Francisco: W. H. Freeman and Company.

MILLER, G. (1983). Children and the congress. *American Psychologist, 38,* 70–76.

MILLER, G. A. (1956). The magical number seven, plus or minus two: Some limits on our capacity for processing information. *Psychological Review, 63,* 81–97.

MILLER, I. V., III, & NORMAN, W. H. (1981). Effects of attributions for success on the alleviation of learned helplessness and depression. *Journal of Abnormal Psychology, 90,* 113–124.

MILLER, N. E. (1969). Learning of visceral and glandular responses. *Science, 163,* 434–445.

MILLER, N. E. (1985). Rx: Biofeedback. *Psychology Today, 19,* (Feb.), 54–59.

MILLON, T. (1969). *Modern psychopathology: A biosocial approach to maladaptive learning and functioning.* Philadelphia: W. B. Saunders.

MILLON, T. (1981). *Disorders of personality: DSM-III: Axis II.* New York: Wiley.

MILNER, B. (1959). The memory defect in bilateral hippocampal lesions. *Psychiatric Research Reports of the American Psychiatric Association, 11,* 43–52.

MILNER, B. (1966). Amnesia following operation on the temporal lobes. In C.W.M. Whitty & O. L. Zangwill (Eds.), *Amnesia.* London: Butterworths.

MILNER, B. (1971). Interhemispheric differences in the localization of psychological processes in man. *British Medical Bulletin, 27,* 272–277.

MILNER, B., CORKIN, S., & TEUBER, H. L. (1968). Further analysis of the hippocampal-amnesic syndrome: 14-year follow-up study of H. M. *Neuropsychologia, 6,* 215–234.

MINDHAM, R. H. (1982). Tricyclic antidepressant and amine precursors. In E. S. Paykel (Ed.), *Handbook of affective disorders.* New York: Guilford Press.

MISCHEL, W. (1968). *Personality and assessment.* New York: Wiley.

MISCHEL, W. (1973). Toward a cognitive social learning reconceptualization of personality. *Psychological Review, 80,* 252–283.

MISCHEL, W. (1979). On the interface of cognition and personality: Beyond the person-situation debate. *American Psychologist, 34,* 740–754.

MITCHEL, J. S., & KEESEY, R. E. (1974). The effects of lateral hypothalamic lesions and castration upon the body weight of male rats. *Behavioral Biology, 11,* 69–82.

MITCHELL, H. E., & BYRNE, D. (1982). Minimizing the influence of irrelevant factors in the courtroom: The defendant's character, judge's instructions, and authoritarianism. In K. M. White & J. C. Speisman, *Research approaches to personality*. Monterey, Calif.: Brooks/Cole.

MONEY, J. (1961). Components of eroticism in man: The hormones in relation to sexual morphology and sexual desire. *Journal of Nervous and Mental Disease, 132*, 239–248.

MONEY, J. (1980). *Love and love sickness*. Baltimore: The Johns Hopkins University Press.

MONEY, J., & EHRHARDT, A. A. (1972). *Man and woman, boy and girl*. Baltimore: The Johns Hopkins University Press.

MONGE, P. T., & KIRSTE, K. K. (1980). Measuring proximity in human organization. *Social Psychology Quarterly, 43*, 10–15.

MOORE-EDE, M. C., SULZMAN, F. M., & FULLER, C. A. (1982). *The clocks that time us*. Cambridge, Mass.: Harvard University Press.

MORAN, B. (1983). What if? *The San Diego Union*, April 24, p. D1, D4.

MOROKOFF, P. J. (1985). Effects of sex guilt, repression, sexual "arousability," and sexual experience on female sexual arousal during erotica and fantasy. *Journal of Personality and Social Psychology, 49*, 177–187.

MORRIS, N. M., & UDRY, J. R. (1978). Pheromonal influences on human sexual behavior: An experimental search. *Journal of Biosocial Science, 10*, 147–157.

MORUZZI, G., & MAGOUN, H. W. (1949). Brain stem reticular formation activation of the EEG. *Electroencephalography and Clinical Neurophysiology, 1*, 455–473.

MOSER, M., & GOLDMAN, A. (1967). *Hypertensive vascular disease—diagnosis and treatment*. Philadelphia: Lippincott.

MUELLER, C., & DONNERSTEIN, E. (1977). The effects of humor-induced arousal upon aggressive behavior. *Journal of Research in Personality, 11*, 73–82.

MUNOZ, R. F., YING, Y. W., & SORENSEN, J. (1985). Prevention of depression in medical outpatients. Presented at the 1985 Annual Meeting of the American Psychiatric Association, Dallas.

MURDOCK, B. B., JR. (1961). The retention of individual items. *Journal of Experimental Psychology, 62*, 618–625.

MURDOCK, B. B., JR. (1962). The second position effect in free recall. *Journal of Experimental Psychology, 64*, 482–488.

MURRAY, H. A. (1938). *Explorations in personality*. New York: Oxford University Press.

MURSTEIN, B. I. (1972). Physical attractiveness and marital choice. *Journal of Personality and Social Psychology, 22*, 8–12.

MYERS, J. J. (1985). Right hemisphere language: Science or fiction? *American Psychologist, 39*, 315–319.

NAKAHO, H. (1979). Emotional behavior and the brain. *Psychotherapy and Psychosomatics, 31*, 156–160.

NAKANO, K., & SACCUZZO, D. P. (1985). Schizotaxia, information processing and the MMPI 2-7-8 code type. *British Journal of Clinical Psychology, 24*, 217–218.

NATIONAL CENTER FOR HEALTH STATISTICS, U.S. DEPT. OF HEALTH AND HUMAN SERVICES. (1980). *Health, United States*. Washington, D.C.: U.S. Government Printing Office.

NATIONAL CENTER FOR HEALTH STATISTICS. (1985). *Final birth statistics for 1983*. Washington, D.C.: U.S. Government Printing Office.

NATIONAL INSTITUTE FOR MENTAL HEALTH (NIMH). (1977). *Psychiatric services and the changing institutional scene. 1950–1985*. (DHEW Publication [ADM] 77-433). Washington, D.C.: U.S. Government Printing Office.

NATIONAL INSTITUTE FOR OCCUPATIONAL SAFETY AND HEALTH (NIOSH) (1978). Occupational stress. Proceedings of the Conference on Occupational Stress, Los Angeles, November 3, 1977. U.S. Department of Health, Education, and Welfare, March 1978.

NATIONAL INSTITUTE OF OCCUPATIONAL SAFETY AND HEALTH (NIOSH). (1980). Coronary heart disease in pink-collar workers. *American Journal of Public Health*. Feb.

NATSOULAS, T. (1978). Consciousness. *American Psychologist, 33*, 906–914.

NATSOULAS, T. (1983). Addendum to "Consciousness." *American Psychologist, 38*, 121–122.

NEISSER, U. (1967). *Cognitive psychology*. New York: Appleton-Century-Crofts.

NELSON, C. A., & DOLGIN, K. G. (1985). The generalized discrimination of facial expressions by seven-month-old infants. *Child Development, 56*, 58–61.

NELSON, D. L., BAJO, M. T., & CASANUEVA, D. (1985). Prior knowledge and memory: The influence of natural category size as a function of intention and distraction. *Journal of Experimental Psychology: Learning, Memory, and Cognition, 11*, 94–105.

NELSON, R., & CRUTCHFIELD, R. S. (1970). Mathematicians: The creative researcher and the average Ph.D. *Journal of Consulting and Clinical Psychology, 34*, 250–257.

NETTELBECK, T. (1982). Inspection time: An index for intelligence? *Quarterly Journal of Experimental Psychology, 34A*, 299–312.

NEUGARTEN, B. L. (1983). Health care, medicare, and health policy for older people: A conversation with Arthur Flemming. *American Psychologist, 38*, 311–315.

NEUGARTEN, B. L., & DATAN, N. (1974). The middle years. In S. Arieti (Ed.), *American handbook of psychiatry*. New York: Basic Books.

NEWCOMB, M. D. (1985). The role of perceived relative parent personality in the development of heterosexuals, homosexuals, and transvestites. *Archives of Sexual Behavior, 14*, 147–164.

NEWCOMB, T. M. (1961). *The acquaintance process*. New York: Holt, Rinehart, & Winston.

NEWCOMB, T. M. (1981). Heiderian balance as a group phenomenon. *Journal of Personality and Social Psy-*

chology, 40, 862–867.

NEWSWEEK. (1983). Living with Jellinek's disease. *Newsweek,* October 17, p. 22.

NICHOLSON, N., COLE, S. G., & ROCKLIN, T. (1985). Conformity in the Asch situation: A comparison between contemporary British and U.S. university students. *British Journal of Social Psychology, 24,* 59–63.

NIES, A., & ROBINSON, D. S. (1982). Monoamine oxidase inhibitors. In E. S. Paykel (Ed.), *Handbook of affective disorders.* New York: Guilford Press.

NILSSON, L-G (Ed.). (1979). *Perspectives on memory research: Essays in honor of Uppsala University's 500th anniversary.* Hillsdale, N.J.: Lawrence Erlbaum Associates.

NISBETT, R. E. (1968a). Birth order and participation in dangerous sports. *Journal of Personality and Social Psychology, 8,* 351–353.

NISBETT, R. E. (1968b). Taste, deprivation and weight behavior. *Journal of Personality and Social Psychology, 10,* 197–216.

NISBETT, R. E. (1972). Hunger, obesity, and the ventromedial hypothalamus. *Psychological Review, 79,* 433–453.

NISBETT, R. E., & ROSS, L. (1980). *Human inference: Strategies and shortcomings of social judgment.* Englewood Cliffs, N.J.: Prentice-Hall.

NOCE, S. F., & WHITMYRE, J. W. (1981). Comparison of MMPI and Mini-Mult with both psychiatric inpatients and screening nursing students. *Journal of Personality Assessment, 45,* 147–150.

NORTON, A. J., & GLICK, P. C. (1979). Marital instability in America: Past, present, and future. In G. Levinger & O. C. Moles (Eds.), *Divorce and separation.* New York: Basic Books.

OBER, B. A., KOSS, E., FRIEDLAND, R. P., & DELIS, D. C. (1985). Processes of verbal memory failure in Alzheimer-Type dementia. *Brain and Cognition, 4,* 90–103.

O'BOYLE, M. W. (1985). Hemispheric asymmetry in memory search for four-letter names and human faces. *Brain & Cognition, 4,* 104–132.

O'DONOHUE, W. T., & GEER, J. H. (1985). The habituation of sexual arousal. *Archives of Sexual Behavior, 14,* 233–246.

ÖHMAN, A., ERIKSON, A., & OLOFSSON, C. (1975). One-trial learning and superior resistance to extinction of autonomic responses conditioned to potentially phobic stimuli. *Journal of Comparative and Physiological Psychology, 88,* 619–627.

OHNOGI, H. (1985). Kindergarteners' selective attention in direct and observational learning. *Perceptual and Motor Skills, 60,* 127–133.

OLDS, J., & MILNER, P. (1954). Positive reinforcement produced by electrical stimulation of septal area and other regions of rat brain. *Journal of Comparative and Physiological Psychology, 47,* 419–427.

OOMURA, Y., ONO, T., OOYAMA, H., & WAYNER, M. (1969). Glucose and osmosensitive neurons of the rat hypothalamus. *Nature, 222,* 282–284.

ORNE, M. T. (1979). On the simulating subject as a quasi-control group in hypnosis research: What, why, and how. In E. Fromm & R. E. Shor (Eds.), *Hypnosis: Developments in research and new perspectives* (2nd ed.). New York: Aldine.

OSAKA, M. (1984). Peak alpha frequency of EEG during a mental task. *Psychophysiology, 21,* 101–105.

OSGOOD, C. E., SUCI, G. J., & TANNENBAUM, P. H. (1957). *The measurement of meaning.* Urbana: University of Illinois Press.

OSKAMP, S. (1977). *Attitudes and opinions.* Englewood Cliffs, N.J.: Prentice-Hall.

OSWALD, I. (1968). Drugs and sleep. *Pharmacology Review, 20,* 273–297.

OVERHOLSER, J., & BECK, S. (1985). Assessing generalization of treatment effects and self-efficacy in the modification of eating styles in obese children. *Addictive Behaviors, 10,* 145–152.

OVERMIER, J. B., & SELIGMAN, M.E.P. (1967). Effects of inescapable shock upon subsequent escape and avoidance responding. *Journal of Comparative and Physiological Psychology, 63,* 28–33.

PAGE, J. D. (1975). *Psychopathology: The science of understanding deviance* (2nd ed.). Chicago: Aldine.

PAGE, R. (1977). Noise and helping behavior. *Environment and Behavior, 9,* 311–334.

PARISH, T. S., & WIGLE, S. E. (1985). A longitudinal study of the impact of parental divorce on adolescents' evaluations of self and parents. *Adolescence, 20,* 239–244.

PARIZKOVA, J. (1973). Body composition and exercise during growth and development. In G. L. Rarick (Ed.), *Physical activity: Human growth and development.* New York: Academic Press.

PARIZKOVA, J. (1977). *Body fat and physical fitness.* The Hague: Martinus Nijhoff.

PARKE, R. D., & WALTERS, R. H. (1967). Some factors influencing the efficacy of punishment training for inducing response inhibition. *Monographs of the Society for Research in Child Development, 32,* (1, Whole No. 109).

PATTERSON, F.G.P. (1979). Linguistic capabilities of a lowland gorilla. Ph.D. dissertation, Stanford University, Stanford, California. University Microfilms International. Ann Arbor, Mich.

PATTERSON, T., WAGGONER, C., SPOHN, H. E., & BOGIA, D. P. (in press for 1986). Thought disorder in schizophrenia conceptualized by linguistic cognitive and neuroscience. *Schizophrenia Bulletin.*

PAVLOV, I. (1927). *Conditioned reflexes.* Oxford, England: Oxford University Press.

PAVLOV, I. (1928). *Lectures on conditioned reflexes* (W. Horsley Gantt, Ed. and trans., 2 vols.). New York: International Publishers.

PEARLMAN, C. A., & BECKER, M. (1973). Brief posttrial REM sleep deprivation impairs discrimination learning in rats. *Physiological Psychology, 1,* 373–376.

PEARLMAN, C. A., & BECKER, M. (1974). REM sleep deprivation impairs serial reversal and probability maximizing in rats. *Physiological Psychology, 2,* 509–512.

PENFIELD, W., & RASMUSSEN, T. (1950). *The cerebral cortex of man.* New York: Macmillan.

PERRIS, C. (1982). The distinction between bipolar and unipolar affective disorders. In E. S. Paykel (Ed.). *Handbook of affective disorders.* New York: Guilford Press.

PERTOVAARA, A., & KOJO, I. (1985). Influence on the rate of temperature change on thermal thresholds in man. *Experimental Neurology, 87,* 439–445.

PETERSON, L. R., & PETERSON, M. J. (1959). Short-term retention of individual verbal items. *Journal of Experimental Psychology, 58,* 193–198.

PETRIE, S. (1974). *Fat destroyer foods.* New York: Parker.

PFEIFFER, G. (1986). Health risk and occupational category. *Employee Assistance Quarterly, 1,* 25–34.

PFOHL, B., & WINOKUR, G. (1983). The micropsychopathology of hebephrenic/catatonic schizophrenia. *Journal of Nervous & Mental Disease, 171,* 296–300.

PFUNGST, O. (1904). *Clever Hans: The horse of Mr. von Osten.* R. Rosenthal (Ed.). New York: Holt, Rinehart & Winston (reprinted 1965).

PIAGET, J. (1929). *The child's conception of the world.* New York: Harcourt, Brace.

PIAGET, J. (1952). *The origins of intelligence in children.* New York: International Universities Press.

PIAGET, J. (1970). Piaget's theory. In P. H. Mussen (Ed.), *Carmichael's manual of child psychology* (Vol. 1). New York: Wiley, 703–732.

PINES, M. (1979). A head start in the nursery. *Psychology Today, 13,* 56–68.

PIOTROWSKI, C. (1984). The status of projective techniques: Or, "Wishing won't make it go away." *Journal of Clinical Psychology, 40,* 1495–1502.

PLUTCHIK, R. (1980a). A general psychoevolutionary theory of emotion. In R. Plutchik & H. Kellerman (Eds.), *Emotion: Theory, research, and experience* (Vol. 1). New York: Academic Press.

PLUTCHIK, R. (1980b). *Emotion: A psychoevolutionary synthesis.* New York: Harper & Row.

POLIT-O'HARA, D., & KAHN, J. R. (1985). Communication and contraceptive practices in adolescent couples. *Adolescence, 20,* 33–43.

POLIVY, J., & HERMAN, C. P. (1985). Dieting and binging: A causal analysis. *American Psychologist, 40,* 193–201.

POLYA, G. (1962). *Mathematical discovery* (Vol. 1). New York: Wiley.

POMERLEAU, O. F., & BRADY, J. P. (1979). Introduction: The scope and promise of behavioral medicine. In O. F. Pomerleau & J. P. Brady (Eds.), *Behavioral medicine: Theory and practice.* Baltimore: Williams and Wilkins.

PORTER, L. J., & KIRBY, E. A. (1986). Effects of two instructional sets on the validity of the Kaufman Assessment Battery for Children—nonverbal scale with a group of severely hearing impaired children. *Psychology in the Schools, 23,* 37–43.

POST, R. M., KOTIN, J., GOODWIN, F. K., & GORDON, E. (1973). Psychomotor activity and cerebrospinal fluid amine metabolites in affective illness. *American Journal of Psychiatry, 130,* 67–72.

POTEGAL, M., BLAU, A., & GLUSMAN, M. (1981). Inhibition of intraspecific aggression in male hamsters of septal stimulation. *Physiological Psychology, 9,* 213–218.

POWERS, R. J., & KUTASH, I. L. (1985). Stress and alcohol. *The International Journal of Addictions, 20,* 461–482.

PREMACK, D. (1976). *Intelligence in ape and man.* Hillsdale, N.J.: Lawrence Erlbaum Associates.

PRENTICE-DUNN, S., & ROGERS, R. W. (1983). Deindividuation in aggression. In R. Geen & E. Donnerstein (Eds.), *Aggression: Theoretical and empirical reviews.* New York: Academic Press.

PRESSMAN, M. R. (1986). Sleep and sleep disorders: An introduction. *Clinical Psychology Review, 6,* 1–10.

PROCTOR, F., et al. (1974). The differentiation of male and female orgasm: An experimental study. In N. Wagner (Ed.), *Perspectives on human sexuality.* New York: Behavioral Publications.

PUJOL, J., MOURET, J., JOUVET, M., & GLOWINSKI, J. (1968). Increased turnover of cerebral norepinephrine during rebound of paradoxical sleep in the rat. *Science, 159,* 112–114.

PYSZCZYNSKI, T. A., & WRIGHTSMAN, L. S. (1981). The effects of opening statements on mock jurors' verdicts in a simulated criminal trial. *Journal of Applied Social Psychology, 11,* 301–313.

RABKIN, J. G. (1980). Stressful life events and schizophrenia: A review of the research literature. *Psychological Bulletin, 87,* 408–425.

RACHMAN, S., & TEASDALE, J. D. (1968). Aversion therapy. In C. M. Franks (Ed.), *Assessment and status of the behavior therapies and associated developments.* New York: McGraw-Hill.

RAJECKI, D. S. (1982). *Attitudes: Themes and advances.* Sunderland, Mass.: Sinauer Associates.

RAMEY, C. T., COLLIER, A. M., SPARLING, J. J., LODA, F. A., CAMPBELL, F. A., INGRAM, D. L., & FINKELSTEIN, N. W. (1976). The Carolina Abecedarian Project: A longitudinal and multidisciplinary approach to the prevention of developmental retardation. In T. Tjossem (Ed.), *Intervention strategies for high-risk infants and young children.* Baltimore: University Park Press.

RATTAN, R. B., & CHAPMAN, L. J. (1973). Associative intrusions in schizophrenic verbal behavior. *Journal of Abnormal Psychology, 82,* 169–173.

RAVELLI, G. P., STEIN, Z. A., & SUSSER, M. W. (1976). Obesity in young men after famine exposure in utero and early infancy. *New England Journal of Medicine, 295,* 349–353.

REED, S. K., DEMPSTER, A., & ETTINGER, M. (1985). Usefulness of analogous solutions for solving algebra word problems. *Journal of Experimental Psychology, 11,* 106–125.

REICH, T., RICE, J. P., & ANDREASEN, N. C. (1985). Familial and genetic aspects of bipolar disorders. Presented at the Annual Meeting of the American

Psychiatric Association, Dallas.

REIS, H. T., SENCHAK, M., & SOLOMON, B. (1985). Sex differences in the intimacy of social interaction: Further examination of potential explanations. *Journal of Personality and Social Psychology, 48,* 1204–1217.

REISER, B. J., BLACK, J. B., & ABELSON, R. P. (1985). Knowledge structures in the organization and retrieval of autobiographical memories. *Cognitive Psychology, 17,* 89–137.

REISS, B. F. (1980). Psychological tests in homosexuality. In J. Marmor (Ed.), *Homosexual behavior.* New York: Basic Books.

REMPEL, J. K., HOLMES, J. G., & ZANNA, M. P. (1985). Trust in close relationships. *Journal of Personality and Social Psychology, 49,* 95–112.

RESICK, P., & ELLIS, E. (1982). Victims of rape: Repeated assessment of depressive symptoms. *Journal of Consulting and Clinical Psychology, 50,* 96–102.

RESNICK, R. B., KESTENBAUM, R. S., & SCHWARTZ, L. K. (1977). Acute systematic effects of cocaine in man: A controlled study by intranasal and intravenous routes of administration. *Science, 195,* 696–698.

RESTAK, R. (1984). *The brain.* New York: Bantam Books.

RESTLE, F. (1970). Moon illusion explained on the basis of relative size. *Science, 167,* 1092–1096.

REVKIN, A. C. (1985). Lunching to win. *Science Digest, 93,* 38–39.

REVUSKY, S. H. (1968). Aversion to sucrose produced by contingent x-irradiation: Temporal and dosage parameters. *Journal of Comparative and Physiological Psychology, 65,* 17–22.

RICE, B. (1985). Why am I in this job? *Psychology Today, 19,* 54–59.

RICHARDSON, J. G., & SIMPSON, C. H. (1982). Children, gender, and social structure: An analysis of the contents of letters to Santa Claus. *Child Development, 53,* 429–436.

RIGBY, B. P. (1977). Higher states of consciousness through transcendental meditation: A literature review. *Journal of Chronic Diseases and Therapeutics Research, 1,* 35–55.

ROCK, I., & KAUFMAN, L. (1962). The moon illusion. *Science, 136,* 1023–1031.

RODIN, J. (1981). Current status of the internal-external hypothesis for obesity: What went wrong? *American Psychologist, 36,* 361–372.

RODNICK, E. H., GOLDSTEIN, M. J., LEWIS, J. M., & DOANE, J. A. (Eds.). (1984). *Children at risk for schizophrenia.* Cambridge: Cambridge University Press.

ROGERS, C. R. (1942). *Counseling and psychotherapy.* Boston: Houghton Mifflin.

ROGERS, C. R. (1951). *Client-centered therapy.* Boston: Houghton Mifflin.

ROGERS, C. R. (1959). A theory of therapy, personality, and interpersonal relationships, as developed in the client-centered framework. In S. Koch (Ed.), *Psychology: A study of a science* (vol. 3). New York: McGraw-Hill.

ROGERS, C. R. (1961). *On becoming a person.* Boston: Houghton Mifflin.

ROGERS, C. R. (1980). *A way of being.* Boston: Houghton Mifflin.

ROGERS, R. W. (1975). A protection motivation theory of fear appeals and attitude change. *Journal of Psychology, 91,* 93–114.

ROKEACH, M., & VIDMAR, N. (1973). Testimony concerning possible jury bias in a Black Panther murder trial. *Journal of Applied Social Psychology, 3,* 19–29.

ROSENFELD, A. H. (1985). Brain chemicals and the gambler's high. *Psychology Today, 19,* 8.

ROSENHAN, D. L. (1973). On being sane in insane places. *Science, 179,* 250–258.

ROSENMAN, R. H., FRIEDMAN, M. F., STRAUS, R., JENKINS, C. D., ZYZANSKI, S. J., & WURM, M. (1970). Coronary heart disease in the Western Collaborative Group Study: A follow-up experience of 4 1/2 years. *Journal of Chronic Diseases, 23,* 173–190.

ROSENTHAL, D. (1977). Searches for the mode of genetic transmission in schizophrenia: Reflections and loose ends. *Schizophrenia Bulletin, 3,* 268–276.

ROSENTHAL, T. L., & ROSENTHAL, R. H. (1985). Clinical stress management. In D. H. Barlow (Ed.), *Clinical handbook of psychological disorders.* New York: The Guilford Press.

ROSETT, H. L., & SANDER, L. W. (1979). Effects of maternal drinking on neonatal morphology and stage regulation. In J. D. Osofsky (Ed.), *Handbook of infant development.* New York: Wiley.

ROSS, L. (1974). Effects of manipulating the salience of food upon consumption by obese and normal eaters. In S. Schachter & J. Rodin (Eds.), *Obese humans and rats.* Washington, D.C.: Erlbaum/Halsted.

ROSS, L. (1977). The intuitive psychologist and his shortcomings: Distortions in the attribution process. In L. Berkowitz (Ed.), *Advances in experimental social psychology* (Vol. 10). New York: Academic Press.

ROSS, L. D., AMABILE, T. M., & STEINMETZ, J. L. (1977). Social roles, social control, and biases in social-perception processes. *Journal of Personality and Social Psychology, 35,* 485–494.

ROSSON, M. B. (1985). The interaction of pronunciation rules and lexical representations in reading aloud. *Memory & Cognition, 13,* 90–99.

ROTH, S., & COHEN, L. J. (1986). Approach, avoidance, and coping with stress. *American Psychologist, 41,* 813–819.

ROTHI, L.J.G., HEILMAN, K., & WATSON, R. T. (1985). Pantomime comprehension and ideomotor apraxia. *Journal of Neurology, Neurosurgery, and Psychiatry, 48,* 207–210.

ROTHWELL, N. A., & STOCK, M. J. (1979). A role for brown adipose tissue in diet-induced thermogenesis. *Nature, 281,* 31–35.

ROTTER, J. B. (1954). *Social learning and clinical psychology.* Englewood Cliffs, N.J.: Prentice-Hall.

ROTTER, J. B. (1966). Generalized expectancies for internal versus external control of reinforcement. *Psychological Monographs, 80,* No. 601.

ROWLAND, N. E., & ANTELMAN, S. M. (1976). Stress-induced hyperphagia and obesity in rats: A possible model for understanding human obesity. *Science, 191,* 310–312.

RUBIN, R. T., REINISCH, J. M., & HASKETT, R. F. (1981). Postnatal gonadal steroid effects on human behavior. *Science, 211,* 1318–1319.

RUSSEK, M. (1971). Hepatic receptors and the neurophysiological mechanisms controlling feeding behavior. In S. Ehrenpreis (Ed.), *Neurosciences Research* (Vol. 4). New York: Academic Press.

RUSSELL, M. J., SWITZ, G. M., & THOMPSON, K. (1977). Olfactory influences in the human menstrual cycle. Paper presented at the meeting of the American Association for the Advancement of Sciences, San Francisco, June.

RUTTER, M. (1979). Maternal deprivation, 1972–1978: New findings, new concepts, new approaches. *Child Development, 50,* 283–318.

SACCUZZO, D. P. (1986). An information-processing interpretation of theory and research in schizophrenia. In R. Ingram (Ed.), *Information processing approaches to psychopathology and clinical psychology.* New York: Academic Press.

SACCUZZO, D. P., & BRAFF, D. L. (1986). Information-processing abnormalities in schizophrenic and psychotic patients: Trait and state dependent components. *Schizophrenia Bulletin* Vol. 12, p. 447–459.

SACCUZZO, D. P., & KAPLAN, R. M. (1984). *Clinical psychology.* Boston: Allyn and Bacon.

SACCUZZO, D. P., LARSON, G. E., & RIMLAND, B. (in press). Visual, auditory, and reaction time approaches to the measurement of speed of information-processing and individual differences in intelligence. *Journal of Personality and Individual Differences.*

SACCUZZO, D. P., & MICHAEL, B. (1984). Speed of information-processing and structured limitations in retarded and dual diagnosis retarded schizophrenic persons. *American Journal of Mental Deficiency, 89,* 187–194.

SACCUZZO, D. P., & SCHUBERT, D. L. (1981). Backward masking as a measure of slow processing in schizophrenia spectrum disorders. *Journal of Abnormal Psychology, 90,* 305–312.

SACK, A. R., BILLINGHAM, R. E., & HOWARD, R. D. (1985). Premarital contraceptive use: A discriminant analysis approach. *Archives of Sexual Behavior, 14,* 165–182.

SADKER, M., & SADKER, D. (1985). Sexism in the schoolroom of the '80s. *Psychology Today, 19,* 54–57.

SADOWSKI, C. J., & BLACKWELL, M. W. (1985). Locus of control and perceived stress among student-teachers. *Psychological Reports, 56,* 723–726.

SAGAN, C. (1980). *Cosmos.* New York: Random House.

SAGHIR, M. T., & ROBINS, E. (1973). *Male and female homosexuality.* Baltimore: Williams & Wilkins.

SALANS, L. B., KNITTLE, J. L., & HIRSCH, J. (1968). The role of adipose cell size and adipose tissue insulin sensitivity in the carbohydrate intolerance of human obesity. *Journal of Clinical Investigation, 47,* 153–165.

SALAPATEK, P. (1975). Pattern perception in early infancy. In L. B. Cohen & P. Salapatek (Eds.), *Infant perception: From sensation to cognition.* Vol 1. *Basic visual processes.* New York: Academic Press.

SALASOO, A., SHIFFRIN, R. M., & FEUSTEL, T. C. (1985). Building permanent memory codes: Codification and repetition effects in word recognition. *Journal of Experimental Psychology: General, 114,* 50–77.

SALZMAN, L. (1982). Obsessions and phobias. In F. G. Guggenheim & C. Nadelson (Eds.), *Major psychiatric disorders.* New York: Elsevier Biomedical. (Reprinted in condensed form from *Contemporary Psychoanalysis,* Journal of the William Alanson White Institute and the William Alanson White Psychoanalytic Society, New York, 1965, 2, 1–25).

SAN DIEGO STATE UNIVERSITY. (1983). Be alert and be responsible. San Diego: San Diego State University Publication.

SANDERS, B., SOARES, M. P., & D'AQUILA, J. (1982). The sex difference on one test of spatial visualization: A nontrivial difference. *Child Development, 53,* 1106–1110.

SARGENT, J. D., GREEN, E. E., & WALTERS, E. D. (1973). Preliminary report on the use of autogenic feedback techniques in the treatment of migraine and tension headaches. *Psychosomatic Medicine, 35,* 129–135.

SATINDER, K. P., & BLACK, A. (1984). Cannabis use and sensation-seeking orientation. *The Journal of Psychology, 116,* 101–105.

SATTLER, J. M. (1982). *Assessment of children's intelligence and special abilities.* (2nd ed.). Boston: Allyn and Bacon.

SCALA, J. (1978). Weight control and the food industry. In G. Bray (Ed.), *Recent advances in obesity research* (vol. 2), *Proceedings of the Second International Congress on Obesity.* London: Newman.

SCHACHTER, S. (1959). *The psychology of affiliation.* Stanford, Calif.: Stanford University Press.

SCHACHTER, S. (1971). Some extraordinary facts about obese humans and rats. *American Psychologist, 26,* 129–144.

SCHACTER, D. L. (1986). Amnesia and crime: How much do we really know? *American Psychologist, 41,* 286–295.

SCHACHTER, S., & GROSS, L. (1968). Manipulated time and eating behavior. *Journal of Personality and Social Psychology, 10*, 98–106.

SCHACHTER, S., & SINGER, J. E. (1962). Cognitive, social, and physiological determinants of emotional stage. *Psychological Review, 69*, 379–399.

SCHAFFER, H. R. (1977). *Mothering*. Cambridge, Mass.: Harvard University Press.

SCHAFFER, H. R., & EMERSON, P. E. (1964). The development of social attachments in infancy. *Monographs of the Society for Research in Child Development, 29*(3).

SCHAIE, K. W. (1982). Knowledge base: Biopsychological. In J. Santos & G. R. VandenBos (Eds.), *Psychology and the older adult: Challenges for training in the 1980s*. Washington, D.C.: American Psychological Association.

SCHALLY, A. V., KASTIN, A. J., & ARIMURA, A. (1977). Hypothalamic hormones: The link between brain and body. *American Scientist, 65*, 712–719.

SCHARF, M. B., & BROWN, L. (1986). Hypnotic drugs: Use and abuse. *Clinical Psychology Review, 6*, 39–50.

SCHIFF, M., DUYME, M., DUMARET, A., & TOMKIEWICZ, S. (1982). How much *could* we boost scholastic achievement and IQ scores? A direct answer from a French adoption study. *Cognition, 12*, 165–196.

SCHIFFMAN, S. S. (1974). Physiochemical correlates of olfactory quality. *Science, 185*, 112–117.

SCHNEIDER, W., & LEWIS, I. A. (1984). The straight story on homosexuality and gay rights. *Public Opinion*, February–March.

SCHNEIDMAN, E. S., FARBEROW, N. L., & LITMAN, R. G. (1970). *The psychology of suicide*. New York: Jason Aronson.

SCHOOLER, C. (1972). Birth order effects: Not here, not now! *Psychological Bulletin, 78*, 161–175.

SCHULTZ, J. H., & LUTHE, W. (1969). *Autogenic therapy*. Vol. 1, New York: Grune and Stratton.

SCOVILLE, W. B., & MILNER, B. (1957). Loss of recent memory after bilateral hippocampal lesions. *Journal of Neurological Neurosurgery and Psychiatry, 20*, 11–21.

SEBEOK, T. A., & ROSENTHAL, R. (Eds.). (1981). *The Clever Hans phenomenon: Communication with horses, whales, apes, and people*. Annals of the New York Academy of Sciences (Vol. 364). New York.

SEGALOWITZ, S. J., & PLANTERY, P. (1985). Music draws attention to the left and speech draws attention to the right. *Brain and Cognition, 4*, 1–6.

SELIGMAN, M. E. P. (1975). *Helplessness: On depression development and death*. San Francisco: W. H. Freeman.

SELIGMAN, M. E. P., & MAIER, S. F. (1967). Failure to escape traumatic shock. *Journal of Experimental Psychology, 74*, 1–9.

SELVINI-PALAZZOLI, M. (1974). *Self-starvation: From the intrapsychic to the transpersonal approach to anorexia nervosa*. London: Chancer.

SELYE, H. (1936). A syndrome produced by diverse noxious agents. *Nature, 138*, 32.

SELYE, H. (1974). *Stress without distress*. Philadelphia: Lippincott.

SELYE, H. (1985). Stress: Eustress, distress, and human perspectives. In S. Day (Ed.), *Life stress* (vol. 3). Cincinnati: Van Nostrand Reinhold.

SENDEN, M. VON. (1960). *Space and sight: The perception of space and shape in the congenitally blind before and after operation*. Peter Heath (Trans.). New York: Free Press.

SHAPIRO, D., SCHWARTZ, G. E., & TURSKY, B. (1972). Control of diastolic blood pressure in man by feedback and reinforcement. *Psychophysiology, 9*, 296–304.

SHAPIRO, D., & SURWIT, S. (1979). Biofeedback. In O. F. Pomerleau & J. P. Brady (Eds.), *Behavioral medicine: Theory and practice*. Baltimore: Williams and Wilkins.

SHAPIRO, D. H. (1983). Meditation as an altered state of consciousness: Empirical contributions of Western behavioral science. *Journal of Transpersonal Psychology, 15*, 61–81.

SHAPIRO, D. H. (1985). Clinical use of meditation as a self-regulation strategy: Comments on Holmes's conclusions and implications. *American Psychologist, 40*, 719–722.

SHAPIRO, E. R. (1978). The psychodynamics and developmental psychology of the borderline patient: A review of the literature. *American Journal of Psychiatry, 135*, 1305–1315.

SHAW, L. B. (Ed.). (1983). *Unplanned careers: The working lives of middle-aged women*. Lexington, Mass.: Lexington Books.

SHAW, M. E. (1981). *Group dynamics: The psychology of small group behavior* (3rd ed.). New York: McGraw-Hill.

SHEPHERD, D. H., & SLOAN, L. R. (1979). Similarity of legal attitudes, defendant social class, and crime intentionality as determinants of legal decisions. *Personality and Social Psychology Bulletin, 5*, 245–248.

SHERIF, M. (1966). *In common predicament: Social psychology of intergroup conflict and cooperation*. Boston: Houghton Mifflin.

SHERIF, M., HARVEY, O. J., WHITE, B. J., HOOD, W. E., & SHERIF, C. W. (1961). *Intergroup conflict and cooperation: The Robber's Cave experiment*. Norman: University of Oklahoma Book Exchange.

SHERROD, D. R., & DOWNS, R. (1974). Environmental determinants of altruism: The effects of stimulus overload and perceived control on helping. *Journal of Experimental Social Psychology, 10*, 468–479.

SHEVRIN, H., & DICKMAN, S. (1980). The psychological unconscious: A necessary assumption for all psychological theory. *American Psychologist, 35*, 421–434.

SHILL, M. (1981). TAT measures of gender identity (castration anxiety) in father-absent males. *Journal of Personality Assessment, 45,* 136–146.

SHORE, E. R. (1985). Alcohol consumption rates among managers and professionals. *Journal of Studies on Alcohol, 46,* 153–156.

SHOTLAND, R. L., & HUSTON, T. L. (1979). Emergencies: What are they and do they influence bystanders to intervene? *Journal of Personality and Social Psychology, 37,* 1822–1834.

SIEGELMAN, M. (1974). Parental background of male homosexuals and heterosexuals. *Archives of Sexual Behavior, 3,* 3–18.

SIGALL, H., & ARONSON, E. (1969). Liking for an evaluator as a function of her physical attractiveness and nature of the evaluations. *Journal of Experimental Social Psychology, 5,* 93–100.

SIMKIN, J. S., & YONTEF, G. M. (1984). Gestalt therapy. In R. J. Corsini (Ed.), *Current psychotherapies* (3rd ed.). Itasca, Ill.: F. E. Peacock.

SIMMONS, F. B. (1970). Monaural processing. In J. V. Tobias (Ed.), *Foundation of modern auditory theory, Vol. 1.* New York: Academic Press.

SIMPSON, A. E., & STEVENSON-HINDE, J. (1985). Temperamental characteristics of three-to-four-year-old boys and girls and child-family interactions. *Journal of Child Psychology and Psychiatry, 26,* 43–53.

SIMPSON, G. E., & YINGER, M. J. (1972). *Racial and cultural minorities: An analysis of prejudice and discrimination* (4th ed.). New York: Harper & Row.

SIMS, E. A. H., DANFORTH, E., JR., HORTON, E. S. (1973). Endocrine and metabolic effects of experimental obesity in man. *Recent Progress in Hormone Research, 29,* 457–496.

SIVACEK, J., & CRANO, W. D. (1982). Vested interest as a moderator of attitude-behavior consistency. *Journal of Personality and Social Psychology, 43,* 210–221.

SKEELS, H. M. (1966). Adult status of children with contrasting early life experiences: A follow-up study. *Monographs of the Society for Research in Child Development.* 31 (3).

SKINNER, B. F. (1938). *The behavior of organisms: An experimental analysis.* New York: Appleton-Century-Crofts.

SKINNER, B. F. (1948). Superstition in the pigeon. *Journal of Experimental Psychology, 38,* 168–172.

SKINNER, B. F. (1953). *Science and human behavior.* New York: Macmillan.

SKINNER, B. F. (1956). A case history in scientific method. *American Psychologist, 11,* 221–233.

SKINNER, B. F. (1978). *Reflections on behaviorism and society.* Englewood Cliffs, N.J.: Prentice-Hall.

SMILLIE, D. (1982). Rethinking Piaget's theory of infancy. *Human Development, 25,* 282–294.

SMITH, D. (1981). Unfinished business with informed consent procedures. *American Psychologist, 36,* 22–26.

SMITH, M. L., & GLASS, G. V. (1977). Meta-analysis of psychotherapy outcome studies. *American Psychol-*

ogist, 32, 752–760.

SMITH, W. M. (1977). Epidemiology of hypertension. *Medical Clinical North American, 61,* 467–486.

SNYDER, M., & KENDZIERSKI, D. (1982). Acting on one's attitudes: Procedures for linking attitude and behavior. *Journal of Experimental Social Psychology, 18,* 165–183.

SNYDER, S. H. (1974). *Madness and the brain.* New York: McGraw-Hill.

SNYDER, S. H. (1977). Biochemical factors in schizophrenia. *Hospital practice, 12,* 133–140.

SNYDER, S. H. (1980). *Biological aspects of mental disorder.* New York: Oxford University Press.

SNYDER, S. H. (1984). Drugs and neurotransmitter receptors in the brain. *Science, 224,* 22–31.

SOLOMON, R. L. (1964). Punishment. *American Psychologist, 19,* 239–253.

SOMMER, B. (1984). PMS in the courts: Are all women on trial. *Psychology Today, 18,* 30–35.

SOMMER, R., & SOMMER, B. A. (1983). Mystery in Milwaukee: Early intervention, IQ, and psychology textbooks. *American Psychologist, 38,* 982–985.

SORENSON, R. (1973). *Adolescent sexuality in contemporary America.* New York: World.

SPEAR, N. E. (1978). *The processing of memories: Forgetting and retention.* Hillsdale, N.J.: Lawrence Erlbaum Associates.

SPEARMAN, C. (1927). *The abilities of man.* London: Macmillan.

SPERLING, G. (1960). The information available in brief visual presentations. *Psychological Monographs, 74,* (11, Whole No. 498).

SPERRY, R. W. (1961). Cerebral organization and behavior. *Science, 133,* 1749–1757.

SPERRY, R. W. (1970). Perception in the absence of the neocortical commissures. In *Perception and Its Disorders,* Research Publications A.R.N.M.D., *48,* 123–128.

SPERRY, R. W. (1974). Lateral specialization in the surgically separated hemispheres. In F. O. Schmitt & F. G. Worden (Eds.), *The neurosciences third study program.* Cambridge, Mass., London: M.I.T. Press.

SPERRY, R. W. (1982). Some effects of disconnecting the cerebral hemispheres. *Science, 217,* 1223–1226.

SPIELMAN, A. J. (1986). Assessment of insomnia. *Clinical Psychology Review, 6,* 11–26.

SPILICH, G. J., VESONDER, G. T., CHIESI, H. L., & VOSS, J. F. (1977). Text processing of domain-related information for individuals with high and low domain knowledge. *Journal of Verbal Learning and Behavior, 18,* 275–290.

SPRING, B. (1983). Mood, Performance and Pain Sensitivity. *Journal of Psychiatric Research, 17,* 49–58.

SPRING, B., & COONS, H. (1982). Stress as a precursor of schizophrenic episodes. In R. W. J. Neufeld (Ed.), *Psychological stress and psychopathology.* New York: McGraw-Hill.

SPRING, B., & ZUBIN, J. (1978). Attention and information-processing as indicator of vulnerability to schizophrenic episodes. In L. C. Wynne, R. L. Cromwell, & S. Matthysse (Eds.), *The nature of schizophrenia: New approaches to research and treatment.* New York: Wiley.

SQUIRE, L. R. (1977). ECT and memory loss. *American Journal of Psychiatry, 134,* 997–1001.

SQUIRE, L. R., SHIMAMURA, A. P., & GRAF, P. (1985). Independence of recognition memory and priming effects: A neuropsychological analysis. *Journal of Experimental Psychology: Learning, Memory, and Cognition, 11,* 37–44.

SROUFE, L. A. (1985). Attachment classification from the perspective of infant-caregiver relationships and infant temperament. *Child Development, 56,* 1–14.

STAFFIERI, J. R. (1967). A study of social stereotypes of body image in children. *Journal of Personality and Social Psychology, 7,* 101–104.

STARK, E. (1985). Breaking the pain habit. *Psychology Today, 19,* 30–36.

STAUB, E. (Ed.). (1978). *Positive social behavior and morality* (Vol. 1). *Social and personal influences.* New York: Academic Press.

STEELE, C. (1986). What happens when you drink too much? *Psychology Today, 20,* 48–53.

STEERS, R. M., & PORTER, L. W. (1975). *Motivation and work behavior.* New York: McGraw-Hill.

STEPHAN, W. G. (1978). School desegregation: An evaluation of predictions made in *Brown* v. *The Board of Education. Psychological Bulletin, 85,* 217–238.

STERLING, S., COWEN, E. L., WEISSBERG, R. P., LOTYCZEWSKI, B. S., & BOIKE, M. (1985). Recent stressful life events and young children's school adjustment. *American Journal of Community Psychology, 13,* 87–98.

STERN, D. (1977). *The first relationship: Mother and infant.* Cambridge, Mass.: Harvard University Press.

STERN, J. S. (1984). Is obesity a disease of inactivity? In A. J. Stunkard & E. Stellar (Eds.), *Eating and its disorders.* New York: Raven.

STERN, P. J. (1976). *C. G. Jung: The haunted prophet.* New York: George Braziller.

STERN, W. (1914). *The psychological methods of testing intelligence.* Baltimore: Warwick & York.

STERNBERG, R. J. (1981). Testing and cognitive psychology. *American Psychologist, 36,* 1181–1189.

STERNBERG, R. J. (1985). *Beyond IQ.* Cambridge: Cambridge University Press.

STEWART, J. E., II. (1980). Defendant's attractiveness as a factor in the outcome of criminal trials: An observational study. *Journal of Applied Social Psychology, 10,* 348–361.

STILES, W. B., SHAPIRO, D. A., & ELLIOTT, R. (1986). Are all psychotherapies equivalent? *American Psychologist, 41,* 165–180.

STIMPSON, D. V., & STIMPSON, M. F. (1979). Relation of personality characteristics and color preferences. *Perceptual and Motor Skills, 49,* 60–62.

STOKOLS, D. (1978a). A typology of crowding experiences. In A. Baum & Y. Epstein (Eds.), *Human response to crowding.* Hillsdale, N.J.: Erlbaum.

STONE, W. F. (1974). *The psychology of politics.* New York: Free Press.

STOUDEMIRE, A., RICHARD, F., KAMLET, M., & HEDEMARK, N. (1985). Depression as a public health problem. Presented at the 1985 Annual Meeting of the American Psychiatric Association, Dallas.

STRICKER, E., & ZIGMOND, M. (1976). Brain cat echolamines and lateral hypothalamus syndrome. In D. Novin, W. Wyrwicka, & G. Bray (Eds.), *Hunger: Basic mechanisms and clinical implications.* New York: Raven Press.

STRUBE, M. J., BERRY, J. M., GOZA, B. K., & FENNIMORE, D. (1985). Type A behavior, age, and psychological well-being. *Journal of Personality and Social Psychology, 49,* 203–218.

STUART, R. B. (1967). Behavioral control of overeating. *Behavioral Research and Therapy, 5,* 357–365.

STUNKARD, A. J. (1972). New therapies for eating disorders. *Archives of General Psychiatry, 26,* 391–398.

STUNKARD, A. J. (1975). From explanation to action in psychosomatic medicine: The case of obesity. *Psychosomatic Medicine, 37,* 195–236.

STUNKARD, A. J. (1979). Behavioral medicine and beyond: The example of obesity. In O. F. Pomerleau and J. P. Brady (Eds.), *Behavioral medicine: Theory and practice.* Baltimore: Williams and Wilkins.

STUSS, D. T., & BENSON, D. F. (1984). Neuropsychological studies of the frontal lobes. *Psychological Bulletin, 95,* 3–28.

SUE, D., SUE, D. W., & SUE, S. (1981). *Understanding abnormal behavior.* Boston: Houghton Mifflin.

SWAP, W. C. (1977). Interpersonal attraction and repeated exposure to rewarders and punishers. *Personality and Social Psychology Bulletin, 3,* 248–251.

SWENSEN, C. H. (1983). A respectable old age. *American Psychologist, 38,* 327–334.

SZYMANSKI, H. V., SIMON, J. C., & GUTTERMAN, N. (1983). Recovery from schizophrenic psychosis. *American Journal of Psychiatry, 140,* 335–338.

TAJFEL, H., & TURNER, J. (1979). An integrative theory of intergroup conflict. In W. G. Austin & S. Worchel (Eds.), *The social psychology of intergroup relations.* Monterey, Calif.: Brooks/Cole.

TALLAL, P. (1980). Language and reading: Some perceptual prerequisites. *Bulletin of the Orton Society, 30,* 170–178.

TALLAL, P. (1981). Learning disabilities in children: Perceptual correlates. *International Journal of Pediatric Otorhinolaryngology, 3,* 1–13.

TAN, L. E. (1985). Laterality and motor skills in four-year-olds. *Child Development, 56,* 119–124.

TAPP, J. L. (1976). Psychology and the law: An overture. *Annual Review of Psychology, 27,* 359–404.

TART, C. T. (1972). *Altered states of consciousness*. Garden City, N.Y.: Doubleday.

TART, C. T. (1975). *Altered states of consciousness*. New York: Dutton.

TART, C. T. (1979). Measuring the depth of an altered state of consciousness, with particular reference to self-report scales of hypnotic depth. In E. Fromm & R. E. Shor (Eds.), *Hypnosis: Developments in research and new perspectives* (2nd ed.). New York: Aldine.

TAVRIS, C., & SADD, S. (1977). *The Redbook report on female sexuality*. New York: Delacorte Press.

TAYLOR, S., & FISKE, S. T. (1978). Salience, attention, and attribution: Top of the head phenomena. In L. Berkowitz (Ed.), *Advances in experimental social psychology* (Vol. 11). New York: Academic Press.

TEASDALE, J. D. (1985). Psychological treatments for depression: How do they work? *Behaviour Research & Therapy, 23*, 157–165.

TEITELBAUM, P. (1955). Sensory control of hypothalamic hyperphagia. *Journal of Comparative and Physiological Psychology, 48*, 156–163.

TEITELBAUM, P., & EPSTEIN, A. N. (1962). The lateral hypothalamic syndrome. *Psychological Review, 69*, 74–90.

TERMAN, L. M. (1916). *The measurement of intelligence*. Boston: Houghton Mifflin.

TERRACE, H. S. (1981). A report to an academy, 1980. In T. A. Sebeok & R. Rosenthal (Eds.), *The Clever Hans phenomenon: Communication with horses, whales, apes, and people. Annals of the New York Academy of Sciences* (Vol. 364). New York.

THIGPEN, C. H., & CLECKLEY, H. (1954). *The three faces of Eve*. Kingsport, Tenn.: Kingsport Press.

THOMAS, A., CHESS, S., & BIRCH, H. G. (1970). The origin of personality. *Scientific American, 223*, 102.

THOMAS, C. B. (1983). Study of healthy personality described in Didato.*

THOMPSON, J. K., JARVIE, G. J., LAHEY, B. B., & CURETON, K. J. (1982). Exercise and obesity: Etiology, physiology, and intervention. *Psychological Bulletin, 91*, 55–79.

THOMPSON, J. L. (1934). Big gains from postponed readings. *Journal of Education, 117*, 445–446.

THORNDIKE, E. L. (1898). Animal intelligence: An experimental study of the associative processes in animals. *Psychological Monographs*, (2, Whole No. 8).

THORNDIKE, E. L. (1905). *The elements of psychology*. New York: Seiler.

THURSTONE, L. L. (1938). Primary mental abilities. *Psychometric Monographs*, No. 1.

TINBERGEN, N. (1951). *The study of instinct*. Oxford, England: Oxford University Press.

TOMKINS, S. (1981). The quest for primary motives: Biography and autobiography of an idea. *Journal of Personality and Social Psychology, 41*, 306–329.

TRAUPMANN, J., PETERSEN, R., UTNE, M., & HATFIELD, E. (1981). Measuring equity in intimate relations. *Applied Psychological Measurement, 5*, 467–480.

TRILLING, L. (1948). The Kinsey Report. In Trilling, L. (Ed.), *The liberal imagination*. New York: Viking Press.

TRIPP, C. A. (1975). *The homosexual matrix*. New York: McGraw-Hill.

TRUAX, C. B., & CARKHUFF, R. R. (1967). *Toward effective counseling and psychotherapy*. Chicago: Aldine.

TRUAX, C. B., & MITCHELL, K. M. (1971). Research on certain therapist interpersonal skills in relation to process and outcome. In A. E. Bergin & S. L. Garfield (Eds.), *Handbook of psychotherapy and behavior change*. New York: Wiley.

TULVING, E. (1962). Subjective organization in free recall of "unrelated" words. *Psychological Review, 69*, 344–354.

TULVING, E. (1972). Episodic and semantic memory. In E. Tulving & W. Donaldson (Eds.), *Organization of memory*. New York: Academic Press.

TULVING, E. (1985). How many memory systems are there? *American Psychologist, 40*, 385–398.

TULVING, E., & PEARLSTONE, Z. (1966). Availability versus accessibility of information in memory for words. *Journal of Verbal Learning and Verbal Behavior, 5*, 381–391.

TULVING, E., & THOMPSON, D. M. (1973). Encoding specificity and retrieval processes in episodic memory. *Psychological Review, 80*, 352–373.

TURKINGTON, C. (1986). High court weighs value of research by social scientists. *The APA Monitor, 17*, 1 & 30.

TURNBULL, C. M. (1961). Notes and discussions: Some observations regarding the experiences and behavior of the Bambute pygmies. *American Journal of Psychology, 7*, 304–308.

TURNER, J. H. (1970). Entrepreneurial environments and the emergence of achievement motivation in adolescent males. *Sociometry, 33*, 147–165.

U.S. NEWS & WORLD REPORT. (1982, Aug. 30). Anorexia: The starving disease epidemic, *93*, 47–48.

UNDERWOOD, B. J. (1957). Interference and forgetting. *Psychological Review, 64*, 49–60.

UNGER, R. K., HILDERBRAND, M., & MADAR, T. (1982). Physical attractiveness and assumptions about social deviance: Some sex-by-sex comparisons. *Personality and Social Psychology Bulletin, 8*, 293–301.

UNGERSTEDT, U. (1971). Stereotaxic mapping of the monamine pathways in the rat brain. *Acta Physiologica Scandinavica, 367*, Supplement 10, 1–48.

UNITED STATES DEPARTMENT OF HEALTH AND HUMAN SERVICES. (1980). *Smoking and health: A report of the surgeon general*. Washington, D.C.: Government Printing Office.

USHER, S., & FELS, M. (1985). The challenge of feminism and career for the middle-aged woman. *International Journal of Women's Studies, 8*, 47–57.

VAILLANT, G. E. (1977). *Adaption to life*. Boston: Little, Brown.

VANDENBOS, G. R. (1986). Psychotherapy research: A special issue. *American Psychologist, 41,* 111–112.

VANDERWOLF, C. H. (1962). Medial thalamic functions in voluntary behavior. *Canadian Journal of Psychology, 16,* 318–330.

VANDERWOLF, C. H. (1963). The effect of medial thalamic lesions on previously established fear-motivated behavior. *Journal of Psychology,* 183–187.

VOSS, J. F. (1979). Organization, structure, and memory: Three perspectives. In C. R. Puff (Ed.), *Memory organization and structure.* New York: Academic Press.

WACHTEL, P. L. (1977). *Psychoanalysis and behavior therapy: Toward an integration.* New York: Basic Books.

WALEN, S. R., DIGIUSEPPE, R., & WESSLER, R. L. (1980). *A practitioner's guide to rational emotive therapy.* New York: Oxford University Press.

WALKER, L. J. (1982). The sequentiality of Kohlberg's stages of moral development. *Child Development, 53,* 1330–1336.

WALL, P. D., & SWEET, W. H. (1967). Temporary abolition of pain in man. *Science, 155,* 108–109.

WALLACE, B., & FISHER, L. E. (1987). *Consciousness and behavior.* Boston: Allyn and Bacon.

WALLACE, H. M., WEEKS, J., & MEDINA, A. (1982). Services for pregnant teenagers in the large cities of the United States, 1970–1980. *Journal of the American Medical Association, 248,* 2270–2273.

WALLACE, R. K., & BENSON, H. (1972). The physiology of meditation. *Scientific American, 226,* 85–90.

WALLACH, M. A. (1976). Tests tell us little about talent. *American Scientist, 64,* 57–63.

WALLERSTEIN, J., & KELLY, J. (1980). *Surviving the breakup: How children actually cope with divorce.* New York: Basic Books.

WALSH, R. N. (1978). Initial meditative experiences. Part II. *Journal of Transpersonal Psychology, 10,* 1–28.

WALSTER, E., ARONSON, V., ABRAHAMS, D., & ROTTMAN, L. (1966). Importance of physical attractiveness in dating behavior. *Journal of Personality and Social Psychology, 4,* 508–516.

WALTERS, J., APTER, M. J., & SVEBACK, S. (1982). Color preference, arousal, and the theory of psychological reversals. *Motivation and Emotion, 6,* 193–215.

WALUM, L. R. (1977). *The dynamics of sex and gender: A sociological perspective.* Chicago: Rand McNally.

WANBERG, K. W., & HORN, J. L. (1983). Assessment of alcohol use with multi-dimensional concepts and measures. *American Psychologist, 38,* 1055–1069.

WARBURTON, D. M. (1975). *Brain, behaviour and drugs: Introduction to the neurochemistry of behaviour.* London: John Wiley & Sons.

WARE, J. C. (1979). The symptom of insomnia: Cures and causes: *Psychiatric Annals, 9,* 27–49.

WATKINS, M. J. (1979). Engrams as cuegrams and forgetting as cue overload. In C. R. Puff (Ed.), *Memory organization and structure.* New York: Academic Press.

WATSON, J. B. (1913). Psychology as a behaviorist views it. *Psychological Review, 20,* 158–177.

WATSON, J. B. (1924). *Psychology from the standpoint of a behaviorist.* Philadelphia: Lippincott.

WEARY, G., & MIRELS, H. L. (1982). *Integrations of clinical and social psychology.* New York: Oxford University Press.

WEBB, W. B. (1975). *Sleep the gentle tyrant.* Englewood Cliffs, N.J.: Prentice-Hall.

WECHSLER, D. (1939). *The measurement of adult intelligence.* Baltimore: Williams & Wilkins.

WECHSLER, D. (1958). *The measurement and appraisal of adult intelligence* (4th ed.). Baltimore: Williams & Wilkins.

WECHSLER, D. (1981). *Wechsler Adult Intelligence Scale-Revised.* New York: Psychological Corporation.

WEIL, A. T. (1972). *The natural mind: A new way of looking at drugs and the higher consciousness.* Boston: Houghton Mifflin.

WEIL, J. L. (1974). *A neurophysiological model of emotional and intentional behavior.* Springfield, Ill.: Charles C Thomas.

WENDER, P. H., ROSENTHAL, D., & KETY, S. S. (1968). A psychiatric assessment of the adoptive parents of schizophrenics. In D. Rosenthal and S. S. Kety (Eds.), *The transmission of schizophrenia.* Oxford: Pergamon Press.

WENDER, P. H., ROSENTHAL, D., KETY, S. S., SCHULSINGER, F., & WELSNER, J. (1974). Cross-fostering. *Archives of General Psychiatry, 30,* 121–128.

WHALEN, R. E. (1976). Brain mechanisms controlling sexual behavior. In F. A. Beach (Ed.), *Human sexuality in four perspectives.* Baltimore: Johns Hopkins University Press.

WHEELER, L., KOESTNER, R., & DRIVER, R. E. (1982). Related attributes in the choice of comparison others: It's there, but it isn't all there is. *Journal of Experimental Social Psychology, 18,* 489–500.

WHITE, B. L., & WATTS, J. C. (1973). *Experience and environment: Major influences on the development of the young child.* Englewood Cliffs, N.J.: Prentice-Hall.

WHITE, J. W., & GRUBER, K. J. (1982). Instigative aggression as a function of past experience and target characteristics. *Journal of Personality and Social Psychology, 42,* 1069–1075.

WHITE, M. J. (1985). On the status of cognitive psychology. *American Psychologist, 40,* 117–119.

WHITT, J. K., & CASEY, P. H. (1982). The mother-infant relationship and infant development: The effect of pediatric intervention. *Child Development, 53,* 948–956.

WHORF, B. L. (1940). Science and linguistics. *Technology Review, 34,* 229–231, 247–248.

WHORF, B. L. (1956). In J. B. Carroll (Ed.), *Language, thought, and reality.* New York: Wiley.

WICKENS, D. D., MOODY, M. J., & VIDULICH, M. (1985). Retrieval time as a function of memory set size, type of probes, and interference in recognition memory. *Journal of Experimental Psychology: Learning, Memory, and Cognition, 11*, 154–164.

WICKWARE, F. S. (1948). Report on the Kinsey Report. *Life*, August, 86–90.

WIERZBICKI, M. (1985). A twin study of childhood depression. Presented at the Fifty-Seventh Annual Meeting of the Midwestern Psychological Association, Chicago.

WIGDOR, A. K., & GARNER, W. R. (1982). *Ability testing: Uses, consequences, and controversies.* (Vol. 1). Washington, D.C.: National Academy Press.

WILDER, D. A. (1981). Perceiving persons as a group: Categorization and intergroup relations. In D. L. Hamilton (Ed.), *Cognitive processes in stereotyping and intergroup behavior.* Hillsdale, N.J.: Erlbaum.

WILKES, J. (1986). A study in hypnosis: Conversation with Ernest R. Hilgard. *Psychology Today, 20*, 22–27.

WILLIAMS, R. L., & LONG, J. D. (1983). *Toward a self-managed life style* (3rd ed.). Boston: Houghton Mifflin.

WILSON, G. (1978). Introversion/Extroversion. In H. London and J. E. Exner (Eds.), *Dimensions of Personality.* New York: Wiley.

WILSON, G., & LAWSON, D. (1976). Effects of alcohol on sexual arousal in women. *Journal of Abnormal Psychology, 85*, 489–497.

WILSON, G. T. (1984). Behavior therapy. In R. J. Corsini (Ed.), *Current psychotherapies* (3rd ed.). Itasca, Ill.: F. E. Peacock.

WILSON, G. T., & RACHMAN, S. J. (1983). Meta-analysis and the evaluation of psychotherapy outcome: Limitations and liabilities. *Journal of Consulting and Clinical Psychology, 51*, 54–64.

WILSON, J. D., GEORGE, F. W., & GRIFFIN, J. E. (1981). The hormonal control of sexual development. *Science, 211*, 1278–1281.

WINE, J. D. (1985). Women's sexuality. *International Journal of Women's Studies, 8*, 58–63.

WINOGRAD, E., & SOLOWAY, R. M. (1985). Reminding as a basis for temporal judgments. *Journal of Experimental Psychology: Learning, Memory, and Cognitions, 11*, 262–271.

WINOKUR, G., CADORET, R., DORZAB, J. (1971). Depressive disease: A genetic study. *Archives of General Psychiatry, 24*, 135–144.

WOLBERG, L. R. (1967). *The technique of psychotherapy* (2nd ed.). New York: Grune & Stratton.

WOLFF, P. H. (1969). The natural history of crying and other vocalizations in early infancy. In B. M. Foss (Ed.), *Determinants of infant behavior* (Vol. 4). London: Methuen.

WOLPE, J. (1958). *Psychotherapy by reciprocal inhibition.* Stanford, Calif.: Stanford University Press.

WOLPE, J. (1981). Behavior therapy vs. psychoanalysis: Therapeutic and social implications. *American Psychologist, 36*, 159–164.

WOLPE, J. (1982). *The practice of behavior therapy.* New York: Pergamon Press.

WOOD, G. (1983). *Cognitive psychology: A skills approach.* Monterey, Calif.: Brooks/Cole.

WOOD, W., & EAGLY, A. H. (1981). Stages in the analysis of persuasive messages: The role of causal attributions and message comprehension. *Journal of Personality and Social Psychology, 40*, 246–259.

WOODWORTH, R. S. (1920). *Personal data sheet.* Chicago: Stoelting.

WOODWORTH, R. S., & SCHLOSBERG, H. (1954). *Experimental psychology.* New York: Holt, Rinehart and Winston.

WYLIE, R. C. (1974). *The self-concept* (vol. 1). Lincoln: University of Nebraska Press.

WYLIE, R. C. (1978). *The self-concept* (vol. 2). Lincoln: University of Nebraska Press.

YARBOROUGH, B. H., & JOHNSON, R. A. (1980). A six-year study of sex differences in intellectual functioning, reading/language arts, achievement, and affective development. *The Journal of Psychology, 106*, 55–61.

YATES, A., LEEHEY, K., & SHISSLAK, C. M. (1983). The obligator runner. *New England Journal of Medicine.**

YERKES, R. M., & DODSON, J. D. (1908). The relation of strength of stimulus to rapidity of habit-formation. *Journal of Comparative Neurology and Psychology, 18*, 459–482.

ZAJONC, R. B. (1968). Attitudinal effects of mere exposure. *Journal of Personality and Social Psychology Monograph Supplement, 9* (2, Part 2), 2–27.

ZAJONC, R. B. (1984). On the primacy of affect. *American Psychologist, 39*, 117–123.

ZATORRE, R. J. (1985). Discrimination and recognition of tonal melodies after unilateral cerebral excisions. *Neuropsychologia, 23*, 31–41.

ZEIGLER, H. P., & LEIBOWITZ, H. (1957). Apparent visual size as a function of distance for children and adults. *American Journal of Psychology, 70*, 106–109.

ZELNIK, M., & KANTNER, J. (1977). Sexual and contraceptive experiences of young unmarried women in the United States, 1976 and 1971. *Family Planning Perspectives, 9*, 55–71.

ZELNIK, M., & KANTNER, J. F. (1979). Reasons for nonuse of contraception by sexually active women aged 15–19. *Family Planning Perspectives, 11*, 289–296.

ZELNIK, M., & KANTNER, J. (1980). Sexual activity, contraceptive use, and pregnancy among metropolitan-area teenagers: 1971–1979. *Family Planning Perspectives, 12*, 230–237.

ZESKIND, P. S., & LESTER, B. M. (1981). Analysis of cry features in newborns with differential fetal growth. *Child Development, 52*, 207–212.

ZILBERGELD, B., & KILMANN, P. R. (1984). The scope and effectiveness of sex therapy. *Psychotherapy, 21*, 319–326.

ZILLMAN, D. (1971). Excitation transfer in communication-mediated aggressive behavior. *Journal of Experimental Social Psychology, 7*, 419–434.

ZILLMAN, D. (1979). *Hostility and aggression.* Hillsdale, N.J.: Erlbaum.

ZIMBARDO, P. G., EBBESEN, E. B., & MASLACH, C. (1977). *Influencing attitudes and changing behavior* (2nd ed.). Reading, Mass.: Addison-Wesley.

ZUCKERMAN, M. (1979). Attribution of success and failure revisited, or: The motivational bias is alive and well in attribution theory. *Journal of Personality, 47,* 245–287.

ZUCKERMAN, M., LAZZARO, M. M., & WALDGEIR, D. (1979). Undermining effects of the foot-in-the-door technique with extrinsic rewards. *Journal of Applied Social Psychology, 9,* 292–296.

ZUECK, V. M., & KATKOVSKY, W. (1985). Self-monitoring, self-evaluation, and self-reinforcement in depressed university students. Presented at the Fifty-Seventh Meeting of the Midwestern Psychological Association, Chicago.

ZYZANSKI, S. J., JENKINS, C. D., RYAN, G. J. (1976). Psychological correlance of coronary angiographic findings. *Archives of Internal Medicine, 136,* 1234–1237.

Name Index

Subject Index